# Elections
## A to Z

CQ'S READY REFERENCE ENCYCLOPEDIA OF AMERICAN GOVERNMENT

# Elections A to Z

John L. Moore

CONGRESSIONAL QUARTERLY INC.
WASHINGTON, D.C.

Book Design by *Kachergis Book Design, Pittsboro, North Carolina.*

*Acknowledgments, cover images*

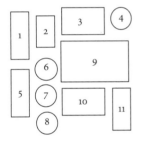

1. Theodore Roosevelt, 1912 campaign, *Harvard University*
2. Republican Convention, *Library of Congress*
3. Harry S. Truman, *St. Louis Mercantile Library*
4. John F. Kennedy campaign button, *The Garrison Studio*
5. Citizens registering, *League of Women Voters*
6. Hubert Humphrey campaign button, *The Garrison Studio*
7. Jimmy Carter 1980 campaign button, *The Garrison Studio*
8. Reagan/ Bush 1984 campaign button, *The Garrison Studio*
9. 1992 Democratic Convention, *R. Michael Jenkins, Congressional Quarterly*
10. Reagans and Bushes, *David Valdez, The White House*
11. Photographer, *Library of Congress*

Frontispiece, *Fred Sons*


Printed and bound in the United States of America.


The paper used in this publication meets the minimum requirements of the American National Standard for Information Sciences—Permanence of Paper for Printed Library Materials, ANSI Z39.48-1984.

LIBRARY OF CONGRESS CATALOGING-IN-PUBLICATION DATA

Moore, John Leo, 1927–
Elections A to Z / John L. Moore.
     p.  cm. — (CQ's ready reference encyclopedia of American government)
    Includes bibliographical references.
    ISBN 1-56802-207-7 (alk. paper)
    1. Elections—United States Encyclopedias.  I. Title.  II. Series.
JK1976 .M57 1999
324.6'0973'03—dc21                        99-25162

# Contents

vi  **Contents**

# Foreword

It is fashionable these days to dismiss elections as boring. When an accountant heard what this book was about, he asked, "How can you stay awake while writing it?" Others responded simply, "Oh." Or, not knowing what else to say—and unwilling to say, "That sounds interesting"—they said nothing or changed the subject.

Yet some of these same individuals, including the accountant, have been active in partisan politics. They have proudly associated themselves with social causes that are very much intertwined with political beliefs and the selection of leaders who share those beliefs. Nevertheless, they reacted as many people do at the very mention of the words *politics* and *elections*.

That is why the last article in the book is entitled "ZZZ," the instantly recognizable symbol for sleep. In this article we examine the sad truth that many Americans today, perhaps a majority, are turned off by politics and apathetic about voting. Many are alienated, feel powerless, and think their vote does not count.

The ZZZ article points out the folly of that belief. There are many instances in U.S. elections where a handful of votes could have reversed the results. But the essay does not preach. To use a popular phrase, it "tells it like it is," and the same is true throughout this book. We have tried to define and explain all the major aspects of the U.S. electoral and political systems, objectively and factually, and not from any point of view.

We have also resisted the urge to editorialize in favor of increased and informed voter participation, even though we are told that voter education and high turnouts ranks right up there in value with apple pie and motherhood. Who could fault us for taking such a safe and comfortable position? No one, probably, even though some patriotic citizens staunchly defend the right *not* to vote, and some political scientists see no great harm in low voter turnouts.

In this foreword, however, we drop all pretense of objectivity about our subject matter. This is, after all, a book about elections. It would be a serious omission not to come right out and say it: elections *are* important. Your vote *does* count. If you are a U.S. citizen eighteen years or older, you have an obligation to register and vote. The government has made it easy for you with the Motor Voter Act. No excuses are acceptable.

Furthermore, if you do vote, you have an obligation to yourself, your family, your community, and your country to learn about the candidates and the issues. That information is easily available in newspapers and magazines, on radio and television, and now through a medium of growing importance, the Internet.

*Elections A to Z* is not a substitute for media information but a supplement that can help you understand it and put it in perspective. It is a treasure trove of useful information about elections and politics, much of it almost impossible to find in any other one-volume encyclopedia. The few such books that exist were consulted during the writing of this book, and in instance after instance subjects covered in some depth here were not mentioned or were dismissed in a sentence or two. Even the major, household-name encyclopedias were found wanting as research sources for elections-related material. By the same token, you will find this book much more helpful than most encyclopedias if you are conducting research or writing a paper on some facet of elections or politics.

Even though elections ultimately are about numbers and percentages—which, while important, do not make for lively reading—you will not find many here. We have included in the appendices the state-by-state re-sults of the 1996 presidential election. If you need more comprehensive results, you can turn to other volumes published by Congressional Quarterly, such as the *Guide to U.S. Elections,* now in its third edition. The *Guide* is the only printed source of all major election re-turns since the founding of the country. Another source for hard data is the *America Votes* series, published every two years. These books give the results of all federal and gubernatorial elections during the period covered.

But, to return to the widespread impression that elections are boring—that is simply nonsense. Like sports events, elections are contests, but they are con-tests for major political offices, with much more at stake than who wins the Super Bowl or the World Series.

Some American elections are more competitive than others, of course, but on the whole they are interesting, often providing drama, conflict, and cliffhanger out-comes. They can be amusing, bizarre, and unpre-dictable. Witness the 1998 election of wrestler Jesse "the

Body" Ventura as governor of Minnesota. Or the use of a poker hand to break a tied mayoral vote in New Mexi-co, which is discussed in the article titled Contested Elections. At this writing, with former White House in-tern Monica S. Lewinsky assured of a place in presiden-tial history, a woman named Monica L. Monica—her real name—is running for Congress in Louisiana. And in Chicago a woman legally changed her name to run for alderman as Carol Moseley-Braun, under protest from the former U.S. senator by that name.

The list could go on and on, but we should not forget why elections are serious business. Our nation's future depends largely on the decisions each individual makes in the polling booth. So never say elections are dull. They can be—and often are—serious, infuriating, fun-ny, and fascinating all at the same time.

John L. Moore
*March 1999*

# Preface

*Elections A to Z*, the newest addition to CQ's Encyclopedia of American Government series, makes the vital but sometimes confusing American electoral process accessible to all readers. Joining its companions in the series—*Congress A to Z, The Presidency A to Z,* and *The Supreme Court A to Z*—this essential reference tool provides a comprehensive guide to understanding the current issues, history, and concepts behind attaining political office in the United States.

Like the other single-volume references in the series, *Elections A to Z* is a useful source for researchers at every level. High school students preparing term papers, college students requiring a quick review, political activists working on an issue or a campaign, and anyone following politics and government will find accurate and interesting information in CQ's Encyclopedia of American Government.

Readers of *Elections A to Z* will discover more than two hundred alphabetical entries on running for the House, the Senate, the presidency, and some statewide offices. There are discussions of the stages in the campaign process and the general election process and the roles played in each by political consultants, the media, and political parties. Topics such as campaign finance, presidential debates, term limits, and the fate of majority-minority districts are thoroughly researched and explained. Included are discussions of the constitutional amendments, legislation, and Supreme Court cases that have shaped the modern electoral process. The expansion of the franchise is explored in articles dealing with voting rights in America, women's suffrage, and youth suffrage. Articles on electoral behavior delve into absentee voting, turnout, and voter apathy ("ZZZ").

Substantial articles cover highlights of presidential and congressional elections, historic milestones in elections, and scandals in elections and campaigns.

Many people, at Congressional Quarterly and elsewhere, deserve acknowledgment for their talent and diligence in the preparation of this volume. John L. Moore, writer and editor of many of Congressional Quarterly's reference works, including *Speaking of Washington,* produced a manuscript that makes *Elections A to Z* not only easy to understand but fun to read. He made bringing this book to press a pleasure. Several other writers made valuable contributions; we thank Ron de Paolo, Kenneth Jost, and Bruce Maxwell. Bits of other CQ publications were adapted for use in *Elections A to Z:* John F. Bibby's *Governing by Consent: An Introduction to American Politics* and articles from *The CQ Researcher* by Charles S. Clark and Nadine Cohodas.

Acquisitions editor Shana Wagger conceived the idea for this book and helped it evolve from brainstorming sessions to manuscript pages. When Shana left CQ, acquisitions editor Patricia Gallagher took over the project and saw it through to completion. Presidential scholar Michael Nelson of Rhodes College reviewed the manuscript and provided expert advice on the book's contents.

Carolyn Goldinger wore two hats as manuscript editor and production editor. Talia Greenberg and Jerry Orvedahl selected and gathered the images that enrich the pages. Those involved in text research include Deborah J. Anderson, Rhodes Cook, Grace Hill, James R. Ingram, Ronald J. Moore, Jon Preimesberger, Robert H. Resnick, and David R. Tarr. Joyce Kachergis and her creative staff at Kachergis Book Design are responsible for the book's design and production.

We hope this volume and the others that make up the Encyclopedia of American Government meet the simple goal we stated at the beginning: to provide readers with accessible, accurate information about the presidency, Congress, the Supreme Court, and the elections that so dramatically influence these institutions.

Kathryn C. Suárez
*Director, Library Reference, CQ Books*

# Elections
## A to Z

# A

## Absentee Voting

Circumstances of all sorts —business travel, illness, military duty, vacation—may keep many registered voters away from the polls on ELECTION DAY. In such cases the states allow the absentee to vote by mail.

Absentee voting began during the Civil War when Union soldiers were caught up in the political struggle and, with Abraham Lincoln's encouragement, wanted to participate in the elections back home. Since then the absentee ballot has become a widely used staple of American elections.

The voter who expects to be away applies for an absentee ballot that must be returned within a designated period, usually by election day or by a certain hour the day after. For the vote to be certified and counted, the voter must carefully follow the CANVASSING BOARD'S instructions, because in a RECOUNT a flawed ballot will be challenged and likely thrown out. Absentee votes have decided many a CONTESTED RESULTS election.

In today's busy world, when voters may not have the time or capability to travel to the polls on a given day, the idea of absentee voting for all is gaining wider acceptance. Even polling officials, who cannot leave their posts during voting hours, must use absentee ballots if they are assigned to a polling station in another district.

About half the states now have an "early voting" option, including "no-fault" absentee voting open to all voters with no need to plead sickness, disability, or any other reason for wanting to vote before election day. And the number of early voters has grown so significantly that candidates are increasingly adapting their CAMPAIGN STRATEGIES to them.

Since 1980 the absentee vote in presidential elections has amounted to almost 10 percent of the total. In a March 1996 California primary 1.42 million absentee votes were cast—24 percent of the total vote.

The availability of absentee voting has long been helpful to Americans living outside the United States. Both major political parties have overseas organizations of absentee voters, Democrats Abroad and Republicans Abroad. At the 1996 Democratic National Convention in Chicago, Democrats Abroad had nine votes divided among twenty-two DELEGATES, including eight SUPERDELEGATES and delegates elected regionally and worldwide.

The VOTING RIGHTS ACT OF 1965 and later amendments interpreted the RIGHT TO VOTE broadly, encompassing the polling place, voters' physical disabilities, language handicaps, and other aspects of the elections process that might deny a person or groups of people access to the ballot box or voting booth. The act directed the Justice Department to determine if state election laws were depriving military personnel of voting rights.

In 1999 the Defense Department was trying to develop a system that would allow military absentee voting over the Internet. The department hoped to have the system in place for the presidential election in 2000.

## Federal Legislation

Men and women in military service make up one of the biggest blocs of absentee voters. Their right to this privilege, as well as that of other Americans living abroad, is protected by two federal statutes: the Federal Voting Assistance Act of 1955 (FVAA) and the Overseas Citizens Voting Rights Act of 1975 (OCVRA).

The FVAA applies to military and merchant marine personnel temporarily stationed outside the United

*Sen. Ron Wyden of Oregon, second from left, reenacts his swearing-in by Vice President Al Gore at the U.S. Capitol February 6, 1996. To Wyden's left is Sen. Mark Hatfield and to his right is Wyden's wife, Carrie. Wyden was the first senator elected by mail. Source: Win McNamee, Reuters*

States, as well as to their spouses and dependents. The OCVRA covers Americans living abroad more or less permanently. Before going overseas they must have voted in the state where they last lived. Most states limit this group to absentee balloting in federal, not state, elections.

Under both acts, application for an absentee ballot is made on the federal postcard application, a postage-free U.S. government form that also serves as a VOTER REGISTRATION form. Most states accept the postcard as a registration or waive their own registration requirement when the postcard is submitted. A few send out their own registration form along with the absentee ballot.

Enactment of the 1975 OCVRA significantly changed the meaning of the term *voting residence* for U.S. citizens living outside the country. Under the act, their state of residence became the last one they voted in, even if they had no home there and no intention to return there.

Previously, under the Constitution, states deter-

mined eligibility for voting, usually defining residence as the place where the voter or a candidate actually lived. In some cases this restriction forced candidates to maintain residences or voting addresses in the district or precinct they represented, even though they lived elsewhere. Gradually, over the years after OCVRA, the Supreme Court struck down the strictest residency requirements, giving more weight to the national right to vote and holding, in effect, that the voter or candidate is the one who decides what to call home for voting purposes.

The lenient definition of residency has caused problems in some jurisdictions, especially those with large military populations. For example, in Val Verde County, Texas, which is 70 percent Hispanic, absentee ballots helped to defeat the Hispanic front-runners for two local offices in a 1997 election. One of the white, non-Hispanic victors allegedly had been a member of the Ku Klux Klan.

Most of the 800 absentee ballots were cast by white military members and their dependents. About 2,900 of

Val Verde County's 42,000 residents live at a nearby air force base. Their votes, both absentee and regular, sometimes conflict with those of the area's Hispanic majority. Also, with eighteen military bases, Texas is popular as a place of residency because there is no state income tax and public college tuition is comparatively low. As permitted by the federal absentee voting law, many military families continue to claim Texas residency for voting and tax purposes long after they have been reassigned to other states or countries.

Permanent residents of Val Verde County complained that the federal law enabled "phantom voters" to thwart the will of the majority. One of the defeated candidates said that the loose residency requirement violated the Supreme Court's ONE-PERSON, ONE-VOTE principle. A federal district judge ruled, however, that the complainants failed to show that absentee ballots had diluted the Hispanic vote. He allowed D'Wayne Jernigan to be sworn in as the county's first Republican sheriff.

## Vote by Mail

Given the success of absentee voting and the dependability of the postal service, various groups have advocated vote-by-mail plans to encourage wider participation in the electoral process, which in the United States has been characterized by a VOTER TURNOUT much lower than in many other industrialized countries. In 1995 and 1996 the vote-by-mail concept was put to the test in two states, Nevada and Oregon, which conducted several elections entirely by mail.

The largest test took place in Oregon, which used mail-in votes to choose a successor to Republican senator Bob Packwood, who had resigned under allegations of sexual harassment. The winner was Democrat Ron Wyden, the first senator elected by mail.

For the SPECIAL ELECTION, both the primaries in 1995 and the general election in early 1996 were conducted by mail. Oregon officials were pleased with the "turnout"—about 57 percent of the eligible 1.8 million voters. The primaries to select contenders for the House seat vacated by Wyden also were conducted by mail, but the special election itself was a conventional voting-booth affair held in conjunction with the Oregon presidential primaries.

Oregon subsequently became the first state to decide to hold all elections by mail. In the 1998 MIDTERM ELECTIONS, Oregon voters approved Ballot Measure 60 requiring vote by mail in biennial primary and general elections. The measure eliminated polling places, but it did not affect current law allowing absentee ballots or voting at the elections office.

In Nevada the 1996 Republican presidential primary was held by mail-in vote. The party's eventual nominee, Robert J. Dole, won, but many votes had been mailed in before another leading candidate, Malcolm S. "Steve" Forbes Jr., dropped out of the race March 14.

A potential for abuse of the vote-by-mail system surfaced in Oregon when candidates were able to obtain from election officials the names of voters who had not yet returned their ballots. Critics said this information left voters open to undue solicitation or even harassment by candidates.

An argument against use of the mails to provide a longer voting period is that it could invite fraud, and indeed there have been instances where the number of votes cast in an election, including absentee ballots, exceeded the number of people living in the community. Another problem with mail-in votes is that duplicate or undelivered ballots could be cast by the wrong persons. But the chances of this particular fraud's being successful are reduced by the standard requirement that the voter's signature be on the envelope.

Proponents argue that the benefits of voting by mail—including convenience, speed, and lower costs—outweigh the disadvantages, including the lost sociability of gathering at the polls, the easing of the procedure to accommodate less civic-minded voters, and the possible abuse of the system.

Mail elections are estimated to cost one-third to one-half less than conventional elections. The U.S. Postal Service in promotional advertising has estimated that the cost of postal voting "can be as much as $1 million lower, because there are no polling personnel to pay, no space to rent, no polling equipment to transport and set up."

In an Oregon survey, 76.5 percent of those polled said they preferred voting by mail over going to a polling place. Women and older voters were strongest in favor of mail voting. Some 66 percent of Oregon's registered voters participated in the 1996 special senatorial election. The figure almost matched the turnout rate for the state's congressional races two years earlier. Although mail voting may be cheaper than a regular election, absentee voting in conjunction with a voting-booth election is more expensive per vote than the polling place balloting. Election officials estimate that absentee ballots require three to four times more labor to process.

Because absentee ballots are assumed to be ripe for fraud, election workers devote considerable time to ensuring that they are legitimate. When the ballot is received, a worker usually checks the name on the envelope to verify that the person is a qualified absentee voter and that the signatures match. The worker also must verify that the person has not already voted.

In many states the ballot may then be entered into a computer that counts it, but by law the ballot cannot actually be tabulated until after the polls close on election day. In contrast, the ballots marked in a voting booth are presumed to be authentic and are counted at the polling place or a central election station when the polls close. Mechanical or computerized VOTING MACHINES provide an immediate tally at each polling place.

Because many absentee voters mail or drop off their ballots at the last minute, election workers already may be swamped with regular returns when the last batches of time-consuming absentee ballots come in. The absentee ballots are usually set aside, sometimes by law, to be dealt with the day after the election—or as long as it takes to verify that they are not fraudulent. If the election is close, it may be days, weeks, or even months before the winner is known.

In California the absentee count may take a few days because of the sheer volume. In other states the process may take two weeks because election workers wait for all ballots postmarked on election day to arrive. In Washington State, for example, officials count qualified absentee ballots received as many as fifteen days after the election, provided the ballot was postmarked on or before election day. California and Oregon count only ballots received before the polls close at 8:00 p.m. on election day.

Postal voting is part of a larger trend since the 1980s toward easier voting, including steps to increase voter registration, such as the federal MOTOR VOTER ACT of 1993, which allows voters to sign up when they obtain or renew their driver's license. A few states such as Colorado, Texas, and Tennessee have experimented with opening voting-style booths before election day in stores or other public places. Most states, however, have simply made absentee ballots available to all, creating a hybrid system that proponents of postal mail decry as "the worst of both worlds," combining the labor-intensive costs of absentee voting with the equipment and location costs of voting booth elections.

More than twenty states have early voting options, with polling stations open as much as twenty-one days before the election. Citizens can use them to vote early without giving a reason, and their votes are counted on election day like regular ballots, causing no delays. Because of their growing numbers, early voters are being courted by candidates as never before. In 1998 California Democrat Lois Capps urged supporters to take advantage of the state's liberal absentee voting law. The eighteen thousand early absentee votes she received helped her to win a difficult race for reelection to the U.S. House.

## Absolute Majority

In electoral or legislative voting, an *absolute majority* is more than 50 percent of all those eligible to vote, regardless of how many actually voted. A *simple majority,* by contrast, consists of a majority of those voting, not of the whole eligible pool.

The U.S. Senate is often used as an example to illustrate these terms because it has exactly 100 members. Therefore an absolute majority of the Senate is fifty-one or more votes. But not all senators vote on every motion or bill. If only sixty-six senators vote on a bill, it passes if there are at least thirty-four "ayes," because that is more than half of the total vote. But it would be only 34 percent of the Senate membership and therefore not an absolute majority.

The same principle holds true in elections. To be elected president or vice president, a candidate must receive an absolute majority of the 538 votes in the ELECTORAL COLLEGE, or at least 270 votes.

Since 1964, when the total number of electoral votes first reached 538 (equal to the 535 members of Congress plus three votes for the DISTRICT OF COLUMBIA), the closest election in terms of electoral votes was the 1976 contest between Gerald R. Ford and Jimmy Carter, the winner with 297 votes or 55.2 percent to Ford's 240 votes or 44.6 percent. (One Republican elector cast his vote for Ronald Reagan instead of Ford.)

The most lopsided electoral vote victory in the same period was Reagan's in 1984, with 525 votes or 97.6 percent to Walter Mondale's 13 votes or 2.4 percent.

There have been three instances when no presidential candidate received the required electoral vote majority. In 1800 and 1824 the presidents were elected by the House of Representatives as provided by the Constitution. In 1876, when the electoral vote total was in dispute, a fifteen-member commission, consisting of five senators, five representatives, and five Supreme Court justices, decided the outcome. (See CONTESTED ELECTIONS; ELECTORAL COLLEGE AND VOTES; ZZZ.)

It is possible for a candidate to achieve an electoral vote majority by winning the right combination of states, while still receiving less than a majority of the POPULAR VOTE. As of the 1996 election there have been seventeen so-called minority presidents. (See table, page 133.)

An absolute majority of the popular vote technically would be 51 percent of the entire voting age population of U.S. citizens. That figure is difficult if not impossible to calculate, however, so the vote percentages of presidential candidates are usually based on their share of the total vote for president. On that basis candidates frequently exceed 50 percent, but that would not be an absolute majority of all those eligible. In 1996, for example, President Bill Clinton came close (49.2 percent)

to getting a majority of all 96.3 million votes cast for president. However, the estimated voting age population that year was 196.5 million. Clinton's 47.4 million votes therefore amounted to only 24.1 percent of the eligible vote—far short of the almost 100.0 million votes needed for an absolute majority.

Similarly, vote percentages for federal, state, and local offices are based on shares of the actual vote rather than on the eligible vote and therefore do not necessarily constitute an absolute majority even if they amount to more than half of the vote. In short, absolute majorities are practicable to calculate only in relatively small bodies where the membership is a fixed number.

---

## America First Party (1992– )

*See* PEOPLE'S PARTY–POPULISTS.

---

## American Independent Party (1968– ) and American Party (1972– )

Both the American Party and the American Independent Party descended from the American Independent Party that served as the vehicle for George C. Wallace's third party presidential candidacy in 1968.

Wallace, governor of Alabama (1963–1967; 1971–1979), burst onto the national scene in 1964 as a Democratic presidential candidate opposed to the 1964 Civil Rights Act. Entering three northern primaries—Wisconsin, Indiana, and Maryland—he surprised political observers by winning between 30 percent and 43 percent of the popular vote in these contests. His unexpectedly strong showing brought the term "white backlash" into the political vocabulary as a description of the racial undertone of the Wallace vote.

In 1968 Wallace broke with the Democrats and launched his second presidential bid under the American Independent Party label. His candidacy capitalized on the bitter reactions of millions of voters, especially whites and blue-collar workers, to the mid-1960s civil rights activism, urban riots, antiwar demonstrations,

*Third parties often signal the public's dissatisfaction with the two major parties. In 1968 Alabama governor George Wallace left the Democratic Party to form the American Independent Party. His supporters included blue-collar workers who were fed up with what they saw as the liberal ideology of the Democrats. Source: Congressional Quarterly*

and the heavy federal spending on "Great Society" programs by President Lyndon B. Johnson's administration. With the help of volunteer groups, Wallace was able to get on the ballot in all fifty states.

The former governor did not hold a convention for his party, but in October he announced his vice-presidential running mate—retired air force general Curtis LeMay—and released a platform. In the November election the Wallace ticket received 9,906,473 votes or 13.5 percent of the popular vote. Wallace and LeMay carried five southern states and won forty-six electoral

votes. The party's showing was the best by a third party since 1924, when Robert M. La Follette collected 16.6 percent of the vote on the Progressive Party ticket.

After his defeat in that election, Wallace returned to the Democratic Party, competing in Democratic presidential primaries in 1972 and 1976. Wallace's American Independent Party began to break into factions after the 1968 election but in 1972 united behind John G. Schmitz, a Republican U.S. representative from California (1970–1973), as its presidential nominee. Thomas J. Anderson, a farm magazine and syndicated news features publisher from Tennessee, was the party's vice-presidential candidate. In many states, the party shortened its name to American Party. In the November election, the Schmitz-Anderson ticket won 1,099,482 votes (1.4 percent of the popular vote) but failed to win any electoral votes.

In December 1972 a bitter fight occurred for the chairmanship of the American Independent Party between Anderson and William K. Shearer, the California chairman of the party. Anderson defeated Shearer, retaining control of the party but renaming it the American Party. Over the next four years, Shearer expanded his California-based group into a new national party. He had kept the name American Independent Party in California and made that the name of the new nationwide group.

By 1976 there were two distinct entities: the American Party headed by Anderson and the American Independent Party headed by Shearer.

The 1976 American Party convention was held in Salt Lake City, Utah, from June 17 to 20. Anderson was nominated for president and Rufus Shackleford of Florida for vice president.

The party's nomination of Anderson followed its failure to enlist a prominent conservative to lead the ticket. Both Gov. Meldrim Thomson Jr. of New Hampshire and Sen. Jesse Helms of North Carolina were approached, but both decided to remain in the Republican Party. With well-known conservatives declining the party's overtures, the convention turned to Anderson. He easily won the nomination on the first ballot by defeating six party workers.

Anderson's campaign stressed the "permanent principles" of the party, augmented by the 1976 platform. These principles included opposition to foreign aid, U.S. withdrawal from the United Nations, and an end to trade with or recognition of communist nations. The platform included planks opposing abortion, gun control, the Equal Rights Amendment, and government-sponsored health care and welfare programs. In general, the party favored limits on federal power and was against budget deficits except in wartime.

The American Party was on the ballot in eighteen states, including eight states where the American Independent Party also appeared. In seven of those eight states, Anderson ran ahead of the American Independent Party ticket. Anderson's strength was spread fairly evenly across the country. His best showings were in Utah (2.5 percent of the vote) and Montana (1.8 percent). He received more than 0.5 percent of the vote in Virginia (1.0), Mississippi (0.9), Minnesota (0.7) and Kentucky (0.7). Anderson's total of 160,773 popular votes (0.2 percent) placed him almost 10,000 votes behind the American Independent Party candidate nationally.

The American Independent Party convention met in Chicago, August 24–27, 1976, and chose former Georgia governor Lester Maddox (1967–1971), a Democrat, as its presidential nominee and former Madison, Wisconsin, mayor William Dyke, a Republican, as its vice-presidential candidate. Maddox won a first-ballot nomination over Dallas columnist Robert Morris and former representative John R. Rarick, a Democrat of Louisiana (1967–1975).

At the convention, a group of nationally prominent conservatives made a bid to take over the party and use it as a vehicle to build a new conservative coalition. Richard Viguerie, a fund raiser for Wallace and a nationally known direct mail expert, was the leader of the group. He was joined at the convention by two leading conservatives—William Rusher, publisher of the *National Review,* and Howard Phillips, the former head of the Office of Economic Opportunity (1973) and leader of the Conservative Caucus, an activist conservative group. Viguerie, Phillips, and Rusher all argued that the American Independent Party should be overhauled, changed from a fringe group to a philosophical home

for believers in free enterprise and traditional moral values. They also hoped they could attract Helms, Thomson, or Rep. Philip M. Crane, Republican of Illinois. When none of these men agreed to run on the American Independent Party ticket, Viguerie and his allies found themselves unable to promote Morris, a lesser-known substitute, successfully.

Many American Independent Party members favored Maddox because they saw him as a colorful personality, one capable of drawing media attention and perhaps of picking up the 5 percent of the national vote needed to qualify the party for federal funding. Maddox never came close to that goal, however, achieving only 0.2 percent of the national vote (170,531). It was 51,098 votes in California, where American Party nominee Anderson was not on the ballot, that enabled Maddox to run slightly ahead of Anderson nationally.

Despite the power struggle between Anderson and Shearer, there was little difference between their two party platforms. Like the American Party, the American Independent Party opposed abortion, gun control, forced busing, foreign aid, and membership in the United Nations.

By 1980 neither party was much of a force in American politics. Both retained the same basic platforms, but each was on the ballot in only a handful of states. The American Independent Party's nominee, former Democrat Rarick, ran in only eight states. Economist Percy L. Greaves Jr., the American Party candidate, was listed in just seven.

The American Independent Party did not field candidates in 1984, while the American Party placed Delmar Dennis, a book publisher from Pigeon Forge, Tennessee, on the ballot in six states.

Dennis also ran under the American Party banner in 1988 and, with his running mate, Earl Jeppson, received 3,475 votes. The American Independent Party did better with their candidates, presidential nominee James C. Griffin and vice-presidential nominee Charles J. Morsa, receiving 27,818 votes.

By 1992 the fortunes of both parties had dwindled. American Party presidential nominee Robert J. Smith and running mate Doris Feimer were on the ballot only in Utah, where they received 292 votes. The American

Independent Party did not appear on any presidential ballots.

---

## American Party–Know-Nothings (1856)

The American Party politicized the nativist, anti-immigrant movement in the mid-1850s, a peak period of European immigration to the United States in the pre–Civil War years. In the decade before the rise of a formal party, the movement took the form of local, secret organizations whose members were sworn to secrecy about their elaborate rituals. To questions about their affiliation, they pleaded ignorance. Hence, the party's popular name: the Know-Nothings.

Many of the millions of immigrants in the mid–nineteenth century were Catholic, and the Know-Nothings were hostile to Catholics. They advocated nominating only native-born American Protestants for political office and requiring a twenty-one-year waiting period before naturalization.

In addition to the great waves of immigrants, the party's meteoric rise was spurred by the increasing polarization of the Democrats and Whigs over the volatile slavery issue. The Know-Nothings benefited from the political situation and attracted members from both of the older parties. In the party's peak years 1854 and 1855, the Know-Nothings elected five U.S. senators, forty-three members of the House, and governors in California, Connecticut, Delaware, Kentucky, Massachusetts, New Hampshire, and Rhode Island.

But as a national party the Know-Nothings, like the Democrats and Whigs, eventually were split by the slavery issue. When a party convention in June 1855 adopted a pro-South position on slavery, antislavery elements bolted, dividing the party and setting the stage for its downfall.

The Know-Nothings held their first and only national nominating convention in February 1856 and selected as their candidate former Whig president Millard Fillmore (1850–1853). The antislavery wing of the party convened separately and endorsed the Republican nominee, John C. Fremont. Fillmore finished third in

*A sheet music cover for a quickstep dedicated to the "Know Nothings," dated 1854. Source: Library of Congress*

the three-way race, receiving 21.5 percent of the popular vote and carrying only one state, Maryland.

Within a year, the bulk of the northern Know-Nothings had joined the Republican Party. By the end of the decade, the party existed only in the BORDER STATES, where it formed the basis for the unsuccessful, antiwar CONSTITUTIONAL UNION PARTY.

---

## Anti-Federalists (1789–1796)

Never a formal party, the Anti-Federalists were a loosely organized group opposed to ratification of the Constitution. With the adoption of the Constitution in 1788, the Anti-Federalists served as the opposition to the Federalists in the early years of Congress.

Anti-Federalists were primarily rural, agrarian men from inland regions who favored individual freedom and states' rights, which they felt would be jeopardized by the new Constitution. After ratification, the efforts of the Anti-Federalists led to adoption of the first ten amendments, the Bill of Rights, which spelled out the major limitations of federal power.

As the opposition faction in Congress during the formative years of the Republic, the Anti-Federalists basically held to a strict interpretation of the Constitution, particularly in regard to the various economic proposals of Treasury Secretary Alexander Hamilton to centralize more power in the federal government.

Although never the majority faction in Congress, the Anti-Federalists were a forerunner of Thomas Jefferson's DEMOCRATIC-REPUBLICAN PARTY, which came into existence in the 1790s and dominated American politics for the first quarter of the nineteenth century.

## Anti-Masonic Party (1832–1836)

Born in the late 1820s in upstate New York, the Anti-Masonic Party focused the strong, anti-elitist mood of the period on a conspicuous symbol of privilege, the Masons. The Masons were a secret fraternal organization with membership drawn largely from the upper class. Conversely, the appeal of the Anti-Masonic movement was to the common man—poor farmers and laborers especially—who resented the secrecy and privilege of the Masons.

The spark that created the party came in 1826, when William Morgan, a dissident Mason from Batavia, New York, allegedly on the verge of exposing the inner workings of the order, mysteriously disappeared and never was seen again. Refusal of Masonic leaders to cooperate in the inconclusive investigation of Morgan's disappearance led to suspicions that Masons had kidnapped and murdered him and were suppressing the inquiry.

From 1828 through 1831, the new Anti-Masonic Party spread through New England and the Middle Atlantic states, in many places establishing itself as the primary opposition to the Democrats. In addition to its appeal to the working classes, particularly in northern rural areas, and its opposition to Masonry, the Anti-Masons displayed a fervor against immorality, as seen not only in secret societies but also in slavery, intemperance, and urban life.

In September 1831 the party held the first national nominating convention in American history. One hundred and sixteen delegates from thirteen states gathered in Baltimore, Maryland, and nominated former attorney general William Wirt of Maryland for the presidency. While Wirt received only 100,715 votes (7.8 percent of the popular vote) and carried only Vermont, the Anti-Masons did reasonably well at other levels, winning two governorships and fifty-three House seats.

But the decline of the Masons, especially in New York, where the number of lodges dropped from 507 in 1826 to 48 six years later, robbed the Anti-Masons of an emotional issue and hastened their decline. The 1832 election was the high point for the Anti-Masons as a national party. In the 1836 campaign the party endorsed Whig candidate William Henry Harrison. Subsequently, the bulk of the Anti-Masonic constituency moved into the WHIG PARTY.

## Apportionment

*See* REAPPORTIONMENT AND REDISTRICTING.

## At-Large

An official elected by an entire jurisdiction rather than a subdivision of it is said to be elected *at-large*. United States senators, two for each state, run statewide and therefore are elected at-large.

Most U.S. representatives, however, are elected from CONGRESSIONAL DISTRICTS that are smaller than an entire state and do not run at-large. The current exceptions are the representatives from the seven states that have only one House seat because of small populations. In their cases the entire state is the district. Those states are Alaska, Delaware, Montana, North Dakota, South Dakota, Vermont, and Wyoming.

The 435 seats in the U.S. House are apportioned on

the basis of population, but under the Constitution each state is entitled to at least one seat, making true PROPORTIONAL REPRESENTATION mathematically impossible. After each ten-year CENSUS the seats are redistributed and states that gain or lose seats must redraw the district lines to make each one as nearly equal in population as possible. (See REAPPORTIONMENT AND REDISTRICTING.)

For more than half a century after the founding of the country, several states had MULTIMEMBER DISTRICTS that elected more than one U.S. representative. Congress abolished the practice in 1842, however, and today all congressional districts are SINGLE-MEMBER DISTRICTS.

At-large elections are common at the local level, such as for city council seats. Within each state there are DISTRICTS, WARDS, AND PRECINCTS for election and voting purposes. Except for Nebraska, which has a UNICAMERAL legislature, each state has a senate and a house of representatives (or its equivalent, such as the Assembly in California, the House of Delegates in Virginia, and the General Assembly in New Jersey). For the election of almost 2,000 state senators and more than 5,400 representatives, the states are divided into districts much like congressional districts only smaller. Under the Supreme Court's BAKER V. CARR ruling in 1962, both houses of a state legislature must be apportioned according to population. In many states the house is twice as large as the senate, and a senate district may comprise two house districts. Unlike Congress, some state legislatures still have multimember districts.

City council districts are often known as wards. Frequently a city council will be made up of some members elected at-large and others elected by the ward he or she represents.

Racial and ethnic minorities tend to oppose at-large election because it makes them less likely to gain representation in the legislative body in question. A MAJORITY-MINORITY DISTRICT, for example, is likely to elect a member of the minority making up the majority if the voting is limited to district residents. But if the election is at-large, the minority's strength in a particular area is diluted by the votes of persons living outside the area.

## Australian Ballot

*See* BALLOT TYPES.

# B

## Baker v. Carr

The Supreme Court's decision in *Baker v. Carr* (1962) began a historic transformation of state legislatures throughout the country. The ruling, which dealt with a Tennessee case, established only the narrow principle that federal courts have jurisdiction to review claims of unconstitutional apportionment of legislative districts. Within two years, however, the Court laid down a sweeping constitutional rule—the ONE-PERSON, ONE-VOTE doctrine—that forced every state legislature in the country except one (Oregon) to redraw legislative districts and give urban and suburban dwellers a proportional voice in legislatures that had been dominated by rural interests because of improper REAPPORTION-MENT AND REDISTRICTING.

Tennessee's legislature had not reapportioned itself in sixty years despite a provision in the state constitution requiring that it be done every ten years. By the 1950s the population shift from the farms to the cities had produced dramatic disparities in the pattern of representation for seats in the Tennessee house and senate. Underrepresented urban dwellers tried but failed to get state courts to enforce the provision. They then filed suit in federal district court in 1959, alleging that the legislature's failure to reapportion itself violated their right to equal protection of the laws under the Fourteenth Amendment. Charles W. Baker, chairman of the Shelby County (Memphis) legislative body, was the lead plaintiff; Secretary of State Joe Carr was the first-named defendant.

The Supreme Court had ruled in a similar case in 1946 that federal courts had no jurisdiction over the "political question" of legislative reapportionment. Following the precedent in *Colegrove v. Green*, the federal

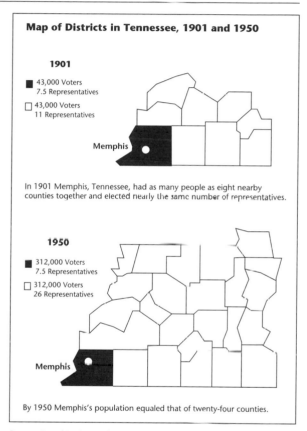

**Map of Districts in Tennessee, 1901 and 1950**

**1901**

■ 43,000 Voters
7.5 Representatives

☐ 43,000 Voters
11 Representatives

Memphis

In 1901 Memphis, Tennessee, had as many people as eight nearby counties together and elected nearly the same number of representatives.

**1950**

■ 312,000 Voters
7.5 Representatives

☐ 312,000 Voters
26 Representatives

Memphis

By 1950 Memphis's population equaled that of twenty-four counties.

Source: *Equal Justice Under Law* (Washington, D.C.: Foundation of the Federal Bar Association, 1965), 108.

district court in Nashville unanimously dismissed the suit. The Tennessee plaintiffs asked the Supreme Court to review the case and reconsider the precedent. The Justice Department, in a brief written by Solicitor General Archibald Cox, supported their plea.

The Court moved cautiously in scrapping the precedent. By a 6–2 vote it held that the plaintiffs' constitutional claims were "justiciable" despite the political-question doctrine. "The mere fact that the suit seeks protection of a political right does not mean it presents a political question," Justice William J. Brennan Jr. wrote in the March 26, 1962, decision. Brennan said the holding did not require the Court to address the merits of the plaintiffs' claim. Three justices—William O. Douglas, Tom C. Clark, and Potter Stewart—wrote concurring opinions. Clark said he would have granted relief to the plaintiffs but also said he would allow some "rational" departures from equal-population districts.

In a dissenting opinion, Justice Felix Frankfurter, who had written the opinion in *Colegrove,* decried the new decision. "There is not under our Constitution a judicial remedy for every political mischief," he wrote. Justice John Marshall Harlan, the second dissenter, called the ruling "an adventure in judicial experimentation."

Within a year, similar reapportionment suits were filed in thirty-six states. Years later, Chief Justice Earl Warren listed *Baker v. Carr* as the most important case decided by the Warren Court.

*Harry Browne, the 1996 Libertarian Party candidate for president, appears on a radio talk show. The Libertarian Party, founded in 1971, has fought hard to achieve and maintain ballot access and has run a candidate in every presidential election since 1972. Source: Reuters*

## Ballot Access

Being listed on the ballot is the basic first step in winning an election, but for THIRD PARTIES, getting on the ballot is not easy. Controversies over ballot access erupt constantly in the United States.

Under the U.S. TWO-PARTY SYSTEM, the Democratic and Republican Parties are ensured a place on the ballot in every partisan election for office. They also control the election bureaucracy in most jurisdictions and frequently resist the listing of splinter groups that could siphon votes from their candidates.

Since the advent of the BALLOT TYPE known as the secret or Australian ballot in the late 1800s, states rather than parties have compiled the official election ballots. This task is one of the major functions of the states in the elections process shared with the federal government. (See STATE AND FEDERAL ELECTION RESPONSIBILITIES.)

## Access Requirements

Ballot access rules vary from state to state, but all states have requirements to keep the ballot from becoming unwieldy and to discourage frivolous candidacies. Usually a third party or INDEPENDENT candidate must submit petitions with valid voters' signatures, which can range from as few as twenty-five in Tennessee to as many as 5 percent of the state's registered voters, which can run into several hundred thousands.

In Florida, for example, a third party or independent candidate for GOVERNOR needs petitions from 3 percent of the voters registered in the previous election, which for 1998 meant more than 242,000 signatures. Because many signatures are likely to be judged invalid, the candidate must obtain several thousand more than the minimum to ensure placement on the ballot. New parties must pay for the validation (ten cents per signature in Florida), which poses another hurdle to candidates outside of the major parties.

Florida is one of the states where reformers have tried for years to ease what they call "unfair and restrictive election laws." No independent candidate for governor of Florida has ever amassed the required number of signatures, according to the state's Fair Ballot Access Committee.

Third parties also complain that in many states they are forced to file too early, weeks or months before they know who their candidates will be. Some states require all parties to hold PRIMARIES to nominate candidates, which small third parties often are not prepared to do, especially early in the election year where the major parties have clustered their primaries. (See FRONT-LOADING.)

The states' right to require petitions for ballot access was upheld by the Supreme Court in *Jenness v. Fortson* (1971). The Court ruled that a state could require separate petitions for each candidate of a new party, with a maximum of signatures from 5 percent of the number of voters registered in the previous election for the office.

States also may specify how the signatures are gathered, such as a minimum percentage from each congressional district; signatures unacceptable from persons who voted in the major party primaries; no solicitation by persons living outside the district; signers required to pledge that they intend to vote for the new party; a limited time period for the signatures collection; or signers required to provide information they are not likely to know, such as their registration number or voting precinct designation.

Richard Winger, publisher of *Ballot Access News*, estimated in 1989 that about 640,000 signatures would be needed to get a new party's presidential candidate on the ballot in all fifty states. In 1992 supporters of independent Ross Perot obtained at least that many signatures to ensure his nationwide candidacy. On the strength of the vote he received in 1992, Perot automatically qualified for the ballot in most states as the Reform Party candidate in 1996. He also qualified for partial PUBLIC FINANCING of his campaign.

Some states require a third party presidential candidate to have a vice-presidential RUNNING MATE on the ballot. A candidate may have a different running mate in each of several states. Persons gathering petition signatures to get the slate on the ballot may not have time to wait until the head of the ticket decides on a national running mate. To meet the state's deadline they may circulate petitions listing a vice-presidential candidate different from the one listed on petitions in another state.

Despite their reserved slots on the ballot, the major parties do not always put up a candidate to fill the slot. In the 1996 elections, 32.7 percent of state legislative races did not have both a Democratic and Republican candidate. Republicans failed to field a candidate in 1,050 of the 5,958 scheduled contests. Democrats had no candidate in 897 races.

## Pressures for Liberalization

In the late 1990s, third parties were disheartened in their efforts to liberalize ballot access laws. They pointed to *Voter Choice '96,* a study by the Brennan Center for Justice at New York University School of Law, as evidence that ballot access had become more difficult in the past century.

Citing the study, the LIBERTARIAN PARTY said that "ballot access laws have doubled, tripled, or quadrupled in difficulty between 1889 and 1996." For example, it said, the petition period for ballot listing has been shortened, the number of signatures needed to get a presidential candidate on the ballot in every state has increased 250–500 percent since 1964, and to stay on the ballot a new party had to receive an average of 3 percent of the presidential vote, compared with 1 percent in 1892.

Although publisher Winger agreed that access laws have become harsher, his newsletter reported some easing in 1997, with bills introduced in seven states and moving closer to passage in seven other states. Changes under consideration included reducing the vote percentage needed to remain on the ballot; lengthening the period for gathering petition signatures; dropping the primary nomination requirement; allowing a new party to qualify before it chooses candidates; and opening petitions to signatures of voters not registered as independents. The Missouri Senate, however, heard arguments on a bill to tighten ballot access. Even Iraqi dictator Saddam Hussein could qualify under the existing law, the sponsor said. The U.S. TAXPAYERS and GREEN Parties testified against the bill.

The Brennan Center study rated the fifty states and the DISTRICT OF COLUMBIA on the difficulty of getting on the primary or general election ballots and their overall treatment of third parties. Failing grades were awarded to states that make it most difficult to get on the ballot. Hawaii, Missouri, Virginia, and Wyoming ranked lowest with "F" grades. Rated "D–" to "D+" were Alaska, Florida, Illinois, Indiana, Minnesota, Montana, New York, Pennsylvania, South Carolina, and Utah. States with "A" grades were Arkansas, Colorado, Kansas, Massachusetts, Mississippi, Tennessee, and Wisconsin.

In advance of the 1997 Virginia elections, writers of letters to the *Washington Post* complained that restrictive laws kept Libertarian, Reform, and other third party candidates off ballots in both Virginia and Maryland. The latter's house of delegates had recently killed a ballot access bill by one vote.

Other letter writers, however, defended the states' policy of keeping new parties off the ballot unless they showed proof of substantial support. One noted that the Libertarians, after qualifying as a party in Massachusetts, had only two candidates in 249 statewide 1996 primaries, putting the state to unnecessary expense. "Ballot access laws in some instances may be unfair," he wrote. "But they exist to ensure that the taxpayer's money and the state's time will not be wasted."

## Changes in Voting Technology

One rationale for the old ballot laws—excessive length—has lost some of its strength because of modern technology. In virtually all jurisdictions of the country, mechanical or computerized VOTING MACHINES have replaced paper ballots, which have inherent limitations on how many candidates or questions can be listed without overwhelming the voter. The machines can handle up to 540 candidates, and in some states the voter can vote a political party's STRAIGHT TICKET by pulling a single lever or marking a single block on a computer readable ballot.

The so-called short ballot gained popularity in the PROGRESSIVE era early in the twentieth century. Voters could make more intelligent choices, the reformers believed, if they had fewer candidates to consider. In the nineteenth century, exponents of Jacksonian democracy, who placed their faith in the common man, favored the long ballot, with many candidates, as a way to involve more people in public affairs.

## Ballot Types

When the first elections were held in Britain's North American colonies, English balloting customs prevailed. In some elections, the colonists cast written ballots. But because many voters could not read, the election official sometimes called for a voice vote or a show of hands. In other elections, voters would make their choice on an issue or candidate by throwing an object symbolic of their choice, for example, a kernel of corn for a yea, a dried bean for a nay, into a receptacle.

During the colonial period the most commonly used methods of voting appear to have been the voice vote or the show of hands. Although there is a record of another kind of ballot—the secret ballot—being used in 1634 by freemen to oust an unpopular English governor, its widespread use in American elections did not happen until more than two centuries later.

From the beginning of the revolutionary period to the early part of the nineteenth century, another method of balloting came into favor. In this system, an eligible voter would write the name of his choice or choices on a slip of paper and then pass it to an election judge who would then drop it in the ballot box.

The increasing growth and subsequent domination of political parties over the political process in the early and middle nineteenth century soon spelled changes in this style of balloting, however. Political operatives have been nothing if not clever over the years about using voting procedures to further their own and their party's interests. Illiteracy or the barest traces of literacy were commonplace in the early United States, and party leaders decided to make it easier for uneducated voters, whose ability to write was likely confined to their signature, and exceptionally useful for themselves. Party representatives would hand out preprinted lists of their party's nominees, which the individual voter could then turn over to the election judge for deposit in the ballot box. The illiterate voter was spared the laborious task of reading or writing out a long list of names (indeed, of reading or writing anything), and the party leader greatly aided his entire slate of nominees, enhancing the party's unity and political power.

Because the list of offices to be voted upon steadily increased through the nineteenth century, getting all the names printed entailed using long strips of paper that resembled the railroad tickets of the day. The list of a party's candidates for a specific election came to be called—and remains—the *ticket.*

The ticket system of voting was tailor-made for corruption and was soon riddled with it. Those who dispensed the ballots outside polling places, it was charged, could easily ensure that their chosen voters voted the way the leaders wanted. Because a voter had to choose a particular ticket before entering the polling place, the leaders or their operatives at the polling place made sure the voter entered with their ticket and no one else's. Intimidation of voters became rife, making a mockery of the democratic voting process. Choices, in short, could not be freely made and expressed; many voters were told how to vote, some were bribed, and others were intimidated, often by the threat or actual use of physical violence.

Any voting system that encouraged the growth of one party's domination of a state or city's political life was guaranteed efforts by that party to preserve it. Abuses, many in the election process, spawned widespread demands for reform down to the most fundamental element of an election—the ballot. The most important innovation introduced by this reform movement was the adoption in the United States of the so-called Australian ballot, which had first been used in South Australia in 1856. Joseph P. Harris, author of a definitive study of the American electoral system, defines the Australian ballot as "an official ballot, printed at public expense, by public officers, containing the names of all candidates duly nominated, and distributed at the polls by the election officers."

Besides ostensibly removing the elements that unduly favored one party over another in the preparation and distribution of earlier ballots, the Australian ballot carried the essential ingredient of secrecy; the voter would cast his ballot in secret and it would be counted in such a way that it was impossible to determine how the voter voted. With this kind of ballot came the shielded voting booth, followed by the VOTING MACHINE, so that the individual voter was free from prying eyes.

After the exceptionally close 1884 presidential election, replete with charges of vote fraud and fears of a deadlocked election, the winner, Grover Cleveland, campaigned hard for the reform measure that eventually became the Electoral Count Act. This measure gave each state final authority in determining the legality of its choice of electors. After its passage, the secret ballot movement gained momentum across the country. The Australian ballot was first adopted by Kentucky in 1888 and soon was in place in all the states except South Carolina, which did not adopt it until 1950.

The Australian ballot form is used in all elections in all states now; and, although the actual forms of the ballot may change considerably from state to state, they must by law fit into one of five major categories. Even with the advent of computerized voting, the electronic ballot form still must conform to these basic types:

• Party Column. In this form, all the candidates of a particular political party are listed in a vertical column. The party lists are arranged side by side and a single vertical column at the left margin displays the office being contested. In this way, the names of all candidates for any particular office are next to each other in a horizontal line that runs across the ballot. This form of ballot, some critics say, encourages "straight-ticket" voting. (See SPLIT- AND STRAIGHT-TICKET VOTING.)

• Office Group. The candidates of all parties running for a particular office are listed in a vertical column with the office being contested listed at the top of the column. This form of ballot was adopted to discourage straight-ticket voting by forcing the voter to read each name for each office and, it was hoped, reflect further on a candidate's individual merit before marking the ballot.

• Party Circle. A political party, on this kind of ballot, will have a circle or box printed at the top of its list of candidates and the voter, by making a mark in the box, signifies that he or she is voting for the party's ticket. In a variation, voters must make a mark next to the name of every individual candidate of his chosen party to vote a straight ticket. Yet another version was called the Massachusetts Plan. In this type, all the names of candidates of all parties for each office are placed in alphabetical order under a heading bearing the name of the office. The voter must then make a mark next to each of his or her choices.

• Party Emblem. Several states allow the printing of some kind of party emblem (the Democrats' donkey, the Republicans' elephant, for example) at either the head of a party's column of candidates or next to the name of each of its candidates. This makes identification of a nominee's party affiliation more obvious to the less-literate voter. Many states do not allow emblems, but some will permit a candidate's party affiliation to be printed under his or her name, particularly when a large number of parties contest a given election.

• Write In. Every state now offers the WRITE-IN VOTE—a means of voting for a candidate not listed on the ballot. Some candidates are left off because they decided to run after the deadline for inclusion on the ballot had passed. In most voting jurisdictions, the ballot has a blank space at the bottom of the list of candidates for a particular office where the voter can write in a name. Some states allow the pasting on of a preprinted label bearing the candidate's name in this space, but this is less common. States that did not permit write-ins or paste-ons were referred to as having "no-Johnny-come-lately" ballots.

Many ballots today also include INITIATIVE, REFERENDUM, REMOVAL FROM OFFICE, and bond-issue questions that require voter approval by a simple "yes" or "no," usually in the form of a check mark. Given the complexity of some of these questions, which are usually couched in formal, legislative language, most initiative or referendum ballots add an "explanatory or interpretive statement" to aid voters in making a fully informed choice.

The style of any state's ballot is set by that state's election laws, those statutes agreed upon by its legislators to impose upon all those involved in the actual election process a firm set of rules and procedures that will leave virtually no room for deviation, whether through chance or an individual election official's discretionary choice. The implementation and oversight of the state's election laws are delegated to a state board of elections, the state's GOVERNOR, or, the most common arrangement, the secretary of state, who also serves as the chief election officer. In voting analyst Harris's definition, the chief election officer "publishes the election laws, receives the official returns and usually tabulates the results for the official CANVASSING BOARD, certifies to the county officers in charge of printing the ballots the names of candidates for state office, certifies the form of the ballot and the working of referendum propositions, and attends to various other clerical details in connection with state elections."

At the next level down, most states' election laws require local officials, such as the county clerk, board of supervisors, or the mayor and city council, to supervise officials of a specific voting district, be it a county or a city. At the lowest level are the only election officials most voters ever see—those present at their particular voting place on ELECTION DAY. Here is where the voters lists and district registers are used to ascertain their eligibility and where the ballots, in whatever form, are cast, counted, and certified. In case of a RECOUNT or CONTESTED ELECTION, further counting and certification takes place later at the election board headquarters, where ABSENTEE VOTING ballots are also counted.

Even though most state laws require these voting-district boards to be nonpartisan, in most jurisdictions the party in the majority gets the majority of positions on the board, which can lead, in some cases, to partisanship or to somewhat less benign treatment of voters from the minority parties. Therefore, the officials that run the actual voting districts, writes Harris, "determine the character of elections."

## Bandwagon Effect

The phrase *bandwagon effect* is used to describe the attraction that successful campaigns have for voters, particularly those who may be undecided as ELECTION DAY nears. If a popular candidate seems to be rolling along to victory, people may "hop on the bandwagon" to be on the winning side.

The term derives from the spectacle of the old-time circus bandwagon coming down Main Street, blaring joyous music and tempting young boys to climb aboard. Indeed, the word *bandwagon* still conjures up visions of bright colors, balloons, and celebration.

POLITICAL CONSULTANTS and campaign managers try to cultivate an image of a confident and happy campaign, even if POLLING shows that their candidate is headed for defeat. They play on voter psychology, knowing that people hesitate to waste votes on a losing cause.

For that reason the bandwagon effect is a serious element in the controversy over the news media's FORECASTING ELECTION RESULTS while the polls are still open in some parts of the country or in parts of a state where a close statewide race is being decided. Some voters, hearing that their candidate is winning, may rush to the polls to be on the bandwagon. Others may stay home thinking the race is over.

Such forecasts are based on EXIT POLLS that have proven highly accurate. In one of their first uses, on election day in 1980, exit polls indicated that Ronald Reagan would defeat incumbent president Jimmy Carter, prompting Carter to concede while polls were

*Candidates and their campaign managers try to orchestrate public appearances that will put the candidate in a favorable light. Richard Nixon appears the hero in this 1968 campaign photo. Source: National Archives*

still open in the West. The bandwagon effect is thought to have caused some western Democratic voters to stay home.

Throughout the campaign, Reagan had projected an image of confidence and optimism, while Carter was dogged by foreign and domestic problems and the memory of his defeatist "malaise" speech. Reagan's CAMPAIGN STRATEGY clearly took advantage of the bandwagon effect.

The Reagan LANDSLIDE also had a related COAT-TAILS effect as Republicans gained seats in the House and won control of the Senate for the first time in twenty-eight years.

## Beauty Contest

A *beauty contest* presidential preference PRIMARY is a sort of popularity STRAW VOTE. It does not affect the allocation of delegates to the Democratic or Republican NATIONAL PARTY CONVENTIONS. (See PRIMARY TYPES.)

Few states still use beauty contest primaries. Of the forty-three Republican presidential primaries held in 1996 (when President Bill Clinton was unopposed for the Democratic nomination) only those in Illinois, Nebraska, Pennsylvania, and West Virginia could be considered the beauty contest type. All four had DIRECT ELECTION of delegates and a nonbinding statewide vote for expressing preference among candidates for the GOP nomination.

Oregon originated the beauty contest primary in 1910, nine years after Florida passed the first presidential primary law. Oregon's was the first in which voters expressed preference for the candidates themselves, rather than for the delegates. The delegates, however, were legally bound to vote for the candidates in accordance with the beauty contest results.

*Gen. Dwight D. Eisenhower, shown here conferring with paratroops prior to the Normandy invasion, was courted by both major parties, despite his initial reluctance to enter politics.*
Source: Courtesy Dwight D. Eisenhower Library

The first-in-the-nation NEW HAMPSHIRE PRIMARY, then a beauty-contest-type vote, attracted national attention in 1952 when World War II general Dwight D. Eisenhower outpolled the leading candidate for the Republican nomination, Sen. Robert Taft of Ohio. Eisenhower's name had been placed on the ballot by Sen. Henry Cabot Lodge of Massachusetts, leader of the "Draft Eisenhower" movement. "Ike" went on to win the nomination and the presidency.

The same year in New Hampshire's Democratic beauty contest, Sen. Estes Kefauver of Tennessee scored a surprise victory over President Harry S. Truman, who later said he had decided before the primary not to seek reelection. The Democratic convention ultimately nominated former governor Adlai E. Stevenson of Illinois, who lost to Eisenhower in the November election.

Since 1952 the New Hampshire primary, no longer a beauty contest, has grown in importance as a crucial first step for presidential aspirants. New Hampshire del-egates of both parties are now divided among the candidates by PROPORTIONAL REPRESENTATION, with each receiving the number reflecting his or her share of the primary vote.

## Bellwether

In politics a *bellwether* is a candidate or place that indicates the likely outcome of an election. It takes its name from shepherds' practice of putting a bell on the lead male sheep to signal which way the flock is heading.

For years Maine enjoyed a reputation as the bellwether in presidential elections. From 1860 to 1932 it voted for the winning candidate in all but three of the nineteen elections, prompting the saying, "As Maine goes, so goes the nation." But that reputation came crashing down in 1936 when Vermont was the only oth-

*Maine lost its reputation as a bellwether in 1936, when it and Vermont were the only states to back Republican nominee Alfred M. Landon.*
Source: Library of Congress

er state that voted for Alfred M. Landon instead of the LANDSLIDE winner, President Franklin D. Roosevelt. "As Maine goes, so goes Vermont," quipped Democratic chairman James A. Farley.

In their book *Forecasting Elections* political scientists Michael S. Lewis-Beck and Tom W. Rice list other states or counties that election watchers regard as bellwethers. Among them is New Mexico, which from 1912 (when it became a state) through 1996 voted only once (1976) for the losing presidential candidate. Another is Delaware, perfect in its predictions from 1964 through 1996. The large states such as California, New York, and Illinois also are frequent predictors of the national preference.

Among counties favored by election forecasters are Crook, Oregon; Laramie, Wyoming; and Palo Alto, Iowa. All three chose the presidential winner correctly from 1916 to 1972. Since then, however, all were wrong in at least one presidential contest through 1996.

Bellwether candidates vary from election to election. Particularly in MIDTERM or off-year elections, journalists and other forecasters will pick a candidate or group of candidates to watch as possible indicators of how other candidates of the same party will fare in the next election.

*Roger Sherman was the most prominent of Connecticut's representatives to the Constitutional Convention of 1787. His delegation presented the outline of "the Great Compromise," which broke the deadlock over representation between large and small states. Source: Library of Congress*

## Bicameral

The U.S. Congress, like the legislatures of every state except Nebraska, is *bicameral*. It consists of two chambers, the Senate and the House of Representatives. A UNICAMERAL legislature has but one house.

When the Constitution was being drafted at Philadelphia in 1787, the founders agreed from the outset that Congress, which they designed to be the heart of the Republic, would be bicameral. They disagreed, however, on how the members of each chamber would be elected. Their debate on the question helps to explain why they favored a two-house lawmaking body rather than a single-house body.

Precedence was one factor. The founders were familiar with bicameralism in the British Parliament, most of the colonial governments, and ten of the thirteen states.

(The remaining three original states eventually converted to bicameral legislatures.)

As Virginia delegate George Mason put it during the Constitutional Convention, the minds of Americans were settled on two points: "an attachment to republican government [and] an attachment to more than one branch in the Legislature." (See REPUBLICAN GOVERNMENT.)

With two branches or houses to the legislature, the delegates were able to resolve a dispute that threatened to break up the convention and the effort to frame a new government. It concerned the fears of small states that they would be dominated by the larger states if seats in both chambers were apportioned according to population, as proposed for the House. The solution, known as the Great Compromise or Connecticut Compromise, was to give each state two senators regardless of population. Even the smallest state was also assured at least one representative.

Convention delegates who were suspicious of a national government preferred election to the House of Representatives by the state legislatures. "The people immediately should have as little to do" with electing the government as possible, said Roger Sherman of Connecticut, because "they want [lack] information and are constantly liable to be misled."

The majority, however, twice defeated election by the legislatures. Popular election for the House was agreed to with only one state dissenting. The government "ought to possess . . . the mind or sense of the people at large," said Pennsylvania delegate James Wilson.

There was little support for the view that the people also should elect the Senate. Nor did the delegates think that the House should choose members of the Senate from among persons nominated by the state legislatures. Election of the Senate by the state legislatures was agreed to with only two states dissenting. DIRECT ELECTION of senators did not become the rule in every state until ratification of the Seventeenth Amendment in 1913.

The lower houses of the state legislatures served as models for the U.S. House. At the time, all the states had at least one chamber elected by popular vote. The three unicameral legislatures—in Georgia, Pennsylvania, and Vermont—also were popularly elected.

The founders intended the Senate to be a restraining influence on the House, and the Senate still claims to be the more deliberative body. George Washington is said to have called the Senate "the saucer where the political passions of the nation are cooled."

## Bilingual Voters

The federal VOTING RIGHTS ACT of 1965, which guaranteed the vote to racial minorities, also protected the rights of millions of bilingual Americans. The act made it illegal to deny the vote to citizens merely because they cannot read or write English, which necessitated the printing of bilingual ballots in areas with heavy concentrations of non–English-speaking people.

Citizens of Hispanic origin make up the largest such group nationally. According to CENSUS Bureau figures, the United States had 18.4 million Hispanics of voting age in 1996. In counties where they numbered ten thousand or more, election officials were required to provide ballots and voting assistance in both Spanish and English. Similar bilingual services were required where Asian and other language minorities met the threshold number.

Hispanics, who may be of any race, were concentrated mostly in the West (45.2 percent) and the South (30.3 percent). The Asian and Pacific Islands population (7.3 million in 1990) lived mostly in the West (55.7 percent) and the Northeast (18.4 percent).

Mexican Americans were the largest Hispanic component (13.3 million), followed by those of Puerto Rican origin (2.7 million). Chinese accounted for the largest Asian segment (1.6 million), followed by Filipino (1.4 million) and Japanese (0.8 million).

Within the 1996 voting age population, 30.0 percent of Hispanics were registered to vote, but only 26.7 percent reported having voted—the lowest VOTER TURNOUT among three racial or ethnic categories cited by the Census Bureau. The other two categories were whites, 56.0 percent, and blacks, 50.6 percent.

The language barrier is part of the reason for Hispanics' lower rate of political participation. Another possible factor is age. Mexican American and Puerto Rican groups have relatively large proportions of young people, who are less likely to vote or otherwise take part in politics.

Asian American participation rates vary by nationality. Chinese Americans, for example, participate at about the same rate as whites. But Japanese, Korean, and Filipino Americans have lower participation rates.

There were indications in the late 1990s that bilingual groups—particularly Hispanics—were becoming more active politically. Reasons included federally mandated changes making it easier to register and vote, and ballot INITIATIVES AND REFERENDUMS directly affecting bilingual voters.

## Effect of Federal Laws

The 1965 Voting Rights Act banned LITERACY TESTS for voting. It also stipulated that a citizen could not be denied the vote because of inability to read or write English, if he or she had successfully completed the sixth grade (or the equivalent depending on state requirements) in a school under the American flag conducted in a language other than English.

In *Katzenbach v. Morgan* (1966) the Supreme Court upheld the provision on accredited American flag schools. It was intended to enfranchise Puerto Ricans educated in such schools, living in the United States, but unable to demonstrate literacy in English.

In 1975 Congress extended the act for seven years and expanded the bilingual provisions. Additional protection was given to persons of Spanish heritage, Asian Americans, and Alaska natives. Federal preclearance of state election law changes was required in any jurisdiction where the Census Bureau had determined the following: more than 5 percent of the voting age citizens were of a single language minority; election materials had been printed only in English for the 1972 presidential election; or fewer than 50 percent of the voting age citizens had registered or voted in the 1972 presidential election.

In 1982 Congress extended the bilingual election provisions to 1992 and the rest of the act to 2007. Ten years later the bilingual requirements also were renewed to 2007. The amendment required that bilingual services be provided in jurisdictions with ten thousand or more non–English speakers, even if they did not make up 5 percent of the population. Among the first to be affected were several counties in the Los Angeles, San Francisco, Chicago, and Philadelphia areas.

The 1993 MOTOR VOTER ACT, enabling citizens to register to vote while obtaining a driver's license, greatly expanded the VOTER REGISTRATION rolls all across the country, including sections where many voters had limited proficiency in English. Affected communities had to recruit and train bilingual poll workers. In some ju-

risdictions outmoded voting systems proved to be inadequate to handle the added requirements.

Santa Clara County, California, for example, had to provide ballots in Vietnamese and Chinese. It also had to seek a replacement for its aged punch-hole system "because the length of the ballot and the use of bilingual ballots has made the continued use of Votomatic impossible." At the same time, the county was leading efforts to register new citizens at naturalization centers. One side effect of immigration and the federal legislation was a quadrupling of the number of Hispanic members of Congress. From 1877 to 1967 there had been no more than four Hispanic members at any one time, and for most Congresses in that period there were none or one or two. After 1967 the number increased gradually, reaching eighteen in the 106th Congress (1999–2001), all in the House (fifteen Democrats, three Republicans).

After the 1990 Census twenty congressional districts in six states (Arizona, California, Florida, Illinois, New York, and Texas) had Hispanic American majorities. Two districts, both in Hawaii, had Asian American majorities.

By 1994 there were 5,459 Hispanic elected public officials, in federal, state, and local governments.

## Growing Involvement

Immigration from Latin America and Asia was changing the POLITICAL CULTURE of the United States, particularly in the West. The Census Bureau projected that by 2015 or 2020 non–Hispanic whites would be a minority in California.

The increasing role of Hispanics and Asians in California politics was intertwined with a debate in 1998 over the future of bilingual education in the state, as well as the after-effect of two earlier ballot propositions that curtailed benefits to minorities. About 30 percent of California's 1.4 million limited-English students were receiving bilingual instruction.

Software maker Ron Unz, sponsor of Proposition 227 to limit bilingual education to one year, challenged Gov. Pete Wilson in the 1994 Republican primary and disagreed with Wilson's anti-immigration views. The split posed a dilemma for the California Republican Party because polls showed surprising support for Unz's proposal in the mostly Democratic Hispanic community.

In the June 1998 election, however, EXIT POLLS indicated that less than 40 percent of Hispanics voted for Proposition 227, which passed easily with 61 percent of the statewide vote. The result was expected to have repercussions all across the country, where some 3 million students were receiving bilingual education. In California's gubernatorial election the following November, Hispanic voters overwhelmingly supported Democrat Gray Davis in his defeat of Wilson's lieutenant governor, Dan Lundgren.

Because Hispanic voters were divided over whether bilingual education helped or hindered their children, the vote did little to clarify the political risks of cutting programs intended to benefit language minorities. A few years earlier that was not the case. Hispanic groups reacted angrily in 1994 when California voters approved Proposition 187, which denied educational and medical benefits to illegal immigrants, and in 1996 when they passed Proposition 209 to curtail affirmative action in combating discrimination.

In backlash against those propositions and eagerness to be heard on the bilingual education proposal, Hispanics showed stronger interest in the political process. Mexican immigrants were applying for citizenship at record rates. The Hispanic turnout in the 1996 presidential election was higher than that for the state's voters as a whole. In the 1998 MIDTERM ELECTIONS, about 5 percent of voters were Hispanics, a record-high proportion.

Although Cuban Americans, who abound in Florida, are strongly anticommunist and tend to be Republicans, Mexican Americans in the West and Southwest are mostly Democratic in their PARTY IDENTIFICATION. They were further alienated from the Republican Party in California by the approval of the proposition denying benefits to illegal immigrants and limiting affirmative action programs.

In advance of the 2000 presidential election, however, Republican leaders were trying to reach out to the Hispanic community. House Speaker Newt Gingrich, for example, spoke Spanish in 1998 at a Cinco de Mayo observance in New Mexico celebrating Mexico's defeat of French invaders on May 5, 1862. Appearing on a platform with a harsh critic of GOP policies toward Hispanics, Gingrich endorsed legislation that would allow descendants of former Mexican citizens to make claims for New Mexican land that the United States seized after the Mexican-American War of 1848.

Earlier, Texas's Republican governor George W. Bush, popular with Hispanics in his state and a possible presidential contender in 2000, visited the Mexican site of the Cinco de Mayo victory. By contrast Democratic president Bill Clinton, mindful of offending the French, pointedly avoided Cinco de Mayo events during a 1997 trip to Mexico.

In another development of special concern to Hispanic voters, Clinton supported a bill to allow Puerto Rico to vote on whether it wants to become the fifty-first state, remain a commonwealth, or choose independence. In March 1998 the Republican-controlled House narrowly approved the bill, subject to further congressional action. First, the House defeated a Republican amendment to make English the official language of the United States, including Puerto Rico if it chose statehood. Both English and Spanish were official languages in the commonwealth.

The Senate did not pass the bill, but it adopted a nonbinding resolution supporting Puerto Rico's decision to hold a referendum on the three options for its future status. On December 13, 1998, Puerto Ricans rejected both statehood and independence. They voted decisively for "none of the above," which in effect retained the status quo even though few voters specifically voted for the commonwealth option on the ballot. The statehood option placed second.

## Black Suffrage

The struggle of blacks for full voting rights in the United States is almost as old as the country itself. For the most part, the struggle ended in 1965 with passage of the historic VOTING RIGHTS ACT. Yet there are still instances where impediments are placed in the way of African Americans' RIGHT TO VOTE.

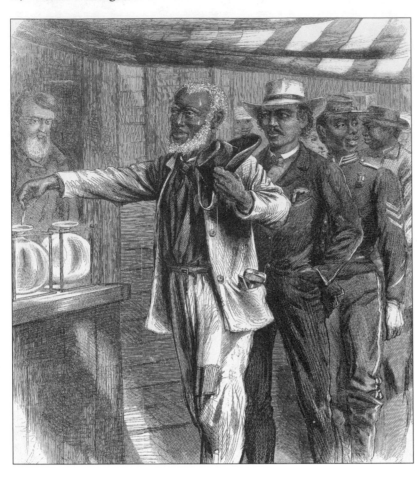

*Blacks, including a Union soldier, are depicted casting their first ballots in an image published November 16, 1867. In fact, it would take about a hundred years to secure voting rights for African Americans.* Source: Library of Congress

In the early days of the Republic, voting was restricted to adult white males, but only about half of them were eligible to vote. States required ownership of property or payment of taxes, which excluded poor white men. Slaves, Indians, and women could not vote. By the early twentieth century most of the ineligible groups had broken down their barriers to the franchise. But voting discrimination against African Americans was the last to be rectified. (See DIRECT ELECTION; WOMEN'S SUFFRAGE.)

The U.S. Constitution sanctioned slavery. The constitutional provision that declared a black person to be three-fifths a person for CENSUS considerations was the ugly codification of what many early Americans considered blacks to be: property. In *Scott v. Sandford* (1857),

popularly known as the *Dred Scott Case*, the Supreme Court confirmed this notion, holding that slaves were property, not included under the word *citizen* in the Constitution, and therefore unable to claim any of the rights and privileges of many white Americans.

Although a tiny fraction of free blacks in the northern states had some voting rights at the beginning of the nineteenth century, they were the exception. In 1861, when the Civil War broke out, twenty seven of the thirty-three states prohibited blacks from voting. Before World War II began, only about 150,000 blacks in the South, or about 3 percent of the estimated population of 5 million blacks of voting age in that region, were registered to vote.

## Slavery and the Civil War

The Civil War was not fought only about slavery, as many popular versions of American history suggest, but also over the issues of states' rights and the North-South balance of power in national politics. When President Abraham Lincoln issued the Emancipation Proclamation on January 1, 1863, it granted freedom to slaves in states fighting the Union. Although the proclamation was questionable legally, and was motivated partly by a hope to enlist blacks as Union soldiers, it led to the extension of the long-denied vote to blacks. Lincoln had openly expressed the desire to move slowly and cautiously on the inclusion of including blacks in the democratic process, however, saying he wished to give priority to "very intelligent" blacks and to blacks who had fought on the Union side.

Black suffrage after the Civil War was seen primarily as a system for the Radical Republicans to control Congress by permanently negating the disproportionate political power of the southern planters. In many southern states, "black codes" had been passed that effectively prohibited blacks from voting and holding office. The Radical Republicans in Congress after the war's end responded to these codes by passing a number of measures to bring blacks into political life, the most important of which was the Reconstruction Act of 1867. The act set up military governments in the states of the Confederacy and tied their readmission to the Union to passage of the Fourteenth Amendment.

Many scholars believe that after the Bill of Rights, the Fourteenth Amendment is the most important addition to the Constitution. The amendment, particularly after expanded interpretations by the Supreme Court in the twentieth century, bans *states* from limiting the "privileges and immunities" of American citizens and orders *states* to respect all citizens' rights to "due process" and "equal protection of the laws." The provisions contained in the Bill of Rights deal with the relationship between a citizen and the federal government, and it took many years before these provisions were made applicable to the states. The Fourteenth Amendment, ratified in 1868, reduces the representation in Congress of states that deny the franchise to any male over twenty-one, a pun-

ishment that has never been carried out. The Fifteenth Amendment, which grants the franchise to all adult males regardless of race or "previous condition of servitude," was passed the following year.

The addition of blacks to the American electorate was a crucial factor in Ulysses S. Grant's slim 300,000-vote margin of victory in the 1868 presidential election, a year in which blacks first won election to state and federal offices as federal troops with ties to the Republican Party enforced their voting rights in the former Confederate states. Between 1870 and 1900, twenty-two southern blacks won election to Congress, and two black Republicans from Mississippi served in the U.S. Senate. (See HOUSE OF REPRESENTATIVES, QUALIFICATIONS; SENATE, QUALIFICATIONS.)

## "Jim Crow" Laws

Between 1858 and 1876, the Republican congressional majority had grown substantially with the addition of seven new northern states. The party also twice benefited from congressional REAPPORTIONMENT. No longer fearful that the "King Cotton" planters would obstruct them, the Republicans abandoned Reconstruction; as part of the political deal that gave the disputed 1876 presidential election to Republican Rutherford B. Hayes, the Republicans agreed to remove federal troops from the South and to allow southern states to enact measures that restricted blacks' ability to participate in politics and the full life of the community. Without federal protection, black voters virtually disappeared.

The states of the old Confederacy kept blacks from voting with an arsenal of racially discriminatory measures known as "Jim Crow" laws. Among these were POLL TAXES, LITERACY TESTS, property requirements, tests of morality, and GRANDFATHER CLAUSES, which exempted poor whites from the measures by guaranteeing the vote to citizens whose ancestors had voted or had served in the state militia.

Another device was the WHITE PRIMARY, which allowed the politically dominant Democratic Party to exclude blacks with the twisted legal argument that the party was a private organization and therefore not covered by the Fourteenth Amendment. Because most blacks who had voted counted themselves as Republicans, most whites were Democrats. Given the measures that kept blacks from the polls and the growing threat of violence for those few who could survive the various barriers and dare to vote, the Democratic SOUTHERN PRIMARY became the region's important election. In the 1944 Supreme Court case, *Smith v. Allwright,* white primaries were struck down in an interpretation that seemed sufficiently broad to forestall any evasion. The marginally increased black participation in southern Democratic primaries, however, did not seriously challenge white political control for another twenty years. Political scientist V. O. Key Jr. estimated that between 400,000 and 600,000 blacks in eleven southern states voted in 1946, only 10 percent to 12 percent of the total population of adult blacks in the region.

In response to the wide range of VOTER REGISTRATION requirements that restricted ballot access to blacks and vulnerable whites, such as illiterates, the total vote in southern states dropped by as much as 60 percent between 1884 and 1904.

## Assault on Voting Discrimination

In the twentieth century, Congress and the federal courts mounted a sustained assault against voting discrimination against blacks. In 1915 the Supreme Court, in *Guinn v. United States,* ruled the grandfather clause unconstitutional. The white primary fell in 1944, and the Court, in the 1966 decision *Harper v. Virginia Board of Elections,* declared state poll tax requirements for voting in state elections unconstitutional.

The CIVIL RIGHTS ACT of 1957 established the Civil Rights Commission, which was empowered to study voter discrimination. The act also greatly expanded the attorney general's power to bring federal lawsuits against anyone restricting blacks' right to vote. A 1960 law gave the Justice Department the power to bring further legal action in cases that disclosed patterns of discrimination. It also authorized the appointment of federal officials to monitor elections. The 1964 Civil Rights Act required states to adopt uniform election procedures for all citizens, mandated that states show sufficient cause for rejecting voters who had completed the

sixth grade or demonstrated an equivalent level of intellectual competence, and made the procedures for federal consideration of voting rights cases easier. Also in 1964 the ratification of the Twenty-fourth Amendment banned the use of the poll tax in federal elections.

In 1965 passage of the sweeping Voting Rights Act suspended literacy tests in seven southern states and parts of one other. It also required federal supervision of voter registration in all states and counties that on November 1, 1964, still had literacy tests or other qualifying examinations and where less than 50 percent of all voting-age citizens had voted in the 1964 presidential election. Jurisdictions under federal supervision henceforth needed Washington's approval for any changes in election procedures. This act alone added an estimated 1 million blacks to the voting rolls.

A 1970 amendment to the Voting Rights Act suspended all literacy tests for five years, whether they were discriminatory or not. Later that year, the Supreme Court upheld the law's constitutionality, and the tests were abolished permanently in 1975. Further, the "trigger" for federal involvement was applied to additional states and jurisdictions by amendments passed in 1970, 1975, and 1982. The 1982 law extended for an additional twenty-five years the provisions requiring nine states and parts of thirteen others to seek Washington's approval for election law changes.

The 1982 amendments to the 1965 Voting Rights Act also allowed states to create MAJORITY-MINORITY legislative districts by concentrating black and Hispanic voters. The Republican Party and the National Association for the Advancement of Colored People (NAACP) became unlikely allies against the measure. Each had favored a different solution. The NAACP wanted creation of guaranteed minority seats, while the Republicans favored separating black voting power from adjacent districts.

Proponents of this so-called stacking of voters noted that minorities were underrepresented in Congress and state legislatures because whites tended to vote against minority candidates. But in the 1993 *SHAW V. RENO* decision, the Supreme Court ruled that such districts could be so "bizarre" in shape that they could be considered unconstitutional RACIAL REDISTRICTING or GERRYMANDERING. Striking down three districts in Texas and one in North Carolina as unconstitutional, the Court ruled in *Bush v. Vera* (1996) that the districts were drawn with race as the overwhelming factor.

At the end of the twentieth century, therefore, disputes remained over methods to give blacks the full power associated with the right to vote and over sporadic but persistent attempts to dilute that power through loopholes in the great body of black suffrage laws. In almost all these battles, the federal courts consistently reinforced black citizens' essential right to vote.

## Blanket Primary

*See* PRIMARY TYPES.

## Blue Dog Democrat

After the Republican Party took control of the U.S. House in 1994, twenty-one conservative Democrats formed a group that allied itself with the moderate Republicans. They called themselves the *Blue Dog Coalition.* The name was a variant of the southern expression "yellow dog Democrat," meaning a loyalist who would vote for a yellow dog so long as it was a Democrat.

The Blue Dogs, however, were not blindly adherent to the Democratic Party or its liberal IDEOLOGY. They shared many of the views of the GOP majority in the House. Five members, in fact, switched in 1995 to the Republican Party, further reducing the already-depleted ranks of Democratic southern conservatives in the House.

As moderates, the Blue Dogs hoped to temper some of the more extreme objectives of the majority party and work with the Republicans to achieve common goals such as a balanced federal budget. After the 1996 elections southern Democrats accounted for only 39 percent of the party's strength in the House. About two-thirds of the Blue Dogs were from southern states.

Republican gains in the South had dramatically altered the once-formidable conservative COALITION of Republicans and southern Democrats. The GOP could now achieve most of its goals without the votes of the Blue Dogs and other conservative Democrats.

That marginalization led some political scientists to dismiss the conservative coalition as a remnant of the era when the South was largely a one-party Democratic monolith. Analysis of the coalition is a waste of time, said one. "It's a concept designed to measure a phenomenon that's no longer out there." Others, however, saw the Blue Dogs as possibly reviving the conservative bipartisanship of the early 1980s, when the self-styled BOLL WEEVIL southern Democrats provided the margin of victory for Republican president Ronald Reagan's tax and spending cuts.

The Blue Dogs use as their logo a painting by New Orleans artist George Rodrigue of a wide-eyed blue dog with the U.S. Capitol in the background.

## Boll Weevil

In the 1980s conservative southern Democrats in the House of Representatives called themselves *Boll Weevils.* Although the boll weevil is a destructive pest in cotton fields, the House Boll Weevils adopted the name because of the insect's southern habitat and resistance to eradication. They often voted with House Republicans to help enact President Ronald Reagan's dramatic economic programs.

The Boll Weevils' opposite number called themselves *Gypsy Moths,* after another destructive and persistent insect. The moderate Republican Gypsy Moths represented mostly northeastern and midwestern districts where gypsy moth infestations had damaged forest areas. House Gypsy Moths often opposed "Reaganomics," which included cutbacks in domestic programs.

With Republicans controlling both chambers of Congress in the 1990s, a new breed of conservative Democrats emerged in the House under the name BLUE DOG DEMOCRATS. The almost two-dozen Blue Dogs were mostly southern Democrats but about a third were from northern states. Some of the Blue Dogs, such as Rep. Charles W. Stenholm of Texas, had been Boll Weevils.

The Boll Weevil term originated in the House during the Eisenhower administration, but it had fallen into disuse until Stenholm revived it during the Reagan presidency.

## Border States

The term *border state* is often used in a political context. Yet most popular dictionaries or encyclopedias do not have an entry under that term. And if a definition is found elsewhere, it is likely to differ from one found in another source.

Originally there were four border states: Delaware, Kentucky, Maryland, and Missouri. Although they were slave states, they did not secede from the Union and they fought on the northern side in the Civil War. When the western counties of Virginia split off and became the state of West Virginia in 1863, a fifth border state was created.

All five technically were southern states because they were below the Mason-Dixon line, the generally accepted demarcation between the North and the South. Surveyors Charles Mason and Jeremiah Dixon established the line in the 1760s as the border between Pennsylvania and Maryland. But the five states came to be called border states rather than southern states because of their proximity to the Confederate border and their loyalty to the Union.

Over the years political scientists, geographers, and statisticians have altered the list of what they consider to be "border states." The U.S. Bureau of the CENSUS, however, does not use the border state classification. It divides the fifty states into four regions (Northeast, Midwest, South, and West) and further divides each of those into two subregions, except for the South which has three subregions. Under the Census Bureau grouping, the five original border states are listed under the South except for Missouri, which is under Midwest.

Congressional Quarterly, the Gallup poll, the *New York Times*/CBS News Poll, and other organizations also define four regions of the country, but without subregions.

For their party competition table in *Vital Statistics on American Politics,* political scientists Harold W. Stanley and Richard G. Niemi define border states as the DISTRICT OF COLUMBIA, Maryland, Missouri, Oklahoma, and West Virginia. But for a school desegregation table they cite another source that adds Delaware and Kentucky to the same list.

In *Vital Statistics on Congress, 1997–1998,* political scientists Norman J. Ornstein, Thomas E. Mann, and Michael J. Malbin define border states as Kentucky, Maryland, Missouri, Oklahoma, and West Virginia.

Another political scientist, Larry Sabato, defines border states in his book *Goodbye to Good-time Charlie: The American Governorship Transformed* as Kentucky, Maryland, Missouri, Oklahoma, Tennessee, and West Virginia.

Oklahoma, which appears on three of these lists, did not become a state until 1907.

## Brass Collar Democrat

A Democrat who votes the straight party ticket is sometimes referred to as a *brass collar Democrat.* Such staunch party loyalists are also called "yellow dog Democrats" because they supposedly would vote for a yellow dog rather than a Republican.

Both are mainly southern expressions that generally applied to conservative Democrats in the days when the so-called solid South was solidly Democratic. Because of Republican inroads that is no longer the case and brass collar or yellow dog Democrats are scarce in the South of today. (See REALIGNMENTS AND DEALIGNMENTS.)

The derivation of brass collar Democrat is unclear, but some language experts believe it, too, may have a canine connection. They surmise that it may refer to the heavy brass collars that made it easier to control strong-willed dogs.

In the mid-1990s moderate to conservative Democrats in the U.S. House of Representatives formed what they called the Blue Dog Coalition. The member BLUE DOG DEMOCRATS, mostly from the South, pledged to form a working relationship with the majority House Republicans in an effort to achieve common goals.

## Brokered Convention

Now a thing of the past, brokered NATIONAL PARTY CONVENTIONS were not unusual after conventions came into general use as presidential nominating devices in the mid–nineteenth century. They were so called because power brokers—influential party leaders, financiers, and FAVORITE SONS—"wheeled and dealed" to steer the nomination to the candidate of their choice, who was not necessarily the first choice of the DELEGATES in the hall.

Two controversial rules, since abolished by the Democrats and never used by the Republicans, made DEMOCRATIC PARTY conventions especially susceptible to manipulation by power brokers. They were the TWO-THIRDS RULE, which required a two-thirds majority vote for nomination, and the UNIT RULE, which enabled the majority of a state delegation to cast all the delegation's votes as a bloc.

The need for a two-thirds majority helped to make multiple balloting a characteristic of Democratic conventions for many years until after the party dropped the rule in 1936. The record was 103 roll calls taken in 1924 before the convention settled on John W. Davis of New York as the party's nominee to oppose the Republican incumbent, Calvin Coolidge.

By contrast, only one GOP convention took more than ten roll calls to nominate a presidential candidate. That was in 1880, when James A. Garfield won on the thirty-sixth ballot.

Many of the Democrats' multiple ballots were used to dispense with favorite son candidates, whose names were placed in nomination by various state delegations. Like brokered conventions, favorite son candidates are now largely relics of a bygone era. Both were

*The nomination of William McKinley (center) as the 1896 Republican candidate was orchestrated well in advance of the convention by power broker Mark Hanna (right). Source: Library of Congress*

outmoded by the rise of PRIMARIES, which diminished the role of the conventions, and by PRESIDENTIAL SELECTION REFORMS that democratized the nominating process. Since 1952 neither of the major parties has taken more than one ballot to nominate a standard bearer.

Although the Democrats' rules made their conventions more vulnerable to domination by party bosses, one of the most famous of brokered conventions was a Republican event—the 1912 convention that pitted the forces of President William Howard Taft against those of former president Theodore Roosevelt.

Because the permanent convention chair would not be filled until the many credentials disputes were settled, the temporary chair was unusually powerful at the divided convention. The post was won by Sen. Elihu Root of New York, whose rulings helped Taft to win the credentials fight and eventually the nomination. Accusing Root of steamroller tactics, Roosevelt supporters rubbed sandpaper and blew horns to imitate the sound of a steamroller. Defeated, Roosevelt launched his own Progressive "Bull Moose" candidacy, which split the GOP vote and helped Democrat Woodrow Wilson to win the presidency.

Wilson's own nomination in 1912 required forty-six roll calls and provided an example of a convention that party leaders were unable to broker in favor of the first ballot leader, House Speaker Champ Clark of Missouri. Clark received a majority on the tenth ballot, but he was never able to win the 730 votes needed for nomination under the two-thirds rule. It was the first time since 1844 that a majority winner ultimately lost the Democratic nomination.

Normally, the absence of a clear FRONT-RUNNER at the outset is the hallmark of a brokered convention. Jockeying for the lead position takes place among the favorite son and other candidates, their supporters, and the power brokers. The Republican convention of 1896, however, was in a sense brokered in advance by industrialist Mark Hanna, who engineered the first-ballot nomination of Ohio governor William McKinley. Hanna, McKinley's mentor and campaign manager, wooed delegates for his candidate for more than a year before the convention. When the opening gavel sounded, McKinley's nomination was almost a foregone conclusion.

*Sen. James L. Buckley, Conservative-Republican from New York, was the lead plaintiff in the lawsuit that set the ground rules of campaign finance for more than two decades. Source: Congressional Quarterly*

---

## Buckley v. Valeo

The Supreme Court's ruling in *Buckley v. Valeo* (1976) limited, on First Amendment grounds, the ability of Congress or other legislative bodies to control campaign spending. But the Court upheld limits on individual contributions, disclosure requirements for expenditures and contributions, and the new system of PUBLIC FINANCING OF CAMPAIGNS for major presidential candidates. The decision created serious gaps in CAM-PAIGN FINANCE laws, but efforts to circumvent or overturn the ruling have not succeeded.

*Buckley* stemmed from a challenge to a 1974 campaign finance law. The plaintiffs included James L. Buckley, who had been elected to the Senate from New York on the Republican and Conservative Party tickets; Eugene J. McCarthy, the former antiwar Democratic senator from Minnesota; the New York Civil Liberties Union; and *Human Events*, a conservative publication. They claimed that the restrictions on individual contributions and on overall campaign spending violated freedom of speech and political association. Francis Valeo, the secretary of the Senate, was named as the lead defendant.

The Court announced its decision in an unsigned,

137-page opinion on January 30, 1976. In its most important ruling, the Court held, 7–1, that proposed spending limits for congressional candidates violated the First Amendment's protections for freedom of speech. "A restriction on the amount of money a person or group can spend on political communication during a campaign necessarily reduces the quantity of expression," the Court stated. Only Justice Byron R. White dissented on that point.

The Court left other important parts of the law standing. The justices upheld, 6–2, the limits on individual contributions to candidates as a permissible means of preventing the risk of corruption. By a different 6–2 vote, they also rejected First Amendment and equal protection challenges to public financing for presidential candidates. The ruling allowed spending limits on candidates who accepted public financing. But it barred ceilings on "independent expenditures" by individuals in connection with federal elections. Finally, the Court unanimously held that the composition of the FEDERAL ELECTION COMMISSION (FEC) violated separation of power principles because the law provided for Congress to appoint some of the commission's members.

Congress moved quickly to reestablish the FEC by providing for the president to appoint all of its voting members, with Senate confirmation. But the other gaps left by the Court's ruling could not be closed. The decision torpedoed the goal of reducing campaign spending. Instead, it allowed unlimited spending by candidates from their own pockets, paving the way for lavish spending by millionaire candidates.

Subsequently, at least three presidential candidates financed their own campaigns after refusing public funding: John B. Connally in 1980, Ross Perot in 1992, and Malcolm S. "Steve" Forbes Jr. in 1996. Perot ran again in 1996, but this time his new REFORM PARTY accepted public financing. Although congressional campaigns were not eligible for public grants, several wealthy Senate candidates financed their own campaigns, which freed them from reliance on individual and POLITICAL ACTION COMMITTEE contributions that were subject to federal limitations.

In addition, *Buckley* opened the way for individuals and groups to spend whatever they wanted as long as they kept their electioneering separate from the candidates' official campaign.

Some individuals and groups disagreed with the Court's reasoning that the First Amendment extended to campaign spending. But the Court reaffirmed the premise in later campaign finance regulation cases.

## Bull Moose

*See* PROGRESSIVE PARTY–BULL MOOSE.

## Bullet Vote

A candidate running AT-LARGE in a MULTIMEMBER DISTRICT, such as a city council, may ask supporters to vote only for him or her and withhold the other votes they may be entitled to cast. That targeted vote is known as a *bullet vote*, and it can enhance the recipient's chances of victory by depriving the other candidates of votes they might have received.

Bullet voting is sometimes used as a strategy by minority candidates to elect one of their number in situations where the other candidates belong to the majority and are more likely to win if they receive support from both the minority and the majority.

In a 1986 Supreme Court case, *Thornburg v. Gingles,* African Americans argued that they were forced to resort to bullet voting in some multimember districts to elect members of the North Carolina legislature. The necessity of surrendering some of the votes they were entitled to cast deprived them of their full rights under section 2 of the 1965 VOTING RIGHTS ACT, they argued.

In its decision the Court did not prohibit multimember districts but it spelled out in detail the steps needed to prove discrimination under section 2. The complainants must be able to show a consistent pattern of being defeated by the majority, the Court said. (See BLACK SUFFRAGE; RACIAL REDISTRICTING; VOTING RIGHTS ACT.)

Bullet voting is advantageous only where several candidates are being elected, such as the top five candidates for at-large seats in a multimember district. Full-slate laws in some communities prohibit the practice, however, by invalidating ballots where voters have omitted some of the votes they were eligible to cast.

---

## Bundling

The gathering together of individual campaign contributions is known as *bundling*. The technique enables a POLITICAL ACTION COMMITTEE (PAC) or party committee to stay within the CAMPAIGN FINANCE laws and still present a candidate with a gift large enough to gain his or her attention and possibly ensure access to the officeholder when the time comes to ask a favor.

Bundling is just one of several methods developed by businesses, INTEREST GROUPS, and others to circumvent the contribution limits imposed by Congress since the 1970s to lessen the influence of big money in campaigns for federal office. Others include SOFT MONEY (unregulated donations to parties) and independent expenditures (a use of regulated HARD MONEY that is permitted if it is spent on a campaign without the candidate's cooperation).

The use of bundling predated the current federal limits on campaign contributions. The Council for a Livable World (CLW) originated the technique in 1962 by soliciting checks payable to George S. McGovern's Senate campaign in South Dakota. In 1995 and 1996 the CLW was among the top fifty nonconnected PACs (those without a sponsoring organization), with receipts of $508,496.

A variation on the bundling system is the "political donor network," pioneered in 1985 as EMILY's List.

EMILY (an acronym for Early Money Is Like Yeast) was formed to raise early campaign money for pro-choice Democratic women candidates. In the 1995–1996 election cycle, EMILY's List ranked first among the nonconnected PACs with receipts of $9.4 million.

Corporate executives use bundling to aggregate their political contributions into larger sums. Like other individuals they may give no more than $2,000 to a single candidate ($1,000 per election, with the primary and general election counted as separate elections). (See CAMPAIGN FINANCE, table.) But if ten executives each give $2,000, the $20,000 bundle would be double the maximum amount ($10,000) that a PAC could contribute to any one candidate over two years. From time to time, the news media have published allegations that some bundled contributions were actually illegal gifts that corporations paid to their executives as "bonuses," with the understanding that they were to be passed on to the candidate the company wished to help.

On April 28, 1992, bundling helped President George Bush set a one-day record for political fund raising. He took in nearly $11 million for his campaign and other Republican Party causes. At a President's Day gala, corporations delivered bundles of $1,500 contributions from employees. The dinner also raised individual soft money gifts of as much as $400,000 for state party activities. The same day as the dinner, which raised $9 million altogether, Bush received $1.9 million in federal funds for PUBLIC FINANCING of presidential campaigns.

---

## By-Election

*See* SPECIAL ELECTION.

# C

## Campaign, Basic Stages of

All political campaigns go through the same basic stages, whether at the ward or national level. The goal is to get elected, and that entails a progression of steps that must be taken over a period of months or even years.

The only major difference between running for alderman and running for president is the degree of elaboration. The higher the office, the larger and more complex the organization required to conduct the campaign. But, as House Speaker Thomas P. "Tip" O'Neill Jr. was fond of saying, "All politics is local," and all campaigns, small or large, boil down to an effort to win the heart and mind of the individual voter.

Studies show that the average voter already has his or her mind made up long before ELECTION DAY. Yet the candidate who takes for granted the allegiance of past supporters, or who writes off a certain bloc as committed to the opposition, does so at considerable peril. Political history is littered with cases of upset victories or defeats.

## The Exploratory Stage

Most stages of a campaign naturally overlap with the STAGES IN AN ELECTION. One shared phase is the exploratory stage. The prospective candidate must decide whether to run for the office and assess the chances of winning. The decision is especially difficult for would-be presidential candidates. (See PRESIDENT, NOMINATING AND ELECTING.)

Voters are little involved in the exploratory stages. They may not even be aware of the potential candidate, let alone be considering which person to support. But the prospective candidate is much aware of the voters at this point.

Rather than guess at the kind of reception to expect from the media and the public, the candidate may send up a trial balloon by letting it be known that he or she is contemplating a run for the office. Or the candidate may hire a POLLING organization to test the market more scientifically.

The prospective candidate may also use family, friends, associates, elected officials, and POLITICAL CONSULTANTS as sounding boards on the advisability of entering the race. Not the least of considerations is money. Even the most modest campaigns entail some expense, and the candidate must take CAMPAIGN FINANCE requirements into account.

Once the decision to run is made, the candidate needs to address the formalities of filing with the state or local elections board, CANVASSING BOARD, or other appropriate authorities. Sometimes a filing fee is charged, or petitions must be submitted with the signatures of a specified number of registered voters.

Candidates for federal office (president, vice president, or Congress) must also register with the FEDERAL ELECTION COMMISSION (FEC) and report periodically on campaign receipts and spending. Almost all states also regulate campaign financing, requiring financial disclosure and, in some cases, limiting contributions by individuals and groups.

## Building an Organization

Election to most offices today is a two-step process. Candidates must first run in PRIMARY or CAUCUS elections to obtain the party's nomination to run in the general election. Under the TWO-PARTY SYSTEM, most primaries and caucuses are held by the DEMOCRATIC and REPUBLICAN Parties. But some THIRD PARTIES also use primaries to select their nominees.

*Lawton Chiles walked the length of Florida—1,003 miles—in 1970 during his successful campaign for the United States Senate. Chiles, who died in December 1998, also served as Florida's governor. Source: AP/Wide World*

Not all primaries are partisan events, however. Many U.S. elections, especially at the local level, are nonpartisan, with no party designation shown on the ballot. Nonpartisan elections often are held in off-years, rather than on the general election day in November of even-numbered years. And even within the two-party system, primaries in some states are open and nonpartisan. (See PRIMARY TYPES.)

The widespread use of the primary system means that campaigns begin earlier than in the past, and can-

didates must start well before the primary to build a political organization of voluntary and paid workers. Recruiting these individuals is one of the major tasks in the early phases of a campaign.

People are needed to compile lists of potential supporters, make and receive phone calls, operate computers and office machines, distribute campaign paraphernalia such as lawn signs and bumper stickers, coordinate the candidate's appearances, devise CAMPAIGN STRATEGIES, plan use of the MEDIA through advertising, seek favorable MEDIA COVERAGE of the campaign, and handle fund raising and myriad other electioneering chores.

Most campaign workers are volunteers. In a large campaign the candidate may hire a campaign manager, a fund raiser, a publicist, and a treasurer but rely on friends and supporters to do all the rest of the necessary work.

The campaign may open a temporary storefront headquarters or a number of strategically located offices to centralize the various operations. Or the campaign headquarters may be the candidate's home.

## Getting Started

To many, if not all candidates, asking for money is distasteful. But unless they are personally wealthy they have to do it, early and often. PUBLIC FINANCING of campaigns is available to presidential candidates, but only if they raise enough money and meet other qualifications for matching grants. Several states also provide some financial assistance to qualifying candidates.

Essentially, however, fund raising is an inescapable aspect of political campaigns. From the outset, candidates spend much of their time sending letters or phoning to request contributions or loans. Some create POLITICAL ACTION COMMITTEES (PACs) to solicit gifts in their behalf. Compliance with federal or state financial disclosure laws may require setting up a special bank account to receive and disburse the funds.

Less tangible than money but helpful to a candidate are endorsements from community leaders, organizations, current officeholders, and other influential persons. Experienced candidates rank the gathering of endorsements as a high priority for fledgling campaigns.

Another early priority of a campaign is learning as much as possible about the DISTRICT or other jurisdiction where the candidate is running. State and local elections boards often sell lists of voters to assist in canvassing. Some candidates begin by touring the entire district to become familiar with its boundaries and characteristics, even if they have lived there all their lives. At the same time they may be looking for strategic locations for campaign signs and posters.

A corollary of knowing the district is defining the issues. The candidate needs to keep abreast of current affairs and address the concerns of his or her particular electorate. Many candidates use PUBLIC OPINION polls to help define the issues and indicate positions to take on them.

## Campaigning Techniques

One of the first things a candidate might do is come up with a catchy CAMPAIGN SLOGAN. Such slogans have been a part of electioneering since the earliest days of the Republic and, since the 1896 presidential election, often appear on CAMPAIGN BUTTONS.

Stump speeches and "pressing the flesh" by shaking the hands of voters are still staples of the campaign art. For many a candidate, the campaign is one long season of greeting voters outside factory gates or shopping malls. Door-to-door canvassing may be feasible in a compact district. An alternative way to reach large numbers of voters is a "live" phone bank of callers asking for voters' support, or an automated phone bank that can play the candidate's recorded appeal if the person called is willing to listen.

Even in large states, candidates have walked great distances to gain attention and meet voters. Lawton Chiles, a Democrat from Florida, earned the nickname "Walkin' Lawton" when he trekked the length of the state, 1,003 miles, in his successful 1970 race for the U.S. Senate. In 1990 Chiles was elected governor of Florida. In 1978 Republican Lamar Alexander donned a red-and-black lumberjack shirt and walked a thousand miles to win the Tennessee governorship. Wearing the same shirt, he tried in vain to win the 1996 NEW HAMPSHIRE PRIMARY by walking across the state.

The extensive travel expected of presidential candidates was once a rarity. William Jennings Bryan started the WHISTLE-STOP tradition in his 1896 race against William McKinley, who won with a front-porch campaign at home in Canton, Ohio.

Today, candidates reach many more voters by television and radio than in person. Ads on television are the largest single expense in many campaigns, and candidates welcome free guest spots on TV and radio news and talk shows. In 1992 Texas billionaire Ross Perot launched his INDEPENDENT bid for the presidency, the strongest ever by an individual, with an "I'm available" remark on the *Larry King Live* TV show.

Televised DEBATES and forums enable voters to compare the IDEOLOGIES, knowledge, and speaking skills of competing candidates. Presidential nominees have debated in every election since 1976, and similar forums have become common in congressional and state elections as well.

Although stations and networks are no longer compelled by the defunct fairness doctrine to give EQUAL TIME on the air to candidates, broadcasters usually try to avoid charges of favoritism. The debate format enables them to give equal exposure to all serious candidates for a given office.

Direct mail is another relatively new technique of grass-roots campaigning. Some political consultants have developed sophisticated methods of targeting mass mailings to voters who share the candidate's political philosophy or are likely to be persuaded by his or her arguments.

Communications with voters are increasingly high-tech. In the 1996 election many parties and candidates had sites on the Internet and its World Wide Web to help disseminate their messages. Bills have been introduced in Congress to ensure that candidates can use the Internet without violating FEC rules. (See Appendix, page 498.)

## The Final Hours

The closing days of political campaigns are the most frantic, with candidates desperately trying to reach as many voters as possible before they go to the polls. For primary losers, the campaign is effectively over, but some remain in the race as independents, and in some states there are RUNOFF elections if no one wins a majority in the primary.

For presidential primary winners the next major events are the NATIONAL PARTY CONVENTIONS, where their nominations are made official by thousands of DELEGATES from all over the country.

For the general election the presidential and vice-presidential nominees, as well as survivors of primaries for other offices, must repeat many of the same steps they completed for the primaries. A major difference is that they may be starting with an existing organization, which the candidate may decide needs to be enlarged or overhauled. In modern presidential politics, the nominee's primary organization is often kept intact, usually taking the place once held by the national party committees in running the campaign.

The traditional time to begin general election campaigns is the Labor Day holiday, but many candidates no longer wait until then. The campaign may start right after the primaries or party conventions and end on election day in the candidate's hometown. In 1996 Republican nominee Robert J. Dole, to dispel the notion that at seventy-three he was too old to be president, finished his campaign with a grueling ninety-six-hour marathon that took him through twenty states and wound up in Russell, Kansas, where he voted looking none the worse for wear.

On election day parties and candidates concentrate on GET-OUT-THE-VOTE activities, making last-minute phone bank calls to urge people to vote. They may offer transportation to the polls if the voters, especially the elderly or disabled, need it. Other campaign workers may be assigned as poll watchers—where this is permitted—to look out for irregularities.

Once the results are in, the winners claim victory and the losers concede defeat. But if it is a close or CONTESTED ELECTION, the speeches might have to wait for a RECOUNT and a tally of the ABSENTEE VOTES.

For the candidates, the end of the campaign is less glamorous than the earlier stages. The headquarters must be emptied, the bills paid, and the organization disbanded. Finally, many communities require the prompt removal of campaign signs and posters.

## Campaign Buttons

The modern political campaign button was born in 1896 when supporters of presidential candidate William McKinley wore his portrait on buttons promising a "full dinner pail." Today campaign buttons are mostly collectors' items because the high cost of POLITICAL ADVERTISING on television leaves little money for manufactured campaign artifacts.

Voters continue to expect buttons, bumper stickers, and other campaign paraphernalia, however, and private vendors help to supply the demand for what parties and candidates can no longer afford. Among them is Nelson Whitman, president of Capitol Stamp and Coin Company in Washington, D.C., who said that parties now hand out buttons only in return for donations.

Americans since George Washington's time have decorated their lapels with printed political statements. But in the early days the items were made of cloth, and most commemorated sitting presidents or events such as the inauguration rather than political campaigns. A forerunner of the McKinley-type button appeared in 1840, when William Henry Harrison and John Tyler won the White House with the CAMPAIGN SLOGAN "Tippecanoe and Tyler Too."

Harrison's buttons were coin-like tokens that could be worn in a buttonhole. By the 1860s, with the invention of photography, black-and-white portraits were added to these metal plate tokens, which were then called "ferrotypes." Within a few elections, photos were commonly being mounted on cardboard or paper that could be pinned to the wearer's clothing.

In 1893 the first patent was granted for a process that wrapped celluloid, a tough plastic, over a metal disk that could be fastened to the lapel by a pin on an attached metal ring. This was the campaign button as it is known today. In the 1920s portrait reproduction was enhanced through the use of lithographs on the buttons. Some new, high-tech buttons feature pop-up or moving parts, blinking lights, holograms, or even tape-recorded messages.

American Political Items Collectors, based in Clear-

*As this pastiche of buttons shows, campaigns, even prior to the media age, were conducted through simple images and slogans.* Source: Fred Sons

water, Florida, publishes a newsletter and magazine and organizes trading conventions. Button collectors have their own jargon, such as *jugate*, meaning a button displaying the faces of two candidates, and *trigate*, which shows three faces, often including a congressional candidate hoping for a COATTAILS effect from the national ticket. Collectors also divide into purists, who insist on official campaign buttons only, and more broadly based collectors who accept "vendor" buttons because official buttons are often colorless and unattractive.

The most valuable button, said to be worth up to $50,000, dates from 1920 and features unsuccessful Democratic presidential candidate James M. Cox and his running mate, Franklin D. Roosevelt.

The most common collectibles are "Nixon Now" buttons from Richard Nixon's 1972 campaign (the Watergate campaign) and a series of Wendell L. Willkie buttons created by the dozens of Willkie clubs that sprang up when the relatively unknown businessman challenged incumbent Roosevelt in the 1940 presidential campaign.

Campaign buttons reveal much about America's past, and not all of it is flattering. When New York governor Alfred E. Smith ran for president in 1928, anti-

Catholic opponents put out an anti-Smith button that called for "A Christian in the White House." Opponents of Roosevelt's groundbreaking bid for a third presidential term produced buttons that read, "Washington Wouldn't. Lincoln Couldn't. Roosevelt Shouldn't."

The national political climate is often reflected in the political button industry. "As America's interest in politics declined after Watergate, so did the frenzy of collectors," writes button expert Mark Warda. "It did not pick up until 1992, when Americans were excited again by the prospect of a serious third party, and Democrats were excited by the first chance in years of regaining the White House."

## Campaign Finance

The cost of political campaigns in the United States has risen sharply since the 1950s, fueling intense controversies about the ways candidates for office at all levels of government raise and spend money. Congress, state legislatures, and local lawmaking bodies have responded by adopting laws requiring disclosure of campaign contributions and expenditures and limiting contributions by individuals and organizations.

The disclosure laws have succeeded in bringing campaign finance practices into the open. But efforts to control the costs of campaigns have been thwarted by a Supreme Court decision that barred mandatory spending limits for candidates or independent groups. In addition, contribution limits, aimed at reducing the influence of wealthy individuals or organizations, have proved difficult to enforce and easy to circumvent.

The earliest campaign finance laws date from the late 1800s and early 1900s. The current wave of reform efforts began in the 1960s and gained strength in the 1970s. The sharp rise in presidential campaign spending led Congress to enact a system of PUBLIC FINANCING of campaigns by major party candidates for president. Then the Watergate scandal during President Richard Nixon's administration resulted in enactment of the current federal law, which places limits on individual contributions to federal candidates. The law also established the FEDERAL ELECTION COMMISSION (FEC) as an independent regulatory agency to enforce its provisions.

*Campaign finance is a complicated subject for many voters, as shown in this 1997 cartoon.*
Source: Jeff MacNelly, Tribune Media Services

**Contribution Limits**

|  | To Cand. per Election[a] per Calendar Year | To Party per Calendar Year | To PAC per Calendar Year | Total per Calendar Year |
|---|---|---|---|---|
| Individual may give | $1,000 | $20,000 | $5,000 | $25,000 |
| Multicandidate committee[b] may give | $5,000 | $15,000 | $5,000 | No limit |
| Other political committee may give | $1,000 | $20,000 | $5,000 | No limit |

*Source:* Federal Election Commission.

a. Because the primary and general election are separate elections, the totals in the first column may be doubled.

b. A qualified multicandidate committee is a political committee with more than fifty contributors that has been registered for at least six months and, with the exception of party committees, has made contributions to five or more candidates.

The 1974 law is blamed by some advocates and experts for an increase in campaign giving by POLITICAL ACTION COMMITTEES (PACs). These organizations are formed by corporations, labor unions, or INTEREST GROUPS to raise money from their employees or members and funnel contributions to candidates. The growth in PACs has raised new fears about the influence of special interests on congressional candidates.

At the federal level, a second source of controversy has been the rise in the use of so-called SOFT MONEY— campaign funds raised by national political parties ostensibly to help finance organizational efforts and voting drives at the state and local level. Congress exempted these funds from federal contribution limits in 1979. Many advocates and experts believe that the growth in soft money spending by both the Republican and the Democratic Parties has undercut the efforts to reduce the influence of campaign contributions in presidential campaigns.

Critics of current campaign finance practices have continued to advocate measures to further limit contributions and to close other gaps in the existing laws. They have also sought to control congressional cam-

paign spending by proposing public campaign financing or other subsidies for candidates for the House and the Senate. From the opposite perspective, some lawmakers, advocates, and experts have criticized the current laws as complex and counterproductive and have dismissed the concerns about the cost of political campaigns as overstated. They have pushed for raising or repealing contribution limits, reducing other regulations, and blocking any expansion of public campaign financing.

At the federal level, both major political parties have called for revising the current laws, but in different ways. Public campaign financing has proved to be politically unpopular, however, and other efforts to tighten the laws have foundered in a partisan stalemate. Some states and localities nevertheless have adopted new laws, some with voluntary spending curbs and limits on individual campaign contributions as low as $100 for certain races.

## Early Reforms

Money—once famously described as "the mother's milk of politics"—has been important to American politics since the early days of the Republic. In those days, some candidates (including George Washington) gave rather than received by rewarding their supporters with whiskey. The spread of popular democracy in the nineteenth century brought with it greater demands for campaign money that were met first by the patronage-based "spoils system" and then after the Civil War by fund raising from corporations and wealthy industrialists.

These practices spawned the first efforts to regulate campaign finance. As part of the country's first federal civil service law in 1883, Congress prohibited the solicitation of political contributions from FEDERAL WORKERS covered by the law. In 1907 Congress followed the lead of several states by passing a law, the Tillman Act, that prohibited banks and corporations from making political contributions to candidates for federal office.

In 1910 Congress passed the Publicity Act, the first federal campaign disclosure law, but the measure required reporting of campaign spending only after elections. Amendments a year later added campaign spending limits for House and Senate candidates. But the ceilings were unrealistically low—$5,000 for House candidates and $10,000 for Senate candidates—and went largely unenforced.

The Supreme Court dealt a blow to congressional efforts to regulate campaign fund raising in 1921 by ruling in *Newberry v. United States* that Congress had no power over party PRIMARIES. Twenty years later, however, the Court reversed itself and allowed regulation of primary elections. (See WHITE PRIMARY.)

In 1925, in the wake of the Teapot Dome scandal, Congress passed the Corrupt Practices Act, which reinforced the campaign spending disclosure requirements and attempted to cap spending at $25,000 for Senate campaigns. But again the provisions went unenforced. A new provision added in 1940 that limited individual contributions to $5,000 also proved to be ineffective; contributors evaded the ceilings by making multiple donations to separate campaign committees for the same candidates, as permitted by the law. In 1943, however, Congress closed one gap by prohibiting labor unions from making direct contributions to candidates for federal office. Three years later, the Congress of Industrial Organizations (CIO) responded by creating a separate political arm—the first political action committee—to raise money from union members to contribute to federal candidates.

## Rising Costs

Political campaign spending, relatively low as late as 1948, began rising with the advent of television advertising in the 1950s. In presidential campaigns, for example, Dwight D. Eisenhower spent $6.6 million in his 1952 race—more than three times the amount spent by the Republican nominee four years earlier. In 1960 Richard Nixon and John F. Kennedy each spent roughly $10 million. In his next two campaigns Nixon set new records for presidential campaign spending: $25.4 million in 1968 and $61.4 million in 1972. Democrats did not keep pace with Republican fund raising, but their spending rose too. Hubert Humphrey spent $11.6 million in 1968; four years later George McGovern spent $30 million.

**Campaign Spending, 1982–1996**

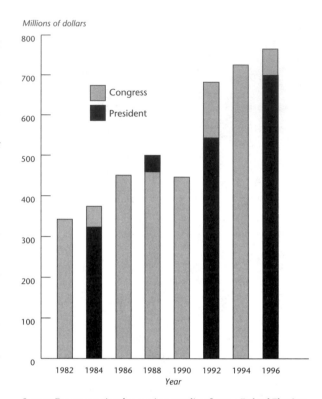

*Sources:* For congressional campaign spending figures, Federal Election Commission press release, April 14, 1997; presidential campaign spending figures courtesy of Herbert E. Alexander, Citizens Research Foundation.

Congressional campaign spending also rose despite the low ceilings prescribed by law. Moreover, the law's disclosure provisions proved to be ineffective. Congress had given the job of maintaining campaign contributions and spending reports to its own officers, the House clerk and Senate secretary. Experts said the reports were of little use, but the lawmakers failed to approve various proposals to create an independent agency to take over the job.

The rising costs, along with discontent with the weak federal legislation, brought calls for reform in the 1950s and 1960s. In 1962 a presidential commission on campaign costs called for raising spending limits, establishing an independent agency to implement the law, and providing matching public funds to presidential candidates. President Kennedy showed little interest in the issue, but in 1966 President Lyndon B. Johnson submitted a campaign finance bill that called for strengthening disclosure requirements and contribution limits and repealing spending limits. The House passed the bill, but it was bottled up in the Senate.

Meanwhile, Sen. Russell Long, a Democrat from Louisiana, managed to get a public financing provision for presidential campaigns enacted into law late in 1966 by attaching it to an unrelated, end-of-session measure. A year later, however, opponents from both parties succeeded in suspending the provision before it could take effect for the 1968 campaign.

## Watergate Scandals

The pressure to strengthen federal campaign finance laws continued after Nixon's election to the presidency in 1968. In 1971 the Democratic-controlled Congress passed two reform measures. The Federal Election Campaign Act strengthened disclosure provisions by requiring reports from political committees, not just candidates, and by requiring identifying information from political contributors. It also limited federal candidates to spending 10 cents per voter on "communications media." Nixon signed the bill into law on February 7, 1972.

Meanwhile, the Revenue Act of 1971 resuscitated public campaign financing for presidential candidates, with funds to come from a $1 checkoff on income tax returns. The bill also provided for a tax credit or deduction to encourage political contributions. Nixon signed the measure, but only after forcing Democrats to agree that public financing was not to take effect until after the 1972 campaign. (The $1 checkoff has since been raised to $3.)

The Watergate scandals that forced Nixon to resign in 1974 exposed a host of fund-raising abuses during Nixon's 1972 reelection campaign. The president's campaign committee used a secret fund—consisting of illegal, laundered corporate contributions and some legal but undisclosed contributions—to finance the break-in at the DEMOCRATIC NATIONAL COMMITTEE head-

quarters on June 17, 1972. In addition, investigations by the special prosecutor and the Senate Watergate Committee after Nixon's reelection showed that campaign funds were also used to pay hush money to the Watergate burglars. (See SCANDALS.)

The political convulsions from these disclosures resulted in a fortified federal campaign finance law signed into law by President Gerald R. Ford two months after Nixon's resignation on August 9, 1974. The new law—titled the Federal Election Campaign Act Amendments—limited individuals to giving $1,000 per candidate per election or a total of $25,000 to all candidates, federal party committees, or federally registered political action committees. It also sought to cap overall spending by limiting spending on congressional races: $140,000 for House races and ceilings for Senate races tied to each state's population, ranging upward from $250,000 for the smallest states. The act also set up public financing for presidential—but not congressional—campaigns, with matching funds for candidates during party primaries and full public funding for the general election. Finally, the act created the Federal Election Commission to administer the law; it specified that the commission would include an equal number of Republican and Democratic members.

Some states followed Congress's lead in enacting similar campaign spending and contribution limits for state campaigns. California voters, for example, approved a ballot INITIATIVE along those lines in 1974.

## Limits of Reform

Just two years after its enactment, the Supreme Court ruled major parts of the new federal law unconstitutional. The Court's ruling in BUCKLEY V. VALEO struck down mandatory candidate spending limits and allowed individuals to make unlimited "independent expenditures" if they had no connection with official campaign organizations. The Court also ruled the composition of the FEC unconstitutional because the law provided for Congress to appoint some of the commission's members.

Congress reestablished the FEC in the spring of 1976 by amending the law to provide for the president to appoint all of its voting members, subject to Senate confirmation. But the Court's ruling left the lawmakers with no evident means of controlling overall campaign spending except by public financing, which was politically unpopular. It also resulted in invalidation of state-enacted campaign spending limits.

Two other major gaps in the law emerged in the next decade. A provision in the 1974 law to allow federal contractors to establish political action committees led to an enormous growth in their number, size, and influence. PAC contributions to congressional candidates rose from $34.1 million for the 1978 election to $201.4 million for the 1996 election. Corporate PACs showed the greatest growth: they increased their contributions more than eight-fold during the period, from $9.5 million to $76.6 million. Labor PACs also increased their giving, but at a considerably slower rate: from $9.9 million to $47.9 million. Multicandidate PACs may give $5,000 to a campaign for each election, compared with a $1,000 limit for individuals. Most PACs qualify as a multicandidate PAC, which must have at least fifty contributors, be registered for at least six months, and contribute to at least five federal office candidates. There is no limit on the total amount PACs may give per year, compared with a limit of $25,000 for individuals. (See, table, page 39.)

Meanwhile, Congress opened a new gap in the law in 1979 by exempting from federal contribution limits any sums given to state and local party committees for general voter registration or mobilization activities so long as they were not aimed at influencing federal elections. The use of soft money was pioneered by Ronald Reagan in his 1980 campaign and grew in importance with each succeeding election, exceeding $120 million for each of the major parties in 1996 and raising renewed demands for stricter campaign finance laws.

"Issue ads," a controversial form of POLITICAL ADVERTISING, also emerged as a major source of interest group money exempt from spending or contribution limits under the *Buckley v. Valeo* ruling. Independent expenditures for ads indirectly supporting a candidate or party were interpreted as free speech protected by the Constitution. In 1998, however, an FEC staff audit determined that many such ads for President Bill Clinton and challenger Robert J. Dole contained a clear "electioneering message" and that their campaigns should return a total of $24 million from their 1996 public funding grants. Overruling its staff, the commission unanimously voted against return of the ad money and upheld the unregulated use of issue ads.

## Partisan Deadlock

Campaign finance reform fell off the congressional agenda in the 1980s with Republicans in control of the White House and the Senate. But when Democrats recaptured the Senate in the 1986 election, they revived the issue with proposals to provide public financing and spending limits for congressional races. Republicans countered with proposals to eliminate or restrict political action committees, which were proving to be a more important source of funds for Democrats than for the GOP. The competing partisan interests produced deadlock.

Democrats brought a bill to the Senate floor in 1988 but failed to break a Republican filibuster. In 1990 the House and the Senate passed somewhat similar Democratic-backed bills late in the session; however, lawmakers never met to try to resolve the differences. Two years later, Democrats succeeded in getting legislation through both houses of Congress. President George Bush vetoed the measure, and the effort to override the veto fell nine votes short in the Senate.

Reformers' hopes for breaking the deadlock were raised with the election of a Democratic president, Bill Clinton, in 1992. Other factors also added to the pressure for reworking the federal law. Campaign costs were continuing to rise. In 1994 congressional campaign spending totaled $724.1 million—four times as much as in 1978. The average House candidate spent about $440,000, while the average Senate race cost $4.4 million. In the 1997–1998 election cycle, direct contributions to congressional candidates and parties topped a record $1 billion, not counting funds received in the last three weeks before the MIDTERM ELECTION.

Many members of Congress admitted that fund raising took up a great deal of time. A variety of public interest groups complained that the high cost of campaigning created advantages for INCUMBENTS, who enjoyed fund-raising advantages over challengers, and for wealthy candidates, who could spend unlimited amounts of their personal funds. In Virginia's 1996 "two Warners" Senate race, for example, Democratic challenger Mark Warner spent $11.5 million in an unsuccessful attempt to unseat Republican John Warner, who spent $5.1 million. In Massachusetts, Sen. John Kerry outspent his Republican challenger, William Weld, $10.7 million to Weld's $7.8 million. Kerry, who married Teresa Heinz, the widow of wealthy senator John Heinz, kept his seat. In 1998 Sen. Harry Reid, a Democrat from Nevada, ran the most expensive race in terms of cost per votes cast. According to a Las Vegas newspaper, Reid spent $22.02 for each vote. His opponent, Republican representative John Ensign, spent $13.14 per vote.

Concerns about the influence of special interest groups rose with the growth in contributions from political action committees. About two-thirds of the 1994 total came from business-oriented PACs. While labor-oriented PACs gave mostly to Democrats, business groups gave equally to candidates of each major party. In the 1995–1996 election cycle, however, with Republicans in control of Congress, business PACs favored GOP candidates. Critics said the tendency of PACs to favor incumbents bolstered their fund-raising edge over challengers.

Despite these factors, the Democratic-controlled Congress failed to give final approval to campaign finance legislation in 1993 or 1994. Both the House and the Senate approved Democratic-sponsored bills in 1993, but House leaders waited until August 1994 to appoint conferees to work out differences between the two bills. With adjournment nearing, Republicans in the Senate then used parliamentary tactics to block a conference.

Prospects for resolving the partisan standoff dimmed after Republicans captured control of both houses of Congress in the 1994 election. Hopes were raised briefly in June 1995 when Clinton and House Speaker Newt Gingrich, a Georgia Republican, agreed in a "town hall" meeting in New Hampshire to create a bipartisan commission to recommend an overhaul of campaign finance laws. The commission was never created, and Clinton and Gingrich blamed each other for the failure.

In Congress, two senators—Republican John McCain of Arizona and Democrat Russell Feingold of Wisconsin—joined in sponsoring a reform measure that called for giving free broadcast time and reduced postage rates to congressional candidates who agreed to campaign spending limits. But supporters fell six votes short in June 1996 of the three-fifths majority needed to cut off debate on the measure. Meanwhile, the House in 1996 rejected competing Republican- and Democratic-sponsored campaign finance bills.

Calls for rewriting campaign finance laws increased during and after the 1996 presidential election, when the two major party nominees each received a federal grant of $61.8 million for their general election campaigns. Both major parties raised hefty amounts of soft money to supplement the federal grant: $122 million for the Democrats, $141 million for the Republicans. Critics said the funds were raised and spent in close coordination with the respective presidential campaigns, undercutting the goal of insulating candidates for the White House from private fund raising.

In 1997 the Democratic National Committee acknowledged receiving millions of dollars in contributions that appeared to have come from foreign individuals or corporations. Federal law prohibits campaign contributions from foreign nationals. Both parties were required to return illegal contributions, leaving the Democrats in particularly serious financial difficulties. The Democrats returned about $3 million, but the controversy did not end there.

The fund-raising scandals dogged President Clinton as he entered his second four-year term in the White House. With Republicans still in control of both houses of Congress, Senate and House committees started investigations of fund-raising practices, focusing on Clinton and the Democratic Party. Damaging disclosures continued. Clinton was found to have worked closely in hosting contributors and potential contributors at White House events, including "coffees" and overnight stays in the Lincoln bedroom.

Vice President Al Gore acknowledged having placed fund-raising calls from his office in the White House. Critics said the practice violated a federal law against soliciting campaign contributions in a federal office building. Gore defended his actions, denying they violated the law, but said he would stop.

Newspaper stories alleged that much of the soft money raised by Gore was converted to HARD MONEY for the Clinton-Gore campaign. Attorney General Janet Reno considered naming an independent counsel to investigate, but decided not to in December 1998.

Senators McCain and Feingold renewed the drive for their bill tying spending limits for congressional races to free television time and low-cost mailings. More than fifty other proposals were also introduced in the early days of the new Congress. But the 105th Congress adjourned without having passed any comprehensive campaign finance legislation.

Despite the stalemate in Washington, several states approved new laws, some of them with voluntary campaign spending limits. Voters in Maine approved a ballot initiative in November 1996 that gave candidates for state office the option of accepting public financing for their campaigns or soliciting private contributions. A voter-approved measure in Colorado created voluntary campaign spending limits and individual contribution limits of $100 for legislative races and $500 for statewide offices; a candidate who agreed to the spending limits was allowed to double the contribution limits if his or her opponent did not agree to the caps.

---

## Campaign Slogans

Elections are not won or lost by campaign slogans, but over the years candidates have used catchy phrases effectively for themselves or against other candidates or causes. Many of those phrases have outlived now-forgotten contests.

As *New York Times* language columnist William Safire observed in his *New Political Dictionary* (1993), "Good slogans have rhyme, rhythm, or alliteration to make them memorable; great slogans may have none of these, but touch a chord of memory, release pent-up hatreds, or stir men's better natures." Another requirement of a campaign slogan is brevity. Modern slogans must be short enough to fit on a campaign button, bumper sticker, placard, or brief television spot—all standard fixtures of present-day electioneering. (See CAMPAIGN, BASIC STAGES OF.)

Oftentimes the phrase identified with a presidential candidate or administration was not issued as a slogan. Rather it may have been buried in a speech and picked up as part of the MEDIA COVERAGE OF ELECTIONS. Examples are Franklin D. Roosevelt's New Deal, which he used in his 1932 acceptance speech (the first delivered in person by a nominee) pledging "a *new deal* for the American people" and John F. Kennedy's acceptance in 1960 noting that "we stand today on the edge of a *new frontier.*"

By contrast, in 1992 Bill Clinton's acceptance speech offer of a *new covenant* for the American people never won wide acceptance as a Clinton hallmark. The most effective and most quoted phrase of the Clinton candidacy, "It's the economy, stupid," was not intended as a slogan. It was campaign strategist James Carville's "war room" sign admonishing staff volunteers to keep in mind the central issue in the fight to unseat President George Bush.

Economic issues figure in several other memorable slogans or speech phrases. For instance, William Jennings Bryan's famed "Cross of Gold" speech at the 1896 Democratic convention condemned opposition to expansion of the money supply through free coinage of silver. "You shall not press down upon the brow of labor this crown of thorns," Bryan roared. "You shall not crucify mankind upon a cross of gold."

The speech won Bryan the presidential nomination, making him at thirty-six the youngest standard bearer of a major party. Despite a strenuous campaign—the first one involving extensive travel—Bryan lost to Republican William McKinley, who campaigned from his front porch with the slogans: "McKinley and the Full Dinner Pail" and "Stop Bryan, Save America."

In the 1932 election the Democrats, led by Franklin Roosevelt, attacked the economic policies of President

*Candidates have long depended on catchy phrases in their campaigns. Some become part of the nation's vocabulary; others do not.*
*Sources: left, courtesy, Dwight D. Eisenhower Library; right, R. Michael Jenkins, Congressional Quarterly*

Herbert Hoover with slogans such as "Sweeping Depression Out" and "Kick Out Depression with a Democratic Vote." For his part, Hoover denied ever making the promise attributed to him: "a chicken in every pot, a car in every garage." As the heir to a sluggish economy left by Republican president Dwight D. Eisenhower, Vice President Richard Nixon was vulnerable in 1960 to Kennedy's promise to "Get the Country Moving Again."

Twenty years later Ronald Reagan turned the tables on Democrat Jimmy Carter by asking the voters, "Are you better off than you were four years ago?" Saddled with double-digit inflation, most voters agreed they were not.

Other notable economic slogans include the 1930s "We Share Our Wealth: Every Man a King" movement of Louisiana's Huey P. Long and George Bush's 1988 pledge, "Read my lips. No new taxes." Like many slogans, Bush's words came back to haunt him after he agreed to a tax increase.

Alliteration is a favorite of sloganeers, and catch phrases that repeat letters or sounds are among the hardest to forget. An example is "Tippecanoe and Tyler Too," the rallying cry in 1840 for the ticket of William Henry Harrison and John Tyler. Harrison, hero of the 1811 Battle of Tippecanoe in Indiana, was the first of

only two Whigs elected president. The other was Mexican-American War hero Zachary Taylor, in 1848.

Other alliterative or rhyming phrases from U.S. political history include "Fifty-four Forty or Fight"; "Rum, Romanism, and Rebellion"; "Ma, Ma, Where's My Pa?"; "Keep Cool with Coolidge"; "Win with Willkie"; and "Dump the Hump."

Republican presidential nominee James G. Blaine was accused of being anti-Catholic in 1884 because he neglected at a New York rally to repudiate a preacher's remark that the Democrats' "antecedents are rum, Romanism, and rebellion." A narrow loss in New York cost Blaine the election.

Blaine's opponent, Grover Cleveland, was the object of the derisive "Ma, Ma, Where's My Pa?" rhyme because he had fathered an illegitimate child. After he won, his supporters added the line, "Gone to the White House, Ha, Ha, Ha."

The "Win with Willkie" slogan evolved from "we want Willkie," a phrase chanted repeatedly at the 1940 Republican national convention by supporters of Wendell L. Willkie for president. Willkie, an Indiana public utilities executive, won the nomination but failed to deny FDR a historic third term.

Similarly, "Dump the Hump" was the rallying cry of

Vietnam War protesters who wanted the 1968 Democratic convention to nominate Minnesota senator Eugene J. McCarthy for president instead of Vice President Hubert H. Humphrey. President Lyndon B. Johnson had dropped out of the race after McCarthy made an impressive second-place finish against LBJ in the NEW HAMPSHIRE PRIMARY.

Like "Dump the Hump," many slogans are negative, aimed more at defeating a specific candidate than at electing a particular opponent. An example at the state level is the slogan aimed at gun control advocate Joseph D. Tydings in 1970, seeking reelection to the U.S. Senate from Maryland. Many gun owners' vehicles sported bumper stickers saying, "If Tydings Wins, You Lose." Tydings lost.

As the first president to seek more than two full terms, FDR was the target of several negative slogans, including in 1940: "No Third Term," "Don't Be a Third Termite," and "No Man Is Good Three Times," and in 1944: "Clean House with Dewey," the slogan of New York governor Thomas E. Dewey. Turning around a familiar negative slogan, the Democrats' presidential nominee in 1952 and 1956, Adlai E. Stevenson, joked that the GOP battle cry appeared to be, "Throw the rascals in."

Some slogans have been alliterative and combative. For example, in the 1840s American expansionists urged warfare unless Britain gave up the whole Pacific northwest as far north as the parallel at fifty-four degrees, forty minutes: hence the slogan, "Fifty-four Forty or Fight." But President James K. Polk compromised with the British, limiting the Northwest Territory to the forty-ninth parallel, now the major boundary between the United States and Canada.

Feisty president Harry S. Truman was often greeted at WHISTLE STOPS by shouts of "give 'em hell, Harry," which became his unofficial slogan. He later said, "I never gave them hell. I just tell the truth and they think it's hell."

The themes of change or stability underlie numerous slogans, particularly regarding war. During the Civil War in 1864 Republicans urged the reelection of Abraham Lincoln. Their rallying cry was, "Don't Change Horses in the Middle of the Stream." Almost a century later, Democrats used the same words to support FDR's wartime reelection in 1944.

Other stay-the-course slogans include "Let Us Continue" and "All the Way with LBJ" (after the assassination of President Kennedy), "Four More Years" and "Re-elect the President" (for Richard Nixon in 1972). On the other hand, "It's Time for a Change" worked for Eisenhower, who pledged "I Shall Go to Korea" if elected in 1952 in an effort to end the Korean War, and for Kennedy and Clinton, who promised new beginnings after years of Republican administrations.

Nicknames provided rhyming slogans for Eisenhower ("I Like Ike") and Nixon ("Click with Dick"). But Nixon could never live down the epithet based on his name: "Tricky Dick."

Optimistic personalities or national moods lend themselves to sloganeering. New York governor Alfred E. Smith, dubbed the Happy Warrior by FDR, was the first Catholic nominated for president by a major party. He lost in 1928. After four years of Ronald Reagan's presidency, Republicans successfully urged his reelection with the feel-good slogan: "It's Morning in America Again." By contrast, Reagan's predecessor, Jimmy Carter, was associated with the pessimistic word *malaise* because of a speech he gave explaining his midterm cabinet shuffle in 1979. Ironically, nowhere in the speech did Carter actually use the word *malaise*.

## Campaign Strategies

All political candidates need a game plan for winning election. As contestants for the biggest electoral prize in the United States, however, presidential candidates require the most developed and comprehensive campaign strategies. Their components are much the same as those for election to other major offices, such as GOVERNOR, HOUSE MEMBER, or SENATOR.

The strategy must cover all CAMPAIGN STAGES, including the earliest phase when the situation must be assessed and a decision made whether to run. If the analyses indicate that there will be sufficient voter sup-

*James Carville, left, chief strategist for Democratic presidential candidate Bill Clinton of Arkansas, hard at work in the national campaign headquarters "war room" in Little Rock, Arkansas, the day before the 1992 election.* Source: AP/Wide World

port and a reasonable chance to win some DELEGATES to the NATIONAL PARTY CONVENTION, then candidacy may be announced and other aspects of the strategy carried forward. The strategy must be dynamic and adaptable, with a mechanism to let the candidate know if he or she is faltering and what corrective action is needed.

Early on the candidate must choose a strategy to use. Political scientists have identified the common types of strategies as *insider, outsider, early knockout, trench warfare, slow buildup,* and *wait and see.* Most of these strategies, or combinations of them, are employed in the prenomination period when the target is not a single opponent but a host of them within the same party.

• The insider strategy, one of the oldest, depends heavily on the endorsements and resources of major party and government figures. This approach was dominant in the period before the PRESIDENTIAL SELECTION REFORMS made by the DEMOCRATIC PARTY beginning in 1968 and subsequently adopted in part by the

REPUBLICAN PARTY. Today, even an insider strategy requires entering and winning most of the primaries.

With greater democratization of the nominating process, reliance on the party power structure lost much of its effectiveness. Nevertheless, candidates of both parties followed the insider strategy as recently as 1996, sometimes with success but not always. The successful candidates included Franklin D. Roosevelt (in 1932, 1936, 1940, and 1944), Harry S. Truman (1948), Robert A. Taft (1952), John F. Kennedy and Richard Nixon (both in 1960), and Hubert H. Humphrey and Nixon (1968). George Bush's 1988 and 1992 campaigns relied on his ties to the GOP establishment as heir to Ronald Reagan.

Bush's 1992 opponent, Bill Clinton, called for change like an outsider but otherwise ran an insider campaign. Clinton's courting of influential party leaders, INTEREST GROUPS, and journalists helped him overcome voters' hesitation about giving the nomination to the governor of a small state. Running for reelection in 1996, Clinton was the quintessential insider. His aggressive use of the DEMOCRATIC NATIONAL COMMITTEE for fund raising resulted in congressional investigation of possible CAMPAIGN FINANCE law violations.

• In the outsider strategy the candidate runs against the entrenched political establishment, offering a fresh face to disenchanted voters. Like the insider approach, the outsider stance has had a mixed record of success. It worked for Jimmy Carter in 1976, Reagan in 1980, and Barry Goldwater in 1964, but not for Eugene J. McCarthy in 1968, or Reagan in 1976 when he lost the GOP nomination to President Gerald R. Ford. Robert F. Kennedy's outsider attempt in 1968 was cut short by his assassination. Jesse L. Jackson in 1984 and 1988 and Edmund G. "Jerry" Brown Jr. and Patrick J. Buchanan in 1992 gave voice to disaffected outsiders but never posed a real threat to the FRONT-RUNNERS.

• Using the early-knockout strategy, front-runners seek a string of early PRIMARY and CAUCUS victories in hopes that the competition will quickly drop out. Nixon in 1968 and Reagan in 1980 both won their nominations early. Walter F. Mondale in 1984 planned an early knockout but was forced to adopt a more gradual approach with the emergence of Gary Hart. George Bush's 1988 and 1992 campaigns won swift victories. Front-runner Robert J. Dole lost the 1996 NEW HAMPSHIRE PRIMARY to Buchanan, but by taking most of the subsequent early primaries Dole quickly eliminated his competition for the GOP nomination.

• The unpopular trench-warfare approach pits two or more strong rivals against each other in the political equivalent of hand-to-hand combat. The objective is to outlast opponents the candidate cannot hope to outdistance. The bitter, debilitating contests often handicap the party nominee in the ensuing general election. The races between Humphrey, McCarthy, and Kennedy in 1968; Humphrey, George S. McGovern, and George C. Wallace in 1972; Ford and Reagan in 1976; Carter and Kennedy in 1980; and Mondale and Hart in 1984 were examples of trench warfare.

• The slow-buildup goal is to avoid early traps and criticism and gain the aura of party savior when other candidates look weak. Had he not been killed, Robert Kennedy might have won the 1968 Democratic nomination using this strategy. He delayed his entry and won the important California primary, then held late in the season. Similarly, Sen. Henry Jackson of Washington tried unsuccessfully to win the 1976 nomination with victories in the late primaries. Today, however, the slow-buildup strategy is obsolete because early losses are now almost always fatal.

• The wait-and-see strategy is also largely obsolete. Presidential nominations no longer are decided at party conventions. Since 1960 all but one have been sewn up beforehand in the primaries and caucuses. Nevertheless, some potential nominees have sat on the sidelines and hoped to emerge as the consensus candidate at a BROKERED CONVENTION if the primaries failed to produce a front-runner. In this way, Humphrey won the 1968 Democratic nomination after a divisive primary season without entering a single contest. The ensuing resentment within the party, however, led to the reforms that have made a repeat of the 1968 situation unlikely.

In 1980 New York governor Hugh Carey joined a movement to free delegates from obligations to vote for a particular candidate with the hope that another candidate might emerge in a deadlocked convention. In 1988 another New York governor, Mario Cuomo, refused to enter the primaries but said he would accept a convention draft, which never materialized. Instead, Dukakis's trench-warfare tactic finally paid off with his nomination on the first ballot.

## Strategies in Action

As a nonincumbent, a candidate may favor an outsider strategy. But if it succeeds, and he or she is elected, the candidate may seek reelection as an insider. Jimmy Carter's campaigns in 1976 and 1980 provide classic examples of both strategies in action at separate times.

As a former Georgia governor looking to the presidency in 1976, Carter followed an outsider script outlined in 1972 by an aide, Hamilton Jordan. He advised Carter to travel abroad to gain exposure to foreign policy problems and to become involved in national politics because, he wrote, Carter will "have to convince the press, public, and politicians that he knows how to run a government."

Although not well known nationally at first, Carter gained publicity and credibility with his anti-Washington campaign. He ran as a "New South" leader who could help heal the wounds of the Watergate scandal and the Vietnam War. By the time MEDIA COVERAGE of Carter's campaign began, including examination of his record in Georgia, Carter had become a strong front-runner.

In contrast, Carter followed an insider strategy to fend off a 1980 nomination challenge from Sen. Edward M. Kennedy of Massachusetts. Besides using his IN-CUMBENCY to line up support from party and business leaders, Carter manipulated the primary and caucus calendar to his advantage. Aides persuaded three southern states—Alabama, Florida, and Georgia—to hold their primaries together on March 11, ensuring a big sweep for Carter. They also managed to avoid a Kennedy sweep on Massachusetts's primary day, March 4, by having neighboring Connecticut switch its primary to March 25. At the Democratic convention, Carter delegates voted down a rules change that would have benefited Kennedy on the first ballot, which Carter won to gain renomination.

In the general election, insider Carter was no match for outsider Reagan. Plagued by the Iran hostage crisis, high inflation, and a national malaise (which he described in a speech without actually using the word), Carter became a one-term president.

## Deciding on a Strategy

With so many strategies to choose from, a candidate must size up himself or herself as well as the number and strengths of the competition, the fund-raising situation, the issues to address, the degree of public acceptance, and the mood of the district, state, or nation.

The strategy chosen for the primary and caucus season may differ from the one used for the general election, when most contests are one-on-one. For presidential candidates, success in the early primaries is crucial. Victories in the New Hampshire primary and IOWA CAUCUS can quickly transform a candidate from DARK HORSE to front-runner in terms of improved POLLING results, delegate counts, endorsements, financial and volunteer backing, and media coverage. Conversely, these contests cause many candidates to drop out before they have a chance to demonstrate their vote-getting ability in home territory.

Once the primaries have winnowed out most candidates, the survivors concentrate on the delegate count. The delegate-selection process is shorter than it used to be, however, because of trend known as FRONT-LOAD-ING or compression of the primary season. Large states such as California, New Jersey, Ohio, and Pennsylvania formerly held their primaries late in the season, which required the candidates to campaign for months to obtain enough delegates to assure nomination.

But because of front-loading the primary season is over quickly. In 1996, when the Democratic presidential nomination was not in question, the Republican primaries in California, Ohio, and Pennsylvania were all held in April, and all the primaries of both parties were over by June 4. By then, Dole already had been the apparent GOP nominee for more than two months.

Front-loading has changed the dynamics of strategic planning for presidential aspirants. Survivors of the early knockout strategy cannot realistically hope to dislodge the front-runner with a slow-buildup strategy. Especially in an age of PROPORTIONAL REPRESENTA-TION, late surges of support are unlikely to undo the mathematics of delegate counts.

For congressional and gubernatorial candidates, primary or caucus success is also essential, but for a different reason. Party primaries or caucuses within a state usually are held on the same day, giving the candidate only one chance to gain the nomination.

Fund-raising ability is a must for all candidates. Presidential candidates can obtain PUBLIC FINANCING of their campaigns, but only if they meet a threshold of fund raising in the primaries and do well enough in the general election popular vote to qualify for funding in the next election. Candidates who accept public financing must also accept federal spending limits. Most candidates set up POLITICAL ACTION COMMITTEES (PACs), which have higher contribution limits than that for individuals.

Congressional elections are not publicly funded but

are subject to federal contribution limits. Most states regulate campaign funding. and some provide partial public financing.

To avoid federal spending limits and disclosure requirements, some wealthy individuals have financed presidential campaigns without accepting public funds. Former Texas governor John B. Connally in 1980 and publishing magnate Malcolm S. "Steve" Forbes Jr. in 1996 spent heavily in the primaries, trying unsuccessfully to win the Republican nomination.

Texas billionaire Ross Perot also passed up federal financing to run as an INDEPENDENT in 1992. His third-place finish with almost 19 percent of the vote was more than enough to qualify his new Reform Party for public funding in the 1996 election.

Most other recent presidential candidates have relied on public funding, and their choice of strategy has been dictated largely by the need to risk resources early in hopes of scoring an electoral breakthrough and attracting more contributions. An exception was former California governor Jerry Brown, who freed himself from fund-raising pressures in 1992 with a "shoestring" campaign for the Democratic nomination. He set a contribution limit of $100 and asked voters to give by calling a toll-free telephone number. The strategy proved effective. Brown placed next to Clinton with 20.1 percent of the total Democratic primary vote.

Another strategy consideration is electability. Although in life "looks aren't everything," in political campaigns appearances are important. In the media age, a candidate's visage must be camera friendly. It need not be Hollywood idol beautiful or handsome (although that quality was an asset to actor Ronald Reagan), but it must at least not be a distraction from the candidate's other strengths, such as intelligence, speaking ability, competence, and experience.

Some analysts believed that Sen. John Kennedy prevailed over Vice President Richard Nixon in 1960 in large part because of his appearance in the first presidential DEBATE. On the black and white television screens of the time, Nixon appeared pale and ill at ease, while Kennedy looked tan and calm. Polls showed that many people who heard the debate on radio thought that Nixon had "won."

Numerous studies have indicated that some voters are so concerned about "wasting" a vote that electability is a major aspect of their decision making. The candidates, too, are concerned about their electability, especially toward the end of the primary season. Then they try even harder to show the public, the media, and political professionals that they would do best against the likely nominee of the other party.

In the general election presidential nominees tailor their strategies to undermine the electability of their opponents and draw as many votes as possible from all regions of the country. They especially want to win the most populous states because these states have the most electoral votes, which go the popular vote winner in each state. To be elected president or vice president, a nominee needs an ABSOLUTE MAJORITY, or at least 270 of the 538 votes in the ELECTORAL COLLEGE. California with its fifty-four electoral votes is the big prize, followed by New York (thirty-three electoral votes), Texas (thirty-two), Florida (twenty-five), Pennsylvania (twenty-three), and Illinois (twenty-two). In 1996 both major party nominees campaigned frequently in those six states, which Clinton won except for Texas.

Sometimes, however, a candidate finds it advantageous to try to assemble a winning combination of smaller states. For example, in the 1960s Republicans, beginning with Barry Goldwater, launched what came to be known as a "southern strategy" to offset Democratic strength in the industrial Northeast and Midwest. To critics the strategy had a racial connotation because it was intended to lure southern white Democrats with opposition to laws by which African Americans were being integrated and gaining voting rights. (See BLACK SUFFRAGE.)

The nominees may also engage in NEGATIVE CAMPAIGNING to reverse a slide in the ratings, as President Bush did in 1988 when the polls indicated he was losing to the Democratic governor of Massachusetts, Michael Dukakis. Bush tried to portray his opponent as unpatriotic, weak on environmental protection, and soft on crime. Bush supporters paid for a TV ad that told the story of a furloughed prisoner from Massachusetts who raped a woman in Maryland. Although the "Willie Horton" ad ran only a few times in southern states, it appeared repeatedly on national TV news because it was so controversial. The Bush campaign's national MEDIA USE strategy thus gained free air time and contributed to Dukakis's subsequent loss of approval.

## Candidate-Centered Campaigns

Political candidates are no longer dependent on the parties' organizational resources. Their CAMPAIGN STRATEGIES are candidate centered and media oriented. Through television, candidates can reach voters without party advertising. They can create their own campaign organizations by hiring POLITICAL CONSULTANTS who specialize in all the techniques of modern campaigning—POLLING, direct mail, creation and placement of TV commercials, and targeted appeals to various voter groups.

Candidates can even deemphasize their party ties when doing so is advantageous. Such candidate-centered campaigning shapes attitudes about the candidates, but it does little to reinforce partisan commitments among the electors and can render PARTY IDENTIFICATION a less powerful influence. Although voters see differences between the DEMOCRATIC and REPUBLICAN Parties, issues and evaluations of the candidates themselves are looming larger in their decisions.

Federalism, the dispersal of authority to a wide array of government units and elected officials, has contributed to the decentralization of power in American politics. Parties must organize not only to win the presidency but also to win offices in the thousands of constituencies found in the fifty states. Each of these election DISTRICTS has its own party organization, elected officials, and candidate organizations. Frequently, their interests and priorities are quite different from those of their party's national leadership.

For example, when the Democratic leader in New York City's Bronx was asked whether he was concerned about the outcome of the 1996 presidential election, he responded: "It doesn't affect our life one bit. National politics—president and such—are too far removed from the bread-and-butter things that matter to local

leaders and mayors and governors. The local leader cares about a senior citizen center, a local concern." By creating thousands of distinct party organizations and separately elected state and local officials, the American brand of federalism has made centralized control of the parties virtually impossible.

The decentralizing effects are reinforced by the manner in which nominations are made and elections are conducted. Party nominations for state, local, and congressional offices are made through a system of PRIMARIES and CAUCUSES. Because the voters, not the party leaders, control the nominating process, the candidates build personal—not party—organizations to compete in the primaries. Knowing that it is their personal campaign efforts and organizations that win primary elections, officeholders rarely feel a strong sense of obligation to their party organization.

Indeed, electoral survival requires building a personal organization and not depending on popular presidents or a party organization to carry one to victory. Individual candidates are responsible for most of their own CAMPAIGN FINANCE needs. Armed with adequate financing, a candidate can then secure the other resources essential to a campaign—media experts, pollsters, computer specialists, direct-mail specialists, accountants, lawyers, campaign managers, and consultants.

INCUMBENCY lends itself to candidate-centered campaigning, particularly for members of Congress. Unlike the president, most GOVERNORS, and many STATE LEGISLATORS, members of Congress are not subject to TERM LIMITS. Efforts by half the states to limit congressional terms have been struck down by the Supreme Court, leaving Congress as a refuge for career politicians.

Campaigning for reelection to Congress has become almost a full-time job. Senators or representatives who win reelection term after term become better known than their CHALLENGERS, have an easier time raising money and obtaining endorsements from other officeholders. They also establish records on which they can run, while the challengers can only promise to do as well or better.

As a campaign strategy, use of incumbency is effec-

*Mary Matalin, right, chief strategist for Republican presidential candidate George Bush, leaves the Oval Office with the president, left, and his campaign manager, Fred Malek, in March 1992. Source: Reuters*

tive. In 1996, for example, 94.0 percent of House members and 90.5 percent of senators seeking reelection were successful. Reelection rates for both chambers have been consistently high for decades.

## The Effect of Image

With the campaign focused on the candidate, his or her image—personality, physical appearance, style, and background—takes on special importance. Nowhere is this more true than in presidential politics, where the candidates are known to the public mostly from the MEDIA COVERAGE of their campaigns.

As in state and local elections, presidential candidates are more independent of their parties than they were in the past. Most nominees go into the general election part of the campaign with the same organization that helped them win the primaries. Beginning in 1976 presidential candidates have received PUBLIC FINANCING, further relieving their dependence on the parties' national committees. Today the parties rely more on the candidates than the other way around. Candidates with a favorable public image can contribute significantly to their party's vote on ELECTION DAY.

Dwight Eisenhower, whose personal appeal transcended partisanship, was a classic example of a candidate whose image added substantially to his total vote. His status as a World War II hero and his personal qualities—sincerity, sense of duty, commitment to family, religious devotion, and sheer likability—all of which were captured in the CAMPAIGN SLOGAN "I like Ike," caused heavy Democratic defections to the Republican Party in 1952 and again in 1956.

In both 1984 and 1988 Democratic nominees were hurt by voters' negative perceptions of them. Reagan benefited in 1984 from public perceptions of Walter Mondale as "a weak leader," "a big spender," and "tied to special interests." In 1988 exit polls showed that voters for George Bush considered Michael Dukakis "too liberal," indicating that the Bush campaign succeeded in defining Dukakis in terms of his IDEOLOGY. Dukakis supporters, on the other hand, said that Bush's NEGATIVE CAMPAIGNING was what they liked least about him.

Candidate images also played a role in the 1992 and 1996 elections. Despite allegations of marital infidelity while he was governor of Arkansas, Democratic challenger Bill Clinton successfully played on public worries in 1992 over the state of the economy. EXIT POLLS showed that the candidate's qualities that mattered most to voters were "will bring about change" (favored Clinton over President Bush 67 percent to 5 percent) and "cares about people like me" (favored Clinton over Bush 64 percent to 11 percent). Bush's most positive qualities were his experience and his ability to handle a crisis.

With the economy healthy in 1996 President Clinton, still fighting off the effects of real estate and sexual harassment SCANDALS from his days as governor, again overcame the character issue to win reelection. His Republican challenger, Robert J. Dole, had image problems of his own, including a reputation for meanness and an alleged affair during his first marriage. Some voters also perceived Dole as too old for the job. At seventy-three, Dole would have been the oldest president at the time of his election.

## Running for Congress

Congressional candidates are largely on their own. They can normally count on only moderate levels of support from their party organizations. They assemble their own campaign staffs, collect their own financial contributions, and emphasize their own records.

Most have been able, through highly personalized campaigning, to insulate themselves from national swings of electoral sentiment. As a result, presidential

COATTAILS (the ability of popular presidential candidates to carry their party's House and Senate candidates into office) have grown extremely short in recent elections.

The three-way 1996 race was no exception. Clinton, Dole, and Reform Party candidate Ross Perot split the POPULAR VOTE, although Perot received no ELECTORAL COLLEGE votes. Because the election did not produce a landslide for Clinton, the coattail effect was limited. The Republicans kept the comfortable margin of congressional control they had gained in the 1994 MIDTERM ELECTIONS, although the Democrats did pick up nine seats in the House and two in the Senate. In 1998, contrary to predictions and historical patterns of presidential party losses at midterm, the Democrats had a net gain of five House seats, cutting the Republicans' margin to twelve, with one INDEPENDENT (in Vermont). The Senate party lineup was unchanged. After the 1998 elections Republicans held thirty-one governorships compared with seventeen for the Democrats and two independents (Maine and Minnesota).

The members of Congress who emerge from this new kind of decentralized and highly personalized electoral atmosphere owe less to their party organizations than did the candidates of old. Most House and Senate members consider themselves loyal party members and generally vote with the party leadership on roll-call votes. But they also recognize that it was their own efforts and the image they conveyed to their constituents—not the party's—that got them elected.

Today's Congress is actually 535 separate political enterprises, all being run simultaneously. It is an institution in which individuals with diverse objectives—reelection, power in the chamber, policy leadership, service to constituents, and even presidential aspirations—pursue their goals, sometimes in conflict with colleagues, and sometimes with their assistance and cooperation. It is a far cry from the days when party leaders hand picked the nominees, and Congress was made up of two large camps—Democratic members and Republican members—all beholden to the local parties that put them there.

## Candidate Image

*See* ELECTORAL BEHAVIOR; PARTY IDENTIFICA-
TION.

## Canvassing Board

A board of canvassers is an official body, usually bipartisan, that has a wide range of responsibilities for
the conduct of elections at the state, county, or local
level.

The name of the board may vary from state to state.
Maryland's, for example, is called the Maryland State
Administrative Board of Election Laws, or SABEL. The
bipartisan board is made up of five members appointed
by the governor for four-year terms. City or county
elections boards in Maryland are called the Board of
Supervisors of Elections.

Counties in some New England states have no government functions outside of the JUDICIAL SYSTEM.
In these states the elections or canvassing boards operate at the state, city, and town levels.

Functions of the canvassing board may include VOT-
ER REGISTRATION, establishing precincts and voting
sites, approving and training precinct officials, preparation and distribution of ballots and voting equipment,
collection of precinct vote counts, certifying the election
results, forwarding certificates of election to the winners, investigating any voting irregularities, and maintaining elections records. (See CONTESTED ELEC-
TIONS; DISTRICTS, WARDS, AND PRECINCTS.)

State elections boards are also responsible for administration of voter registration in compliance with
the National Voter Registration Act of 1993, popularly
known as the MOTOR VOTER ACT. Other aspects of
elections are shared with the federal government. (See
STATE AND FEDERAL ELECTION RESPONSIBILI-
TIES.)

## Caucus

A political caucus is a meeting of party members to
act on official business, chiefly the nomination of candidates. In the PRIMARY-dominated era of presidential
politics, however, caucuses have survived almost as an
anachronism in the nominating process. As the number
of primaries has grown, caucuses have lost much of
their former significance.

As late as 1968, candidates sought to run well in primary states mainly to gain a bargaining chip with
which to deal with powerful leaders in the caucus states.
Republicans Barry M. Goldwater in 1964 and Richard
Nixon in 1968 and Democrat Hubert H. Humphrey in
1968 all built up solid majorities among caucus-state
delegates that carried them to their parties' nominations. Humphrey did not even enter a primary in
1968.

In subsequent presidential elections, candidates
placed their principal emphasis on primaries. Democratic candidate George S. McGovern in 1972 and both
Republican president Gerald R. Ford and Democratic
challenger Jimmy Carter in 1976 won nomination by securing large majorities of the primary-state DELE-
GATES. McGovern's campaign benefited from a surprise win in the IOWA CAUCUS, but neither he nor Ford
won a majority of the caucus-state delegates. Carter was
able to win a delegate majority only after his opponents'
primary campaigns collapsed.

Carter's victory in Iowa transformed caucuses into
the means of attracting national publicity. Later DARK-
HORSE candidates—Republicans George Bush in 1980
and Marion G. "Pat" Robertson in 1988 and Democrats
Gary Hart in 1984 and Richard Gephardt in 1988—attracted attention because of their wins or surprisingly
strong showings in the Iowa contests.

### Complex Method

Compared with a primary, the caucus system is
complicated. Instead of focusing on a single primary
election ballot, the caucus presents a multitiered system that involves meetings scheduled over several

*Republican caucus voters stretch to place their ballots into a bucket at Indian Hills Junior High School in West Des Moines, Iowa, February 12, 1996. Senate majority leader Bob Dole was the winner, and Patrick J. Buchanan came in second.* Source: Jim Bourg, Reuters

weeks, sometimes even months. There is mass participation only at the first level (the so-called first-round caucuses), with meetings often lasting several hours and attracting only the most enthusiastic and dedicated party members.

Operation of the caucus varies from state to state, and each party has its own set of rules. Most begin with PRECINCT caucuses or some other type of local mass meeting open to all party voters. Participants, often publicly declaring their votes, elect delegates to the next stage in the process. In smaller states, such as Delaware and Hawaii, delegates are elected directly to a state convention, where the NATIONAL PARTY CONVENTION delegates are chosen. In larger states, such as Iowa, there is at least one intermediate step. Most frequently, precinct caucuses elect delegates to county conventions,

which then choose the national convention delegates.

Voter participation, even at the first level of the caucus process, is much lower than in primaries. Caucus participants usually are local party leaders and activists. Many rank-and-file voters find a caucus complex, confusing, time-consuming, even intimidating.

In a caucus state the focus is on one-on-one campaigning. Time, not money, is the most valuable resource. Because organization and personal campaigning are so important, an early start is far more crucial in a caucus state than in a primary. And because only a small segment of the electorate is targeted in most caucus states, candidates tend to use POLITICAL ADVERTISING sparingly.

Although the basic steps in the caucus process are the same for both parties, the rules that govern them are

## Delegate Selection Calendar for 1996

| | | | |
|---|---|---|---|
| January 25–31 | Hawaii (R) | March 16 | Michigan (D) |
| January 27–29 | Alaska (R) | March 19 | **Illinois** |
| February 6 | Louisiana (R) | | **Michigan (R)** |
| February 10 | Guam (R) | | **Ohio** |
| February 12 | Iowa | | **Wisconsin** |
| February 20 | **New Hampshire** | March 23 | Wyoming (D) |
| February 24 | **Delaware** | March 25 | Utah |
| February 27 | **Arizona (R)** | March 26 | **California** |
| | **North Dakota (R)** | | **Nevada (R)** |
| | **South Dakota (R)** | | **Washington (R)** |
| March | Virginia (R) | March 29 | North Dakota (D) |
| March 2 | **South Carolina (R)** | March 30 | Virgin Islands (D) |
| | Wyoming (R) | April 2 | **Kansas** |
| March 3 | **Puerto Rico (R)** | April 13, 15 | Virginia (D) |
| March 5 | **Colorado** | April 23 | **Pennsylvania** |
| | **Connecticut** | May 4 | Guam (D) |
| | **Georgia (D)** | May 7 | **District of Columbia** |
| | Idaho (D) | | **Indiana** |
| | **Maine** | | **North Carolina** |
| | **Maryland** | May 14 | **Nebraska** |
| | **Massachusetts** | | **West Virginia** |
| | Minnesota | May 21 | **Arkansas** |
| | **Rhode Island** | May 28 | **Idaho (R)** |
| | South Carolina (D) | | **Kentucky** |
| | **Vermont** | June 4 | **Alabama** |
| | Washington (D) | | **Montana (D)** |
| | American Samoa (D) | | **New Jersey** |
| March 7 | Missouri (D) | | **New Mexico** |
| | **New York** | June 5–13 | Montana (R) |
| March 9 | Alaska (D) | August 12–15 | Republican national |
| | Arizona (D) | | convention in San Diego |
| | Missouri (R) | August 26–29 | Democratic national |
| | South Dakota (D) | | convention in Chicago |
| March 9–11 | Democrats Abroad (D) | | |
| March 10 | Nevada (D) | | |
| | **Puerto Rico (D)** | | |
| March 12 | **Florida** | | |
| | Hawaii (D) | | |
| | **Louisiana** | | |
| | **Mississippi** | | |
| | **Oklahoma** | | |
| | **Oregon** | | |
| | **Tennessee** | | |
| | **Texas (R)** | | |
| | Texas (D) | | |

*Source:* Rhodes Cook, "1996 Presidential Primary and Caucus Calendar," *Congressional Quarterly Weekly Report,* January 13, 1996, 98–99.
*Note:* States that selected Democratic and Republican delegates on different dates in 1996 are designated by a "D" or an "R." States listed in normal type held caucuses; states listed in **bold** type held primaries.

vastly different. Democratic rules have been revamped substantially since 1968, establishing national standards for grass-roots participation. Republican rules have remained largely unchanged, with the states given wide latitude in drawing up their delegate-selection plans.

In some states, one party holds caucuses while the other holds primaries. Even if both parties hold caucuses, they might not be on the same date. In 1996 Democrats in Texas and Republicans in Louisiana and Washington used both a primary and caucus to elect delegates.

## Caucuses 1980–1996

For both the Republican and Democratic parties, the percentage of delegates elected from caucus states declined sharply throughout the 1970s. But the Democrats temporarily broke the downward trend and elected more delegates by the caucus process in 1980 than in 1976. Between 1980 and 1984 six states switched from a primary to a caucus system; none went the other way.

Since 1984 the trend has turned back toward primaries. In 1996 primaries were held by one or both parties in forty-four states, the District of Columbia, and Puerto Rico. The Democrats elected 65.3 percent of their national convention delegates in primaries, against only 16.8 percent in caucuses. (The remaining 17.9 percent were SUPERDELEGATE party and elected officials.) The Republicans in 1996 chose 87.9 percent of delegates in primaries and the rest in caucuses, with no superdelegates.

Events in 1984 and 1988 pointed up weaknesses in the caucus system. A strong caucus-states showing by Walter F. Mondale in 1984 led many Democrats to conclude that caucuses are inherently unfair. More than primaries, the complicated, low-visibility world of caucuses is open to takeover by insiders. In Mondale's case, a mainstream Democratic coalition of party activists, labor union members, and teachers had dominated the caucuses in his behalf.

In 1988 the Iowa Democratic caucus was seen as an unrepresentative test dominated by liberal INTEREST GROUPS. And the credibility of the caucus was shaken by the withdrawal from the race of the two winners—

### Iowa, New Hampshire, and Beyond

Following is a list of the Iowa and New Hampshire winners since 1980 and the eventual nominee. In most cases, that nominee has been the winner in New Hampshire, not Iowa, although for the Democrats in 1992, it was neither.

| Year | Party | Iowa Winner | N.H. Winner | Nominee |
|---|---|---|---|---|
| 1996 | Democrats | Clinton | Clinton | Clinton |
| | Republicans | Dole | Buchanan | Dole |
| 1992 | Democrats | Harkin | Tsongas | Clinton |
| | Republicans | No vote | Bush | Bush |
| 1988 | Democrats | Gephardt | Dukakis | Dukakis |
| | Republicans | Dole | Bush | Bush |
| 1984 | Democrats | Mondale | Hart | Mondale |
| | Republicans | No vote | Reagan | Reagan |
| 1980 | Democrats | Carter | Carter | Carter |
| | Republicans | Bush | Reagan | Reagan |

Source: Congressional Quarterly Weekly Report, February 17, 1996, 403. (Updated after nominees were chosen.)

Democrat Richard Gephardt and Republican Robert J. Dole—within a month after the caucus was held. Furthermore, several other state caucuses were marked by vicious infighting between supporters of various candidates.

In 1992 the presence of a FAVORITE SON candidate, Sen. Tom Harkin of Iowa, among the leading Democratic candidates for president further diminished the Iowa caucus's significance as a rival to the NEW HAMPSHIRE PRIMARY in predicting the parties' eventual nominees. Harkin easily won the caucus, but he soon dropped out after fading in the primaries.

With the field for the GOP nomination wide open in 1996 for the first time since 1980, Senator Dole again prevailed in Iowa, winning 26.3 percent of the vote. But he subsequently lost the New Hampshire primary to his chief Iowa opponent, Patrick J. Buchanan.

President Bill Clinton, unopposed for renomination, was the first eventual nominee since Jimmy Carter in

1980 to win both the Iowa caucus and the New Hampshire primary.

## Caucus Pros and Cons

Besides its complexity and tendency toward domination by party professionals, a major complaint about the caucus process is that it does not involve enough voters. The low turnouts are thought to be less representative of voter sentiment than a higher-turnout primary.

Staunch defenders, however, believe a caucus has party-building attributes a primary cannot match. They note that several hours at a caucus can involve voters in a way that quickly casting a primary ballot does not. The state party comes away from caucus meetings with lists of thousands of voters who can be tapped to volunteer time or money, or even to run for local office. And, while the multitiered caucus process is often a chore for the state party to organize, a primary is substantially more expensive.

---

# Census

Every ten years since 1790 a census has been taken of the U.S. population. The process turns up much valuable information about American society, but its constitutional purpose is to determine how many members each state will have in the House of Representatives. The size of the House has been fixed at 435 since Arizona and New Mexico joined the Union in 1912 (except for a temporary addition of two seats in 1959 when Alaska and Hawaii became states).

After each census Congress uses another process, REAPPORTIONMENT, to redivide the 435 House seats among the states according to population. As the population shifts, some states gain representatives at the expense of others. Then the affected state legislatures use the census data for REDISTRICTING—redrawing CONGRESSIONAL DISTRICTS as well as state legislative DISTRICTS to make their populations as nearly equal as possible.

Equality among districts within a state is required by the Supreme Court's ONE-PERSON, ONE-VOTE decision handed down in *Gray v. Sanders* (1963). Until then, some rural-dominated legislatures had drawn the lines to make farm districts much smaller in population than urban districts, in effect giving city dwellers less representation in the legislature. In 1964 the Court applied the same one-person, one-vote standard to Congress in *Wesberry v. Sanders.*

New computer technology, as well as legislation requiring more equitable representation of minority groups, greatly affected the redistricting process. Some congressional districts became so weirdly contorted that they gave new meaning to the term GERRYMANDER, the shaping of districts to benefit a particular politician, party, or minority group.

Efforts to get an accurate census count of African Americans and other minorities, and then link their neighborhoods through RACIAL REDISTRICTING, have proven to be particularly difficult and controversial. One congressional district in North Carolina, the Twelfth, included nearly every black neighborhood in the 175 miles between Durham and Charlotte and at times was no more than a strip along the Interstate 85 highway.

Conventional census methods usually undercount minorities and the poor. Many in those groups do not receive or respond to the forms mailed out by the U.S. Bureau of the Census. The 1990 census, for example, missed an estimated 4.7 million people.

For the 2000 census, the Census Bureau proposed to use statistical sampling techniques—like those used in POLLING—to solve the undercount problem. Ninety percent of households would be covered by questionnaire, telephone, or census visit. Enumerators would visit one in ten of the remaining households, and the additional data would be extrapolated from those surveys. Such sampling, the bureau said, could reduce the undercount from 2.1 percent to one-tenth of 1 percent.

The Democratic administration of President Bill Clinton supported the plan, but the Republican-controlled Congress tried to block it. Republicans believed that sampling would benefit Democrats because mi-

*The national census is conducted every ten years to determine, among other things, how many representatives each state will have in Congress. Here a census taker prepares to collect information in person. Source: R. Michael Jenkins, Congressional Quarterly*

norities, the homeless, and young people away from home tend to vote for Democratic candidates. They contended that the Constitution requires an actual head count. Some members of Congress sued to stop the sampling and largely succeeded. The Court ruled 5–4 in January 1999 that sampling estimates could not be used for reapportionment. The Court, however, did not foreclose using sampling numbers for redistricting within states. The Census Bureau said it would release both the actual and estimated numbers.

The controversy was not the first one caused by the census. After the 1920 census Congress, for the first time, could not agree on a reapportionment plan for the House. The 1910 allocation of seats remained the same until after the 1930 census, when farm states lost the seats they should have lost earlier because of the U.S. population shift to the cities.

## Constitutional Mandate

The Constitution made the first apportionment of the House because no reliable figures on the population were available at the time. The constitutional formula produced a House of sixty-five members divided among the thirteen original states. This apportionment was in effect for the First and Second Congresses, 1789–1793. (See HOUSE OF REPRESENTATIVES, ELECTING; HOUSE OF REPRESENTATIVES, QUALIFICATIONS.)

Article I, section 2, clause 3, of the Constitution called for a decennial census beginning in 1790 on which to base future apportionments of House seats. It states: "The actual Enumeration shall be made within three years after the first Meeting of the Congress of the United States, and within every subsequent Term of Ten years, in such manner as they shall by Law direct." Each state was guaranteed at least one representative.

Federal marshals, going from house to house on foot or horseback, took the early national censuses. The first census in 1790 took nine months and counted 3,929,214 people. By comparison, the 1990 census counted the U.S. population at 248,709,873.

In the early years of the Republic, a slave was counted as three-fifths of a person for House apportionment purposes. Slaves, women, and many white males who did not pay taxes or own property could not vote. Although they were counted for purposes of representation, they lacked true representation in Congress for many years until they gained the FRANCHISE. Gradually all religious, property, race, sex, and other adult voting restrictions fell. (See BLACK SUFFRAGE; NATURE OF REPRESENTATION; RIGHT TO VOTE; WOMEN'S SUFFRAGE; YOUTH SUFFRAGE.)

In 1850 census takers began recording every inhabitant by name, classified for the first time by age, sex, race, place of birth, and other categories. Thirty years later a census office in Washington took over the marshals' duties as enumerators. In 1902 Congress created the Bureau of the Census in what is now the Department of Commerce.

With every census, the bureau has expanded its coverage and analyses of the U.S. population, economy, and other facets of American life. Besides the national census, the bureau makes special interim censuses of regions, states, and cities. It also gathers all manner of statistics on agriculture, education, elections and voter turnout, law enforcement, manufacturing, and other areas that affect the nation as a whole. The bureau publishes the information in numerous reports, notably its annual and historical versions of the *Statistical Abstract of the United States.*

Much of the updated information is available on the Census Bureau's World Wide Web site on the Internet: *http://www.census.gov.* Scholars complained, however, that the Census Bureau was shifting emphasis to the Internet at the expense of its printed reports. In 1997 and 1998 the number of reports was down sharply from the 1,035 published in 1992, and in some cases census data was not available as quickly by computer as it had been in print form. Census officials attributed some of the changes to pressure from Congress to cut costs and narrow its areas of study. For the census on April 1, 2000, the bureau planned to ask only seven questions on its short-form questionnaire, down from twelve in 1990. For the long form, which about 20 percent of households would receive, the census would drop five subjects and add one—asking whether grandparents are caregivers for their grandchildren.

## Count and Consequences

The seemingly straightforward task of counting noses is more complex and subject to dispute than are most activities of government agencies. So much depends on the census findings that the losers seldom give up without a fight and the winners are only too willing to claim their rewards.

Prized above all in the fallout from the census is full representation in Congress and the state legislatures. Many battles over U.S. House or state legislative seats have been fought in the capitals or courts, usually with the underrepresented gaining some ground in their struggle for equal rights.

A case in point is the prolonged dispute over the landmark census of 1920. Although the rural states managed to stave off the consequences for a full decade, California and other states with large urban populations ultimately gained the seats to which they were entitled according to the census figures.

In the 1960s a number of lawsuits pointed up the great disparities of apportionment in the state legislatures and the U.S. House, culminating in decisions that nudged the legislatures closer to the Supreme Court's one-person, one-vote standard.

The lopsidedness was worst in the state capitals. By 1960 no state legislative body had less than a 2-to-1 population disparity between the most and least heavily populated districts. In some it was far greater. The disparity was 242–1 in the Connecticut house, 223–1 in the Nevada senate, 141–1 in the Rhode Island senate, and 9–1 in the Georgia senate.

In congressional districts the census showed that one Texas district had one-fourth as many inhabitants as the largest district. Arizona, Maryland, and Ohio each had at least one district with three times as many inhabitants as the least populated. But in contrast to the 1920s situation it was the suburbs—not the cities—that were most underrepresented. After World War II the population shifted away from the central cities, but again the legislatures were slow to make apportionment mirror reality.

They were no longer able, however, to ignore the problem of malapportionment. As a result of the 1960s Court decisions in cases such as *Gray v. Sanders* and BAKER V. CARR, nearly every state was forced to redraw its district lines. By the 1990s the effects were obvious. Most states came close to population equality among districts. After the 1990 census all thirty congressional districts in Texas, for example, had the same population: 566,217.

Most census-related disputes in the 1990s arose from questions of who to count and how to do it. With the United States' growing racial diversity, legal and illegal immigration, and unsolved gaps between the rich and the poor, it was not easy for the Census Bureau to avoid controversy over methodology.

In addition to its role in congressional reapportionment, the census supplies the data for drawing state and local district boundaries and for distributing certain federal funds. If that distribution favors one group over another, the Census Bureau likely takes the blame. Some public officials complain that the bureau's effort to count all people living in the United States has unfair political ramifications.

The inclusion of illegal aliens in the population figures is one area of dispute. The Fourteenth Amendment, ratified in 1868, changed the Constitution's original census wording to require apportionment based on a count of "the whole number of persons in each State, excluding Indians not taxed." To the Census Bureau this phrase means including illegal aliens, a policy troubling to states that fear losing House seats to states such as California and Texas that have high rates of illegal immigration. Defenders of the policy say that any questions used to separate out illegal aliens could discourage others from responding and undermine the accuracy of the census.

Census Bureau efforts to address the undercounting of minorities has produced even more heated debate. In 1991, during the Bush administration, the Commerce Department refused to adjust the 1990 census despite the apparent 2.1 percent undercount. In 1996 the Supreme Court upheld a lower court's ruling against New York City and others in support of Commerce's decision to make no adjustment.

A postcensus survey by the National Research Council, an affiliate of the National Academy of Sciences, found that more than 9.0 million people had not been counted, while several million had been counted erroneously, for an estimated net undercount of about 5.3 million people. According to the survey, blacks were undercounted by 4.8 percent, American Indians by 5 percent, and Hispanics by 5.2 percent. The 5.3 million undercount estimate was later revised to 4.7 million.

A related problem arose from the difficulty of racial identification. With the multiplicity of races in the United States, many people do not fit neatly into any one category such as "white," "black," Asian, or Latino. They may be a blend of several such categories, making it difficult for them to find the right block to check on the census form.

To make it easier for them, and make the census more accurate, the Clinton administration announced that the 2000 census, for the first time, would allow Americans to check off as many categories as they like to describe their race. The administration rejected, however, the creation of a single "multiracial" category, as proposed by some multiracial advocacy groups.

Another long-standing question, whether to count overseas military personnel and dependents, was decided in their favor for the 1990 census. Reversing policy, the Census Bureau included them in 1990 and counted 923,000, who, for purposes of reapportionment, were assigned to the state each individual considered home. Americans stationed abroad had also been counted once before, in the 1970 census during the Vietnam War. Congress later made permanent provision for the counting of overseas personnel. (See ABSENTEE VOTING.)

## Challenger

In political races the challenger is the person seeking the office already held by an INCUMBENT. As a rule, the challenger faces an uphill battle in trying to unseat an officeholder.

Incumbents have advantages in name recognition, fund raising, staff, news MEDIA COVERAGE, and a proven record to run on. The record in office can be a disadvantage, however, if it includes actions or issue positions that have angered the voters.

Under the TERM LIMIT imposed by the Twenty-second Amendment, presidents can be incumbents for no more than two full terms. Challengers therefore have only one opportunity to unseat a sitting president. Since the amendment became effective in 1951, only three challengers have been successful: Jimmy Carter against Gerald R. Ford in 1976, Ronald Reagan against Carter in 1980, and Bill Clinton against George Bush in 1992. During the same period, five incumbents survived election challenges (Dwight D. Eisenhower in 1956, Lyndon B. Johnson in 1964, Richard Nixon in 1972, Reagan in 1984, and Clinton in 1996). Although many factors enter into the unseating of a president, all three of the losing incumbents undoubtedly were hurt by problems with the economy during their administrations.

Governors are particularly vulnerable to challengers if they have succeeded in raising taxes or failed to cut them when the state's economy improved. POCKET-BOOK VOTING is perhaps more common in state elections than federal elections because people are more immediately affected by state and local taxes.

Although there are many "tax-loss governors" it is not entirely clear that challengers always benefit from state tax increases. Political scientist Gerald Pomper surveyed thirty-seven states in the 1960s and concluded that "voters do not evidence a consistent concern for fiscal issues."

More recent evidence shows that challengers usually fail to dislodge incumbent governors. From 1970 to 1991, 180 governors ran for reelection, and 131 or 73 percent won. Put another way, challengers were successful in only 27 percent of these races.

The trend to four-year terms for governors has reduced the opportunities to be elected to this office. Although the longer tenure is somewhat offset by term limits in many states, the turnover in statehouses is lower than in the past. From 1900 to 1910, each state elected an average of 3.3 new governors. In the 1980s the average state had only 1.1 new governors.

In congressional elections since 1988, challengers' success rate in Senate races dropped, while the rate for House challengers improved. In 1988, 13 percent of Senate incumbents were defeated, compared with only 1 percent for House incumbents. By 1996 only 5 percent of Senate incumbents were defeated, and House incumbent defeats had risen to 5 percent.

CAMPAIGN FINANCE reports filed with the FEDERAL ELECTION COMMISSION showed a direct correlation in 1996 between challengers' spending and their successes or failures in the general election. Successful challengers for House seats spent an average of more than $1 million on their campaigns. It was the first time since 1986 that challengers spent as much money as the incumbents they defeated.

In 1996 Senate campaigns, challengers spent 26 percent less than the $4.2 million spent by the average incumbent senator.

---

## Checkoff Fund

*See* CAMPAIGN FINANCE; PUBLIC FINANCING.

---

## Chronology of Presidential Elections

The American system of presidential selection has evolved over the years with little guidance from the nation's founders. The Constitution contained no provisions for organizing political parties, for nominating candidates, or for campaigning for office. Furthermore, the original provision for balloting by the ELECTORAL COLLEGE was flawed and had to be superseded by the Twelfth Amendment in 1804. Following are brief descriptions of elections that proved to be turning points in the evolution of presidential selection.

### Election of 1789

In 1789 there was no formal nomination of candidates. It had been obvious since the close of the Constitutional Convention that George Washington would be president, even though he was not eager to serve. The only real question was who his vice president would be. Most Federalist leaders ultimately decided to support John Adams of Massachusetts.

Federalist leader Alexander Hamilton disliked Adams and so plotted to siphon votes away from him. He feared that Adams could become president because, under the Constitution as originally written, each member of the electoral college was to vote for two persons, with no distinction between votes for president or vice president. Hamilton's strategy worked. When the electoral votes were counted, Washington had been elected president unanimously, with all sixty-nine votes. As the

*There was no formal nomination of candidates in 1789 because at the close of the Constitutional Convention it was obvious that George Washington, the Revolutionary War hero, would be elected president. Source: Library of Congress*

next highest vote getter, Adams became vice president with thirty-four electoral votes; the others were divided among several candidates.

## The First Contest: 1796

Washington won a second term in 1792 but chose not to run again in 1796. With Washington out of the race, the United States witnessed its first partisan contest for president. Once again the defects of the electoral college system were evident. It was still possible for the two top candidates to receive the same number of votes, which would throw the election into the House of Representatives. And again it was also possible that the candidate for vice presidency—through fluke or machination—could end up with the most votes and be elected president.

The two presidential candidates were Federalist John Adams and Democratic-Republican Thomas Jefferson. Hamilton once again sought to thwart Adams's ambitions by urging northern electors to divide their votes between Adams and his running mate, Thomas Pinckney of South Carolina. Because Adams was unpopular in the South, Hamilton expected that Pinckney would win more votes there and, with northern electors divided, Pinckney would win the election.

Hamilton's plot backfired, however, when eighteen northern electors voted not for Pinckney but for other Federalist candidates. As a result, Adams was elected president with seventy-one electoral votes, and Thomas Jefferson was named vice president with sixty-eight votes. Pinckney came in third. Neither the Federalists nor the Democratic-Republicans seemed unduly concerned that the president and vice president were of opposing parties. Both sides felt that they had prevented the opposition from gaining total victory.

## The Jefferson-Burr Contest: 1800

The election of 1800 was notable for two reasons. It was the first in which both parties used congressional caucuses to nominate candidates for their tickets, and it was the first presidential election to be decided in the House of Representatives.

The Federalists named Adams and Maj. Gen. Charles Cotesworth Pinckney, older brother of Thomas Pinckney, to their ticket. Jefferson and Aaron Burr were the nominees of the Democratic-Republicans. Hamilton again sought to use the defect of the electoral college system to defeat Adams and give Pinckney the presidency. But when the votes were counted it turned out that Jefferson and Burr were tied for first place. The election was thrown into the Federalist-controlled House of Representatives.

Some Federalists felt that Burr was the lesser of two evils and plotted to elect him president instead of Jefferson. Hamilton helped to squelch that idea, but thirty-six ballots were taken before Jefferson received a majority. The crisis—which could have fatally wounded the new nation by calling into question the legitimacy of the president—was over.

The near disaster led to the passage of the Twelfth

Amendment to the Constitution in September 1804. It called for electors to vote for president and vice president on separate ballots, thus eliminating the possibility of a tie between the principal candidate and his running mate.

## The Death of King Caucus: 1824

With Jefferson's election, the Federalist Party began to fade away, leaving only one party. That meant that nomination by the Democratic-Republican caucus, or King Caucus as it was known, was tantamount to election. In 1824 the Democratic-Republicans were still the only party, but several candidates within it were seeking the presidential nomination: Secretary of State John Quincy Adams, Sen. Andrew Jackson, Secretary of War John C. Calhoun, House Speaker Henry Clay, and Secretary of the Treasury William H. Crawford.

Crawford was the early leader, and it was assumed that he would win the nomination if a congressional caucus were held. For that reason, supporters of the other candidates refused to attend a caucus. When it was finally convened, only sixty-six members of Congress were present, virtually all of them Crawford supporters. Although Crawford was suffering from the debilitating effects of a stroke, he won the nomination. The other candidates immediately criticized the caucus as being unrepresentative of the party and refused to abide by its results.

That incident put an end to the caucus as a mechanism for naming presidential nominees. But it did not end the drama of the 1824 election. Calhoun dropped his race to join forces with Crawford, but Adams, Clay, and Jackson all continued to campaign. When none of the four received a majority of the electoral votes, the names of the top three candidates—Jackson, Adams, and Crawford—were placed before the House. Clay, who came in fourth, helped tip the balance when he announced that he would support Adams. Adams narrowly won the House election, even though Jackson had won the most popular votes and the most electoral votes. Rumor had it that Adams had promised to name Clay secretary of state, as in fact he did. The events of 1824 kindled the flame of popular democracy and set

the stage for a rematch between Adams and Jackson in 1828.

## Jackson's Rise: 1828

The hold of the so-called Virginia dynasty on U.S. politics was loosened in 1828 when Jackson's broad appeal among farmers and common laborers, especially in the West, gave him an easy victory. As the nation expanded economically and geographically, Jackson's appeal for democratic processes to replace elite maneuverings was bound to receive a sympathetic hearing.

Under the tutelage of Vice President Martin Van Buren of New York, Jackson developed a strong national Democratic Party based on patronage. Strict party organization soon became a prerequisite for competition in national politics. The Whigs' 1836 presidential campaign was the last in which a party eschewed a unified national ticket. Van Buren easily defeated the Whigs that year.

## The Fateful Election of 1860

The regional differences that had torn the nation apart for decades reached their peak in 1860. Four major candidates sought the presidency. None could compete seriously throughout the nation, and it was probable that a candidate from the North would win because that region had the most electoral votes.

The two northern candidates were Abraham Lincoln, a former U.S. representative from Illinois, and Stephen Douglas, a Democrat who had defeated Lincoln for the Illinois Senate seat in 1858. Southern Democrats who had defected from the party nominated Vice President John Breckinridge of Kentucky as their candidate for president. The CONSTITUTIONAL UNION PARTY— which developed as an attempt, although an unsuccessful one, to repair the nation's geographic divisions— nominated John Bell of Tennessee.

Lincoln was the consensus compromise choice of the Republican Party, which had developed in the 1850s out of disgruntled elements from several parties. Above all else, the Republicans stood against the extension of slavery into new territories. By accepting slavery where it already existed but warning against nationalization of

*After the antislavery Abraham Lincoln won the 1860 presidential election, seven southern states seceded from the Union and formed the Confederate States of America. Source: Library of Congress*

the system, the Republicans divided the Democrats and picked up support from an array of otherwise contentious factions—abolitionists, moderate abolitionists, and whites who feared for their position in the economy.

Lincoln won easily, with 40 percent of the popular vote and 180 electoral votes. Although Douglas came in second with the electorate, winning 29.5 percent, he won only 12 electoral votes. Breckinridge received 72, and Bell 39.

Southerners had vowed to secede from the Union if Lincoln won the presidency. After the election South Carolina, Louisiana, Mississippi, Alabama, Georgia, Texas, and Florida seceded and in February 1861 formed the Confederate States of America. After a protracted standoff between Union soldiers who held Fort Sumter in Charleston, South Carolina, and the Confederate sol-

diers who controlled the state, the Confederates fired on the fort. Virginia, Arkansas, North Carolina, and Tennessee then joined the Confederacy, and the Civil War had begun.

## The Compromise of 1876

Little more than ten years after the Civil War ended, disputed election results in the contest between Republican Rutherford B. Hayes and Democrat Samuel J. Tilden created a constitutional crisis and raised fears that another civil war was imminent. Hayes, the three-time governor of Ohio, lost the popular vote and had a questionable hold on the electoral college vote, but he managed to win the presidency when the election was settled by a special commission created by Congress. (Hayes won 4.0 million votes to Tilden's 4.3 million.)

The problem arose when the vote tallies in Florida, South Carolina, and Louisiana were called into question. There was good reason to be suspicious of any vote count in these and other southern states. Although the Republicans controlled the balloting places and mounted vigorous drives to get newly enfranchised blacks to the polls, the Democrats used physical intimidation and bribery to keep blacks away.

When state election board recounts and investigations did not settle the issue, Congress appointed a commission composed of five senators, five representatives, and five Supreme Court justices; eight commission members were Republican, seven Democratic. The crisis was resolved after weeks of bargaining that gave the Republicans the presidency in exchange for a pledge to pull federal troops out of the states of the Confederacy and to commit federal money to making internal improvements in the South.

The compromise did more than settle the partisan dispute between Hayes and Tilden; it also established a rigid alignment of political interests that would dominate U.S. politics for the next half century. Although Democrats won occasional victories, the Republican, eastern, conservative, business-oriented establishment held sway over the system until Franklin Roosevelt's election in 1932. At the same time, southern politics was left in the hands of many of the same figures who led or,

*Franklin D. Roosevelt was the first candidate to appear before the convention that nominated him and the only president to be elected four times. Source: AP/Wide World*

later, honored the Confederacy. Within months, southern states were erecting a powerful edifice of racial discrimination that would last until the 1960s.

## The Republicans Self-Destruct: 1912

Between 1860 and 1932, only two Democrats won the presidency—Grover Cleveland in 1884 and 1892, and Woodrow Wilson in 1912.

In Wilson, a former university professor and governor of New Jersey, the Democrats nominated a true liberal. During his presidency Wilson left a lasting legacy in domestic and foreign affairs and also in the style of presidential leadership. But Wilson probably would not have won the general election in 1912 without a battle in the Republican Party that pitted the incumbent William Howard Taft against the popular former president Theodore Roosevelt.

The Taft-Roosevelt feud stemmed largely from Roosevelt's feeling that Taft had betrayed the trust-busting, conservation, and foreign policies that Roosevelt had pursued between 1901 and 1908. Roosevelt was a proud advocate of the "bully pulpit," and Taft was ill suited to the rough-and-tumble nature of public controversies.

Although Roosevelt challenged Taft in the Republican primaries—the first instance of a popular campaign for the nomination—Wilson plotted and plodded his way to the Democratic nomination. He won the nomination on the forty-sixth ballot. Wilson then took to the hustings, urging Americans to seek a moral awakening and to approve a program of liberal reforms.

But Wilson's campaigning alone might not have been enough to win him the presidency. The margin of victory was provided when Roosevelt bolted the Republican Party to run his own third party campaign. (See

PROGRESSIVE PARTY–BULL MOOSE.) Wilson won the election with 41.8 percent of the vote. Roosevelt finished second, with 27.4 percent, and the incumbent, Taft, brought up the rear with 23.2 percent. It was a most unusual result, with a newly created third party outpolling the incumbent, and both losing to a candidate with little political experience.

## Dawn of the New Deal: 1932

After three years of Republican Herbert C. Hoover's uncertain leadership following the stock market crash of 1929, Democrat Franklin D. Roosevelt won the presidency and oversaw the greatest shift in political alignments in U.S. history.

Roosevelt, who won the Democratic nomination on the fourth ballot, was the first candidate to appear before the convention that nominated him. In his acceptance speech, he made passing reference to a "new deal" that his administration would offer Americans. After an active fall campaign, Roosevelt won 57.4 percent of the vote, 42 of the 48 states, and 472 of 531 electoral votes.

The Democratic coalition that began to form during that election brought together a disparate group of interests. Until the New Deal, the party's base in the North had consisted of laborers and the poor, immigrants and Catholics; in the South, the Democrats were the party of white supremacy and agricultural interests. In 1932 blacks moved en masse to the Democratic Party from their traditional position in the "Party of Lincoln," partly because of Hoover's failure, but also because of the inclusive rhetoric of the New Deal. Jews, who had traditionally voted Republican, turned to the Democrats as they became the more liberal party.

Political scientist Samuel Beer has argued that with the New Deal, the Democratic Party was able to combine its traditional concern for local, individual interests with a national vision. By bringing "locked out" groups into the system, the Democrats contributed both to the building of the nation and to individual freedoms.

The political genius of the New Deal was not just that it offered something to everyone, but also that it created a situation in which everyone's interest lay in growth. The potentially divisive competition over restricted and unequally distributed resources was avoided with a general acceptance of growth as the common goal. When there was growth, everyone could get a little more. That public philosophy remained part of American political discourse.

Roosevelt's coalition and leadership were so strong that he became the only president to win more than two elections. Roosevelt's four electoral triumphs caused Republicans to fume about his "imperial" presidency.

In his second run for the White House, Roosevelt won 60.8 percent of the popular vote and increased the number of Democrats in both the House and the Senate. His percentages dropped in the next two elections—to 54.7 percent in 1940 and 53.4 percent in 1944—but in neither election did his Republican challenger receive more than ninety-nine electoral votes.

Harry S. Truman, who succeeded to the presidency when Roosevelt died less than two months after his fourth inauguration, had a much tougher time of it in 1948. Truman ran against not only Republican Thomas E. Dewey, who had lost to Roosevelt in 1944, but also two candidates backed by the left and right wings of his own party. The Dixiecrats, under the leadership of South Carolina's governor, J. Strom Thurmond, left the Democratic convention to run a states' rights campaign in the South. Henry Wallace was the candidate of the Democratic left, campaigning against Truman's Marshall Plan, military buildup, and confrontational stance toward the Soviet Union. Truman squeaked by with 49.5 percent of the vote to Dewey's 45.1 percent. Each of the breakaway Democrats won 2.4 percent.

Truman's political fortunes worsened after the 1948 election, and he belatedly decided against seeking a second full term. In 1952, for the first time in twenty-four years, neither party had an incumbent president as its nominee.

## Eisenhower's Victory: 1952

In Dwight Eisenhower the Republicans were able to recruit a candidate with universal appeal who was coveted by both parties. Eisenhower, who had just left the presidency of Columbia University to take charge of the forces of the North Atlantic Treaty Organization, won the Republican nomination on the first convention ballot. He selected as his running mate Sen. Richard Nixon of California, a young conservative who had won national recognition for his role in the controversial House Committee on Un-American Activities.

The eventual Democratic nominee was Adlai Stevenson, governor of Illinois and the grandson of Grover Cleveland's second vice president. Stevenson's campaign was an eloquent call to arms for liberals and reformers. Years later, Democrats would recall how the campaign inspired the generation that would take the reins of power under John F. Kennedy. But Stevenson did not stand a chance against the popular Eisenhower.

The campaign's biggest controversy developed when newspaper reports alleged that Nixon had used a "secret fund" provided by California millionaires to pay for travel and other expenses. Nixon admitted the existence of the fund but maintained that he used the money solely for travel and that his family had not accepted personal gifts.

Eisenhower refused to back his running mate, and Nixon decided to confront his accusers with a television speech, even though campaign aides told him he would be dropped from the ticket if public reaction was not favorable. The speech was remarkable. Nixon denied that he had accepted gifts, such as a mink coat for his wife, Pat, saying that she wore a "Republican cloth coat." Nixon acknowledged receiving a pet dog named Checkers from a Texas admirer: "And you know, the kids love that dog, and I just want to say this right now, that regardless of what they say about it, we're going to keep it." His folksy message and appeal for telegrams created a wave of sympathy, which Eisenhower rewarded with a pledge of support. The crisis was over.

Eisenhower swept into office in a personal victory, since surveys showed that the nation still favored the programs of the New Deal and simply wanted to put the cronyism of the Truman years and the Korean War behind it. Ike won 442 electoral votes and 55.1 percent of the popular vote.

The 1956 election was nearly a repeat of the 1952 match. Despite his age and a heart attack, Eisenhower once again trounced Stevenson, this time winning 457 electoral votes and 57.4 percent of the popular vote. Overall, the campaign was marked by little conflict or desire for change. In an unprecedented development, however, both houses of Congress went to the opposition.

## Kennedy and the Politics of Change: 1960

The periodic national desire for change took its toll on the Republicans in 1960, when Sen. John F. Kennedy of Massachusetts became the youngest person elected president. Kennedy defeated Vice President Nixon in one of the tightest elections in history.

The presidential election took shape in the 1958 midterm election. The Democrats made impressive gains in Congress, which gave them 64 of 98 Senate seats and 283 of 435 House seats. A recession and the election of several younger and more liberal Democrats to Congress created the first major shift toward liberalism since the administration of Franklin Roosevelt.

Running against senior party leaders such as senators Lyndon B. Johnson of Texas, Hubert H. Humphrey of Minnesota, and Stuart Symington of Missouri, Kennedy seemed more likely to win the vice-presidential nomination. Well financed and backed by a skilled campaign staff headed by his younger brother Robert, Kennedy used the primaries to allay fears both that he was too conservative and that his Catholic religion would affect his loyalty to the nation. With primary victories over Humphrey in the crucial states of Wisconsin and West Virginia, Kennedy was able to win the nomination on the first ballot. His surprise choice of Johnson for a running mate raised doubts even among Kennedy supporters, but the selection of the southerner was a classic ticket-balancing move.

Vice President Nixon was the overwhelming choice for the Republican nomination, and he selected United Nations ambassador Henry Cabot Lodge as his running mate.

Nixon's campaign stressed the need for experience in a dangerous world and tried to portray Kennedy as an inexperienced upstart. Kennedy's campaign was based on a promise to "get the nation moving again" after eight years of calm Republican rule. The high point of the campaign came on September 26, 1960, when the candidates debated on national television before 70 million viewers. It was the first presidential DEBATE in the nation's history and the last until 1976. Kennedy was well rested and tan. Nixon was tired from two solid weeks of campaigning. His five o'clock shadow reinforced the political cartoonists' image of him as darkly sinister. Polls found that Nixon had "won" the debate in the minds of radio listeners but that Kennedy had captured the TV audience. "It was the picture image that had done it," wrote historian Theodore H. White, "and in 1960 it was television that had won the nation away from sound to images, and that was that."

The candidates held three more debates, but none of them had the effect of the first, which had neutralized Nixon's incumbency advantage. Nor was Nixon greatly helped by President Eisenhower, who did not campaign for his vice president until late in the race.

The election results were so close that Nixon did not concede his defeat until the afternoon of the day following the election. Just 115,000 votes separated Kennedy from Nixon in the popular vote tally. A shift of eleven thousand to thirteen thousand votes in just five or six states would have given him the electoral vote triumph. As it was, Kennedy won 303 electoral votes to Nixon's 219. (Democratic senator Harry F. Byrd of Virginia attracted 15 electoral votes.)

## Johnson and the Great Society: 1964

Kennedy's presidency was cut short by his assassination on November 22, 1963. Lyndon Johnson, his vice president, faced no serious opposition for the 1964 Democratic nomination. The Republicans, however, were bitterly divided between the conservatives, led by Sen. Barry Goldwater of Arizona, and the liberal wing of the party, led by New York governor Nelson A. Rockefeller. Goldwater had lined up most of the delegate support he needed even before the primaries began, and key primary victories, including his defeat of Rockefeller in California, ensured that he would receive the nomination.

There was never a real contest between the two presidential nominees in the fall campaign. Johnson's landslide was the largest in U.S. history. He won 61 percent of the popular vote to Goldwater's 38 percent and won 486 electoral college votes to Goldwater's 52.

## The Breakup of Consensus: 1968

A long period of uncertainty in U.S. politics began after Johnson's landslide victory in 1964. There was rising opposition to the Vietnam War, combined with a conservative reaction to Johnson's Great Society programs and to the riots in many of the nation's cities. These issues seriously divided the nation and the Democratic Party. After Sen. Eugene McCarthy of Minnesota ran surprisingly well against Johnson on an antiwar platform in the New Hampshire primary, the beleaguered president withdrew from the campaign. Vice President Hubert Humphrey became the administration's candidate but decided not to enter any primaries. New York senator Robert F. Kennedy entered the race as an antiwar candidate and appeared to be leading McCarthy when he was assassinated in a Los Angeles hotel the night of his victory in the California primary.

The Democratic convention in Chicago was marred by skirmishes on the convention floor and bloody confrontations between police and antiwar and civil rights demonstrators outside. Democrats nominated Humphrey on the strength of endorsements from state party organizations. The nomination of a candidate who had not entered a single primary led to major changes in the way Democrats selected their delegates and ultimately to the proliferation of presidential primaries.

The Republicans united behind Richard Nixon. The former vice president's fall campaign was well financed and well organized, and the Republican candidate capitalized on the national discontent. Alabama governor George C. Wallace also made use of national sentiment, mounting one of the strongest third party campaigns in U.S. history. Wallace ran as an antiestablishment conservative, railing at desegregation, crime, taxes, opponents of the Vietnam War, social programs, and "pointy head" bureaucrats. Wallace's campaign stirred fears that neither major party candidate would receive a majority of the electoral college votes and that the election would be thrown into the House of Representatives.

The election was one of the closest in U.S. history. Nixon attracted 31.8 million votes, to Humphrey's 31.3 million and Wallace's 9.9 million. But Nixon won 301 electoral votes, a clear majority. Humphrey picked up 191, and Wallace won only 46.

President Nixon and his vice president, Spiro T. Agnew, were nominated in 1972 with barely a peep out of other Republicans. On the Democratic side, though, twelve serious contenders announced their candidacy. Senator George S. McGovern of South Dakota led the pack at the end of a grueling primary season and was nominated at the convention.

Under the best of circumstances, the liberal Democrat would have been an underdog in the race against Nixon. But McGovern was badly damaged when his choice for vice president, Thomas F. Eagleton of Missouri, withdrew from the ticket after it was revealed that he had been treated for nervous exhaustion. McGovern replaced Eagleton with R. Sargent Shriver, but he never overcame the appearance of confusion that surrounded the Eagleton affair.

Nixon won all but Massachusetts and the District of Columbia in the fall election, gaining 520 electoral votes to 17 for McGovern.

## Effects of the Watergate Affair: 1976

Revelations that people associated with Nixon's campaign committee had been arrested for breaking into Democratic headquarters in the Watergate Hotel in June 1972 had little effect on the 1972 election. Eventually, the investigation of the burglary and the subsequent cover-up by President Nixon and his aides drove the president from office in August 1974. Less than a year earlier, Agnew had resigned after pleading no contest to charges that he had accepted bribes while he was governor of Maryland and vice president. Nixon named House minority leader Gerald R. Ford, a longtime Republican Party stalwart, to become vice president under the Twenty-fifth Amendment. When Nixon resigned, Ford became the first president in U.S. history who had never run in a presidential election.

Although he started out with the support of the American public, Ford soon ignited a firestorm of criticism when he granted Nixon a full pardon for any crimes he might have committed as president. Combined with nagging economic problems and a stubborn, but losing, primary campaign waged by California governor Ronald Reagan, the pardon left Ford and the Republican Party vulnerable in the 1976 election.

The Democrats appeared headed for a long and bitter nomination struggle for the third time in a row. But former Georgia governor Jimmy Carter, whose support as measured by national polls was extremely low when the campaign began, executed a brilliant campaign strategy. He was elected on the first ballot and went on to defeat Ford by a slim margin, winning 297 electoral votes to Ford's 240.

The 1976 election was notable in two ways. For the first time, the presidential campaigns were partially financed with public funds. And for the first time since 1960 the presidential nominees took part in televised debates. (See CAMPAIGN FINANCE; DEBATES.)

## The Reagan Revolution: 1980

Carter's presidency was troubled by inflation and unemployment, his own inability to work with a Democratic Congress, an energy crisis, and the Iran hostage crisis. He nonetheless managed to win renomination on the first ballot, putting down a serious challenge from Massachusetts senator Edward M. Kennedy. But the Democratic ticket garnered little enthusiasm from the rank and file.

The Republicans united early behind the conservative Reagan. By the time of the convention Reagan was the consensus candidate, and he improved party unity by adding George Bush, his only serious primary challenger, to the fall ticket. Rep. John B. Anderson of Illinois, a moderate who dropped out of the Republican race, ran an independent campaign.

Although polls before election day predicted a close race, Reagan won all but six states and took the White House in an electoral landslide, 489 electoral votes to 49. The Republicans also gained control over the Senate.

The extraordinarily popular former movie actor was

*Ronald Reagan easily won the 1980 presidential election against Jimmy Carter, whose presidency was plagued with troubles. Reagan won all but six states, with an electoral landslide of 489 votes to 49.* Source: National Archives

able to parlay his claims of an electoral mandate into wide-ranging changes in tax, budget, and military policies. Although Reagan's popularity fell during a recession early in his first term, he recovered, and there was no serious challenge to his renomination in 1984.

Jimmy Carter's vice president, Walter F. Mondale of Minnesota, was the early front-runner for the Democratic nomination and won it on the first ballot. Mondale named Rep. Geraldine Ferraro of New York as his RUNNING MATE, the first woman ever to receive a major party nomination for national office. Ferraro's nomination was probably a drag on the ticket, not because of her gender but because of her lack of government experience and a controversy that surrounded her husband's finances. The Mondale-Ferraro campaign never caught fire, and Reagan rolled to an easy victory, winning 525 electoral votes to the Democrats' 13.

## The Election of 1988

In 1988, for the first time since 1968, the incumbent president was not a candidate, since Reagan was completing his second and final term. With no major figure and no major issues, the campaign was a tumultuous affair. As fourteen candidates struggled to make themselves known to the voters during the parties' nominating contests, the campaign lurched from one symbolic issue to the next.

Massachusetts governor Michael S. Dukakis won the Democratic nomination, but only after a long and initially shaky primary season. His only competitor at the end was civil rights leader Jesse Jackson, who attracted support from blacks and from farmers and blue-collar workers disgruntled with the economy. When Dukakis passed over Jackson to choose Texas senator Lloyd M. Bentsen Jr. for vice president, Jackson complained both publicly and privately. But he eventually embraced Bentsen for the sake of party unity.

Vice President Bush was an early favorite on the Republican side, and he overcame a loss in the Iowa caucus to win the nomination. He was hurt by his controversial choice of Dan Quayle, a youthful senator from Indiana, as his running mate, but benefited from Dukakis's inability to pull together his own inconsistent and confusing campaign strategy. The Bush-Quayle ticket won handily, capturing 54 percent of the vote to the Democrats' 46 percent. A negative campaign and limited voter-registration efforts resulted in the one of the lowest VOTER TURNOUT rates in modern times. Barely 50 percent of all eligible citizens voted for president in 1988.

## Clinton Victory: 1992

Democrat Bill Clinton broke what seemed like a Republican lock on the White House when he defeated incumbent President George Bush in 1992. Republicans had won five of the six previous presidential elections. And for a while it did not seem as if 1992 would be any different.

Just a year before the campaign began, Bush seemed poised for one of the smoothest reelections in White House history. After he led the nation to victory in the brief 1991 Persian Gulf War, Bush's popularity soared. But in the months that followed, the economy went into what even the president called a "free fall." So, too, did Bush's popularity. And not much the White House did before or during the campaign helped revitalize either the economy or the president's political standing.

A majority of American voters listened to Clinton's call for change and turned Bush out of office. Clinton carried thirty-two states and the District of Columbia, won 370 of 538 electoral votes and outscored Bush by 5 percentage points—43 percent to 38 percent.

Clinton was only the second Democrat to gain the White House in the nearly three decades since Lyndon Johnson's lopsided victory in 1964. Clinton's win was especially important to the Democratic Party, which had made dismal showings in the three national elections since Carter was in office in the late 1970s. With the election of Clinton at age forty-six and Tennessee senator Albert Gore Jr., age forty-four, Americans for the first time chose a president and vice president from the so-called baby-boom generation—they were both born after World War II.

The widespread desire for change in government also benefited independent candidate Ross Perot, a Texas billionaire who spoke bluntly of the need to reduce the federal budget deficit. Perot won 19 percent of the popular vote, the largest vote total for an independent candidate in presidential election history and the biggest vote share since 1912, when Theodore Roosevelt ran under the Progressive Party banner.

## Divided Government Retained: 1996

The election of 1996 was significant in several ways. Clinton became the first Democrat elected to a second full term since Franklin Roosevelt in 1936. But unlike FDR, whose party controlled Congress throughout his twelve-year tenure, Clinton would continue to preside over a divided government. And from the rubble of Ross Perot's second try for the presidency, a new political party emerged as an option to voters fed up with the two-party system.

After a lackluster first two years in which he failed to deliver his promised health care reform, Clinton was an easy target for House Republicans led by Newt Gingrich of Georgia. Campaigning on a ten-point "Contract with America," the GOP won control of the House in the 1994 MIDTERM ELECTIONS and elected Gingrich as Speaker. The Democrats also lost control of the Senate, and Robert J. Dole of Kansas became the majority leader.

As the first Democratic president since Truman forced to deal with a Congress entirely controlled by the opposition party, Clinton faced an uphill fight to govern, and his chances of reelection looked slim. But after a series of budget battles that closed down the government briefly in 1995, Gingrich became the lightning rod for public apprehension about Congress's intent. Congressional Democrats played on fears that the Republicans would end Social Security and Medicare, both targeted for "reform" in the Contract with America.

By late 1996, with the economy healthy, Clinton's approval ratings had improved and he enjoyed a strong lead in the polls over his Republican challenger, Dole. At seventy-three, Dole faced doubts about his age as well as his reputation for having an acerbic tongue. For his part, Gingrich kept a low profile during the campaign.

Meanwhile, Ross Perot had converted his independent candidacy, financed with his own money, into a bona fide new political party, the REFORM PARTY. As its nominee, Perot accepted federal campaign funding, which limited spending from his own pocket and from outside sources. In the election Perot and running mate Pat Choate, an economist, won only 8.5 percent of the popular vote and no electoral votes. But as the first third party to qualify for public funding of its general election campaign, the Reform Party remained a potential force in future presidential elections.

Although Clinton's reelection was no surprise in light of the polls, his coattails proved weaker than expected. For what was believed to be the first time, the electorate consciously voted for divided government, keeping the White House in Democratic hands and Congress in Republican hands as a check on one another.

The "status quo election," as it came to be called, gave the Clinton-Gore team 379 electoral votes to 159 for Dole and his running mate, former House member Jack Kemp of New York. The election was also dubbed the "whatever" election because of voter apathy. The voter turnout was the lowest in seventy-two years. Only 48.8 percent of the voting age population participated, depriving Clinton of any kind of mandate. Clinton fell short of his personal goal of winning more than 50 percent of the popular vote. He thus became a "minority president" for the second time, raising his 1992 total of 43 percent to 49 percent in 1996.

## Citizens Party (1979–1984)

Organized in 1979 as a coalition of dissident liberals and populists, the first Citizens Party convention chose author and environmental scientist Barry Commoner as its 1980 presidential candidate and La Donna Harris, wife of former Democratic senator Fred R. Harris of Oklahoma, as Commoner's running mate. The Citizens Party ticket ran on the central theme that major decisions in America were made to benefit corporations and not the average citizen. The party proposed public control of energy industries and multinational corporations, a halt to the use of nuclear power, a sharp cut in military spending, and price controls on food, fuel, housing, and health care.

Commoner ran in all of the large electoral vote states except Florida and Texas. He made his biggest push in California, Illinois, Michigan, New York, and Pennsylvania, where party leaders believed they could tap a "sophisticated working-class population" and appeal to political activists who had been involved in the environmental and antinuclear movements that had arisen in the late 1970s.

The Commoner/Harris ticket was on the ballot in twenty-nine states and the District of Columbia in 1980. Party leaders asserted that it was the largest number of ballot positions attained by any third party in its first campaign. In addition to its presidential ticket, the Citizens Party fielded twenty-two candidates for other offices, including two for the U.S. Senate and seven for the House. The Citizens Party won 234,294 votes, or 0.3 percent of the 1980 vote.

As its 1984 presidential nominee the Citizens Party chose outspoken feminist Sonia Johnson of Virginia. Johnson first attracted national attention in 1979, when the Mormon Church excommunicated her for supporting the Equal Rights Amendment. In 1982 she staged a thirty-seven-day hunger strike in an unsuccessful effort to pressure the Illinois legislature to approve the ERA. The Citizens Party selected party activist Richard J. Walton of Rhode Island to accompany Johnson on the ticket. Winning 72,200 votes in 1984, the ticket garnered 0.1 percent of the vote.

## Citizenship and Voting

A primary right of every American citizen age eighteen and over is the RIGHT TO VOTE, the "first liberty," as historians and political scientists have called it. But what defines the nature of citizenship? What exactly is a citizen?

The first four articles of the Constitution mention the words *citizen* and *natural born citizen*. Article I requires that members of both houses of Congress be U.S. citizens. Article II says the president must either be a U.S. citizen "at the time of Adoption of this Constitution" or be a "natural born citizen." Articles III and IV

*Deprived of many of their civil rights during World War II, Japanese Americans could still vote. In November 1942 citizens of Japanese descent wait to have their absentee ballots notarized at the Tule Lake Relocation Center in Newell, California.*
Source: National Archives

concern questions of federal courts' jurisdiction over citizens and the extension of rights from all states to citizens of any particular one. But nowhere does the Constitution define the word *citizen.*

Constitutional scholars and historians agree that the phrase "natural born citizen" represents the framers' intent to impose an ancient doctrine called *jus soli* or "right of land or ground," meaning that citizenship arises from place of birth. An opposing concept, *jus sanguinis,* "right of blood," implies that citizenship derives from one's parents.

*Jus soli,* or birthright citizenship as it has come to be called, represented, beyond the concept of citizenship alone, several utilitarian ideas to the framers: it helped to clarify property rights in the new land and to mitigate or eliminate jurisdictional disputes between citizens of different states. Perhaps most important, it helped to lessen the very real fear of massive expatriation during wartime, a phenomenon that many of the framers had witnessed firsthand during the War of Independence as crown loyalists fled to Canada or back to England, there to oppose the Revolution.

Despite the adoption of the "right of land or ground" concept in deciding citizenship, several groups of native-born Americans were excluded from citizenship and hence from the political processes of the new nation: women; second-generation slaves born on American soil; and Native Americans, who, under the "right of land" concept, should have been the first citizens of the young country.

The *Dred Scott* decision of 1857 *(Scott v. Sandford),* the most famous (or infamous) attempt to define citizenship before the onset of the Civil War, ruled that a black person could not be a citizen. According to Chief Justice Roger B. Taney, who wrote the opinion for the 7–2 majority, the Constitution did not intend the black to be included under the term *citizen* and therefore no black could claim any of the rights and privileges held by U.S. citizens. Slaves or their descendants, Taney wrote, "are not included, and were not intended to be included, under the word 'citizen' in the Constitution."

## Constitutional Amendments

In its very first phrase the Fourteenth Amendment, ratified eleven years later after the slavery crisis had convulsed the nation in civil war, reversed the *Scott* decision with the ringing declaration that

All persons born or naturalized in the United States and subject to the jurisdiction thereof, are citizens of the United States and of the State wherein they reside. No State shall make or enforce any law which shall abridge the privileges or immunities of citizens of the United States; nor shall any State deprive any person of life, liberty, or property, without due process of law; nor deny to any person within its jurisdiction the equal protection of the laws.

For Native Americans, even with the passage of the Fourteenth Amendment, the road to full citizenship, which blacks had seemingly won with the amendment's ratification, proved more difficult. In an 1884 case, *Elk v. Wilkins,* the Court ruled that even though Native Americans were indeed born in the United States, they as members of tribes or Indian nations were not wholly "subject to the jurisdiction" of the U.S. government. Under the decision, Native Americans living in tribes remained an exception to the Fourteenth Amendment until 1925, when Congress enacted a law saying they are subject to U.S. jurisdiction and therefore entitled to citizenship.

The jurisdiction question was raised in the 1898 decision in *United States v. Wong Kim Ark,* which concerned a person born in the United States to resident-alien Chinese parents. The case arose when Wong Kim Ark was denied readmission after a visit to China.

The decision came at a time when anti-Chinese sentiment was running high. Waves of immigrants from the Far East had raised fears of economic dislocation among many working-class Americans, most of them white Europeans. Congress in 1882 had specifically barred Chinese from becoming citizens through the naturalization process, and Congress's right to discriminate in this fashion had been upheld by the Court. The

authorities therefore said that Wong Kim Ark could not be a citizen because his parents could not become citizens.

In deciding that Wong Kim Ark was indeed a citizen, the Court applied an English common law principle—allegiance to the king. Under that principle children of aliens born in England were natural-born subjects, as were children of England's ambassadors and diplomats born abroad because they owed obedience to the king, the opinion said. The law had been applied to all English colonies before the Declaration of Independence and would apply now. *Jus sanguinis,* which said the child's citizenship was that of his parents, did not.

After the Fourteenth Amendment was ratified, the issues of citizenship and voting were addressed in several other amendments. The Fifteenth, ratified in 1870 in the middle of the Reconstruction Era, provided for BLACK SUFFRAGE: "The right of citizens of the United States to vote shall not be denied or abridged by the United States or by any State on account of race, color, or previous condition of servitude." The Nineteenth Amendment, ratified in 1920, finally guaranteed WOMEN'S SUFFRAGE. The Twenty-third, ratified in 1961, extended the right to vote for president to the citizens of Washington, D.C., the nation's capital. The Twenty-fourth, ratified in 1964, abolished the POLL TAX, one of the more noxious and lingering legal devices (known as the "Jim Crow laws") that had been enacted by the southern states after Reconstruction to deprive blacks of the vote. Finally, the TWENTY-SIXTH AMENDMENT, ratified in 1971 after a campaign that featured the slogan "Old enough to fight and die, old enough to vote," lowered the voting age for American citizens to eighteen. (See YOUTH SUFFRAGE.)

However, not all citizens—be they native-born, black, female, Native American, eighteen-year-olds, or naturalized citizens—are allowed to vote: convicted felons and persons ruled legally insane are barred from voting. Yet the Supreme Court has ruled in *Schneiderman v. United States* (1944) and in *Trop v. Dulles* (1958) that U.S. citizenship is so prized and valuable an asset that the federal government would be guilty of "cruel and unusual punishment" in depriving even those citizens who espouse antithetical political views or, in the *Trop* case, desert in wartime, of what the Court recognized as their "status in organized society." Another 1958 decision, *Perez v. Brownell,* said that Congress had the power to remove the citizenship of a person who had voted in a foreign election. But in a 1967 case, *Afroyim v. Rusk,* the Court overruled the *Perez* decision, holding that citizenship could be relinquished only voluntarily.

## Naturalization Process

The United States was founded by immigrants and their descendants and has remained a refuge for many from other countries. American citizenship, with all its implicit and explicit rights, is available to those new arrivals who enter into the naturalization process. To qualify, an applicant must be eighteen or older and have been a lawful resident of the United States for a continuous period of five years. For spouses of U.S. citizens, the period is three years. During the five-year period, the applicant must have been physically present in the United States for at least half the required residence period.

An applicant for naturalization must demonstrate an understanding of the English language, including an ability to read, write, and speak words in ordinary usage (although exceptions are made for applicants over fifty-five who have been lawful residents for at least fifteen years). Applicants must have demonstrated "good moral character, attached to the principles of the Constitution and well disposed to the good order and happiness of the United States" for five years prior to making their applications. They must also demonstrate, in a personal interview with an examiner from the U.S. Immigration and Naturalization Service, that they have a "knowledge and understanding of the fundamentals of the history, and the principles and form of government, of the United States." If, at the conclusion of the process, a favorable decision to grant citizenship is made, an applicant becomes a citizen after swearing an oath of allegiance to the United States. The new citizen is then eligible to vote as soon as he or she registers to do so.

One legal scholar writes that the Supreme Court's actions on citizenship are notable in their "remarkably limited scope. This is so since, while one must be a citizen to vote or to hold federal office, most of the Constitution's key rights and liberties do not extend to citizens only. No less than the entire Bill of Rights applies to 'the people'—citizen and the noncitizen alike."

The Supreme Court has steadfastly defined citizenship by the *jus soli* or birthright citizenship doctrine and made it exceptionally difficult for the government to wrest citizenship away from individuals. It is on the issues of voting and of holding elected office that the Court's predominating concern with the Constitution's provisions for equal protection has tended to focus citizenship questions.

---

## Civil Rights Acts

During the ten-year Reconstruction period immediately following the Civil War, the reunified United States tried to secure voting and other civil rights for the freed slaves. But the determination of many whites in southern states to block BLACK SUFFRAGE, together with restrictive interpretations by the U.S. Supreme Court, held African American voting to a trickle.

Among the Reconstruction-era remedies approved by Congress and the states were three amendments to the U.S. Constitution and seven pieces of implementing legislation. None, however, brought about significant permanent change in the racial composition of southern voting. Not until 1965 did a sweeping VOTING RIGHTS ACT finally provide the means and security for large numbers of African Americans to go to the polls in southern states.

The first of the three Civil War amendments, the Thirteenth, ratified in 1865, simply abolished slavery. The next two extended civil rights to the former slaves and proved to be more difficult to carry out.

Historians have asserted that the Supreme Court's narrow interpretation of the Fourteenth and Fifteenth amendments provided an environment that made possible the long denial of full voting rights to African Americans. The Fourteenth Amendment, ratified in 1868, made blacks citizens and prohibited states from

*Long lines of black voters in Cobb County, Georgia, casting ballots for the 1946 Democratic primary elections showed that when the government removed obstacles to voting, blacks turned up at the polls in large numbers. A 1944 Supreme Court decision,* Smith v. Allwright, *opened party primaries to all voters. Source: Bettmann*

denying citizens due process and equal protection of the laws; the Fifteenth Amendment, ratified two years later, prohibited the federal and state governments from denying the right to vote to citizens on the basis of race, color, or previous condition of servitude. The voting rights provisions of both amendments applied only to men at that time. (See WOMEN'S SUFFRAGE.)

By 1875, when the Reconstruction period was drawing to a close, Congress had passed seven statutes, each entitled "Civil Rights Act," to implement and enforce the three amendments. Most of the seven acts did not deal directly with voting rights but rather conferred rights and protections already enjoyed by white citizens. Taken as a whole, however, the acts made it clear that the Reconstruction Congress, controlled by the so-called Radical Republicans, intended the Fourteenth and Fifteenth Amendments to provide the RIGHT TO VOTE to black citizens. The Radical Republicans, who disagreed with Abraham Lincoln's lenient policy toward the defeated South, saw the black vote as a way to thwart the return to political power of white southerners who had strongly backed the Confederate cause.

The Civil Rights Act of 1870, known as the Enforcement Act, set criminal penalties for interfering with suffrage under the Fifteenth Amendment or the Civil Rights Act of April 9, 1866. The latter, passed over President Andrew Johnson's veto, gave blacks full equality under the law "as is enjoyed by white citizens." Debate over the constitutionality of the 1866 law, which provided for enforcement by federal troops if necessary, led to the Fourteenth Amendment.

The Civil Rights Act of 1871, an amendment to the Enforcement Act, called for the appointment of election supervisors and deputy marshals in cities over twenty thousand population if two citizens requested them in writing to a federal judge. The supervisors were to watch for abuses of voting rights.

All or parts of the post–Civil War civil rights acts

were nullified by state or federal courts. The last of the seven, the Civil Rights Act of 1875, outlawed racial discrimination in hotels, theaters, transportation, or jury selection. The Supreme Court nullified it in 1883 (*Civil Rights Cases*).

As time went on, the southern states were able, with increasingly greater effectiveness, to evade those parts of the laws that the courts did not invalidate. The states used so-called exclusionary devices such as LITERACY TESTS, the GRANDFATHER CLAUSE, the WHITE PRIMARY, and POLL TAXES to keep blacks from voting. Outside the law, white groups, including the Ku Klux Klan, kept blacks from voting by terrorizing them, sometimes through violence. Thus, the voting rights guarantees of the Fourteenth and Fifteenth Amendments represented an unkept promise to African Americans in the southern states until the second half of the twentieth century when, in the environment of a great civil rights movement, Congress moved decisively to fulfill the old guarantees.

On the heels of the Civil Rights Act of 1957, which created the Civil Rights Commission, and the wide-ranging Civil Rights Act of 1964, which bars discrimination in public accommodations and employment, Congress enacted the Voting Rights Act of 1965. In upholding the Voting Rights Act and later amendments, the Supreme Court invoked the Fourteenth and Fifteenth Amendments that the Court of the previous century had so narrowly construed.

## The Court's New Attitude

Two rulings, both issued on March 27, 1876, had pointed the direction in which the Supreme Court would take the voting rights issue for decades into the future. In *United States v. Reese,* the Court held that the Fifteenth Amendment did not give anyone the right to vote. It simply guaranteed the right to be free from racial discrimination in the exercise of the right to vote, a right granted under state laws. Therefore, Congress exceeded its power to enforce the Fifteenth Amendment when it enacted laws that penalized state officials who denied blacks the right to vote, refused to count votes, or obstructed citizens from voting.

In the second ruling, *United States v. Cruikshank,* the Court dismissed indictments brought against Louisiana citizens accused of using violence and fraud to prevent blacks from voting. Because the indictments did not charge that the actions were motivated by racial discrimination, they were not federal offenses.

In the two rulings, the Court laid down the doctrine that the amendments did not authorize the federal government to protect citizens from each other but only from discriminatory state legislation and that they gave protection only where such legislation discriminated because of race and color.

From the end of Reconstruction until well into the twentieth century, Congress took virtually no action that might have fostered black suffrage. Moreover, the courts generally avoided taking an activist role in interpreting the Fifteenth Amendment or in applying Reconstruction laws pertaining to voting rights.

According to the U.S. Civil Rights Commission, by 1910 every state of the former Confederacy had either disenfranchised African Americans or had otherwise deprived them of political effectiveness through the use of exclusionary devices. In the case of literacy tests, a prospective voter was required to read, and sometimes to explain, a passage from a state constitution. Grandfather clauses exempted a voter from the literacy test if his ancestor had voted in 1866, which included hardly any former slaves or their ancestors. Finally, in allowing the Democratic Party to restrict PRIMARIES to whites, many states argued that political parties were private clubs or associations and that primary elections were functions of the parties, not the states.

In a precedent-setting literacy test case, *Williams v. Mississippi,* which the Supreme Court decided in 1898, Henry Williams, a black man, had been indicted for murder by an all-white jury. The jurors were selected from a list of registered voters who had, among other qualifications, passed a literacy test. Williams challenged the test as unconstitutional. His attorneys argued that his conviction was invalid because the laws under which the grand jury was selected allowed discrimination in voter registration, violating the Equal Protection Clause of the Fourteenth Amendment. Writing for the

Court's majority, Justice Joseph McKenna refused to find the Mississippi statutes in violation of the Equal Protection Clause. The "evil" was not in the laws themselves, he wrote, because they did not on their face discriminate against blacks. The only evil resulted from the effect of their discriminatory administration.

In 1915 in *Guinn v. United States* the Supreme Court began to move toward a broader interpretation of the Fifteenth Amendment. In a unanimous ruling, the Court struck down Oklahoma's voting system, which combined a literacy test with a grandfather clause, as an unconstitutional violation of the Fifteenth Amendment. The decision was the first voting rights case in which the Court looked beyond the nondiscriminatory form of a law to scrutinize its discriminatory intent.

A 1921 Court decision involving CAMPAIGN FINANCE in *Newberry v. United States* seemed to say that Congress lacked the power to regulate primaries. Twenty years later, however, in *United States v. Classic,* the Court overruled *Newberry* and said that the white primary was an integral part of the election process, and therefore subject to federal regulation. But it was only in 1953, in *Terry v. Adams,* that the Court ended a resourceful effort by Texas Democrats to maintain the white primary in that state. Because the DEMOCRATIC PARTY for many decades was dominant in southern states, voting in primary elections was more important than voting in the general election.

The last exclusionary device to fall was the poll tax. Early in the country's history, poll taxes had been levied as a less burdensome requirement for voting than landholding. But, for the most part, those poll taxes had been eliminated by the time of the Civil War. The tax was revived in the 1890s as an additional way to restrict suffrage in the southern states to whites. Officials, however, usually described poll taxes as merely a means to "cleanse" the rolls of ineligible voters and prevent ELECTION FRAUD.

In 1937 the Supreme Court upheld the constitutionality of the poll tax against a challenge that it violated the equal protection guarantee of the Fourteenth Amendment. Proposals to abolish the tax were introduced in every Congress from 1939 to 1962. In August

1962 Congress approved a constitutional amendment outlawing poll taxes in federal elections. The states completed ratification of the Twenty-fourth Amendment on January 23, 1964. Two years later, the Supreme Court held that the poll tax also was an unconstitutional requirement for voting in state and local elections.

## Voting Rights Act of 1965

Congress passed the comprehensive Voting Rights Act of 1965 against a disturbing backdrop of attacks by southern whites on peaceful marches by blacks demonstrating for voting rights. The law was designed to close all the legal loopholes that had for so long allowed state and local officials to block VOTER REGISTRATION of blacks. Earlier, President Lyndon B. Johnson had asked a joint session of Congress to pass the sweeping measure. He said, "No law that we now have on the books . . . can ensure the right to vote when local officials are determined to deny it."

The law suspended all literacy tests and provided for appointment of federal voting registrars in states that had such tests together with low voting rates. The provisions applied to six southern states and part of a seventh state. The act also required covered states or counties to obtain federal approval before changing their voting laws or procedures.

Enactment of the Voting Rights Act of 1965 resulted in a marked increase in the number of blacks registering, voting, and running for office in southern states. The Civil Rights Commission in 1968 reported that registration of African Americans had climbed to above 50 percent of the black voting age population in every southern state. In the first ten years the act was in force, an estimated 2 million African Americans were added to voting rolls in the South.

The Voting Rights Act was immediately challenged as infringing upon state power to oversee elections. In *South Carolina v. Katzenbach* the Supreme Court in 1966 upheld the power of Congress to pass the law and also upheld all of its major provisions, including the suspension of literacy tests. Delivering the opinion for the Court, Chief Justice Earl Warren wrote that the provision suspending the tests "was clearly a legitimate response to the problem, for which there is ample precedent in Fifteenth Amendment cases."

With a single exception, the Court in all challenges upheld the law and interpreted it broadly. The exception was *Mobile v. Bolden* (1980). In that case, the Court ruled that the act did not reach a voting system that had a discriminatory effect unless there was also evidence of a discriminating intent. The ruling upheld an at-large system of electing city commissioners in Mobile, Alabama. African Americans said the system diluted their right to vote by effectively preventing the election of blacks. In a 1982 revision of the law, Congress responded by deleting any requirement of discriminatory intent.

The first extension of the law, for five years, was approved by Congress in 1970. States and local governments were forbidden to use literacy tests or voter qualifying devices through 1975. When the act was again renewed and amended, in 1975, supporters won a seven-year extension. They also gained two major provisions designed to give greater protection to certain "language minorities," defined as persons of Spanish heritage, American Indians, Asian Americans, and Alaskan natives. (See BILINGUAL VOTERS.)

A third extension of the act was approved in 1982. The amended law that year was given strong backing from members of both the House and Senate, including legislators from southern states. More than twice as many southern Democrats in both chambers of Congress voted for passage in 1982 than when the law was initially approved in 1965. Observers said the change reflected, among other things the addition of many new black voters in southern constituencies.

The 1982 legislation extended for twenty-five years provisions of the law requiring nine states and portions of thirteen others to obtain Justice Department approval for alterations in their election laws and procedures.

## Closed Primary

*See* PRIMARY TYPES.

## Coalition

A coming together of distinct parties or people of different IDEOLOGIES is called a *coalition*. In a TWO-PARTY SYSTEM, formation of a coalition is often required to elect candidates or enact legislation.

One of the oldest and best known U.S. coalitions is the conservative coalition of southern Democrats and Republicans in Congress. Now in decline because many southern conservatives have switched from the Democratic Party to the Republicans, the coalition operated for more than half a century as a formidable obstacle to CIVIL RIGHTS ACTS, the VOTING RIGHTS ACT, and other legislation on the liberal agenda.

A newer alliance is the BLUE DOG Coalition of moderate to conservative Democrats, mostly from the South, who organized in 1995 to form a working relationship with the Republican majority in the House of Representatives. Unlike the conservative coalition the Blue Dog Coalition is a formal organization with officers and a statement of purpose.

The conservative coalition is an ad hoc grouping formed automatically in Congress whenever a majority of southern Democrats joins with a majority of Republicans to oppose a majority of northern Democrats. Analysis of the conservative coalition is one of several voting studies compiled regularly by Congressional Quarterly.

Some political scientists believed, however, that continued analysis of the conservative coalition was a waste of time. Because the South was so solidly Republican, the GOP could achieve its goals without the help of the few remaining conservative southern Democrats. Reflecting that REALIGNMENT, during 1996 the conservative voting bloc came together on only 89 of 760 roll call votes in the second session of the 104th Congress. Its appearance rate was 11.7 percent, compared with 30.0 percent twenty-five years earlier. When it did come together, however, the conservative coalition was as effective as ever. The coalition was on the winning side of 98.9 percent of the votes on which it came together in 1996.

The conservative coalition first appeared in the late

1930s in opposition to another famous alliance, President Franklin D. Roosevelt's Democratic coalition of southern Protestants, Jews, blacks, blue-collar workers, farmers, and urban Catholics. Powerful southern committee chairmen joined with Republicans to fight Roosevelt's New Deal policies.

In the 1950s and 1960s the conservative coalition began to lose ground against the initiatives of civil rights leaders and urban liberals. But it revived with vigor in the 1980s as southern Democrat BOLL WEEVILS joined with Republicans to help pass President Ronald Reagan's tax and domestic spending cuts.

## Coattails

A popular candidate who sweeps other candidates to victory along with him or her is said to have "long coattails." Congressional and state candidates might ride the coattails of a strong presidential candidate. A candidate for governor might gain votes for the party's candidates for state and local offices.

In 1980 the coattail effect of Ronald Reagan's popularity helped Republicans win a majority in the Senate for the first time since 1955. On the other hand, an unpopular president can have "reverse coattails" and be a drag on the rest of the ticket, as Herbert Hoover was to the Republicans in 1932.

Although his own approval ratings were high in 1996, Bill Clinton became the first Democratic president reelected without leading his party to control of either chamber of Congress. The Republicans who took over in the 1994 MIDTERM ELECTIONS retained their majorities in the Senate and House of Representatives. Despite the possibility of gridlock, voters often seem to prefer divided government—split-party control of the executive and legislative branches of government.

INCUMBENCY is frequently a stronger factor in elections than the popularity of the candidate heading the ticket. Incumbents usually win and CHALLENGERS usually lose.

Independence also weakens the coattail effect, and modern campaigns are mostly CANDIDATE-CENTERED.

The candidates form their own organizations and run largely on their own with little reliance on the party organizations or help from the ticket leader.

Most states elect their governors and other state officials in nonpresidential election years, to minimize the effect of national politics on state and local elections. By one estimate, a strong national candidate could add as much as 5 percent to the votes of statewide candidates.

Abraham Lincoln, then a U.S. representative from Illinois, is credited with popularizing the coattails metaphor. Responding on the House floor in 1848 to an accusation that he and others were taking shelter under Zachary Taylor's "military coat tail," Lincoln noted that the Democrats were still running under the coattails of another war hero, former president Andrew Jackson.

## Communist Party (1924– )

In 1919, shortly after the Russian Revolution, Soviet communists encouraged American left-wing groups to withdraw from the Socialist Party and to form a communist party in the United States. After several years of internal dissension, a new political organization named the Workers' Party of America was established in 1921 at the insistence of Moscow. The goal of the new party was revolutionary—to overthrow capitalism and to create a communist state ruled by the working classes.

William Z. Foster, a labor organizer, was the party's first presidential candidate, in 1924. National tickets were run every four years through 1940 and from 1968 through 1984, but the party's peak year at the polls was 1932, when Foster received 103,253 votes (0.3 percent of the popular vote).

The communists have a distinctive place in American political history as the only party to have had international ties. In 1929 a party split brought the formal creation of the Communist Party of the United States, with acknowledged status as a part of the worldwide communist movement (the Communist International).

The Communist International terminated during World War II, and in 1944 the party's leader in America, Earl Browder, dissolved the party and committed the

*Communist leader Gus Hall, candidate for president on the Communist Party ticket in the 1976 presidential election, speaks at a press conference at the party's national headquarters. Source: UPI/Bettmann*

movement to operate within the two-party system. In the 1944 campaign the communists endorsed President Franklin D. Roosevelt, who repudiated their support.

However, with the breakup of the U.S.-Soviet alliance after World War II, the Communists reconstituted themselves as a political party. They supported Henry Wallace's Progressive Party candidacy in 1948, but they were limited in the cold war period of the 1950s by restrictive federal and state legislation that virtually outlawed the party.

With the gradual easing of restrictive measures, the Communist Party resumed electoral activities in the late 1960s. In a policy statement written in 1966, the par-

ty described itself as "a revolutionary party whose aim is the fundamental transformation of society."

The party's success at the polls, however, continued to be minimal. Its presidential candidates in 1968, 1972, 1976, 1980, and 1984—the last year that they appeared on the ballot—each received less than one-tenth of 1 percent of the vote.

## Compression

*See* FRONT-LOADING.

## Compulsory Voting

*See* INTERNATIONAL AND U.S. ELECTIONS COMPARED.

## Congressional District

The 435 congressional DISTRICTS in the United States resemble a gigantic jigsaw puzzle. In fact, the dual processes of REAPPORTIONMENT AND REDISTRICTING—adjusting the districts after each ten-year CENSUS—have aptly been described as "jigsaw politics."

The districts come in all shapes and sizes. Some are rich, some are poor. Some are crowded, some are sparsely settled. Some in one area have little in common with those in another area, except that they are all the foundation blocks of the American system of representative DEMOCRACY.

Congressional districts have physical shapes, yet they are not about geography but about people. As such, the districts have been the subject of some of the most fiercely fought political battles in U.S. history. In politics, people mean votes, and votes mean power. And power is at the heart of more than two centuries of haggling over where the district lines are drawn to benefit this or that party, this or that rural or urban area, this or that racial group, and even this or that individual member of Congress.

Under the Constitution as interpreted since 1964 by the Supreme Court, each congressional district must be as nearly equal as possible in population to every other district in that state. This requirement ensures adherence to the principle of ONE PERSON, ONE VOTE. Computer technology has helped the states to meet the Court's rigid mathematical guidelines.

Even in the most heavily populated state, California, the districts drawn after the 1990 census show remarkably little variance in population—from 573,082 in District 1, north of San Francisco, to 573,203 in District 52, on the Mexican border. Yet equality of population does not always tell the full story, here or elsewhere.

Debate still rages about the legality of political GERRYMANDERING, the artful drawing of district lines to benefit a particular party or candidate. Until 1986 the Supreme Court avoided this particular "political thicket," considering it a matter for the elected branches, not the courts. But that year the Court ruled in *Davis v. Bandemer*, a case originating in Indiana, that such gerrymandering is indeed subject to constitutional review. However, it let stand the districting plan drawn by the Republican dominated legislature at issue in the case.

Three years later, the Court declined to become involved in a challenge to California's districting plan, which was widely regarded as a textbook example of political gerrymandering. The map based on the 1980 census was the legacy of Phillip Burton, a Democratic representative who served from 1964 to 1983. It featured several oddly shaped districts, drawn neither compactly nor with respect to community boundaries, but all with nearly equal populations. As one writer described it, "Burton carefully stretched districts from one Democratic enclave to another—sometimes joining them with nothing but a bridge, a stretch of harbor, or a spit of land . . . avoiding Republicans block for block and household for household."

Adopted by the Democratic-controlled state legislature, the Burton plan helped California Democrats to gain six House seats in the 1982 elections, prompting a lawsuit from one of the minority Republicans. By a 6–3 vote the Supreme Court refused in 1989 to overturn the Burton plan, agreeing with a lower court that California

Republicans had not proven a general pattern of exclusion from the political process.

In one area, however, the Court has not hesitated to enter the gerrymander thicket. It has outlawed racial gerrymandering where the "predominant factor" is the fashioning of districts either to ensure or to make more likely the election of a minority representative. (See RACIAL REDISTRICTING.)

## District Characteristics

Equality of population within a state has not erased the diversity of congressional districts in other respects or across state lines. The lone House member from Montana, for example, represents many more people than any one of California's fifty-two representatives. Because Montana is entitled to only one member, that person represents the state's entire population—799,065 in the 1990 census. On the other hand, the Wyoming representative has only 453,588 constituents. In all, seven states have one House member elected AT-LARGE. The other five are Alaska, Delaware, North Dakota, South Dakota, and Vermont. The District of Columbia's non-voting delegate is also elected at-large.

The state of Alaska is also the largest congressional district, covering 570,374 square miles or a little more than one square mile for every Alaskan. By contrast, New York's District 11 in central Brooklyn has 580,337 residents packed within ten square miles.

Although the U.S. House is sometimes referred to as the "lower" chamber of Congress (erroneously because the House and Senate have equal legislative power), a representative in one state may have more constituents than a U.S. senator in another state. Maine's two House members, for example, each represent 613,900 people—more than the entire population of Alaska, Vermont, or Wyoming.

According to Census Bureau data, Maryland's District 8 in the Washington, D.C., suburbs was the richest in 1990, with a median family income of $64,199. The poorest was New York's District 16, with family income of $16,683. The same district had the highest percentage of families (39.5) living below the government's poverty line.

The district with the highest percentage of African American residents was New York's 11th, with 74.0 percent. California's District 33 just east of Los Angeles had the highest density of Hispanic population, 83.7 percent.

The average district after the 1990 census had 573,394 residents, making congressional districts among the world's largest electoral units. To maintain a semblance of personal contact with so many constituents, virtually all House members maintain one or more district offices in addition to their Washington, D.C., offices. Most visit their district offices frequently and also keep in touch with their staff and constituents by telephone, radio and television, press releases, direct mail, and the Internet.

## Shifts in the 1990s

Reapportionment after the 1990 census took nineteen House seats away from thirteen slow-growing states, mostly in the Northeast and Midwest. Those seats were shifted to eight states, mainly in the South and West, where population increased sharply in the 1980s.

California alone gained seven seats. Its total of fifty-two seats was the most any state ever held in the House. Texas moved up three seats to thirty, almost knocking New York from its perch as the second most populous state. New York lost three seats, more than any other state, to end up with thirty-one seats. Florida's phenomenal growth moved it up to fourth in the delegate count; it added four seats for a total of twenty-three, surging past Pennsylvania, Illinois, and Ohio, each of which lost two seats.

The population shifts among and within states required state legislatures to revise substantially congressional district maps that had been in place for a decade. The easiest change came in Montana, which, because of its reduction from two seats to one, did not have to decide how to redistrict.

Across the country, some two dozen House members found themselves remapped into the same district with another incumbent. And numerous other members saw their reelection prospects complicated by maps that gave them thousands of new constituents.

The prospects of campaigning against a House colleague or facing unfamiliar faces at the polls contributed to the large number of incumbent retirements in the 1992 campaign cycle: fifty-two members did not seek another House term. That exodus helped create opportunities for newcomer candidates, and the 1992 election produced the biggest crop of House freshmen—110—since the election of 1948. That number included twenty-five freshman women, bringing the number of female House members to an all-time high of forty-eight.

A congressional district carried by the president with less than 50 percent of the vote (a PLURALITY) is considered a marginal "swing district" that could go for or against the president's party in the next election. In 1996 President Clinton produced 101 swing districts, sixty-one held by Republicans, forty by Democrats. Political scientists are fond of watching such districts as BELL-WETHERS indicating possible voting patterns in the next election. In the 1998 midterm elections, seventeen House districts changed hands, including nine of the 101 swing districts. That left the new swing district ratio at sixty-two Republican and thirty-nine Democratic. Overall, however, the Democrats gained five House seats in 1998, reducing the GOP majority edge from twenty-one seats to eleven (with one independent).

---

## Congressional Elections

Congressional elections are the world's oldest broadly popular elections. The House of Representatives was elected by POPULAR VOTE in 1788, forty years before most presidential electors were chosen that way. House elections have come to be considered a close second behind presidential elections in determining national political trends and in conferring legitimacy upon those who exercise political power in the United States. (See HOUSE OF REPRESENTATIVES, ELECTING; REALIGNMENTS AND DEALIGNMENTS.)

Although popular election of the Senate did not come along until early in the twentieth century, the biennial House elections alone justify the claim that modern democratic popular elections originated with congressional elections. The American vote for House candidates in 1832 was higher than Britain's vote the same year in that country's parliamentary election, even though Britain had five times the U.S. population.

The first two congressional elections, in 1788 and 1790, confirmed popular willingness to give the new Constitution and national government a chance to function. The FEDERALISTS, supporters of President George Washington, won majorities in the House.

But 1792 was a premature modern election fought along party lines. Thomas Jefferson's DEMOCRATIC-REPUBLICANS (forerunners of today's Democrats), having organized on a national basis, were able to capture the House while Washington was reelected. The rise of the Democratic-Republicans to overwhelming majority power after 1800 caused popular interest to focus on factional contests for the presidency.

## Nineteenth Century

Congressional elections were comparatively undramatic for the next three decades. The Federalists declined, and Democratic-Republicans held the presidency and both chambers of Congress from 1800 to 1840.

In 1824 the presidential election went to the House because no candidate won an electoral vote majority. The House elected John Quincy Adams, even though Andrew Jackson had led a four-way race. Jackson and his allies organized the modern DEMOCRATIC PARTY and made the 1826 MIDTERM ELECTION a referendum on the legitimacy of the Adams administration. The Jacksonians won. Jackson defeated Adams in 1828, and all future midterm congressional elections became in large part a referendum on the incumbent presidential administration.

In 1848 the WHIG PARTY—anti-Democratic successors to Adams's NATIONAL REPUBLICAN PARTY—lost Congress while succeeding for their second and last time in electing a war hero president, Zachary Taylor. It was the only time between 1792 and 1956 that a president-elect's party failed to capture the House. The setback preordained the Whigs' disintegration over the slavery issue.

Although Democrats elected presidents in 1852 and 1856 on platforms of preserving the Union by attempting to compromise on the slavery issue, anti-Democratic "Free Soil" COALITIONS won the 1854 and 1858 midterm elections, choosing a Free Soil Speaker of the House both times after many ballots.

The Senate, elected for staggered terms by state legislatures, tended to be isolated from popular turmoil. It was more Democratic than the House from 1800 to 1860, and later tended to be more Republican than the House from 1860 to 1914, when popular election of senators began. (See DIRECT ELECTION and SENATE, ELECTING.)

But the 1858 Senate race in Illinois between Stephen A. Douglas, a Democratic leader of the Senate, and former representative Abraham Lincoln of the newly organized REPUBLICAN PARTY, became the single most important congressional race in American political history. The Lincoln-Douglas DEBATES turned into a national debate on the people's right to prevent the expansion of slavery into new territories. Lincoln won the popular vote, but Democrats gained a majority in the Illinois legislature, which reelected Douglas.

## Civil War and Aftermath

In 1860 the Republicans, led by Lincoln, gained complete control of the national government and held it for fourteen years through civil war, Lincoln's assassination, and postwar Reconstruction. From 1874 through 1890 the Democrats won every midterm House election on issues such as ending Reconstruction without guarantees of civil rights for newly freed blacks, civil service reform, low tariffs, and farm relief.

The Democrats took the presidency and Congress in 1892 for the first time since 1856, but they proved completely unable to handle an ensuing financial panic and farmers' revolt. The Republicans gained more House seats in 1894 than in any election until that time, and they held control of the government from 1896 to 1910.

But when the Progressive spirit of the age faltered within the Republican Party, it found a new home with the Democrats, who controlled the presidency and Congress from 1912 to 1918 and had the most successful reform administration (Woodrow Wilson's) since Lincoln's first term. The Progressive era ended in bitterness and disillusionment after the 1917–1918 World War. A Republican era of quiet economy suited the national mood during the "Roaring Twenties."

The Republican failure to handle the Great Depression that began in 1929 gave the Democrats the chance to be the majority party on a platform of relief, recovery, and reform. They captured the House after the 1930 election and held it for sixty of the next sixty-four years. After winning the Senate in 1932, the Democrats held it for fifty-two of the next sixty-two years. President Franklin D. Roosevelt's first term (1933–1937) marked another period of successful domestic reform.

## The Postwar Years

After World War II the two parties became more competitive in presidential elections, but the Democrats remained dominant in Congress. In 1956 Republican Dwight D. Eisenhower was reelected president, but he also became the first presidential victor since 1848 to fail to carry his party to control of Congress.

In the postwar period the ideological conflicts of the 1930s were softened, and it was possible for the two major parties to argue more about means and less about basic national aims. The main issue usually was which party could best provide for the needs of the people in a steadily expanding economy and at the same time provide firm, reliable leadership for the United States and the free world in the protracted cold war with the communist bloc.

By and large the Democrats were more successful than the Republicans in presenting themselves as the party better able to carry out the national consensus. Three Democrats were elected to the presidency—Harry S. Truman, John F. Kennedy, and Lyndon B. Johnson—while only one Republican, Eisenhower, was successful, and then primarily because of his status as a hero of World War II.

Of the ten Congresses elected in the postwar period, eight had Democratic and only two had Republican majorities. The political movements demonstrated a rapidly changing and ambiguous electoral mandate: the

Republicans scored major victories in 1946 and 1952, but the Democrats achieved significant and far-reaching successes in 1948, 1958, and 1964. (See Appendix table, PARTY AFFILIATIONS IN CONGRESS AND THE PRESIDENCY, 1789–2001.)

Even in the years of party sweeps, voters showed an increasing tendency to vote for the candidate rather than the party. The trend toward SPLIT-TICKET VOTING was especially evident in 1956, when Eisenhower was reelected by a LANDSLIDE but the Democrats held Congress, and in 1964, when numerous Republican candidates eked out narrow victories in their districts despite Lyndon Johnson's massive defeat of Barry Goldwater.

The postwar era might be remembered as one in which both American parties became truly national. Democrats extended their power and influence into midwestern and northern New England territory that had been unwaveringly Republican. Republicans made significant new breakthroughs in the growing industrial South and in their best years won the votes of millions of Americans who had never voted Republican before.

The 1964 election, at the end of the era, left the Democratic Party in control of most of the power centers, from the presidency to the state legislatures. But many Republicans, noting the somber outcome of an election in which their party had moved far to the right and by implication had repudiated the national stance on most matters, began to work to return the party to a centrist course. By underlining the strength of the American consensus on vital issues of domestic economy, civil rights, and foreign policy, the 1964 election had demonstrated anew the broad opportunities for a party willing to offer solutions to national needs.

## The Vietnam War Years

The 1960s and 1970s were some of the most turbulent decades in the nation's history. With the Vietnam War, urban riots, and the rise of the baby-boom generation, the seeds of great upheavals already were sprouting before President John F. Kennedy's death in November 1963.

Through the 1964 election, the nation had enjoyed remarkably stable two-party politics for almost two decades. When Barry Goldwater was repudiated at the polls in 1964, the post–New Deal consensus seemed to have been reaffirmed. Indeed, the year 1965 saw the last major burst of legislative accomplishments and national optimism for some time.

With the large majorities created by the Johnson landslide, the Democratic Congress enacted federal aid to education, a national health insurance program for the elderly (Medicare) and for the poor (Medicaid), and the VOTING RIGHTS ACT. But the Johnson administration's fortunes soon changed. The decision to commit massive American ground forces to Vietnam resulted in increased opposition to the war, stimulating student and racial unrest. Blacks burst forth in anger and rioted in American cities. Martin Luther King Jr. and Sen. Robert F. Kennedy were assassinated in 1968.

The Democratic Party coalition broke apart under these strains, and Republican Richard Nixon was elected president. The Democrats kept control of Congress, however, and Nixon, like Johnson, had to deal with antiwar demonstrations. His gradual withdrawal of American troops, climaxing with the peace settlement of January 1973, finally removed the war from the top of the American political agenda.

Just as things began looking better, the nation was hit by a fresh series of calamities, including an oil crisis and steep inflation. Throughout 1973 and 1974 the Watergate SCANDAL implicated several top public officials, including the president, in illegal activities. The immediate result was Nixon's resignation, the first presidential resignation in U.S. history, but deeper ramifications could be found in the American people's weakening of confidence in their government and leaders.

President Gerald R. Ford, with his low-key personality and image of personal integrity, helped calm the country after these misfortunes. But he was not seen by many as a strong leader, and by 1977 the Democrats again had control of the White House as well as both chambers of Congress.

## Years of Uneasy Peace

In large part Jimmy Carter's victory in 1976 stemmed from the voters' weariness with the usual political leadership of the country and their search for a new start. But however great the hopes, President Carter soon became embroiled in national problems and Washington politics. Even with a Congress controlled by his own Democratic Party, Carter was unable to push through much of his legislative program.

By mid-1979 few were optimistic that the energy shortages and double-digit inflation would be resolved any time soon. In November 1979 the nation's confidence was shaken further when Iranian militants seized the U.S. Embassy in Tehran, taking Americans hostage. The crisis cast a pall over the remainder of Carter's term, ending when the hostages were released as Ronald Reagan replaced Carter as president.

Besides sweeping Carter from office in 1980, Reagan provided COATTAILS for a Republican takeover of the Senate, while the Democrats remained in control of the House. Reagan became the first GOP president since Eisenhower to have his party in a majority position in either chamber.

Easily reelected in 1984, Reagan nevertheless lost GOP control of the Senate in the 1986 midterm elections. The setback came in the wake of a major White House scandal involving the sale of arms to Iran, in an attempt to free American hostages in Lebanon, and the illegal siphoning of the sale proceeds to help the contra guerrillas in Nicaragua.

Reagan left the presidency as an apostle of superpower disarmament, welcoming the U.S.-Soviet summitry that he had once disdained. Perhaps Reagan's ultimate accolade from the nation's voters was their elevation of his vice president and preferred successor, George Bush, to the Oval Office. Once again, however, the electorate chose to keep Congress in Democratic hands.

## The Post–Cold War Era

In the early 1990s the world watched as, one by one, the countries of the Warsaw Pact broke away from the Soviet Union to turn toward democracy and market economies and then as the Soviet Union itself broke apart. Seemingly overnight, the superpower rivalry that had dominated U.S. defense and foreign policy for nearly half a century was over.

"MINE! MINE! ALL MINE!"

*Source: © 1994 by Herblock*

For many Americans, however, these astounding events were overshadowed by an economic recession. Faced with slow economic growth and high levels of unemployment, more and more people began to fear that they and their children would never be able to realize the American dream of a continually improving standard of living.

Those fears were to make Republican George Bush a one-term president. Bush saw his public approval ratings soar to record heights after the successful U.S.-led military action against Iraq in 1991. But Bush was never able to persuade voters that he had a credible plan for rejuvenating the economy or addressing other domestic problems, including a failing health insurance system and the huge budget deficits caused in part by the Reagan-Bush economic policies.

The Democratic-controlled Congress gave the president little quarter. Although they cooperated on some significant legislation, more often than not Congress clashed with the Republican White House, with legislative gridlock the result. This perceived ineptitude combined with numerous scandals to drive congressional approval ratings to record lows.

The military victory in Iraq was the crowning moment of George Bush's presidency. But the euphoria was fleeting. Almost as soon as the war had ended, Democrats succeeded in turning the nation's attention to the economy's miserable performance.

The single action that may have dealt the biggest blow to Bush's political fortunes occurred in 1990 when Bush broke his 1988 campaign promise not to raise taxes. Concerned that a hemorrhaging deficit could severely damage the economy and his own reelection chances in 1992, Bush sought the help of Democrats to work out a deficit-reduction package that included some tax increases.

## End of an Era in the House

By late 1994, two years after the Democrats won back the presidency while keeping control of Congress, an end-of-an-era atmosphere had settled over the Capitol. Democrats were in disarray in the House of Representatives, which they were about to lose. They had held the House since 1954, when they regained a narrow majority midway through Eisenhower's first term. In 1956 Eisenhower won reelection in a landslide, but it was not enough to recapture the House for his party. In the years to come American voters elected a Republican president and a Democratic House five more times: in 1968, 1972, 1980, 1984, and 1988.

One theory offered to explain this pattern emphasized the role of the cold war, which seemed a permanent fact of life for nearly half a century. During those years the electorate as a whole seemed more comfortable having Republican presidents handle the defense and foreign policy issues of the presidency. At the same time, the voters consistently elected Democratic majorities in Congress who could be counted on to create and sustain popular domestic programs.

When the cold war ended in 1991, national security seemed less salient as an issue—as President Bush was to learn when he lost to former Vietnam War protester Bill Clinton in 1992. At the same time, Democrats were finding their four-decade formula for holding the House less reliable as well.

They seemed beset by rising resentment of federal tax levels and increasing hostility toward government in general as expensive, overbearing, and inefficient. Led by Newt Gingrich of Georgia, congressional Republicans capitalized on the voters' mood and the Democrats' confusion in the 1994 midterm elections. They succeeded in ending the Democrats' long rule in the House and eight-year tenure in the Senate. Two years later, in what appeared to be a deliberate affirmation of this new kind of divided government—Democratic president, Republican Congress—the voters reelected President Clinton while keeping both chambers in GOP hands. Clinton became the first Democratic president reelected without carrying either chamber of Congress for his party.

With the economy healthy and the nation at peace, Clinton's public approval ratings were high in early 1998 despite his involvement in a major sex scandal. His popularity remained high through the midterm elections even though House Republicans were preparing to impeach him for lying to a federal grand jury about his relations with a White House intern, Monica S. Lewinsky. In an apparent backlash against impeachment, voters sent five more Democrats to the House, narrowing the GOP margin of control. Clinton became the first president since Franklin D. Roosevelt in 1934 to gain House seats at midterm. The embarrassing setback prompted Gingrich to resign as Speaker and leave the House. It also reinforced the Republican majority's resolve to impeach Clinton, which it did on December 19, 1998. (See REMOVAL FROM OFFICE.)

In the subsequent Senate trial of President Clinton, the nation's anti-impeachment mood made it difficult for the Republicans to secure the two-thirds majority needed to convict him. The electorate appeared ready to punish either party if it ignored the people's will.

## Conservative

See IDEOLOGY.

## Constituency

The people who elect a government official make up his or her constituency. They may be all the people of the United States, in the case of the president; or they may be the residents of a small community, in the case of a town council member.

Constituency service is an important aspect of elective office, especially in lawmaking bodies such as Congress or a state legislature. Most constituents are voters, and legislators who ignore the voters do so at their own peril.

The high reelection rates of INCUMBENTS indicate that few officeholders neglect the needs of their constituents. Well over 90 percent of U.S. representatives win reelection, many with more than 60 percent of the vote. Senators and other incumbents also usually win if they seek reelection.

In a 1977 House study, 79 percent of members described their job as "constituency servant," second only to the 87 percent who mentioned "legislator" when asked the same question. Caseworkers make up a large part of congressional staffs. They help constituents obtain Social Security and veterans benefits, navigate through the bureaucratic maze for various problems, appeal decisions of executive agencies, and do all manner of other favors for the people they serve.

Keeping in touch with their constituents is something many lawmakers feel is too important to be left entirely to their staffs. All members of Congress have offices in their state or DISTRICT, as well as in Washington. Many return home every weekend and frequently schedule "town meetings" to hear what is on constituents' minds.

Political scientist Richard F. Fenno Jr. observed that the "home styles" of House members in their districts often differ from their styles at work in Washington.

The differences stem from the contrast in the lawmakers' minds between their geographic constituency and their personal constituency of loyalists, supporters, and intimates. To deal successfully with the different constituencies, House members devise styles suited for each one.

Although civil service and other restrictions on FEDERAL WORKERS have limited the government jobs that members of Congress can dispense, patronage remains an important service they can provide. But today the jobs are less likely to be on the government payroll than they are to be supplied indirectly through a large defense contract or public works project in the state or district.

Congress's ability to award so-called pork barrel projects to favored regions was jeopardized for a time in the 1990s by a law giving President Bill Clinton the authority to veto individual items in appropriations bills. But the Supreme Court invalidated the line-item veto as an unwarranted delegation of Congress's own powers under the Constitution.

## Constitutional Union Party (1860)

The short-lived Constitutional Union Party was formed in 1859 to promote national conciliation in the face of rampant sectionalism, which included southern threats of secession. The party appealed to conservative remnants of the American (Know-Nothing) and Whig Parties, who viewed preservation of the Union as their primary goal.

The Constitutional Union Party held its first and only national convention in Baltimore in May 1860. For president the party nominated John Bell of Tennessee, a former senator and Speaker of the House of Representatives, who previously had been both a Democrat and a Whig. The convention adopted a short platform, which intentionally avoided controversial subjects, most notably the divisive slavery issue. Instead, the platform simply urged support for "the Constitution, the Union and the Laws."

In the fall election, Bell received 590,901 votes (12.6 percent of the popular vote) and won Kentucky, Tennessee, and Virginia. However, the Bell ticket finished last in the four-way presidential race and, together with the sectional split in the Democratic Party, was a prominent factor in the victory of Republican Abraham Lincoln.

In the months after the 1860 election the Constitutional Union Party continued to urge national conciliation, but with the outbreak of the Civil War the party disappeared.

## Contested Elections

VOTER TURNOUT is low in many elections, partly because of a common belief that an individual's vote does not make a difference. Yet U.S. elections occasionally are so close that a few votes one way or the other could change the outcome. In such cases losing candidates frequently contest the result, sometimes successfully.

The RECOUNT may show that election officials mistabulated the paper ballot or VOTING MACHINE totals. Or there may be evidence of ELECTION FRAUD, with a change of result if enough votes are invalidated. ABSENTEE VOTING may be the deciding factor in a close vote, and the counting of absentee ballots may take days or weeks as the disputants and their lawyers pore over each vote.

Even presidential elections can be extremely close. Although the ELECTORAL COLLEGE system ensures that every president and vice president can claim an electoral vote majority, sixteen presidents have been elected with less than 50 percent of the POPULAR VOTE. They included Bill Clinton in both 1992 and 1996. (See table, page 133.)

Other presidents attained a slight majority, including John F. Kennedy in 1960, but won by such slim margins that a few thousand votes difference in four or five pivotal states could have changed the result. The 1968 and 1976 elections also were in that category.

In 1960 the vote was 34.2 million for Kennedy and 34.1 million for Richard Nixon, a margin of about one-tenth of 1 percent or 115,000 votes. It was so close that Nixon delayed his concession until the afternoon of the next day. But after considering the option during a vacation, Nixon decided against demanding a recount, saying it would take "at least a year and a half" and would throw the federal government into turmoil.

Below the presidential level, contested elections are commonplace. The House and Senate, invoking their constitutional authority to judge the qualifications and elections of their own members, have settled hundreds of contested elections— usually in favor of the candidate of the party in power.

The House, with 435 elections every two years, is governed in elections disputes by the Federal Contested Election Act of 1969. The act defines candidates as those listed on the ballot or as bona fide WRITE-IN candidates, thereby eliminating challenges from most candidates denied BALLOT ACCESS by their state. PRIMARY elections are not covered by the act. The Senate, which elects one-third of its one hundred members every two years, has no comparable legislation.

Several disputes arose from congressional, state, and local races in the 1996–1998 election cycle. In the Miami mayoral race such a dispute ended with a reversal of the initial result.

Tightened federal and state laws have reduced the likelihood of vote fraud as a factor in close elections. More recent cases of contested elections have centered on racial and ethnic bias rather than outright fraud as a possible distorting factor.

## President

Only once in U.S. history have popular vote irregularities been at the heart of a contested presidential election. That race was between Republican Rutherford B. Hayes of Ohio and Democrat Samuel J. Tilden of New York in 1876. The dispute centered on rival sets of electoral votes that resulted from popular vote controversies in three southern states.

Tilden won in the popular vote, 4.3 million or 51 percent to Hayes's 4.0 million or 49 percent. By the following morning, however, it became apparent that if the Republicans could hold South Carolina, Florida, and Louisiana, Hayes would be elected with 185 electoral votes to 184 for Tilden. But if a single elector in any of these states voted for Tilden, the vote would throw the election to the Democrats. Passions on both sides were so high some feared a new civil war.

Popular vote tallies in all three states were called into question, intensifying the situation. As historian Eugene H. Roseboom described the circumstances:

The Republicans controlled the state governments and the election machinery, had relied upon the Negro masses for votes, and had practiced frauds as in the past. The Democrats used threats, intimidation, and even violence when necessary, to keep Negroes from the polls; and where they were in a position to do so they resorted to fraud also. The firm determination of the whites to overthrow carpetbag rule contributed to make a full and fair vote impossible; carpetbag hold on the state governments made a fair count impossible. Radical reconstruction was reaping its final harvest.

Both parties pursued the votes of the three states with little regard for propriety or legality, and in the end all three states sent double sets of elector returns to Congress. The Constitution gives no guidance on what to do in such cases.

Between 1865 and 1876 Congress had a Republican-sponsored rule—the Twenty-second Joint Rule—that might have helped resolve the Hayes-Tilden dispute. It provided that when Congress met in joint session to count electoral votes, no votes objected to could be counted except by the concurrent votes of both the Senate and House. The rule had lapsed at the beginning of 1876, however, when the Senate refused to readopt it because the House was in Democratic control. Had the Twenty-second Joint Rule remained in effect, the Democratic House could have objected to any of Hayes's disputed votes. Instead, Congress had to find some new method of resolving electoral disputes.

It created a joint committee to work out a plan, resulting in the Electoral Commission Law of 1877, which applied only to the 1876 electoral vote count. The law established a fifteen-member commission made up of five senators (three majority party Republicans and two minority Democrats), five representatives (three majority, two minority), and five Supreme Court justices (two

*To resolve the disputed returns in the presidential election of 1876, Congress created an electoral commission, shown here deliberating by candlelight. Made up of five senators, five House members, and five Supreme Court justices, the commission voted 8–7 to give Republican candidate Rutherford B. Hayes the disputed electoral votes.* Source: Library of Congress

from each party and one independent). Because the independent justice was appointed to a Senate seat, he disqualified himself, and the Democrats accepted a Republican they regarded as somewhat independent. He voted with the Republicans on every dispute, however, ensuring Hayes's victory.

A Democratic threat to block the month-long count until after Inauguration Day, then March 4, was not carried out because of an agreement reached between the Hayes forces and southern Democrats. The southerners agreed to let the electoral count continue without obstruction. In return Hayes agreed that, as president, he would withdraw federal troops from the South, end Reconstruction, and make other concessions. The south-

erners, for their part, pledged to respect black rights, a pledge they did not carry out.

The compromise enabled the Senate president to announce at 4:00 a.m. March 2, 1877, that Hayes had been elected president with 185 electoral votes, as against 184 for Tilden. Because March 4 fell on a Sunday, Hayes was sworn in privately at the White House. His formal inauguration followed on Monday. The country acquiesced, ending the crisis that brought the nation to the brink of domestic upheaval.

In 1887 Congress enacted permanent legislation on the handling of disputed electoral votes. The Electoral Count Act of that year gave each state final authority in determining the legality of its choice of electors and required a concurrent majority of both the Senate and House to reject any electoral votes. It also established procedures for counting electoral votes in Congress.

## Senate

The closest Senate election since 1913, when DIRECT ELECTION of senators began, was the 1974 New Hampshire contest between Republican Louis C. Wyman and Democrat John A. Durkin. In the initial tally Wyman held a slight lead over Durkin, who contested the result.

After two recounts the state's final tally showed Wyman the winner by only two votes, 110,926 to 110,924 for Durkin, who had led the first recount by ten votes. Durkin then challenged Wyman's right to the seat vacated by retiring Republican Norris H. Cotton. After seven months of wrangling and forty-one roll-call votes, the Senate for the first time declared itself unable to decide an election contest. It declared the seat vacant, and Durkin asked for a new election, which was held September 16, 1975.

Durkin easily won the rerun with 140,788 votes to Wyman's 113,007. Meanwhile, retired senator Cotton returned briefly (August 8–September 18, 1975) to his old seat as an interim appointee pending the results of the special election.

An even longer dispute over a Senate election ended in October 1997 when the Senate Rules and Administration Committee concluded it had no grounds to overturn the election of Mary L. Landrieu, Louisiana Democrat. Her Republican opponent, Louis "Woody" Jenkins, had contested the election held eleven months earlier.

Jenkins asked the Senate to unseat Landrieu and order a new election because of what he called widespread vote fraud, including vote buying and multiple voting. But by a bipartisan 16–0 vote, the Republican-controlled committee said it had "not found a cumulative body of evidence of fraud, irregularities or other errors." No further Senate action was needed to end the investigation.

The action was consistent with most of the approximately one hundred contested elections judged by the Senate in its history. In only nine cases, including Wyman-Durkin, had the Senate denied a seat to the state-certified winner. Louisiana's Republican governor Mike Foster had certified Landrieu the winner by a 5,788-vote margin out of 1.5 million votes cast.

The Supreme Court has ruled only once on whether a state law can interfere with Congress's constitutional right to judge the election returns of its own members. *Roudebush v. Hartke* (1972) concerned a Senate election dispute between Republican challenger Richard L. Roudebush and incumbent Vance Hartke, Indiana Democrat. Hartke won but tried to block a recount sought by Roudebush. The Court ruled that the state recount, which did not change the result, "does not prevent the Senate from independently evaluating the election any more than the initial count does. The Senate is free to accept or reject the apparent winner in either count, and, if it chooses, to conduct its own recount."

## House

In 1965 the House settled an unusual challenge to the election of the so-called Mississippi Five, four Democrats and one Republican certified as winners in 1964. The Democrats were Thomas G. Abernethy, William M. Colmer, Jamie L. Whitten, and John Bell Williams. The Republican was Prentiss Walker.

Their right to be seated was contested by a biracial group, the Mississippi Freedom Democratic Party, originally formed to challenge the seating of the state's all-white delegation to the Democrats' 1964 NATIONAL PARTY CONVENTION. Unsuccessful in getting its candidates on that year's congressional ballot, the group conducted a rump election in which Annie Devine, Virginia Gray, and Fannie L. Hamer were the winners.

When the three women tried to enter the House floor, they were barred. Because of the dispute, however, Speaker John W. McCormack, Massachusetts Democrat, asked the regular Mississippi delegation to stand aside while the other House members were sworn in.

William F. Ryan, New York Democrat, contended that the official congressional election in Mississippi had been invalid because of interference with BLACK SUFFRAGE. African Americans had been systematically prevented from voting, Ryan said.

The House, however, decided in favor of the white males. On January 4, 1965, it adopted by voice vote a resolution to seat the regular Mississippi delegation. Later that year, Congress enacted the VOTING RIGHTS ACT of 1965, which contained strict sanctions against states that practiced discrimination against minority voters. In 1969 Representative Ryan objected to passage of the Federal Contested Elections Act, noting that under it the three women in the Mississippi Five case would have been ineligible to challenge the election because their names were not on the official ballot.

Losers in three close House races in 1984 contested the results. One of the three, in Indiana, became what appeared to be the closest House contest in the twentieth century. It led to four months of acrimony between Democrats and Republicans. Debate on the election took up far more time than almost any other issue the House considered in 1985.

Incumbent Frank McCloskey, a Democrat, apparently had won reelection to his District 8 seat by seventy-two votes. But correction of an arithmetical error (ballots in two precincts had been counted twice) gave Republican challenger Richard D. McIntyre an apparent thirty-four-vote victory. On that basis, the Indiana secretary of state certified McIntyre the winner.

But when Congress convened on January 3, 1985, the Democratic-controlled House refused to seat McIntyre pending an investigation of alleged vote fraud. Three times after that, Republicans pushed the seating of McIntyre to a vote, losing each time while picking up no more than a handful of votes from the Democrats.

A recount showed McIntyre's lead had increased to 418 votes, after more than 4,800 ballots were thrown out for technical reasons. But a task force of the Committee on House Administration, with auditors from the congressional General Accounting Office, conducted its own recount and, on a 2–1 partisan split, found McCloskey the winner by 4 votes. Republicans then tried to get a new election by declaring the seat vacant. Their attempt lost, 229–200. Nineteen Democrats joined with 181 Republicans in voting for a new election.

After Republicans tried unsuccessfully to have the majority reverse itself and count thirty-two absentee ballots, the House voted 236–190 (including ten Democrats) to seat McCloskey. GOP members walked out of the House in protest, accusing the Democrats of stealing the election.

The Supreme Court subsequently refused to get involved in the dispute. It let stand a lower court's ruling against McIntyre that the House had a constitutional right to judge its own membership. In a 1986 rematch, McCloskey handily defeated McIntyre. (See HOUSE OF REPRESENTATIVES, QUALIFICATIONS.)

In February 1998 thirteen months of acrimonious debate with ethnic overtones ended when the Republican-led House refused to overturn the defeat of California Republican Robert K. Dornan by Democrat Loretta Sanchez, a Hispanic woman. Dornan charged the election was stolen by the illegal votes of noncitizens, mostly Hispanics.

A special three-member task force said it found evidence of 748 noncitizen votes, not enough to offset Sanchez's 984-vote victory in 1996. Rep. Steny H. Hoyer of Maryland, the lone Democrat on the task force, supported the dismissal but criticized the process as contrary to the Federal Contested Elections Act and "an unprecedented intrusion into the privacy of hundreds of thousands of persons who did no wrong." He said the 740 included naturalized citizens and persons who may have inadvertently violated California's absentee voting law.

Dornan, an outspoken conservative who often clashed with Democrats during his twelve years in the House, accused Sanchez and her supporters of impeding the investigation by noncooperation. Dornan's former Orange County district, once a Republican stronghold, had become a swing district through legal and illegal immigration. In the 1998 election, Sanchez kept her seat by fighting off a challenge from Dornan.

## State and Local

Numerous elections for governor have been contested since the nation was founded, with rival governments existing in several southern states during the Civil War. In modern times one of the most celebrated disputes took place in Georgia after the death in 1946 of governor-elect Eugene Talmadge. The courts invalidated the legislature's attempt to name Talmadge's son Herman as the replacement, which elevated the lieutenant governor to the vacancy. (See GOVERNOR.)

Courts have reversed or invalidated several gubernatorial elections. In 1956, after weeks of vote counting, Rhode Island governor Dennis J. Roberts, Democrat, appealed his defeat by Republican Christopher Del Sesto. The state supreme court threw out some five thousand absentee ballots on a technicality, making Roberts the winner by 711 votes. Complaining that the election was stolen, Republicans got their revenge two years later when Del Sesto decisively defeated Roberts.

Minnesota governor Elmer L. Anderson, Republican, had to relinquish his title after three months in office when the state supreme court reversed his 1962 election. Democrat Karl F. Rolvaag became the winner by ninety-one votes out of almost 1.25 million cast.

In one of the most bitterly contested gubernatorial elections in recent history, Republican Ellen R. Sauerbrey refused for months to concede her 1994 defeat in Maryland by Democrat Parris N. Glendening. After the official canvass announced Thanksgiving Eve showed her losing by 5,993 votes out of 1.4 million cast, Sauerbrey snapped, "Everybody knows that turkeys weren't the only thing that was being stuffed in Baltimore city this month."

She charged fraud, including votes by thirty-seven dead people. But *Washington Post* reporters quickly found most of them alive, and a county court concluded that Sauerbrey had not proved that fraud or procedural errors changed the election result.

The bitterness continued in 1998 with a Glendening-Sauerbrey rematch marked by massive NEGATIVE CAMPAIGNING on both sides. Media analysts ranked the attack ads as among the most negative in a MIDTERM ELECTION year characterized by "carpet bombing" of harsh ads in many contests coast to coast. Sauerbrey lost again and this time conceded defeat on election night.

At the municipal level, Florida courts reinstated Joe Carollo as mayor of Miami in March 1998 because of alleged fraud. Carollo had been narrowly defeated in a RUNOFF ELECTION with Xavier L. Suarez. (See ELECTION FRAUD.)

The same month in a much smaller community, Estancia, New Mexico (population 792), a tie vote for mayor was broken in novel fashion—by a poker game. With an ace-high flush, incumbent James Farrington defeated JoAnn Carlson, who had tied with him at sixty-eight votes in a field of five candidates. New Mexico law requires municipal election ties to be settled by a game of chance.

## Cross-Filing

*See* FUSIONISM.

## Crossover Voting

Voting in the PRIMARY of an opposing political party is called crossover voting. It is permitted in states with open primaries and is possible in closed primaries provided the voter changes his or her party registration before the specified deadline. (See PRIMARY TYPES.)

Most crossover voting takes place when the other party's primary is more interesting than one's own, or when the voter genuinely wants to support a candidate of the party to which he or she does not belong. There have been instances, however, of a practice known as "raiding"—partisans crossing over to try to help nominate the weakest opponent. Political scientists agree that raiding, a nefarious type of SOPHISTICATED VOTING, is not very prevalent.

A larger factor in the rise of crossover voting and the trend to open primaries is the decline of PARTY IDENTIFICATION. With voters less attached to one party or the other, there is more demand for the opportunity to choose among candidates regardless of party labels. About thirty-five states have open primaries or CAUCUSES for one or both parties, including California which held its first open primary in June 1998.

California and a few other states, notably Washington, have the most open type of primary, known as a "blanket" or "jungle" primary in which all the candidates appear on the same ballot, with their parties designated. A voter may vote for a Democratic candidate for one office and a Republican for another office. But voting for candidates of more than one party for the same office is prohibited.

Advocates of open primaries argue that they bring the large pool of independent voters into the nominating process. The independents are a moderating influence, they contend, because partisan voters tend to nominate candidates whose IDEOLOGY is more extreme than that of a party's average member.

The political parties understandably dislike crossover voting. They feel that it weakens party allegiance and makes it more difficult to discipline errant members elected to office by denying them renomination. The parties also resent the intrusion of outsiders into their affairs.

In California's first open primary, for example, Democratic votes helped state treasurer Matt Fong to defeat businessman Darrell Issa for the Republican nomination to oppose Sen. Barbara Boxer, the Democratic incumbent. Issa, a car alarm manufacturer, spent heavily in the primary and may have been a stronger candidate, at least financially, against Boxer, who defeated Fong in the general election.

In May 1997 the Supreme Court upheld Alaska's open primary law against a Republican challenge, but in earlier rulings it recognized the parties' right, within limits, to restrict their primaries to registered members. In *Rosario v. Rockefeller* (1973), the Court upheld New York's eight- to eleven-month time limit between switching registration and participating in the other party's closed primary.

But later the same year in *Kusper v. Pontikes* it struck down an Illinois law denying the primary vote to anyone who voted in another party's primary within the previous twenty-three months. The Court ruled that locking the voter into an affiliation for almost two years was an unconstitutional deprivation of the right to free political association.

## Cumulative Voting

An alternative election system that improves minority groups' chances of obtaining a greater share of seats in a legislative body is called *cumulative voting*. The system works only in MULTIMEMBER DISTRICTS where each voter has more than one vote.

In conventional voting, a nine-member county council, for example, may have six seats elected by district and three seats elected AT-LARGE by all the county voters. If a minority group makes up one-third of the county population but is clustered in one district, it has little chance of electing any of the council candidates running countywide on a WINNER-TAKE-ALL basis. Assuming the group succeeds in electing one of its own in the district where it is a majority, it would still be two seats shy of the three seats needed to equal its one-third share of the county population.

In cumulative voting, however, all nine seats might be filled at-large. Each voter would have nine votes to distribute among the candidates or to concentrate on one or a few. The nine top vote getters would be the winners. If the minority group put up several candidates and concentrated its votes on them it would have a good chance of electing two or more, thereby gaining partial or full PROPORTIONAL REPRESENTATION on the council. This strategy is similar to BULLET VOTING, in which a voter entitled to vote for several candidates instead votes only for one, depriving the other candidates of votes they might have received.

Under current federal law, cumulative voting is not possible for CONGRESSIONAL ELECTIONS. Each member of the House of Representatives is elected from a single district. The only at-large voting for House members takes place in the seven states that are entitled to only one seat because of their low populations. Even in those states, each voter may vote for only one candidate for representative. (See HOUSE OF REPRESENTATIVES, ELECTING.)

Cumulative voting has been used in state and local elections, however, and some reformers advocate a law change to permit its use in congressional elections. A 1993 RACIAL REDISTRICTING case in North Carolina drew renewed attention to the cumulative voting concept as an alternative to the drawing of MAJORITY-MINORITY DISTRICTS to ensure minority representation. The Supreme Court ruling in SHAW V. RENO reinstated a challenge to the two North Carolina districts, but the dispute was resolved without any effort in Congress to allow cumulative voting. As one of fourteen states required by the VOTING RIGHTS ACT to obtain federal approval of election law changes, North Carolina had created the oddly shaped majority-minority districts in an attempt to satisfy the Justice Department.

Also in 1993 the writings of law professor Lani Guinier in favor of cumulative voting helped to kill her nomination by President Bill Clinton to head the Justice Department Civil Rights Division. The incident demonstrated that the idea of cumulative voting has the potential to be explosively controversial. Opponents contend that it violates the Supreme Court's ONE-PERSON, ONE-VOTE standard and in effect imposes quotas for membership in legislatures.

In April 1994 a federal judge ordered Worcester County, Maryland, to institute cumulative voting in electing its commissioners to correct racial discrimination perpetuated by the county's district-based elections. Although African Americans made up 21 percent of the county population, none had ever sat on the five-member commission. Four seats were elected by districts and one was elected countywide. The five commissioners, all white, appealed the federal judge's order and won a partial victory. Instead of cumulative voting, the county redrew the five districts, making each one as nearly equal in population as practicable, including one where African Americans were in the majority. The new majority-minority district elected the county's first African American commissioner.

For more than one hundred years (1880 to 1982) cumulative voting was used to elect the Illinois legislature. A variation called *limited voting* has been used at various times in Boston, Indianapolis, New York, and Philadelphia. In limited voting voters have multiple votes but fewer than the number of officials to be elected.

# D

## Dark Horse

A political dark horse is a candidate who comes out of nowhere to receive serious consideration as a compromise recipient of a party's nomination.

The first dark-horse candidate actually elected president was James K. Polk of Tennessee, who won the Democratic nomination in 1844 and went on to defeat the Whig candidate, Henry Clay of Kentucky. Polk was also the first and only former House Speaker ever elected president.

Early NATIONAL PARTY CONVENTIONS were open and deliberative. Party leaders often arrived with no idea who would eventually head the ticket, a situation that allowed dark-horse candidates to emerge with some frequency. What happened at the Democrats' 1844 convention was a little different. Former president Martin Van Buren of New York was the FRONT-RUNNER for the nomination, and Lewis Cass of Michigan was the second leading contender. But Van Buren opposed the extension of slavery and the annexation of Texas, and his view cost him his front-runner status. It was also Clay's position and an unpopular one with the Democrats, who needed southern support to defeat Clay.

In the convention voting, delegates soon deadlocked between Van Buren and Cass. Neither could muster the votes required under the Democrats' now-abandoned TWO-THIRDS RULE. On the eighth ballot Polk was suggested as a compromise, and on the next ballot he won the nomination.

Other presidents who began as dark horses were Franklin Pierce in 1852, Rutherford B. Hayes in 1876, Warren G. Harding in 1920, and Jimmy Carter in 1976. Carter owed his dark-horse success to the PRIMARY system's replacement of the national conventions as the

*James K. Polk is generally considered the first dark-horse candidate in American history to win the presidency. Source: Library of Congress*

way presidential nominations have been decided since the 1960s.

Origins of the term *dark-horse* are as obscure as some of the dark-horse candidates were before they gained celebrity. *New York Times* language columnist

William Safire cites a source for the first printed use of the term, a reference to Abraham Lincoln in 1860. Safire also notes that a STALKING HORSE is a different animal from a dark horse.

## Debates

Debates between presidential contenders have become a mainstay of political campaigns, both in the PRIMARY season and in the fall campaigns after the parties have chosen their nominees. Now almost taken for granted, the debates are a relatively recent phenomenon. Until the second half of the twentieth century, White House aspirants did not debate face-to-face. Even now, when the debate has become an election tradition, some presidential candidates still choose not to debate.

The first debate between major party nominees Richard Nixon and John F. Kennedy on September 26, 1960, is often referred to as the first "televised" debate, as if there were earlier presidential debates, just not on television. There were none. When Abraham Lincoln and Stephen Douglas held their famed debates, they were Senate candidates; they did not face off as presidential candidates in 1860. When the first debate took place a hundred years later, television did play an important role. Nixon is widely considered to have "lost" the debate to Kennedy, in part because of his poor makeup and haggard appearance.

Unlike formal, academic debates, the presidential confrontations have been loosely structured, with a panel of journalists or audience members asking the questions in the early years. Beginning in 1992 debate sponsors have experimented with various formats, with the moderator questioning the candidates and the audience sometimes allowed to participate. Throughout, there have been no judges to award points and therefore no way to determine who "won" or "lost" except by samplings of PUBLIC OPINION through POLLING. Media commentators make immediate assessments of winners and losers, however, and their judgments undoubtedly influence the public's opinion about which candidate won the debate.

*Candidates Ross Perot and Bill Clinton shake hands with President George Bush following the second televised presidential debate of the 1992 campaign, held at the University of Richmond. Source: Library of Congress*

American-style debates generally have not been copied among candidates for high office in INTERNATIONAL ELECTIONS. In Britain's 1997 parliamentary elections it had been announced that Prime Minister John Major, the Conservative leader, would debate his Labour Party opponent, Tony Blair. The debate never took place, however, and with Labour's victory Blair succeeded Major as head of the government.

In the United States the debate tradition is not confined to presidential candidates. Candidates for GOVERNOR and Congress debated numerous times in the 1998 campaigns, usually on television. In addition to the coverage provided by commercial and public networks and stations, C-SPAN (Cable-Satellite Public Affairs Network), broadcast 103 of the gubernatorial and congressional debates.

## Incumbents' Reluctance

INCUMBENT presidents and FRONT-RUNNERS—before 1960 but more so afterwards—resisted agreeing to debates because they feared giving their opponents a boost in stature by appearing on the same stage with them. They also feared that a less-than-perfect performance might undermine their advantages in the polls or give opponents ammunition for the campaign trail.

In 1976, however, President Gerald R. Ford decided to challenge Jimmy Carter to a series of televised debates. Far behind in the polls, Ford was generally perceived to be a poor stump performer but well prepared for debates. Ford and his advisers calculated that he had little to lose and much to gain by debating.

The outcome was mixed. Surveys taken immediately after the second debate indicated that viewers, by almost a two-to-one margin, thought that Ford had won. However, subsequent media attention to Ford's misstatement that Eastern Europe was not dominated by the Soviet Union dramatically reversed that opinion within three days.

In recent years front-runners have been obliged to take part in debates to avoid the charge that they were "hiding" from their opponents. President Ronald Reagan agreed to debate Democrat Walter Mondale in 1984 despite Reagan's huge leads in the polls. For the next election the chairs of the Democratic and Republican national committees secured their candidates' commitments a year in advance to participate in debates.

Although debates are a vehicle for transmitting policy positions, viewers often seem to be more impressed by the style of the debaters than by their stands on the issues. Nixon's appearance in 1960 is a case in point. People who heard the debate on radio thought that Nixon had won, but television viewers were impressed with Kennedy's manner and his healthier appearance. Likewise, Ronald Reagan won against Jimmy Carter in 1980 largely because of his style. He conveyed a warm image through his use of folksy anecdotes, his rejoinders to the president ("There you go again . . ."), and his answers, which were structured in easy-to-understand terms.

The importance of style was again illustrated by the 1992 debates in which Republican George Bush, Democrat Bill Clinton, and INDEPENDENT candidate Ross Perot participated. There were three debates, each with different rules and format—each favoring one of the candidate's speaking styles. Clinton, for example, was most effective in the format that allowed the candidates to stroll around the platform and speak directly to audience members.

In 1996 Perot, this time running as the nominee of his new REFORM PARTY, was closed out of the debates by a presidential debates commission. Clinton and his Republican challenger, Robert J. Dole, debated twice without generating much excitement. With Clinton far ahead in the polls, Dole partisans urged him to use the debates to assail Clinton on what they perceived as his weakest point: character. But Dole refrained from mentioning the scandals swirling around Clinton's administration, such as an independent counsel's investigation of the Whitewater land deal in Arkansas while Clinton was governor, allegations against him of adultery and sexual harassment, and newly disclosed campaign contributions from foreign nationals in apparent violation of CAMPAIGN FINANCE laws.

Part of Dole's reticence may be attributed to his campaign's awareness that the *Washington Post* had interviewed a woman who claimed to have had an affair with Dole while he was still married to his first wife. According to accounts published afterward, the Dole camp feared that the *Post* would reveal the story before the election, delivering what one aide said would be a "mortal threat" to Dole's candidacy. But the *Post* did not publish the story, and against strong criticism its editors defended the decision to withhold the information from the voters. (See MEDIA COVERAGE OF CAMPAIGNS.)

But cleaner debates also meant duller debates, and it showed in the ratings. Television viewership for the debates was down sharply. An estimated 28.4 million households tuned in for the first 1996 debate, as compared with 43.1 million households for the second 1992 debate.

The effect of debates is hard to measure, especially because—as in the 1976 Ford-Carter match—they are quickly followed by a barrage of media commentary and speculation over who won. Nevertheless, it appears that debates usually do not significantly alter voters' perceptions of the candidates.

## Vice-Presidential Debates

The vice-presidential debates might have greater, if longer-range, impact. Experts closely watch those debates not only because the VICE PRESIDENT could become president by succession but also because the vice-presidential nominees could be future party leaders regardless of the election outcome.

Except for 1980, vice-presidential nominees have debated since 1976 when Republican Dole faced Democrat Mondale. Both men were highly partisan, but some experts thought that Dole's acerbic style damaged the Ford-Dole ticket, perhaps enough to have caused its defeat in the close election.

The 1984 vice-presidential debate featured Democrat Geraldine Ferraro, the first woman nominated by a major party, and Republican George Bush. Bush boasted afterward that he had "kicked ass" and won, but polls showed the public was evenly divided about the victor.

Republican Dan Quayle, Bush's RUNNING MATE in 1988, did not fare well against the rhetoric of Democratic senator Lloyd M. Bentsen Jr. When the youthful Quayle sought to compare his experience in Congress with that of John F. Kennedy, Bentsen uttered one of the most famous of all debate quotes. "Senator, I served with Jack Kennedy," he said. "I knew Jack Kennedy. Jack Kennedy was a friend of mine. Senator, you're no Jack Kennedy."

James Stockdale, independent candidate Perot's running mate, was included in the 1992 vice-presidential debate but was often reduced to the role of bystander as Quayle and Al Gore bickered. Hampered by a balky hearing aid, Stockdale seemed confused and out of his element.

As the incumbent in 1996, Gore debated Jack Kemp, Dole's running mate, only once. Pat Choate, the Reform Party vice-presidential candidate, was excluded from the showdown. With Clinton barred from seeking a third term if he won, media attention focused on Gore

as a likely Democratic nominee in the year 2000. Press accounts indicated that Gore performed adequately against Kemp, but as with the Clinton-Dole debates the television audience was far smaller than in the past.

## Prenomination Debates

Debates in the primary and CAUCUS season, when candidates are trying to win their party's nomination, have become common since the number of primaries increased in the 1970s. These debates may be the most useful in helping voters and political pundits sort out and get to know the candidates of each party. Especially in the early stages of a campaign, debates are important because they offer the only large event at which candidates can be judged.

Debates among party contenders have been prominent parts of every presidential campaign since 1980. Debates in Iowa and New Hampshire that year were considered crucial turning points in the Republican nominating process. Ronald Reagan became vulnerable in Iowa when he refused to debate his opponents; he fell from 50 percent to 26 percent in the public opinion polls between December and the day after the January 5 debate.

Just weeks later, Reagan's bluntness in the Nashua, New Hampshire, debate gave his campaign an important lift. Reagan invited other Republican candidates to join a one-on-one debate he had scheduled with George Bush. When Bush resisted the inclusion of the others and debate moderator Jon Breen ordered Reagan's microphone cut off, Reagan, misstating Breen's name, declared angrily: "I paid for this microphone, Mr. Green." The self-righteous declaration won applause for Reagan and made Bush appear stiff and uncompromising.

The 1984 Democratic debates first chipped away at former vice president Mondale's status as front-runner, then dealt a devastating blow to Gary Hart's candidacy. Mondale's mocking of Hart's "new ideas" campaign with an allusion to a popular television commercial ("Where's the beef?") left the Colorado senator on the defensive in a major Atlanta debate.

Early in the 1988 campaign, candidates started a trend that has since become commonplace—appearing together on radio and television talk shows. In the summer of 1987, several Democratic hopefuls debated under the auspices of the TV show *Firing Line.* The Republicans debated on the same program in the fall. The 1988 campaign also included televised one-on-one matchups.

In 1992 Clinton used talk shows to help dispel the notion that his experience as a small-state governor did not qualify him to be president. Debating former California governor Jerry Brown on the *Donahue* show, Clinton demonstrated his mastery of national-level policy minutiae.

## Presidential Debate Commission

Beginning in 1976, most of the broadcast debates were sponsored by the television networks and/or the League of Women Voters. The league had pioneered in sponsoring debates as voter education in congressional and state elections of the 1920s. There were no presidential debates in the elections of 1964, 1968, or 1972 because of incumbents' or front-runners' reluctance to help publicize their opponents' campaigns.

As debates among nominees became the norm after the Carter-Ford appearances, the formats basically were similar in the next three elections: a moderator, journalists as questioners, a time limit on candidates' responses, and opportunities for rebuttal by candidates and follow-up questions by the reporters.

Increasingly, however, squabbles arose over who should sponsor debates and who should decide on the ground rules. In 1980 the nonpartisan League of Women Voters tried to arrange a debate that would include Democratic president Carter, Republican challenger Reagan, and independent John B. Anderson. The White House objected, and Reagan debated Anderson alone. The second debate featured Carter and Reagan, without Anderson.

After the 1984 debates, which again pointed up the league's difficulties in coping with White House efforts to dictate debate terms, two formal studies were undertaken—in 1985 by the Commission on National Elections in Washington and in 1986 by the Twentieth Century Fund at Harvard. Both recommended a change to a permanent, independent debate sponsor.

As an outgrowth of the studies, the two major parties cooperated in creating the Commission on Presidential Debates (CPD) in 1987 under leadership of the national party chairs, Frank J. Fahrenkopf Jr., Republican, and Paul G. Kirk Jr., Democrat. Both continued to chair the CPD after leaving their party posts. They and eight other men and women make up the CPD board of directors.

The commission retained the moderator/reporters format for the 1988 debates. A question asked at the second of those debates, however, may have contributed to the commission's subsequent decision to use a single-moderator format for the 1992 and 1996 debates.

The controversial question was asked at the opening of the October 13, 1988, debate between George Bush and Michael S. Dukakis. The reporter, Bernard Shaw of Cable News Network, who was also the moderator, addressed the first question to Dukakis, who was widely regarded as the winner of the first debate. Shaw asked Dukakis if he would favor the death penalty if his wife, Kitty Dukakis, were raped and killed. Dukakis said no. His unemotional explanation did little to counteract the Bush campaign's efforts to portray Dukakis as soft on crime. Largely because of Dukakis's impassive answer, most commentators rated Bush as the winner.

After the first 1992 debate the commission dropped the panel of reporters, with all questions asked by the moderator or, in some cases, audience members in a town hall format. The commission settled on Jim Lehrer of public television's *Newshour with Jim Lehrer* as moderator of all the 1996 debates.

As with the League of Women Voters, the White House did not always cooperate with the commission. The first Clinton-Dole debate, scheduled for September 25 in St. Louis, had to be canceled because Clinton was speaking to the United Nations the day before and at a fund-raiser the night of the debate. Similarly, George Bush rejected the first scheduled debate of 1992.

In 1996 the CPD sponsored DebateWatch '96, a focus group effort to assess the debates and improve their effectiveness. Several corporations provided financial support. The CPD site on the Internet provided transcripts and other information about the debates.

## Third Party Participation

In 1996 the CPD made its most controversial decision to date by barring Ross Perot from the Clinton-Dole debates, even though he took part in the 1992 debates, won 19 percent of the vote, and had qualified for nearly $30 million in PUBLIC FINANCING for his second candidacy. As an independent in 1992 Perot had avoided federal limits on campaign spending by not taking public money.

The CPD accepted the recommendation of its advisory board, which said Perot should be excluded because he lacked a "realistic chance" to win. That was the only criterion applied, the board said. Critics said the decision proved what some had claimed all along, that sponsorship by a bipartisan commission biased the debate system against THIRD PARTIES. Some recommended restructuring to make the commission more nonpartisan than bipartisan.

Rebuffed, Perot fell back on talk show appearances and paid *infomercials* (part information, part selling) to get his message across. The networks were reluctant to sell him the air time, however, because the infomercials drew relatively few viewers. In the end, Perot fell far short of his 1992 mark, winning only 8.4 percent of the 1996 vote.

Perot and Ralph Nader of the GREEN PARTY declined to take part in a debate on C-SPAN with three other third party candidates—Harry Browne, LIBERTARIAN; Jon Hagelin, NATIONAL LAW; and Howard Phillips, U.S. TAXPAYERS.

In a decision that will affect third party candidates' future access to televised debates, in 1998 the Supreme Court, 6–3, agreed that networks have discretion to exclude independent or minor party candidates from debates they sponsor. The case arose from a suit brought by Ralph P. Forbes, an independent candidate for Congress in Arkansas, who was barred from a 1996 debate sponsored by the state's Educational Television Network. The editors concluded that Forbes was not a serious candidate and therefore not eligible to participate with the Democratic and Republican candidates. A federal appeals court upheld Forbes's position. The FEDERAL ELECTION COMMISSION sided with the Arkansas network, contending that public television licensees would likely abandon their sponsorship of political debates if the lower court ruling were upheld. Writing for the Court, Justice Anthony M. Kennedy said that the decision to exclude Forbes was a "reasonable, viewpoint-neutral exercise of journalistic discretion" because the exclusion was based on the candidate's "objective lack of support," and not on his political views.

## Delegates

The process of selecting delegates to the NATIONAL PARTY CONVENTIONS has changed dramatically since 1968. Most delegates of both major parties now win their seats through PRESIDENTIAL PRIMARY elections—a development that has vastly enhanced the influence of rank-and-file voters in choosing the party's nominee and greatly diminished the influence of party leaders.

Although the DEMOCRATIC PARTY spearheaded the transformation with formal rules changes requiring broader representation of women and minorities, the proliferation of primaries also has affected the REPUBLICAN PARTY's delegate selection process.

Only 116 delegates from thirteen states attended the first national nominating convention held by the ANTI-MASONIC PARTY in 1831, but with the addition of more states and the adoption of increasingly complex voting-allocation formulas by the major parties, the size of conventions spiraled, especially since the 1960s. The expanded size reflected the democratization of modern conventions, with less command by a few party leaders and dramatic growth among youth, women, and minority delegations. (See figure, Republican and Democratic Convention Delegates, 1932–1996.)

With the larger size of conventions has come a formalization in the method of delegate selection, which at first was often haphazard. At the Democratic convention in 1835, for example, Maryland had 188 delegates to cast the state's ten votes. In contrast, Tennessee's fifteen votes were cast by a traveling businessman who happened to be in the convention city at the time.

**Republican and Democratic Convention Delegates, 1932–1996**

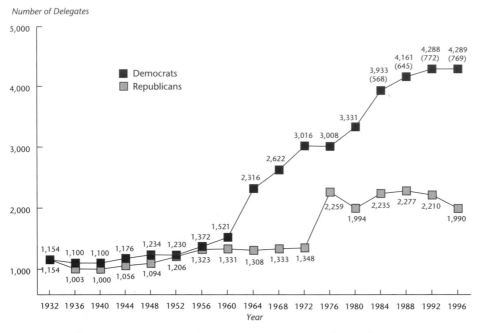

*Number of Delegates*

■ Democrats
□ Republicans

*Source: National Party Conventions, 1831–1996* (Washington, D.C.: Congressional Quarterly, 1997).
*Note:* Numbers in parentheses represent superdelegates.

In those days delegates were handpicked by party leaders and nomination deals often were made in so-called smoke-filled rooms off the convention floor. More recently, under the CAUCUS system, delegates were named at state party conventions. Some states, notably Iowa, still hold caucuses, but since the early twentieth century the trend has been toward the use of primaries to choose delegates and allow party members to vote their presidential preference. (See IOWA CAUCUS.) Nevertheless, the continued dominance of conventions by party bosses prompted calls for changes in the way delegations were formed.

## Democratic Rules Changes

The PRESIDENTIAL SELECTION REFORMS were an aftermath of the violence-marred 1968 Democratic convention in Chicago. That convention nominated Vice President Hubert H. Humphrey over antiwar activist Sen. Eugene J. McCarthy of Minnesota even though Humphrey had not participated in a single primary. State delegations that opposed Humphrey felt excluded. They complained that the delegate-selection process was unfair and that party leaders had manipulated the outcome of the convention.

As a result, in February 1969 the party established the Commission on Party Structure and Delegate Selection, chaired by Sen. George S. McGovern of South Dakota and later by Rep. Donald M. Fraser of Minnesota. (The commission came to be known as the McGovern-Fraser Commission.) A little more than a year later, the commission issued eighteen detailed guidelines to be followed in the state delegate-selection process.

The mandatory guidelines condemned discrimination due to race, color, creed, sex, or age and required that affirmative steps be taken to give delegate slots to women, minorities, and young people in proportion to

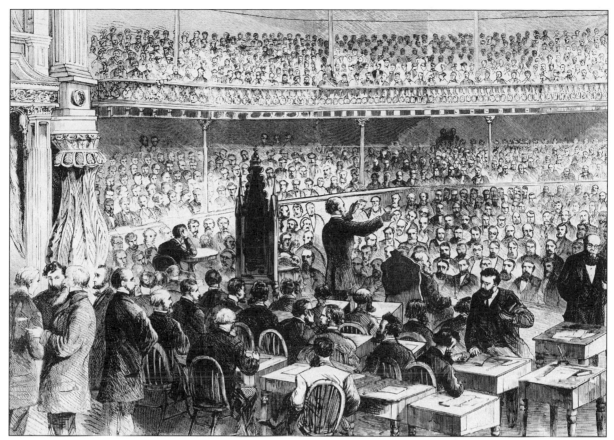

*Early in American history, nominating conventions were wide-open affairs at which almost anything could happen, including the nomination of dark-horse candidates. Over time, changes in the nominating system have turned national conventions into rubber stamps. Pictured is the 1868 Republican convention in Chicago. Source: Library of Congress*

their population in each state. They also barred restrictive fees and petition requirements for delegate candidates. The guidelines banned the UNIT RULE, followed by the party since its inception, under which all delegates had to vote as the majority of the delegation voted. They also limited the influence of party committees in the selection of convention delegates.

In addition, the guidelines urged a move toward PROPORTIONAL REPRESENTATION. Under this system, delegates are assigned in proportion to the percentage of the total that each presidential candidate receives in the primary. The major alternative is a WINNER-TAKE-ALL system, in which the candidate who wins the plurality of the popular vote receives all of the delegate votes.

By democratizing the process substantially, these delegate-selection reforms had a considerable impact. At the same time, they greatly reduced the power of party leaders, prompting some to complain that the party had been dismantled.

Although states were largely in compliance with the guidelines by 1972, there was considerable resistance to the reforms. To address these concerns, the Democrats created commissions in 1972 (when McGovern was the party's presidential nominee) and again in 1976. But neither the commission headed by Barbara A. Mikulski of Maryland (1972) or by Morley Winograd of Michigan (1976) changed the McGovern-Fraser rules significantly, and the notion of fair representation became generally accepted.

Concern that the reforms had gone too far in reducing the influence of party leaders still ran high. So in 1980 the party created yet another commission, this one chaired by North Carolina governor James B. Hunt Jr. The main recommendation made by the Hunt Commission was to increase the number of delegate slots reserved at the national convention for party leaders and elected officials—or SUPERDELEGATES, as they have come to be called. Every state is now guaranteed enough slots to accommodate its "core" Democratic officials, defined as the governor, members of Congress, and mayors of cities with populations of more than 250,000.

## Effect on Primaries

As a result of the reforms, the number of primaries ballooned. Most state party leaders thought that the adoption of a presidential primary was the easiest and surest way to conform to the rules and prevent challenges to their convention delegations.

Primaries almost tripled between 1968 and 1996, while the number of caucuses shrank. Of the 1,990 delegates to the 1996 Republican convention in San Diego, 1,750 or 87.9 percent were selected in primaries, compared with 240 or 12.1 percent chosen in caucuses. The much larger Democratic convention in Chicago saw 2,802 or 65.3 percent of the 4,289 delegates selected in primaries, against 719 or 16.8 percent from caucus states. The remaining 769 Democratic delegates (17.9 percent) were superdelegates. One or both parties held primaries in forty-three states, the District of Columbia, and Puerto Rico.

The reforms also transformed the presidential nominating convention itself. Many thought that the use of proportional representation would enhance the role of the convention by creating a situation in which there were many candidates but no FRONT-RUNNERS. That has not happened. Instead, the convention has become a rubber stamp, formally adopting a decision that has already been made by the popular vote of the rank and file.

The proliferation of primaries that accompanied the Democratic reforms also affected the Republicans. The Republican Party, however, did not experience the same sort of wrenching pressures to reform as did the Democratic Party, mostly because the Republicans were a smaller, more ideologically cohesive party than the Democrats. The Republican Party also had far fewer minority members, which meant there was less demand for equal representation of minorities within its ranks. Furthermore, the Republicans had already instituted several of the reforms sought by the Democrats. For instance, use of the unit rule had been banned at Republican conventions since the mid-nineteenth century.

## Allocating the Seats

When the convention system began in the nineteenth century, the Democrats and the Republicans distributed delegate seats based on each state's ELECTORAL COLLEGE strength, which is equal to the state's representation in Congress—two senators for each state plus the number of representatives in the House.

Under this method, the South was overrepresented at GOP conventions in relation to the number of Republican voters in that region. After the divisive 1912 convention at which President William Howard Taft defeated former president Theodore Roosevelt for the nomination, the party made the first major deviation from the electoral college ratio. Taft's almost solid support from the South pointed up the disparity in representation, prompting the party to reduce the allocation for southern states at the 1916 convention.

At their 1924 convention the Republicans applied the first bonus system, by which states were awarded extra votes for supporting the Republican presidential candidate in the previous election. The Democrats first used a bonus system in 1944, completing a compromise arrangement with southern states for abolishing the party's controversial two-thirds nominating rule. Since then both parties have used various delegate allocation formulas.

From 1932 through 1960 the Democratic and Republican conventions were about the same size, roughly 1,200 to 1,300 delegates. But in 1964 the Democrats added about a thousand delegates and its total number climbed steadily until the 1992 and 1996 elections, when it leveled off at about 4,290.

At their 1972 convention the Republicans added more than 900 new delegate slots, bringing the total to 2,259 for 1976. The Ripon Society, an organization of liberal Republicans, sued to have the new rules overturned. They argued that, because of the extra delegates awarded to states that voted Republican in the previous presidential election, less-populous southern and western states were favored at the expense of the more populous but less Republican eastern states. The challenge failed when the Supreme Court in February 1976 refused to hear the case and let stand a U.S. court of appeals decision upholding the rules. Republican conventions have remained stable in size ever since.

## Credentials Disputes

Selection as a delegate does not automatically guarantee admittance to the convention floor as a voting participant. The parties examine the credentials of each delegate to make sure he or she has a right to be there. In the past the credentials process often was used to exclude certain delegations in favor of others, producing some historic political disputes.

Before the opening of a convention the national committee compiles a temporary roll of delegates. The roll is referred to the convention's credentials committee, which holds hearings on the challenges and makes recommendations to the convention, the final arbiter of all disputes.

In the twentieth century most of the heated credentials fights concerned delegations from the South. In the Republican Party the challenges focused on the power of the Republican state organizations to dictate the selection of delegates. The issue was hottest in 1912 and 1952, when the party throughout most of the South was a skeletal structure whose power was restricted largely to selecting convention delegates.

The furious 1912 struggle centered on Roosevelt's effort to wrest the Republican nomination from President Taft. The Roosevelt forces brought seventy-two delegate challenges to the floor, but the test of strength between the two candidates came on a procedural motion. By a vote of 567 to 507, the convention tabled a motion by the Roosevelt forces to bar the delegates under challenge from voting on any of the credentials contests. All the credentials challenges were settled in favor of the delegates for Taft, who won the nomination. Roosevelt went on to run as an independent, and the split cost the Republicans the election.

The 1952 GOP dispute arose over the seating of delegations from Georgia, Louisiana, and Texas as retired general Dwight D. Eisenhower and Sen. Robert A. Taft of Ohio contested for the nomination. The national committee, controlled by Taft forces, had voted to seat delegations from the three states that were friendly to Taft. But the convention voted 607 to 531 to seat a Georgia delegation favorable to Eisenhower. It then seated Eisenhower delegates from Louisiana and Texas without roll calls. Eisenhower won the nomination on the first ballot.

After the 1952 dispute the Republicans established a subcommittee of the national committee to review credentials challenges in advance of the convention. Within the Democratic Party the question of southern credentials emerged after World War II on the volatile issues of civil rights and party loyalty. Important credentials challenges on these issues occurred at the 1948, 1952, 1964, and 1968 Democratic conventions.

There were numerous credentials challenges at the 1972 Democratic convention, but, unlike those at its immediate predecessors, the challenges involved delegations from across the nation and focused on violations of the party's newly adopted guidelines. After their divisive 1968 convention the Democrats also created a formal credentials procedure to review all challenges before the opening of the convention.

Equally important to the settlement of credentials challenges are the rules under which the convention operates. The Republican Party adopts a new set of rules at every convention. Although large portions of the existing rules are enacted each time, general revision is always possible. The Democratic Party's first set of formal rules were those adopted at the 1972 convention on rec-ommendation of the McGovern-Fraser Commission.

## Results

By the end of the 1990s, the Democrats' tinkering with delegate selection had produced a set of nominating rules characterized by the following: primaries and caucuses restricted to a three-month "window" in election years (basically March through May, exempting the earlier NEW HAMPSHIRE PRIMARY and Iowa caucus); participation restricted to party members; proportional representation required, with bans on all types of contests where primary victors win all or extra delegates; candidates entitled to approve delegates loyal to their candidacy; delegations allowed to have both pledged and uncommitted superdelegates; delegations divided equally between men and women; and representation by youth and minorities encouraged.

Through tradition rather than formal rules, the Republicans likewise made their nominating process more open and representative of the party as a whole. At its 1996 convention in San Diego the GOP changed its rules to lock in some of those guarantees, beginning with the 2000 presidential election. The changes required states to submit delegate-selection plans by July 1, 1999, to avoid last-minute jockeying for early primary positions; set a primary and caucus period in 2000, from the first Monday in February to the third Tuesday of June, with extra delegates awarded states voting later in that period, beginning March 15; and took steps to minimize chances of non-Republicans dominating GOP primaries in states where all parties appear on a single ballot.

As a result of the reforms, the typical convention delegate today is more apt than in the past to be a woman or an African American, but political IDEOLOGY is still apparent in their distribution. Delegate polls for 1996 show more women at the Democrats' convention (53 percent) than at the Republicans' (46 percent). Black Democratic delegates far outnumbered black Republican delegates (17 percent to 3 percent). Labor union members as Democratic delegates (24 percent) were more numerous than their GOP counterparts (4 percent). Both parties had about the same percentage of lawyer delegates—Democrats, 10 percent and Republicans, 11 percent. In 1944, 38 percent of Democratic and 37 percent of Republican delegates were lawyers.

Forty-three percent of Democratic delegates in 1996 considered themselves liberal, versus zero percent of Republican delegates. The proportions were the reverse when delegates were asked if they were conservative. Only 5 percent of Democratic delegates said yes, compared with 70 percent of the GOP delegates. At the Republican convention, Protestants outnumbered Catholics 62 percent to 25 percent. Among Democratic delegates the ratio was closer, 47 percent to 30 percent. Jews made up only 3 percent of GOP delegates, 6 percent of Democrats.

---

## Democracy

The term *democracy* means rule by the people. It is derived from two Greek words *demos* (people) and *krato* (rule or power). Democratic government basically has two forms: *direct* or *pure* democracy and *representative* or *indirect* democracy. The United States is a representative democracy.

In a pure democracy like those of ancient Greece and today's New England town meetings, citizens participate directly in making government decisions. In many states citizens also can make or review laws through INITIATIVES AND REFERENDUMS. But for the most part, government decisions in the United States and most Western nations are made by men and women elected by the people to represent them.

The American type of representative democracy features a presidential system in which a chief executive is elected independently of the national legislature. In the parliamentary systems of most European nations, the majority party or coalition of parties in the national legislature selects the chief executive, who is called a prime minister, premier, or chancellor.

Democracies also differ in how they divide power between the national government and regional governments. Australia, Canada, Germany, and the United States are organized on a federal basis—that is, they divide power between the national government and states. But in Britain and France all government authority resides with the national government.

Whatever its form, democracy is not perfect. "Indeed," Prime Minister Winston Churchill told the House of Commons in 1947, "it has been said that democracy is the worst form of government except all those other forms that have been tried from time to time."

## Control of Leadership

Despite their significant differences, the Western democracies all meet a basic test of a democracy: their citizens have a relatively high degree of control over what their leaders do. Citizens' efforts to influence political leaders are expected, accepted, and frequently successful. This sets Western democracies in stark contrast to regimes such as the People's Republic of China, where open opposition to government policies is not permitted.

Achieving an orderly succession—the transfer of government authority without serious disruptions—has been a long-standing problem of governance. The conventional democratic solution to this problem is routine elections, ensuring that leadership positions will become vacant at periodic intervals without beheadings or revolutions. In the United States, succession is accomplished without elections in case of death in the most powerful offices—PRESIDENT to VICE PRESIDENT and GOVERNOR to LIEUTENANT GOVERNOR.

Democratic procedures operate best when there is an expectation that policy changes in the short run will be modest and relatively narrow, and there will be no wholesale changes in the economic order or the system

*Harry S. Truman takes the oath of office after the death of Franklin D. Roosevelt. The smooth transition from president to president, whether through election or succession, is a hallmark of democracy. Source: National Park Service—Abbie Rowe; Courtesy Harry S. Truman Library.*

*A hallmark of democracy is the right to protest without fear of reprisal. At this demonstration, anti–Vietnam War protesters brand President Lyndon B. Johnson a war criminal.* Source: *Library of Congress*

of government. Losers of an election need not fear being liquidated or deprived of their liberty without due process of law. They know that all concerned will be able to continue the struggle in the next election. There is, in other words, a societal consensus on the limits of the political struggle.

Americans, for example, operate on the assumption that politics will continue to function within the existing constitutional order. They further assume that the economic system will be primarily a free-enterprise one. But within these areas of fundamental agreement, Americans dispute narrower issues such as the level of the minimum wage, the need to take military action in various parts of the world, appropriate sentences for convicted drug dealers, and the amounts to be spent on defense, health care, and education.

In a democracy, there is not only the freedom to dissent, but also the expectation that peaceful protests will be heard and considered, though not necessarily heeded, and that no reprisals will be taken against the protesters. The freedom to dissent is accompanied by the right to join with others to seek redress of grievances by ousting officeholders through the electoral process.

No single set of institutions is required for a democratic order. All Western-style democracies, however, supplement the executives, courts, and councils found in any government—nondemocratic as well as democratic  with institutions and processes that link the ruled with the rulers, permit consultation with the governed, manage succession of authority, and reconcile competing interests within society. Although the exact nature of the institutions and processes that carry out these functions varies from one representative democracy to another, most democratic orders have the following elements in common:

• Political parties to contest elections, mobilize public support for or opposition to the government's policies, and handle the succession of power.
• An elected legislature to serve as the agent and advocate of the representatives' constituents, to symbolize consultation with the governed, and to act as a conduit for the communication of approval of and dissent from official policy.

• Electoral procedures to express mass approval or disapproval of government policy, to set limits on the course of government policy, and to renew leaders' terms of office or dismiss them.
• Nonparty associations and groups (INTEREST GROUPS) to supplement the formal system of representation in the legislature, to communicate their members' views to government officials, and to act as a means of consultation between the governed and the governors.
• Additional linkages between the government and its citizens to provide supplementary means of communications through guarantees of freedom of the press, the right to petition the government for redress of grievances, and protection against official reprisals for dissent against government actions.

## Constitutional Framework

American politics always functions within the shadow of the Constitution, which sets the legal framework for the government. The Constitution obliges the national government to guarantee to the states a REPUBLICAN GOVERNMENT, a term the framers used to distinguish the American system from either a monarchy or a direct democracy.

The educated men who wrote the Constitution in 1787 (twenty-six of the fifty-five delegates had college degrees) were well acquainted with the IDEOLOGY of democracy, the British and French political philosophers who espoused it, and the efforts to achieve it abroad, notably in France. As delegates they were intent on drafting a written constitution because the unwritten British constitution had not protected the colonists' basic rights.

The delegates also were wary of pure democracy, which they equated with mob rule. They were aware that historically many pure democracies had disintegrated as tyrannies. Although not a delegate himself, John Adams of Massachusetts voiced the sentiments of the times when he wrote, "Remember, democracy never lasts long. It soon wastes, exhausts, and murders itself. There was never a democracy yet that did not commit suicide." Instead, the delegates created a *republic* in which liberty and representative government were combined.

But by itself the founders' handiwork, the Constitution, does not explain America's unique brand of representative democracy or its stability. Other nations, especially in Latin America, have copied the U.S. constitutional system, but they have not developed stable democratic political orders. Rather, some of these countries may enjoy occasional periods of free elections and civilian rule, but then suffer military coups, authoritarian rule, and instability.

At the time the United States was founded, circumstances were favorable to the development of democracy. The vast American subcontinent, with its abundant natural resources and fertile land, had no history of feudalism, no titled aristocracy, and no monopoly of landownership by a privileged few.

In the early years of settlement and nationhood, governments imposed few limitations on those seeking to improve their lots in life. For those for whom opportunities seemed limited, the vast western frontier was available for starting a new life.

But the frontier and the prospect of free land and a new life in the West did not last forever. By 1900 the western frontier was largely closed, and the United States was becoming an industrialized nation whose people were increasingly crowded into teeming cities. Yet despite these and more recent challenges, American democracy has shown a remarkable capacity for adaptability and durability.

The forces molding the uniquely American brand of politics involve more than geophysical conditions, accidents of history, and a remarkable constitution, although each of these has affected and continues to affect politics. American politics is also shaped by the cultural and socioeconomic environment of the nation: the values and attitudes that people have, the size and composition of the population, the distribution of wealth and income, the class structure, where people live, living patterns, and the issues that unite as well as divide the people. (See POLITICAL CULTURE IN AMERICA.)

## Democratic National Committee

The chief administrative body of the DEMOCRATIC PARTY is the Democratic National Committee (DNC). With almost four hundred members, the DNC is twice the size of its major party counterpart, the REPUBLICAN NATIONAL COMMITTEE.

In both parties, the NATIONAL PARTY CONVENTION is the highest governing authority. But between the four-year conventions the national committees and their staffs carry out the parties' day-to-day business.

Formed in 1848, the DNC is the oldest national party committee. Since 1984 it has operated from its first permanent home, a $6.5 million office building on Capitol Hill at 430 South Capitol Street, S.E., in Washington, D.C. Previous locations in New York and Washington (including the Watergate offices burglarized by Republican operatives in 1972) were rented.

The national committee is responsible for issuing the *Call for the National Convention,* which sets forth the method of allocating delegates to each state. The *Call* establishes the convention's standing committees and temporary rules.

The DNC assists in conducting the party's presidential campaign, works to elect Democrats to state and local offices, and plays a major role in formulating and disseminating party policy. To help with these duties the DNC employs a staff that usually numbers at least forty. Since the 1976 election, however, the nominees of both major parties have relied mostly on their own PRIMARY campaign organizations to conduct their general election campaigns. The PUBLIC FINANCING of presidential campaigns, which began in 1976, required candidates to set up primary campaign committees to receive funds needed to qualify for the federal grants. Such committees continued into the general election period and usually became the nominees' main campaign organizations. (See PRESIDENT, NOMINATING AND ELECTING.)

The DNC is a large organization, numbering 398 members including the 9 officers. Each state or territorial chair and the next highest officer, who must be of the

*Interviewed on election night, November 11, 1972, Jean West wood was the first woman to serve as the chair of a major party. Source: Library of Congress*

*Ron Brown, the first African American to head a major party committee, held the post from 1989 to 1993. Source: Library of Congress*

opposite sex—a total of 112 from 56 jurisdictions—serve four-year terms. Two hundred additional memberships are allocated to the same jurisdictions based on population, with at least two members for each state or territory, leaving eighty-eight seats to be divided among the larger jurisdictions. All these delegations must be equally divided between men and women.

Democratic U.S. senators, House members, and a group called the College Democrats each are represented by two seats on the committee. Affiliated party groups—governors, mayors, state legislators, county officials, municipal officials, Young Democrats, and the National Federation of Democratic Women—each elect three DNC members. The DNC chair appoints fifty at-

large members to ensure broad representation of the party as a whole.

Sub-units of the DNC are the executive committee and three standing committees: credentials, rules and bylaws, and resolutions. Fifty four men and women make up the executive committee: the national chair and eight other officers, twenty regional representatives, ten at-large members elected by the DNC, and fifteen others representing Democratic affiliates. The DNC normally meets twice a year, in the spring and fall. In presidential election years, it also meets after the national convention.

Through its rules and PRESIDENTIAL SELECTION REFORMS, the Democratic Party has pioneered in expanding participation by women and minorities. It requires national convention delegations to be equally divided between men and women. It was the first major party to have a woman chair, Jean Westwood of Utah in 1972, and a woman vice-presidential candidate, Geraldine Ferraro in 1984. And it was the first party to have an African American national chair, Ronald H. Brown, 1989–1993. Brown, credited with helping to put Bill Clinton in the White House, was killed in an airplane crash while on a European mission as secretary of commerce in 1996.

Brown's successor as chair, David Wilhelm, resigned after enduring two years of heavy criticism, especially after the Republican takeover of Congress in the 1994 MIDTERM ELECTION. Wilhelm was succeeded by a dual chairmanship of Donald L. Fowler of South Carolina, who had chaired a DNC reform study group, the Fairness Commission, and Sen. Christopher J. Dodd of Connecticut, who held the title of general chair.

In both major parties the position of chair formerly was part time, often filled by a member of Congress. Now it is a full time, salaried position. But both Republican Ronald Reagan and Democrat Clinton circumvented the rule by naming a tandem general chair.

Fowler and Dodd led a highly effective fund-raising operation that helped Clinton win reelection in 1996. Their success, however, was marred by SCANDALS. Shortly before the election it was disclosed that the DNC had accepted large contributions from Asian and other foreign business interests, which by law are barred from participation in U.S. elections. Some major contributors, including foreigners, were invited to White House coffees with President Clinton. In all, the Democrats raised $122.3 million in so-called SOFT MONEY from corporations and individuals for party building, advertising, and other activities that indirectly benefited Clinton's reelection campaign.

Although the DNC denied any illegality, it later returned almost $3 million in suspect contributions and wound up heavily in debt. It was also reported that the communist government of China planned to buy influence in the 1996 election, but that the U.S. intelligence community's warning was not passed on to President Clinton. In mid-1997 the Republican-controlled Congress began investigating these and other allegations to determine whether either party had broken CAMPAIGN FINANCE laws.

Both Fowler and Dodd had announced their intention to resign after the election, and they did so. Clinton chose Colorado governor Roy Romer to succeed Dodd as general chair and party spokesman. Steve Grossman, a Massachusetts businessman, was named national chair. Grossman planned to step down in 1999, but Clinton did not immediately name a successor. (See Appendix, National Party Chairs, 1848–1998.)

National party chairs traditionally subordinate their own political ambitions to that of the president when the party is in power. Democratic chair James A. Farley, however, broke with that tradition in 1940 after a falling out with President Franklin D. Roosevelt. Farley unsuccessfully challenged Roosevelt's bid for a third-term nomination. During FDR's first two terms Farley also served as postmaster general, a practice now prohibited by the Hatch Act's restrictions on FEDERAL WORKERS' POLITICAL ACTIVITY.

Other Democratic aspirants have gained the party chair after their own national office candidacies failed. In 1960 nominee John F. Kennedy considered two senators, Lyndon B. Johnson of Texas and Henry M. Jackson of Washington, as potential RUNNING MATES. After his first choice, Johnson, accepted the offer, Kennedy named Jackson to head the DNC. In office himself after Kennedy was assassinated, Johnson became the only modern president who never appointed a party chair. (Technically, the chair is elected by the DNC. But traditionally, especially among the Democrats, the committee ratifies the president's selection.)

In 1968 Hubert H. Humphrey chose Edmund S. Muskie of Maine over Sen. Fred Harris of Oklahoma as his running mate. Harris then lost out briefly as party chair to Lawrence F. O'Brien, who both preceded and followed Harris in the DNC job in the 1968–1972 period. In 1992 national chair Ronald Brown was mentioned as a possible running mate to Bill Clinton, who settled instead on Sen. Al Gore of Tennessee.

Party rules empower the DNC to fill the vacancy if a

nominee resigns or dies before the election. This situation arose in 1972 when Thomas Eagleton withdrew as George S. McGovern's running mate after it was disclosed that Eagleton had a past history of clinical depression. The DNC then ratified McGovern's choice of a successor, R. Sargent Shriver of Maryland.

## Democratic National Convention

*See* NATIONAL PARTY CONVENTION.

## Democratic Party (1832– )

There is no precise birth date for the Democratic Party. It developed as an outgrowth of Thomas Jefferson's Democratic-Republican Party, which splintered into factions in the 1820s. The group led by Andrew Jackson took the name Democratic-Republican, but after 1830 dropped the second half of the label and became simply the Democratic Party. The new party encouraged and benefited from the increasing democratization of American politics that began in the 1820s. Andrew Jackson became a symbol of this mass democracy, and when he was elected in 1828 a period of Democratic dominance began that lasted until the Civil War.

The Democrats were a national party, with a particular appeal among workers, immigrants, and settlers west of the Alleghenies. The success of the party in the pre–Civil War period was due in part to a national organization stronger than that of its rivals. In 1832 the Democrats were the first major party to hold a national nominating convention, and in 1848 they became the first party to establish an ongoing national committee.

Between 1828 and 1860 the party held the White House for twenty-four years, controlled the Senate for twenty-six years, and controlled the House of Representatives for twenty-four years. Leadership in the party generally resided in Congress. The Democrats' two-thirds nominating rule, adopted at the 1832 convention and retained for a century, gave the South veto power over the choice of a national ticket. The result, not only

*The Democratic Party traces its lineage to President Andrew Jackson.* Source: Library of Congress

in the pre–Civil War years but until the rule was eliminated in 1936, was the frequent selection of conservative candidates for president.

The early philosophy of the Democratic Party stressed a belief in a strict interpretation of the Constitution, states' rights, and limited spending by the federal government. While party members throughout the nation accepted these basic tenets, there was no national consensus on the volatile slavery issue, which strained the party in the mid–nineteenth century and finally divided it geographically in 1860. Two separate Democratic tickets were run in the 1860 election—one northern, one southern. The party division aided the election of the candidate of the new antislavery Republican Party, Abraham Lincoln, who received less than 40 percent of the popular vote.

During the Civil War the northern wing of the party was factionalized. One group, the Copperheads, were hostile to the Union war effort and favored a negotiated peace with the Confederacy. The stance of the Copperheads, coupled with the involvement of many southern Democrats in the Confederate government, enabled the Republicans for a generation after the Civil War to denounce the reunified Democratic Party as the "party of treason."

The Democrats were a national party after the Civil War, but they were displaced as the majority party by the Republicans. The strength of the Democrats was in the South, which voted in large majorities for Democratic candidates. Party strength outside the South was scattered, being most noticeable among urban ethnics and voters in the BORDER STATES. The period of Republican dominance lasted for nearly three-quarters of a century, 1860 to 1932. The Democrats occupied the White House for sixteen of these seventy-two years, controlled the House of Representatives for twenty-six years, and controlled the Senate for ten years.

The Great Depression, which began in 1929, dramatically altered American politics and provided the opportunity for the Democrats to reemerge as the majority party. The Democrats swept to victory behind Franklin D. Roosevelt in 1932 and, with widespread popular acceptance of his New Deal programs, a new coalition was formed, which has remained largely intact. The new majority coalition combined the bulk of the black electorate, the academic community, and organized labor with the party's core strength among urban ethnic and southern voters.

Between 1932 and 1980 the Democrats occupied the presidency thirty-two of forty-eight years and controlled both houses of Congress for forty-four years. The acceptance of Roosevelt's New Deal, coupled with the abolishment of the TWO-THIRDS RULE for nominating candidates and the decline of southern power, resulted in more liberal party leadership. The liberal stance of most party leaders included belief in a broad interpretation of the Constitution and increased use of federal power and government spending to combat the problems of society.

From time to time since 1932 the party's unity has been threatened from both the inside and outside. As a party of diverse elements, its strength traditionally was undermined by southern Democrats' loose alliance with Republicans. (Since the 1970s the South, once solidly Democratic, has tended to vote Republican in congressional and presidential elections.) At the national level the Democrats were split by explosive issues such as the Vietnam War, which prompted violent protest demonstrations at the 1968 Democratic convention in Chicago.

In the 1970s the party began revising its delegate-selection rules to give minorities and women more representation in the party's national nominating convention. The effect of the rules changes was largely negated, however, by the growth of PRIMARIES and the resultant evolution of the convention into an event where nominations are merely formalized.

The Democrats remained the majority party during the 1970s, despite the impact of divisive issues and conservative members' defections to the Republicans, particularly in presidential elections. The 1980 election brought signs of a power shift, however, as the Republicans regained the presidency and won control of the Senate for the first time in twenty-eight years. The 1982 MIDTERM ELECTIONS swept twenty-six new Democrats into the House and strengthened the Democrats' control of that chamber. According to a Gallup poll taken in the spring of 1983, when the nation was beginning to recover from the most serious recession since the depression of the 1930s, more than twice as many people described themselves as Democrats (46 percent) than as Republicans (23 percent).

As the economy rebounded under the leadership of Republican president Ronald Reagan, the Democratic Party lost ground, according to a Gallup poll taken in August 1984. By this time the percentage of people who identified themselves as Democrats had dropped to 42 percent, while the Republican share increased to 28 percent. In the 1984 election Democratic presidential nominee Walter F. Mondale won 40.6 percent of the popular vote and only 13 of the 538 electoral votes. Mondale's running mate, Rep. Geraldine A. Ferraro, New York, was the first woman to receive a major party nomination for national office.

By late 1986 the Democratic Party rejuvenated. Congressional elections gave the Senate back to the Democrats with a 55–45 majority. Some experts speculated that the "forgotten middle class" and other groups that suffered from federal budget cuts voted Democratic in hope of finding a voice there. A Democratic Congress paired with a Republican president limited the GOP's power.

The Democrats were not able to rally enough support in 1988 to elect their candidates—Michael S. Dukakis and Lloyd Bentsen. The Democratic ticket received 45.6 percent of the popular vote and 111 electoral votes. In Congress, meanwhile, the Democrats held on to their majority. In the midterm elections of 1990, they even picked up eight seats in the House and one seat in the Senate.

In 1992 the Democrats paired for the first time two southern moderates, Bill Clinton of Arkansas and Albert Gore Jr. of Tennessee, on the presidential ticket. Widespread dissatisfaction with government and the lingering effects of the recession of 1990 and 1991 helped the Democrats regain the presidency after twelve years. Clinton campaigned as a "new Democrat" who declared that "the era of big government is over." The presence of a strong INDEPENDENT candidate, Ross Perot, although not substantially affecting the outcome, resulted in Clinton's being elected without a majority. The Clinton-Gore ticket took 43.0 percent of the popular vote and received 370 electoral votes.

The flush of victory was short-lived, however. While the Democrats were winning back the White House they were losing ten seats in the House. Party strength in the Senate remained unchanged. Two years later the midterm elections were even more disastrous for the party. It lost control of Congress, ending forty years of Democratic rule in the House and eight in the Senate. From 1995 to 1996, as the Republican Congress led by Speaker Newt Gingrich tried to dismantle decades-old social programs, President Clinton adopted more moderate positions and fought successfully to maintain his budget priorities.

Boosted by his budget stand against the Republican Congress and buoyed by continued good economic news, Clinton defeated his Republican challenger, former Senate majority leader Robert J. Dole, in the 1996 presidential race. Clinton won reelection with 49.2 percent of the POPULAR VOTE and 379 electoral votes. Although Perot was again a candidate, he won only 8.4 percent of the popular vote—less than half of what he won four years earlier. Despite holding onto the White House, the Democrats did not regain control of Congress. In the congressional elections, the Democratic Party lost two seats in the Senate while picking up nine seats in the House.

In the 1998 midterm elections, with Clinton under threat of impeachment, the Republicans hoped to make substantial gains in Congress and the statehouses. But it was not to be. The ratio of Republican to Democratic governors remained almost unchanged from 1996; Minnesota, which formerly had a Republican governor, elected an independent. The Democrats took the biggest prize—California. In the Senate the Republicans made no gains, while in the House the Democrats picked up five seats.

## Democratic-Republican Party (1796–1828)

The Democratic-Republican Party developed in the early 1790s as the organized opposition to the incumbent Federalists and successor to the Anti-Federalists. The Anti-Federalists were a loose alliance of elements initially opposed to the ratification of the Constitution and subsequently to the policies of the George Washington administration, which were designed to centralize power in the federal government.

Thomas Jefferson was the leader of the new party, whose members as early as 1792 referred to themselves as Republicans. This remained their primary name throughout the party's history, although in some states they became known as Democratic-Republicans, the label used frequently by historians to avoid confusing Jefferson's party with the later Republican Party, which

*From Thomas Jefferson's election in 1800, the Democratic-Republican Party dominated national politics until 1828.*
Source: National Portrait Gallery

began in 1854. Party members were called Jeffersonian Republicans as well.

The Democratic-Republicans favored states' rights, a literal interpretation of the Constitution, and expanded democracy through extension of suffrage and popular control of the government. The party was dominated by rural, agrarian interests, intent on maintaining their dominance over the growing commercial and industrial interests of the Northeast. The principal strength of the party came from the southern and mid-Atlantic states.

The Democratic-Republicans first gained control of the federal government in 1800, when Jefferson was

elected president and the party won majorities in both houses of Congress. For the next twenty-four years the party controlled both the White House and Congress, the last eight years virtually without opposition. For all but four years during this twenty-four-year period, there was a Virginia–New York alliance controlling the executive branch, with all three presidents from Virginia—Jefferson, James Madison, and James Monroe—and three of the four vice presidents from New York. Lacking an opposition party, the Democratic-Republicans in the 1820s became increasingly divided. In 1824, when four party leaders ran for president, John Quincy Adams won the election in the House of Representatives, although Andrew Jackson had received more popular votes.

The deep factionalism evident in the 1824 election doomed the Democratic-Republican Party. The two-party system revived shortly thereafter with the emergence of the National Republican Party, an outgrowth of the Adams faction, and the Democratic-Republican Party, the political organization of the Jackson faction. After 1830 the Jacksonians adopted the name Democratic Party.

## Direct Election

Almost all political offices in the United States are filled by direct election. More specifically, holders of these offices are chosen by direct *popular* election. That is, the people make their choices at the polls, and the winners are elected then and there.

Not so with the highest offices in the land. The president and vice president are indirectly elected through the mechanism known as the ELECTORAL COLLEGE. When they vote for those two offices, the voters are actually choosing electors who will later assemble in each state and elect the president and vice president.

Until the early twentieth century U.S. senators also were indirectly elected, although in a different manner. Before the Seventeenth Amendment to the Constitution won final approval in 1913, the legislature in each state elected the state's two senators. Some states, however, began direct election of senators before the amendment made it mandatory. (See SENATE, ELECTING.)

In the early years of the country, presidential elections were even more indirect than they are today. The Constitution left it to the states to decide the method of choosing presidential electors, and most states chose to have their legislature name the electors.

That method was in keeping with the intent of the framers of the Constitution, who were wary of the general public's ability to select a president having the right qualities of leadership, character, and intelligence. It was thought that the electors should be the wisest and most educated men in each state, who would in turn be capable of selecting the man most qualified to be president or vice president. (Until the system was changed by the Twelfth Amendment in 1804, the electors did not ballot separately for vice president. The runner-up for president became the vice president. See PRESIDENT, NOMINATING AND ELECTING.)

At the time, virtually all voters were adult white males who owned property. States could have permitted women to vote, but none did so. All thirteen original states limited the FRANCHISE to property owners and taxpayers, which meant that less than half the adult white male population was eligible to vote in federal elections. Gradually the barriers to voting fell, and today almost all Americans over age eighteen are eligible to vote. (See POPULAR VOTE; RIGHT TO VOTE; WOMEN'S SUFFRAGE; YOUTH SUFFRAGE.)

Gradually, too, the selection of presidential electors moved from state legislatures to the voters. Even in the first presidential election, in 1789, four states chose electors by direct popular election: Delaware, Maryland, Pennsylvania, and Virginia. Two others, New Hampshire and Massachusetts, used a combination of legislative and popular election. Legislatures made the choices in four states: Connecticut, Georgia, New Jersey, and South Carolina. A dispute prevented the New York legislature from choosing electors. And two states, North Carolina and Rhode Island, had not yet ratified the Constitution and so could not participate in the first election.

The rise of political parties after 1800 accelerated the trend toward popular election of presidential electors. Several states switched back temporarily to legislative election, but all finally settled for popular election. By 1836 only the South Carolina legislature was still choosing electors. Not until after the Civil War did South Carolina institute popular voting for presidential electors.

Awarding of each state's electoral college votes (now totaling 538: equal to the size of the House of Representatives, 435; the size of the Senate, 100; and 3 for the DISTRICT OF COLUMBIA) has evolved into a WINNER-TAKE-ALL system. The presidential ticket that wins the largest share of the popular vote in a state (not necessarily a majority) receives all of the state's electoral votes.

The exceptions are Maine and Nebraska, which distribute electoral votes on the basis of special presidential election DISTRICTS. The districts coincide with the congressional districts (two in Maine and three in Nebraska), and the plurality winner in each district wins that electoral vote. The other two votes in each state go to the statewide plurality winner. Although it is conceivable for the electoral vote to be split under such a system, Maine and Nebraska have consistently cast all their electoral votes for a single candidate.

Electors pledged to the presidential ticket on which they were elected cast their votes for that ticket. There have been cases of so-called faithless electors who vote for another candidate, but in recent years there have been no true cases of a state's electoral votes being split between two candidates. The most recent instance of a state's electoral vote being split, other than by the action of a single faithless elector, was in 1960 when six "unpledged Democrats" in Alabama voted for Sen. Harry F. Byrd of Virginia, rather than for the state's popular vote winner, John F. Kennedy.

From time to time, most recently in the 1970s, efforts have been made to eliminate the electoral college or at least revise the presidential selection system to ensure that the person elected is indeed "the people's choice" and not a candidate who happened to win because of a splintered vote. Even under the electoral college system, with its requirement of a majority vote, there have been several instances of so-called MINORITY PRESIDENTS winning with less than a majority of the popular vote.

(See ELECTORAL ANOMOLIES; ELECTORAL COLLEGE AND VOTES.)

But because it almost always works out that the popular vote winner is also the electoral vote winner, most people have been satisfied with the status quo and have found little incentive to support major changes in the indirect election system.

## District of Columbia

Throughout most of the history of the District of Columbia, residents have been deprived of voting rights enjoyed by citizens of all the states of the Union. In the post–World War II era, largely as a result of unrelenting political pressure, District residents regained the RIGHT TO VOTE for president and vice president and for mayor and other local officials. They also won the right once again to send a nonvoting delegate to the U.S. House of Representatives.

In the same period, however, District residents failed in their push to achieve the right to elect a full congressional delegation. A constitutional amendment providing for that advance in suffrage, although approved by Congress, failed when presented to the states for ratification. Then too, the partial self-government residents gained in 1973 was diminished in 1995 when, with the District of Columbia virtually insolvent, Congress imposed on elected leaders a financial control board, whose chairman and members were unelected.

The unique status of the District of Columbia with respect to both voting and governance was established under Article I, section 8, clause 17, of the U.S. Constitution. The clause says it is in the power of Congress "to exercise exclusive Legislation in all Cases whatsoever, over such District . . . as may, by Cession of particular States, and the Acceptance of Congress, become the Seat of Government of the United States."

Moreover, after the Civil War issues of race and partisan politics were impediments to the enlargement of suffrage. African American residents constituted about one-third of the population in 1870, and that proportion increased in coming decades. In the latter part of

*Many residents of the District of Columbia resent the lack of voting representation in Congress. Source: R. Michael Jenkins, Congressional Quarterly*

the twentieth century, there were far more Democrats registered to vote in the District than Republicans, leading to a belief that if residents could vote they would elect only Democratic candidates.

## Nineteenth Century

In the very early years of the nineteenth century, voters in the area now covered by the District of Columbia had the right to vote in many elections. For example, they voted in the presidential election of 1800 but had no electoral votes. Also in the early years, although the mayor was appointed by the president, voters in the City of Washington (at the heart of the District of Columbia) cast ballots for a twelve-member council and an eight-member board of aldermen. In 1820 Congress permitted them to elect the mayor.

BLACK SUFFRAGE was established in the District of Columbia in 1867, three years before ratification of the Fifteenth Amendment, which prohibits voting discrimination on the basis of race. Congress granted suffrage at that time "without any distinction on account of color or race" to male citizens twenty-one years of age and older who had resided in the District of Columbia for at least one year. President Andrew Johnson vetoed the legislation, but both houses of Congress overrode his veto.

Blacks quickly became influential in local politics, and in a short time they controlled both the city council and the board of aldermen. With the support of black voters, the Republican candidate for mayor won a narrow victory in 1868. When projects initiated by the mayor resulted in heavy debt and when his successor as mayor of Washington also ran into difficulties, Congress looked for another way to govern the federal city.

The plan Congress chose was a modified territorial form. It provided for the appointment of a GOVERNOR by the president and for the election of a nonvoting delegate to the U.S. House of Representatives. It called for a territorial assembly consisting of an eleven-member council appointed by the president and a twenty-two-member house of delegates elected by the voters. Finally, it established a five-member board of public works, its members appointed by the president. The act of Congress setting up the territorial system also stipulated that the entire District would be considered a single entity for political purposes.

Actions by the powerful board of public works led in four years to the end of the territorial experiment. The board put in water mains and a sewerage system, paved the streets, and developed parks. But the cost was high. When in 1873 President Ulysses S. Grant appointed the board's executive officer, Alexander Shepherd, as gover-

nor, Congress was alarmed. A joint congressional committee reported that the government was weakened by graft and mismanagement. Abolishing the board of public works, the assembly, and the nonvoting delegate to the House, Congress established a three-member commission to administer the city. And it took on the District's legislative functions itself. Made permanent by Congress on July 1, 1878, the three-commissioner system stayed in place until 1967. Historians have pointed to hostility to black suffrage as a major reason the three-commissioner form was prolonged. They have said that white residents of the city preferred to do without the right to vote rather than share it with the black residents.

## Post–World War II

A step toward restoration of voting rights in the District was taken in 1955, when Congress approved legislation setting up the federal city's first election machinery in eighty-one years. The measure, signed into law by President Dwight D. Eisenhower on August 12, authorized the election of members of the national committees of both political parties along with delegates to the NATIONAL PARTY CONVENTIONS. A year earlier, Eisenhower had vetoed a somewhat similar bill because it would have allowed FEDERAL WORKERS in the District to engage in partisan political activity, a violation of the Hatch Act. That provision was omitted in the bill that became law.

The admission of Alaska and Hawaii to the Union as the forty-ninth and fiftieth states was seen as a catalyst for approval by Congress in 1960 of a proposed amendment to the U.S. Constitution permitting District residents to vote in presidential elections. That action was a major milestone in the long effort District residents made to obtain the voting rights taken for granted by residents of the states. The proposed amendment gave the District of Columbia three electors in the ELECTORAL COLLEGE. As introduced, it also would have given residents a nonvoting delegate in the House. District advocates later dropped that provision to clinch congressional approval and to increase the likelihood that the amendment would be ratified.

Submitted to the states in June 1960, the Twenty-third Amendment was ratified in less than a year, on March 29, 1961. Most of the opposition to the amendment came from the South, and it was motivated, historians have said, by the issue of race. (The District of Columbia at the time was more than 50 percent black.)

Then too, some Republican legislators in the states worried that the District would automatically vote Democratic because blacks had been strongly pro-Democratic since the 1930s. As it turned out, Kansas, with a Republican legislature, was the thirty-eighth state to approve the amendment, giving it the required three-fourths of the states for ratification.

To implement the amendment, President John F. Kennedy advocated enlarging the vote to include YOUTH SUFFRAGE, by setting the D.C. minimum voting age at eighteen. He also recommended a minimum residence requirement of only ninety days. But the bill Congress passed and Kennedy signed set the minimum age at twenty-one and the residence requirement at one year.

In the 1960s the civil rights movement provided another spur to the enlargement of suffrage in the District of Columbia. The District was in effect governed by members of Congress, many of whom were from the South. Responding to those pressures, and to controversies over local school programs, Congress in 1968 authorized the election of an eleven-member board of education. District residents cast their votes for members of the board in November 1968. For sixty-two years under a 1906 act of Congress, the board had been chosen by judges of the U.S. District Court of the District of Columbia.

Two years later, in 1970, Congress approved legislation providing for the election of a nonvoting delegate to the U.S. House. District residents had not been represented by such a delegate since 1875. While bills providing for a nonvoting delegate had been introduced repeatedly after the demise of the territorial form in 1884, up until the 1950s they had made little headway in Congress.

The nonvoting delegate plan had received a boost in 1969 when President Richard Nixon advocated the delegate as a temporary measure until ratification of an amendment providing for full congressional representation in Congress could be completed. Nixon signed the nonvoting delegate measure into law on September 22, 1970.

District voters on March 23, 1971, elected Walter E. Fauntroy, a Democrat, as the first nonvoting delegate from the District of Columbia since Norton F. Chipman, a Republican, left the House at the final adjournment of the Forty-third Congress on March 4, 1875.

Established in 1874, the three-commissioner government in the District lasted for ninety-three years. In 1967 President Lyndon B. Johnson replaced the three commissioners with a single commissioner and a city council. The president appointed the commissioner and council members. Three years later, President Nixon raised hopes of home-rule advocates when he sent a message to Congress calling for partial self-government. The right to vote for local officials would greatly extend suffrage in the District.

Many bills calling for HOME RULE had been introduced in Congress over the years. One reached the floor of the House in 1948, but it was killed by southern Democrats. For the next twenty-four years the House District of Columbia Committee kept similar legislation bottled up in committee. Elections in 1972, however, freed up the process as the committee chairman and five other committee members, all southerners, either retired or were defeated for reelection.

## Partial Home Rule

Legislation providing for partial home rule was approved by the House District Committee on July 31, 1973, by a 20–4 vote. The legislation provided for an elected mayor and an elected thirteen-member council. The Senate cleared the bill on December 19, 1973, and President Nixon signed it into law December 24. Under the law, Congress reserved the right to legislate for the District of Columbia at any time and established a procedure by which it could veto any action taken by the city council. Still, despite the restrictions on the city government, District voters at last were able to elect their political leaders.

All of the first four elected mayors were African Americans, beginning with Walter E. Washington in 1975. He was succeeded in 1978 by Marion S. Barry Jr., a civil rights activist whose long tenure as mayor was marred by the city's financial problems and a national SCANDAL surrounding Barry's 1990 arrest and subsequent conviction for cocaine possession. After a four-year hiatus, including six months in jail, Barry was re-elected mayor in 1994, succeeding Sharon Pratt Kelly. When Barry decided against seeking another term in 1998, Anthony A. Williams resigned as the city's financial officer and was elected mayor.

In 1995, with the District of Columbia heading toward bankruptcy, Congress passed nonpartisan legislation creating a powerful financial control board to oversee the elected government. The control board would continue to function until the District government produced four consecutive balanced budgets. President Clinton signed the legislation into law on April 17, 1995.

In 1997 Congress enabled the control board to strip power from the District's elected officials and to reorganize the city bureaucracy. Thus, during a period of uncertain duration, District residents could vote for mayor and for members of the city council and board of education, but the power of those officials was greatly reduced. As a vote of confidence for mayor-elect Williams, the control board in December 1998 restored most of the powers it had stripped from Mayor Barry.

## Proposed Amendment

District of Columbia advocates in the 1970s continued to press for a full congressional delegation of two senators and one or two representatives, depending on population. It was a goal residents had formally sought twenty-three times without success. Full congressional representation could be achieved only by amending the Constitution. That was so because the Constitution provided that the House was to be composed of "Members chosen . . . by the People of the several States" and that the Senate was to be composed of "two Senators from each State." Furthermore, Supreme Court decisions beginning in 1805 made it clear that the District of Columbia was not a state.

Congress in 1978 narrowly approved such an amendment. In the Senate the vote was 67–32, just one more than the required two-thirds. As proposed, the amendment treated the District as a state for purposes of congressional and electoral college representation, for representation in presidential elections, and for ratification of proposed constitutional amendments.

Sent to the states for ratification, the proposed amendment died seven years later, on August 22, 1985, when the statutory deadline for ratification expired. Only sixteen states had ratified it, well short of the thirty-eight required. Mayor Barry's well-publicized problems were widely cited as a major factor in the District's failure to win equal status with the fifty states.

## Districts, Wards, and Precincts

For purposes of voting and representation, the United States is made up of many jurisdictions of various sizes. They range from whole states to compact neighborhoods. Each is important in its own way to the political structure of the country.

The nation as a whole votes only for two offices: president and vice president. Although they appear on state ballots as a team, the two top officers are elected separately in the ELECTORAL COLLEGE.

All other federal, state, and local officials are elected in sub-units of the United States. In Congress, each state is entitled to two senators regardless of population, and they are elected statewide in all cases. The House of Representatives is based on population, and each member is elected by his or her CONGRESSIONAL DISTRICT. Other types of districts serve as representational areas for state, city, and county legislatures.

## District

A congressional district is the geographical area represented by a single member of the House of Representatives. For states with one representative, the entire state is the congressional district. As of 1998, seven states had only one representative (Alaska, Delaware, Montana, North Dakota, South Dakota, Vermont, and

Wyoming). These members are elected AT LARGE by voters of the whole state.

The 435 seats in the House are allocated on the basis of population after each ten-year CENSUS. In the forty-three states with two or more representatives, the state legislature divides the state into congressional districts, depending on the number of House members the state is entitled to. Under the Supreme Court's ONE-PERSON, ONE-VOTE rulings, each district must be as nearly equal in population as possible. (See REAPPORTIONMENT AND REDISTRICTING.)

Computer technology enables redistricters to make congressional districts almost exactly equal in population. After the 1990 census, for example, each of Colorado's six congressional districts had roughly 549,000 residents, with a variance of only sixteen persons from the largest district to the smallest.

Although the Supreme Court requirements for population equality have made redistricting much less arbitrary than it used to be, the process is still largely political. Parties try to win the state governorships and legislative majorities so that they can control the redrawing of district lines following the decennial census. Even within the confines of the Court rulings, it is possible to draw district lines to benefit the political party in power. This practice is known as GERRYMANDERING.

In recent years legislatures also have used a type of gerrymandering, called RACIAL REDISTRICTING, to achieve a racial balance in the state's representation in the House. In such cases, lines are drawn to create districts where the racial minority is in the majority and therefore more likely to elect someone from that group to represent them in Washington. Several of these districts have been created to satisfy Justice Department mandates. The Supreme Court, however, has rejected some oddly shaped minority-majority districts, requiring the lines to be redrawn.

States also are divided into districts for the election of state legislators. Only one state, Nebraska, has a unicameral (one chamber) legislature. All the others are bicameral, with one body usually known as a senate and another body called a house or assembly. Unlike the U.S. Senate, where both senators represent the entire state, state senates are elected from senatorial districts much like house districts, but larger. About a fourth of state legislatures still have MULTIMEMBER DISTRICTS, which are no longer permitted in U.S. House elections.

State legislatures use U.S. Census Bureau data in drawing their own district lines. Those districts, too, must conform to the Supreme Court's one-person, one-vote doctrine if the seats are apportioned on the basis of population.

Districts, congressional or state legislative, are often part of the political party organizational framework within a state. The Democratic and Republican Parties, for example, may have a state central committee and a separate, smaller committee for each congressional district.

## Ward

A ward is a form of district usually associated with city council and other municipal elections. A large city may be divided into numerous wards, each with its own political party committee. Some wards are multimember districts, with two or more city or county council members elected to represent that ward.

The term *ward heeler* is a somewhat derogatory name for rank-and-file party workers. It is derived from the practice of training a dog to follow obediently at the heels of its master. In the past more than today, ward heelers unquestioningly did the bidding of big city political bosses. Many cities now hold nonpartisan elections for local offices, which diminishes the influence of party organizations or leaders.

Most city councils are elected at large, or by wards with some members elected at large. Minority groups favor the ward system because they seldom can gain adequate representation in citywide elections. A disadvantage is that wards tend to emphasize the interests of neighborhoods rather than the community as a whole.

## Precinct

The precinct is the smallest unit of the American electoral system. It is where grassroots political activity is practiced and nurtured. Districts and wards are divided into precincts for voting purposes. After the 1990 census there were some 147,000 precincts in the United States, each with a polling place serving 200 to 1,000 or more voters.

Precincts serve as the basic building block for political organization. Each party normally appoints a precinct captain as party leader in the neighborhood and as its representative on the larger city or county party committee. Precincts may also elect delegates to city or county party conventions.

In the IOWA CAUCUS, the first of its kind in presidential election years, party members vote in precinct caucuses for the candidates they want to receive their party's nomination. The same system is used in other states that use the CAUCUS rather than the PRIMARY system.

Before the development of the welfare system, the needy often looked to the political parties for help in obtaining food, clothing, and shelter, and the precinct captain was the person to see for such requests. Today the precinct captain's job is mostly one of education and organization: to explain the benefits of party membership, register voters, and lead GET OUT THE VOTE efforts on ELECTION DAY.

## Dixiecrats

*See* STATES' RIGHTS DEMOCRATIC PARTY.

## DO Committee

*See* PRESIDENTIAL SELECTION REFORMS.

# E

## Election Cycle in America

The basic election cycle in the United States is determined primarily by the length of terms the Constitution set for the president and members of Congress. By staggering the terms and varying their length, the framers of the Constitution ensured that it would be virtually impossible for the entire government to be turned out in any single election. The election cycle therefore serves as part of the system of checks and balances that prevents any one branch of the federal government from assuming tyrannical powers.

Article I, section 2, states that the House of Representatives "shall be composed of Members chosen every second year by the people of the several States." Section 3 says, "The Senate of the United States shall be composed of two Senators from each State for six years." Senators, the article provides, are to be divided into three classes, with one class being elected every second year. Article II, section 1, says, "The executive Power shall be invested in a President of the United States of America. He shall hold his Office during the Term of four Years," as would, the article says, the vice president. (See HOUSE OF REPRESENTATIVES, ELECTING; PRESIDENT, NOMINATING AND ELECTING; SENATE, ELECTING.)

Requiring House members to face the electorate every two years made them more answerable to their constituents than a longer term would and presumably made them more responsive to the people's needs and wishes.

The Senate's longer term of service, constitutional scholars have noted, gave its members a certain distance from the day-to-day concerns that House members must confront in their biennial worries about reelection. The lessening of reelection requirements would allow senators the time and freedom to deliberate longer-range concerns; and the staggering of the Senate's classes ensured continuity of experience, expertise, and, it was hoped, statesmanship. As has become obvious over the years, the Senate serves as a brake on its sister house, on the president, and even on the judiciary, not least because its members are insulated from the urgent press of reelection.

Although the Supreme Court has struck down efforts in a number of states to impose TERM LIMITS on their members of Congress, the Twenty-second Amendment to the Constitution (1951) limits the president to two four-year terms. Only Franklin D. Roosevelt, who died in 1945 at the start of his fourth term, served more than eight years as president.

By law, federal elections are held on the first Tuesday after the first Monday in November of even-numbered years. The Supreme Court has ruled that states may not deviate from this date for presidential and congressional elections. (See ELECTION DAY.)

In the name of economy and efficiency, most states also hold their elections for state and local officials in November along with the balloting for federal offices. Some states, however, elect their governor and other state officials in odd-numbered years to prevent national issues and candidacies from influencing the outcome of state contests.

PRIMARY or CAUCUS elections to nominate candidates for congressional, state, and local offices are usually held anywhere from two to six months before the general election. State legislatures set the dates for these elections, as well as those for the PRESIDENTIAL PRIMARIES held in about forty states. The scheduling of primaries has altered the election cycle in recent years as states jockey for an earlier primary position to exert greater influence on the presidential selection process. (See FRONT-LOADING; NEW HAMPSHIRE PRIMARY.)

Special elections to fill a vacated Senate or House seat can be called by a state GOVERNOR, who, if empowered by the state legislature or constitution, may make a temporary appointment of a senator until an election is held. In some states a special RUNOFF PRIMARY is held outside the normal election cycle if no candidate receives a majority of the vote.

Another type of election outside the normal cycle is one allowed under the provisions of the recall laws effective in several states. Under these laws, if a specified percentage of voters sign a recall petition, a special election must be held to decide whether that particular incumbent can complete the term or must leave office immediately.

At the federal level, the impeachment process allows the removal of the president or other officials impeached by the House and convicted by the Senate. (See REMOVAL FROM OFFICE.)

# Election Day

For more than a century the day for state and federal elections has been the first Tuesday after the first Monday in November in even-numbered years. For many voters Tuesday is inconvenient, and some scholars think elections should be held on a weekend day, as in many European countries, to encourage higher VOTER TURNOUT.

A simple act of Congress could move the date. No constitutional amendment would be required because the election day is not fixed in the Constitution. Article I, section 4, allows the states to set the "Times, Places and Manner of holding Elections for Senators and Representatives," but it adds that "the Congress may at any time by Law make or alter such Regulations."

For presidential elections, Article II, section 1, provides that Congress may determine the time of choosing electors and the day on which they give their votes, "which Day shall be the same throughout the United States."

## Legislative History

In 1792 Congress set the date for presidential electors (the ELECTORAL COLLEGE) to meet, but it left some leeway in the time period for appointing electors. The act designated the first Wednesday in December of election years for electors to meet and cast their votes for president and vice president. But the act permitted states to appoint the electors any day within thirty-four days before the December date on which the electors were to convene and vote.

Problems arose because of the lack of a specific day for choosing electors. States selected electors on different dates, sometimes influencing the choices in neighboring states that had not yet made their appointments.

Congress moved to rectify the situation with an act in January 1845 that said electors must be selected on the "Tuesday next after the first Monday in the month of November of the year in which they are to be appointed." The same Tuesday in November of even-numbered years became House of Representatives election day under an act of Congress in 1872. After the Seventeenth Amendment mandated popular election of senators in 1913, Congress amended the act to include Senate elections.

The sponsor of the 1872 Uniform Federal Election Day Act, Rep. Benjamin Franklin Butler, Massachusetts Republican, argued during floor debate that Indiana, Ohio, and Pennsylvania held an "undue advantage" in electing their representatives in October. He recalled that in 1840 the news from Pennsylvania and other states that had already held House elections settled the November presidential election "as effectively as it was afterward done."

The legislative history of the 1845 and 1872 acts indicates that Congress weighed several factors in choosing the month and day for all federal elections. November was agreed upon because weather is temperate then, and, with the harvest in, farmers are more likely to vote. The first and last days of the month met objections because they might complicate the closing out of business accounting books. As to the day, religious objections ruled out Sunday and possibly Monday as well, because Monday voting might require Sunday travel to the polls in large states. Tuesday and Wednesday were acceptable.

*John Chancellor and David Brinkley of NBC News show the progress of House and Senate races on election day in 1976. To prevent election results from the East influencing voters in western states, broadcasters have volunteered to hold off their election calls until most polls have closed. Source: National Broadcasting Company*

Thursday was dismissed because it was Britain's election day. Friday was the end of the work week, and Saturday was shopping day.

Why Tuesday was chosen is unclear. One theory is that it was the day when people were likely to be in town for court sessions or farmers' markets. But the first Tuesday was rejected because it might fall on the first of the month. Therefore the first Tuesday after the first Monday emerged as Congress's choice.

The Supreme Court has upheld Congress's power to override state attempts to hold federal elections at other times. In *Foster v. Love* (1997) the Court nullified Louisiana's unique open PRIMARY as it applied to federal elections. The law permitted U.S. senators and rep-

resentatives to be elected in October if they received a majority vote in the Louisiana primary. If no candidate received a majority, the two top finishers would compete in the November "general election" on federal election day. This system conflicted with Congress's intention of preventing early elections from influencing the vote of later elections, the Court said. (See PRIMARY TYPES.)

## Proposals for Change

Some argue that an election day geared to the mostly rural pace of nineteenth-century America is an anachronism that no longer meets the needs of a fast-paced, high-tech country entering a new millennium.

They contend that bold change is needed to reverse the decline in voter participation and the widespread disenchantment with the U.S. electoral process. (See zzz.)

Proponents of change note that some foreign countries make election day a holiday or hold weekend elections to make it easier for people to vote without losing work time. Some also make voting mandatory by imposing small fines on nonvoters. (See INTERNATIONAL AND U.S. ELECTIONS COMPARED.)

Some states have experimented with expanded ABSENTEE VOTING by mail to reduce the need to vote on a fixed day. Others have tried mobile or storefront voting to bring the polls closer to the users. Critics say that polling hours (thirteen to fourteen hours in most states) leave too small a "window" for voting when many Americans are working longer hours or on unconventional schedules. NBC newscaster Tom Brokaw has suggested that polls be open twenty-four hours on a rolling basis across the country, so that all close at the same time. His plan, however, would increase expenses for poll workers and for their security in some areas.

Congress has considered but not enacted uniform polls closing bills to alleviate the problem of western voters' being influenced by the networks' early calling of election results on the basis of EXIT POLLS taken in the East. Broadcasters have eased the problem in recent years by voluntarily holding off their election calls until most polls have closed.

Voting by telephone or the Internet has been suggested as another way to make election day more convenient. Computerized VOTING MACHINES can report their totals through modems, and with passwords and other security precautions they could receive the voters' choices just as easily.

---

# Election Fraud

Fraud is an ever-present danger in elections. Authorities go to great lengths to prevent it through VOTER REGISTRATION and other restrictions, yet allegations of vote fraud arise in virtually every election cycle.

ABSENTEE VOTING is particularly vulnerable to abuse, despite stringent requirements in all the states to ensure that the ballots are mailed to the proper voter, signed on the outside of the envelope to protect privacy of the vote, and returned by the specified deadline. Absentee ballots have been central to the settling of numerous CONTESTED ELECTIONS.

An example was Miami's 1997 mayoral race, in which a Florida grand jury found "outright fraud" in absentee voting. Ballots allegedly were tampered with or sold, voted in the names of dead persons or nonresidents, cast for confused elderly voters, or given to persons who were paid to vote.

Overturning a lower court that ordered a new election, an appeals court invalidated all four thousand absentee ballots and reinstated Miami mayor Joe Carollo, who had lost a close RUNOFF election to Xavier L. Suarez. To do otherwise, the court said, "would be sending out the wrong message that the worst that would happen in the face of voter fraud would be another election."

## Reforms and Technology

Fraud in conventional voting at the polling place is less common than it was in the late nineteenth and early twentieth centuries during the heyday of big city political bosses such as William M. "Boss" Tweed in New York, James M. Curley in Boston, and Frank Hague in Jersey City. In those days, tales were told of underlings instructed to "vote early and often," of jobless men paid a dollar or two for each vote, obituary pages used as voting lists, and wardens entering voting booths in the guise of giving assistance and pulling the STRAIGHT-TICKET lever for the party in power.

With the waning of the urban political machines, reforms reduced the chances of overt fraud. Tighter regulation, screening of polling place officials, bipartisan verification of voters' identification, opening of the polls to election watchers, and other monitoring activities have made fraudulent voting at the polling place more difficult than in the past. But it is still not impossible, and in the late 1990s fourteen states required some form of voter identification. Several communities were considering photo identification of all prospective vot-

*The late nineteenth century was rife with big city political bosses whose stock in trade was election fraud. Thomas Nast's 1871 cartoon depicts "Boss" Tweed and his cronies.*
Source: American Antiquarian Society

ers. The city council of Annapolis, Maryland, voted to require photo ID beginning with the city election in 2001.

The widespread replacement of paper ballots by mechanical VOTING MACHINES also reduced the opportunities for tampering with votes or spoiling them with a surreptitious mark. The machines had a vote counter that wardens could read as soon as the polls closed, and

that could be impounded for later verification in case of a RECOUNT.

In the late 1990s, however, many communities replaced the old lever-operated machines with electronic systems that conservative conspiracy theorists viewed with suspicion. They contended that modems in the machines for transmission of electronic data could be rigged by liberals in favor of their candidates.

Although no hard evidence of such fraud was produced, the skeptics campaigned on the Internet and in newsletters for the return of paper ballots, which they contended are more difficult to falsify and easier to verify and recount. Computers, they argued, left no tamper-proof physical record of how many votes were cast for each candidate.

The paper-ballot proponents were particularly leery of a system manufactured by the Sequoia Pacific Voting Equipment Company of Jamestown, New York. They circulated a Jack Anderson newspaper column about a 1995 incident that happened during a Sequoia Pacific demonstration after an election in Jefferson Parish, Louisiana. When a defeated candidate pressed her name on the ballot, according to Anderson, her opponent's name appeared instead. Sequoia Pacific defended its product and said the error was a fluke that may have happened because the candidate "rolled her finger," causing her to push two buttons at the same time. That explanation, however, failed to satisfy the critics.

To commit another type of election fraud, unscrupulous political operatives have used computer technology to doctor photographs. Several POLITICAL CONSULTANTS have been fired or rebuked for rearranging still or video images to discredit opponents. (See NEGATIVE CAMPAIGNING.)

## Watchdog Activities

In 1996 a new organization, Voter Integrity Project (VIP), began soliciting reports of vote fraud and recruiting retired investigators to look into the allegations. One of its first inquiries concerned the 1996 Polk County, Florida, commission race between a Democratic incumbent and Republican challenger. Although VIP found no evidence of conspiracy, it criticized the count process and concluded, "We may never know the truth about the actual vote counts in this election."

The group gained more visibility in the investigation of possible fraud in Louisiana's contested 1996 Senate election between Mary L. Landrieu and Louis "Woody" Jenkins. A Senate committee settled the dispute in Landrieu's favor. In San Francisco VIP sought to overturn a REFERENDUM that approved a new stadium for the

49ers football team. The lawsuit alleged that polls were opened early in pro-stadium precincts.

VIP, based in Arlington, Virginia, and headed by Deborah Phillips, described itself as a "national, non-partisan citizens' coalition organized to protect the American electoral process." University of Virginia political scientist Larry Sabato, however, told a Florida newspaper, "It's clearly a conservative Republican organization." VIP disputed Sabato's description.

Besides electronic voting machines, another target of vote watchers is the Clinton administration's MOTOR VOTER ACT of 1993, which allows motorists to register to vote while obtaining a driver's license. The *Wall Street Journal,* in a March 1998 editorial, said the law "created lax registration and voting procedures" because "forty-seven states don't require proof of legal U.S. residence much less citizenship for such a license."

In the DISTRICT OF COLUMBIA, the editorial noted, voter registration went from 58 percent to 86 percent even though the city had lost 100,000 residents since 1980. "Felons, dead people, non-residents and fictitious registrations clog the rolls in Washington, where anyone can walk up and vote without showing I.D."

On the other hand, the *Washington Post* reported that stricter procedures instituted in compliance with the Motor Voter Act had helped Maryland to avoid a repetition of its disputed 1994 gubernatorial election, when the loser alleged fraud caused by inaccurate voting lists. The 1998 contest between the same candidates produced the same winner but no claims of fraud.

## Electoral Anomalies

The American political system sometimes produces a result that deviates from what normally would be expected. One such anomaly is the phenomenon of "minority" presidents—the sixteen presidents elected without receiving a majority of the POPULAR VOTE.

Three of those candidates actually lost the popular vote to their opponents and still won the presidency: John Quincy Adams in 1824, Rutherford B. Hayes in 1876, and Benjamin Harrison in 1888.

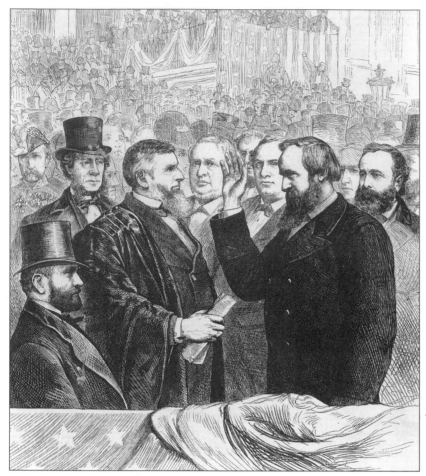

*Chief Justice Morrison R. Waite administers the oath of office to Rutherford B. Hayes on March 4, 1877. Hayes was one of three candidates who lost the popular vote to their opponents but still won the presidency. Source: Library of Congress*

In Adams's case, the election was thrown to the House of Representatives after he and three other candidates failed to gain the required majority of ELECTORAL COLLEGE votes. Under the Twelfth Amendment, the House had to choose from among the three highest vote-getters. It chose Adams, who had run second to Andrew Jackson in both popular and electoral votes. The third contender, Treasury Secretary William H. Crawford, was paralyzed from a recent stroke. Speaker Henry Clay, who ran fourth and was therefore out of the running, helped swing the House vote to Adams.

Only one other presidential election was decided by the House. That was in 1800 when Thomas Jefferson and his intended vice president, Aaron Burr, tied in the electoral vote before the Twelfth Amendment required separate voting for president and vice president. The House chose Jefferson on the thirty-sixth ballot to succeed John Adams, father of John Quincy Adams, and Burr became vice president.

In 1876 Democrat Samuel J. Tilden outpolled Republican Hayes, but his electoral vote total was one short of a majority, with the votes of three southern states in dispute. To resolve the crisis Congress set up a special fifteen-member commission, which decided the disputed votes in Hayes's favor, giving him a bare majority victory of 185 votes to Tilden's 184. Under a compromise that broke the impasse, Hayes agreed to remove federal troops from the South after he took office, ending the

## "Minority" Presidents

Under the U.S. electoral system, there have been seventeen presidential elections (decided by either the electoral college itself or by the House of Representatives) where the victor did not receive a majority of the popular votes cast in the election. Three of these future presidents—John Quincy Adams in 1824, Rutherford B. Hayes in 1876, and Benjamin Harrison in 1888—actually trailed their opponents in the popular vote.

The table shows the percentage of the popular vote received by candidates in the seventeen elections in which a "minority" president (designated by boldface type) was elected.

| Year Elected | Candidate | Percentage of Popular Vote | Candidate | Percentage of Popular Vote | Candidate | Percentage of Popular Vote | Candidate | Percentage of Popular Vote |
|---|---|---|---|---|---|---|---|---|
| 1824 | Jackson | 41.34 | **Adams** | 30.92 | Clay | 12.99 | Crawford | 11.17 |
| 1844 | **Polk** | 49.54 | Clay | 48.08 | Birney | 2.30 | | |
| 1848 | **Taylor** | 47.28 | Cass | 42.49 | Van Buren | 10.12 | | |
| 1856 | **Buchanan** | 45.28 | Fremont | 33.11 | Fillmore | 21.53 | | |
| 1860 | **Lincoln** | 39.82 | Douglas | 29.46 | Breckenridge | 18.09 | Bell | 12.61 |
| 1876 | Tilden | 50.97 | **Hayes** | 47.95 | Cooper | .97 | | |
| 1880 | **Garfield** | 48.27 | Hancock | 48.25 | Weaver | 3.32 | Others | .15 |
| 1884 | **Cleveland** | 48.50 | Blaine | 48.25 | Butler | 1.74 | St. John | 1.47 |
| 1888 | Cleveland | 48.62 | **Harrison** | 47.82 | Fisk | 2.19 | Streeter | 1.29 |
| 1892 | **Cleveland** | 46.05 | Harrison | 42.96 | Weaver | 8.50 | Others | 2.25 |
| 1912 | **Wilson** | 41.84 | T. Roosevelt | 27.39 | Taft | 23.18 | Debs | 5.99 |
| 1916 | **Wilson** | 49.24 | Hughes | 46.11 | Benson | 3.18 | Others | 1.46 |
| 1948 | **Truman** | 49.52 | Dewey | 45.12 | Thurmond | 2.40 | Wallace | 2.38 |
| 1960 | **Kennedy** | 49.72 | Nixon | 49.55 | Others | .72 | | |
| 1968 | **Nixon** | 43.42 | Humphrey | 42.72 | Wallace | 13.53 | Others | .33 |
| 1992 | **Clinton** | 43.01 | Bush | 37.45 | Perot | 18.91 | Others | .64 |
| 1996 | **Clinton** | 49.24 | Dole | 40.71 | Perot | 8.40 | Others | 1.65 |

Reconstruction era that had bitterly divided the nation. Southern whites gained domination of Congress, and Republican industrial interests solidified a hold on presidential politics that lasted until Franklin D. Roosevelt was elected in 1932.

## Electoral Vote Effect

All other instances of a president's being elected with less than a majority of the popular vote (including Benjamin Harrison in 1888) were attributable to the electoral college system, which tends to exaggerate narrow victories and permit a minority president to claim something of a mandate to enact the administration's legislative agenda.

In 1888 Republican Harrison trailed Democratic president Grover Cleveland in the popular vote, 48.6 percent to 47.8 percent, with other candidates sharing the 3.6 percent remainder. But by winning New York and other populous states of the North and West, Harrison took 58.1 percent of the electoral vote, a clear majority. Four years later the ousted Cleveland defeated Harrison to become the only president to serve two nonconsecutive terms.

With his 49.2 percent popular vote reelection victory in 1996, Bill Clinton became only the third president in history to win two terms with less than half the vote each time. (He won in 1992 with 43.0 percent.) The other two were Cleveland, 1884 and 1892, and Woodrow Wilson, in 1912 and 1916.

An electoral vote anomaly of another sort arose in 1872 when famed newspaper editor Horace Greeley, the Democratic/Liberal Republican presidential candidate, died after losing the election to Ulysses S. Grant. Electors from the six states he won divided their votes among other candidates. Three of the electors voted for Greeley anyway, but Congress did not recognize their votes.

In another unusual circumstance, Vice President James S. Sherman died shortly before the 1912 election that he and President William Howard Taft lost to Woodrow Wilson and Thomas R. Marshall. It was too late for Sherman's name to be changed on the ballots in every state, so his electoral votes went to his replacement, Nicholas Murray Butler. (See RUNNING MATE.)

## Oddities in Congressional Elections

CONGRESSIONAL ELECTIONS have produced a number of anomalies, particularly in the South, where slavery, the Civil War, Reconstruction, and racial antagonisms created special problems in the electoral process. The counting of slaves for the apportionment of House seats posed an especially difficult problem.

Under a compromise adopted in the Constitution (Article I, section 2) every five slaves would be counted as three persons. After the Civil War and the emancipation of slaves, the Fourteenth Amendment required that blacks be fully counted for apportionment purposes. On this basis, several southern states tried to claim additional representation on readmission to the Union. Tennessee, for example, elected an extra U.S. representative in 1868, claiming that adding the full slave population entitled the state to nine instead of eight House members. Virginia and South Carolina followed suit. But the House refused to seat the additional representatives, requiring the states to wait for the regular reapportionment after the 1870 census for any changes in their representation.

A formula in the Fourteenth Amendment, designed to coerce southern states to accept black voting participation by reducing House seats wherever voting rights were abridged, never was implemented because of its complexity. Instead, the Republican-controlled House unseated Democrats from districts in former Confederate states where abuses of the RIGHT TO VOTE were charged. Between 1881 and 1897, the House unseated eighteen Democrats on this basis.

Another anomaly, of a different sort, arose from the 1930 MIDTERM ELECTION, when the beginning of the Great Depression threatened to end the Republicans' seventeen-year domination of the House. On election night in November it appeared that the Republicans had nevertheless retained the House by a narrow margin. The tally showed 218 Republicans elected, against 216 Democrats and one independent. But in those days, before the Twentieth Amendment moved up the convening date, thirteen months elapsed between the election and the convening of the new Congress. During that interval, an unusually large number of deaths (fourteen) occurred among the newly elected representatives.

In SPECIAL ELECTIONS to fill the vacancies, several had no effect on the political balance because the same party retained the seat. But in three cases Republicans who died were replaced by Democrats, tipping the balance to the Democrats' favor in time for them to organize the new Congress in December 1931. A fourth Republican vacancy went to the Democrats in early 1932.

When the Seventy-second Congress convened on December 7, 1931, House Democrats held the edge, 219 to 215, with one independent. As the majority, they were able to elect as Speaker John Nance Garner of Texas. In 1932 Garner was elected as Franklin D. Roosevelt's first vice president.

Even without the special election gains, control of the House likely would have passed to the Democrats in 1931. Immediately after the 1930 general election, a group of Farm Belt Republicans announced that they would withhold their votes from veteran Speaker Nicholas Longworth of Ohio and allow the Democrats to organize the House, which they did. The vote for Garner as Speaker was 218 to 207, a margin greater than the three seats the Democrats gained during the preceding thirteen months.

The 1972 House election oddity resulted from the preelection disappearance of two House Democrats, Majority Leader Hale Boggs of Louisiana and Nick Begich of Alaska, during an Alaskan airplane trip. Despite their absence, both were reelected. Boggs's wife, Lindy, was elected to succeed him after he was declared legally dead in 1973. Begich was declared legally dead after the 1972 election, and a special election to replace him was held in 1973.

## Electoral Behavior

Many factors shape the choices a voter makes on ELECTION DAY. Collectively, the voters' decisions constitute the electorate's political behavior, which may vary from one election to another.

Political scientists generally agree that PARTY IDENTIFICATION exerts the strongest influence on the voter's choice among candidates. Although the proportion of INDEPENDENTS is rising, most Americans still identify themselves as Democrats or Republicans. As a rule, when they step into the voting booth, they support their party's nominee for the office at stake.

Other factors, however, may outweigh party affiliation under certain circumstances. This is particularly true in PRIMARY elections, when the candidates are all of the same party and vying for a group's nomination. In such cases, the candidate's public image—looks, personality, background, grasp of the issues, inspirational qualities, and the like—may be the chief determinant.

In the television age, candidates usually run independently of the parties, making image all the more important. In such CANDIDATE-CENTERED CAMPAIGNS, especially for the presidency, the voter is unlikely to be personally acquainted with those who are running. All he or she is likely to know about the candidate comes from MEDIA COVERAGE of the campaign or MEDIA USE by the campaign through interviews, talk-show appearances, and POLITICAL ADVERTISING. This information in turn helps to shape the voter's perception of the candidate's image as negative or positive.

POLLING measures the public's attitude toward the candidates leading up to the election. Often the approval ratings fluctuate. Both major party nominees for president usually receive a POSTCONVENTION BOUNCE in the ratings.

In the 1996 election, for example, President Bill Clinton was consistently ahead in the polls, even though he was under investigation by an independent counsel for his role in the Arkansas Whitewater real estate deal before he became president. He was also facing an unprecedented sexual harassment trial in a civil suit brought by Paula Jones, a former Arkansas state employee. Yet Republican challenger Robert J. Dole could not match Clinton's overall approval ratings from the American public.

Four years earlier, in his successful bid to oust President George Bush, Clinton also had benefited from a positive candidate image. Although Bush had recently enjoyed record-high approval ratings for his leadership in the Persian Gulf War against Iraq, his candidate image soon turned negative.

In part Bush was a victim of RETROSPECTIVE VOTING, another major aspect of electoral behavior. The voters looked back on Bush as vice president and then successor to the popular Ronald Reagan, and they found Bush wanting in comparison with Clinton. INCUMBENCY and previous service did more harm than good to Bush's reelection chances. Voters apparently doubted Bush's ability to handle the worsening economy.

To an unusually strong degree, ISSUE VOTING also helped Clinton, particularly in the 1996 campaign. His stands on abortion rights, health care, child care, education, and other so-called women's issues made him especially popular with women voters. Even after his affair with Monica Lewinsky, a former White House intern, became public in 1998, Clinton continued to draw strong support in the polls from women.

Political scientists have charted the ups and downs of presidential candidates' images in the public mind and found that neither party has a monopoly on positive or negative evaluations. Although the Republican nominee was viewed more positively in eight of the twelve elections from 1952 to 1996, that did not always bring electoral success. Sometimes the evaluations were too closely matched to make a difference.

The GOP candidate had the higher image rating in 1952 and 1956 (Dwight Eisenhower); 1960, 1968, and 1972 (Richard Nixon); 1980 and 1984 (Ronald Reagan); and 1988 (George Bush). The public's perception of the

Democratic candidate was higher in 1964 (Lyndon Johnson), 1976 (Jimmy Carter), and in 1992 and 1996 (Bill Clinton). Nixon lost in 1960 to John Kennedy, although he had a more favorable image than Kennedy according to the polls. Reagan, despite his impressive popularity as president, was considered too old by some voters. His candidate image rated higher than Carter's in 1980 and Walter Mondale's in 1984, but not by much.

The age of the voters also affects their electoral behavior. Older people have higher VOTER TURNOUT rates than young people, particularly those in the eighteen to twenty-one age group. ABSENTEE VOTING makes it possible for people who are away from home or have difficulty getting to the polls to participate in elections. Some states are experimenting with elections conducted entirely by mail.

The public's POLITICAL SOCIALIZATION remains one of the most enduring factors in determining how people vote. Lessons learned in childhood, or remarks overheard from parents, help to shape the IDEOLOGY that will likely guide the voter for a lifetime.

## Electoral College and Votes

The election of a president and vice president is accomplished through the electoral college system, which the framers of the Constitution conceived as a compromise between selection by Congress and DIRECT ELECTION by POPULAR VOTE. Each state has as many members in the college as it does in Congress, and it is their votes that actually elect the government's two top officers.

Few of the framers' actions have been more criticized. Thomas Jefferson decried the indirect election system as "the most dangerous blot on our Constitution," and people have been calling for reform ever since.

The compromise made a great concession to the less-populous states because it assured them of three electoral votes (two for their two senators and at least one for their representative) no matter how small their populations might be. The plan also left important powers with the states by giving complete discretion to state legislatures to determine the method of choosing electors.

The system finally agreed upon (Article II, section 1, clause 2) grew out of problems arising from diverse state voting requirements, the slavery problem, big-state versus small-state rivalries, and the complexities of the balance of power among different branches of the government. Moreover, it was probably as close to a direct popular election as the men who wrote the Constitution thought possible and appropriate at the time.

Direct election was opposed because it was felt generally that the people lacked sufficient knowledge of the character and qualifications of possible candidates to make an intelligent choice. Many delegates also feared that the people of the various states would be unlikely to agree on a single person, usually casting their votes for FAVORITE SON candidates well known to them.

The term *electoral college* itself does not appear in the Constitution. It was first used unofficially in the early 1800s and became the official designation for the electoral body in 1845.

## How the System Works

When Americans vote for a particular presidential candidate, they are in fact voting for a slate of electors pledged to that candidate. Each state is allocated as many electors as it has representatives and senators in Congress. The winning electors in each state then meet in their state capital on the first Monday after the second Wednesday in December to cast their votes for president and vice president. A statement of the vote is sent to Washington, D.C., where Congress counts the votes January 6. A majority of electoral votes (270 out of a total of 538 in recent years) is needed to elect.

Counting the electoral votes is a ceremonial function. But if no candidate wins a majority, or in case of a tie, the House of Representatives must choose the president. Each state delegation in the House has one vote, and a majority of states is required for election. (The Senate chooses the vice president if no candidate wins a majority of the electoral college vote.) The House has chosen the president only twice, although several cam-

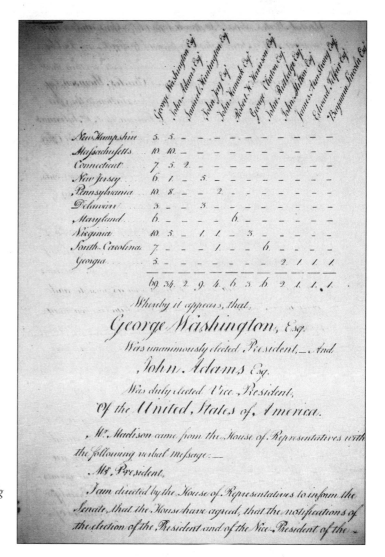

Page 7 of the Senate Journal, April 6, 1789, showing the electoral vote in the first presidential election, which awarded George Washington a unanimous vote. *Source: National Archives*

paigns have been deliberately designed to throw elections into the House.

Originally, no distinction was made between electoral college ballots for president and vice president. That caused confusion when the TWO-PARTY SYSTEM developed and parties began to nominate party tickets for the two offices. All the electors of one party tended to vote for their party's two nominees. But with no distinction between the presidential and vice-presidential nominees, there was danger of a tie vote. That actually happened in the election of 1800. The election was thrown into the House of Representatives, which was forced to choose between running mates Thomas Jefferson and Aaron Burr. In 1804 the Twelfth Amendment was added to the Constitution, requiring separate votes for the two offices. The amendment kept the constitutional requirement that the electors vote for at least one candidate who "shall not be an inhabitant of the same state with themselves," which in effect ensured that the president and vice president would be

## Faithless Electors

One cause for splits in a state's electoral vote is the so-called "faithless elector." Legally, electors are not bound to vote for any particular candidate; they may cast their ballots any way they wish. But in reality electors are almost always faithful to the candidate of the party with which they are affiliated.

But at times in U.S. political history, electors have broken ranks to vote for candidates not supported by their parties. In 1796 a Pennsylvania Federalist elector voted for Democratic-Republican Thomas Jefferson instead of Federalist John Adams. In 1820 a New Hampshire Democratic-Republican elector voted for John Quincy Adams instead of the party nominee, James Monroe.

There was no further occurrence until 1948, when Preston Parks, a Harry S. Truman elector in Tennessee, voted for Gov. Strom Thurmond of South Carolina, the States Rights Democratic Party (Dixiecrat) presidential nominee. Since then, there have been the following instances:

• In 1956 W. F. Turner, a Stevenson elector in Alabama, voted for Walter B. Jones, a local judge.
• In 1960 Henry D. Irwin, a Nixon elector in Oklahoma, voted for Sen. Harry F. Byrd, Democrat of Virginia.
• In 1968 Dr. Lloyd W. Bailey, a Nixon elector in North Carolina, voted for George C. Wallace, the American Independent Party candidate.
• In 1972 Roger L. MacBride, a Nixon elector in Virginia, voted for John Hospers, the Libertarian Party candidate.
• In 1976 Mike Padden, a Ford elector in Washington State, voted for former governor Ronald Reagan of California.
• In 1988 Margaret Leach, a Dukakis elector in West Virginia, voted for Dukakis's running mate, Sen. Lloyd Bentsen of Texas.

*Source: Presidential Elections, 1789–1996 (Washington, D.C.: Congressional Quarterly, 1997), 15.*

from different states. (See CHRONOLOGY OF PRESI- DENTIAL ELECTIONS.)

The only unanimously elected president was the first one, George Washington. In 1789, before the system was changed and each elector had two votes, Washington received 100 percent of the electoral votes it was possible for one candidate to receive. Under the system as revised by the Twelfth Amendment, two candidates came close to unanimous election: James Monroe in 1820 received 98.3 percent of the electoral vote, and in 1936 Franklin D. Roosevelt received 98.5 percent.

Until the Twentieth Amendment was adopted in 1933, there were no rules for parceling out electoral votes of a candidate who died after the election. This ELEC- TORAL ANOMALY happened in 1872 when the Demo- cratic/Liberal Republican candidate, Horace Greeley, died after losing the popular vote to Ulysses S. Grant. Left to their own judgment, the sixty-six Democratic electors divided their votes among four candidates.

Three Georgia electors insisted on casting their votes for the deceased Greeley, but Congress refused to count them.

Presumably the Twentieth Amendment (the so-called Lame Duck Amendment) would apply if a future candidate should die after winning electoral votes. The amendment states that the vice president-elect becomes president if the president-elect dies before taking office. It also empowers Congress to decide what to do if the president-elect and the vice president-elect both fail to qualify by the date prescribed for commencement of their terms, and it gives Congress authority to settle problems arising from the death of candidates in cases where the election is thrown to the House (president) or Senate (vice president).

If a presidential or vice-presidential nominee resigns or dies after the NATIONAL PARTY CONVENTION but before ELECTION DAY, the vacancy on the ticket is filled by the DEMOCRATIC NATIONAL COMMITTEE or the

REPUBLICAN NATIONAL COMMITTEE. Both major parties have had to replace vice-presidential nominees. (See RUNNING MATE; VICE PRESIDENT.)

## Method of Choosing Electors

The Constitution stipulates that each state shall specify how its electors are to be chosen. Initially, the norm was for state legislatures to appoint electors, although a handful of states used direct popular election. After the first three presidential elections, popular vote increasingly became the preferred method for choosing electors. Since 1860, the only state to use legislative appointment was Colorado in 1876.

After 1832 electors came to be chosen by what is known as the *general ticket.* Electors for each party are grouped together on a general party ticket and are elected as a bloc. In all but a few states, electors' names do not even appear on the ballot. Instead, voters cast their ballot for a particular party's presidential ticket, and the winner of the popular vote wins all of the state's electors, in what is known as WINNER TAKE ALL. Maine and Nebraska are exceptions. They allocate their electors by presidential-election districts that match their CONGRESSIONAL DISTRICTS (two in Maine and three in Nebraska). The plurality winner wins the district electoral vote and the statewide plurality winner receives the other two electoral votes (equal to the two senators in each state).

Under the Constitution, electors are free to vote as they please, but electors who do so are rare and are known as *faithless electors.* Some states prohibit faithless voting, but the constitutionality of such laws has not been tested. The most recent instance of a faithless elector was in 1988, when a West Virginia Democratic elector reversed her votes, choosing Lloyd Bentsen for president and Michael Dukakis for vice president, instead of the other way around.

The Constitution did not say what to do if there

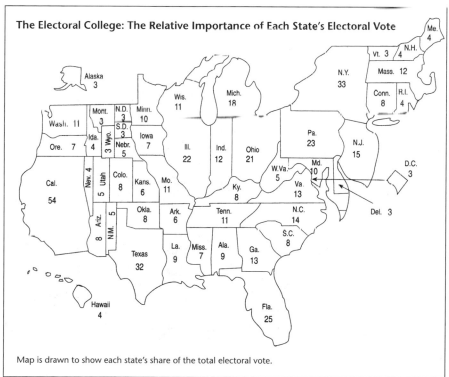

**The Electoral College: The Relative Importance of Each State's Electoral Vote**

Map is drawn to show each state's share of the total electoral vote.

*Source:* John Bibby, *Governing by Consent: An Introduction to American Politics,* 2d ed. (Washington, D.C.: CQ Press, 1995), 237.

were disputes about electors' ballots. That issue became a critical concern following the 1876 election when, for the first time, the outcome had to be determined by decisions on disputed electoral votes. The 1876 campaign pitted Republican Rutherford B. Hayes against Democrat Samuel J. Tilden. Tilden led in the popular vote by more than 250,000 votes but fell one vote short of a majority in the electoral college; the votes of three southern states were in dispute. After Republicans agreed to withdraw federal troops from the South, a special commission awarded all the disputed electoral votes to Hayes.

In 1887 Congress passed permanent legislation for the handling of disputed electoral votes. The 1887 law, still in force, authorized each state to determine the legality of the choice of electors. Majorities of both the House and Senate are needed to reject any disputed electoral votes. If the two chambers cannot agree, the electors certified by the governor are accepted.

## Other Anomalies

The complicated and indirect system of presidential selection has led to anomalies other than the Horace Greeley situation. In 1836, for example, the Whigs sought to take advantage of the electoral system by running different presidential candidates in different parts of the country. William Henry Harrison ran in most of New England, the mid-Atlantic states, and the Midwest; Daniel Webster ran in Massachusetts; Hugh White of Tennessee ran in the South. The theory was that each candidate would capture electoral votes for the Whig Party in the region where he was strongest. Then the Whig electors could combine on one candidate or, alternatively, throw the election into the House, whichever seemed to their advantage. The scheme did not work, however, because Martin Van Buren, the Democratic nominee, captured a majority of the electoral votes.

Critics of the electoral college system point out several possible sources of an electoral crisis. First, a candidate who loses the popular vote may still be elected president. That has happened three times in the nation's history. John Quincy Adams in 1824, Rutherford B.

Hayes in 1876, and Benjamin Harrison in 1888 won the presidency with a smaller popular vote than their opponents received.

In the 1824 election, Andrew Jackson, hero of the War of 1812, ran ahead of Adams in both the popular and electoral voting, but he fell short of the necessary majority, throwing the election to the House, which chose Adams. Other than the 1800 election when the House selected Jefferson over Burr, it was the only time the House has been called upon to decide an election. (The Hayes-Tilden contest of 1876 was a unique case, with the dispute settled by a special commission of House, Senate, and Supreme Court members. See CHRONOLOGY OF PRESIDENTIAL ELECTIONS; CONTESTED ELECTIONS.)

In 1888 Benjamin Harrison won about 100,000 fewer votes (of almost 12 million cast) than President Grover Cleveland, but he won the electoral college vote by 233 to 168 because he won in larger states that had more electoral votes.

Only once has the Senate elected a vice president because no candidate won an electoral vote majority. Richard M. Johnson, Martin Van Buren's running mate on the Democratic ticket, fell one vote short in 1837 after Van Buren won the presidency. Objecting to Johnson's alleged affairs with slave mistresses, Virginia's electors gave their votes to another candidate. Limited by the Twelfth Amendment to a choice between the two top contenders, the Senate voted along party lines for Johnson over Francis Granger, a Whig.

Because a presidential ticket takes all of a state's electoral votes by winning most of the state's popular vote (a PLURALITY) and not necessarily a majority (more than 50 percent), the system permits lopsided electoral vote victories and the election of so-called minority presidents. Since 1824 there have been seventeen minority presidents, including three elected twice with less than a majority of the popular vote: Grover Cleveland (1884 and 1892), Woodrow Wilson (1912 and 1916), and Bill Clinton (1992 and 1996). (See table, "Minority" Presidents, page 133.)

Clinton's 1996 win provided a vivid example of how the electoral system can exaggerate the margin of victory. Although Clinton won only 49 percent of the popular vote, he gained 70 percent of the electoral vote (379), against 30 percent (159) for Republican challenger Robert J. Dole. Dole won 41 percent of the popular vote, and Reform Party candidate Ross Perot won 8 percent, with no electoral votes.

Clinton targeted the largest states and the strategy paid off. He took California (54 votes), New York (33 votes), and six of the other states in the top-ten electoral vote category. Of the top ten he lost only Texas (32 votes) and North Carolina (14 votes).

## Reform Efforts

Although the electoral college system prevents the smaller states from being completely left out, it has not stopped the megastates from dominating the presidential election process. To correct the imbalance, numerous reforms have been proposed, including elimination of the electoral college altogether.

Concern also has been expressed about a possible deadlock in the electoral college if the election involves more than two candidates. If a third-party candidate won one or two states in a close race, he or she could try to play an important "broker" role either in the electoral college or, if one candidate did not receive a majority in the electoral college, in the House.

George Wallace's candidacy on the American Independent Party ticket in 1968 presented such a threat. Republican Richard Nixon and Democrat Hubert Humphrey ran one of the closest races in history. Despite earlier hopes of winning the whole South, Wallace won only five states and forty-six electoral votes. If Nixon had lost just California or two or three smaller states that were close, he would have been denied an electoral majority.

Proposals to change or do away with some of the obsolete and odd features of the electoral college system have included direct election of the president, bonus electors for the winner of the national popular vote, and proportional allocation of a state's electoral vote, which would lead to more frequent congressional selection of the president.

None of the reforms has been adopted. Each would need a constitutional amendment, requiring a two-thirds vote of Congress. During the Ninety-fifth Congress (1977–1979) the Senate voted to abolish the electoral college as proposed by President Jimmy Carter, but the proposed amendment did not receive a two-thirds majority.

For all its supposed faults, the electoral college system has withstood repeated assaults for several reasons. Some states, large or small, fear that they would lose out if the president were elected directly by the people. And despite its potential for failure, the system has defenders who hold to the adage, "If it ain't broke, don't fix it." They point out that, for the most part, the system has worked for more than two hundred years, with scant evidence that it will not continue to work just as well in the twenty-first century.

---

## Entrance Polls

Entrance polls, as the name indicates, are similar to EXIT POLLS, a device the news media use on ELECTION DAY to speed the reporting of election results. While exit polls are based on interviews of people leaving voting places, entrance polls collect data from people entering them.

Exit polls are more widely used because people usually leave the polling place singly or in pairs, making them easy to approach for interviews. Entrance polls are used in events—a CAUCUS, for instance—where the participants leave in groups, making it difficult for interviewers to take a scientific sampling of the overall vote.

Both entrance polls and exit polls are used to find out not only how people intend to vote (or actually voted) but also their reasons for doing so. In addition, they are used to obtain demographic information about the supporters of a particular candidate, such as age, sex, religion, and perhaps their stand on a controversial issue, such as abortion. In the 1996 IOWA CAUCUS, for example, the Voter News Service (VNS) conducted entrance polls at Republican precinct caucuses around the state. The results showed that the winner, Robert J. Dole, had constructed a demographic coalition of older and ideologically moderate voters. He ran better in small towns and farm areas than in large population centers.

Patrick J. Buchanan, who finished second among the nine candidates seeking Iowa's GOP delegates, campaigned largely on social issues. His best showing was in strongly antiabortion Catholic and Dutch Calvinist areas.

VNS is a cooperative venture of the Associated Press and the ABC, CBS, CNN, Fox, and NBC networks. It has been the polling and vote counting arm of the AP and broadcast networks since 1990.

## Equal Time and Rebuttal Rules

The First Amendment's protection of press freedom extends to all forms of news media. Unlike print media, however, the electronic media are subject to some government regulation, including a few rules that affect elections. The most important of these are the *equal time* and related *right of rebuttal* rules, ensuring balance in air time given to political candidates.

Access to the airwaves, television especially, has become vital to campaigns for major elective offices in the United States. Television is the dominant medium by which candidates try to "sell" themselves to the voters and convey their positions on issues. In the 1996 presidential campaign, television advertising was the largest single expense for the major contenders, President Bill Clinton and challenger Robert J. Dole. Between them they spent $112.9 million for POLITICAL ADVERTISING, almost all of it on television.

Under the equal time rule, a station that gives time to one candidate for a specific office must make the same opportunity available to other candidates for the same office. But the rule does not apply to regular news programs, most talk shows, or DEBATES between candidates. The right of rebuttal rule requires stations to make their facilities available to any person who has been assailed on radio or television for purposes of rebutting the criticism.

In practice, commercial radio and television stations rarely give free air time because it opens them to equal time demands from numerous INDEPENDENT and THIRD PARTY candidates. But if a candidate buys time to attack an opponent, the broadcaster is obliged to try to schedule rebuttal time if the opponent wishes to buy it. With the increase in NEGATIVE CAMPAIGNING since the 1980s, "attack ads" have become commonplace, resulting in expensive barrages and counterbarrages of political commercials.

Public radio and television stations, which sometimes give air time to candidates, won the right in 1998 to exclude certain candidates from their broadcast debates. Ruling in *Arkansas Educational Television v. Forbes,* the Supreme Court voted 6–3 to affirm public TV's right to limit debate participants to those it believes have sufficient public support.

## First Amendment Considerations

Newspapers, magazines, and other publications also play critical roles in MEDIA USE BY CAMPAIGNS and MEDIA COVERAGE OF CAMPAIGNS. For the most part they, too, try to provide balanced coverage of political campaigns. Unlike the electronic media, however, newspapers and magazines are not required by law or government regulation to provide equal news or advertising space to opposing viewpoints. The Supreme Court has upheld the print media's exemption from such regulation under the free press and free speech protections of the First Amendment. In *Miami Herald Publishing Co. v. Tornillo* (1974) the Court unanimously struck down a Florida law that required newspapers to grant political candidates equal space to reply to criticism of their public records.

The Court on the other hand has upheld the government's authority to regulate the broadcast industry. Citing the limited number of radio and television frequencies available, the Court in 1943 sustained the power of the Federal Communications Commission (FCC) to determine who receives licenses to use the airwaves. It emphasized, however, that the FCC must award licenses on the basis of neutral principles that do not favor one applicant over another because of an applicant's particular views.

FCC regulations fall into three categories: (1) rules limiting the number of stations controlled by a single organization; (2) rules calling for examination of the goals and performances of stations as part of their periodic licensing; and (3) rules guaranteeing fair treatment of individuals.

Under the Communications Act of 1934, the FCC for years sharply limited the number of radio and television stations a single organization could own in the same media market or nationally. In a comprehensive rewriting of the telephone and broadcast laws, however, Congress in 1996 relaxed the limits on ownership of multiple radio and television stations. The new law also made it easier for broadcasters to renew their licenses. The Telecommunications Act of 1996 (PL 104-104) extended the license period to eight years, with no consideration of competing applications required unless the owner had not served the public or had violated laws or FCC regulations.

A company could own unlimited AM (amplitude modulation) or FM (frequency modulation) radio stations nationally so long as they did not exceed the multiple ownership limits that apply in individual markets; these limits vary, depending on the size of the market. A network or other company also could own an unlimited number of TV stations, provided their signals did not reach more than 35 percent of the nation's households. The new law also removed a prohibition against cross-ownership of cable systems and TV stations in the same market.

Source: © 1998 by Herblock in The Washington Post

## Regulation Controversies

Federal law requires broadcasters to "serve the public interest, convenience, and necessity." This rather vague standard gives the FCC little guidance to determine whether to renew a station's license other than to review the mix of programs presented, the proportion of public service offerings, and the inclusion of programs for selected groups. But the agency does not try to scrutinize program content in any detail. With its limited staff, the FCC has been neither inclined nor able to rigorously define and enforce rules on programming for the public interest.

In principle, the equal time and rebuttal rules are related to—but different from—the now-abandoned fairness doctrine that caused almost four decades of controversy in broadcast and political circles. The FCC developed the fairness doctrine in the late 1940s to require licensees to devote a reasonable percentage of time to coverage of public issues and to provide an opportunity for presentation of contrasting points of view on those issues. Broadcasters challenged the doctrine, however, as a violation of their right to determine program content free from government interference.

In 1969 the Court in *Red Lion Broadcasting Co. v.*

*Federal Communications Commission* upheld the government's authority to impose such regulations. Again citing the scarcity of broadcast frequencies, the Court said that a broadcaster "has no constitutional right to be the one who holds the license or to monopolize a radio frequency to the exclusion of his fellow citizens."

Broadcasters continued to fight the fairness doctrine. They contended that it actually worked against presentation of different viewpoints on public policy issues. Instead, they pointed out, the fairness doctrine encouraged stations to avoid controversial programming. The proliferation of third parties made compliance even more difficult.

There also was evidence that the broadcast media, wishing to comply with the fairness doctrine and not risk losing their licenses, assumed that every political issue has two sides and only two sides, when in fact many issues are more complex than that. As CBS correspondent Bill Plante put it during the 1980 campaign, "If you have somebody who's calling the president an idiot, you then almost have to have somebody who's saying, 'Well, no, he's not, he's a great statesman.'"

In 1987, however, broadcasters finally won their battle. They gained a sympathetic hearing from President Ronald Reagan, who vetoed a congressional attempt to convert the fairness doctrine from FCC policy into statutory law. After the veto, the FCC promptly voted 4–0 to abolish the thirty-eight-year-old doctrine. The commission emphasized, however, that the action did not affect its enforcement of the equal time or right of rebuttal requirements.

After the fairness doctrine was repealed, congressional oversight and potential litigation still maintained pressure on broadcasters to continue airing opposing viewpoints. For example, the broadcast of rebuttals after presidential, gubernatorial, and mayoral addresses dealing with major public issues is now commonplace.

In the 1990s "issue advertising" emerged as a controversial form of political debate. Keyed to ISSUE VOT-ING, issue ads provided a means to circumvent contribution limits of CAMPAIGN FINANCE laws. Instead of contributing directly to an antiabortion candidate, for example, the candidate's supporters could spend without limit on antiabortion ads. If the opponent was pro-choice, the ads would by implication endorse the abortion foe without naming him or her.

The Supreme Court ruled in *Columbia Broadcasting System v. Democratic National Committee* (1973) that broadcasters could refuse to sell commercial time for issue-related advertising. In *CBS, Inc. v. Federal Communications Commission* (1981) it upheld a law that required broadcasters to provide candidates for federal office with "reasonable access" to buying commercial time.

Although cable systems transmit signals by wire rather than the airwaves, the FCC began regulating cable television in the 1960s, in part to protect broadcasters from unfair competition and to require cable operators to serve local community needs. In 1986 the Court for the first time held that the First Amendment applies to the cable franchising process. The ruling in *City of Los Angeles v. Preferred Communications Inc.* allowed an unsuccessful applicant for a franchise to pursue a claim that the city violated his press freedom rights and antitrust law by granting only one franchise in the area to be served.

Generally the FCC regulates the electronic media with a light hand. With its vague statutory mandate and small staff, as well as its constant buffeting by conflicting industry, congressional, and administration pressures, the agency has earned the reputation of a benign regulator. Even so, the broadcasting industry is vulnerable to government pressures in a way that the print industry is not.

In 1998, for example, FCC chairman William Kennard—reportedly with President Clinton's backing—proposed that commercial broadcasters be compelled to provide free air time to political candidates. The rule, he said, would be "minimally intrusive and doesn't trample anyone's First Amendment rights."

Broadcasters and their allies insisted such a rule could come only from Congress, where they were prepared to lobby against the potential loss of revenue. They argued that owners pay heavy fees for their licenses and that candidates already receive discounts and special access to broadcast advertising under federal law. With Kennard arguing that the FCC had the power to act on its own, a court case over jurisdiction appeared likely if the commission imposed a free air time rule before the 2000 presidential election.

## Exit Polls

Exit polls are a relatively new technique in the science of POLLING, which has become an indispensable tool in modern American politics. Through 1996, exit polls had been widely used in only four presidential elections.

By interviewing many thousands of citizens just after they have voted, pollsters can accurately predict election results without waiting for the official vote count. They also can gain some insight into why the voters acted as they did, along with indications of how the vote divided along lines of age, sex, race, religion, and income.

Television networks and wire services use exit polls on ELECTION DAY mainly to help them find out who won—and why—as quickly as possible. As such, exit polls are almost exclusively a part of MEDIA COVERAGE OF CAMPAIGNS. The major PUBLIC OPINION pollsters such as Gallup, Harris, or Roper rarely conduct exit polls on their own without being hired by a news organization.

Since the 1990 MIDTERM ELECTIONS the networks have pooled their exit polling and vote counting to reduce costs. Now known as the Voter News Service (VNS), the cooperative includes the Associated Press and the ABC, CBS, CNN, Fox, and NBC networks.

VNS has also used ENTRANCE POLLS for the same purposes as exit polls. Entrance polling is more practicable when it is easier to interview people going into a voting place than leaving it. This is generally the case with CAUCUSES, where the voters trickle in but leave all at once when the caucus ends, making it difficult for reporters to interview a representative sampling of the participants.

## Brief History

The origins of exit polls are somewhat obscure, but by most accounts they are the brainchild of Warren Mitofsky, a former CENSUS statistician who developed them for CBS beginning in 1967. NBC had used a form of exit poll in the 1964 California primaries, but it was less scientific than today's version.

Mitofsky organized the first full-fledged exit poll in Kentucky's gubernatorial contest in 1967, the same year CBS hired him to set up the first polling operation within a news organization. Previously, the networks, sometimes working with professional pollsters, had relied on precinct voting and past voting patterns to project the winners on election night.

Under Mitofsky's direction the CBS team devised a systematic sampling technique of interviewing voters at specific intervals, such as every third voter, as they left the voting place. The interviewers were stationed in precincts selected to provide a cross-section of the electorate. These early exit polls were mostly for internal use by the reporters and forecasters. The results were not made public as a general rule.

Having tested it in the Kentucky race, CBS used the exit poll in the 1968 presidential contest between Hubert H. Humphrey and Richard Nixon, again only as a check against actual vote counts. Exit polls were conducted in twenty states, with voters asked some demographic information as well as how they voted.

By 1980 other networks were using exit polls, and some were more aggressive than CBS in basing projections on them. CBS was still using exit polls mostly for analysis and verification of the early vote counts.

As a result, NBC and ABC beat CBS in projecting Ronald Reagan's LANDSLIDE victory over Jimmy Carter. Exit polls by all three networks showed that Reagan would be big winner in what had been expected to be a close race. But the CBS unit, still led by Mitofsky, did not project the winner until after Carter conceded.

Carter's decision to concede at about 10:00 p.m. eastern standard time, while polls were still open in California, aroused controversy about exit polls and the networks' decisions to "declare" winners early. Many think these results discouraged voters who had not yet cast their ballots because they believed their votes would not make a difference.

Some states subsequently tried to ban exit polls by creating so-called no-First-Amendment zones near voting places, making it difficult if not impossible for poll takers to identify and interview people who had just voted. But the courts ruled that First Amendment free speech and free press rights cannot be excluded from certain areas.

On Capitol Hill, the House and Senate held hearings on exit polls but made no attempt to prohibit their use. Congress did adopt resolutions before the 1982 and 1984 elections, however, asking the networks to refrain from projecting results until all polls had closed except in Alaska and Hawaii.

The election news cooperative, then called Voter Research and Surveys (VRS) and headed by Mitofsky, received its first test in the 1990 elections. Despite some start-up problems and complaints that the monopoly meant no other exit polls to check on VRS, the system has been refined, renamed, and used in all subsequent major elections.

## Accuracy

With one notable exception, exit polls have been remarkably accurate. The exception was the November 1996 U.S. Senate race in New Hampshire, when VNS projected that Republican Bob Smith had lost his Senate seat to Democrat Dick Swett. Using VNS figures, TV networks flashed "news" of the "upset" shortly after 7:00 p.m. Vice President Al Gore even called Swett to congratulate him. "N.H.'s Smith Defeated," headlined the next day's *Washington Post*.

Within hours red-faced journalists had to retract their erroneous reports as Smith emerged the winner. The final, official results showed Smith reelected by 14,907 votes. He received 242,304 votes or 49.2 percent of the total to Swett's 227,397 or 46.2 percent. The reddest faces were at VNS. There the executive in charge said it was "the largest error in any exit poll estimate" he had seen in fifteen years of directing the poll. It was the only wrong call by VNS in 110 races covered that night, in-

cluding the race between President Bill Clinton and Robert J. Dole. Out of 2,100 races called by VNS or its forerunners since 1968, only 5 had been wrong before the Senate contest in New Hampshire.

VNS had randomly asked 2,355 voters about their choices as they left the polls in twenty-five New Hampshire PRECINCTS selected to be representative of the state as a whole. The expected margin of error was plus or minus 3 percent. Most of the polls had closed when VNS released its estimate, but they were still open in twenty communities, including the industrial areas of Nashua, Merrimack, and Exeter. Some residents complained that they planned to vote but decided not to bother after hearing Swett had "won."

The error in New Hampshire brought renewed calls for laws or voluntary restraint to delay FORECASTING ELECTION RESULTS before all the polls are closed. Premature projections diminish VOTER TURNOUT in areas that are still voting while winners are declared on the basis of exit polls taken earlier.

Conservative media critics point to VNS's almost unerring accuracy as "proof" that the Associated Press and the networks are in "total cooperation" rather than being competitive with each other in the reporting of election returns. They charge that computerized VOTING MACHINES somehow enable the news media to manipulate election results.

## Purpose

Television viewers and radio listeners rarely hear mention of the Voting News Service. Broadcasters prefer to label the VNS data, which they are helping to pay for, as their own. Newscasters therefore say, "ABC finds this race too close to call," or, "NBC lists (blank) the winner."

Political scientists Michael W. Traugott and Paul J. Lavrakas in their 1996 book *The Voter's Guide to Election Polls* give three main reasons why news organizations conduct their own polls:

First, they like to have editorial control over the content and timing of the surveys, exercising their own judgment over news decisions and values. Second, they enjoy the professional prestige that comes from their peers' acknowledgment of the quality of their polls. This occurs when other news organizations pick up their stories or cite their poll results in stories they produce. Third, they use poll results to inform and structure their subsequent reporting of the campaign.

Concerning the controversy over early vote projections and their influence on West Coast voting, Traugott and Lavrakas say, "There are no studies that have proved an unequivocal relationship between election night broadcasts and levels of turnout or margin of vote for a particular candidate." But they note there are indications that some people will stay home when the result is known and that others either will be affected by the BANDWAGON EFFECT or will want to help the underdog in the race.

# F

## Fairness Commission

*See* PRESIDENTIAL SELECTION REFORMS.

## Fairness Doctrine

*See* EQUAL TIME AND REBUTTAL RULES.

## Faithless Electors

*See* ELECTORAL COLLEGE AND VOTES.

## Favorite Son

A favorite son (or favorite daughter) candidate is not usually a serious candidate for political office. In presidential politics, the favorite son generally is a candidate who hopes to hold his state's delegation together to make it a bargaining bloc at the NATIONAL PARTY CONVENTION.

In the age of the PRIMARY, which has dramatically diminished the role of the nominating convention, the favorite son is almost an anachronism. The term was much more common in the era of BROKERED CONVENTIONS, where favorite sons diluted the strength of the leading candidates, enabling party bosses to negotiate deals.

Brokered conventions were more likely in the DEMOCRATIC PARTY before 1936 because the old TWO-THIRDS RULE often necessitated numerous ballots until a candidate obtained the two-thirds majority vote required for nomination. Republican nominations have always been made by a simple majority.

PRESIDENTIAL SELECTION REFORMS have made brokered conventions and favorite son candidacies unlikely but not impossible. Since 1972 the Democrats have required names placed in nomination to have the written support of at least fifty delegates from three or more states, with no more than twenty signatures from any one delegation.

By rule or practice, the parties have also limited the number and length of seconding speeches for nominations. A primary aim of conventions today is to hold the huge television viewing audience, and one of the surest ways to lose it is to allow boring, long-winded oratory in support of favorite sons to go unchecked.

The framers of the U.S. Constitution saw the favorite son concept as basic to the PRESIDENTIAL NOMINATING AND ELECTING system. They expected that the states would put forth their most qualified candidates as favorite sons, and that the wise and learned ELECTORAL COLLEGE members would choose the two best candidates, with the winner becoming president and the second-place finisher becoming vice president.

But with adoption of the Twelfth Amendment, requiring separate balloting for president and vice president, and with the trend toward popular election of electors rather than appointment by state legislatures, the role of favorite son changed. Instead of creating a pool of likely presidents, it became more of an honorary position with some potential for influencing the final outcome of the nominating process.

## Federal Election Commission

The Federal Election Commission (FEC), an independent agency created by Congress in 1975, administers and enforces the CAMPAIGN FINANCE law affecting candidates for federal office. The law, basically the Federal Election Campaign Act of 1971 (FECA) and amendments, requires disclosure of sources and uses of funds for presidential and congressional campaigns, limits the size of contributions, and provides for partial PUBLIC FINANCING OF CAMPAIGNS for the presidency.

Candidates and their campaign committees, party committees, and POLITICAL ACTION COMMITTEES (PACs) formed to support one or more candidates must register with the FEC once they cross a certain threshold of financial activity. They then must report periodically to the FEC on their campaign receipts and expenditures. Individuals and committees contributing to or making independent expenditures for or against a candidate also must file reports. The FEC makes the reports available to the public.

FEC staff members review the reports for omissions. If any are found the commission may request additional information from the candidate or committee. If the FEC finds an apparent law violation, it has the authority to seek a conciliation agreement and impose a fine. If a conciliation agreement cannot be reached, the FEC may sue for enforcement in U.S. District Court. The commission may refer to the Justice Department any matter that involves a willful violation.

The FEC also administers the Presidential Election Campaign Fund, which makes possible the public funding of PRESIDENTIAL PRIMARIES, NATIONAL PARTY CONVENTIONS, and presidential general elections. (See PRESIDENT: NOMINATING AND ELECTING.) Each year the fund receives almost $100 million from the optional $3 checkoff on individual income tax returns.

The FEC found itself at the center of controversy in the 1996 presidential election and aftermath because of its inaction in the face of numerous allegations of campaign funding irregularities.

## Background

There had been several attempts to reform campaign financing before the 1971 statute was enacted. As early as 1907 President Theodore Roosevelt recommended public financing of federal elections and a ban on private contributions, with little success. The Corrupt Practices

Act of 1925 was intended to force public disclosure of campaign finances, but it was difficult to enforce.

The campaign finance system remained riddled with loopholes until passage of the 1971 act. Soon after came the Watergate SCANDAL of the Richard Nixon administration, stemming from a burglary at the DEMOCRATIC NATIONAL COMMITTEE headquarters in the Watergate Hotel complex and the subsequent attempted cover-up that drove President Nixon from office. The scandal involved the role of money in politics and spurred further reforms. Congress in 1974 passed the most significant overhaul of campaign finance legislation in the nation's history. Creation of the FEC was a part of the overhaul.

The Supreme Court in 1976 in *BUCKLEY V. VALEO* declared unconstitutional several parts of the 1974 amendments, including the method for selecting members of the FEC. The Court said the method violated the separation of powers clauses of the Constitution because four commissioners were appointed by congressional officials but exercised executive powers. Amendments passed in 1976 reconstituted the FEC as a six member commission appointed by the president and confirmed by the Senate.

The commissioners serve staggered six-year terms, and no more than three commissioners may be members of the same political party. Commissioners are limited by law to one term.

The clerk of the House and secretary of the Senate served as nonvoting ex officio members until 1993 when a federal court ruled the practice unconstitutional. The FEC then reconstituted itself without the ex officio members.

## Operations

The FEC offices are located at 999 E Street, N.W., in Washington, D.C., 20463. Many of the commission's reports and compilations are available on the FEC World Wide Web site on the Internet: *http://www.fec.gov*. (See Appendix, Election-Related Web Sites.)

FEC chairman Joan D. Aikens, a Pennsylvania Republican, was the only member of the original commission still serving when she retired in September 1998. Because of the new one-term limit, Aikens's twenty-four-year record of service was unlikely to be surpassed.

In December 1998 the commission elected Democrat Scott E. Thomas, serving his third term, as chairman and Republican Darryl R. Wold, a first-term member, as vice chairman. FECA requires the chairman and vice chairman, elected annually, to be of different political parties.

Senior FEC staff members include a staff director, general counsel, commission secretary, and assistant staff directors for audit, reports analysis, public disclosure, information, and administration.

The FEC's evenly divided makeup (three Democrats and three Republicans) was intended by Congress to ensure bipartisanship. Instead, the membership has frequently stalemated, resulting in little action and much criticism of the agency. Many complaints of system abuse have been dropped after long delays because the commissioners split along party lines and could not reach a decision.

The commission cited lack of resources as another reason why many of its investigations are "dumped" without resolution. In 1997, for example, 208 of 508 cases, or 41 percent, were dropped. The commission said its $32 million appropriation was inadequate to deal with the workload.

On February 12, 1997, the *Washington Post* detailed some of the FEC's problems in a front-page story headlined "The Little Agency That Can't." "Once hailed as the two-fisted enforcer that would protect the body politic from future Watergate scandals and the corrupting scourge of unregulated campaign cash, the commission has proved to be weak, slow-footed and largely ineffectual," the article said.

The *Post* article, and many others like it, appeared in the wake of the FEC's biggest challenge to date: the frenzied raising of millions of dollars in unregulated SOFT MONEY by the political parties for the 1996 contest between President Bill Clinton and his Republican challenger, Robert J. Dole.

Meant to be used for party-building activities, much of the so-called soft money reportedly was used to support the Clinton and Dole candidacies, even though each received $61.8 million from the public fund and was limited by law to spending only that amount. An FEC staff audit found that both campaigns had benefited from millions of dollars in Democratic and Republican national committee expenditures for "issue ads" that amounted to spending in excess of the federal grants. The FEC, however, rejected the staff recommendation that the campaigns be required to return the excess to the federal Treasury.

Much of the questionable soft money was obtained from foreign nationals, who are barred from contributing to U.S. elections. Clinton and Vice President Al Gore reportedly made some fund-raising calls from their offices, in violation of a law prohibiting such activity on federal property. Generous donors were entertained at White House coffees and some were invited for overnight stays in the residence guest quarters.

The Democratic National Committee returned several millions of dollars in possibly tainted receipts, and both major parties ended the 1996 election in considerable debt: $17.4 million for the Democrats and $15.0 million for the Republicans.

The allegations and counterallegations touched off Senate and House investigations, while Attorney General Janet Reno considered appointing an independent counsel to investigate and prosecute possible law violations. In December 1998 Reno announced her decision against launching an independent counsel investigation.

The FEC indirectly exposed some of the 1996 irregularities through its required disclosure reports. But for the most part the agency remained silent and passive during the investigations. Then-chairman John Warren McCarry described the FEC as "underfunded and overworked." Others called the FEC "a joke."

Both parties pledged to support reforms to strengthen the FEC and tighten the campaign finance system. But no such legislation emerged from the 105th Congress, 1997–1999.

## Federal Matching Funds

*See* PUBLIC FINANCING.

## Federal Workers' Political Activity

Limitations on political activity by federal government employees were eased in 1993 when President Bill Clinton signed into law a revision of the 1939 Hatch Act. The legislation affected the nearly 3 million federal and postal workers as well as state and local government employees in jobs largely funded by federal grants.

Although the Hatch Act originally was intended to protect government workers from being fired or demoted unless they gave to political campaigns, many chafed under the provisions as too restrictive. Passage of the new law climaxed a two-decade effort by congressional Democrats to grant the requested relief.

In the MIDTERM ELECTION of 1994 Clinton and the Democrats lost control of both chambers of Congress. But with the revision enacted into law, "un-Hatched" federal workers of both parties were able for the first time to serve as DELEGATES to the 1996 NATIONAL PARTY CONVENTIONS. They also were able in some instances to run for local office and take part in other long-prohibited political activities.

The act named for Sen. Carl A. Hatch, New Mexico Democrat, is actually two statutes. The second Hatch Act, enacted in 1940, contained the provisions that apply to federally financed state and local workers.

Senator Hatch proposed restrictions on federal workers after a Senate committee found that political appointees in the Works Progress Administration had coerced employees into contributing to political campaigns. At the time, fewer than 32 percent of the 950,000 federal workers were career public servants. The rest were political appointees.

Today about 55 percent of 2.3 million employees are in the civil service system. The total does not include the Central Intelligence Agency or the National Security Agency, whose employment figures are secret. The CIA, NSA, and several other agencies, including the FEDERAL ELECTION COMMISSION, remained subject to the pre-1993 restrictions.

Under the original law, federal workers could not actively participate in partisan campaigns. They could, however, take part in nonpartisan elections such as those for school boards or city councils. They could give money to candidates but not stuff envelopes or work on GET-OUT-THE-VOTE drives for a particular candidate or party. They could wear campaign buttons and have bumper stickers on their cars.

## Loosening the Reins

Critics argued that the Hatch Act denied federal workers the right of political expression guaranteed to other citizens, that it was outdated because the federal workforce was made up mostly of career professionals, and that the jumble of rules and regulations was contradictory and confusing. Opponents to revising the act argued that doing so would politicize the workforce. They noted that the Supreme Court had twice, in 1947 and 1972, upheld the constitutionality of the Hatch Act.

Republican presidents Gerald R. Ford, Ronald Reagan, and George Bush had used the veto or veto threats to block earlier Democratic sponsored efforts in Congress to soften the act. They and others feared that liberalization would enhance the ability of employee unions to help elect Democrats. In 1996 federal workers contributed $312,000 to Clinton's reelection campaign but only $80,000 to Republican CHALLENGER Robert J. Dole, according to the Center for Responsive Politics.

The Hatch Act does not apply to employees of the Executive Office of the President, to individuals appointed by the president and confirmed by the Senate, or to members of the armed forces, whose conduct is governed by separate Defense Department rules. The act covers most DISTRICT OF COLUMBIA employees but not the mayor or city council. The 1993 revision permitted more political activity by covered D.C. government employees.

Under the revised rules, according to the independent U.S. Office of Special Counsel (OSC), covered federal employees are permitted to

• be candidates for public office in nonpartisan elections;
• register and vote as they choose;
• assist in VOTER REGISTRATION drives;

*President James A. Garfield was elected in 1880. His assassination by a job seeker less than eight months into his administration led his successor, Chester A. Arthur, to sign into law the Pendleton Civil Service Reform Act. Source: Library of Congress*

• express opinions about candidates and issues;

• contribute money to political organizations;

• attend political fund-raising functions;

• attend and be active at political rallies and meetings;

• join and be an active member of a political party or club;

• sign nominating petitions;

• campaign for or against INITIATIVE AND REFERENDUM questions, constitutional amendments, and municipal ordinances;

• campaign for or against candidates in partisan elections;

• make campaign speeches for or against candidates in partisan elections;

• distribute campaign literature in partisan elections; and

• hold office in political parties or clubs.

According to the same OSC advisory, federal employees are *not* permitted to

• use official authority or influence to interfere with an election;

• solicit or discourage political activity of anyone having business before their agency;

• solicit or receive political contributions (which may be done in limited situations by federal labor or other employee organizations);

• be candidates for public office in any partisan elections;

• engage in political activity while on duty, in a government office, wearing an official uniform, or using a government vehicle; or

• wear political buttons on duty.

Permitted activities for covered state and local employees include running for public office in nonpartisan elections; campaigning for and holding office in political organizations; actively campaigning for candidates in partisan and nonpartisan elections; and contributing money to political organizations and attending fund-raising functions.

Covered state and local employees are not permitted to be a candidate for public office in a partisan election; use official authority or influence to interfere with or affect the results of an election or nomination; or directly or indirectly coerce contributions from subordinates in support of a political party or candidate.

Penalties for Hatch Act violations are dismissal or (for federal employees) a minimum thirty-day suspension without pay or (for state or local employees) forfeiture by the affected government of the federal assistance equal to two years of the charged employee's salary.

## Earlier Acts

The Civil Service Act of 1883, known as the Pendleton Act for its sponsor, Sen. George H. Pendleton, Ohio Democrat, barred government employees from soliciting political contributions and protected them from coerced assessments for campaigns. The act marked the first significant effort by Congress to control the so-called spoils system of substantial turnover in patronage jobs with each new administration.

The assassination of President James A. Garfield in 1881 by a deranged federal job seeker, Charles J. Guiteau, stimulated popular support for reforming the civil service and taming the spoils system. The Pendleton Act created the bipartisan Civil Service Commission and a merit employment system that gradually covered most career federal employees.

The arrival of Franklin D. Roosevelt's New Deal in 1933 brought to Washington many new federal workers who owed their jobs to Roosevelt and the Democratic Party. To forestall abuses by the grateful officeholders, a COALITION of Republicans and conservative Democrats passed the Hatch Act (officially the Political Activities Act) in 1938.

By 1948 nearly 84 percent of federal workers were in classified civil service positions and therefore subject to the Hatch Act restrictions. But enforcement of the act fell under the same agency that administered the civil service system, a situation unacceptable to President Jimmy Carter when he took office in 1977.

At Carter's behest Congress enacted the most sweeping reform of the civil service system since the Pendleton Act. The Civil Service Reform Act of 1978 abolished the Civil Service Commission and split its functions among the Office of Personnel Management (OPM), the Merit Systems Protection Board (MSPB), and the Federal Labor Relations Authority.

The independent Office of Special Counsel was created in 1979 to investigate and prosecute personnel practices, including Hatch Act violations, before the MSPB. Under the Whistleblower Protection Act of 1989 the OSC and MSPB are charged with protecting employees from reprisals for reporting suspected violations.

The approximately 45 percent of federal employees who are not under the OPM's competitive merit system fall under the excepted service, which includes the FBI, or the Senior Executive Service of officials who have less job security than employees in the OPM system.

In addition to the CIA, NSA, and FEC, the Office of Special Counsel listed itself, the MSPB, and several other agencies as those whose employees are prohibited from partisan political activity under the pre-1993 restrictions. They include the Justice Department Criminal Division; Defense Intelligence Agency; FBI; National Security Council; Internal Revenue Service Office of Criminal Investigation; Customs Service Office of Investigative Programs; Bureau of Alcohol, Tobacco, and Firearms Office of Law Enforcement; Secret Service; and certain Senior Executive Service employees.

## Federalist Party (1789–1816)

The Federalist Party grew out of the movement that drafted and worked for the ratification of the Constitution of 1787, which established a stronger national government than that in operation under the existing Articles of Confederation. Supporters of the new constitutional government were known as Federalists, and in the formative first decade of the Republic they controlled the national government. With President George Washington staying aloof from the development of political parties, Alexander Hamilton and John Adams exercised the leadership of the Federalists. The party's basic strength was among urban, commercial interests, who were particularly drawn to the Federalists because of the party's belief in a strong federal economic policy and the maintenance of domestic order—viewpoints based on a broad interpretation of the Constitution.

The Federalists were perceived widely as a party of the aristocracy, a decided liability in the late eighteenth and early nineteenth centuries, when the right to vote was being widely extended to members of the middle and lower classes. Never so well organized as the Democratic-Republicans, the Federalists were unable to compete for support of the important rural, agrarian elements that made up the majority of the electorate.

*John Adams (left) and Alexander Hamilton were the driving forces behind the Federalist Party, which failed to win the presidency or either house of Congress after 1800. Source: Library of Congress*

The election of Thomas Jefferson in 1800 ended Federalist control of both the White House and Congress. After 1800 the Federalists did not elect a president or win a majority in either house of Congress. The party's strength was largely limited to commercial New England, where Federalists advocated states' rights and were involved in threats of regional secession in 1808 and again during the War of 1812.

The party soon began to lose its energy, and in 1812 the Federalists held their last meeting of party leaders to field a presidential ticket. Four years later there were no nominations, but Federalist electors were chosen in three states. Although this marked the last appearance of the party at the national level, the Federalists remained in existence at the local level until the mid-1820s.

## Fifteenth Amendment

*See* VOTING RIGHTS ACT.

## Forecasting Election Results

In the highly competitive news industry, timely reporting is essential. Nowhere is this more evident than in the predicting of electoral outcomes.

At intervals before an election, the news media use various POLLING techniques to help them determine who is ahead in the race and report that information to their readers, viewers, or listeners. Candidates and their parties, INTEREST GROUPS, POLITICAL CONSULTANTS, as well as large segments of the general public

*Harry S. Truman gleefully holds up a newspaper announcing, incorrectly, his defeat in the 1948 presidential election. Since then, election forecasting has improved tremendously in methodology and accuracy.* Source: St. Louis Mercantile Library

follow the poll reports closely—sometimes out of curiosity and sometimes because they have a vested interest in how the election turns out.

The scientific sampling methods used today are far more sophisticated than those once used by newspapers. Old-time reporters relied on their instincts and "seat-of-the pants journalism" to help them identify the likely winners. They were assisted at times by their newspapers, which early in the nineteenth century began taking what came to be known as a STRAW VOTE before elections. The straw vote or poll began simply, with reporters asking train or steamship passengers about their candidate preferences. By the 1930s some

straw votes had become elaborate affairs, involving extensive mailings of returnable ballots.

At about the same time an Agriculture Department analyst named Jerzy Heyman developed the systematic sampling techniques that are at the heart of modern polling. The Survey Research Center of the Interuniversity Consortium for Political and Social Research at the University of Michigan is an outgrowth of the Agriculture program. (See NATIONAL ELECTION STUDIES.)

Pioneer pollsters George Gallup, Elmo Roper, and Archibald Crossley soon adopted the sampling methodology and used it successfully to predict Franklin D.

Roosevelt's LANDSLIDE victory over Alfred M. Landon in 1936. Twelve years later the still-young polling industry received a black eye with its almost unanimous prediction that Thomas E. Dewey would unseat President Harry S. Truman in the 1948 election.

The setback was only temporary; pollsters learned from their mistakes, and the activity grew into a respected and valued profession. It would be another two decades, however, before the news media began taking full advantage of the professional pollsters' generally successful methods of forecasting election results. *Washington Post* political reporter David S. Broder recalls in his 1987 book *Behind the Front Page* that in 1960 he camped out for a week in Beckley, West Virginia, to try to sense PUBLIC OPINION in the crucial presidential PRIMARY between Democrats John F. Kennedy and Hubert H. Humphrey. Although Humphrey was expected to defeat Kennedy in the state, which had only a 5 percent Catholic population, Broder found considerable support for Kennedy and he reported it in the paper he was then working for, the *Washington Star*.

Although Kennedy's "surprise" defeat of Humphrey vindicated his reporting, Broder wrote, "I wish now I had used 'newspaper interviews' rather than 'polling' to describe what I did, for there was nothing scientifically random about the selection of those 112 people [I interviewed]."

Broder had used methods pioneered by Samuel Lubell, a journalist who knocked on doors in selected precincts to sample public opinion in an election. At that time the major pollsters such as Gallup and Roper were still developing their highly accurate methods of political polling, and few newspapers used their services.

Today the television networks and most large newspapers have their own polling operations, sometimes in association with another media company or a professional polling organization. The *Washington Post* began systematic polling in 1977.

Scientific polling has not entirely replaced informal means of gauging how people feel about candidates. The print and electronic media still use straw polls or *man-in-the-street* interviews for that purpose, even though they have little validity as genuine polls.

A *preference poll*, also known as a *trial heat*, is another unscientific type of opinion sampling. It usually takes the form of a mock election in which people are asked who they would vote for if the election were held tomorrow. As commonly used today, trial heat usually refers to a contest between candidates of opposing parties. Preference polls measure public attitudes toward candidates of the same party, as in a primary.

A notorious type of "poll," the PUSH POLL, is not a poll at all but rather a form of NEGATIVE CAMPAIGNING. Candidates or their consultants may employ the technique to discredit opponents. They use computer technology to dial hundreds or thousands of voters in the guise of a poll and ask the respondents if they would vote for the opponent if they knew he or she was a communist, a child abuser, or some other disreputable type of person, whether or not that characterization has any basis in fact.

Most of the legitimate types of polls are used to forecast results weeks or months in advance of an election. Two other types, EXIT POLLS and ENTRANCE POLLS, do not come into play until ELECTION DAY. Then the news media send representatives to ask people leaving the polls how they voted, or people approaching the voting station or caucus auditorium how they plan to vote.

Exit polls, the more common of the two, came into widespread use in the 1980s. In recent years exit polling has been a joint effort of the Associated Press and the broadcast networks through an organization called the Voter News Service and using the logo VNS.

Because they are based on responses from people who have actually voted, or are on their way to vote, exit and entrance polls are highly accurate and are controversial for that very reason. There have been complaints that they influence the outcome of the election if they are broadcast while some polls are still open.

## Fourteenth Amendment

*See* BLACK SUFFRAGE.

# Franchise

The American electorate has changed markedly over the years as it has grown in size. Since the early days of the nation, when the franchise—eligibility to vote—was limited to the property-owning class of males, one voting barrier after another has fallen to pressures for wider suffrage.

First unpropertied males, then black men, all women, and finally young people pushed for the franchise. By the early 1970s almost every restriction on voting had been removed, and virtually every adult citizen eighteen years of age and older had won the RIGHT TO VOTE. (See BLACK SUFFRAGE; WOMEN'S SUFFRAGE; YOUTH SUFFRAGE.)

During the first few decades of the Republic, all thirteen of the original states limited the franchise to property holders and taxpayers. Seven states required ownership of land, or a life estate as opposed to a leased estate, as a qualification for voting. The other six states permitted persons to qualify by substituting either evidence of ownership of certain amounts of personal property or payment of taxes.

The framers of the Constitution apparently were content to have the states limit the right to vote to adult males who had a real stake in good government. This meant, in most cases, persons in the upper economic levels. Not wishing to discriminate against any particular type of property owner (uniform federal voting standards inevitably would have conflicted with some of the state standards), the Constitutional Convention of 1787 adopted without dissent the recommendation of its Committee of Detail that the states be allowed to set their own qualifications for voting. As embodied in the Constitution, this provision (Article I, section 2) states that persons eligible to elect the House of Representatives "shall have the Qualifications requisite for Electors of the most numerous Branch of the State Legislature."

Under this provision, with states controlling the qualifications, fewer than half of the adult white men in the United States were eligible to vote in federal elections. Because no state made women eligible (although states were not forbidden to do so), only one white adult in four qualified to go to the polls. Slaves—black or Indian—were ineligible, and they formed almost one-fifth of the American population as enumerated in the CENSUS of 1790. Also ineligible were white indentured servants, whose status during their period of service was little better than that of the slaves.

Actually, these early state practices represented a liberalization of restrictions on voting that had prevailed at one time in the colonial period. Roman Catholics had been disfranchised in almost every colony, Jews in most colonies, Quakers and Baptists in some. In Rhode Island Jews remained legally ineligible to vote until 1842.

For half a century before the Civil War there was a steady broadening of the electorate. The new western settlements supplied a stimulus to the principle of universal male suffrage for whites, and Jacksonian democracy encouraged its acceptance. Gradually, the seven states making property ownership a condition for voting substituted a taxpaying requirement: Delaware in 1792, Maryland in 1810, Connecticut in 1818, Massachusetts in 1821, New York in 1821, Rhode Island in 1842, and Virginia in 1850. By the middle of the nineteenth century most states had removed even the taxpaying qualifications, but some retained LITERACY TESTS and the POLL TAX well into the twentieth century.

On the federal level the Constitution has been amended five times to override state qualifications denying the franchise to certain categories of people. The Fourteenth Amendment, ratified in 1868, directed Congress to reduce the number of representatives from any state that disfranchised adult male citizens for any reason other than commission of a crime. No such reduction was ever made, even though a number of states effectively prevented African American men from voting by literacy tests, intimidation, and other means.

The Fifteenth Amendment, ratified in 1870, prohibited denial of the right to vote "on account of race, color or previous condition of servitude," and the Nineteenth Amendment in 1920 prohibited denial of that right "on account of sex."

The Twenty-fourth Amendment, which came into effect in 1964, barred denial of the right to vote in any

*A print commemorating a celebration held in Baltimore on May 19, 1870, in honor of the Fifteenth Amendment, which had been ratified February 3. The intent of the constitutional amendment was subverted for nearly a century, especially in the South, through poll taxes, literacy tests, and intimidation. Source: Library of Congress*

federal election "by reason of failure to pay any poll tax or other tax." The poll tax, especially in the South, posed a significant barrier to voting by the poor, both black and white. Finally, in 1971 the Twenty-sixth Amendment lowered the voting age to eighteen in federal, state, and local elections.

Congress in the 1950s and 1960s enacted a series of statutes to enforce the Fifteenth Amendment's guarantee against racial discrimination in voting. The most significant was the VOTING RIGHTS ACT of 1965, which resulted in a sharp increase in VOTER REGISTRATION and VOTER TURNOUT among African Americans.

A federal law passed in 1970 nullified state residence requirements of longer than thirty days for voting in presidential elections, suspended literacy tests for a five-year period (the suspension was made permanent in 1975), and lowered the minimum voting age to eighteen years from twenty-one, the requirement then in effect in all but a few states.

A 1970 Supreme Court ruling upheld the voting-age change for federal elections but invalidated it for state and local elections. In the same decision the Court upheld the provision on residence requirements and sustained the suspension of literacy tests with respect to both state and local elections. The Twenty-sixth Amendment was ratified six months after the Court's decision, ensuring the same minimum age for all elections.

The right to vote in presidential elections was extended to citizens of the DISTRICT OF COLUMBIA by the Twenty-third Amendment, ratified in 1961. Residents of the nation's capital had been disfranchised from national elections except for a brief period in the 1870s when they elected a nonvoting delegate to the House of Representatives.

In general, by the two hundredth anniversary of the nation in 1976, the only remaining restrictions prevented voting by the insane, convicted felons, and otherwise eligible voters who were unable to meet short residence requirements. By 1992 the American electorate, as measured by the 104 million people who voted for president, had exceeded 100 million for the first time. (See table, Growing Franchise in the United States, 1930–1996, page 460.)

*In 1848 the Free Soil Party nominated former Democratic president Martin Van Buren for the presidency.* Source: Library of Congress

## Free Soil Party (1848–1852)

Born as a result of opposition to the extension of slavery into the newly acquired Southwest territories, the Free Soil Party was launched formally at a convention in Buffalo, New York, in August 1848. The Free Soilers were composed of antislavery elements from the Democratic and Whig Parties as well as remnants of the Liberal Party. Representatives from all the northern states and three BORDER STATES attended the Buffalo convention, where the slogan "free soil, free speech, free labor and free men" was adopted. This slogan expressed the antislavery sentiment of the Free Soilers as well as the desire for cheap Western land.

The convention selected former Democratic president Martin Van Buren (1837–1841) as the party's presidential candidate and Charles Francis Adams, the son of President John Quincy Adams (1825–1829), as his running mate.

In the 1848 election the Free Soil ticket received 291,501 votes (10.1 percent of the popular vote) but was unable to carry a single state. The party did better at the congressional level, winning nine House seats and holding the balance of power in the organization of the closely divided new Congress.

The 1848 election marked the peak of the party's influence. With the passage of compromise legislation on slavery in 1850, the Free Soilers lost their basic issue and began a rapid decline. The party ran its second and last national ticket in 1852, headed by John Hale, who received 155,210 votes (4.9 percent of the popular vote). As in 1848 the Free Soil national ticket failed to carry a single state.

Although the party went out of existence shortly thereafter, its program and constituency were absorbed by the Republican Party, whose birth and growth dramatically paralleled the resurgence of the slavery issue in the mid-1850s.

---

## Freeholder

Possession of property was a common requisite for the RIGHT TO VOTE in the formative years of the United States. The Constitution left it to the states to determine who could vote, and all states at first restricted that right to white men. Many states also limited the vote to men of property or freeholders.

Property qualifications had existed in all the colonies and endured afterward, although they varied from state to state. Colonial restrictions tended to be harsher than those adopted by the states and often were based on a measure of real estate ownership. It was widely thought that only a man with a "stake in society" would vote responsibly, and property was tangible evidence that he held such a stake.

Actual ownership of real estate was not always required. Lifetime tenure as a leaseholder sometimes sufficed. In Virginia—the home of some of the most important members of the 1787 Constitutional Convention and four of the first five presidents—property possession had been a prerequisite for voting since 1677. From 1705 until 1736 the laws were quite liberal: any male tenant who held land for life (his own or that of another person such as his wife or child) was considered a freeholder and could vote. Leasing property for the duration of one's own lifetime or for that of a family member was the equivalent of owning property.

From 1736 onward, the Virginia definition of freeholder was more restrictive. To vote, a man living in the country had to hold twenty-five acres of cultivated land with a house, or one hundred acres (changed to fifty in 1762) of uncleared land. A man living in town had to hold a house with a lot. By the standards of the time, those requirements were not excessive.

The American Revolution brought no suffrage reform to Virginia, although it did to other states. The Virginia Constitution of 1776 stated that voting requirements "shall remain as exercised at present." Even those

who paid taxes or fought in the militia could not vote unless they held the requisite amount of land. By 1800 Virginia was one of five states that retained real estate property qualifications. (At the other extreme, four states had established universal suffrage by 1800.) While various other states allowed the ownership of personal property, such as a horse-drawn carriage, or the payment of taxes to substitute for holding real estate, Virginia held on to its old property qualifications until 1830.

Property requirements of one kind or another were not abandoned by all the states until 1856. But because the United States was predominantly a middle-class society with fairly widespread ownership of property, such qualifications were not so significant a limit to voting as they may first have appeared.

---

## Front-Loading

The clustering of PRIMARY and caucus elections early in the presidential election year has come to be known as *front-loading.* Opinion on whether it is a healthy or unhealthy trend depends largely on how it affects the candidate or state at hand.

Candidates who start early and begin to build up a BANDWAGON EFFECT with primary or caucus victories tend to benefit from front-loading, although it may force them to conduct a campaign in many places at once. Those who delay entering a race may find the opportunity lost because the crucial primaries are past.

States that resist the trend and schedule late primaries, which give the voters more time to study the candidates and the issues, may reduce their influence on presidential nominations. On the other hand, smaller states that join in front-loading may be ignored by candidates who need to concentrate on certain contests, especially the important NEW HAMPSHIRE PRIMARY and IOWA CAUCUS, which traditionally lead off the schedule and weed out the weaker candidates.

Whatever its benefits or detriments, front-loading has resisted all efforts to reverse it. In 1968 seventeen states held presidential primaries, with only New

Hampshire's held before April. In 1996 there were forty-two primaries, with most (twenty-nine) held in March or before. The last few primaries were held June 4.

By March 26 Robert J. Dole had locked up the Republican nomination against President Bill Clinton, who was unopposed for renomination. Both nominations were known more than four months before the NATIONAL PARTY CONVENTIONS, even though thirteen states had yet to elect the convention DELEGATES who, technically, would decide on the nominations.

As the major parties prepared for the last presidential election of the twentieth century, at least one of them clearly regarded front-loading as a detriment. As the loser in the presidential elections of 1992 and 1996, while keeping the control of Congress won in 1994, the REPUBLICAN PARTY set its sights on the front-loading phenomenon. Even before the 1996 primary season was over, the GOP national committee created a task force to consider changes in the nominating process, including a less compressed primary schedule.

Haley Barbour, who was chairman of the Republican National Committee, said, "If the process is so compressed . . . voters don't have time for reflection. Compression and front-loading [work] to the benefit of the best-known candidates."

Republican action on the primary schedule marked a departure from the party's laissez faire approach to the nominating process. Since 1968 the Democrats had pioneered reforms in the process, with the GOP and the states compelled to follow suit in many cases. (See PRESIDENTIAL PRIMARIES; PRESIDENTIAL SELECTION REFORMS.)

But in the 1990s the Democrats seemed content with the status quo, while the Republicans chafed under it. The 1996 Republican convention approved a rule change dealing with front-loading or "March Madness" as it was also called. The new rule awards bonus delegates to states that schedule primaries or caucuses later in the spring. Waiting until March 15 earns a 5 percent bonus in seats; waiting until April 15 earns 7.5 percent; and states holding primaries May 15 or later gain 10 percent more delegates. The delegate bonus, however, apparently had little appeal for California, where the departing Republican governor, Pete Wilson, signed legislation moving the state's 2000 presidential primary to March 7.

The front-loaded schedule, said Mark Siegel, former executive director of the Democratic National Committee, was tailor-made for "someone who is well known and well financed and can compete in thirty-five states in twenty-eight days." Little-known, DARK-HORSE candidates were unlikely to successfully challenge the FRONT-RUNNER for the Democratic nomination, as did George McGovern in 1972 and Jimmy Carter in 1976. Back then, the primary schedule was more spread out, giving the less well known candidates more time to raise money and achieve momentum after doing well in the early rounds.

The longer primary season was a mixed blessing. It was also more divisive, exhausted the candidates, and caused the voters to lose interest, prompting the Democratic Party in 1980 to restrict the delegate-selection period to three months, ending in early June. The new rule exempted the New Hampshire primary and Iowa Caucus, allowing them to be held before the "window" opened.

A group of mostly southern states soon began holding their primaries on the same day a few weeks after the New Hampshire primary. Dubbed SUPER TUESDAY, the cooperative effort peaked in 1988 with twenty-two states participating. In 1996 Super Tuesday (seven primaries on March 12) was surpassed by the ill-named JUNIOR TUESDAY, with eight primaries on March 5. Two southern states moved up the GOP primaries: South Carolina Republicans voted on March 2, a Saturday, and Georgia Republicans voted on Junior Tuesday.

The biggest change in 1996 was California's shift of its primary from June to March 26. The change increased the importance of early fund raising to help pay for candidates' television advertising in the most populous state.

In all, 13,992,204 voters took part in Republican primaries in 1996, and 10,962,552 voted in the uncontested Democratic primaries. Of the total GOP primary votes, 64.5 percent were cast before April. Only 23.1 percent of the Democratic vote was cast before April. The disparity helps to explain the Republicans' heightened concern over front-loading.

The early contests have a winnowing effect that quickly narrows the field of candidates. In 1996 the New Hampshire primary attracted eight major candidates hoping to dislodge Clinton from the White House in November: Lamar Alexander, Patrick J. Buchanan, Robert J. Dole, Robert K. Dornan, Malcolm S. "Steve" Forbes Jr., Phil Gramm, Alan Keyes, and Richard G. Lugar. By the time of the Pennsylvania primary—the only one in April—all but Buchanan, Dole, Dornan, and Keyes had dropped out of the race.

For contributors, the winnowing process serves a useful purpose. It helps to indicate which candidates have a chance of staying the course and therefore are worth an investment in his or her campaign. Dole lost the New Hampshire primary to Buchanan, but he won most of the others after that, giving him a fund-raising advantage. Buchanan and Forbes were the only other candidates to win any of the Republican primaries or first-round caucuses.

## Front-Runner

The leading candidate in a political race is called the *front-runner*. Usually the term is applied when there are several candidates, as in a PRIMARY contest for a party's nomination, rather than in a general election face-off between the two major party candidates.

*Thomas E. Dewey was a perennial front-runner for the Republican presidential nomination and for the presidency. In May 1948, while campaigning in Grants Pass, Oregon, he was escorted by members of the Oregon Cavemen Club. Source: AP/Wide World*

Becoming the front-runner can be a mixed blessing. A candidate wants to be perceived by the voters and political activists as a winner. But if he or she emerges from the pack as the candidate to beat, the other candidates are likely to "gang up" and try to take away the leader's front-runner status.

In presidential politics a perennial front-runner was Thomas E. Dewey, the crime-busting district attorney who was elected the Republican governor of New York in 1942. Two years earlier Dewey, then thirty-eight years old, was a prime contender for the GOP nomination to oppose Franklin D. Roosevelt's unprecedented bid for a third term as president. At the NATIONAL PARTY CONVENTION, Dewey won the first ballot but lost on the second and steadily weakened after that. His candidacy for the 1940 nomination ultimately was overwhelmed by the DARK HORSE popularity of Indiana businessman Wendell L. Willkie.

As governor in 1944, Dewey was the clear front-runner for his party's presidential nomination, which he won with only one dissenting convention vote. But Roosevelt defeated Dewey to gain a fourth term, which he did not live to complete.

In 1948 Dewey was again the front-runner for the nomination, and he won it after his opponents withdrew following the second ballot. Although Dewey was widely favored to win the November election, President Harry S. Truman embarrassed the forecasters with a surprise victory. Dewey was never again a front-runner for national office.

Jimmy Carter in 1976 is an example of a candidate who successfully turned the front-runner position into an asset. As an obscure former governor of Georgia, Carter pursued an outsider CAMPAIGN STRATEGY to attract public attention and establish his credentials as a potential national leader. After winning the NEW HAMPSHIRE PRIMARY and other early primaries and caucuses, Carter arrived at the Democratic convention with the nomination locked up.

Similarly in 1992 another relatively unknown southern governor, Bill Clinton of Arkansas, dubbed himself the "comeback kid" after he lost the important New Hampshire primary and still managed to become the front-runner for the Democratic presidential nomina-

tion. He went to the convention with enough delegates for a first-ballot victory.

## Fund Raising

*See* CAMPAIGN FINANCE; HARD MONEY; SOFT MONEY.

## Fusionism

In modern American politics the term *fusionism*—meaning candidates running under several party labels at the same time—is associated chiefly with New York. State law there permitted multiple-party nominations after other states prohibited them.

For most of the twentieth century the Democratic machine known as Tammany Hall so dominated New York City politics that reform candidates had little chance of election unless they formed a COALITION with other parties. Between 1901 and 1933 New Yorkers elected three fusion mayors, in addition to two elected in the late 1800s.

The most famous of the five was Fiorello La Guardia, a Republican who won in 1933 with 446,833 votes in the GOP column and 421,689 in the City Fusion Party column. La Guardia was reelected in 1937 and 1941, but in those elections the City Fusion Party votes added insignificantly to his victory margin.

The last Fusion Party candidate appeared on New York mayoral ballots in 1957. In 1981, however, former U.S. representative Edward I. Koch was elected mayor as the nominee of both the Democratic and Republican parties. Multiple-party candidacies are still common in New York elections for Congress and state offices.

In 1900 the Democratic nominee for president, William Jennings Bryan, was also the candidate of the PEOPLE'S (POPULIST) PARTY's Fusionist Faction. The Populists' Anti-Fusionist Faction opposed joining with the Democrats in 1896 and ran its own candidate, Wharton Barker, in 1900. Republican William McKinley defeated Bryan in both elections.

As in New York, THIRD PARTIES find it advantageous to ally themselves with another party in nominating a candidate. The Supreme Court, however, has upheld an antifusion statute similar to those on the books in forty states. The Court ruled in a 1997 Minnesota case, *McKenna v. Twin Cities Area New Party,* that the state's ban on fusionism does not interfere with the free association rights of third party members. A federal district court had held that the prohibition on multiple-party nominations violated the First Amendment.

Fusionism is related to the practices of cross-filing (seeking the nomination of more than one party) and cross-endorsing (a party's endorsing of another party's candidate). (See PARTY ENDORSEMENT OF CANDIDATES.)

California permitted cross-filing until 1959. In 1946, for example, Republican governor Earl Warren also won the Democratic nomination and easily won reelection.

Because cross-filing and fusionism tend to weaken PARTY IDENTIFICATION BY VOTERS, the political parties that dominate the American TWO-PARTY SYSTEM often exert pressure to have state legislatures prohibit such practices.

# G

## Gerrymander

The term *gerrymander* originated in 1812 to describe the practice of manipulating election DISTRICT boundaries to benefit a certain INCUMBENT or political party. Today the term is most often used in connection with controversies over RACIAL REDISTRICTING.

Gov. Elbridge Gerry of Massachusetts, a former vice president of the United States, inadvertently gave the practice his name. When his DEMOCRATIC-REPUBLICAN PARTY carved out a misshapen Essex County district, artist Gilbert Stuart penciled a head, wings, and claws onto the district map and exclaimed, "That will do for a salamander!" Whereupon editor Benjamin Russell replied, "Better say a Gerrymander!"

In the ensuing 1812 election the opposing FEDERALISTS, packed largely into the outlying district, won 51 percent of the vote but gained only eleven of forty Senate seats. Politicians ever since have tried to emulate Gerry's success with the mapping process.

Whether gerrymandering is legitimate, however, has never been settled. By one argument it is unconstitutional because it can deprive voters of the right to make an effective choice between candidates of both parties. If a district is set up to make election of a Democrat virtually inevitable, then Republicans there have lost the right to cast anything more than a symbolic vote for their candidate.

The Supreme Court has been reluctant to address gerrymandering directly, viewing the issue as a political question for governors and legislatures to address. So long as districts are sufficiently similar in population, the Court has been reluctant to judge whether they were unfairly gerrymandered, except where racial discrimination is at issue.

Until the 1960s the Court avoided all types of REAPPORTIONMENT AND REDISTRICTING cases. In *Colegrove v. Green* (1946) Justice Felix Frankfurter wrote, "It is hostile to a democratic system to involve the judiciary in the politics of the people. . . . Courts ought not to enter this political thicket."

But by 1962 the Court had changed its collective mind. In BAKER V. CARR it ruled that malapportionment is a matter for judicial review, while leaving open the standards to be applied in such cases. A year later, in *Gray v. Sanders,* the Court began spelling out the most basic of those standards: ONE PERSON, ONE VOTE. Different-sized populations in a state's legislative districts violate the principle of equal protection of the laws under the Fourteenth Amendment and therefore are unconstitutional, the Court said. In 1964 it extended the one-person, one-vote test to congressional elections, and the federal VOTING RIGHTS ACT of 1965 further reinforced the notion of equality in districting.

In 1986, however, the Supreme Court indicated that gerrymandering was subject to constitutional challenges even where the one-person, one-vote standard had been met, or at least was not at issue. In *Davis v. Bandemer,* a case involving Indiana's state legislative districts, the Court ruled that gerrymanders may be challenged for unfairly discriminating against political parties. In this case, the Court ruled, the Indiana plan would stand because it takes more than one election to prove that such a plan is discriminatory.

The *Davis* case arose from the redistricting plan adopted by the Indiana General Assembly in 1981. The Republican Party, in control of the governorship and both chambers of the legislature, redrew election districts based on 1980 CENSUS data. Acting in secret with computerized data on the political makeup of each re-

*Before the Massachusetts election of 1812, Gov. Elbridge Gerry signed a bill redrawing the state senatorial districts so that his party, the Democratic-Republicans, would be likely to win more seats than their actual numbers warranted. One of the new districts looked like a salamander and was quickly dubbed a "gerrymander," a term that continues to be used to describe a redistricting plan designed to benefit one party. Source: Library of Congress*

gion, the Republicans offered a plan two days before the end of the legislative session and passed it by a party-line vote. No public hearings were held, and Democratic legislators had no opportunity to participate in the design process. They were given only forty hours to come up with their own plan for the state's four thousand precincts.

Republicans were frank about what they had done. "The name of the game is to keep us in power," one member said. The legislators announced that the plan was designed to yield fifty-six "safe" Republican seats and thirty Democratic seats in the lower house, with the remainder being "tossups." In the state senate the Republicans expected the plan to give them thirty seats to the Democrats' eight to ten.

On appeal by the Democrats, the federal district court examined the extent of the plan's manipulations.

New election districts dissected counties and townships into strange shapes lacking common political bonds, "with no concern for any adherence to principles of community interest," the court said. Nor did the new boundaries for senate districts necessarily coincide with the districts for house seats, adding to potential voter confusion. The MULTIMEMBER districts established for some house seats stacked Democrats into districts where their majority would be overwhelming, while fragmenting other traditionally Democratic districts, so Republicans would stand a better chance in WINNER-TAKE-ALL contests among multiple candidates.

The 1982 elections demonstrated the success of the plan, with all one hundred seats up for election. Although Democratic candidates received about 53 percent of the popular vote and Republicans, 48 percent, Democratic candidates took only forty-three seats compared with fifty-seven for the Republicans. In some areas where Democrats received 47 percent of the vote, they won only three of twenty-one seats.

The special three-judge district court panel invalidated the 1981 reapportionment on grounds that it violated the principle of equal protection of the laws and presented a controversy that courts could settle. The court ordered the legislature to prepare a new plan for future elections.

Because the jurisdiction of federal courts does not extend to political questions, the first issue addressed by the Supreme Court in *Davis* was whether the Court could decide the case. By a 6–3 vote, the Court found "such political gerrymandering to be justiciable," but it reversed the district court ruling as having applied "an insufficiently demanding standard in finding unconstitutional vote dilution."

The opinion by Justice Byron R. White reviewed *Baker v. Carr* and other one-person, one-vote rulings to establish that it had previously indicated that reapportionment cases could present justiciable issues. "Our past decisions also make clear that even where there is no population deviation among the districts, racial gerrymandering presents a justiciable equal protection claim," the Court added. Acknowledging that it had often upheld lower courts when they dismissed political cases as nonjusticiable, the Court said that "we are not bound by those decisions." The decision resolved the apparent inconsistency in favor of justiciability, whether the violation of the equal protection claim is made by a political or by a racial group.

Justice Sandra Day O'Connor dissented in part. She argued that judicial review of purely political redistricting cases will "lead to political instability and judicial malaise. If members of the major political parties are protected by the Equal Protection Clause from dilution of their voting strength, then members of every identifiable group that possesses distinctive interests should be able to bring similar claims."

By a separate 7–2 vote the Court decided against invalidating the Indiana reapportionment scheme. It disagreed with the district court finding of an equal protection violation based on the results of a single election. Indiana is a swing state, White noted. "Voters sometimes prefer Democratic candidates, and sometimes Republicans." The district court did not rule out the possibility that in the next few elections the Democrats could win control of the assembly. "Nor was there any finding that the 1981 reapportionment plan would consign the Democrats to a minority status throughout the 1980's. . . . Without findings of this nature, the District Court erred in concluding that the 1981 Act violated the Equal Protection Clause," the Court said.

Although *Davis v. Bandemer* was expected to open the door to other challenges to political gerrymandering plans, the Court declined to become involved in 1989 when it reaffirmed without comment a lower court's decision to uphold California's congressional map, widely recognized as a classic example of a partisan gerrymander. As of early 1999 the Court had not taken up any other such challenges. Unlike malapportionment, nonracial gerrymandering still had not been definitively prohibited by law.

## Get Out the Vote

The low VOTER TURNOUT rate in U.S. elections prompts widespread efforts to get more people to the polls on ELECTION DAY, either on their own initiative or with some incentive such as a free ride to the voting station. National, state, and local organizations sponsor get-out-the-vote drives before elections, sometimes with success but more often with little appreciable effect on the numbers of participating voters.

Political scientists cite voter apathy and lack of interest as the major causes of persistent low turnout rates. PUBLIC OPINION polls show that many Americans find politics boring. (See zzz.)

Presidential elections generally spark more interest than MIDTERM ELECTIONS, yet with few exceptions the turnout in presidential elections has been dropping steadily since 1960 when 62.8 percent of the voting age population voted. In 1996 the figure fell to 49.0 percent. (See table, Growing Franchise in the United States, 1930–1996, page 460.)

To combat the trend, political parties and organizations such as the League of Women Voters appeal to the public's sense of civic duty with a wide array of advertising campaigns in the print and electronic media. Readers and viewers are bombarded with messages urging, "Vote for the Candidate of Your Choice. But Vote!"

With their large numbers of officials and members, labor unions have been able to operate phone banks that blanket areas with calls asking people to vote and sometimes offering transportation to the polls. The AFL CIO, as part of its COALITION with the Democratic Party, has for years conducted drives to get out the vote, almost exclusively for Democratic candidates.

With the rise of POLITICAL ADVERTISING on television large-scale campaign parades and rallies, once major components of get-out-the-vote efforts, have become largely things of the past. The televised NATIONAL PARTY CONVENTIONS are among the few remaining collective events used to whip up enthusiasm for candidates and voting.

Individual candidates, sometimes with party assistance, tailor get-out-the-vote activities to their own needs, concentrating their resources in areas where their supporters are most numerous. Federal CAMPAIGN FINANCE law permits the parties to use unlimited SOFT MONEY contributions for get-out-the-vote drives and

*A bus provided by the Sixth Avenue Baptist Church of Birmingham, Alabama, gets African American voters to the polls on primary election day in 1972. Low voter turnout prompts widespread efforts, such as free rides, to get more people to the polls.* Source: National Archives

other party-building activities not associated with any particular candidate.

Such drives are generally thought of as patriotic, public service endeavors because nonvoting is considered undemocratic and unhealthy for the electoral process. But that view is not universally accepted. Some authorities on government feel that uninterested persons should not be cajoled into voting because they are apt to make poor choices if they have not taken the time to study the issues and the candidates' qualifications.

## Governor

Next to the president, governors are the most powerful elected officials in the United States. Some preside over a state, such as Ohio, that is larger than many foreign countries. Some deal with a legislature, such as New Hampshire's, that has almost as many members as the U.S. House of Representatives.

Many regard executive experience as a governor as more akin to that of the president than service as a legis-

lator, military commander, or business leader, which helps to explain why three of the four presidents since 1977 were governors or former governors. In all, sixteen U.S. presidents have been state governors.

Like the president, a governor must depend on political skills to achieve a record of accomplishment in office. Many have served as a STATE LEGISLATOR and therefore are acquainted with the legislative process. Of the 225 elected governors in office between 1970 and 1994, forty-three or 19 percent had been state legislators just prior to becoming governor.

As political scientist Larry Sabato has observed, today's governors are a far cry from the glad-handing "good-time Charlies" of the past. He described the new breed as being, for the most part, "vigorous, incisive, and thoroughly trained leaders."

Governors' duties vary in detail from state to state, but basically they are the same. Most state constitutions today have the "strong governor, weak legislature" system, which is the reverse of the situation that prevailed in the "good-time Charlie" era, the first half of the twentieth century.

*Nellie Tayloe Ross, right, director of the Bureau of the Mint, is all smiles as Vice President and Mrs. Alben Barkley present President Harry S. Truman with the gold medal for distinguished service in Congress. Ross was one of the first two female governors elected in the United States, both in 1924. Source: Harry S. Truman Library*

The governor's chief responsibility is to enforce the laws of the state. Other duties include reporting to the legislature on the "state of the state"; preparing the state's operating and capital budgets, along with a tax budget to provide the revenue; appointing department heads and other officials, often subject to legislative confirmation; signing or vetoing new laws; participating in the federal grant-in-aid system; issuing pardons of criminals, sometimes in conjunction with a pardoning board; and commanding the state militia.

Unlike the federal system, in which the president makes major appointments subject to Senate confirmation, some state appointments are made by the legislature or other officials, subject to confirmation by the governor. Political scientist Thad L. Beyle, using Council of State Governments data, found that in most states in 1994 someone other than the governor appointed top officials in six major areas—corrections, education below college level, health, highways, public utilities regulation, and welfare—with the approval of the governor, the legislature, or both. Only in Ohio could the governor appoint all six of these officials with no confirmation needed; in Pennsylvania, four of the six required senate confirmation.

Most governors have long had a power that the president gained only recently (and temporarily)—the line-item veto, which is the authority to disapprove individual items in an appropriations bill without vetoing the whole bill. As president, former California governor Ronald Reagan was denied the line-item veto by a Democratic Congress. But a Republican Congress granted it to Democratic president Bill Clinton, former governor of Arkansas. The U.S. Supreme Court ruled the presidential line-item veto unconstitutional in 1998.

Unlike the U.S. Constitution, most state constitutions require governors to sign a balanced budget. President Reagan, whose "supply-side economics" resulted in record-high federal deficits, often called for a balanced budget amendment for the United States, as did the congressional Republicans' "Contract with America" in 1994. Proposals for such an amendment did not receive the required two-thirds approval of Congress. (See MIDTERM ELECTIONS.)

Governors' salaries range from a high of $130,000 (New York) to a low of $58,310 (Montana). California, the most populous state (29.8 million), pays its governor $120,000. Wyoming, the smallest state in population (453,588), pays the governor $95,000. The Arkansas governor ranks second to the lowest in salary.

Campaigns for governor seats are expensive. In 1990 the average cost of thirty-six gubernatorial elections was $10.6 million. The California election alone cost $58.8 million; in Texas it was $55.9 million. Almost half the states (twenty-three) have some form of PUBLIC FINANCING of elections. Even more states (thirty-two) have CAMPAIGN FINANCE limitations on individual contributions, and forty-four limit corporate party contributions.

Governors in some states are elected in tandem with the LIEUTENANT GOVERNOR. Five states in 1994 had a governor and lieutenant governor elected as a team, much like the ballot pairing of the president and VICE PRESIDENT. The remaining forty-five states had either a governor–lieutenant governor ballot team that included other elective officials, such as the attorney general, or they had no team election.

## Governorship History

In the formative years of the United States, Americans looked with suspicion on the office of governor. To them, these officials were reminders of the British-appointed governors who symbolized the mother country's control and tyranny during the colonial era.

Colonial legislatures, on the other hand, had been able to assert control over appropriations and in this way became champions of colonial rights against the governors. After the Revolutionary War, when drawing up their constitutions, states gave most of the power to the legislative bodies and placed restrictions on the governors, including the term of office and the method of election.

For all their power today, governors still are on a tighter leash from the people than most other officials elected under our federal system of government. Presidents have been limited to two terms since 1951 by constitutional amendment, but the Supreme Court has nullified state efforts to impose TERM LIMITS on their members of Congress. By contrast, almost four-fifths of the states limit their governors to a single term or two consecutive terms. Almost all, however, have abandoned

### Party Lineup of Governors

The figures below show the number of governorships held by the two major parties after each election since 1950.

| Year | Democrat | Republican | Independent |
|------|----------|------------|-------------|
| 1950 | 23 | 25 | 0 |
| 1952 | 18 | 30 | 0 |
| 1954 | 27 | 21 | 0 |
| 1956 | 29 | 19 | 0 |
| 1958 | 35 | 14 | 0 |
| 1960 | 34 | 16 | 0 |
| 1962 | 34 | 16 | 0 |
| 1964 | 33 | 17 | 0 |
| 1966 | 25 | 25 | 0 |
| 1968 | 19 | 31 | 0 |
| 1970 | 29 | 21 | 0 |
| 1972 | 31 | 19 | 0 |
| 1974 | 36 | 13 | 1 |
| 1976 | 37 | 12 | 1 |
| 1978 | 32 | 18 | 0 |
| 1980 | 26 | 24 | 0 |
| 1982 | 34 | 16 | 0 |
| 1984 | 34 | 16 | 0 |
| 1986 | 26 | 24 | 0 |
| 1988 | 28 | 22 | 0 |
| 1990 | 27 | 21 | 2 |
| 1992 | 30 | 18 | 2 |
| 1994 | 19 | 30 | 1 |
| 1996 | 18 | 31 | 1 |
| 1998 | 17 | 31 | 2 |

*Sources: Book of the States, 1996–1997*, vol. 31 (Lexington, Ky.: Council of State Governments, 1996); *Congressional Quarterly Weekly*, November 7, 1998, 3000.

the original one- or two-year terms in favor of four-year terms that required fewer elections and permitted more stability in the nation's statehouses.

For years Democrats held most governorships, but the reverse has been the case since 1994. After the 1998 election thirty-one governors were Republicans, seventeen were Democrats, and two (in Maine and Minnesota ) were independents. (See table, Party Lineup of Governors.)

The first female governors were elected in 1924, four years after the Nineteenth Amendment granted WOMEN'S SUFFRAGE in every state. Elected that year to succeed their husbands were Nellie Tayloe Ross of Wyoming and Miriam "Ma" Ferguson of Texas, both Democrats.

The first popularly elected African American governor was L. Douglas Wilder of Virginia, Democrat, who served from 1990 to 1994. The first two Hispanic governors were elected in 1974: Jerry Apodaca in New Mexico and Raul Castro in Arizona, both Democrats. Gary Locke, a Democrat of Chinese descent, became the first Asian American governor with his election in Washington in 1996.

## Length of Terms

As of 1789, the four New England states—Connecticut, Massachusetts, New Hampshire, and Rhode Island (Vermont was admitted in 1791 and Maine in 1820)—held gubernatorial elections every year. Some of the Middle Atlantic states favored somewhat longer terms;

**Length of Governor Terms**

| State | 1900 | 1996 | Year of Change to Longer Term | State | 1900 | 1996 | Year of Change to Longer Term |
|---|---|---|---|---|---|---|---|
| Alabama | 2 | 4 | 1902 | Montana | 4 | 4 | — |
| Alaska[1] | — | 4 | — | Nebraska | 2 | 4 | 1966 |
| Arizona[1] | — | 4 | 1970 | Nevada | 4 | 4 | — |
| Arkansas | 2 | 4 | 1986 | New Hampshire | 2 | 2 | — |
| California | 4 | 4 | — | New Jersey | 3 | 4 | 1949 |
| Colorado | 2 | 4 | 1958 | New Mexico[1] | — | 4 | 1970 |
| Connecticut | 2 | 4 | 1950 | New York | 2 | 4 | 1938 |
| Delaware | 4 | 4 | — | North Carolina | 4 | 4 | — |
| Florida | 4 | 4 | — | North Dakota | 2 | 4 | 1964 |
| Georgia | 2 | 4 | 1942 | Ohio | 2 | 4 | 1958 |
| Hawaii[1] | — | 4 | — | Oklahoma[1] | — | 4 | — |
| Idaho | 2 | 4 | 1946 | Oregon | 4 | 4 | — |
| Illinois | 4 | 4 | — | Pennsylvania | 4 | 4 | — |
| Indiana | 4 | 4 | — | Rhode Island[3] | 1 | 4 | 1912, 1994 |
| Iowa | 2 | 4 | 1974 | South Carolina | 2 | 4 | 1926 |
| Kansas | 2 | 4 | 1974 | South Dakota | 2 | 4 | 1974 |
| Kentucky | 4 | 4 | — | Tennessee | 2 | 4 | 1954 |
| Louisiana | 4 | 4 | — | Texas | 2 | 4 | 1974 |
| Maine | 2 | 4 | 1958 | Utah | 4 | 4 | — |
| Maryland | 4 | 4 | — | Vermont | 2 | 2 | — |
| Massachusetts[2] | 1 | 4 | 1920, 1966 | Virginia | 4 | 4 | — |
| Michigan | 2 | 4 | 1966 | Washington | 4 | 4 | — |
| Minnesota | 2 | 4 | 1962 | West Virginia | 4 | 4 | — |
| Mississippi | 4 | 4 | — | Wisconsin | 2 | 4 | 1970 |
| Missouri | 4 | 4 | — | Wyoming | 4 | 4 | — |

Sources: Book of the States, 1996–1997, vol. 31 (Lexington, Ky.: Council of State Governments, 1996); Congressional Quarterly Weekly, November 7, 1998, 3000.

1. Oklahoma was admitted to the Union in 1907, Arizona and New Mexico in 1912, and Alaska and Hawaii in 1959. Oklahoma, Alaska, and Hawaii have always had four-year gubernatorial terms; Arizona began with a two-year term and switched to four years in 1970. New Mexico (1912) began with a four-year term, changed to two years in 1916, and back to four years in 1970.

2. Massachusetts switched from a one-year term to a two-year term in 1920 and to a four-year term in 1966.

3. Rhode Island switched from a one- to a two-year term in 1912 and to a four-year term in 1994.

New York and Pennsylvania had three-year terms for their governors, although New Jersey instituted a one-year term. The BORDER and southern states had a mix: Maryland and North Carolina governors served a one-year term, South Carolina had a two-year term, and Delaware, Virginia, and Georgia had three-year terms. No state had a four-year term.

Over the years states have changed the length of gubernatorial terms. With some occasional back and forth movement, the general trend has been toward longer terms. New York, for example, has changed the governor's term of office four times. Beginning in 1777 with a three-year term, the state switched to a two-year term in 1820, back to a three-year term in 1876, back to a two-year term in 1894, and to a four-year term beginning in 1938.

Maryland provides another example of a state that has changed its gubernatorial term several times. Beginning with one year in 1776, the state extended the term to three years in 1838, then to four years in 1851. Regular gubernatorial elections were held every second odd year from then through 1923, when the state had one three-year term so that future elections would be held in even-numbered years, beginning in 1926. Thus, the state held gubernatorial elections in 1919, 1923, and 1926 and then every four years after that.

The trend toward longer gubernatorial terms shows up clearly by comparing the length of terms in 1900 and 1998. Of the forty-five states in the Union in 1900, twenty-two, almost half, had two-year terms. One (New Jersey) had a three-year term, while Rhode Island and Massachusetts were the only states left with one-year terms. The remaining twenty states had four-year gubernatorial terms.

By mid-1998, forty-three of those same states had four-year terms, as did the five states admitted to the Union after 1900—Oklahoma (1907), Arizona and New Mexico (1912), Alaska and Hawaii (1959). This left only two states with two-year terms: New Hampshire and Vermont. Arkansas, one of the last holdouts, voted in 1984 to switch to a four-year term, effective in 1986. Rhode Island voters in 1992 approved a constitutional change to a four-year term beginning with the 1994 election. (See table, Length of Governor Terms.)

## Elections in Nonpresidential Years

Along with the change to longer terms for governors came another trend—away from holding gubernatorial elections in presidential election years. The separation reduces the likelihood that presidential politics will influence the choice of state officials.

Except for North Dakota, every state that switched in the twentieth century to four-year gubernatorial terms scheduled its elections in nonpresidential election years. That left only nine states—Delaware, Indiana, Missouri, Montana, North Carolina, North Dakota, Utah, Washington, and West Virginia—holding quadrennial gubernatorial elections at the same time as the presidential election. New Hampshire and Vermont still have two-year terms, so every other gubernatorial election in these two states occurs in a presidential election year.

Four states—Louisiana, Mississippi, New Jersey, and Virginia—elect governors in odd-numbered years.

## Methods of Election

Yet another way in which Americans of the early federal period restricted their governors was by the method of election. In 1789 the only states in which the people directly chose their governors by popular vote were New York and the four New England states. In the remaining eight states, state legislatures chose the governors, which enhanced the power of the legislatures in their dealings with the governors.

But several factors—including the democratic trend to DIRECT ELECTION, the increasing trust in the office of governor, and the need for a stronger and more independent chief executive—led to the gradual introduction of popular votes in all the states. By the 1860s the remaining eight original states all had switched to popular ballots. Pennsylvania was first, in 1790, followed by Delaware in 1792, Georgia in 1824, North Carolina in 1835, Maryland in 1838, New Jersey in 1844, Virginia in 1851, and South Carolina in 1865, after the Civil War.

All the states admitted to the Union after the original thirteen, with one exception, made provision from the very beginning for popular election of their governors. The exception was Louisiana, which from its admission in 1812 until a change in the state constitution in 1845 had a unique system of gubernatorial elections. The people participated by voting in a first-step popular election. In a second step, the legislature was to select the governor from the two candidates receiving the highest popular vote.

Because of the domination of the Democratic Party in the South for many years after the Civil War, the Democrats' SOUTHERN PRIMARY was more important than the general election in the selection of governors and other officials in some southern states. Victory in the party's primary often was tantamount to election, with the winner facing weak or token Republican opposition in the November election.

Although the so-called Solid South has become more of a two-party region in recent decades, the South continues to produce some anomalies in the election of governors. Louisiana, for example, holds an open primary for governor in every fourth odd-numbered year.

Candidates from all parties run on the same ballot. Any candidate who receives a majority is elected. If no candidate receives 50 percent, a RUNOFF is held in November between the two top finishers.

## Number of Terms

Another limitation placed on governors is a restriction on the number of terms they are allowed to serve. In the early years at least three states had such limitations. Governors of Maryland were eligible to serve three consecutive one-year terms and then were required to retire for at least one year. Pennsylvania allowed its governors three consecutive three-year terms and then forced retirement for at least one term. In New Jersey, according to the constitution of 1844, a governor could serve only one three-year term before retiring for at least one term.

In 1998 most states—thirty-seven—placed some sort

### Limitations on Governor Terms

In most states with limits of one or two consecutive terms, governors may serve again after a one-term hiatus. Thus, in a state with a two-term limitation, the governor must retire after two consecutive terms. After a one-term interim, he or she may serve again.

| State | Maximum Number of Consecutive Terms (as of 1996) | State | Maximum Number of Consecutive Terms (as of 1996) | State | Maximum Number of Consecutive Terms (as of 1996) |
|---|---|---|---|---|---|
| Alabama | 2 | Louisiana | 2 | Ohio[1] | 2 |
| Alaska | 2 | Maine | 2 | Oklahoma | 2 |
| Arizona | 2 | Maryland | 2 | Oregon[2] | 2 |
| Arkansas[1] | 2 | Massachusetts | 2 | Pennsylvania | 2 |
| California | 2 | Michigan | 2 | Rhode Island | 2 |
| Colorado | 2 | Minnesota | No limit | South Carolina | 2 |
| Connecticut | No limit | Mississippi[1] | 2 | South Dakota | 2 |
| Delaware[1] | 2 | Missouri[1] | 2 | Tennessee | 2 |
| Florida | 2 | Montana[3] | 2 | Texas | No limit |
| Georgia | 2 | Nebraska | 2 | Utah | 3 |
| Hawaii | 2 | Nevada | 2 | Vermont | No limit |
| Idaho | No limit | New Hampshire | No limit | Virginia | 1 |
| Illinois | No limit | New Jersey | 2 | Washington[4] | No limit |
| Indiana[2] | 2 | New Mexico | 2 | West Virginia | 2 |
| Iowa | No limit | New York | No limit | Wisconsin | No limit |
| Kansas | 2 | North Carolina | 2 | Wyoming[3] | No limit |
| Kentucky | 2 | North Dakota | No limit | | |

*Source: Book of the States, 1996–1997*, vol. 31 (Lexington, Ky.: Council of State Governments, 1996), Table 2.1.

1. Arkansas, Delaware, Mississippi, Missouri, and Ohio have absolute two-term limits. That is, no person may serve more than two gubernatorial terms in his or her lifetime.

2. Indiana and Oregon prohibit a person from serving more than eight years in any twelve-year period.

3. Montana and Wyoming prohibit a person from serving more than eight years in any sixteen-year period.

4. Washington prohibits a person from serving more than eight years in any fourteen-year period.

of limitation on the number of consecutive terms the governor could serve. Only Virginia limited its governor to one term. Utah had a three-term limit. Thirty-five states permitted reelection once but required that the governor step down after two terms for an interval of at least one term. Five states—Arkansas, Delaware, Mississippi, Missouri, and Ohio—imposed an absolute two-term limit. That is, a governor could serve only two terms, however spaced, in his or her lifetime. The remaining thirteen states imposed no limits on the number of consecutive terms a governor could serve. (See table, Limitations on Governor Terms.)

## Majority Vote Requirement

A peculiarity of gubernatorial voting that has almost disappeared from the American political scene is the requirement that the winning candidate receive a majority of the popular vote. Otherwise, the choice devolves upon the state legislature or, in one case, a runoff between the two highest candidates is required.

Centered in New England, this practice was used mainly in the nineteenth century. All six New England states, plus Georgia, had such a provision in their state constitutions at one time. New Hampshire, Vermont, Massachusetts, and Connecticut already had the provision when they entered the Union between 1789 and 1791. Rhode Island required a majority election but did not adopt a provision for legislative election until 1842. Maine adopted a majority provision when it split off from Massachusetts to form a separate state in 1820. Georgia put the majority provision in its constitution when it switched from legislative to popular election of governors in 1825.

The purpose of the majority provision appears to have been to safeguard against a candidate's winning with a small fraction of the popular vote in a multiple field. In most of New England, the provision was part of the early state constitutions, formed largely in the 1780s, before the development of the TWO-PARTY SYSTEM.

The emergence of two major political parties diminished the prospects of multiple candidates for the same office. Nevertheless, each of these states had occasion to use the majority provision at least once. Sometimes, in an extremely close election, minor party candidates received enough of a vote to keep the winner from getting a majority of the total vote. And at other times strong THIRD PARTY movements or disintegration of the old party structure resulted in the election's being thrown into the state legislature.

Vermont retains the majority vote provision, although its legislature has not elected a governor since 1912. Mississippi has a majority vote provision under the 1890 state constitution, but the provision has not been used because one candidate always received a majority (through 1987 it was always the Democratic nominee; in 1991 and 1995 it was the Republican).

Georgia maintains the requirement for a majority vote for governor but, instead of legislative election, provides for a runoff between the top two contenders three weeks after the general election. Although the Georgia Constitution contained a majority vote requirement as early as 1825, it was not used until the twentieth century. In 1966, with an emerging Republican Party, a controversial Democratic nominee, and an independent Democrat all affecting the gubernatorial race, no candidate received a majority. The legislature chose Democrat Lester Maddox. It was the controversy surrounding this experience that led to Georgia's change from legislative choice to a runoff between the top two contenders.

Earlier, in 1946, the Georgia legislature also attempted to choose the governor, under unusual circumstances not covered by the majority vote requirement. The governor-elect, Eugene Talmadge, Democrat, died before taking office. When it met, the legislature chose Talmadge's son, Herman E. Talmadge, as the new governor. Herman Talmadge was eligible for consideration because he had received enough WRITE-IN VOTES in the general election to make him the second-place candidate, but the outgoing governor and the lieutenant governor-elect, Melvin E. Thompson, disputed the legislature's action. Talmadge seized the governor's mansion by force and held it for sixty-seven days before being thrown out of office by the Georgia Supreme Court, which voided the legislature's choice and declared that Thompson should be governor. Two years later Talmadge, unopposed, won a special election to serve the remainder of his father's term.

## Removal from Office

Term limits ensure a steady turnover of governors in most states. Elections every four years also enable the voters to replace an unpopular governor. In addition, governors guilty of unethical conduct or crimes and misdemeanors may be removed from office through impeachment or RECALL.

Recall, which requires the holding of a SPECIAL ELECTION if enough voters petition for removal of an official, has been used only once against a governor. In 1921 North Dakota voters ousted Gov. Lynn J. Frazier, Republican and National Prohibition Party, who had been forced into a special election with Ragnvald A. Nestos, Independent Republican. Frazier was in his third two-year term when he was removed, along with two cabinet members. The following year Frazier was elected to the U.S. Senate, where he served until 1941.

Impeachment by the state legislature, similar to the federal system in which the House impeaches (charges) and the Senate acquits or convicts, was used five times in the twentieth century to remove governors. The most recent case was that of Arizona governor Evan Mecham, Republican, who was impeached and convicted in January 1988. He was found guilty of obstructing an investigation and improperly using official funds. Mecham's removal through impeachment ended a recall movement against him.

Other governors have resigned after being convicted in the JUDICIAL SYSTEM. Among such cases is that of Maryland governor Marvin Mandel, Democrat, who served time in prison while suspended from office after his 1977 conviction on federal mail fraud charges. After his conviction was reversed he served the remaining few hours of his term.

Alabama governor Guy Hunt, Republican, was removed from office in 1993 after he was convicted of diverting inaugural funds to personal use. Jim Guy Tucker, who as lieutenant governor succeeded President Bill Clinton as governor of Arkansas, resigned in 1996 after being convicted of bank fraud conspiracy in connection with the Whitewater real estate SCANDAL. In September 1997 Arizona governor J. Fife Symington III, Republican, resigned after being convicted of making false statements to obtain loans for his real estate business.

---

## Grandfather Clause

In the parlance of politics and elections, the term *grandfather clause* has two principal meanings—one dealing with voting rights, and the other with campaign funds.

The older use of the term refers to the laws passed in seven southern states after the Civil War that exempted illiterate whites from the LITERACY TESTS for voters. They were "grandfathered" because in most cases their ancestors had voted before 1867. Few blacks could meet that test because they were descendants of slaves who had not been eligible to vote.

The Supreme Court ruled in 1915 that these grandfather clauses violated the Fifteenth Amendment to the Constitution, which prohibited denial of the RIGHT TO VOTE on account of race. (See VOTING RIGHTS ACT.)

The modern grandfather clause concerned a loophole in the 1979 CAMPAIGN FINANCE law that permitted House members to pocket leftover campaign funds. The law barred personal use of excess campaign funds except by grandfathered members—those who were in office on January 8, 1980. Under House rules they could make personal use of the money after leaving Congress. The funds became taxable as income, but once the members disclosed the conversion of the money to personal use their reporting obligations ended. Senate rules prohibited personal use of excess campaign money by members past or present.

Congress closed the grandfather clause loophole with a provision in a 1989 ethics and pay law. House members were forced to leave Congress before the beginning of the 103d Congress in 1993 or lose the right to take the money. At the beginning of the 101st Congress in 1989, 191 House members were eligible to take advantage of the so-called grandfather clause.

Between 1980 and the beginning of 1989, grandfathered members converted to personal use at least $862,000, including more than $710,000 in cash. Another $115,000 was borrowed or used to retire personal loans unconnected with their former campaigns. At least $37,000 went for cars, furniture, travel, and other services.

Exempt retirees who had left Congress since 1980 had access to more than $2 million in surplus campaign money. Most of it, $1.5 million, was controlled by members whose service ended with the 100th Congress (1987–1989).

## *Gray v. Sanders*

*See* ONE PERSON, ONE VOTE.

## Green Party (1996– )

With famed consumer activist Ralph Nader heading its ticket, the Green Party made an impressive debut in U.S. presidential politics in 1996. Nader received 684,872 votes to finish a distant fourth behind the Reform Party's Ross Perot, the most successful third party candidate in eighty-four years.

Nader was on the ballot in twenty-two states, including California and several other western states. His running mate was Winona LaDuke of the White Earth reservation in Minnesota. A Harvard graduate, LaDuke was active as an advocate and writer on human rights and Native American environmental causes.

Although new to the United States, the Green Party was part of a decentralized worldwide movement for peace, social justice, and the environment. Until the collapse of international communism and the fall of the Berlin Wall, the Greens were best known for their political inroads in Germany. The party lost ground after opposing reunification, but has since returned to the German parliament.

Nader spoke at the Green Party convention in Los Angeles in August 1996 and agreed to be its candidate. He refused campaign contributions, however, and left the organizational work to the party.

## Greenback Party (1876–1884)

The National Independent or Greenback-Labor Party, commonly known as the Greenback Party, was launched in Indianapolis, Indiana, in November 1874 at a meeting organized by the Indiana Grange. The party grew out of the Panic of 1873, a post–Civil War economic depression, which hit farmers and industrial workers particularly hard. Currency was the basic issue of the new party, which opposed return to the gold standard and favored retention of the inflationary paper money (known as greenbacks), first introduced as an emergency measure during the Civil War.

In the 1876 presidential election, the party ran Peter Cooper, a New York philanthropist, and drafted a platform that focused entirely on the currency issue. Cooper received 75,973 votes (0.9 percent of the popular vote), mainly from agrarian voters. Aided by the continuing depression, a Greenback national convention in 1878 effected the merger of the party with various labor reform groups and adopted a platform that addressed labor and currency issues. Showing voting strength in the industrial East as well as in the agrarian South and Midwest, the Greenbacks polled more than 1 million votes in the 1878 congressional races and won fourteen seats in the U.S. House of Representatives. This marked the high point of the party's strength.

Returning prosperity, the prospect of fusion with one of the major parties, and a split between the party's agrarian and labor leadership served to undermine the Greenback Party. In the 1880 election the party elected only eight representatives and its presidential candidate, Rep. James B. Weaver of Iowa, received 305,997 votes (3.3 percent of the popular vote), far less than party leaders expected.

The party slipped further four years later, when the Greenbacks' candidate for president, former Massachusetts governor Benjamin F. Butler, received 175,096 votes (1.7 percent of the popular vote). With the demise of the Greenbacks, most of the party's constituency moved into the Populist Party, the agrarian reform movement that swept the South and Midwest in the 1890s.

# H

## Hard Money

Enactment of laws in the 1970s to regulate the flow of cash to and from political campaign chests led to an unofficial differentiation between "hard" and "soft" money. The term *hard money* refers to federal election campaign funds that are limited as to contributions, spending, or both. This money is *hard* in the sense that it is stringently controlled. SOFT MONEY means unregulated funds given to political party committees, ostensibly for worthy purposes such as voter registration and turnout drives.

Of the two, soft money has proven to be the more troublesome. Both major parties have taken full advantage of it as a way to circumvent the tight CAMPAIGN FINANCE restrictions imposed by the Federal Election Campaign Act of 1971 (FECA) and later amendments.

Hard money, by comparison, has produced relatively few headlines since the FEDERAL ELECTION COMMISSION (FEC) began administering and enforcing FECA in 1976. The bipartisan commission relies mostly on voluntary compliance with the act's contribution and spending limits, although it has the authority to investigate suspected violations and, if necessary, to impose fines and order repayment of public funds.

The act requires disclosure of receipts and expenditures by candidates for federal office. Individuals and political committees are limited in how much they can give annually to candidates, parties, or POLITICAL ACTION COMMITTEES (PACs). The limit is $25,000 for individuals. (See table, page 39.)

Presidential candidates who accept PUBLIC FINANCING must abide by overall spending limits in their campaigns, although they may spend up to $50,000 of their own money in addition in the general election campaign. Because there is no public funding of House or Senate campaigns, congressional candidates are subject to the contribution limits but not spending limits.

Besides giving soft money, interest groups and wealthy individuals have used other means to get around the hard money contribution limits. One is BUNDLING—the collection of a number of checks, each within the legal gift limit, that are sent as a single package to a candidate under the auspices of a PAC or party committee. The group gets the credit, and presumably access, and, because the bundle is made up of individual legal-sized donations, it is within the law.

Another technique that skirts the limits is the so-called independent expenditure—money spent on a candidate's own campaign or by another person or group on the candidate's behalf without his or her collusion. The Supreme Court ruled in *BUCKLEY V. VALEO* (1976) that such spending is a form of free speech protected by the First Amendment to the Constitution. If it is truly independent, the Court said, it may not be restricted.

Independent expenditures survived further challenges in the Supreme Court in 1980 and 1985. During the next campaign year, 1986, independent expenditures—which must be disclosed to the FEC—peaked in congressional races at $9.4 million, with more than half ($5.3 million) going to Senate campaigns. In the 1994 MIDTERM ELECTION, when Republicans won control of Congress, independent expenditures amounted to $4.6 million, again with the larger share ($2.5 million) spent for or against Senate candidates.

## Hatch Act

*See* FEDERAL WORKERS' POLITICAL ACTIVITY.

## Historic Milestones in U.S. Elections

Few aspects of the American democratic system have changed so much as the elections process. Because the Constitution has little to say on the subject, the rules for choosing government leaders have developed gradually through events, legislation, and court opinions. Following are some major milestones in the course of that development.

### 1787

The "Great Compromise" at the Constitutional Convention in Philadelphia pacifies less-populous states by giving each state two senators and a House delegation based on population, assuring even the smallest state at least three votes in Congress (and in the ELECTORAL COLLEGE). Senators are to be elected by the state legislatures (changed in 1913 to POPULAR VOTE election by the Seventeenth Amendment) for six-year terms. Representatives are to be popularly elected to two-year terms.

### 1789

George Washington wins the first U.S. presidential election on February 4. The election is tantamount to unanimous as Washington receives the maximum possible number of electoral votes, sixty-nine. (New York's sixteen electoral votes are not cast because of a dispute

*George Washington set many precedents during his two terms, often consciously so. Here, he delivers his inaugural address, in April 1789. Source: Library of Congress*

in the state legislature; North Carolina, fourteen votes, and Rhode Island, six votes, also are not eligible because they have not yet ratified the Constitution.) John Adams, second with thirty-four votes, wins the vice presidency. Washington is inaugurated on April 30 in New York City.

## 1796

John Adams, Federalist, wins the first two-party presidential election. Thomas Jefferson, Democratic-Republican, is second and therefore is elected vice president.

## 1800

Thomas Jefferson and Aaron Burr tie in electoral votes for the presidency. The election devolves to the House of Representatives, which elects Jefferson. The unforeseen possibility of a tie vote leads to adoption of the Twelfth Amendment to the Constitution (1804), requiring separate electoral college voting for president and vice president. (See PRESIDENT, NOMINATING AND ELECTING.)

## 1807

Jefferson formalizes Washington's two-term precedent for presidents. Jefferson sets forth his reasons in a December 10 letter to the Vermont state legislature, which had asked him to run for a third term. Seven other states sent similar letters.

## 1824

"King Caucus" dies, ending the decades-long system of presidential candidate selection by congressional party caucuses. State legislatures nominate four candidates representing different factions of the DEMOCRATIC-REPUBLICAN PARTY. Andrew Jackson of Tennessee wins the popular vote but falls short of the required electoral vote majority, throwing the election to the House for the second time in U.S. history. The House elects John Quincy Adams of Massachusetts, who placed second in both the electoral and popular vote. Jackson's loss leads to his election in 1828 and formation of the present-day DEMOCRATIC PARTY.

## 1831

The first NATIONAL PARTY CONVENTIONS are held in Baltimore. The Anti-Masons nominate William Wirt in September, and the National Republicans nominate Henry Clay in December. Both lose to President Andrew Jackson in 1832.

## 1832

The Democrats hold their first national convention, also in Baltimore, and adopt a TWO-THIRDS RULE for presidential nomination. Jackson is nominated for re-election by the required two-thirds majority vote.

## 1837

For the first and only time, the Senate decides a vice-presidential election as the Constitution provides. Democrat Martin Van Buren's RUNNING MATE, Richard M. Johnson, falls one vote short of the required majority because Virginia's Democratic electors object to his moral character. The Senate nevertheless votes along party lines (33 to 16) to elect Johnson.

## 1840

Van Buren and Johnson become the first sitting president and vice president defeated for reelection. They lose to Whigs William Henry Harrison and John Tyler. Harrison dies April 4, 1841, after just one month in office, and Tyler establishes the precedent for the vice president's becoming president rather than just the "acting president."

## 1844

The Democrats nominate the first DARK HORSE presidential candidate, James K. Polk, who wins the election.

## 1854

Antislavery sympathizers opposed to the expansion of slavery into the western territories gather at Ripon, Wisconsin, and form the REPUBLICAN PARTY. With the Whigs torn over the slavery issue, the Republicans soon emerge as the Democrats' counterpart in the nation's TWO-PARTY SYSTEM.

*Abraham Lincoln was the first successful candidate of the Republican Party.* Source: *Library of Congress*

## 1856

Democrat Franklin Pierce becomes the only elected president denied renomination by his own party. He had alienated fellow northerners by signing legislation that made the Kansas territory a bloody battleground over the slavery issue. James Buchanan wins the nomination and the presidency.

## 1860

The new Republican Party elects its first president, Abraham Lincoln, and the divided nation advances toward Civil War. The election is the last in which at least one state (South Carolina) has no popular voting for president; instead, South Carolina's electors are chosen by the legislature. (South Carolina allows popular voting after the war, when it and other former Confederate states resume participation in presidential elections.)

## 1865

Abraham Lincoln is assassinated six weeks after beginning his second term. He dies on April 15 after being shot the night before by John Wilkes Booth. Vice President Andrew Johnson succeeds to the presidency and immediately comes into conflict with the radical northern Republicans who plan harsh postwar treatment of the rebel states. The Radical Republicans gain control of Congress in the 1866 MIDTERM ELECTIONS and later impeach Johnson, who narrowly escapes conviction.

## 1870

The Fifteenth Amendment, enfranchising newly freed slaves, is ratified on February 3. The first blacks are elected to Congress: Republican Hiram R. Revels of Mississippi serves in the Senate from 1870 to 1871. Mississippi Republican Blanche K. Bruce is elected to the Senate in 1874 and is the first black member to serve a full term in that chamber.

## 1874

The donkey and elephant emerge as symbols of the Democratic and Republican Parties after drawings by cartoonist Thomas Nast. They are important as guides to illiterate and semiliterate voters and are a boon to editorial cartoonists.

## 1876

A special commission decides a CONTESTED presidential election for the first and only time. Democrat Samuel J. Tilden wins the popular vote against Republican Rutherford B. Hayes, but the electoral vote outcome hangs on the disputed votes of three southern states. Congress appoints a commission that reaches a compromise on March 2, 1877, and awards the votes to Hayes in return for his pledge to remove federal troops from the South. He wins, 185–184.

Cartoonist Thomas Nast created the enduring symbols of the two major parties: the Democratic donkey and Republican elephant. *Source: Library of Congress*

## 1881

On July 2, only four months after taking office, President James A. Garfield is shot by Charles J. Guiteau in Washington, D.C. The bullet lodges near Garfield's spine, and he dies on September 19. He is succeeded by Vice President Chester A. Arthur, who fails to win the Republican nomination in 1884.

## 1887

Congress enacts the Electoral Count Act, which charges states with resolving future electoral vote disputes similar to the one that followed the Tilden-Hayes contest in 1876.

## 1890

Wyoming enters the Union as the first state to enfranchise women. As a territory, Wyoming had given the vote to women in 1869.

## 1892

A mechanical VOTING MACHINE built by Jacob H. Myers is used for the first time at Lockport, New York. Inventor Thomas A. Edison had received his first patent for a similar machine twenty-three years earlier.

## 1901

The first presidential PRIMARY law is passed in Florida. The primary gets its biggest impetus when the 1904 Republican convention refuses seating to backers of Wisconsin governor Robert M. La Follette, leader of the GOP's Progressive wing. In 1905 La Follette successfully promotes legislation in his state that provides for primary election of delegates to national party conventions.

Six months after his inauguration, President William McKinley is shot in Buffalo, New York, by Leon Czolgosz, an anarchist disturbed by social injustice. The president dies a week later, on September 14, and is succeeded by Vice President Theodore Roosevelt. In 1904 Roosevelt is elected to a full four-year term, the first presidential successor ever to do so.

## 1912

Former president Theodore Roosevelt deserts the Republican Party to run on his own PROGRESSIVE "BULL MOOSE" ticket. He attains the highest THIRD PARTY vote in history, but the split in the GOP helps to elect Democrat Woodrow Wilson.

## 1913

Popular election of senators becomes the norm when the Seventeenth Amendment is ratified, replacing election by state legislatures. Some states institute popular election of senators before it becomes mandatory, beginning with the 1914 midterm elections.

## 1916

The first woman, Jeannette Rankin, Montana Republican, is elected to the U.S. House, four years before the Nineteenth Amendment ensures WOMEN'S SUFFRAGE in all states. During her two terms (1917–1919; 1941–1943) Rankin becomes the only member of Congress to vote against both World Wars.

## 1918

Socialist Party leader Eugene V. Debs is sentenced to ten years in prison for his antiwar statements. He nevertheless receives almost a million votes (3.4 percent of the vote) in 1920, his last election. President Warren G. Harding frees him in 1921.

## 1920

The Nineteenth Amendment, giving full voting rights to women, is ratified on August 26. Some states allowed women to vote earlier. By 1918 fifteen states had enfranchised women.

## 1923

Harding dies in office August 2. Vice President Calvin Coolidge becomes president.

## 1924

The first women governors are elected: Miriam "Ma" Ferguson in Texas and Nellie Tayloe Ross in Wyoming.

Ross succeeded her husband, who had died; Ferguson's husband had been impeached and removed from office.

## 1928

The first Roman Catholic, New York governor Alfred E. Smith, is nominated for president on a major party ticket (Democratic). The urbanite Smith favors repeal of Prohibition, opposes the Ku Klux Klan, and is an unabashed liberal—all considered "alien traits" by much of the still rural, dry United States. He loses to Republican Herbert C. Hoover.

## 1932

At the Democratic National Convention in Chicago, Franklin D. Roosevelt becomes the first major party candidate to accept the presidential nomination in person. In his acceptance he promises a "new deal" for the American people. The Democrats win control of the White House and Congress as the nation battles the Great Depression, the worst in U.S. history. Roosevelt's first three and a half months in office produce an unprecedented flood of economic legislation and establish the "hundred-day" yardstick for measuring the initial success of future presidents.

## 1934

The second session of the Seventy-third Congress meets for the first time on January 3 in accordance with the Twentieth Amendment (the so-called Lame Duck Amendment) to the Constitution. The amendment, rat-

*Franklin D. Roosevelt, seen here in the back seat of a car surrounded by supporters, made an indelible mark on the nation in winning four successive presidential elections. Source: Franklin D. Roosevelt Library*

ified in 1933, also fixes January 20 as the beginning of each four-year presidential term, effective in 1937. Previously it had been March 4, by statute.

## 1936

At their convention, Democrats abolish the two-thirds majority rule for presidential or vice-presidential nomination, which previously resulted in protracted balloting. The South objects because the rule had assured the region virtual veto power over any nominee. To make up for the loss, the South is given more votes at later conventions.

## 1940

FDR breaks the traditional two-term limit for presidents when he is elected for a third term. His popular margin of victory narrows from four years earlier, however, in part because some voters object to his disregard of the unwritten "no-third-term" rule.

The Republicans hold the first televised national convention, in Philadelphia. The viewing audience is quite small.

## 1944

The Supreme Court in *Smith v. Allwright* outlaws WHITE PRIMARIES. Previously, political parties as "private" organizations, particularly in the South, were permitted to exclude blacks from membership and participation.

## 1945

Roosevelt dies in office April 12 and is succeeded by Vice President Harry S. Truman.

## 1948

President Truman fools the pollsters and defeats his Republican challenger, Thomas E. Dewey. The upset produces a historic photo of Truman gleefully holding up the erroneous *Chicago Daily Tribune* banner headline, "Dewey Defeats Truman."

## 1951

The Twenty-second Amendment, setting a two-term limit for presidents, is ratified February 27. Truman, who became president in 1945 on Roosevelt's death and was elected in his own right in 1948, was exempted from the law.

## 1952

In danger of being dumped as Dwight D. Eisenhower's running mate, Richard Nixon saves himself with an emotional address to the nation September 23. The address becomes known as the "Checkers speech" because Nixon refers to a little gift dog he refuses to give up.

## 1954

Strom Thurmond of South Carolina becomes the only senator ever elected by a WRITE-IN VOTE.

## 1960

The first DEBATE between presidential candidates, Democrat John F. Kennedy and Republican Richard Nixon, is televised in Chicago, Illinois, on September 26. The 1960 general election is the first in which television plays a major role in MEDIA COVERAGE of the candidates and issues. With a narrow victory over Nixon, Kennedy becomes the first Catholic president.

## 1961

Ratification of the Twenty-third Amendment on March 29 gives DISTRICT OF COLUMBIA residents the RIGHT TO VOTE in presidential elections.

## 1962

The Supreme Court in BAKER V. CARR permits federal court suits to require REAPPORTIONMENT AND REDISTRICTING of state legislative districts that violate the principle of ONE PERSON, ONE VOTE. The Court later extends the requirement to CONGRESSIONAL DISTRICTS.

## 1963

*Gray v. Sanders,* the first major one-person, one-vote Supreme Court decision, is handed down on March 18. The Court rules that Georgia's "county unit" system of electing officers to state posts violates the equal protection guarantee of the Fourteenth Amendment by giving

*John F. Kennedy used the relatively new medium of television to defeat Richard Nixon in the 1960 presidential election.* Source: National Archives

more weight to the votes of persons in rural counties than in urban counties.

President Kennedy is assassinated by Lee Harvey Oswald November 22 in Dallas, Texas. Kennedy is succeeded by Vice President Lyndon B. Johnson, a former Senate majority leader who wins approval of much of Kennedy's "New Frontier" legislative program.

## 1964

The Twenty-fourth Amendment is ratified on February 4, abolishing the POLL TAX as a requisite to voting in primary or general elections for president and other federal officials. The controversial tax had often been a bar to voting, especially among poor blacks.

The Supreme Court hands down a decision in *Wesberry v. Sanders* February 17, extending the one-person,

one-vote doctrine to congressional districts. The Court rules that substantial disparity in a state's district populations results in unequal representation in the U.S. House. Congressional districts should be as nearly equal in population "as is practicable."

Lyndon B. Johnson scores the largest popular vote LANDSLIDE in history, taking 61.1 percent of the vote against Barry Goldwater. LBJ's percentage surpasses FDR's 60.8 percent against Alfred M. Landon in 1936.

Congress passes the CIVIL RIGHTS ACT of 1964, which prohibits discrimination in employment, public accommodations, and federally funded programs.

## 1965

Passage of the Civil Rights Act of 1964 helps pave the way for the VOTING RIGHTS ACT of 1965, which provides protections for African Americans wishing to vote.

## 1967

The Twenty-fifth Amendment, ratified February 10, sets procedure in case of presidential disability or vacancy in the office of vice president.

## 1968

Urban riots break out in response to the April 4 assassination of civil rights leader Martin Luther King Jr. in Memphis.

Widespread opposition to the Vietnam War prompts President Johnson to decline renomination. Robert F. Kennedy, a leading candidate for the nomination, is assassinated in Los Angeles by Sirhan Sirhan on June 6. Riotous protests against the candidacy of Johnson's handpicked successor, Hubert H. Humphrey, mar the Democratic convention at Chicago, and the party split helps to elect Republican Richard Nixon.

At their convention the Democrats drop the controversial UNIT RULE allowing convention delegations to vote as a whole despite minority objections.

In the general election, former Democratic governor George C. Wallace of Alabama runs on the AMERICAN INDEPENDENT PARTY ticket and draws conservative support from Nixon. Wallace wins five southern states and 13.5 percent of the vote.

In congressional elections, New York Democrat Shirley Chisholm becomes the first black woman elected to the U.S. House.

## 1969

*Powell v. McCormack,* the landmark Supreme Court decision handed down on June 16, prohibits the House of Representatives from adding to the constitutional qualifications for House membership. The Court rules that the House lacked the authority to exclude a duly elected representative who met the constitutional qualifications of age, residence, and citizenship. The decision reinstates Adam Clayton Powell, New York Democrat, who was excluded for misconduct and misuse of public funds. (See HOUSE OF REPRESENTATIVES, QUALIFICATIONS.)

## 1971

The Twenty-sixth Amendment lowers the voting age to eighteen nationally. Ratification takes only 107 days, less than half the time required for any other constitutional amendment. It is spurred by an unusually large number of young people in the population, together with the Vietnam War and conscription into the army for eighteen-year-olds.

Congress passes the Federal Election Campaign Act of 1971, which creates the FEDERAL ELECTION COMMISSION, limits spending for POLITICAL ADVERTISING by candidates for federal office, and requires full disclosure of campaign contributions and expenditures. Major amendments are enacted in 1974 and 1976. The spending limits are later (in 1976) found unconstitutional except for presidential candidates who accept PUBLIC FINANCING of their campaigns.

## 1972

George Wallace, reelected as Alabama governor in 1970, is shot May 15 at a Laurel, Maryland, shopping center while campaigning for the Democratic presidential nomination. Partially paralyzed, he withdraws as a candidate.

The Democrats adopt McGovern-Fraser Commission proposals opening the party to more participation by rank-and-file voters. The commission's guidelines are designed to counteract rules and practices that inhibited access to the states' delegate-selection process or diluted the influence of those who had access. The PRESIDENTIAL SELECTION REFORMS bring about a proliferation of primaries in subsequent presidential election years.

The former head of the commission, Sen. George S. McGovern of South Dakota, wins the Democratic presidential nomination. His running mate, Sen. Thomas F. Eagleton of Missouri, withdraws after the convention and is replaced on the ticket by R. Sargent Shriver of Maryland. (See RUNNING MATE.)

President Richard Nixon easily defeats McGovern to win the election that culminates in the first presidential resignation. A preelection burglary at the DEMOCRATIC NATIONAL COMMITTEE headquarters in Washington's

Watergate Hotel is traced to Republican operatives. Investigation discloses Nixon's active role in the subsequent attempted cover-up.

## 1973

Vice President Spiro T. Agnew resigns on October 10 as part of a plea bargain with federal prosecutors. Agnew faced trial on corruption charges from his years as governor of Maryland. In the first use of the Twenty-fifth Amendment (1967) to fill a vacancy in the vice presidency, President Nixon nominates Gerald R. Ford, who wins confirmation by Congress.

## 1974

Facing near-certain impeachment in the Watergate SCANDAL, President Nixon resigns August 9 and is succeeded by Vice President Ford, the first president to take office without being elected by the electoral college.

## 1976

BUCKLEY V. VALEO, a major Supreme Court campaign finance decision, is handed down January 31. It sanctions PUBLIC FINANCING of presidential elections but bars spending limits for candidates who reject federal funding. The decision also removes ceilings on contributions to one's own campaign.

The first debate of vice-presidential candidates, Democrat Walter F. Mondale and Republican Robert J. Dole, is televised October 15 in Houston, Texas.

## 1981

The Iranian hostage crisis that plagued the presidency of Jimmy Carter ends January 20 when the Americans held hostage for 444 days are freed as Ronald Reagan becomes president. Reagan is wounded in an assassination attempt March 30 outside a Washington hotel.

## 1984

Democratic presidential nominee Mondale chooses Geraldine Ferraro of New York as his running mate. Ferraro, a three-term House member, becomes the first woman nominated on a major party presidential ticket.

*Richard Nixon leaving the White House. His resignation in 1974 was unprecedented.* Source: Nixon Project, National Archives

## 1988

Republican George Bush defeats Democrat Michael S. Dukakis to become the first sitting vice president since Martin Van Buren (in 1836) to win the presidency.

## 1989

Virginia elects the first African American governor, L. Douglas Wilder, Democrat.

## 1990

Kansas elects Joan Finney, Democrat, as governor. Kansas is the first state to have a woman governor, senator (Nancy Landon Kassebaum, Republican), and House member (Jan Meyers, Republican) at the same time.

## 1992

Bush, also like Van Buren, is defeated after a single term in office. Texas billionaire Ross Perot mounts the strongest-ever individual presidential campaign and receives 18.9 percent of the popular vote as an INDEPENDENT. Democrat Bill Clinton is elected.

Carol Moseley-Braun of Illinois wins election as the first black woman U.S. senator. California becomes the first state to have two woman senators, Barbara Boxer and Dianne Feinstein.

## 1994

In a midterm setback to the Democratic administration of President Clinton, the Republican Party wins control of both chambers of Congress for the first time in forty years. The House GOP strategy engineered by Newt Gingrich of Georgia centers on his proposed "Contract with America." The House elects Gingrich as Speaker. (See MIDTERM ELECTION, Contract with America box.)

## 1995

Ruling in an Arkansas case, *U.S. Term Limits Inc. v. Thornton*, the Supreme Court May 22 strikes down state attempts to impose TERM LIMITS on House and Senate members. Only a constitutional amendment can change the qualifications for service in Congress, the Court says.

## 1996

President Clinton is the first Democrat elected to a second full term since Franklin Roosevelt in 1936. Newt Gingrich of Georgia is the first Republican reelected as Speaker of the House in sixty-eight years.

The election results are historic. For only ten years out of more than two hundred has the country had a Democratic president and Republican Congress. The election also clearly establishes the South as the GOP's new bastion. With the Plains and Rocky Mountain states, half the country is strongly Republican. The other half, made up of the Northeast, Midwest, and Pacific Coast states, is strongly Democratic. (See REALIGNMENTS AND DEALIGNMENTS.)

Some states, notably Oregon, conduct the first experiments with elections by mail, other than those associated with ABSENTEE VOTING.

## 1998

The nation is stunned in January by revelation of a sex scandal that threatens the Clinton presidency. Clinton is accused of having an affair from 1995 to 1997 with Monica S. Lewinsky, who was a twenty-one-year-old White House intern when the relationship began. Clinton at first denies the allegations, both to the news media and under oath in court depositions, then later admits to having sexual relations with Lewinsky.

Clinton nevertheless remains popular in the polls and his party gains seats in the House, a rarity in midterm elections. Republican leader Newt Gingrich resigns as House Speaker and leaves Congress. His heir apparent, Robert Livingston of Louisiana, confesses to marital infidelity and declines to run for Speaker. He, too, announces his intention to resign, as the House prepares to vote on impeachment of Clinton.

After considering Independent Counsel Kenneth W. Starr's report to Congress, the House impeaches Clinton December 19 on charges of perjury and obstruction of justice. (See REMOVAL FROM OFFICE and SCANDALS.)

## 1999

The Senate February 12 acquits Clinton on both impeachment charges. With a two-thirds majority (67 votes) needed for conviction, neither article receives even a simple majority (51 votes). The historic Senate trial, with Chief Justice William H. Rehnquist presiding, included excerpts from Monica Lewinsky's videotaped deposition as a witness.

## Home Rule

The power of a local government, usually a city, to write its own charter and manage its own affairs is called *home rule*. The term derives from British usage in the long controversy over self-government for Ireland.

In U.S. national politics the issue of home rule pertains mostly to the question of self-government for the DISTRICT OF COLUMBIA. As the nation's capital, the District has unique status as a federal enclave carved out of Maryland and controlled by Congress.

The framers of the Constitution kept the District separate so that the policy makers of the national government would not be subordinate to the legislators of the state where the capital happened to be located. Although the District has had a nonvoting delegate to Congress since 1971, its efforts to gain statehood have been thwarted. A constitutional amendment to give the District full representation in Congress failed because too few states ratified it by the 1985 deadline.

Congress granted limited home rule to the District in 1973 but retained the power to overrule actions of the city government. The city subsequently elected its first mayor and city council. In 1995, however, Congress installed a powerful control board to oversee the District's near-bankrupt financial affairs. It increased the board's authority in 1997, further weakening the District's already limited home rule. In December 1998, as the District was preparing to swear in Anthony Williams as its new mayor, the control board restored most of the powers of the mayor's office.

The Twenty-third Amendment to the Constitution, ratified in 1961, gave District residents the RIGHT TO VOTE in presidential elections.

Outside of the District of Columbia, states may confer home rule on their cities and counties under the method specified by the individual state constitution. Once home rule is granted, the affected jurisdiction appoints a commission to draft a charter that is subject to approval by the voters. Most American cities enjoy a degree of freedom from interference by the state legislature.

## House of Representatives, Electing

The framers of the U.S. Constitution intended the House of Representatives to be the branch of government closest to the people. The members would be popularly elected; the terms of office would be two years so that the representatives would not lose touch with their homes; and the House would be a numerous branch, with members having relatively small constituencies.

Today, more than two hundred years later, the House is still the people's branch, with members elected much as the framers intended. Unlike SENATE ELECTIONS, which were fundamentally changed by the Seventeenth Amendment, House elections remain basically the same, except that the legislature itself has grown along with the population, bringing added expense and complexity to the electoral process.

From 65 seats in the First Congress, the House has swelled to its current size of 435 seats, beginning in 1911. The Senate, fixed at two senators for each state regardless of population, has grown from the original twenty-six members to one hundred.

The Constitution set few qualifications for House membership. To be eligible, one must be at least twenty-five years old, a U.S. citizen for at least seven years, and a resident of the state from which elected. From time to time the states, and even the House itself, have tried to add to those requirements, but the Supreme Court has invalidated such efforts as unconstitutional. (See HOUSE OF REPRESENTATIVES, QUALIFICATIONS.)

*Pat Danner (left), a Democrat from the Sixth District of Missouri, greets a constituent. Source: CQ file photo*

## Term Length and Limits

The two-year term for House members was a compromise at the Constitutional Convention in 1787. Many delegates wanted annual elections, believing they would make the House more responsive to the wishes of the people. James Madison, however, had argued for a three-year term, to allow representatives time to gain knowledge and experience in national and local affairs before they had to stand for reelection.

Proposals have been made to extend the term to four years; the last time was in 1966 when President Lyndon B. Johnson urged it in his State of the Union message. With House members making up the largest part of the House chamber audience, Johnson's proposal received loud applause. Afterward, however, critics argued that making the terms coincide with the president's four-

year term would create a House of "coattail riders" and end the minority party's traditional gains in MIDTERM ELECTIONS. The proposed constitutional amendment never emerged from committee.

During the 1990s another concern arose—that House members serve too long, despite having to run for reelection every two years. INCUMBENCY, in the view of many observers, leads to stagnation of ideas, concentration of power among a few individuals, and a shift from party-centered campaigns to CANDIDATE-CENTERED CAMPAIGNS where the challenger is at a disadvantage. Turnover in the modern House elections is low, unlike in the pre–Civil War era when about half the members were newcomers after each election.

To offset the advantages of incumbency, twenty-three states voted in the 1990s to impose TERM LIMITS on their members of Congress. The Supreme Court, however, struck down such limits, ruling May 22, 1995, in an Arkansas case that states may not add to the qualifications for Congress spelled out in the Constitution. The landmark 5–4 decision in *U.S. Term Limits Inc. v. Thornton* effectively nullified congressional term limit statutes enacted by these states.

Term limits, however, had already affected an election. In 1994 the congressional Republicans' "Contract with America" pledged "A first-ever vote on term limits to replace career politicians with citizen legislators." In the elections that fall, Washington State voters ousted the Democratic House Speaker, Thomas S. Foley, a fifteen-term veteran. Over Foley's strong opposition, his state had approved term limits in 1992. When the GOP-controlled Congress was seated in January 1995, Rep. Newt Gingrich of Georgia, architect of the Contract with America, replaced Foley as Speaker. The House voted down a constitutional amendment to overturn the Supreme Court's term limits decision. The proposal would have limited House members to three two-year terms.

## Size of the House

The Constitution specified (Article I, section 2) that the original House would have sixty-five representatives, with each state entitled to at least one. It also directed that the House be apportioned according to population after the first CENSUS in 1790.

Until then the thirteen states were to have the following numbers of representatives: Connecticut, five; Delaware, one; Georgia, three; Maryland, six; Massachusetts, eight; New Hampshire, three; New Jersey, four; New York, six; North Carolina, five; Pennsylvania, eight; Rhode Island, one; South Carolina, five; and Virginia, ten. This apportionment of sixty-five seats remained in effect during the First and Second Congresses (1789–1793). (Seats allotted to North Carolina and Rhode Island were not filled until 1790, after those states had ratified the Constitution.)

Originally the Constitution limited the House to one representative for every thirty thousand inhabitants, with three-fifths of a state's slave population added to the whole number of free citizens in the state. This concession to the South, where slavery was prevalent, helped to produce anomalies in House elections that continued through the emancipation of slaves and into the Reconstruction era after the Civil War. The House refused to seat some southern representatives because of disputes over the apportionment of seats after former slaves were fully counted as part of the population. (See ELECTORAL ANOMALIES.)

In its apportionment measure after the first census, Congress in April 1792 set the ratio at one member for every 33,000 inhabitants and fixed the exact number of representatives to which each state was entitled. Thereafter, Congress enacted a new apportionment measure, including the mathematical formula to be used, every ten years (except 1920, when Congress could not agree on a plan) until a permanent apportionment method became effective in 1929.

If the Constitution's original allotment of one representative for every 30,000 persons were still in use, the House would have had about 8,500 members after the 1990 census. But with changes in the apportionment formula and a limit on size of the House, each of the 435 members now represents an average of about 588,000 people.

The size of the House has been fixed at a maximum of 435 since Arizona and New Mexico joined the Union in 1912. (Two seats temporarily were added from 1959 to 1963 after Alaska and Hawaii became states.) (See REAPPORTIONMENT AND REDISTRICTING.)

House members are elected from CONGRESSIONAL DISTRICTS. State legislatures redraw the district lines after each census. Under the Supreme Court's ONE-PERSON, ONE-VOTE DOCTRINE, the LEGISLATORS are obligated to make the districts as equal in population size as possible.

## Majority Elections

House members today are elected by plurality, with victory going to the candidate winning the largest share of the votes. But at one time or another five New England states required a majority share—more than 50 percent—to win a seat in the U.S. House. If no candidate gained a majority, new elections were held until one contender succeeded.

The provision was last invoked in Maine in 1844, in New Hampshire in 1845, in Vermont in 1866, in Massachusetts in 1848, and in Rhode Island in 1892. Sometimes, multiple races were necessary because none of the candidates could achieve the required majority. In the Fourth District of Massachusetts in 1848 and 1849, for example, twelve successive elections were held to try to choose a representative. None of them was successful, and the district remained unrepresented in the House during the Thirty-first Congress (1849–1851).

Under the current system, House elections sometimes are decided by a few votes, with the apparent loser or losers calling for a RECOUNT. In such elections the ABSENTEE VOTES, which are not usually counted until after ELECTION DAY, often determine the winner. (See CONTESTED ELECTIONS.)

Districts in some states formerly elected more than one representative. Congress abolished these MULTI-MEMBER DISTRICTS in 1842.

Seven states have populations so small they are entitled to only one representative, who is elected AT-LARGE to represent the entire state. Pending the 2000 census, the single-member states were Alaska, Delaware, Montana, North Dakota, South Dakota, Vermont, and Wyoming. Despite being the smallest state geographically, Rhode Island had a population that entitled it to two House members.

## Elections in Odd-Numbered Years

Like multimember districts, House elections in odd-numbered years have faded from general usage. Before ratification of the Twentieth (lame duck) Amendment in 1933, which, among other things, specified January 3 as the end of one congressional term and the beginning of the next, regular sessions of Congress began in December of odd-numbered years. There were, therefore, eleven months in the odd-numbered years to elect members before the beginning of the congressional session.

In 1841, for example, twelve states held general elections for representatives for the Twenty-seventh Congress, convening that year: Alabama, Connecticut, Illinois, Indiana, Kentucky, Maryland, Mississippi, New Hampshire, North Carolina, Rhode Island, Tennessee, and Virginia.

Although it faded well before the Twentieth Amendment took effect, the practice of odd-year elections continued until late in the nineteenth century. In 1875 four states still chose their representatives in regular odd-year elections: California, Connecticut, Mississippi, and New Hampshire. But by 1880 all members of the House were being chosen in even-numbered years (except for special elections to fill vacancies).

One major problem encountered by states choosing their representatives in odd-numbered years was the possibility of a special session of the new Congress being called before the states' elections were held. Depending on the date of the election, a state could be unrepresented in the House. For example, California elected its House delegation to the Fortieth Congress (1867–1869) on September 4, 1867, in plenty of time for the first regular session scheduled for December 2. But Congress already had met in two special sessions—March 4 to March 20 and July 3 to July 20—without any representation from California.

## Special Elections

When a vacancy occurs in the House, the usual procedure is for the governor of the affected state to call a special election. Such elections may be held at any time throughout the year, and there are usually several during each two-year Congress. Senate vacancies often are filled by gubernatorial appointment, sometimes followed by a special election. (See SENATE, ELECTING.)

At times there are delays in the calling of House special elections. One of the longest periods in which a congressional district went unrepresented occurred in 1959 and 1960, following the death on April 28, 1959, of Rep. James G. Polk, Democrat, of Ohio's Sixth District.

The election to replace Polk did not take place until November 1960. It was held simultaneously with the general election for the same seat, and the winner, Ward M. Miller, Republican, served only the two months remaining in the term. For the full term, the Republican and Democratic Parties nominated candidates different from those who ran for the short term.

In the days of the lame-duck sessions of Congress, elections for the remainder of a term quite often were held simultaneously with the general election, because the session following the election was an important working meeting that lasted until March 4. However, since the passage of the Twentieth Amendment and the ending of most lame-duck sessions, elections for the remaining two months of a term have become less common. Miller, for example, never was sworn in because Congress was not in session during the brief period for which he was elected.

Usually states are more prompt in holding special House elections than was Ohio between 1959 and 1960. One of the most rapid instances of succession occurred in Texas's Tenth District in 1963. Democratic representative Homer Thornberry submitted his resignation on September 26, 1963, to take effect December 20. On the strength of Thornberry's postdated resignation, a special election was held in his district—the first election was held November 9 and the RUNOFF on December 17. The winner, J. J. Pickle, Democrat, was ready to take his seat as soon as Thornberry stepped down. Pickle was sworn in the next day, December 21, 1963.

## Campaign Costs

Unlike presidential campaigns, congressional election campaigns receive no PUBLIC FINANCING and therefore are not subject to spending limits. House and Senate campaigns are, however, restricted by contribution limits and disclosure requirements administered by the FEDERAL ELECTION COMMISSION (FEC).

FEC figures for the 1995–1996 election cycle showed that CAMPAIGN FINANCE expenditures for House elections escalated sharply in the last two decades of the twentieth century. Adjusted for inflation, spending on House races rose from about $340 million in 1982 to $478 million in 1996.

Median spending by incumbents who won was $928,000 among Republicans, who retained the majority won in 1994, and $856,000 among Democrats. Five reelected House members, including Speaker Gingrich and Majority Whip Tom DeLay of Texas, received more than $1 million in contributions from POLITICAL ACTION COMMITTEES (PACs). DeLay received two-thirds of his campaign money from PACs, the highest ratio among the House's top ten PAC recipients.

Under the Federal Election Campaign Act (FECA) an individual's contributions to a federal candidate may not exceed $1,000 for each primary or general election, with annual limits of $20,000 to a national party committee, $5,000 to a state party committee, $5,000 to a PAC, with an overall limit of $25,000. PACs may give $5,000 per election to a candidate, with annual limits of $15,000 to a national party committee and $5,000 to other PACs, with no overall yearly limit.

In the original 1971 version of FECA, Congress tried to limit spending on congressional races. But the Supreme Court ruled in BUCKLEY V. VALEO (1976) that such limits are unconstitutional without public funding of campaigns. In the revised law, contribution limits were kept, but spending limits were dropped, except for presidential candidates who accept the public grants.

## Party Shifts in the House

Until the Republican takeover of Congress in the 1994 midterm elections, the House had been a Democratic bastion for forty years (1955–1995). For twenty-six of those years (1955–1981), the Democrats also held the Senate majority for a record of thirteen consecutive Congresses controlled by the same party.

Since 1901 Republicans have held control of the House for only five relatively brief periods 1901–1911, 1919–1931, 1947–1949, 1953–1955, and 1995–2001 (through the 106th Congress). Most of those periods coincided with Republican presidencies. The exceptions, during Democratic presidencies, were 1947–1949 (Harry S. Truman) and 1995–1999 (Bill Clinton).

After the Democrats led by Franklin D. Roosevelt gained the White House and Congress in the Great Depression year of 1932, Republicans controlled the House for only two Congresses until the 1990s—the Eightieth Congress (1947–1949, which Truman called the "do-nothing" Congress) and the Eighty-third Congress

(1953–1955) during the first half of President Dwight D. Eisenhower's first term.

Regionally, the makeup of the House majority strength shifted dramatically in the latter half of the twentieth century. The South, once called the "Solid South" because of its solidarity with the Democratic Party, now forms the core of Republican electoral strength in presidential and congressional elections. The Northeast, once a GOP stronghold, now provides much of the Democratic base of support.

## House of Representatives, Qualifications

Article I, section 2, of the Constitution set few requirements for election to the U.S. House of Representatives: a member had to be at least twenty-five years of age, have been a U.S. citizen for seven years, and be an inhabitant of the state from which elected. Qualifications for Senate membership are similar. (See SENATE, ELECTING; SENATE, QUALIFICATIONS.)

Besides age, citizenship, and residency, there were other de facto requirements for House election in the early days of the Republic. They included race, sex, and property. Since the Constitution left it to the states to determine who could vote, this in effect limited House membership to propertied white males.

At first, most states had some kind of property requirement for voting. But the democratic trend of the early nineteenth century swept away most property qualifications, producing practically universal white male suffrage by the 1830s. It would be about forty more years, however, before anyone other than a white male citizen could gain membership in the House.

Gradually, several changes in the Constitution broadened the FRANCHISE (the RIGHT TO VOTE) in ways that affected House elections. The Fifteenth Amendment (1870) extended the franchise to newly freed slaves; the Nineteenth Amendment (1920) granted WOMEN'S SUFFRAGE; the Twenty-fourth Amendment (1964) abolished the POLL TAX; and the Twenty-sixth Amendment (1971) broadened YOUTH SUFFRAGE, lowering the voting age to eighteen from twenty-one. In 1965 Congress passed the VOTING RIGHTS ACT to remove barriers several states and localities had erected to keep blacks and other minorities from voting. Other laws and Supreme Court decisions affected BLACK SUFFRAGE and RACIAL REDISTRICTING.

## House Characteristics

The average House member in the 105th Congress (1997–1999) was slightly more than fifty-one years, seven months old. But over the years the age of individual U.S. representatives has ranged from below the legal minimum to almost eighty-five.

The youngest representative was William Charles Cole Claiborne of Tennessee, who took office in 1797 when he was three years under the minimum age of twenty-five. Apparently no one challenged his being underage.

The oldest representative was Jamie L. Whitten, Mississippi Democrat, who served longer in the House (more than fifty-three years) than anyone else. He was eighty-four years and eight months old when he retired in January 1995. He died nine months later.

A close second to Whitten in age was William H. Natcher, Kentucky Democrat, who was also eighty-four when he died in office on March 29, 1994. Natcher was best known for having an unbroken string of 18,401 House votes, a record number, until he became inactive because of illness shortly before his death.

The first black representative was Joseph H. Rainey, South Carolina Republican, who served from 1870 to 1879. Another African American, John W. Menard of Louisiana, had won a seat in 1868 but the House excluded him because of an election dispute.

Jeannette Rankin, Montana Republican, was the first woman elected to Congress. She served in the House twice, 1917–1919 and 1941–1943, and was the only member of Congress to vote against U.S. entry into both World Wars.

The first black woman in the House was Shirley Chisholm, New York Democrat, who served from 1969 to 1983. The first Jewish woman member was Bella S. Abzug, New York Democrat, who served three terms after being elected in 1970.

*Adam Clayton Powell Jr. was at the center of a Supreme Court ruling,* Powell v. McCormack, *that prevented the House from adding qualifications for membership in Congress to those enumerated in the Constitution. Source: Library of Congress*

At the beginning of the 105th Congress fifty-one representatives were women, including a number of African Americans. In all, more than one hundred fifty women had been elected to the House through 1996.

African Americans held thirty-seven House seats in the 105th Congress. They brought the total of black representatives since 1870 to more than one hundred.

## Qualification Disputes

One of the most important Supreme Court decisions regarding qualifications for House membership concerned a black representative, New York Democrat Adam Clayton Powell Jr., but his race ostensibly was not the issue. It was Powell's flamboyant conduct and apparent disregard for the law that led to his being excluded from the House on March 1, 1967.

A House member since 1945, Powell had risen to the chairmanship of the Education and Labor Committee. But as his power grew, Powell came under increasing criticism for absenteeism, income tax evasion, libel, contempt of court, and other offenses alleged or proven.

After his reelection in 1966, Powell was stripped of his chairmanship and recommended for censure and a fine for "gross misconduct." Instead, the full House voted 307–166 to deny Powell his seat.

Powell sued, arguing that he met the constitutional qualifications of age, citizenship, and residency. The Supreme Court agreed and on June 16, 1969, ruled 7–1 in *Powell v. McCormack* that Powell had been improperly excluded. Powell, who meanwhile had been reelected in 1968, lost interest in Congress and rarely attended sessions. He lost the 1970 Democratic primary for his seat and died in April 1972.

Another type of effort to add to the qualifications for Congress swept the nation in the 1990s in the form of TERM LIMITS. These, too, were struck down by the Supreme Court as unconstitutional.

Twenty-three of the fifty states had enacted some form of limitation on the number of terms their senators and representatives could serve. Advocates viewed long INCUMBENCY as dangerous to democratic government. Opponents argued that experience makes better lawmakers and that, besides, the voters are entitled to choose their own representatives so long as they meet the constitutional requirements.

The Court ruling against state-imposed term limits for Congress came in a May 1995 decision in *Term Limits Inc. v. Thornton*. By a 5–4 majority the Court declared that Arkansas may not add to the qualifications for Congress enumerated in the Constitution. (See HOUSE OF REPRESENTATIVES, ELECTING; TERM LIMITS.)

Basically, the Constitution makes clear that Congress has exclusive authority to judge the qualifications of its members. Article I, section 5, states in part: "Each House shall be the Judge of the Election, Returns and Qualifications of its own members."

From time to time this authority conflicts with the right of the people to decide who will represent them. But in the thirty-five cases involving qualifications for House membership since 1789, the House admitted the challenged representative in twenty-two cases.

Only twelve of the thirty-five cases involved the three qualifications set by the Constitution: age, citizenship, or residency. The only person excluded for one of those reasons was John Bailey, independent, unseated in 1823 as not being a resident of the Massachusetts district that elected him, even though the Constitution requires only that the person elected reside in the state. He subsequently was elected to the same seat and served until 1831.

Four exclusions were for disloyalty during the Civil War. The Fourteenth Amendment to the Constitution, ratified in 1868, barred from Congress anyone who "engaged in insurrection or rebellion" against the United States. The four men denied seats had been elected from southern states in 1867. Other exclusions from the House have been for malfeasance, polygamy, and sedition.

## Hunt Commission

*See* PRESIDENTIAL SELECTION REFORMS.

# I

## Ideology

An organized and coherent set of attitudes about government and public policy is known as a political ideology. The word *ideology,* or science of ideas, originated in eighteenth century France during the intellectual Age of Enlightenment that produced the American form of DEMOCRACY.

In contemporary America people with a *liberal* ideology traditionally have supported a strong national government that actively promotes social welfare and equality and intervenes to regulate the economy. Holders of a *conservative* ideology, by contrast, have believed that government should have a limited role in regulating the economy and providing social services. They have stressed that people are primarily responsible for their own welfare.

People who fall between the liberal and conservative viewpoints are considered *moderates.* Other, more extreme, ideologies such as *communism, fascism,* and *socialism* have gained adherents and controlled governments in other countries, as communism does today in China and Cuba. But in the United States only the SOCIALISTS, who advocate collective ownership of production and distribution, have had any measurable and sustained popularity as a THIRD PARTY.

Americans generally find a home in the two major political parties, liberals in the DEMOCRATIC PARTY and conservatives in the REPUBLICAN PARTY, with a wide range from left to right in both. For most of the twentieth century, southern Democrats were highly conservative and, by joining with the Republicans, they often formed a potent conservative COALITION on many votes in Congress. With the GOP's growth in the South, the coalition's importance has waned.

## Ideological Self-Identification

Americans' descriptions of their own ideological positions changed relatively little from the 1970s to the 1990s. Although conservative sentiment grew somewhat in the 1980s, the proportions of the public considering themselves liberal, moderate, or conservative tended to remain stable, with moderates consistently making up the largest category and liberals the smallest.

The significance of such ideological self-identification data is limited, however, because many people do not agree on the meaning of the categories. For example, some self-identified conservatives support supposedly "liberal" policies such as increased federal spending for health, the elderly, and education.

Another difficulty in sorting out people's ideological self-identification stems from the way political discourse changed in the latter half of the twentieth century. During the 1950s and until the mid-1960s liberalism and conservatism pertained primarily to the scope of government involvement in the economy and society. Since the 1960s, however, the traditional distinction between the two ideologies has been overlaid with additional policy dimensions. In foreign policy, for example, conservatism is now also equated with supporting military expenditures, showing a greater willingness to use military force in international affairs, and giving the president the primary role in formulating policy in international affairs. By contrast, liberalism is also equated with giving less priority to military expenditures, exhibiting greater reluctance to use military power, and giving Congress a substantial role in the shaping of foreign policy.

There is also a social policy dimension to use of the terms *liberalism* and *conservatism.* On so-called lifestyle

*Sen. Robert F. Kennedy epitomized liberal ideology for many Americans in the 1960s. Source: Senate Historical Office*

issues—abortion, law and order, prayer in the public schools, women's rights, gay rights, pornography—conservatives show a greater willingness to permit government intervention to regulate human conduct than do liberals.

The multidimensional nature of both ideologies makes it difficult for people to place themselves on a liberal-conservative continuum. It also means that a person might take a traditionally liberal position on issues relating to the government's social welfare responsibilities, yet at the same time support conservative lifestyle positions such as advocating prayer in the public schools, taking a hard line on law and order, and opposing abortion. Or the person might be a liberal on social issues and conservative on fiscal matters, favoring a balanced budget and tight controls on government spending.

Indeed, it was lifestyle issues that gave Republican presidential candidates Richard Nixon, Ronald Reagan, and George Bush an opening wedge with which to split off traditional Democratic voters from their party. In 1992, however, because of people's anxiety over the state of the economy, the Republicans' attempt to place lifestyle issues within the context of "family values" proved much less effective in motivating Democrats to defect from their party. Bill Clinton played to those concerns, then and again in 1996, pledging to control spending and reduce the federal deficit.

## Extent of Ideological Thinking

Although students of PUBLIC OPINION have engaged in a lively debate about the extent of the ideological thinking of the American public, the evidence indicates that it is not high. In 1988 only 18 percent of the voters used terms such as *liberal* or *conservative* in evaluating candidates and issues; the number was even lower—12 percent—in 1956. Surveys in the 1960s and 1970s had found a higher level of ideological awareness among Americans, with voters' use of ideology-based evaluations of presidential candidates and parties hitting levels of 27 percent in 1964, 26 percent in 1968, and 22 percent in 1972. GOP conservatives claimed victory in the 1994 MIDTERM ELECTION, but whether their congressional win was an ideological coup for the Contract with America or an electoral rebuke of the policies of the first Clinton administration or a combination of both factors is unclear. The picture became even cloudier in 1998 when the Democrats gained seats in the House instead of losing them, as is normally the case, especially in the middle of a president's second term. Some analysts interpreted the result as a backlash against the Republicans for their conservative policies and their determination to impeach Clinton over the Monica Lewinsky SCANDAL despite his continued popularity in the polls.

The reasons for the rise in ideological thinking are not altogether clear, but it is likely that the high-voltage political environment of the 1960s and 1970s had an impact. The 1964, 1968, and 1972 elections took place in the supercharged and often polarizing atmosphere of civil rights demonstrations, urban riots, and the Vietnam War. Moreover, these elections were characterized by sharp policy differences between the presidential candidates.

For example, the 1964 Republican nominee, conservative senator Barry Goldwater of Arizona, offered Americans "a choice, not an echo" as he campaigned against a committed liberal Democrat, President Lyndon B. Johnson. Goldwater even sought to capitalize on criticism that his brand of conservatism was too extreme. "I would remind you that extremism in the defense of liberty is no vice," he said in accepting his nomination. "And let me remind you also that moderation in the pursuit of liberty is no virtue."

Two decades later, under the cheery conservatism of Ronald Reagan, it was the liberals who were on the defensive. Even the most committed liberals avoided the label, and comedians joked that they were afraid to use "the L word." From about 25 percent in 1976 the percentage of self-described liberals plunged to about 15 percent in 1981, about where it remained in the 1990s.

Not all public opinion analysts, however, are prepared to acknowledge that Americans became more ideological in the 1960s and 1970s. Some skeptics believe that reworded survey questions were responsible for the findings of an increased incidence of ideological thinking.

This controversy is just one more indication of the complexity and changing nature of public opinion. Although some analysts claim that ideological thinking has been on the rise, the thrust of political science research is that most Americans do not view politics from an ideological perspective. To the extent that they do, however, education is a contributing factor. An educated citizen understands political issues, the government's role in society, and the links between issues.

Although Americans are more likely to consider an issue from the perspective of individual or group self-interest, it is important to make a distinction between the mass public and the political elites—individuals active and influential in political decision making. Candidates, for example, are more likely than the average citizen to have coherent views on current political affairs. They are also more likely to rely on ideological criteria in evaluating issues and political events.

Analysts have discovered as well that, in their ideologies, political activists are less moderate than average voters. This difference is shown by a comparison of the ideologies of the DELEGATES to the NATIONAL PARTY CONVENTIONS and those of the rank-and-file voters. According to POLLING data, not only is there a major "ideology gap" between Republican and Democratic national convention delegates, but Republican delegates are considerably more conservative than rank-and-file Republicans, and Democratic delegates are more liberal than their party's voters.

*Sen. Barry M. Goldwater, well known for his conservative principles, accepts his party's nomination for president in 1964.*
Source: Library of Congress

This situation has implications for presidential nominating politics. Republican presidential aspirants must demonstrate their conservative credentials to have a chance of being nominated. Even George Bush, an incumbent president, was forced to stress conservative themes in 1992 while fending off the right-wing challenge of Patrick Buchanan. By the same token, Democratic candidates for presidential nominations must certify their liberal bona fides. Even Bill Clinton, who proclaimed himself to be a "new kind of Democrat," also made it a point in 1992 and 1996 to cultivate support among liberal constituencies (such as organized labor, feminists, African Americans, and gays and lesbians) with substantial influence over the nominating process.

## Ideology in Operation

The functioning of American politics is profoundly influenced by the scant attention most people pay to ideological concerns and their failure to divide themselves neatly into distinct liberal or conservative groups. Instead of a situation in which liberals and conservatives stand united against each other, people tend to fall into either the liberal or conservative camp depending on the domestic or foreign policy issue at stake.

Economically liberal auto workers, for example, may fight business interests on issues such as raising the minimum wage or requiring health insurance for workers. Later, however, they may find themselves arm-in-arm with the major auto makers in jointly opposing tougher government clean air standards for auto emissions because they believe these standards pose an economic threat to American auto manufacturers. So people who are at odds on one issue today may find themselves allied on another issue tomorrow, making it difficult for cumulative antagonisms to build up through a series of confrontations. The overlapping and inconsistent belief systems that characterize the American public, therefore, reduce the intensity of political conflict. At the same time, however, these overlapping belief systems make it hard to form political alliances based on common attitudes. This in turn contributes to the government's frequent difficulty in reaching policy decisions.

The public's lack of ideological perspectives on many issues also has meant that voters often settle for the easier route of simple PARTY IDENTIFICATION. Party allegiance is an important component of the political thought process for many voters and a basis for their ELECTION DAY decisions.

## Impeachment

*See* REMOVAL FROM OFFICE.

## Incumbency

For a political candidate, nothing succeeds like success. Once in office, the incumbent has a better-than-average chance of being reelected. For presidents, the reelection rate has been about 66 percent. It is even higher for other elective offices, particularly the U.S. House of Representatives, where about 90 percent of members return every two years if they want another term. The Senate return rate is also high, if somewhat less consistent.

Incumbency gives the candidate an edge in name recognition, fund raising, attracting news coverage, using the powers and perquisites of office, and the freedom to campaign without losing income.

The advantages usually far outweigh the disadvantages, but incumbency can have liabilities. They include the possibility of mistakes or failure, the occasional need to take unpopular actions or stands, the inevitable tie to a record that the incumbent may wish to bury, and the blame for events that were beyond the incumbent's control.

## Presidency

The best indication that incumbency gives an advantage to the sitting president is the success rate of those who sought reelection or election in their own right if they had succeeded to the presidency. Of the thirty attempts (including Franklin D. Roosevelt's in 1936, 1940, and 1944) twenty were successful, through and including Bill Clinton's in 1996.

*Making frequent television appearances is one of the advantages of incumbency. Here President Bill Clinton voices his opinion during an ESPN panel discussion on issues of sports and race April 14, 1998, in Houston, Texas. With him is former NFL star Jim Brown. Source: Win McNamee, Reuters*

Other recent history, however, has shown that renomination is not inevitable. Harry Truman, Lyndon Johnson, Gerald Ford, Jimmy Carter, and George Bush all faced strong challenges when they sought to run again. Truman in 1952 and Johnson in 1968 ultimately decided against seeking renomination, and they are not included in the thirty presidential reelection efforts. Since 1951, when the Twenty-second Amendment was ratified, the second-term incumbent president has been barred from running again. The amendment exempted Truman in 1952, but he chose not to seek a second full term.

If the incumbent appears at all vulnerable, another candidate likely will emerge to contend for the nomination. The decline of PARTY IDENTIFICATION and the rise of CANDIDATE-CENTERED CAMPAIGNS and IN-

TEREST GROUPS can make an incumbent appear vulnerable if economic or foreign policy crises develop.

Nevertheless, incumbency offers advantages. The president can dominate MEDIA COVERAGE, divert attention from domestic problems with foreign policy initiatives, and make use of budgetary and regulatory powers. So great is the prestige of the office that most party members are reluctant to reject an incumbent. No president since Chester A. Arthur in 1884 has lost a renomination effort at a NATIONAL PARTY CONVENTION.

When it appeared in 1980 that he might become the first president since Arthur to lose the convention vote, Carter embarked on a CAMPAIGN STRATEGY that overwhelmed challenges by Massachusetts senator Edward Kennedy and California governor Jerry Brown. Carter

won renomination by using the powers of incumbency. He stayed at the White House occupied with the Iranian hostage crisis, trying to appear above the partisan fray. At the same time he was deeply engaged in the primary strategy—persuading southern states to push their primaries to the early part of the schedule.

Incumbents play to the natural reluctance of voters to exchange a known commodity for a newcomer. Their CAMPAIGN SLOGANS stress stability rather than change. The Carter-Mondale slogan in 1980 was "A Tested and Trustworthy Team." Similarly, pointing to a healthy economy and peace abroad, Clinton and Vice President Al Gore campaigned on a "don't rock the boat" theme in 1996.

As the president, the incumbent can take advantage of the job title in campaign activities and literature. In 1972 Republicans called the Richard Nixon reelection organization the "Committee for the Reelection of the President." Nixon won handily even though the committee soon became known as "CREEP."

Deciding whether and how to participate in televised DEBATES with their challengers is an important tactical decision for an incumbent president. As a rule challengers have more to gain in debates because they are put on an equal footing with the president and have a chance to demonstrate that they can deal with substantive issues.

In 1976 President Ford's Rose Garden strategy included challenging his opponent, Carter, to a series of televised debates. With their man behind in the polls, Ford's advisers calculated that he had little to lose and much to gain. There had been no such debates since 1960, and they were bound to be a decisive element in the campaign. They were, but not to Ford's advantage. Ford's gaffe in saying that the Soviet Union did not dominate Eastern Europe hurt him and helped Carter. Nevertheless, presidents since Ford have consented, sometimes reluctantly, to debates with their opponents. The negotiations about format, moderators, and the inclusion of THIRD PARTY candidates can sometimes be almost as interesting as the debates.

In debates and other venues, incumbents are easily placed on the defensive because they are tied to their records and their policies. They may become the victims—or beneficiaries—of RETROSPECTIVE VOTING as citizens judge from their records whether they should be kept in office or replaced. Presidents are blamed for failures as well as remembered for successes. They are even saddled with events beyond their control. Oil shortages, regional conflicts abroad, and adverse economic conditions may arise through no particular fault of the incumbent president.

In other ways the two major party nominees are on equal footing in the general election campaign. Since 1976 these nominees have received identical PUBLIC FINANCING grants to underwrite their campaigns. The news media cover the two candidates on a roughly equal basis. Even when third party or INDEPENDENT candidates—such as George Wallace in 1968, John Anderson in 1980, or Ross Perot in 1992 and 1996—run for the presidency, the spotlight usually stays trained on the Democratic and Republican nominees.

But if one of the two is a sitting president the balance of power can tilt. The president benefits from the public's reluctance to reject a tested national leader for an unknown quantity. The people's emotional bond with the president is an important, if unquantifiable, factor in the equation. Perhaps the outstanding examples in recent years are Lyndon Johnson's 1964 reelection, which benefited from the nation's deep desire for continuity in the wake of President John Kennedy's assassination, and President Ronald Reagan's evocation of patriotic themes in his 1984 campaign for reelection.

The defeats of Presidents Ford, Carter, and Bush demonstrate that incumbency does not guarantee victory. Negative perceptions of actions or abilities—such as Ford's pardon of the disgraced president Nixon and Carter's handling of economic and foreign policy crises—can doom an incumbent. Both Ford and Carter suffered from bitter struggles for their party nominations.

## Congress

A seat in the House or Senate carries with it advantages that help the occupants gain reelection, sometimes for many terms. Incumbents have the franking privilege, which allows them to send supposedly nonpolitical mailings to constituents without paying postage. They have the use of video and audio recording studios for taping news releases for the hometown radio and television stations. They have a work schedule that allows for campaigning and a travel allowance that permits them to be back in their home districts every weekend.

The result of these and other perquisites of office is that turnover is low, although the entire House and one-third of the Senate come up for election every two years. Most House elections since 1949 have brought fewer than 80 new members to that 435-member body. The 100-member Senate also has relatively low turnover. The 1998 election produced an exceptionally low turnover, with only 40 freshmen in the House in 1999.

A *safe seat,* usually in the House, is one in which turnover is unlikely from one election to another. Some seats are safe because the incumbent is popular. Others are safe for a particular political party because most of the voters in the district almost invariably cast their ballots for its candidate. Often a safe seat incumbent wins by a wide margin. In 1994, for example, 63 percent of House incumbents were reelected with 60 percent or more of the vote. For senators it was 48 percent.

Almost half the states tried to ensure more rotation in their congressional delegations by imposing TERM LIMITS on the members. But in 1995 the Supreme Court ruled that the Constitution does not permit states to impose such limits on qualifications for Congress.

Since the end of World War II the success rate for House members seeking reelection has been about 90 percent. It was 98.3 percent in 1998. Even in 1994, when thirty-seven Democrats were defeated in the Republicans' MIDTERM ELECTION takeover of Congress, the rate was 90.2 percent for those seeking reelection or 80.0 percent of the House membership. About 10 percent of the incumbents did not seek reelection that year.

The Senate reelection rate for the same period has been somewhat lower, although 89.6 percent of the incumbent candidates in 1998 won another six-year term. Four senators retired that year.

Congressional incumbents also enjoy a significant advantage in CAMPAIGN FINANCE. POLITICAL ACTION COMMITTEES (PACs) overwhelmingly favor incumbents over challengers because if reelected they can help the special interests in committee and on the floor. Challengers represent a risk because they likely will not win.

In the 1995–1996 election cycle, according to the FEDERAL ELECTION COMMISSION, incumbents received 67 percent ($146.4 million) of the $217.8 million that PACs contributed to congressional campaigns. The remaining 33 percent went to challengers ($31.6 million) or candidates for open seats ($39.8 million).

Despite the margin of safety it provides, incumbency is often of little protection to members caught in SCANDALS. In the FBI's 1980 Abscam sting operation, in which federal agents posing as Arab sheiks offered fake bribes to members, six House members and one senator were convicted. After the next election, all seven were gone, including one expelled from the House.

The subsequent House bank scandal took an even higher toll. Of the 269 members who had penalty-free overdrafts on their personal accounts, 77 or 25 percent resigned or were defeated in the 1992 election.

## State Officers and Legislators

GOVERNORS, other statewide officers, and state legislators also benefit from incumbency. The average reelection rate of governors from 1968 through 1994 was 77 percent. For LIEUTENANT GOVERNORS and other offices elected statewide, the average was 89 percent. State representatives seeking reelection had the highest success rate: 90 percent. The average for state senators was 86 percent.

Like presidents, who can serve no more than two four-year terms, many governors are subject to term limits. As of 1998, thirty-eight states placed some limit on the number of terms their governor could serve. (See term limits table, page 173.) In most states the limit was two consecutive four-year terms, but some permitted longer service if the terms were not consecutive.

Unlike members of Congress, exempted from term limits by the Constitution, legislators in twenty states are subject to some form of term limits, usually eight two-year terms. Most of the legislature term limits were enacted after 1990 and over time will have an effect on incumbency. Although they may not affect the percentage of incumbents winning reelection if they are eligible, they will increase turnover and reduce the percentage of the legislature returning after each election. It has been reported that some state legislatures are already feeling the effects of term limits—the members lack expertise and institutional memory.

## Independent

An independent candidate or voter is one not affiliated with a political party. Few people run as independents in U.S. elections, and fewer still are successful.

Between 1979 and 1991 there were no independents in Congress. In 1999 there was one, Rep. Bernard Sanders of Vermont, reelected to his fifth two-year term in 1998.

Since 1951 only four states have had independent governors, including two in Maine: James B. Longley (1975–1979) and Angus King (1995– ). The others were Lowell P. Weicker Jr. of Connecticut (1991–1995), Walter J. Hickel of Alaska (1990–1994), and Jesse Ventura of Minnesota (1999– ).

No independent has been elected president, but there have been some interesting attempts. Texas billionaire Ross Perot was the most successful independent presidential candidate. In 1992 he received 18.9 percent of the POPULAR VOTE in his self-financed contest with incumbent Republican George Bush and Democrat Bill Clinton, the victor. Four years later Perot ran again, this time as the nominee of his new REFORM PARTY, but won only 8.4 percent of the vote. Another major independent presidential candidacy was that of Illinois Republican representative John B. Anderson, who received 6.6 percent of the vote running as an independent in 1980. (See table, page 438.)

In America's TWO-PARTY SYSTEM independent candidates are at a disadvantage. Unlike Democratic and Republican candidates, independents are not automatically placed on the ballot. To gain BALLOT ACCESS

they must meet each state's requirements. Perot in 1992, for example, employed an army of paid and volunteer workers to gather hundreds of thousands of signatures to get his name on the ballot in all fifty states.

It is sometimes difficult to tell the difference between an independent candidate and the nominee of a minor THIRD PARTY. Some third parties appear to be single-person entities calling themselves parties to give their campaigns credibility or to satisfy ballot requirements. In the 1996 presidential election, for example, candidates of four parties with the word *independent* in their titles received four hundred or more votes apiece. A scattering of other votes, including WRITE-INS, went to independent or minor party candidates in some states.

Ohio formerly required every candidate to be the nominee of a major political party. But in *Williams v. Rhodes* (1968) the Supreme Court invalidated an Ohio statute requiring a candidate or new party to obtain voters' signatures equal to at least 15 percent of the vote in the previous gubernatorial election. This requirement and others essentially had limited the Ohio ballot to Democratic and Republican nominees.

In 1971, however, the Court in *Jenness v. Fortson* upheld a Georgia law that kept independent and nonparty candidates off the ballot unless they filed a nominating petition signed by at least 5 percent of those eligible to vote in the previous election. In its decision the Court took note of its Ohio decision and said that Georgia's restrictions were reasonable while Ohio's had been unconstitutionally burdensome.

In *Storer v. Brown,* a 1974 case, the Court upheld California's right to require a candidate to break with a political party at least a year before the election in which he or she planned to run as an independent.

The sizable Perot vote in 1992 highlighted a trend toward more independence and less PARTY IDENTIFICATION among voters. Based on NATIONAL ELECTION STUDIES data, 22 percent of voters in 1994 described themselves as independents, with 10 percent leaning Democratic and 12 percent leaning Republican.

According to state election officials, the 1993 MOTOR VOTER ACT accelerated the trend to independent VOTER REGISTRATIONS. In Kentucky, for example, annual independent registrations jumped from 5 percent to 25 percent in the first year after the Motor Voter Act made registering easier throughout the country.

## Independent Expenditures

*See* HARD MONEY.

## Indirect Election

*See* DIRECT ELECTION.

## Infomercials

*See* MEDIA USE IN CAMPAIGNS; POLITICAL ADVERTISING.

## Initiatives and Referendums

A ballot initiative is a form of direct DEMOCRACY in which the people propose new laws subject to approval by all the state's voters. A referendum is similar, except that it usually originates with the legislature.

Ballot initiatives have become increasingly important in recent years, especially in California, where they are called propositions. California has permitted such questions to be on the ballot since 1912. The state's campaigns over issues such as bilingual education in 1998 have attracted national attention and often are copied in other states. INTEREST GROUPS frequently spend millions of dollars for POLITICAL ADVERTISING in initiative campaigns, which are professionally managed by POLITICAL CONSULTANTS.

About half the states allow initiatives to pass laws or amend the state constitution. All states require referendums on amendments to the state constitution, including the sixteen states that allow such amendments to originate as initiatives. Because the U.S. Constitution does not permit Congress to delegate its responsibili-

ties, there are no initiatives or referendums on federal laws.

Twenty-four states permit the legislature to submit questions for voter approval. In the case of bond issues or major debt authorization, nineteen states require referendum approval. Twenty-three states allow citizens to petition for a referendum on a law already passed by the legislature.

A *plebiscite* is a type of referendum on a political entity's boundaries or form of government. In 1998, for example, the U.S. House of Representatives approved the holding of a plebiscite in the Commonwealth of Puerto Rico on whether it should remain a commonwealth, become independent, or become a Spanish-speaking state of the United States. (The voters in effect chose to remain a commonwealth. See BILINGUAL VOTERS.)

States vary widely in the number of signatures needed to place an initiative on the ballot. Generally it ranges from 5 percent to 15 percent of the number of votes for governor in the previous election. Amendments to the state constitution require more signatures than proposals for state laws. Often the petitioning is a two-step procedure: first, the sponsors must petition for permission to circulate a ballot question; then, if enough signatures are obtained, they must circulate a petition to place the initiative on the ballot.

Ten states use the *indirect initiative*, which sends the proposed law to the legislature for its consideration. If it is not passed, the initiative can then be put before the voters. California abandoned indirect initiative in 1966. Four states (Nevada, Ohio, Utah, and Washington) allow both the direct and indirect initiative.

### California Example

The most famous initiative, California's Proposition 13 in 1978, rolled back property taxes to 1 percent of 1975–1976 home values and capped further increases at 2 percent a year until the house was sold. The measure won 65 percent approval.

Sponsored by antitax activists Howard Jarvis and Paul Gann, Prop 13, as it came to be known, had far-reaching consequences. Although it gave homeowners a tax break, it forced cutbacks in government services and led to a complex fee system to make up for the lost revenue. Other states followed suit, with some of the same results.

Above all, Prop 13 reinvigorated the initiative process. Between 1912 and 1978, Californians had voted on 153 ballot measures. In the twenty years after Prop 13, they faced decisions on 109 measures. Only 91 of the 262 total measures, or 34.7 percent, won approval.

## Initiatives Industry

A corps of advertising, political, POLLING, public relations, and other types of consultants has grown up around the business of persuading voters to approve or disapprove ballot questions. Even the gathering of sig-

nature petitions can be contracted out to firms specializing in that activity.

California law gives initiative sponsors 150 days in which to gather 433,000 valid signatures of registered voters to put a statute proposal on the ballot; 693,000 signatures are needed for a constitutional amendment. Faced with such numbers, based on a percentage of the gubernatorial vote, sponsors must turn to signature companies for help. Estimated costs range from $700,000 to $1 million or more. For an Indian tribe gambling initiative in 1998, collectors were paid $1.50 per signature.

Overall costs of an initiatives campaign can rival those for governor or Congress. California's insurance industry reportedly spent $80 million in a futile effort to

*Skip Cook, left, and Tim Jacob of Arkansans for Governmental Reform speak at a news conference on a 1992 ballot measure to limit the terms of the members of the Arkansas congressional delegation. The Supreme Court declared such measures unconstitutional in 1995. Source:* Arkansas Democrat-Gazette

prevent a rollback of auto insurance prices. Other multimillion-dollar campaigns have been waged by tobacco companies against antismoking initiatives, technology companies against a law making it easier to sue for securities fraud, and organized labor against curtailment of union dues for political purposes.

In these and other initiatives contests, special interests were on one or both sides of the issue. In Washington State in 1997, the National Rifle Association spent $3 million, much of it raised out of state, to defeat a handgun safety initiative. Supporters spent $800,000. The same year in Oregon a consortium of Christian groups spent $4 million in an unsuccessful campaign for an initiative to repeal Oregon's assisted suicide law, the first such state law in the nation.

Controversial ballot issues also affect races for elective office. Candidates often take a stand for or against the question, and that influences voters' choices of candidates. Arkansas voters in 1996 approved a law to label candidate ballots with their stances on TERM LIMITS, but the state supreme court invalidated the law as unconstitutional. The U.S. Supreme Court let the ruling stand.

California's Republican governor Pete Wilson staked his prestige on passage in 1998 of Proposition 226, the so-called paycheck protection initiative requiring annual, written permission to use union members' dues for political purposes. Although Wilson was leaving office, the proposition's defeat may have hurt his presidential ambitions.

*First lady Hillary Rodham Clinton addresses a bipartisan fund raiser supporting California's Proposition 10 on October 30, 1998, in Los Angeles. Proposition 10, the California Children and Families Initiative, would add a 50 cent tax to each pack of cigarettes sold in the state to fund antismoking education and programs for early childhood development. Source: Rose Prouser, Reuters*

## Growing Popularity

The number of statewide initiatives that reached the ballot rose from 67 in 1992 to 106 in 1996, according to a compilation by a Nevada signature-gathering firm. Among the reasons put forth for such growth are public frustration with inaction and partisan bickering in legislatures, the imitation of successful initiatives, and interests groups' bypassing of legislatures to go directly to the people.

An additional reason is that initiative campaigns have become lucrative businesses. In 1998 there were a half-dozen signature-gathering firms in California and

Nevada, operating as far away as Florida and Massachusetts. By one estimate those companies accounted for 90 percent of the initiatives that reached the ballot. Typically, a company will be circulating petitions for several initiatives at the same time.

In a January 1999 case, *Buckley v. American Constitutional Law Reform,* the Supreme Court struck down as "excessively restrictive of political speech" three Colorado limits on petition circulators. A badge requirement was struck down 8–1. Nullified 6–3 were rules that the signature collectors be registered voters and that sponsors disclose their names and pay.

## Interest Group

Whether condemned as a special interest or cherished as a special way that citizens can have their say in government, the interest group is an integral part of the American political process. An interest group, or lobby, is an organized body of individuals who share goals and try to influence public policy. The operative elements of this definition are "organized" and "influence public policy." African Americans, farmers, manufacturers, and workers are not interest groups in and of themselves. Being unorganized, they are interests and *potential* interest groups. But the National Association for the Advancement of Colored People (NAACP), the American Farm Bureau Federation (AFBF), the National Association of Manufacturers (NAM), and the AFL-CIO *are* organized groups seeking to influence government policy.

Not all interest group activity is carried on by huge groups such as the AFL-CIO or AFBF. Some organizations consist only of a small staff backed by financial patrons. For example, the Media Access Project is a public interest law firm concerned about the public's access to government information.

Most interest groups have lobbyists on their staffs, or at least on a retainer to represent the group. The latter category includes the so-called hired guns—Washington lawyers, public relations consultants, and other professionals, who, for a fee, try to influence government policy for their clients.

Interest groups receive a lot of bad press. Yet they perform an essential function in American DEMOCRACY: they are one way in which people who share the same attitudes or interests can be represented informally before Congress, executive agencies, and state and local legislative or regulatory bodies. This informal system of group representation supplements the formal system of geographic area representation used in Congress—states in the Senate and districts in the House of Representatives.

In their representational roles, interest groups provide policy makers with specialized information that otherwise might not be readily available. Interest groups also are an avenue for more effective political participation than is likely to be achieved by a lone person picketing in front of the White House.

## Composition and Growth

Since the 1960s there has been a virtual explosion in the number and diversity of interest groups operating in Washington. As the scope of government activities has grown, more and more groups have recognized the benefits of having a presence in the nation's capital.

The composition of the interest group system has changed as well. The traditional farm, union, professional, and business groups must now compete with a vast array of citizens' groups organized around an idea or cause and having no occupational basis for membership. In addition, individual corporations, states, cities, counties, and universities have gravitated toward Washington to advance or protect interests that can be dramatically affected by government policy.

Business-oriented groups are among the strongest of the Washington lobbies. The largest of these are the so-called peak business organizations that seek to represent general business interests. These include the U.S. Chamber of Commerce, the National Association of Manufacturers, and the Business Roundtable. NAM is made up of large manufacturing concerns, and the Business Roundtable includes approximately two hundred of the nation's largest companies such as IBM, General Motors, GTE, and Shell Oil.

The more specialized business groups, called trade associations, are composed of companies in the same line of business. Trade associations range from the American Bankers Association with its thirteen thousand member banks to the much smaller International Association of Refrigerated Warehouses and the Pet Food Institute.

Individual corporations also try to influence policy making. More than eight hundred have Washington offices, and those without an office frequently hire a law firm or lobbyist to look out for their interests. In a sense, many corporations have multiple representation in Washington: their own corporate representation as well as the resources of groups such as the U.S. Chamber of Commerce and the trade associations to which

*The power of interest groups in the political process has long been observed. In this nineteenth century cartoon by Joseph Keppler, the Senate is watched over by fat-cat "monopolists" who crowd through an open door while the "people's entrance" is locked shut.*
Source: Library of Congress

they belong. Large corporations engaged in several lines of business may belong to more than twenty lobbying organizations.

Labor unions have a larger base of individual members than do business organizations. The largest and most influential union is the AFL-CIO, a confederation of operating unions such as the United Steel Workers, United Auto Workers, and United Brotherhood of Carpenters and Joiners of America. (Not all unions are affiliated with the AFL-CIO. For example, the highly politicized National Education Association, a union of teachers, operates independently of the AFL-CIO, as do various railroad employee unions. In 1998 the NEA membership resisted offers to merge with the AFL-CIO's American Federation of Teachers.)

As the industrial sector of the economy has declined since the 1950s so have the memberships of the longtime AFL-CIO unions representing industrial and building trades workers. The auto workers, steel workers, and carpenters unions are no longer the largest. They have been replaced by white-collar and service sector unions such as the Teamsters and the American Federation of State, County, and Municipal Employees.

Agriculture, another economic sector, is organized to reflect general farm interests as well as those of specific commodity producers. The largest of the general farm interest groups is the American Farm Bureau Federation, which tends to represent the larger, more efficient producers and to support a relatively conservative political agenda.

On many issues the AFBF is opposed by the politically weaker National Farmers Organization and National Farmers Union, who represent the dwindling number of small producers. Major powers in agricultural policy making are the organizations that promote the interests of specific commodity growers and processors—for example, the National Peanut Council, Tobacco Institute, National Association of Wheat Growers, and agribusiness corporations such as Ralston Purina, Cargill, and Archer-Daniels-Midland.

Finally, professional associations represent many of the individuals whose occupations demand technical training and expertise. Political involvement is greatest among those professional groups heavily regulated by government or dependent on government for financing. Examples are the American Bar Association and the American Medical Association.

Nonprofit organizations represent the interests of people as citizens, consumers, and taxpayers, or as the elderly, disadvantaged, handicapped, and minorities. Many of these organizations—particularly those for consumers, the environment, minorities, and the poor—are commonly called public interest groups, although their "public interest" label has stirred the resentment of those who oppose them and have a different conception of the public interest.

One of the most prominent and influential of the public interest groups is Common Cause. It has called for government reforms in areas such as CAMPAIGN FINANCE, lobbying, government ethics, congressional organization, and VOTER REGISTRATION. Persons linked by IDEOLOGY have found outlets in the interest group system as well. For liberals, there is the Americans for Democratic Action, and for conservatives, the American Conservative Union.

Religious and government organizations also maintain a strong presence in Washington. Religious groups were in the forefront of the CIVIL RIGHTS and anti–Vietnam War movements, and some actively oppose abortion. Protestant church groups, however, often split along ideological lines. The mainline National Council of Churches generally takes liberal positions and has been opposed by the fundamentalist groups of the Christian Coalition. They clashed, for example, over the 1987 Supreme Court nomination of Judge Robert Bork, an outspoken conservative.

In the public sector, nearly all of the states have federal liaison offices, and many cities, counties, and state universities as well have their own Washington offices or law firms or lobbyists representing them. Major associations representing the government sector include the National Governors' Association, the National Association of Counties, and the U.S. Conference of Mayors.

## Foreign Lobbying

Foreign governments also try to influence U.S. public policy. Some of this activity is carried out by foreign ambassadors and their staffs, but, increasingly, high-priced Washington lobbyists and law firms are representing foreign government and corporate clients.

Such practice is highly controversial, however, because the foreign interests may run counter to those of the United States. Representatives of a "foreign principal" are required to register with the Justice Department under the Foreign Agents Registration Act, but the act relies more on disclosure than on penalties and enforcement. Originally enacted in 1938 to guard against Nazi propaganda, the law was revised in 1966 to place more emphasis on protecting "the integrity of the decision-making process of our government."

Federal law prohibits foreign nationals from making campaign contributions in U.S. elections. Alleged violations of those laws produced a major SCANDAL regarding FUND RAISING for the 1996 presidential election. Both parties had to return foreign contributions but the DEMOCRATIC NATIONAL COMMITTEE returned the larger amount. Congress in 1997 and 1998 investigated allegations that some of the Asian contributions to President Bill Clinton's reelection campaign were part of an effort by the People's Republic of China to influence U.S. policy.

Not all interest group activity in behalf of foreign countries is initiated by their governments or hired agents in Washington. Some nations have home-grown support organizations. For example, Israel has benefited from having an organization of Americans, the American Israel Public Affairs Committee, devoted to protecting its interests.

## Interest Groups and Elections

Elected officials cannot wage credible election campaigns without money, and interest groups are often willing to provide campaign cash. The chosen vehicle for these financial contributions is the POLITICAL ACTION COMMITTEE (PAC). The Federal Election Campaign Act (FECA) amendments of 1971 and 1974 allow a political committee created by an interest group to solicit funds for distribution to candidates. The act allows corporations and unions, which cannot legally give from their treasuries to candidates, to set up PACs that may solicit funds from stockholders or members.

Independent PACs abound as well, made up of like-minded people interested in promoting a particular ideology or policy position—for example, the National Abortion Rights Action League PAC, EMILY's List (supports prochoice Democratic women candidates), the National Right to Life Committee, the National Congressional Club (a conservative PAC formed by supporters of Sen. Jesse Helms, North Carolina Republican), and the liberal National Committee for an Effective Congress.

PACs must comply with federal regulations calling for regular reports of receipts and limits on contributions of $5,000 per candidate in the primary and general election, for a total of $10,000. The FECA also sets individual limits for contributions to federal candidates and spending limits for presidential campaigns that receive public funding. (See CAMPAIGN FINANCE; PUBLIC FINANCING OF CAMPAIGNS.)

Campaign funds are not the only kind of campaign assistance interest groups make available to candidates. Mass membership organizations can mobilize their members to vote for and work in behalf of preferred candidates. Organized labor, for example, operates phone banks during election campaigns, contacting union households to get out the vote for union-endorsed candidates (almost exclusively Democrats).

But group members often have other commitments and beliefs that conflict with those of the group, and they may not vote in accordance with the official position of their leaders. Indeed, in spite of organized labor's vigorous support of Democratic presidential nominee Clinton in 1992, 45 percent of voters in union households cast their ballots instead for either his Republican opponent, George Bush, or independent Ross

Perot. Exit polls taken during the 1996 election indicated that among union households 50 percent supported Clinton, 30 percent supported the Republican candidate, Robert Dole, and 9 percent voted for Perot. In June 1998, however, strong labor and Democratic opposition helped to defeat California's Proposition 226 INITIATIVE, which would have prohibited withholding of wages or union dues for political contributions without written, annual permission from the employee or union member.

Interest groups may even take the more extreme measure of reaching beyond their membership and publicizing the record—often in a negative manner—of a public official. Environmental Action, for example, periodically announces its "Dirty Dozen," incumbent members of Congress who, in its view, had the worst records on environmental issues. And interest groups, particularly large and well-financed organizations such as the American Medical Association PAC and the Realtors' PAC, have made independent expenditures to bolster the campaigns of supportive members of Congress or to defeat those who have opposed them. Such expenditures, if truly independent, are exempt from the contribution limits to federal candidates.

Corporations, unions, and nonprofit sector groups often supplement their lobbying and PAC activities with POLITICAL ADVERTISING. This technique is especially evident when an interest group believes its political influence as well as its public image could benefit from a little polishing.

In the 1996 elections, "issue ads" emerged as a controversial way for groups or individuals to spend lavishly for or against candidates for Congress without running afoul of the FECA contribution limits. Ostensibly a discussion of the issues rather than the candidates, issue ads can be none-too-subtle boosts for a specific candidate if his or her views on the issue differ sharply from those of the opposing candidate.

Direct marketing by mail and telephone—targeting past and potential supporters with an appeal to join a group, contact public officials, and contribute money to an organization—is another means of mobilizing mass support for a cause or a candidate. One large-scale practitioner of this method is right-wing organizer Richard Viguerie, who claims to have the addresses of millions of conservative voters on file in his northern Virginia office.

## Regulation

The term *lobbyist* goes back to the early 1800s when favor seekers jammed the lobbies, cloakrooms, and hallways of legislatures. Initially, these hallway denizens were called "lobby agents," a designation that was shortened to lobbyists in the 1830s.

Although the term *lobbying* was not yet in vogue when the Constitution was written, the right to lobby was made explicit by its First Amendment, which provides that "Congress shall make no law . . . abridging . . . the right of the people . . . to petition the Government for a redress of grievances."

About three-quarters of the more than 14,500 lobbyists in Washington work as officers and other employees of interest groups. The rest are attorneys or consultants, who represent clients and in return receive a fee or retainer. But lobbyists, who need support to do their jobs, constitute only a small fraction of the interest group workforce in Washington. An estimated eighty thousand people work in the capital for associations seeking to influence government policy.

Concern about the undue influence of this army of special interest troops has led Congress to enact regulatory legislation. Under the Federal Regulation of Lobbying Act passed in 1946, groups and individuals seeking to influence legislation are required to register with the clerk of the House and the secretary of the Senate and to file quarterly financial statements. As it has been interpreted, however, the act has little practical impact. The Supreme Court has held that the law applies only to groups or individuals involved in direct lobbying and whose "principal purpose" is lobbying. As a result, not all groups register, and grassroots lobbying is not covered by the law. In addition, it does not apply to attempts to influence the executive branch.

Although the lobby disclosure statements do not give a complete picture, a computerized study of them in 1998 indicated that $100 million a month is spent on Washington lobbying. The study, described as the first of its kind, was a joint effort of the Associated Press and the nonpartisan Center for Responsive Politics.

There is broad support for the notion that the public is entitled to more information than the current law permits about the activities of interest groups. But proposals to strengthen the reporting and disclosure provisions of the law have raised serious issues of privacy, burdensome red tape, and the constitutional rights of free speech and petition to redress grievances.

---

## International and U.S. Elections Compared

Any comparison of U.S. elections with those of other nations must take into account the differences in both the rights and privileges of the citizens and in the structure and function of government. What passes for an "election" in a totalitarian regime might be a mere sham in the sense of an election in the United States and in other democracies.

In 1995, for example, Iraq held a REFERENDUM on whether President Saddam Hussein was performing up to his people's expectations. When the results were announced, Hussein had won 99.96 percent of the vote. In the old Soviet Union and in its then-satellite countries, similar high percentages were routinely chalked up for the candidates put forth by the COMMUNIST PARTY. In both the Iraqi and Soviet situations, virtually every eligible voter turned up at the polls to cast a ballot.

These elections clearly were not meaningful in any sense of expressing the people's will by offering them alternatives and the freedom of choice. And the remarkably high VOTER TURNOUTS, while on their face admirable and useful for propaganda purposes, meant nothing, given the nature of political and economic coercion that these monolithic states brought to bear on their citizens to ensure high percentages.

Among the democratic countries, the United States ranks poorly in voter participation. Only 49 percent of voting age Americans took part in the 1996 presidential election, and turnout, as it usually is, was even lower (about 37 percent) in the 1998 MIDTERM ELECTION. In

*Japanese citizens cast their ballots as voting starts in Kokubunji, west of Tokyo, October 20, 1996 —the first general election for three years. Japan has looser campaign finance regulations than the United States, but appears to have fewer campaign finance problems. Source: Eriko Sugita, Reuters*

other democracies participation is traditionally higher in nearly all forms of elections held—from national to local. A study conducted during the 1980s found that the average turnout in eighteen of twenty countries was well above 75 percent, ranging as high as 91 percent in Australia (it rose to 96 percent in 1996). Only Switzerland ranked behind the United States.

Although some political scientists see dire omens in the U.S. turnout percentages, others point out that there are differences that make direct comparisons difficult. When those factors are considered, the American voter participation rate compares more favorably with those of other free nations.

In sixteen of the twenty countries in the 1980s study, for example, VOTER REGISTRATION is automatic, done for the voter by the state. In Australia and New Zealand, registration is mandatory. Only in the United States, which has no national registration system, and France is the initiative to register placed entirely on the individual voter. Any American who wants to vote must make the effort to register (except in North Dakota, which has no formal registration).

Studies have indicated that voter turnout in U.S. presidential elections could rise as much as 15 percent if registration were made simpler. But the MOTOR VOTER ACT of 1993, which made voter registration forms readily available at many government offices and resulted in the registration of 10 million new voters in time for the 1996 presidential election, did not increase voter turnout.

Elections in fourteen of the countries studied are held on "rest" days, not work days, making it easier for most voters to find time to go to the polls. Holding elections on weekends or holidays may also help better focus the collective attention of prospective voters. In addition, most of these countries schedule as many elections as they can, from the national to the local level, on the same day, again reinforcing the idea that the citizen's vote is an institution vital to all levels of government. Some American states have experimented with weekend elections, but by law the federal ELECTION DAY is on a Tuesday. Many states schedule state and local elections to coincide with federal elections.

In many democracies the ballot choices are far more limited than in the United States. In Great Britain, for example, a voter must cast only one vote for a candidate to Parliament, and in Germany one vote is cast for a representative to the Bundestag and one for a political party. Researchers have found, however, that the existence of a large number of political parties depresses voter turnout. Besides being confusing, the array of names indicates to voters that the real struggle for political power will take place in the legislature as parties jockey to form majority coalitions.

Another finding by researchers is that democracies with a UNICAMERAL legislature have higher voter turnouts than those with a BICAMERAL system that includes a strong upper house, as in the U.S. Congress. Voters apparently believe that elections in a single-chamber system are likely to produce significant results. In the United States, only Nebraska has a unicameral legislature.

## Mandatory Voting

Some democracies make voting compulsory—a coercion that likely would not find favor in the United States, with its strong traditions of individualism and independent action. In countries where voting is mandatory, nonvoters are fined. Rigorous enforcement is difficult and expensive, however, and the fines are small—about the equal of those for a parking ticket. Nevertheless, compulsory voting has produced exceptionally large voter turnouts in all the countries that have made it the law.

But even though a government can mandate that a citizen show up at a polling place and accept a ballot, and even drop it into a ballot box, it cannot compel a voter to mark the ballot. As the political scientist Arend Lijphart writes, "Secret ballots mean that nobody can be prevented from casting an invalid or blank one."

Despite his recognition of its shortcomings, Lijphart is a strong advocate of compulsory voting. He argues that it reduces elections costs because parties do not have to spend as much to get voters to the polls. It might also reduce so-called "attack ads" and other forms of NEGATIVE CAMPAIGNING, which polls show depress voter participation. With compulsory voting, Lijphart writes, attack ads might prove to be "no longer worth the effort."

Compulsory voting in the United States, other scholars contend, might violate individual freedom. Such a finding led the Netherlands to abolish it in 1970, resulting in a drop of nearly 40 percentage points in voter turnout. Conservative parties generally have opposed compulsion, according to Lijphart, because "high turnout is not in their partisan self-interest, . . . unequal turnout favors privileged voters, who tend to be conservative."

In the United States, the better educated are far more likely to vote than the less educated; in a matching corollary, higher-income Americans are more likely to vote than those with lower incomes. In other democracies, the better educated are only slightly more likely to vote than the less educated, perhaps because registration and voting are easier or required.

## Money and Elections

Despite the laws governing CAMPAIGN FINANCE, irregularities in fund raising have been a major problem in U.S. elections. The situation apparently worsened in the 1996 presidential election. Other major democracies, such as Great Britain and Japan, appear to have fewer such problems, even though they have looser regulations that allow much higher contributions to candidates. Unlike the United States, where corporations and unions can contribute to candidates only through their POLITICAL ACTION COMMITTEES, unions and companies in Canada can give directly to parties and candidates. There are regulations, however, on how much candidates and parties can spend.

In Russia legal spending limits are barely enforced. In Mexico, which has higher contribution limits than the United States, the long-dominant ruling party still managed to spend above the limits by illegally giving secret government funds to its nominees.

Political candidates in Britain, Germany, and Mexico get free television time during the campaign. Similar proposals were before Congress in 1998. The U.S. Federal Communications Commission has EQUAL TIME AND REBUTTAL RULES that require broadcasters to let candidates reply to attacks on them, but candidates must pay for POLITICAL ADVERTISING on television and radio. Advocates of free air time argue that it would result in cleaner elections because candidates would be less pressed for money to buy TV time, the largest single expense of modern U.S. campaigns.

## Iowa Caucus

The Iowa CAUCUS shares with the NEW HAMPSHIRE PRIMARY special status as the first major delegate-selection events in presidential election years. And it ranks close to the first primary as the early maker or breaker of presidential aspirations. Yet the Iowa caucus is a relative newcomer to the important place it now holds in the nominating process.

The New Hampshire primary has been around since 1913, but the Iowa caucus as we know it today sprang from the new politics that captured the Democratic Party in the late 1960s and early 1970s. The grassroots activism of Iowa's precinct caucuses provided fertile ground for that new breed of politics.

For decades Iowans held precinct caucuses in January every four years to begin the process of selecting delegates to the Democratic and Republican national conventions. But in the old days the process was firmly in the hands of party regulars, pragmatic politicians who selected delegates to county conventions and therefore controlled eligibility for national convention delegates.

Sometimes these decisions would be made in the context of broader political deals between important state bosses and particular candidates. But often they would not have anything to do with a delegate's preference for the presidential nomination. The county convention delegates were expected to represent their localities; the job of choosing the nominee could be left to later convention delegates.

Rank-and-file voters were not involved. Typically, the county chairman of a party would meet with a few political cronies to choose delegates to the county convention. Sometimes the local bosses did not even meet in caucus, because few party members were interested enough to attend. The leaders would simply run the requisite advance notice in the local newspaper, then meet amongst themselves to select county convention delegates.

All that changed with the Vietnam War. Angered and politically energized by the war in 1968, ordinary voters showed up in droves at precinct caucuses across the state. They overwhelmed the political bosses and sent their own antiwar delegates to the county conventions. Their champion was the antiwar insurgent, Sen. Eugene J. McCarthy of Minnesota.

The politicians fought back at the county conventions and reclaimed the levers of power and decision making. But the die was cast. When Sen. George S. McGovern of South Dakota, another antiwar Democrat, headed up a commission to transform party rules for the 1972 campaign, he ensured that the bosses would never again dominate the process. The ensuing PRESIDENTIAL SELECTION REFORMS forced the regulars into retreat; the activists came into their own.

Thus was born the present-day Iowa caucus. What began as an outlet for Democratic Party activism soon became a testing ground for Republican presidential aspirants as well. Only the Democrats, however, protect the Iowa caucus's first-in-the-nation status. The Republican Party, with fewer restrictive rules generally, permits other states to hold earlier party caucuses. In 1996 the Iowa caucuses of both parties were held on February

12. But GOP caucuses had already taken place in Hawaii, Alaska, Louisiana, and Guam. Caucuses generally, however, have declined in number and prestige. Most national convention delegates are now chosen in primaries.

By building strong organizations in both states, former Georgia governor Jimmy Carter used the Iowa caucus and New Hampshire primary in 1976 to advance his long-shot candidacy to FRONT-RUNNER status. He won both contests, sidelining eight other Democratic contenders, most of them better known than Carter. It would be twenty years before another candidate of either party—Bill Clinton in 1996—won both the Iowa caucus and New Hampshire primary before going on to win election or reelection as president. (As the incumbent in 1984, Ronald Reagan won the New Hampshire primary, but there was no presidential caucus vote in Iowa that year.) Before winning his first term in 1992, Clinton lost Iowa to Sen. Tom Harkin of that state, then lost New Hampshire to former senator Paul Tsongas of Massachusetts. As the self-styled "comeback kid," Clinton recovered from those defeats to win the nomination and the presidency.

Among Republicans, Iowa's second-place finisher (Ronald Reagan in 1980) and third-place finisher (George Bush in 1988) both won in New Hampshire and then went on to clinch the nomination and the presidency.

In 1996 Senate Majority Leader Robert J. Dole of Kansas won the Iowa caucus but lost the New Hampshire primary to television commentator Patrick J. Buchanan. Dole then won all twenty-five primaries in March and quickly locked up the GOP nomination. Dole also had won the Iowa caucus in 1988, but in New Hampshire he lost to Bush.

## Issue Ads

*See* MEDIA USE IN CAMPAIGNS; POLITICAL ADVERTISING.

## Issue Voting

Americans are constantly urged to acquaint themselves with the issues in an election and vote accordingly. Yet, studies of ELECTORAL BEHAVIOR show that voters choose among candidates largely on the basis of PARTY IDENTIFICATION and candidate image, with issues playing a minor role.

That way of approaching an election may be changing, however. In the relatively calm 1950s, studies showed voters paying scant attention to issues. In the more turbulent and divisive decades since then, newer research indicates that issues figure somewhat larger in voters' choices.

Voters care, for example, about taxes, jobs, and other issues that affect them directly, and these issues can influence their choice of candidates. Candidates can capitalize on such issues without sophisticated policy statements, as the Bill Clinton campaign did in 1992 with its unofficial CAMPAIGN SLOGAN, "It's the economy, stupid." (See POCKETBOOK VOTING.)

Another so-called hot-button issue among voters is abortion. In a *Los Angeles Times* EXIT POLL of 7,300 voters on ELECTION DAY 1996, 9 percent said that abortion was the most important factor determining their vote for president. From that, syndicated columnist Mark Shields extrapolated that 8.3 million Americans chose antiabortion Robert J. Dole over prochoice President Bill Clinton, or 60 percent to 34 percent. To those voters, Shields wrote, "abortion was quite relevant."

By contrast, voters usually ignore foreign policy issues, which they tend to find has little relevance to their own lives. So-called issue voting is further diminished by some voters' tendency to project their personal issue positions onto their preferred candidates, regardless of the candidates' actual positions.

In 1968, for example, people on both sides of the debate over U.S. military involvement in the Vietnam War (hawks and doves) were found among the supporters of Richard Nixon and his Democratic opponent Hubert Humphrey. Because the candidates were less than explicit about their Vietnam policies, voters who saw a difference in their positions were responding to their own

*For some voters a candidate's stand on abortion may be the most important factor in an election decision. Source: R. Michael Jenkins, Congressional Quarterly*

wishes and not engaging in issue voting. It is also possible for voters to adopt issue positions because their preferred candidate has taken that position.

An issue determines voter choice only when (1) voters are informed and concerned about the issue; (2) candidates take distinguishable stands on it; and (3) voters perceive how the candidate stands in relation to their own concerns. In the 1972 presidential contest between President Nixon and Democratic challenger George McGovern, issues clearly had an effect. On eleven of fourteen issues studied the voters felt closer to Nixon than to McGovern, and there was a close correlation between people's perceptions of where the candidates stood and the candidate for whom they voted. Only on issues related to the environment and urban unrest did McGovern appear to be closer to citizens' positions. Nixon was viewed as closer on issues such as

Vietnam, marijuana, desegregation, and campus unrest.

With most voters tending to be moderate or centrist in their orientations, and with each party made up of people with diverse viewpoints, there may be little incentive for candidates to take strongly opposing stands. They may instead straddle issues, making issue-based voting difficult for the average citizen. This is less true in PRIMARY elections, where competing candidates within the same party need to take clear-cut positions to differentiate themselves from their opponents.

Voters' decisions are made easier when an incumbent is seeking reelection. Having had an opportunity to judge the candidate's performance, voters can render a verdict on his or her behavior in office. This process of electoral decision making is called RETROSPECTIVE VOTING.

# J

## Judicial System

As the ultimate authority on interpretation of the Constitution, the Supreme Court is a crucial power center in the American political system. At several points in U.S. history, the Court's decisions have helped to produce HISTORIC MILESTONES IN U.S. ELECTIONS.

Using the power of judicial review, federal and state courts also have had a significant effect on the nation's electoral process. Acts of Congress, orders of the executive branch, or state laws cannot be put into effect if the courts declare them unconstitutional. But it is when the Supreme Court takes a case for review that the outcome can have the broadest and most lasting repercussions. Its decisions about the meaning of the Constitution can be changed only through its own later reinterpretation or through the difficult and time-consuming process of constitutional amendment.

The Constitution created a federal system of government in which both the national and state governments exercise significant legislative, executive, and judicial powers. Fifty state judicial systems, therefore, operate side by side with the federal court system. Each system has its own personnel and jurisdiction, and each interprets and enforces its own constitution and laws. Although the two court systems are separate and distinct, they do overlap: the constitutional principle of federal supremacy enables the federal courts to throw out state actions they deem to be in violation of the U.S. Constitution or acts of Congress.

Both the federal and state systems have trial courts and appellate courts. Trial courts are the tribunals in which a case is first heard—that is, they are courts of original jurisdiction. Cases in trial courts may be heard before a jury, or a judge may render the verdict. Appel-

late courts hear cases on appeal from lower courts. But appellate courts have no juries; all cases are decided by a panel of judges. These courts are concerned primarily with whether the lower courts correctly interpreted the applicable laws and followed the proper judicial procedures in deciding a case. Appellate courts normally do not consider new factual evidence because the record of the lower court constitutes the basis for judgment.

In contrast to the federal government's process, in which all judges are appointed by the president and confirmed by the Senate, the states use a variety of selection procedures, depending on their constitutions and statutes. Both appointment and election are used. Almost half the states follow a mixed appointment and election process, such as the Missouri plan, in which the GOVERNOR appoints judges from a list of candidates approved by a judicial commission, and a REFERENDUM is held on each appointee's performance at the next general election.

## Origins of Judicial Review

Basic though it is to the U.S. system of government, judicial review is not mentioned in the Constitution. Rather, it was asserted by the Supreme Court in the case of *Marbury v. Madison* (1803), which arose on the heels of the election of 1800.

After losing the election, President John Adams appointed a number of federal judges in an effort to control the judiciary once his successor, Thomas Jefferson, took office. One of these appointees, William Marbury, was designated a justice of the peace for the District of Columbia. The outgoing Adams administration neglected to give Marbury his commission to office, however, and the new secretary of state, James Madison, re-

*Chief Justice John Marshall (left) set a crucial precedent in 1803 when he claimed for the Court the right to review federal legislation. The case,* Marbury v. Madison, *was brought by William Marbury (right), a federal appointee. Sources: Library of Congress, Maryland Historical Society*

fused to do so. Marbury then brought suit in the Supreme Court asking that Madison be required to give him his commission. Marbury took his case directly to the Supreme Court because an act of Congress, the Judiciary Act of 1789, had made such an issue part of the Court's original jurisdiction. The act authorized the Court to issue writs of mandamus, which compelled a federal officer to carry out his duty.

Chief Justice John Marshall's opinion for the Court stated that Marbury was indeed entitled to his commission and that Madison had erred in denying it to him. The Court ruled, however, that it lacked the power to order Madison to give Marbury his commission because the Court did *not* have jurisdiction over the case. It added that the provisions in the Judiciary Act of 1789

giving the Court jurisdiction over such cases were an unconstitutional extension by Congress of the Court's original jurisdiction, which had already been provided for in Article III, section 2.

## Sparing Use

Judicial review is a power the Court has used sparingly in cases involving federal law. After *Marbury v. Madison* it was fifty-four years before another act of Congress was declared unconstitutional. This occurred in *Scott v. Sandford* (1857), a case that had later implications in the fight for BLACK SUFFRAGE.

Dred Scott, a slave, claimed to be free when his master took him to a territory where slavery was banned. The Court ruled, however, that the Missouri Compromise of 1820, which outlawed slavery in the northern territories, was unconstitutional because it took the slaveowner's property without due process of law. In declaring that free Negroes were not citizens and without constitutional rights, the Court in the *Scott* case created a public furor and helped to precipitate the Civil War.

Since it asserted its power of judicial review, the Supreme Court has declared state laws or provisions of state constitutions unconstitutional more than a thousand times. But out of more than 95,000 laws passed through 1992, only 141 were declared unconstitutional in whole or in part.

## The Court and Equality of Vote

Many of the Supreme Court's farthest reaching decisions have dealt with inequities in civil rights and voting rights through discriminatory practices such as malapportionment of legislative seats, RACIAL REDISTRICTING or GERRYMANDERING, or LITERACY TESTS that excluded African Americans from SOUTHERN PRIMARIES or the now-outlawed WHITE PRIMARIES.

In addressing the REAPPORTIONMENT AND REDISTRICTING issue, the Supreme Court announced in *BAKER V. CARR* (1962) that henceforth the judiciary would interject itself into the redistricting process to ensure that DISTRICTS were equal in size and adhered to the Court's ONE-PERSON, ONE-VOTE principle. This decision dramatically changed how Americans were represented in their state legislatures and Congress.

In 1986 the Court took a step farther into this politically charged area when it stated that it would review instances of partisan gerrymandering to determine whether a political minority had suffered substantial and long-standing harm in violation of the Fourteenth Amendment's Equal Protection Clause. The Court's controversial role in redistricting policy was expanded again in 1993 when it ruled in *SHAW V. RENO* that it would consider whether majority-minority congressional districts created under the VOTING RIGHTS ACT of 1965 could deprive white voters of the equal protection of the laws.

The case involved a North Carolina plan that created two districts, one of them severely contorted, with black majorities. Both elected black representatives in 1992, and white voters challenged the plan as discriminatory. In a second opinion, *Shaw v. Hunt,* the Court ruled in 1996 that the state could not justify the plan on the basis of either possible past discrimination against a minority or compliance with the 1965 act.

## The Court and Elections

Supreme Court decisions are not self-enforcing; rather the Court must rely on others—notably the attorney general—to implement its decisions. When the issue is clear-cut and the order is directed at one person, compliance is prompt. This was the case in 1974 when the Court ordered President Richard Nixon to turn over to a lower federal court taped Oval Office conversations about the Watergate cover-up.

The Watergate SCANDAL arose from a June 1972 burglary at the DEMOCRATIC NATIONAL COMMITTEE headquarters in Washington's Watergate Hotel complex. Although the purpose of the break-in was never determined, the burglars and others involved were quickly linked to the Republican Party and the Nixon reelection committee. Investigators speculated that the burglars may have been attempting to plant listening devices in the DNC office or find information that would be detrimental to Nixon's opposition in the November election. Although Nixon denied any complicity in the burglary or the cover-up, the tapes proved otherwise. On July 24, 1974, the Court in *United States v. Nixon* dismissed the president's claim of executive privilege and ordered him to turn over the tapes, which revealed that Nixon was aware of plans to pay "hush money" to the burglars. Facing impeachment by the House, Nixon resigned on August 9, 1974.

The resignation resulted in the first turnover of the presidency without either a death or an election. Nixon's successor, Gerald R. Ford, had been nominated by Nixon and approved by both houses of Congress under the terms of the Twenty-fifth Amendment following the resignation of Vice President Spiro T. Agnew. With the similar election of Nelson A. Rockefeller to succeed Ford, the nation for the first time had a president and vice president not elected by the ELECTORAL COLLEGE.

In the wake of the Watergate affair, Congress passed the Federal Election Campaign Act (FECA) amendments of 1974. These revised older CAMPAIGN FINANCE restrictions and established a PUBLIC FINANCING system for presidential elections.

Ruling on a challenge to the new law, the Court in BUCKLEY V. VALEO (1976) invalidated the spending limits as infringing on political speech, but it upheld the limits on contributions to federal candidates. Congress subsequently amended the FECA to conform to the decision.

Two years later the Court struck down a Massachusetts law that forbade corporations to spend money to influence voters' decisions on referendum issues. In the case, *First National Bank of Boston v. Bellotti*, the Court said that laws barring corporate gifts to candidates might be justified in preventing corruption. On that basis, it ruled in *Austin v. Michigan Chamber of Commerce* (1990) that states can bar corporations from giving to political campaigns without setting up a POLITICAL ACTION COMMITTEE for that purpose.

Earlier, in *Williams v. Rhodes* (1968), the Court struck down an Ohio law that limited BALLOT ACCESS to THIRD PARTY candidates. The Court held that the law denied equal protection of the laws to candidates and voters. Since then the Court has treated other state laws in similar fashion. In 1992, for example, it invalidated an Illinois law that required a new political party in Chicago to obtain twenty-five thousand signatures in both the city and the suburbs to place candidates' names on a countywide ballot.

In two other 1992 cases, however, the Court rejected First Amendment challenges to election laws. It upheld a Hawaii law that blocked WRITE-IN VOTES in state elections. And it affirmed a Tennessee law that prohibited electioneering within one hundred feet of the entrance to a polling place.

## The Court and Political Parties

Early in the twentieth century, as the PRIMARY system came into widespread use, the courts regarded such elections as internal political party affairs not subject to government interference. But in a 1941 Louisiana case,

*United States v. Classic,* the Supreme Court reversed the precedent and ruled that Congress may regulate primaries for federal elections. Although it was not a racial discrimination case, *Classic* led to the abolition of primaries that excluded blacks under the pretext that the parties running them were private organizations.

Several rulings in the 1970s and 1980s dealt with the states' power to protect the parties' membership rolls and nominating procedures. The decisions reflected an effort to balance the rights of political parties to run their own affairs and the rights of voters to participate in party nominating elections.

In a significant decision, *Cousins v. Wigoda* (1975), the Court ruled that parties, like individuals, have a constitutional right to political association. The case stemmed from a dispute between rival Illinois delegations to the 1972 Democratic NATIONAL PARTY CONVENTION, one pledged to the candidacy of George S. McGovern and the other led by Chicago mayor Richard J. Daley. The losing Daley delegation appealed, but the Supreme Court ruled that the state courts would have had no jurisdiction because in such instances the parties settle their own claims.

Several decisions in 1973 and 1974 set out the Court's view of the permissible restrictions a state might place on persons wishing to change political parties as voters or candidates. In *Rosario v. Rockefeller* (1973) the Court upheld a state requirement that voters who wished to vote in a party's primary have enrolled in that party at least thirty days before the previous general election.

To protect voters' rights, the Court ruled, also in 1973, that states cannot impose unreasonable deadlines for party registration to vote in a primary. The case, *Kusper v. Pontikes,* involved a law that forbade voting in a party primary if the voter had participated in a primary of another party within the previous twenty-three months. But the next year the Court upheld in *Storer v. Brown, Frommhagen v. Brown* a state law that barred people from running as INDEPENDENTS or candidates of new parties unless they had disqualified themselves from any other party at least one year before the election.

The Court also respected the autonomy of the political parties in two decisions involving open and closed primaries. In open primaries any registered voter may participate, but closed primaries accept only registered party members. (See PRIMARY TYPES.)

A 1981 decision, *Democratic Party of the United States v. La Follette,* allowed Wisconsin to require an open primary but said the state could not require the national party organization to recognize the results. A year later the Court struck down Ohio's law requiring candidates to disclose the names and addresses of campaign contributors. By a 6–3 vote the Court held in *Brown v. Socialist Workers '74 Campaign Committee* that such disclosure, particularly of contributors to minor parties, might subject the donors to harassment, violating their freedom of association.

In 1986 in *Tashjian v. Republican Party of Connecticut* the Court held that states could not compel parties to hold closed primaries; parties could make those decisions themselves.

By unanimous vote in *Foster v. Love* (1997) the Court struck down a type of open primary used only in Louisiana. Under it, a congressional candidate was elected if he or she received a majority of votes in the primary. That short cut, the Court said, undermined Congress's intent in setting a uniform ELECTION DAY for federal elections.

---

# Jungle Primary

*See* PRIMARY TYPES.

---

# Junior Tuesday

The compression or FRONT-LOADING of presidential primaries into a narrow window early in the delegate-selection season reached a new dimension in 1996, giving rise to the term *Junior Tuesday.*

Used to distinguish it from the older, mostly southern SUPER TUESDAY, Junior Tuesday was somewhat of a misnomer. There were eight primaries on Junior Tues-day, March 5, compared with seven on Super Tuesday, March 12. But the latter included larger states, such as Florida and Texas, with more delegates at stake and a total vote almost twice the 1.6 million votes cast in the Junior Tuesday Republican primaries.

Election watchers, however, counted primaries close to March 5 as part of Junior Tuesday *Week,* including South Carolina's on March 2 and Puerto Rico's on March 3, which added a half-million votes to the Junior Tuesday Week total. New York's March 7 primary was also included, but that was for delegate election with no direct vote for candidates. Two states held caucuses during Junior Tuesday Week: Wyoming on March 2 and Minnesota on March 5.

Except for New Hampshire, which is required by state law to hold its primary before any other state, all the New England states held primaries on Junior Tuesday: Connecticut, Maine, Massachusetts, Rhode Island, and Vermont. The other participants were Colorado, Georgia, and Maryland.

After losing the NEW HAMPSHIRE PRIMARY on February 20, Robert J. Dole of Kansas quickly regained FRONT-RUNNER status by winning all of the Junior Tuesday Week Republican primaries and caucuses. Democratic presidential primaries in 1996 lacked interest because President Bill Clinton faced no serious opposition for the nomination.

From the introduction of Super Tuesday in 1988, the presence of Massachusetts and Rhode Island had diluted the mix of what would have been an all-southern regional primary. With the departure of those two states to Junior Tuesday, along with Georgia and Maryland, Super Tuesday regained much of its southern orientation. Oregon was the only northern state holding a primary on Super Tuesday 1996.

The holding of so many primaries on Junior Tuesday, only two weeks after the New Hampshire primary, exacerbated the compression problem that already had political analysts worried. In an effort to stretch out the delegate-selection season, the Republican Party moved to award bonus delegates to states holding later primaries in 2000.

# L

## Lame Duck

An officeholder weakened by the impending expiration of his or her term is said to be a lame duck. INCUMBENTS defeated, not seeking reelection, or barred by law from succeeding themselves fall into this category.

The term originated with the British as an uncharitable description of bankrupt business owners. By the early nineteenth century it was being applied in the United States to "politically bankrupt" elected officials. Patronage jobs they hand out shortly before leaving office are called "lame-duck" appointments.

The Twentieth Amendment to the Constitution, ratified in 1933, was named the "lame-duck amendment." It eased the lame-duck problem by shortening the intervals after presidents and members of Congress are elect-

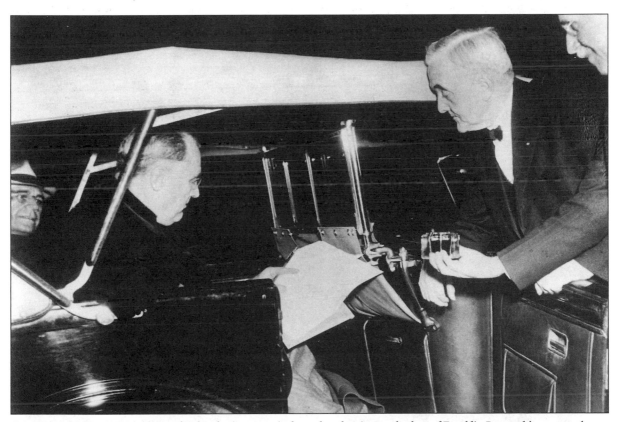

*Sen. George W. Norris, Republican of Nebraska (1913–1943), shown here leaning on the door of Franklin Roosevelt's car, was the leading advocate of a constitutional amendment, the so-called lame-duck amendment, to move the start of the new Congress and administration from March to January. Source: Senate Historical Office*

ed and actually take office. (See PRESIDENT, NOMI-NATING AND ELECTING; SENATE, ELECTING; VICE PRESIDENT, QUALIFICATIONS.)

Formerly, presidents and vice presidents had to wait about four months, from ELECTION DAY in November until inauguration on March 4, before they were sworn in. The Twentieth Amendment moved up the swearing-in to January 20, beginning in 1937.

The waiting period for newly elected members of Congress was even longer—thirteen months, from election day to the first Monday in December of the following year. The Twentieth Amendment specified that both sessions of each two-year Congress would begin on January 3, greatly reducing the postelection lame-duck period.

Reelected presidents in effect are lame ducks throughout their whole second term. Under the Twenty-second Amendment, ratified in 1951, no president can serve more than two terms. Even if reelected in a

LANDSLIDE, the president must deal with a Congress that is aware the president cannot run again and therefore is hampered in building popular support for initiatives and programs that many in Congress oppose. The situation is even more difficult for the second-term president if the opposing party controls Congress, as happened to President Bill Clinton beginning with the MIDTERM ELECTION of 1994 and continuing after his reelection in 1996.

## Landslide

A lopsided election victory that buries the defeated candidate under the winner's votes is called a *landslide*. What constitutes a landslide is not precisely known, but in presidential politics it generally means 60 percent or more of the POPULAR VOTE.

By that measure only four presidents can claim land-

*Lyndon B. Johnson's 61.1 percent of the popular vote in 1968 is the record for highest margin in U.S. presidential elections. Source: Lyndon Baines Johnson Library*

slide victories: Republican Warren G. Harding in 1920, Democrat Franklin D. Roosevelt in 1936, Democrat Lyndon B. Johnson in 1964, and Republican Richard Nixon in 1972.

Johnson's landslide was the largest. He polled 61.1 percent of the vote to Republican Barry Goldwater's 38.5 percent and won by about 15.9 million votes. Johnson's margin surpassed the previous record set in 1936 when Franklin Roosevelt defeated Republican challenger Alfred M. Landon, 60.8 percent to 36.5 percent for an 11.1 million-vote margin.

Harding received 60.3 percent of the popular vote for a margin of 7.0 million over Democrat James M. Cox. Nixon took 60.7 percent for a 17.9 million-vote margin over Democrat George S. McGovern. Nixon's popular vote margin was the largest ever.

Roosevelt's 523 ELECTORAL COLLEGE vote total in 1936 (out of the total 531 at the time, when there were only forty-eight states) remains the largest electoral vote percentage (98.5) after George Washington's 100 percent in 1789.

Republican Ronald Reagan won 525 electoral votes in his 1984 defeat of Democrat Walter F. Mondale, but Reagan's 97.6 percent of the 538 electoral vote total still ranked behind Roosevelt's 98.5 percent.

Reagan's two presidential victories are often called landslides, but both fell short of the 60 percent benchmark. Reagan defeated incumbent Democrat Jimmy Carter with 50.7 percent or a margin of 8.4 million in 1980, and he was reelected with 58.8 percent in 1984, for a margin of 16.8 million votes over Mondale.

The electoral college system, which requires an ABSOLUTE MAJORITY for presidential election, tends to exaggerate the margin of success. The right combination of large-state victories can turn a popular vote plurality into an electoral vote landslide. For example, in 1996 Democrat Bill Clinton won reelection over Republican Robert J. Dole with only 49.2 percent of the popular vote. But Clinton won 379 of the 538 electoral votes, or 70.4 percent. (See table of "minority presidents," page 133.)

Landslide presidents sometimes claim a MANDATE from the voters to carry out whatever program they promised during the campaign. Frequently, however, the mandate is not clear or the victory turns sour for some reason, cutting short the president's tenure. This was the case with Johnson, who decided against seeking another term in 1968, and Nixon, who resigned two years after being reelected in 1972. Had Harding not died in office in 1923, the SCANDALS during his administration likely would have denied him a second term.

## Liberal

*See* IDEOLOGY.

## Liberal Republican Party (1872)

Dissatisfied with President Ulysses S. Grant's first term in office, a faction of the Republican Party split off in 1872 to form a new party. Composed of party reformers, as well as anti-Grant politicians and newspaper editors, the new party focused on the corruption of the Grant administration and the need for civil service reform and for an end to the Reconstruction policy in the South.

The call for the Liberal Republican national convention came from the state party in Missouri, the birthplace of the reform movement. The convention, meeting in Cincinnati, Ohio, in May 1872, nominated Horace Greeley, editor of the *New York Tribune*, for president and Missouri governor B. Gratz Brown as his running mate. Greeley, the choice of anti-Grant politicians but suspect among reformers, was not popular among many Democrats either, who recalled his longtime criticism of the Democratic Party.

With the hope of victory in the fall election, however, the Democratic National Convention, meeting in July, endorsed the Liberal Republican ticket and platform. The coalition was an unsuccessful one, as many Democrats refused to vote for Greeley. He received 2,834,761 votes (43.8 percent of the POPULAR VOTE) but carried only six states and lost to Grant by more than 750,000 votes out of nearly 6.5 million cast. Greeley died shortly after the election.

Underfinanced, poorly organized, and dependent on

*Newspaper editor Horace Greeley was the only presidential nominee of the short-lived Liberal Republican Party. Source: Library of Congress*

the Democrats for their success, the Liberal Republicans went out of existence after the 1872 election.

## Libertarian Party (1971– )

In the brief period of four years, 1972 to 1976, the Libertarian Party leaped from a fledgling organization on the presidential ballot in only two states to the nation's largest THIRD PARTY. As of 1996, although its candidate ran fifth in the presidential race, the Libertarians still claimed to be the largest third party, with more than twenty-one thousand paying members nationwide.

Formed in Colorado in 1971, the party nominated John Hospers of California for president in 1972. On the ballot only in Colorado and Washington, Hospers garnered 3,673 votes (including WRITE-IN votes from other states). But he received a measure of national attention when a Republican presidential elector from Virginia, Roger MacBride, cast his electoral vote for the Libertarian presidential nominee.

MacBride's action made him a hero in Libertarian

circles, and the party chose him as its 1976 standard-bearer at its August 1975 convention in New York City. MacBride had served in the Vermont legislature in the 1960s and was defeated for the Republican gubernatorial nomination in that state in 1964. In the 1970s he settled on a farm near Charlottesville, Virginia, and devoted himself to writing and party affairs. He was co-creator of the television series *Little House on the Prairie.*

Making a major effort in 1976, the Libertarians got on the ballot in thirty-two states, more than Eugene J. McCarthy—who ran independent of any political party—or any other third party candidate. The reward was a vote of 173,011, more than for any other minor party candidate but far below McCarthy's total and only 0.2 percent of the national vote. MacBride's strength was centered in the West; he received 5.5 percent of the vote in Alaska and 1.0 percent or more in Arizona, Hawaii, and Idaho. He also ran well ahead of his national average in California (0.7 percent) and Nevada (0.8 percent). His running mate was David P. Bergland, a California lawyer.

In 1980 the Libertarian Party appeared on the ballot in all fifty states and the DISTRICT OF COLUMBIA for the first time. The party also fielded about 550 candidates for other offices, a number that dwarfed other third party efforts. The party nominees, Edward E. Clark of California for president and David Koch of New York for vice president, garnered 921,299 votes or 1.1 percent of the vote nationwide. Again, the major support for the Libertarians came from western states.

Of all minor party presidential candidates running in 1984, the Libertarians appeared on the greatest number of ballots: thirty-eight states and the District of Columbia. David Bergland, who had run in 1976 for the second slot, was the party's presidential candidate, and Jim Lewis, a Connecticut business executive, his running mate. In 1988 the Libertarian presidential and vice-presidential nominees—Ron Paul and Andre V. Marrou, respectively—were on the ballot in all fifty-one jurisdictions save four and received 432,179 votes.

In 1992 Nevada real estate broker Marrou was the presidential nominee with RUNNING MATE Nancy Lord, a Georgia lawyer. The pair was on the ballot in all states and the District of Columbia and had a campaign budget of $1 million. Marrou received 291,627 votes in a fourth-place finish behind Ross Perot, who stole most of the third party candidates' thunder that year. The Libertarians maintained their strong western base, especially in California, Nevada, and Hawaii, where they also ran candidates for most House seats.

In 1996 the Libertarians regained voting strength but nevertheless dropped to fifth place in the presidential race behind Ralph Nader of the new Green Party. The Libertarian candidate, financial analyst Harry Browne of Lafayette, California, and running mate Jo Anne Jorgensen of Greenville, South Carolina, drew 485,120 votes or 0.50 percent of the total. It was the party's best showing since 1980. Besides being on the presidential ballot in all states, Libertarians were congressional candidates in thirty-three states.

Individual responsibility and minimal government interference were the hallmarks of the Libertarian philosophy. The party favored repeal of laws against so-called victimless crimes—such as pornography, drug use, and homosexual activity—the abolition of all federal police agencies, and the elimination of all government subsidies to private enterprise. In foreign and military affairs, the Libertarians advocated the removal of U.S. troops from abroad, a cut in the defense budget, and the emergence of the United States as a "giant Switzerland," with no international treaty obligations. Libertarians also favored repeal of legislation that they believe hindered individual or corporate action. They opposed gun control, civil rights laws, price controls on oil and gas, labor protection laws, federal welfare and poverty programs, forced busing, compulsory education, Social Security, national medical care, and federal land-use restrictions.

## Liberty Party (1840–1848)

Established in 1839, the Liberty Party was the product of a split in the antislavery movement between a faction led by William Lloyd Garrison that favored action outside the political process and a second led by James

*James G. Birney, twice the nominee of the Liberty Party, failed to carry a state in 1840 or 1844 on an antislavery platform.*
Source: *Library of Congress*

G. Birney that proposed action within the political system through the establishment of an independent antislavery party. The Birney faction launched the Liberty Party in November 1839. The following April a national convention with delegates from six states nominated Birney for president.

Although the Liberty Party was the first political party to take an antislavery position, and the only one at the time to do so, most abolitionist voters in the 1840 election supported the Democratic or Whig presidential candidates. Birney received only 6,797 votes (0.3 percent of the popular vote).

Aided by the controversy over the annexation of slaveholding Texas, the Liberty Party's popularity increased in 1844. Birney, again the party's presidential nominee, received 62,103 votes (2.3 percent of the popular vote) but, as in 1840, carried no states. The peak strength of the party was reached two years later in 1846, when in various state elections Liberty Party candidates received 74,017 votes.

In October 1847 the party nominated New Hampshire senator John P. Hale for president, but his candidacy was withdrawn the following year when the Liberty Party joined the broader-based FREE SOIL PARTY.

## Lieutenant Governor

The lieutenant governor of a state is roughly the equivalent of the U.S. VICE PRESIDENT. His or her most important duty is to be prepared to take over as chief executive should the governorship become vacant.

As the "standby" GOVERNOR, the lieutenant governor has been the butt of jokes about the job's lack of substance. "I'm the lieutenant governor," Calvin Coolidge once told a Massachusetts woman who asked his occupation. When she excitedly asked him to tell her all about it, Coolidge replied, "I just did."

But as it was for "Silent Cal," the lieutenant governorship can be a steppingstone to higher office. In his 1983 study of the 357 governors in office from 1951 to 1981, political scientist Larry Sabato found that sixty-two lieutenant governors had become chief executive through election or, less frequently, through succession. Since 1980 several lieutenant governors have won election as governors. Among them, elected in 1996, was Frank L. O'Bannon, Democrat, in Indiana.

Even for lieutenant governors who do not aspire to anything higher, the job in most states today is more rewarding and challenging than it was in Coolidge's day. States have added to the lieutenant governor's duties and responsibilities, just as modern presidents have found more meaningful tasks for their vice presidents than flying to funerals of foreign dignitaries.

One of O'Bannon's predecessors as governor of Indiana, Paul McNutt, began the practice of delegating executive functions to the lieutenant governor. In 1933 McNutt placed his lieutenant in charge of the state's Commerce and Industries Department. Now, according to Sabato, thirty states empower the governor to assign executive tasks to the lieutenant governor. Governors in other states have done the same on their own authority.

In contrast to the past when lieutenant governor was a part-time job in the legislative branch, it is now a full-time job in most of the states that have the position. Twelve states have placed the lieutenant governor entirely in the executive branch. Like the vice president, who is president of the U.S. Senate, the lieutenant governor in most states presides over the state senate and votes only to break a tie.

Eight states have no elected lieutenant governor: Arizona, Maine, New Hampshire, New Jersey, Oregon, Tennessee, West Virginia, and Wyoming. In Arizona and Wyoming the secretary of state is designated the lieutenant governor. In Maine and Oregon, the state senate president succeeds the governor. In Tennessee the state senate elects one of its members as the dual lieutenant governor and senate Speaker. The remaining three states without lieutenant governors fill gubernatorial vacancies through acting governors, legislative elections, or special elections.

Almost half the states jointly elect the governor and lieutenant governor, as a team by themselves or a team in combination with other elective officers such as the attorney general. Team elections offer greater prospects of harmony between the two highest officers in their working relationship, as well as policy continuity if the governor dies or otherwise leaves office.

Feuds between the governor and lieutenant governor are not unusual. Some state constitutions provide that the lieutenant governor becomes acting governor when the governor is outside the state, which can lead to mischief or worse if the two leaders are not on good terms.

When Edmund G. "Jerry" Brown Jr. was the Demo-cratic governor of California in the early 1980s, he had a Republican lieutenant governor, Mike Curb, who would embarrass Brown by making appointments or issuing executive orders while the governor was absent. Other governors have had the same experience.

After Lt. Gov. Jim Guy Tucker succeeded Bill Clinton as Arkansas governor in 1992, he was invited to Clinton's inauguration. While Tucker was in Washington, the acting governor, senate president pro tem and fellow Democrat Jerry Jewell, pardoned two prison inmates. Later, while Tucker was in Minnesota, his Republican lieutenant governor, Mike Huckabee, signed a heritage week proclamation that Tucker had declined to sign.

*L. Douglas Wilder, the grandson of slaves, was elected lieutenant governor of Virginia in 1985. Source: Mannie Garcia, Reuters*

Tucker himself was forced from office by his conviction in connection with the Whitewater SCANDAL, and Huckabee became governor by succession.

New York lieutenant governor Elizabeth McCaughey Ross defected to the Democrats after Gov. George E. Pataki dumped her from the GOP ticket for the 1998 election. She had infuriated Pataki in 1996 by standing behind him as he addressed the legislature, diverting the television cameras away from him.

In January 1998 John H. Hager, Republican, became the first lieutenant governor of Virginia—and perhaps of any state—to take office with a disability. He uses a wheelchair.

One of Hager's predecessors as lieutenant governor of Virginia, Democrat L. Douglas Wilder, elected in 1985, was the first African American elected to statewide office in the South since Reconstruction. In the 1989 election Wilder became the first African American governor.

The first woman elected lieutenant governor was Democrat Mary Anne Krupsak of New York, in 1974. Another woman had earlier served as lieutenant governor, but she had been appointed to fill an unexpired term.

---

## Literacy Tests

In the South during much of the twentieth century, literacy tests were among methods used to limit the FRANCHISE to whites. Other such devices included the POLL TAX, complex VOTER REGISTRATION laws, and supposedly private WHITE PRIMARIES.

Under the literacy test method, voters were required to read aloud and/or write a passage correctly—usually a section of the state or federal Constitution. Sometimes, voters who could not pass the test could have the material read to them, to see if they could "understand" or "interpret" it correctly. This allowed local voting officials, inevitably whites, to judge whether voters passed the tests and usually resulted in whites passing and blacks failing.

As descendants of former slaves, many African Americans also had difficulty answering questions about family background, age, and birthplace. Their often-illiterate forebears may not have had access to such information or kept records. Some southern states passed so-called GRANDFATHER CLAUSES that exempted most whites from the literacy test because they—unlike many blacks—could show that their ancestors were eligible to vote in 1866. The Supreme Court ruled in *Guinn v. United States* (1915) that grandfather clauses violated the Fifteenth Amendment, ratified in 1870, which forbade denial of the RIGHT TO VOTE on account of "race, color, or previous condition of servitude." It was the first voting rights decision based on a law's discriminatory aspects.

Earlier, in *Williams v. Mississippi* (1898), the Court had upheld literacy tests as a qualification. Henry Williams was an African American indicted for murder by an all-white grand jury chosen from the pool of registered voters. All had passed a literacy test, which Williams contended was an unconstitutional requirement because it allowed discrimination in voting registration, and therefore violated his equal protection rights under the Fourteenth Amendment. The Court, however, ruled that the Mississippi voting laws did not on their face discriminate but rather were used administratively for a discriminatory result.

For decades afterward the literacy tests went unchallenged. But as more blacks became educated and able to pass the tests, some southern states supplemented the "understanding and interpretation" requirements for registration. Voters had to meet standards of good citizenship, good character, and other subjective qualifications.

In 1959 in a North Carolina case, *Lassiter v. Northampton County Board of Elections,* the Supreme Court upheld the state's right to ensure an independent and intelligent electorate. How the state achieved that objective was outside its purview, the Court said.

Gradually, however, literacy tests and other formal and informal bars to voting in the South began to fall. In *Louisiana v. United States* (1965) the Court struck down Louisiana's understanding and interpretation test, calling it "not a test but a trap." The same year Congress in the VOTING RIGHTS ACT banned literacy tests and other interference with the right to vote.

Within five years, two-thirds of all southern blacks were registered, and the number of black elected officials began to climb. By 1993 there were almost eight thousand African American officials in the United States, more than half of them in the eleven states of the Old Confederacy: Alabama, Arkansas, Florida, Georgia, Louisiana, Mississippi, North Carolina, South Carolina, Tennessee, Texas, and Virginia.

## Loophole Primaries

*See* PRIMARY TYPES.

## *Louisiana v. United States*

*See* LITERACY TESTS.

# M

## McGovern-Fraser Commission

*See* PRESIDENTIAL SELECTION REFORMS.

## Majority-Minority District

The term *majority-minority district* is relatively new in the lexicon of politics. It came into general usage in the 1990s to describe electoral DISTRICTS specifically drawn to have majority populations of African American or Hispanic minorities.

RACIAL REDISTRICTING to create majority-minority CONGRESSIONAL DISTRICTS took place in many areas of the country following the 1990 CENSUS as legislators tried to comply with the antidiscriminatory provisions of the VOTING RIGHTS ACT OF 1965. The efforts had some success, resulting in unprecedented numbers of minority members in the U.S. House of Representatives. (See tables, pages 525–527.)

White candidates, however, particularly in the South, challenged some of the oddly shaped districts as illegal forms of racial GERRYMANDERING and reverse discrimination. In several decisions the Supreme Court agreed with the challengers and ordered the districts redrawn.

Six majority-minority districts in Florida, Georgia, Louisiana, and Texas that had elected African Americans were redistricted to have white majorities. Nevertheless, five of the six redistricted black members (all Democrats) were reelected in 1996 and 1998. The sixth did not seek another term in 1996 and was succeeded by a white Republican who won reelection in 1998.

Critics pointed to the 1996 and 1998 results as evidence that majority-minority districts are not needed to

*Rep. Cynthia A. McKinney, Democrat of Georgia, with a supporter. McKinney was elected twice from the Eleventh District, which as a Georgia house member she helped create. Thrown into a new Fourth District in 1995 after the Supreme Court voided the old district lines, she won reelection from her new district in 1996, tailoring her campaign to a biracial contest.*
Source: Deborah Kalb, Congressional Quarterly

ensure minority representation in Congress. The reelected black INCUMBENTS, however, took issue with that conclusion. They said their earlier election from majority-black districts gave them the name recognition and financial support needed to retain their seats in districts that were changed to mostly white.

"My victory says more about the power of incumbency than anything," said Rep. Cynthia A. McKinney, Democrat, of Georgia's Fourth District. "Proof of this lies in the fact that all of Georgia's incumbents were re-elected" (including House Speaker Newt Gingrich, who resigned his seat before the beginning of the 106th Congress).

McKinney's old Eleventh District, 60 percent black, was changed to the Fourth, making her the only black woman in the South to win from a 65 percent majority-white district.

Writing in the *Washington Post* after the 1996 election McKinney concluded, "Don't use my victory to gut the Voting Rights Act, because I am a product of the Voting Rights Act!"

## Mandate

Mandates are usually associated with LANDSLIDE victories, particularly in presidential elections. A candidate who wins big is said to have a mandate to carry out the will of the people as expressed in the election results. Often, weaker candidates on the same ticket also win, riding into office on the winner's COATTAILS.

Lyndon B. Johnson's overwhelming defeat of Barry Goldwater in 1964, for example, was interpreted as a go-ahead for Johnson to propose his Great Society legislation. Although Johnson was largely successful with his legislative program, the unpopularity of his Vietnam War policies eventually undercut whatever mandate he may have had. He declined to seek reelection.

It is not clear, in any case, what margin of victory constitutes a mandate, or what the mandate was for if there was one. John F Kennedy did not hesitate to claim a mandate for his New Frontier proposals, despite his thin margin of victory over Richard Nixon in 1960. The very fact that he won—even if it had been by one vote—was taken by Kennedy as a mandate, according to his aide, Theodore Sorensen.

What the real or imagined mandate implied is even more difficult to interpret. If the voters were approving a specific course of action, presumably they were basing their decisions on the ideas and proposals the candidate put forth during the campaign. Election studies show, however, that ISSUE VOTING is a minor factor in most contests, compared with PARTY IDENTIFICATION, candidate image, and other considerations.

Campaign promises nevertheless offer some indication of what the mandate was about, if indeed there was one. Although the public dismisses such promises as so much campaign oratory, successful candidates do try to act on them. Political scientist Jeff Fishel found that presidents from Kennedy through Ronald Reagan's first term tried through bills or executive orders to make good on about two-thirds of their campaign pledges.

But candidates do not always indicate clearly what their policies will be once elected. Kennedy's promise to "get this country moving again," for example, was vague enough to cover a wide range of voters' hopes but gave little indication of the policies he intended to follow to achieve economic growth.

Even when candidates are clear about their intentions, the voters may base their decisions on other grounds. In 1980 Reagan was forthcoming with specific proposals on taxation, government expenditures, and national security policy. PUBLIC OPINION surveys, however, indicated that the voters did not base their decisions on Reagan's conservative policies. Rather, the election was primarily a case of RETROSPECTIVE VOTING—a referendum on the performance of Jimmy Carter's administration, particularly its handling of the economy.

The meaning of signals the voters send in congressional elections is even harder to discern. With so many issues and so many different voter groups involved, parties and candidates tend to collect votes for different, and even conflicting, reasons.

In the MIDTERM ELECTION of 1994, the voters seemed to be giving a mandate to the Republicans and their conservative "Contract with America" agenda. Although the president's party almost always loses seats at midterm, the Democrats' loss of fifty-two House seats was the greatest in five decades. And indeed the Republican-controlled Congress was able to enact some of the Contract with America over the next two years. (See box, page 246.)

Parts of the contract passed on a bipartisan basis with Clinton's help. But other parts were not passed, notably constitutional amendment proposals for congressional TERM LIMITS and a mandatory balanced budget. By the end of Clinton's first term both sides could claim successes. Clinton was reelected, but the Republicans retained control of Congress. In the 1998 congressional elections, contrary to the historical pattern, the president's party gained seats in the House, although both chambers of Congress remained in GOP control. Some analysts saw the results as a protest against the House's impending impeachment of a popular president. (See REMOVAL FROM OFFICE.)

The electorate in 1994, 1996, and 1998 appeared to be endorsing the concept of divided government rather than any specific legislative agenda. Although many had decried the twelve years of deadlock between Republican presidents and a Democratic Congress, the voters ordered a return to divided government (albeit with the parties reversed) to have the White House and Congress serve as a check on one another. That in itself may have been a form of mandate.

## Mandatory Voting

*See* INTERNATIONAL AND U.S. ELECTIONS COMPARED.

## Media Coverage of Campaigns

There is much about elections that is exciting. The opportunity to do volunteer work in a campaign that you believe in. The chance to shake hands with a well-known candidate. The color and hoopla of the nominating conventions. And, finally, the suspense on election night as the names of the winners and losers are revealed.

On the other hand, there is much about elections that the public finds boring. The long speeches. The NEGATIVE CAMPAIGNING that seems to get worse with every election. The constant appeals for money for this or that campaign. And, finally, the sheer length of the campaign seasons, which are longer in the United States

than in almost any other democratic country and perhaps much longer than they need to be to ensure that the voters have sufficient information to make intelligent choices. (See INTERNATIONAL AND U.S. ELECTIONS COMPARED; ZZZ.)

What separates the exciting from the boring is chiefly the presence or absence of drama, and that in turn helps to determine the amount of attention a campaign receives from the news media, especially television. In the highly competitive news business, the media are looking for a larger audience share or greater readership. What the producers and editors think will gain the most viewers or readers may have little to do with what the individual voters find exciting about politics and elections.

Because drama thrives on conflict, the news coverage often emphasizes the "horse-race" aspects of an election, rather than the candidate's qualifications or positions on issues. CAMPAIGN STRATEGY, momentum, competition, and error are emphasized at the expense of candidates' records and policy pronouncements.

Journalists covering presidential DEBATES, for example, are more concerned with who "won" than with the issues articulated. Issues are subordinated to personalities, and electoral outcomes focus on the individual's personal victory or defeat rather than on the process and its implications for the country, state, or region. Thus the media can impinge on the ability of candidates to set the policy agenda and articulate their positions.

By exposing a flaw in the person's history the media can derail a candidacy long before the election. In 1972 Thomas Eagleton was forced to give up the Democratic vice-presidential nomination after his past treatment for depression was disclosed. Gary Hart and Joseph Biden abandoned fledgling presidential bids in 1987 after receiving adverse publicity. Hart was caught in an extramarital relationship, and Biden had engaged in plagiarism.

SCANDAL, however, is not necessarily the kiss of death to a campaign. In 1992 Arkansas governor Bill Clinton, with his wife at his side, weathered Gennifer Flowers's assertions that she had been Clinton's mistress

*George Bush had a love-hate relationship with the press, which found his policy statements dull but made much of his pithy catch phrase, "Read my lips. No new taxes." Source: National Archives, Bush Presidential Materials Project*

for twelve years. And in 1996, on the day Clinton accepted the Democratic presidential nomination for the second time, the media disclosed that one of his chief POLITICAL CONSULTANTS, Dick Morris, had a long-term relationship with a prostitute.

At the same time, Clinton himself was still under investigation by an independent counsel for the Whitewater real estate scandal in Arkansas, was fending off a sexual assault civil suit by former Arkansas employee Paula Jones, and was under fire for receiving illicit campaign contributions from foreign nationals.

Clinton's Republican challenger, Robert J. Dole, had his own brush with scandal, over an extramarital affair he had during his first marriage. For weeks he and his advisers were afraid the tabloid press would expose the affair before the election, forcing the mainstream press to follow suit, as in the Flowers-Clinton case. The feared headline explosion never took place, however. Although a tabloid disclosed the affair in October, major publications all but ignored the story until after Dole had been defeated.

Incidents such as these still make headlines, but they are perhaps less damaging than in the past. One reason is that the modern media—and the campaign funds to use them—provide candidates with ways to bypass reporters and take their message directly to the people. Television, in particular, has transformed electoral politics. Cutting across all socioeconomic divisions, television reaches nearly 98 percent of all households in the continental United States. One study shows that as re-

*The press is interested in every aspect of a campaigner's life, even their pets. In November 1992 photographers in Little Rock, Arkansas, surround Socks, the cat belonging to the family of president-elect Bill Clinton. Source: Mike Nelson, Agence France Presse*

cently as 1982 more American homes had televisions than refrigerators or indoor plumbing.

Computers and modems, too, are increasingly common, and politicians were quick to latch on to the Internet. Both major parties, several THIRD PARTIES, and many candidates at all levels had World Wide Web sites for disseminating information in the 1996 elections. One survey indicated that 9 percent of voters, or about 8.5 million people, were influenced by information they found on the Internet. (See page 498.)

## Types of Messages

There are times, however, when candidate messages must be filtered, in whole or in part, through the jour-

nalistic media. Political scientists David Paletz and Robert Entman have identified three types of media content: unmediated messages, partially mediated messages, and mostly mediated messages. *Unmediated messages* are those, usually paid advertising, over which the candidates exercise total control. *Partially mediated messages* are those delivered in televised press conferences, debates, talk shows, interviews, and other formats where candidates cannot totally control the content. They may air their views but are constrained by the questioning of journalists or, in debates, the responses of opposing candidates. *Mostly mediated messages* are those that the candidates control the least, such as news stories that are constructed by the media about the candidate. (For discussion of unmediated messages, see POLITICAL ADVERTISING; for partially mediated messages, see DEBATES; MEDIA USE BY CAMPAIGNS.)

Paletz and Entman contend that mostly mediated messages have the greatest effect on PUBLIC OPINION precisely because the candidates do not appear to control their content. Candidates' campaign staffs therefore use a wide variety of techniques to try to influence such coverage, including timing and staging events, restricting reporters' access to the candidate, and controlling the flow of information from the campaign organization.

INCUMBENCY particularly lends itself to efforts to attract coverage through such activities. Only an incumbent president, for example, can schedule an event in the Rose Garden or the East Room of the White House, or participate in foreign "summit meetings" as Richard Nixon did in 1972.

These "visuals" are often criticized for lack of substance and avoidance of issues. But journalists' efforts to expose their shallowness can backfire, as CBS's Lesley Stahl discovered in 1984. Ronald Reagan's strategists relied on emotional, visual advertising with lots of American flags flapping in the breeze, which gave rise to a famous episode in the continuing clash between political handlers and the press. In 1984 Stahl broadcast a hard-hitting report on alleged hypocrisy in the Reagan campaign. Her spot juxtaposed footage of a Reagan speech on mental disabilities given at a Special Olympics event with a voice-over pointing out that Reagan had cut funding for mental health. According to Stahl, White House aide Richard Darman subsequently called her to praise her work. The puzzled reporter replied, "Did you hear what I said? I killed you."

"You people in Televisionland haven't figured it out yet, have you?" Darman countered. "When the pictures are powerful and emotional, they override if not completely drown out the sound. Lesley, I mean it. Nobody heard you."

Later, when Stahl replayed the tapes with the sound turned off, she realized that she had prepared a "magnificent montage of Reagan in a series of wonderful, upbeat scenes, with flags, balloons, children, and adoring supporters—virtually an unpaid commercial."

Both as a challenger and as the incumbent, Bill Clinton proved adept at using visuals to obtain free publicity. He played the saxophone on the late night *Arsenio Hall Show* while running for the 1992 Democratic presidential nomination. After he won it, he and RUNNING MATE Al Gore boarded buses for a much-photographed tour of several states, forsaking the traditional postconvention campaign break until Labor Day. In 1996 Clinton WHISTLE-STOPPED again, this time by train to the convention, evoking images of Harry S. Truman.

As president, Clinton gave new meaning to the term *photo op.* He tried to ensure that each time he faced the cameras, he would appear on the front page or the nightly news. Throughout his reelection campaign, the hands of pollsters and other consultants were evident in the Clinton strategy. Taking his cues from a 1995 Mark Penn poll, Clinton reportedly tailored remarks, gestures, and even his bearing to suit the public taste. Instead of strolling off *Air Force One,* he began striding off in a military manner.

## Emphasis on the "Horse Race"

News stories about candidates and campaigns—the "mostly mediated" category—have become even more mediated in the past four decades. Instead of merely reporting the "who" and "what" of elections, today's reporters feel obliged to analyze events for their readers and viewers. They focus more than in the past on the "why" aspect, and in so doing they not only outline the competitors' agendas but also help to set them.

Political scientist Thomas E. Patterson discerned the changed pattern by comparing random *New York Times* front-page stories about presidential races from 1960 through 1992. He found that coverage of the Kennedy-Nixon race in 1960 was about equally balanced between stories on policy or issues and those on the horse race or strategic aspects of the contest. By 1972 as PRIMARIES began lengthening the nominating process, the emphasis had shifted heavily away from policy to strategy. Twenty years later in the Bush-Clinton-Perot coverage, more than 80 percent of the stories were about what the candidates were doing to move up in the race. While almost all the 1960 stories were descriptive, most of those in 1992 were attempts to analyze the campaign strategies, devoting little space to the candidates' own statements (their unmediated messages).

Nor was the *New York Times* alone in its concentration on strategy in 1992. Another media scholar, Matthew Robert Kerbel, found that more than half the political stories on CNN's *Prime News* and more than a third on ABC News were strategy based. "Collectively, the 1992 coverage amounted to a personalized, politicized, self-interested account of the election, running like a narrative through the campaign," Kerbel wrote.

In an informal study of five news sources, Kerbel found more of the same in 1996. After quoting at length a *Washington Post* account of a Dole trip to California, Kerbel said that it was "analysis with a vengeance . . . seen through the eyes of an observer intent on finding thematic significance in mundane political acts."

But Kerbel also found some self-conscious awareness in the media of too much strategy-based coverage. He noted that *CBS Evening News* anchor Dan Rather went through a period where he tried to work the word *substance* into every election story. "But he said 'substance' when he really meant 'horse race,'" Kerbel commented.

Reporters usually do not find candidates' policy statements particularly newsworthy. They prefer pithy, slogan-like statements on issues that are clear-cut rather than complex and difficult to summarize. It has been argued, for example, that the 1988 presidential campaign reached a turning point when President Bush (or his handlers) came up with the catch phrase, "Read my lips. No new taxes."

In that campaign, strategists dealt with the "issues" by having their candidates visit flag factories or ride in an army tank, or by raising racial fears by highlighting the case of Willie Horton, the furloughed black prisoner who raped a white woman.

It was then that substance hit an all-time low, according to veteran journalist Marvin Kalb, director of the Joan Shorenstein Center on the Press, Politics, and Public Policy at Harvard University. The unfortunate "new fact of campaign life," he said, is that reporters are always looking for "small, behind-the-scenes issues of who's doing what to whom."

Bush's 1988 opponent, Michael S. Dukakis, recalled a time during the campaign when he gave a major environmental speech at Rutgers University, only to see the evening news focus instead on the flat tire one of his Secret Service cars got. "You can't blame consultants," Dukakis said. "It's the craziness of an election, and the media's incessant search for the new and the visual."

In 1996 Dole tumbled off a platform when a railing gave way as he was reaching down to shake hands with voters. He was not hurt, but it was the fall—not what he said that day—that made the evening TV news.

## Media "Bias"

Candidates from all points on the IDEOLOGY spectrum have complained about the media's so-called bias. In complaining about liberal bias, Republicans cite surveys showing that reporters regularly vote for Democrats. Democrats complain about the subtle pressure from conservative editorial boards and media owners on reporters in the field.

Media bias depends on the circumstances of the race. In 1980, for example, reporters appeared to treat Republican Ronald Reagan more favorably than Jimmy Carter, whose Democratic administration was plagued by the Iranian hostage crisis, high inflation, and other problems. In 1992 the media produced more negative reports about Republican George Bush than Democrat Bill Clinton. The nonpartisan Center for Media and Public Affairs reported that 78 percent of Bush's preconvention coverage on the evening news was negative, compared with 59 percent of Clinton's. Bush, in fact, endured twenty-three consecutive weeks of negative coverage.

Dole in 1996 was only the latest GOP candidate to rail against "liberal bias," declaring, "We're not going to let the media steal this election." And although a Freedom Forum–Roper Center survey of 139 reporters showed that 89 percent had voted for Clinton, most journalists, asserting their professionalism, defended their coverage as unbiased. The same press that Dole complained about, they noted, had disclosed the Clinton-Gore campaign's zealous pursuit of SOFT MONEY campaign contributions.

Media critics attributed inadequate coverage of Dole's ideas, such as his proposed 15 percent tax cut, to curtailed overall coverage and a perception that the election was dull. The Freedom Forum's Media Studies Center said network (ABC, CBS, NBC) coverage on the evening newscasts had dropped 51 percent in eight years, from 1,929 minutes in 1988 to 988 minutes in 1996 (both periods running from Labor Day to the following July 31).

The networks also cut back coverage of the national nominating conventions, limiting it to about sixty to ninety minutes a night, instead of gavel to gavel as in the past. And reporters' commentaries used up most of that time—taking about twelve times more than the convention speakers, according to the Center for Media and Public Affairs. The study covered only the three major commercial networks, however. Interested viewers could find additional coverage on CNN (Cable News Network) and C-SPAN (Cable-Satellite Public Affairs Network).

Most of the stories dealt with strategy rather than issues. The Dick Morris scandal on the last day of the Democratic convention accounted for fourteen stories—about as many as any single issue had received at either major convention. When it came to bias, however, the study showed that the reporters were evenhanded in their comments. They were equally negative at both conventions.

Other studies showed that between 1968 and 1992 the average length of a statement made by a presidential candidate on the evening network news broadcasts fell from forty-two seconds to less than nine seconds. In campaigns for state and congressional offices, local stations also severely restricted the air time devoted to the statements of candidates.

## Media Influence on Voters

In the 1940s, before the introduction of television into political campaigning, the media apparently had little influence on voters' decisions. Researchers believed that the media mainly *reinforced* the voters' partisan loyalties.

But partisan considerations today are less important in guiding voter choices than they were in the 1940s and 1950s. PARTY IDENTIFICATION OF VOTERS is down, which seemingly would make the media more influential in voter choices. Research has found, however, that regular viewing of network news has little or no effect on voters' awareness of candidates; yet viewing of political commercials is associated with higher voter awareness of candidates' issue stances. The simple explanation for the difference is that political commercials contain more information about the issues than do nightly news stories.

The tendency of approximately two-thirds of voters to decide on their choice for president before the general election campaign officially begins further limits the media coverage's effect on voter choice. In close elections, however, media coverage that sways even a small percentage of voters can be crucial.

Although the media may not directly affect voter choice to any great degree, they do play a significant role in setting the agenda for an election. This was demonstrated in 1990 and early 1991 during the Persian Gulf War. The prominent play the media gave to defense and foreign policy concerns meant that for this period the most important criterion for evaluating the president was his performance in foreign affairs.

In this context of military success, President Bush was accorded high marks. But after the war, when media coverage emphasized economic adversity at home and policy gridlock in Washington, the evaluation criteria shifted to domestic concerns, and the president received poor grades. The content and emphasis of news reporting therefore are significant because they help to create the context within which voters' choices are made.

Voter attitudes and moods are part of that context. If voters are turned off by negative advertising, CAMPAIGN FINANCE abuses, too little emphasis on substance, and other unsavory aspects of U.S. elections, they become cynical and disinterested. VOTER REGISTRATION and VOTER TURNOUT drop, leading to more lamentations about public apathy and the decline of our electoral system.

Thus begins what Joseph A. Cappella and Kathleen Hall Jamieson of the Annenberg School of Communications call "the spiral of cynicism." Their in-depth study of news coverage included experiments with different versions of the same print or broadcast stories about a Philadelphia mayoral race and the national health care reform debate—one version was strategy based and the other, issue based.

The responses led Cappella and Jamieson to conclude in their 1997 book, *Spiral of Cynicism: The Press and the Public Good,* that the media's near-obsession with strategy coverage initiates citizen dissatisfaction that in turn breeds still more disinterest and lack of confidence in the electoral process.

They wrote: "A public that has accepted the belief that officials are acting in their own self-interest rather than in the interests of the common weal can be easily primed to see self-promotion in every political act. When journalists frame political events strategically they activate existing beliefs and understandings; they do not need to create them."

## Media Use by Campaigns

The news and advertising media have become the primary sources of information about candidates and elections for most Americans. As a result, television, radio, newspapers, and magazines have helped to determine the type of candidate who is likely to succeed. Increasingly, the emphasis has been on style, image, and an ability to communicate well on television.

To take advantage of news coverage, daily campaign activities are geared to getting impressive visual "bites" or sound bites on national and local news programs. Strategists try to adapt the day's "news" events to reinforce the campaign's overall themes and POLITICAL ADVERTISING appeals.

The candidates use television and radio throughout the PRIMARY season and again in the fall to publicize their campaigns. The pace quickens at the end of October, when many voters first begin to pay close attention to the election.

Depending on their standing in the POLLS, and on whether they are running for or against the party in

power, the candidates switch back and forth between appeals to bolster their own image and ads to undermine their opponent's credibility. In 1984 President Ronald Reagan's reelection campaign used "feel good" commercials with imprecise images of Americana because it wanted to reinforce a positive mood in the nation.

In 1988 George Bush built and maintained an advantage over Massachusetts governor Michael Dukakis throughout the fall campaign by emphasizing his own conservative IDEOLOGY, portraying the Democrat as a liberal out of step with the mainstream. Many criticized the vice president for his tactics, but few questioned their effectiveness. For example, Bush targeted Dukakis's veto of a state law requiring teachers to lead their pupils in reciting the Pledge of Allegiance. "What's his problem with the Pledge?" Bush asked again and again, implying that Dukakis was unpatriotic.

These examples and most of those that follow are from presidential races. On a smaller scale, congressional and gubernatorial campaigns make similar use of the media. But because presidential campaigns are the most studied and analyzed, they provide the most readily available illustrations of media strategies at work in the technological age.

### Peaks and Valleys

Ideally, a candidate would like to keep his or her name before the voters in a favorable light throughout the campaign period. But realistically that is not always possible. Voters' interest surges and wanes at several points during the election year. Candidates and their advisers conserve their advertising budgets for periods when circumstances justify the purchase of time for expensive television spots. The Federal Communications Commission's EQUAL TIME AND REBUTTAL RULES ensure that all candidates have equal opportunities for use of broadcast or cable television.

During the nominating season, presidential candidates may spend heavily for commercial spots in New England in an effort to win the first-in-the-nation NEW HAMPSHIRE PRIMARY. That contest and the early IOWA CAUCUS have eliminated much of the competi-

*Candidates are increasing their use of sites on the World Wide Web, some with splashy graphics, to enlist volunteers and win over "connected" voters. Source: Patt Chisholm, Congressional Quarterly*

tion in subsequent PRESIDENTIAL PRIMARIES. For the remaining primaries, the candidates concentrate their travel and advertising dollars on the states needed to clinch the nomination.

In recent elections the major party nominees have in effect been chosen well ahead of the NATIONAL PARTY CONVENTIONS where the nominations are formalized. Despite their declining importance, the conventions still inform, educate, and entertain millions of viewers. Polls by the Media Studies Center/Roper Survey showed that 49 percent of Americans got most of their information about the 1996 conventions by watching them live on TV, compared with 17 percent who learned about

them from news stories. And 39 percent thought TV coverage was fairer than newspaper coverage (19 percent).

Both major party nominees usually receive a POST-CONVENTION BOUNCE from the MEDIA COVERAGE, emerging from the conventions with higher poll ratings than when they went in. After Labor Day, the traditional start of the campaign, the polls become the most important part of the "horse-race" aspect of the election. Usually, the leader in the polls after the convention wins in November if the lead is maintained until then.

Chances are that last-minute changes will not affect the outcome. Most voters make up their minds well be-

*Former independent presidential candidate Ross Perot, right, who had announced his candidacy on* Larry King Live, *proclaims the launching of an effort to create a national independent party, now called the Reform Party, September 25, 1995. Source: Dan Groshong, Reuters*

fore ELECTION DAY. In the presidential elections from 1960 to 1996, more than 60 percent of the voters, on average, made up their minds before or during the conventions. Late deciders, however, can swing the ELECTORAL COLLEGE votes of pivotal states, which are often won by margins of less than 5 percentage points. For example, in 1992 Bill Clinton carried eleven states (106 electoral votes) by a margin of less than 5 percentage points, so that a late surge of support for President Bush or Ross Perot conceivably could have reversed the election outcome.

Clinton's 1996 Republican opponent, former Senate majority leader Robert J. Dole, counted on a late surge of support that never came. In the final ninety-six hours before the election, he waged a nonstop, twenty-state campaign. Exit polls showed that Dole defeated Clinton 41 percent to 35 percent among those who decided dur-

ing the last week of the campaign. But that group accounted for only 17 percent of the voters.

## Getting the Message Across

As the challenger in 1992 Clinton provided an example of skillful use of the media to overcome the advantages enjoyed by the INCUMBENT, President Bush. But part of Bush's advantage was lost because of weaknesses in his reelection organization. Some of the people who had directed his successful 1988 campaign were no longer there: strategist Lee Atwater had died; media guru Roger Ailes was doing commercial advertising; and the campaign already was in serious trouble when James Baker took over its direction in late August. The 1992 team was afflicted with organizational bickering and unable to develop a theme and consistent focus for the campaign.

In contrast, the Clinton team was cohesive and disciplined, with a competitive edge that had been honed during the presidential primaries. Many of its leaders (top strategist James Carville and media consultants Frank Greer and Mandy Grunwald) had sharpened their skills in southern elections and, unlike the 1988 Dukakis campaign, had mastered the art of rebutting conservative attacks. Clinton's staff also included experienced Washington hands, such as campaign chairman Mickey Kantor and communications director George Stephanopoulos. Carville's "war room" personnel reveled in their reputations as "tough Democrats" as they scanned the news wire services and satellite feeds for attacks on their candidate, priding themselves on the speed of their responses while at the same time, firing off their own first strikes.

In 1988 the Bush campaign had shown the same awareness of the need to coordinate PUBLIC OPINION polling, media advertising, candidate appearances, and use of the free media. Polls were taken every night with the results available for chairman Baker's daily 7:30 a.m. senior staff meeting.

At these meetings campaign activities were carefully planned to stress the campaign message of the day or week. Media consultants even inserted snappy lines into Bush's speeches—tested in advance—to ensure that they were picked up as sound bites on TV news programs.

To complete the media package, television commercials were designed to back up the chosen message. The Bush campaign also sought to limit news conferences with reporters, lest the free-wheeling and often adversary nature of these sessions resulted in the wrong messages being communicated to the voters. The campaign was thus designed to exert maximum control over what the voters would see and hear about the candidate on television, the people's most important and trusted source of news.

## Refinement and Innovation

The 1992 Clinton and Perot campaigns used many of the same time-tested techniques plus innovative ones to get their messages across. In seeking favorable free cov-erage, the Clinton organization took full advantage of the news media's alleged distaste for the NEGATIVE CAMPAIGNING that they said had excessively dominated the 1988 campaign. With the national press corps continually looking for distortions in the charges leveled by one candidate against another, the Clinton campaign adopted a strategy of reacting quickly to Republican attacks. If a staff response promptly faxed to the media did not do the job, Clinton frequently responded in person, in the process gaining extensive media coverage and blunting the GOP charges.

The Clinton campaign also tried to use the local television news more fully by providing local reporters in pivotal media markets with access to the candidate through satellite feeds. From one location the candidate often did five to six interviews for local evening news programs.

Using the local media had the added advantage of bypassing the national press corps with its often critical "gotcha" style of journalism. And local reporters, because they were less familiar with the details of national policy, were more likely to allow the candidate to get his message out without journalistic tinkering or mediation. Going one step further, the Democratic organization did its own filming of Clinton campaign appearances and then sent the footage via satellite feeds to local stations for use on news programs.

One of the most distinctive features of 1992 was the "talk-show campaign." Ross Perot was the first to discover this format as an effective way to bypass national political reporters and speak directly to the public. His campaign quite literally began on *Larry King Live*, where Perot said that, after the New Hampshire primary, he would run if "volunteers" put his name on the ballot.

Perot, financing his own campaign, also revived the use of paid half-hour infomercials to promote his candidacy and explain his policy proposals with the help of charts, graphs, and other visual props. These marathon campaign commercials had been used frequently in the 1950s and 1960s.

Clinton was the first of the major party candidates to follow the Perot example and exploit the talk shows with appearances on nontraditional candidate venues such as the MTV and ESPN networks, as well as the Phil Donahue, Arsenio Hall, and Larry King shows. The early morning network broadcasts such as *Today* and *Good Morning America* even brought the candidates to the nation's breakfast tables. President Bush at first resisted participating in what he characterized as these "weird talk shows," but he too eventually followed the trend.

Unlike the tough questions posed by national political reporters about campaign tactics, polls, and inconsistencies in policy positions, the less-confrontational questions posed on talk shows concerned how the candidates would solve the problems on the minds of callers or members of the studio audience. This kind of platform, on which Clinton was highly effective, gave him an opportunity to reach voters on subjects they cared about without having his message mediated by reporters. Information (and some misinformation) was also disseminated over the Internet, a development that seems likely to have an increasing—and as yet unpredictable—influence as more and more Americans hook up their computers to the World Wide Web.

## Participation in Candidate Forums

Televised DEBATES now go hand in hand with presidential and other American elections. For nonincumbent and underdog candidates, such debates are potentially advantageous because they place these candidates on an equal footing with a president, governor, or frontrunning candidate for any office. On an unadorned stage, the candidates stand alone as equals. Not only are incumbents robbed of the aura of the White House or statehouse, but also their claims of superior experience can be quickly eroded during the debate by challengers who are credible and clever, which most are.

Because the news media give prime-time coverage to debates, candidates tend to see them as the make-or-break events. In fact, extended negotiations among campaign managers over debate formats are usually the rule—all aimed at preventing the opposition from gaining any procedural advantage.

Wrangling over the number, timing, and format of the presidential debates in 1992 lasted until late September, with incumbent president Bush unenthusiastic about debating Clinton, who was generally considered more articulate and practiced in the debate format. The final agreement resulted in the first three-way presidential debates, with Bush, Clinton, and Perot taking part.

In 1996, however, the new Commission on Presidential Debates limited the two debates to Clinton and Dole. Frozen out, Perot reverted to his infomercials to offset some of his lost exposure.

---

## Midterm Election

The election that falls at the halfway mark of four-year presidential terms is known as the *midterm* or, less precisely, *off-year* election. Every seat in the House of Representatives and one-third of the Senate seats are at stake in this election. In every midterm election in the twentieth century, except in 1934 and 1998, the president's party has lost seats in the House. Because of the smaller number of Senate seats contested every two years, the midterm election has less effect on the make-up of that body.

To some extent the midterm election serves as a referendum on the president's performance during the previous two years. If the economy is poor, if lives are being lost in an unpopular war, or if the president has a low approval rating in the PUBLIC OPINION polls, it is likely that the president's party will lose congressional seats—perhaps enough to change control of one or both chambers.

A prime example was the DEMOCRATIC PARTY's loss of Congress in 1994 after four decades of control in the House and eight years in the Senate. The party leader, President Bill Clinton, accepted partial blame for the stunning setback.

Clinton was on shaky ground midway through his first term. He had been elected in 1992 with less than a majority of the popular vote, making him one of sixteen so-called "minority presidents." On taking office he put forth an ambitious agenda, including an overhaul of the nation's health care system, a formidable undertaking that he delegated to his wife, Hillary. The effort failed.

*Democratic senator Barbara Boxer and nominee Gray Davis display their readiness for their general election battles in the 1998 Senate and gubernatorial races in California.* Source: Fred Prouser, Reuters

Clinton angered religious conservatives with a policy supporting rights of homosexuals in the military. At the same time, his personal character was under constant scrutiny because of alleged infidelity, sexual harassment, and the Whitewater real estate deals in Arkansas while he was governor. Other SCANDALS involved firings in the White House travel office and the suicide of a top aide, Vincent Foster.

In light of these problems, congressional Democrats felt burdened by the Clinton White House. Republicans, on the other hand, rallied around Rep. Newt Gingrich of Georgia and his ten-point Contract with America, which proposed a balanced-budget amendment to the Constitution, TERM LIMITS on members of Congress, a line-item veto for the president, an anticrime package, tax cuts, and other reforms.

The results on ELECTION DAY 1994 showed GOP gains of fifty-two seats in the House and eight seats in the Senate, shifting both chambers from Democratic to Republican control. Gingrich became House Speaker, and Robert J. Dole of Kansas became Senate majority leader.

Two years later Clinton won reelection (again with less than a majority, making him the seventeenth "minority president"), defeating Republican nominee Dole and Reform Party nominee Ross Perot. Although the

# Contract with America

| Congressional Process | Enacted? Y/N/P |
|---|---|
| **Preface** | |
| End Congress's exemption from eleven safety and other laws. | Y |
| Cut House committees, limit terms of chairs, require three-fifths majority vote for tax increases. | Y |
| **1. Balanced Budget and Line-Item Veto** | |
| Send states a proposed balanced-budget amendment. | N |
| Give president power to veto an appropriation or tax break. | Y |
| **2. Anticrime Package** | |
| Restitution for victims, prison construction grants; limit death row appeals, reform certain laws. | P |
| **3. Welfare** | |
| Require work after two years of welfare, other reforms. | Y |
| **4. Families and Children** | |
| Parental consent for children to take part in surveys. | N |
| Tax benefits for adoption and home care. | Y |
| Increased penalties for sex crimes against children. | Y |
| Stronger enforcement of child support orders. | Y |
| **5. Middle-Class Tax Cut** | |
| $500 per-child tax credit, expand IRAs, ease "marriage penalty." | P |
| **6. Defense Policy** | |
| Bar U.S. troops in UN missions under foreign command, prohibit defense cuts for social programs. | N |
| **7. Social Security** | |
| Repeal increase in benefits subject to income tax; raise earnings ceiling for recipients. | P |
| **8. Capital Gains and Regulations** | |
| Cut capital gains taxes, adjust other provisions. | P |
| Reduce unfunded mandates to states. | Y |
| Reduce federal paperwork. | Y |
| Require agencies to assess costs/benefits of regulations. | P |
| **9. Civil Law and Product Liability** | |
| National product liability law with punitive damage limits. | N |
| Restrict investor suits against companies. | Y |
| Apply "loser pays" rule to certain federal cases. | Y |
| **10. Term Limits** | |
| Constitutional amendment limiting congressional terms. | N |

Key: Y = Yes; N = No; P = Partly.

*For New York's Columbus Day Parade on October 12, 1998, Republican senator Alfonse D'Amato brought out top party members, including Mayor Rudolph Giuliani and Gov. George E. Pataki, to help him in his race against Democrat Charles E. Schumer.*
Source: Suzanne Tobias, AP

Republicans retained control of Congress, they gave up some of their 1994 midterm gains in the House. The more subdued GOP congressional leadership was able to reach a balanced-budget agreement with Clinton in mid-1997, fulfilling, in effect, a major objective of the Contract with America. (See CHRONOLOGY OF PRESIDENTIAL ELECTIONS.)

## Return to the Past

The 1994 Democratic losses were a throwback to the way the midterm election used to be, when the president's congressional strength ebbed and flowed dramatically. Eight times between the end of the Civil War and the end of World War II, the party occupying the White House lost more than fifty House seats in the midterm election. But until 1994 it had been twenty years since the president's party lost more than forty seats at midterm.

In 1946 postwar voters were ready for a change. Democrats under Franklin D. Roosevelt and Harry S. Truman had held control of the White House and Congress for fourteen years. Republicans won both chambers of Congress as Democrats lost fifty-five seats in the House and twelve in the Senate. But the GOP domination was short-lived. Truman waged a feisty campaign against the "Do-Nothing" Eightieth Congress and a feeble Republican response. The Democrats not only retained the White House—in a surprise victory for Truman against Thomas E. Dewey—but also regained control of both chambers in 1948.

**Midterm Election Results, 1902–1998**

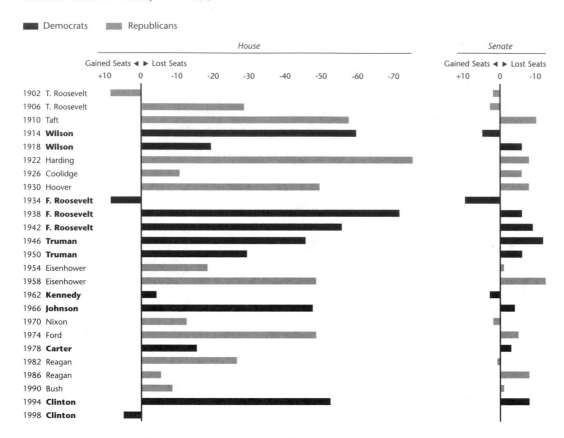

*Sources:* Norman J. Ornstein, Thomas E. Mann, and Michael J. Malbin, *Vital Statistics on Congress, 1997–1998* (Washington, D.C.: Congressional Quarterly, 1998), Table 2–4; 1998 Election data from *CQ Weekly,* November 7, 1998.

In 1958 economic recession, low farm prices, and labor agitation against right-to-work laws partly offset President Dwight D. Eisenhower's personal popularity. Against Democratic gains in the Midwest and blue-collar regions, Republicans lost forty-eight House and thirteen Senate seats. Two years later they lost the White House to John F. Kennedy.

The election of 1966, two years after President Lyndon B. Johnson's landslide election and the launching of his "Great Society" programs, dealt Democrats their worst midterm losses in twenty years. Amid mounting dissension over the Vietnam War, Johnson scaled back his campaigning for Democrats in Congress. Although it retained control, his party lost forty-seven House seats and four Senate seats. Two years later, Johnson declined renomination, and Republican Richard Nixon won the presidency.

Reelected in a landslide in 1972, Nixon himself encountered the midterm losses phenomenon in 1974. By then he had suffered precipitous drops in public standing because of the damaging revelations of the Watergate scandal. Voters also were disgruntled by an economic downturn, and Republicans had trouble raising money and persuading strong candidates to run for office. Democrats were roused to action by Watergate, in part because the offenses had been directed against Democratic Party leaders. Their offices in the Watergate Hotel were burglarized before the 1972 election, and the White House was implicated in the subsequent cover-up. As a result, Democrats at all levels were motivated to run for office, donate money, and work to defeat Republicans.

At the same time, an unusually large number of legislators, most of them Republican, decided to retire in 1974, opening up more seats and enhancing the Democratic challengers' chances. Facing impeachment by the House because of Watergate, Nixon resigned on August 9, 1974, further damaging the Republicans' campaigns for the congressional election three months later. The net result for the Democrats was a gain of forty-nine seats in the House and four in the Senate, solidifying their hold on Congress.

Second-term losses by the president's party tend to be more severe than first-term losses. But, like Roosevelt in 1934, Clinton and his party defied the seemingly inevitable in 1998. Instead of losing more House seats, the Democrats had a net gain of five seats. The 106th Congress had 228 Republicans, 206 Democrats, and 1 independent. The Senate division remained unchanged at fifty-five Republicans and forty-five Democrats.

Facing the loss of his speakership over the unexpected setback, Gingrich stepped down and left the House. In a surprising development, his apparent successor, Louisiana Republican Robert L. Livingston, also declined the post and resigned his seat. Livingston confessed to marital infidelity as the House prepared to impeach Clinton for perjury and obstruction of justice in connection with his illicit affair with Monica S. Lewinsky, then a White House intern. The House subsequently elected Illinois Republican Dennis Hastert as the new Speaker.

Clinton's popularity apparently was a factor in the Democrats' gains and the ripple effect in the GOP House leadership. The rebuff to the Republicans was widely interpreted as an anti-impeachment signal from the voters. Even after the House impeached Clinton and his trial began in the Senate, his job approval rating in the polls remained high. (See POLLING; REMOVAL FROM OFFICE.)

## Effect on Turnout

Compared with presidential contests, the midterm congressional election lacks interest for many voters. The relative apathy is reflected in the lower VOTER TURNOUT figures for election years not having a presidential election.

The turnout for the 1994 midterm election was significantly lower than in 1992 when President George Bush and challengers Bill Clinton and Ross Perot were at the top of their respective tickets. The turnout in 1998, although somewhat higher than expected, was lower than it was in 1996 when Clinton won reelection. Based on the actual vote as a percentage of the voting age population, the 1994 turnout was 36.0 percent, against 55.2 percent in 1992. The 1998 turnout also was 36.0 percent, against 49.0 percent in 1996.

In midterm elections, a gauge of the nationwide turnout is the total vote cast for the House of Representatives, because the entire House comes up for election every two years. In the 1992 presidential election year, 96.4 million votes were cast for U.S. representatives, or 50.8 percent of the voting age population. In the midterm election of 1990, however, only 61.5 million voted for House members, or 33.0 percent of the voting age population, which was estimated at 185.8 million for that year.

Even in presidential election years, fewer people vote for House candidates than for presidential candidates. As noted, the 1992 House races drew a 50.8 percent turnout, while the presidential race on the same day had a participation rate of 55.2 percent. Although the presidential vote was low compared with the turnout in many INTERNATIONAL ELECTIONS, it tied with 1970 as the highest in the United States since the 60.9 percent recorded in 1968. The 1992 election was also the first in which more than 100 million Americans voted.

Factors that help explain the difference in participation between the two types of elections include the greater MEDIA COVERAGE of presidential campaigns, the lower significance that voters attach to congressional offices, the relative importance of the issues raised in the campaigns, the attractiveness of the candidates, and the degree of competition in the contests, which in many congressional districts may be slight.

## Presidential Involvement

It is often to the president's advantage to campaign vigorously in the midterm election for congressional candidates of the president's own party. The stronger the president is in Congress the easier it is for the White House to carry out its legislative program. But in practice the level of presidential enthusiasm for midterm campaigning varies widely. President Eisenhower said in 1954 that a president should try to provide an "umbrella of accomplishment" under which party members can run, rather than participate "too intensively and directly in off-year congressional elections."

Because it is all but inevitable that the president's party will lose House seats in the midterm election, there is almost no way for the president to look good by getting closely involved. The most he can hope to do is minimize losses. If the president is under siege within his own party, as Lyndon Johnson was in 1966, there is even more incentive for the president to keep a low profile at midterm, as Johnson did.

Midterm campaigning that inflames partisan opposition may make it harder for the president to work with the new Congress, especially if the opposition party controls it. Some presidents have also found members of the opposition party to be more supportive than their own partisans. As a result, they have naturally been reluctant to campaign against those members.

## Effect on State Elections

Like House elections, gubernatorial elections are affected by national issues and conditions. For that reason, most states elect their GOVERNORS in the middle of presidential terms, rather than at the same time as the president, when the White House race is likely to overshadow battles for the statehouses. (The term *off-year,* as used by Eisenhower, has been largely replaced in usage by *midterm election.* This helps to avoid confusion with some state and many local elections that are held in odd-numbered years to further insulate them from being influenced by debates over national issues or candidates.)

But the move to midterm elections has not prevented state contests from being caught up in national partisan politics. The president's party loses governorships in midterm elections as consistently, and sometimes in larger percentages, than it loses House seats.

Except for 1962, when there was no net change, and 1986, the president's party lost governors in every midterm election from 1950 to 1994. In 1986, midway in President Ronald Reagan's second term, the Republicans made a net gain of eight governors. A relatively strong economy and stable international scene kept voters focused on close-to-home issues, with Reagan's personal popularity giving an edge to GOP candidates. Also, Democrats in 1986 were defending more statehouse seats than the Republicans. The Democrats, however, regained control of the Senate that year. Their heavy losses in Congress in 1994 were matched by their loss of twelve governorships in those midterm elections.

Midterm elections of state legislators also consistently result in losses for the president's party. The losses of seats in these elections are more likely to result in change of party control of one or both chambers than in presidential election years.

---

## Mikulski Commission

*See* PRESIDENTIAL SELECTION REFORMS.

---

## *Miller v. Johnson*

*See* RACIAL REDISTRICTING.

---

## Minority Presidents

*See* ELECTORAL ANOMALIES; ELECTORAL COLLEGE AND VOTES.

## Motor Voter Act

Registering to vote in the United States became easier beginning May 20, 1993, when President Bill Clinton signed into law the so-called Motor Voter Act (PL 103-31). The law required states to provide all eligible citizens the opportunity to register when they applied for or renewed a driver's license. It also required states to allow mail-in registration and to provide VOTER REGISTRATION forms at agencies that supplied public assistance, such as welfare checks or help for the disabled. Compliance with the federally mandated program was required by 1995. Costs were to be borne by the states.

Partly as a result of the legislation, a record number of new voters, some 10 million, signed up in the first three years following implementation of the act. The FEDERAL ELECTION COMMISSION reported to Congress in 1996 that the United States had 143 million registered voters, or 72.8 percent of the voting age population. The percentage was the highest since 1960, when national registration figures first became available.

For years, political activists had tried both to simplify the process of registering to vote and to shorten the length of time (the residency requirement) that many states mandated before deeming that citizens had the right to register to vote. Efforts to increase voter registration had begun in a handful of states by the mid-1980s, with state legislatures ordering motor vehicle departments to provide voter registration forms. By 1992 twenty-seven states had some type of motor voter practices in place. But state programs varied in their degree of sophistication and their effect on VOTER TURNOUT.

In most Western nations, government agencies sign up voters, but the United States places the burden for qualifying for electoral participation on the citizen. Although the procedure is still somewhat cumbersome, the Motor Voter Act along with other federal legislation has made voter registration more convenient.

The motor vehicle itself helped to create one of the obstacles to registration. As American society became more mobile, some potential voters encountered difficulty with residency requirements. Many states had required residency for as long as two years before a citizen could register to vote. The 1970 Voting Rights Act Amendment guaranteed the vote in presidential elections if the citizen had lived in the voting district for at

*President Bill Clinton signs the Motor Voter Bill during a ceremony at the White House May 20, 1993. Standing behind him are, left to right, Rep. Al Swift, Sen. Mark Hatfield, University of New Hampshire student Joel Shulkin, secretary of the board of Human Serve Frances Fox Privin, executive director of Human Serve Richard Cloward, NAACP Director Benjamin Chavis, and League of Woman Voters President Becky Cain. Source: Win McNamee, Reuters*

least thirty days prior to the election. This measure, analysts have estimated, made approximately 5 million people eligible to vote in the 1972 presidential election.

In 1973 the Supreme Court ruled in *Marston v. Lewis* that states could not deny the full FRANCHISE to people who had not lived in a state for a year and in a county for three months. By 1980 seventeen states had no residency requirement, and all but one had requirements of thirty or fewer days.

President Jimmy Carter proposed several bills that would have allowed voters to register on ELECTION DAY, but they were not enacted. By the late 1980s, however, most Americans lived in states that allowed registration by postcard. Two states, Oregon and Wisconsin, allow registration on election day, a factor that likely accounts for their voter participation rates being about ten percentage points higher than the national average.

The Motor Voter Act (technically the National Voter Registration Act of 1993) was passed shortly after President Clinton took office and while his party, the Democrats, still controlled both houses of Congress. Congressional Republicans had opposed the legislation on political grounds, namely that it would allow citizens of traditional Democratic constituencies—the urban poor and minorities, among others—easier access to the voting booth and therefore provide a new source of votes for the Democrats. Opponents, including President George Bush, also argued that easier registration could lead to ELECTION FRAUD. Bush had vetoed a motor voter bill in 1992, citing possible fraud as one of his reasons.

President Clinton's signing of the 1993 Motor Voter Act initially did not benefit him as Republicans swept to victory in the 1994 MIDTERM ELECTIONS, taking control of both houses of Congress for the first time in forty years. Although Clinton was reelected in 1996, the increase in registered voters did not translate into an increase in those actually voting. Only 49 percent of the electorate voted, a decrease of 6 percentage points from 1992. The 1998 turnout, although somewhat higher than expected, was only 30 percent, the lowest since 1942. In 1998, however, the Democrats gained five House seats,

making Clinton the first president since Franklin D. Roosevelt in 1934 to win seats at midterm instead of losing them.

The 1998 election provided some indication that the Motor Voter Act reduced chances of fraud instead of increasing it. In Maryland, for example, aides to defeated Republican gubernatorial candidate Ellen R. Sauerbrey said that the act helped to solve the problem of nonvoters clogging the rolls. In her previous loss to Democrat Parris N. Glendening in 1994, Sauerbrey charged in court that some fifty thousand votes were cast illegally—some in the name of persons who should have been purged from the voting rolls because they had not voted in years. A state judge ruled in Sauerbrey's CONTESTED ELECTION case that, although he found some questionable votes, there were not enough to have changed the result. In her 1998 rematch with Glendening, Sauerbrey lost by a wide margin and did not challenge the result.

Maryland election officials said the voting rolls were cleaner as a result of the Motor Voter Act procedures. They said the changes required them to contact voters by mail and place their names on an inactive list if they fail to respond to two mailings. If those on the inactive list do not vote in the next four years their names are removed from the rolls.

## Mugwump

One of the more colorful epithets of American politics—*mugwump*—has survived its rather narrow meaning. It originally referred to a Republican who refused to support the presidential candidacy of James G. Blaine in 1884. Now seldom used, it means someone who bolted his or her political party in favor of another candidate.

Blaine offended some GOP stalwarts with his ethics problems, including allegations that he had accepted bribes from Crédit Mobilier, the Union Pacific subsidiary building the transcontinental railroad. Blaine, then Speaker of the House, avoided censure, but the stain of scandal hurt his later candidacy. Supporters of

*House Speaker James G. Blaine's ethics problems, and the rift they caused in the Republican Party, helped coin the term "mugwump" in 1884. Source: Library of Congress*

Democrat Grover Cleveland chanted: "Blaine, Blaine, James G. Blaine! Continental liar from the state of Maine!" Cleveland won, despite his admission that he was supporting an illegitimate son.

*Mugwump* comes from the Algonquin word for chief. A more facetious derivation is attributed to a Princeton University president, Harold Willis Dodds, who said a mugwump "is a fellow with his mug on one side of the fence and his wump on the other." Given wide circulation by the media, Dodds's definition has endured as a secondary meaning of mugwump: a person who cannot make up his or her mind.

## Multimember Districts

In the early days of the House of Representatives several states had at least one CONGRESSIONAL DISTRICT that elected more than one member. The multimember system permitted multiple representatives to be allotted to the more populous area of a state—or perhaps the one with the most political clout—without drawing the district lines to achieve that result.

For example, in 1824 Maryland's Fifth District chose two representatives, while the remaining seven districts chose one each. And in Pennsylvania two districts (the Fourth and Ninth) elected three representatives each, and four districts (the Seventh, Eighth, Eleventh, and Seventeenth) chose two representatives each.

As late as 1840, New York still had as many as five multimember congressional districts: one (the Third) electing four members and four (the Eighth, Seventeenth, Twenty-second, and Twenty-third) choosing two each. But the practice ended in 1842 when Congress enacted a law that said "no one district may elect more than one Representative." The SINGLE-MEMBER DISTRICT provision was a part of the REAPPORTIONMENT legislation following the CENSUS of 1840.

At the state and local levels, multimember districts remained commonplace into modern times. Until the 1970s about a third of state legislature house members and a sixth of state senators were elected from multimember jurisdictions. Voters in many city council districts could vote for as many seats as were up for election. Seats in multimember districts are almost always filled by AT-LARGE elections in which voters of the whole city, county, or other jurisdiction are eligible to participate.

Protests from racial and other minorities have diminished the use of multimember districts. Opponents contended that such districts diluted minorities' voting strength and violated the principles of PROPORTIONAL REPRESENTATION. Multimember districts were particularly prevalent and controversial in the South until those found discriminatory were struck down as unconstitutional by the Supreme Court in *White v. Regester*, a Texas case, in 1973.

Earlier, in the VOTING RIGHTS ACT of 1965, Congress had acted against multimember districts and other discriminatory practices by requiring federal preclearance of election law changes in southern states. In 1975 the provision was extended to states outside the South.

In a 1986 case, *Davis v. Bandemer,* the Supreme Court struck down Indiana's multimember districting plan as an illegal form of political GERRYMANDERING. Democrats protested that the Republican-controlled legislature had drawn the district lines to dilute the Democrats' voting strength, especially in urban areas.

A form of at-large voting, called CUMULATIVE VOTING, has gained some adherents as a means for minorities to achieve proportional representation by concentrating their votes on candidates from their minority group. Cumulative voting, however, has not been widely adopted in the United States.

# N

## National Democratic Party (1896)

A conservative faction in favor of the gold standard, the National Democrats bolted from the Democratic Party after the 1896 convention adopted a pro-silver platform and nominated William Jennings Bryan. With the nation in the midst of a depression and the Populists in the agrarian Midwest and South demanding monetary reform, currency was the dominant issue of the 1896 campaign. This produced a brief REALIGNMENT in American politics.

The Republican Party was controlled by leaders who favored maintenance of the gold standard, a noninflationary currency. Agrarian Midwestern and Southern Democrats, reflecting a Populist philosophy, gained control of the Democratic Party in 1896 and committed it to the free coinage of silver, an inflationary currency demanded by rural elements threatened by debts. The Democrats attracted pro-silver bolters from the Republican Party, but gold standard Democrats, opposed to the Republicans' protectionist position on the tariff issue, established an independent party.

Meeting in Indianapolis in September 1896, the National Democrats adopted a platform favoring maintenance of the gold standard and selected a ticket headed by seventy-nine-year-old Illinois senator John M. Palmer.

Democratic president Grover Cleveland and leading members of his administration, repudiated by the convention that chose Bryan, supported the National Democrats. During the campaign the National Democrats encouraged conservative Democrats to vote either for the National Democratic ticket or for the Republican candidate, William McKinley. The Palmer ticket received 133,435 votes (1.0 percent of the popular vote), and McKinley defeated Bryan.

*The nomination of William Jennings Bryan in 1896 splintered the Democratic Party, leading conservative party members to form the National Democratic Party.* Source: Library of Congress

In the 1890s returning prosperity and the Spanish-American War overshadowed the currency issue, and the intense Democratic Party factionalism that produced the National Democratic Party ended.

## National Election Studies

In the last quarter of the twentieth century, social scientists in the United States and around the world benefited from a systematic examination of U.S. elections by the National Election Studies (NES). The work of the NES is highly regarded by political scientists and other scholars who need objective, factual information on American political behavior.

The NES describes its mission as follows: "To produce high quality data on voting, public opinion, and political participation that serve social scientists, policy makers, teachers, and students concerned with the theoretical and empirical foundations of mass politics in a democratic society." To that end, the NES conducts national surveys of the U.S. electorate in presidential and MIDTERM election years. During odd-numbered years it carries out research and development work through pilot studies.

The NES "time series" are made up of pre- and post-election studies in presidential election years and post-election studies in MIDTERM ELECTION years. The lengthy time span covered helps scholars to spot and understand long-term trends and changes in PUBLIC OPINION, political values and behavior, and the political and social composition of the electorate.

## Background

The U.S. National Science Foundation established the NES in 1977 as a national resource for data on voting, public opinion, and political participation. It began funding NES data collections the following year. As of March 1998 the NES time series encompassed twenty-three biennial election studies spanning five decades.

The NES is located within the Center for Political Studies at the University of Michigan's Institute for Social Research at Ann Arbor. The institute's Inter-university Consortium for Political and Social Research (ICPSR), established in 1962, disseminates NES data in several different ways, including the Internet and CD-ROM. The CD-ROM disk contains all the major time-series datasets, as well as major panel and special studies

(including a special Senate study), and the 1952–1996 cumulative data file.

The address for the NES home page on the Internet's World Wide Web is *http://www.umich.edu/~nes*. The ICPSR home page address is *http://www.icpsr.umich. edu*.

Any user at any educational institution can access the NES time-series studies datasets for on-line interactive use. Most NES documents on the Web page, as well as some not yet available on the Web, are available for anonymous retrieval from the NES FTP server (*ftp.nes.isr.umich.edu*).

ICPSR maintains what it calls "the world's largest repository of social science data." Among its holdings is the Historical Elections Returns File resulting from a massive data collection effort begun in 1962 with support of the Social Science Research Council and the National Science Foundation. Scholars in all the states participated in the data search for returns on presidential, congressional, and gubernatorial elections.

Through 1973 the collection included 25,000 individual elections and the names of almost 115,000 candidates. ICPSR's continued collection of election returns was supported by more than three-hundred member colleges and universities.

In cooperation with ICPSR, Congressional Quarterly published the original historical returns file in 1975 as *Congressional Quarterly's Guide to U.S. Elections.* Popular returns in the book began in 1824 for presidential, gubernatorial, and U.S. House elections and in 1913 for Senate elections. For subsequent editions in 1985 and 1994, Congressional Quarterly provided the most recent election returns.

## Methodology

For twenty-five years before the NES came into existence, the Survey Research Center and the Center for Political Studies carried out national studies of the American electorate. They covered all thirteen presidential and midterm elections from 1952 through 1976. The NES took over the projects in 1978 under direction of its Board of Overseers, made up of eleven social scientists representing various disciplines.

The board, one of three NES components, defines the core data needed for the time series and reviews recommendations of the other two components. They are the Principal Investigators and Project Staff and the 2,600 social science researchers who rely on NES data. Social scientists from around the country participate in NES activities by helping to identify subject areas needing attention and advising on study design and questions to be asked.

Unlike other voting behavior studies of the 1940s–1950s period, the early "Michigan studies" were national in scope, conducted just before and just after an election rather than periodically throughout the campaign year. They focused on the role of intra-individual social psychological processes on vote decisions, rather than on outside influences such as group membership or the mass media.

Emphasis of the Michigan studies gradually shifted from attitudes toward candidates, political parties, and major issues to measurements of partisanship, candidate evaluations, issue preferences, and political behavior. The goal was to plumb "the deeper issues of political socialization: what effects were generational, which life-cycle, and which resulted from the context of a particular slice of time?" Also in this period, more attention was paid to issues and their effect on voter participation.

For its first election study, of the 1978 congressional election, the NES introduced changes it said "brought about an explosion of research that led to a revolution in our understanding of congressional elections." Although a random cross-section of citizens was interviewed, as in past surveys, the 2,304 respondents were broken down into small samples of 108 congressional districts. This feature was dropped after the 1980 election, but other innovations of the 1978 study were retained and refined for subsequent studies.

Except after the 1984 election, when half of the preelection respondents were reinterviewed by telephone, all NES time-series interviews have been face-to-face with the respondents. In presidential elections they are interviewed twice, once between Labor Day and ELECTION DAY, and again after the election up to about mid-January.

## Scope

The National Election Studies cover a wide range of subject areas concerning elections and campaigns, opinions on social and political issues (such as affirmative action, gun control, and health care), values (such as patriotism and religious attitudes), and social and economic characteristics (such as age, sex, race, and education). The *NES Guide to Public Opinion and Electoral Behavior* provides access to tables and graphs based on NES studies from 1952 to 1996. The displays are grouped into nine topics including Political Involvement and Participation in Politics, Partisanship and Evaluation of the Political Parties, and Vote Choice.

Data from each of the biennial election studies, 1948–1996, have been merged into a single file, *NES Cumulative Data File,* available from ICPSR. The compilation is useful for tracking changes in Americans' opinions, individual characteristics, and political behavior. The cumulative file contains only data from the time-series studies, not NES special studies or panel studies. In January 1999 work began on the postelection study of the 1998 midterm election.

One of the largest special studies examined the presidential nomination process in light of the growth of PRESIDENTIAL PRIMARIES resulting from the party reforms of the 1970s. The study consisted of three coordinated data collections, beginning with the 1980 primary campaigns. Each data collection focused on citizens and changes in their interest in the campaign, candidate assessments, party allegiance, and candidate preferences.

To complement the 1980 study, NES conducted a "rolling cross-section study" with weekly interviews of randomly selected citizens throughout the 1984 midterm campaign. The technique provided the continuous monitoring needed to follow the public's responses to campaign events and MEDIA COVERAGE.

The third component of the nomination process study became known as the SUPER TUESDAY Study. It was designed around the Super Tuesday cluster of primaries held March 8, 1988, and focused on how voters learn about the viability of the candidates, how quickly the learning takes place, and how the information is used in vote decisions.

Another major special study, the Senate Study, sought to overcome the shortcomings of national surveys in helping to understand Senate elections. Because state size matters a great deal in Senate races, national surveys tend to obscure the role of small states. The NES study carried out in 1988, 1990, and 1992 was designed to correct the problem with interview samples of about equal size in all fifty states.

NES pilot studies make use of panel study techniques—that is, repeatedly interviewing the same individuals to ascertain change in political behavior over time. Unlike the biennial election studies that are so-called two-wave panels, with the same individuals interviewed before and after the election, the pilot studies are three- and four-wave panels. In 1991, for example, the pilot study originally intended as research and development for the 1992 election was extended to a second wave to cover political consequences of the Persian Gulf War and then to a third wave to examine the disintegration of what had appeared to be an invincible coalition for President George Bush.

## National Party Conventions

Although they have lost much of their importance in the presidential nominating process, national conventions remain major public relations and mobilizing events for the political parties. They conclude the process with extravaganzas of color, socializing, and occasional drama, sometimes centering on the nominees' selection of their RUNNING MATES.

By the time the Democratic and Republican DELE-GATES gather every four years, party members almost always have already chosen the nominees in state PRI-MARY and CAUCUS elections where the delegates themselves have been elected. Yet the nominations are not official until the convention goes through the motions of approving the two people who will carry the party's banner into the fall election and, if successful in November, into the White House.

The convention delegates also agree upon a statement of party principles and issue stances, or PLAT-FORM, on which the party's nominees can run. The gathering serves as a massive rally, where rival factions can be conciliated and unified, and enthusiasm generated, in preparation for the fall election campaign.

Since the adoption of delegate-selection reforms by both major parties in the 1970s, national conventions have been more media events than deliberative bodies. Much of the once-spontaneous activity is now carefully orchestrated to appeal to the television audience. More show than substance, conventions have gained the derisive nickname "balloon drops," for the thousands of balloons—almost always red, white, and blue—that cascade from the ceiling as the proceedings end.

Seldom does the previous days' balloting hold any real suspense. Since 1952 every Democratic and Republican nominee for president has been nominated on the first ballot. More recently, every presidential nomination has been won in the primaries, leaving the convention vote as a mere formality. Nonetheless, a stirring keynote or acceptance speech can still inspire party regulars and television viewers. The convention gives the presidential and vice-presidential nominees a forum to kick off the general election campaign and to demonstrate their leadership qualities to the party and the public.

### Multiple Functions

Despite its diminished role, the convention has survived because of its decision-making and public relations purposes. For almost two centuries it has been the nominating body that the Democrats, Republicans, and most of the principal third parties have used to choose—or at least ratify—their candidates for president and vice president. Besides being platform writers, delegates form the organization's supreme governing body and as such they make major decisions on party affairs. Between conventions, such decisions are made by the national committee with the guidance of the party chair.

The convention is an outgrowth of the American political experience. Nowhere is it mentioned in the

*Barbara Jordan, a Democratic representative from Texas, was the first black woman to deliver the keynote address at a convention. Source: R. Michael Jenkins, Congressional Quarterly*

*Clare Boothe Luce, a representative from Connecticut, coined the term "G.I. Joe" at the 1944 Republican convention. Source: Library of Congress*

Constitution, nor has the convention's authority ever been a subject of congressional legislation. Rather, the convention has evolved along with the rest of the PRESIDENTIAL SELECTION process. It replaced the so-called King Caucus, the partisan congressional groupings that controlled nominations until they began to dissipate in the 1820s as state legislatures, state conventions, and mass meetings challenged the caucuses' power. The 1828 election of Andrew Jackson, nominated by the Tennessee legislature, signaled the death of King Caucus.

Its successor, the convention, has been the accepted nominating method of the major political parties since the election of 1832, but internal changes within the convention system have been massive since the early, formative years.

## Locations and Financing

Choosing a location is the first major step in convention planning. The national committees of the two parties select the sites about a year before the conventions are to take place.

Before the Civil War, conventions frequently were held in small buildings, even churches, and attracted only several hundred delegates and a minimum of spectators. Transportation and communications were slow, so most conventions were held in the late spring in a

## Sites of Major Party Conventions, 1832–1996

The chart lists the twenty-one cities selected as the sites of major party conventions and the number of conventions they have hosted from the first national gathering for the Democrats (1832) and the Republicans (1856) through the 1996 conventions. The Democrats have hosted a total of forty-three conventions; the Republicans thirty-six.

| | Total Conventions | Democratic Conventions | | Republican Conventions | |
|---|---|---|---|---|---|
| | | Number | Last Hosted | Number | Last Hosted |
| Chicago, Ill. | 25 | 11 | 1996 | 14 | 1960 |
| Baltimore, Md. | 10 | 9 | 1912 | 1 | 1864 |
| Philadelphia, Pa. | 7 | 2 | 1948 | 5 | 1948 |
| St. Louis, Mo. | 5 | 4 | 1916 | 1 | 1896 |
| New York, N.Y. | 5 | 5 | 1992 | 0 | — |
| San Francisco, Calif. | 4 | 2 | 1984 | 2 | 1964 |
| Cincinnati, Ohio | 3 | 2 | 1880 | 1 | 1876 |
| Kansas City, Mo. | 3 | 1 | 1900 | 2 | 1976 |
| Miami Beach, Fla. | 3 | 1 | 1972 | 2 | 1972 |
| Cleveland, Ohio | 2 | 0 | — | 2 | 1936 |
| Houston, Texas | 2 | 1 | 1928 | 1 | 1992 |
| Atlanta, Ga. | 1 | 1 | 1988 | 0 | — |
| Atlantic City, N.J. | 1 | 1 | 1964 | 0 | — |
| Charleston, S.C. | 1 | 1 | 1860 | 0 | — |
| Dallas, Texas | 1 | 0 | — | 1 | 1984 |
| Denver, Colo. | 1 | 1 | 1908 | 0 | — |
| Detroit, Mich. | 1 | 0 | — | 1 | 1980 |
| Los Angeles, Calif. | 1 | 1 | 1960 | 0 | — |
| Minneapolis, Minn. | 1 | 0 | — | 1 | 1892 |
| New Orleans, La. | 1 | 0 | — | 1 | 1988 |
| San Diego, Calif. | 1 | 0 | — | 1 | 1996 |

centrally located city. Baltimore, Maryland, was the most popular convention city in this period, playing host to the first six Democratic conventions (1832 through 1852), two Whig conventions, one National Republican convention, and the 1831 Anti-Masonic gathering—America's first national nominating convention. With the nation's westward expansion, the heartland city of Chicago, Illinois, became the most frequent convention center. Since its first one in 1860, Chicago has been the site of twenty-five major party conventions (fourteen Republican, eleven Democratic).

Advances in transportation, particularly jet aircraft, have affected the scheduling and placement of conventions. In the nineteenth century, conventions were sometimes held a year or more before the election and at the latest were completed by late spring of the election year. With the ability of people to assemble quickly, conventions now are held later in the election year, usually in July or August.

Geographic centrality is no longer the primary consideration in site selection. With the conventions drawing between 2,200 and 4,300 delegates and tens of thou-

# Highlights of National Party Conventions, 1831–1996

1831 First national political convention held in Baltimore by Anti-Masonic Party.

1832 Democratic Party met in Baltimore for its first national convention.

1839 Whig Party held its first national convention.

1840 Democrats set up committee to select vice-presidential nominees, subject to approval of convention.

1844 Democrats nominated James K. Polk—first "dark horse" candidate—after nine ballots. Silas Wright declined the vice-presidential nomination. First time a convention nominee refused nomination.

1848 Democrats established continuing committee, known as "Democratic National Committee."

1852 Democrats and Whigs both adopted platforms before nominating candidates for president, setting precedent followed almost uniformly ever since.

1856 First Republican national convention held in Philadelphia.

1860 Democrats met in Charleston, S.C. After ten days and deadlocked on a presidential nominee, delegates adjourned and reconvened in Baltimore. Benjamin Fitzpatrick, the Democrats' choice for vice president, became the first candidate to withdraw after convention adjournment and be replaced by a selection of the national committee.

First Republican credentials dispute took place over seating delegates from slave states and voting strength of delegates from states where party was comparatively weak.

1864 In attempt to close ranks during Civil War, Republicans used the name "Union Party" at convention.

1868 For the first time, Republicans gave a candidate (Ulysses S. Grant) 100 percent of vote on first ballot.

Susan B. Anthony spoke before Democratic convention urging support of women's suffrage.

1872 Victoria Clafin Woodhull, nominated by the Equal Rights Party, was first woman presidential candidate. Black leader Frederick Douglass was her running mate.

1880 Republicans nominated James A. Garfield for president on 36th ballot—party's all-time record number of ballots.

1884 Republican representative John Roy Lynch of Mississippi became first black elected temporary chairman of national nominating convention.

1888 Frederick Douglass was first black to receive a vote in presidential balloting at a major party political convention (Republican).

1900 Each party had one woman delegate.

1904 Florida Democrats selected delegates in first-ever presidential primary election.

1920 For first time, women attended conventions in significant numbers.

1924 Republicans adopted bonus votes for states that went Republican in previous election. GOP convention was first to be broadcast on radio.

John W. Davis was nominated by Democrats on record 103d ballot.

1932 Republicans began tradition of appointing party leader from House of Representatives as permanent convention chairman.

Democrat Franklin D. Roosevelt became first major party candidate to accept presidential nomination in person.

1936 Democratic Party voted to end requirement of two-thirds delegate majority for nomination.

1940 Republican convention was first to be televised.

1944 Democrats adopted bonus votes for states that went Democratic in previous election.

Thomas E. Dewey became first Republican candidate to accept nomination in person.

1948 Democrats began appointing Speaker of the House as permanent chairman.

Republicans renominated Thomas E. Dewey—first time GOP renominated a defeated presidential candidate.

1952 Adlai E. Stevenson was chosen as Democratic nominee in one of few genuine "drafts" in history.

1956 Democrats use party loyalty provision in selecting delegates for first time.

1960 Democrats adopted civil rights plank that was strongest in party history.

Republican nominee Richard Nixon was party's first vice president nominated for president at completion of his term.

1964 Sen. Margaret Chase Smith was nominated for presidency at Republican convention—first time a woman placed in nomination by a major party.

1968 Democratic Party voted to end unit rule. Outside the Chicago convention, antiwar protests erupt in violence.

1980 Democratic delegates were composed of an equal number of men and women.

1984 Democrats nominated Rep. Geraldine A. Ferraro of New York for vice president—the first woman placed on national ticket by a major party.

1996 The Reform Party conducted its first convention in a two-stage process that allowed balloting by mail, electronic mail, or phone.

sands more of alternate delegates, reporters and news media technicians, party officials, guests, vendors, and others, the choice of a site is limited to the relatively few cities capable of handling such a large temporary population.

In addition to adequate hotel and convention hall facilities, the safety of the delegates and other attendees is a major consideration in selection of a national party convention site. The island location of Miami Beach, for example, made it easier to contain Vietnam War protest demonstrators and reportedly was a factor in its selection by the Republicans in 1968 and by both parties in 1972. For the party that controls the White House, often the overriding factor in site selection is the president's personal preference—as in the GOP's decision to meet in 1992 at President George Bush's adopted home city of Houston.

Since 1976 presidential elections have received PUBLIC FINANCING, and parties have depended on host cities to supplement the amount they could legally spend on their conventions. In 1996 that amount was $12.4 million, which each major party received from the optional checkoff on federal income taxes for presidential campaigns. (Congress raised the original $1 checkoff to $3 per taxpayer beginning in 1993.)

The Federal Election Commission has ruled that host-city contributions are not prohibited contributions, and this has enabled the parties to far exceed the technical limit on convention spending. In 1996, for example, both host cities—San Diego for the Republicans and Chicago for the Democrats—sought to match or exceed the $12.4 million federal grant. Set up as private organizations, the host committees could receive cash or in-kind contributions from businesses and other donors. At least a dozen major corporations gave $100,000 or more to each convention, on top of their POLITICAL ACTION COMMITTEE gifts to candidates of both parties and their so-called soft-money gifts to the parties themselves. In the case of Philip Morris/Kraft, these combined donations amounted to $2.4 million. Those from American Telephone & Telegraph Co. (AT&T) totaled almost $2 million. Many of the corporate sponsors benefit from tax breaks or other provisions of federal law, giving rise to criticism that convention support is a way for the companies to buy access and political influence.

No breakdown of the 1996 convention costs was available, but major outlays typically go for construction, administration, office space, convention committees, and police and fire protection.

In 1996 the new REFORM PARTY held a two-phase convention in Long Beach, California, and Valley Forge, Pennsylvania. During the week-long interval between the two meetings, members voted by phone, mail, or e-mail to nominate party founder Ross Perot as their presidential candidate.

## Call of the Convention

The second major step in the quadrennial convention process follows several months after the site selection with announcement of the convention call, the establishment of the three major convention committees—credentials, rules, and platform (resolutions)—the appointment of convention officers and finally the holding of the convention itself. While these basic steps have undergone little change over the years, there have been major alterations within the nominating convention system.

The call to the convention sets the date and site of the meeting and is issued early in each election year, if not before. The call to the first Democratic convention, held in 1832, was issued by the New Hampshire legislature. Early Whig conventions were called by party members in Congress. With the establishment of national committees later in the nineteenth century, the function of issuing the convention call fell to these new party organizations. Each national committee currently has the responsibility for allocating delegates to each state. (See DELEGATE; PRESIDENTIAL PRIMARIES; PRESIDENTIAL SELECTION REFORMS.)

## Controversial Rules

Although it did not have a formal set of rules before 1972, the Democratic Party operated from its inception with two controversial practices never used by the Republicans: the UNIT RULE and the TWO-THIRDS RULE.

The unit rule, which enabled the majority of a delegation to cast the delegation's entire vote for one candidate or position, even if there were dissenters, lasted the longest. The Democrats did not abolish it until their 1968 convention.

The two-thirds nominating rule required any candidate for president or vice president to win not just a simple majority but a two-thirds majority. Because the "solid South" was heavily Democratic at the time, the rule gave the region a virtual veto over any possible nominee. Nevertheless, after trying unsuccessfully in 1932, supporters of President Franklin D. Roosevelt won abolition of the rule in 1936. In return, the South received more delegate votes at later conventions.

In its century of use, the two-thirds rule frequently produced protracted, multiballot conventions, often giving the Democrats a degree of turbulence that the Republicans, requiring only a simple majority, did not have. Between 1832 and 1932, seven Democratic conventions took more than ten ballots to select a presidential candidate. In contrast, in their entire convention history, the Republicans have had just one convention that required more than ten ballots to select a presidential candidate. That was in 1880, when James A. Garfield was nominated on the thirty-sixth ballot over former president Ulysses S. Grant and other candidates.

A number of presidential nominations, particularly of Democratic candidates under the two-thirds rule, were made at so-called BROKERED CONVENTIONS dominated by party bosses who controlled the proceedings and selected the nominees behind closed doors. Much of the protracted balloting on the convention floor dealt with the elimination of FAVORITE SON candidates put forth by state delegations even though they had no realistic chance of being nominated. PRESIDENTIAL SELECTION REFORMS by the major political parties have made brokered conventions and favorite son candidacies largely obsolete.

One such reform survived a controversial vote at the 1980 Democratic convention. The vote concerned a new rule that bound delegates to vote on the first ballot for the candidates under whose banner they had been elected. Most of these delegates were obliged to vote for President Jimmy Carter because of his primary and caucus victories. Supporters of Sen. Edward M. Kennedy of Massachusetts, however, wanted to open the convention and pry the nomination away from Carter. They tried but failed to defeat the binding rule and improve Kennedy's first-ballot standing. The rule won approval, 1,936.42 to 1,390.58. Passage ensured Carter's renomination. Shortly afterward Kennedy announced that his name would not be placed in nomination.

## Convention Officers

Credentials, rules, and platform are the three major convention committees, but each party has additional committees, including one in charge of convention arrangements. Within the Republican Party the arrangements committee recommends a slate of convention officers to the national committee, which in turn refers the names to the committee on permanent organization. The officers chosen by the committee are then subject to approval by the convention. In the Democratic Party, this function is performed by the rules committee.

In both parties, the presiding officer during the bulk of the convention is the permanent chairman, usually the party's leader in the House of Representatives. However, this loose precedent was broken in the Democratic Party by a rule adopted at the 1972 convention requiring that the presiding officer position alternate every four years between the sexes. In 1976 Rep. Lindy Boggs of Louisiana became the first female convention chairman.

## Platform Writing

The job of writing a document of party principles falls to the platform committee. Although the major party philosophies usually do not change drastically in four years, the platform committee begins anew with each convention, and its product lasts until the party's next national convention.

Sometimes there are bitter convention fights over a particular plank, even though the platform is not binding on the party's presidential candidate, and the document is often viewed as inconsequential rhetoric. In 1948, for example, Mississippi and Alabama delegates walked out after the Democratic convention adopted a strong civil rights plank. Several days later dissidents from thirteen southern states nominated Gov. Strom Thurmond of South Carolina for president under the States' Rights (Dixiecrat) banner. In 1964 Thurmond switched to the Republican Party.

In 1996 both parties adopted their platforms without any serious divisions among the delegates. In 1992 the Democratic convention defeated, 2,287 to 953, a minority plank sponsored by former senator Paul E. Tsongas of Massachusetts, recommending that a middle class tax cut be delayed until the federal deficit was under control. Gov. Bill Clinton of Arkansas, who pledged a tax cut, defeated Tsongas and former California governor Jerry Brown for the presidential nomination.

The drafting of the platform begins well ahead of the convention. Like the other standing committees—credentials and rules—platform is a preconvention committee, selected at the end of the delegate-selection process. Positions are allocated on the basis of the candidates' success in the primaries and caucuses, allowing the FRONT-RUNNER to dominate the proceedings.

Both major parties use similar systems. For example, the Democratic platform committee (like the party's other two standing committees) has 186 members; the Republican version has 107. Members of the Democratic standing committees are allocated to states according to their population and party strength. Most members are convention delegates, but they need not be.

A separate seventeen-member platform drafting committee, appointed by the Democratic national chair, is charged with preparing a working draft for the platform committee. The full committee holds preconvention hearings in the convention city or elsewhere (Pittsburgh and Kansas City in 1996). The final draft is voted on the second day of the convention. (See Major Platform Fights, page 503; PLATFORM.)

## Filling Vacancies

An important convention function that rarely has to be used is to anticipate possible vacancies at the top of the ticket. The Republicans faced this problem in June 1912 when they renominated President William Howard Taft and Vice President James S. Sherman. Because Sherman was in failing health, the convention authorized the national committee to fill any vacancy that might occur. When Sherman died October 30, just before ELECTION DAY, the GOP national committee selected Nicholas Murray Butler, president of Columbia University, as Taft's running mate. Sherman's name remained on the ballot, but the GOP lost to the Democratic ticket of Woodrow Wilson and Thomas R. Marshall in an election marked by a strong showing from former president Theodore Roosevelt running as a Progressive. The ELECTORAL COLLEGE subsequently awarded Sherman's eight votes to Butler.

Today, standing rules of both major parties call for the national party committee to fill the vacancy if a nominee dies or resigns after the convention but before election day, or after the election but before Congress counts the electoral votes.

The Democratic Party was faced with this situation in 1972 when Sen. Thomas F. Eagleton of Missouri resigned as the vice-presidential nominee after it was disclosed that years earlier he had undergone electroshock therapy for depression. Sen. George S. McGovern of South Dakota then chose R. Sargent Shriver of Maryland as his running mate, and the national party committee confirmed the substitute nomination.

## Oratory and Coverage

The invention of new means of communication, particularly television, has significantly affected the nominating convention system. No longer are the thousands of people in the hall the primary concern of party leaders. Now their challenge is to attract and hold the attention of millions of viewers nationally and around the world.

Radio coverage of conventions began in 1924, and television coverage sixteen years later. One of the first changes inspired by the media age was the termination of the custom that a presidential candidate did not appear at the convention but accepted his nomination in a ceremony several weeks later. Franklin D. Roosevelt was the first major party candidate to break this tradition when in 1932 he delivered his acceptance speech in person before the Democratic convention at Chicago. His offer of a "new deal" for the American people coined the unofficial name for his record-long presidency. Twelve years later FDR's final rival, Thomas E. Dewey, became the first Republican nominee to give his acceptance speech to the convention, also in Chicago. Since then the final activity of both the Democratic and Republican conventions has been the delivery of the acceptance speeches by the vice-presidential and presidential nominees.

With an eye on the viewing public, party leaders in recent years have streamlined the convention schedule. The result has been shorter speeches and generally fewer roll calls than at pre television conventions. An exception to the short-speech rule was the thirty-five-minute nominating speech Bill Clinton gave for Michael Dukakis at the 1988 Democratic convention. In 1992, as the nominee himself, Clinton began his acceptance speech by joking that he wanted "to finish that speech I started four years ago." He went on to speak even longer: sixty-six minutes.

Convention leaders try to put the party's major selling points—the highly partisan keynote speech, the nominating ballots, and the candidates' acceptance speeches—on in television's prime evening viewing time. (The effort to put acceptance speeches on in prime time has been especially strong since 1972, when Democratic nominee McGovern was forced to wait until 3 a.m. EDT to make his speech.)

H. L. Mencken once wrote that convention speakers are "plainly on furlough from some home for extinct volcanoes." And indeed most convention oratory is quickly forgotten, but there are exceptions.

William Jennings Bryan, for example, electrified the 1896 Democratic convention with his "Cross of Gold" speech condemning GOP and Gold Democrat opposition to expansion of the money supply by free coinage of silver. The gold plank was defeated, and Bryan won the nomination on the fifth ballot. He lost the election but later recorded his famed speech on Thomas Edison's invention, the phonograph.

Keynoters, public figures known for their oratorical skills, are expected to whip up enthusiasm early in the convention. Until the 1950s the temporary chair gave the keynote address, but Democrats abolished the position, and Republicans began dividing the two jobs. In recent years military or space heroes, and current or former governors or members of Congress, including women, have been popular choices, sometimes with more than one keynoter at the same convention. (See Appendix, pages 506, 507.)

Rep. Barbara C. Jordan, a Texas Democrat, the first black woman to keynote a convention, did it twice, in 1976 and, after she left the House, in 1992. In 1988 Texas treasurer Ann Richards poked keynote fun at GOP candidate George Bush as having "been born with a silver foot in his mouth." She was elected governor in 1990, but Bush had the last laugh; his son George W. Bush defeated Richards in 1994.

Although not a keynote speaker, playwright Clare Boothe Luce, then a member of Congress from Connecticut, made history at the 1944 Republican convention by coining the term "G.I. Joe."

Other convention "firsts":

• Civil War general Ulysses S. Grant won the 1868 Republican nomination on the first ballot with 100 percent of the vote.

• The first woman nominated for president at a convention was Victoria Claflin Woodhull, in 1872. Her running mate on the Equal Rights Party ticket was black leader Frederick Douglass. At the 1888 GOP convention Douglass became the first black to receive a vote for presidential nomination.

• Republican Rutherford B. Hayes of Ohio and Democrat Samuel J. Tilden of New York were the first sitting governors nominated for president, in 1876.

• The first conventions to have women delegates were in 1900, when each party had one.

• The 1904 Republican convention nominated Theodore Roosevelt, the first former vice president nominated in his own right after succeeding a deceased president.

• Democrats held the longest national party convention—seventeen days in New York in 1924. It took a record 103 roll calls to nominate Wall Street lawyer John W. Davis over another New Yorker, Gov. Alfred E. Smith. Four years later Smith became the first Roman Catholic nominated for president by a major party.

• The first woman nominated for vice president was Geraldine Ferraro of New York, Democrat, in 1984.

Just as they try to put their candidate's best foot forward during prime time, party leaders try to keep evidence of bitter party factionalism—such as explosive credentials and platform battles—confined to the daytime hours when fewer people are watching. The aim is to make the party look unified and enhance the candidate's POSTCONVENTION BOUNCE in the public opinion polls. Sometimes this bounce is enough to reverse the nominees' standings, but usually the one who was ahead in ratings before the convention goes on to win the general election.

In the media age the appearance of fairness is important, and in a sense the need to look fair and open has assisted the movement for party reform. Some influential party leaders, skeptical of reform of the convention, have found resistance difficult in the glare of television.

Before the revolution in the means of transportation and communication, conventions met in relative anonymity. Today they are held in all the privacy of a fishbowl, with every action and every rumor closely scrutinized. They have become media events and as such are targets for incidents and demonstrations that can embarrass the party or cause security problems.

On the eve of President Clinton's 1996 acceptance speech, for example, Dick Morris, one of his top POLITICAL CONSULTANTS, was exposed as having an affair with a prostitute. News of the scandal somewhat overshadowed the president's speech.

Most recent conventions, however, have had more problems with boredom than with excitement. In 1996 ABC News anchor Ted Koppel caused a stir halfway through the Republican convention by declaring there was so little news that he was pulling his *Nightline* show out of San Diego. Later, at the Democratic convention, veteran ABC newsman David Brinkley called Clinton "a bore" and said his speech was "one of the worst things I've ever heard.... Everything in there he's already said." Brinkley, covering his last convention before retirement, thought his intemperate farewell remarks were off the air.

None of the major networks offered gavel-to-gavel coverage of the conventions, forcing hard-core political fans to rely on CNN or cable television's C-SPAN for broadcasts of routine proceedings. NBC teamed up with the Public Broadcasting System (PBS) for its abbreviated coverage of the conventions. The networks said poor ratings justified their cutbacks. In 1988 network convention coverage drew 47 percent of the audience; by 1992 it had dropped to 37 percent.

Part of the 1996 network curtailment was made up by the so-called new media, offering on-line computer users convention news over the Internet and its World Wide Web. All of the major parties and candidates, as well as newspapers and news magazines, provided web sites or e-mail addresses. By one survey some 8.5 million voters found Internet information that influenced their vote. (See page 498.)

In spite of its difficulties in a changing world, the convention system has survived. As the nation has developed since 1832, the convention has evolved as well, altering its form but retaining its variety of functions. Criticism has been leveled at the convention, but no substitute has yet been offered that would nominate a presidential ticket, adopt a party platform, act as the supreme governing body of the party, and serve as a massive campaign rally and propaganda forum. In addition to these functions, a convention is a place where compromise can take place—compromise often mandatory in a major political party that combines varying viewpoints.

---

## National Republican Party (1828–1832)

The Democratic-Republican Party splintered after the 1824 election into two factions. The group led by Andrew Jackson retained the name Democratic-Republicans, which eventually was shortened to Democrats; the other faction, headed by President John Quincy Adams, assumed the name National Republicans. Reflecting the belief of President Adams in the establishment of a national policy by the federal government, the new party supported a protective tariff, the Bank of the United States, federal overview of public lands, and national programs of internal improvements. But Adams's belief in a strong national government contrasted with the prevailing mood of populism and states' rights.

The Adams forces controlled Congress for two years, 1825 to 1827, but, as party structures formalized, the National Republicans became a minority in Congress and suffered a decisive loss in the 1828 presidential election. Running for reelection, Adams was beaten by Jackson. Adams received 43.6 percent of the popular vote and carried eight states, none in the South. Henry Clay, the party's candidate against Jackson four years later, had even less success. He received only 37.4 percent of the popular vote and carried just six states, none of which, again, were in the South.

Poorly organized, with dwindling support and a heritage of defeat, the National Republicans went out of existence after the 1832 election, but their members provided the base for a new anti-Jackson party, the WHIG PARTY, which came into being in 1834.

## National Unity Party
## (Independent John B. Anderson)
## (1980–1988)

Republican representative John B. Anderson of Illinois formed the National Unity Campaign as the vehicle for his INDEPENDENT presidential campaign in 1980. Anderson began his quest for the presidency by trying to win the Republican Party nomination. But, as a liberal in a party coming under conservative control, he won no primaries and could claim only fifty-seven convention delegates by April 1980. Anderson withdrew from the Republican race and declared his independent candidacy.

Anderson focused his campaign on the need to establish a viable THIRD PARTY as an alternative to domination of the political scene by the Republican and Democratic Parties. The National Unity Campaign platform touted the Anderson program as a "new public philosophy"—more innovative than that of the Democrats, who "cling to the policies of the New Deal," and more enlightened than that of the Republicans, who talk "incessantly about freedom, but hardly ever about

*John B. Anderson, an independent presidential candidate in 1980, formally established the National Unity Party in 1983. The party dissolved without ever nominating a candidate.
Source. Congressional Quarterly file photo*

justice." In general, the group took positions that were fiscally conservative and socially liberal. Anderson and his running mate, former Democratic Wisconsin governor Patrick J. Lucey, tried to appeal to Republican and Democratic voters disenchanted with their parties and to the growing bloc of voters who classified themselves as independents.

The National Unity Campaign ticket was on the ballot in all fifty states in 1980, although Anderson had to wage costly legal battles in some states to ensure that result. In the end, the party won 6.6 percent of the presidential vote, well over the 5 percent necessary to qualify for retroactive federal campaign funding.

In April 1984 Anderson announced that he would not seek the presidency in that year. He said that instead he would focus his energies on building the National Unity Party, which he established officially in December 1983. He planned to concentrate initially on running candidates at the local level. On August 28 Anderson endorsed Walter F. Mondale, the Democratic nominee for president, and his running mate, Geraldine A. Ferraro.

The National Unity Party did not run a presidential candidate in the 1988 race and by 1992 was no longer a political party.

## Natural Law Party (1992– )

Improving on its first outing, the Natural Law Party claimed more than 2 million votes nationwide for its candidates in 1996. The presidential candidate, John Hagelin of Fairfield, Iowa, received 113,659 votes, almost tripling his 1992 total of 39,179. Among third parties, Hagelin's vote was fifth highest in 1996.

Hagelin was on the ballot in forty-four states. In all, the party had some four hundred candidates in federal, state, and local races. Because it fulfilled the necessary requirements, Natural Law was assured automatic BALLOT ACCESS in ten states in the next election.

Hagelin, a Harvard-trained quantum physicist, was born in Pittsburgh in 1954 and grew up in Connecticut. He became associated with Maharishi International University in Iowa in 1983. His RUNNING MATE was fellow Maharishi scientist Mike Tompkins, a Harvard graduate and specialist in crime prevention programs.

Natural Law described itself as "the fastest growing grassroots party," standing for the environment, education, economic growth, job creation, and lower taxes. Despite its title, the party seemed to have little connection with the philosophic concept of natural law, which holds that some rules of society—such as the prohibition against murder—are so basic and inherent that they must be obeyed whether or not they are legislated.

Hagelin and the party advocated prevention-oriented government and meditative, tension-relieving programs "designed to bring national life into harmony with natural law."

## Nature of Representation

The word *representation* has come to mean "to present again by standing in the place of another." The British political philosopher John Stuart Mill described *representative government* as what "the whole people, or some numerous portion of them, exercise through deputies [representatives] periodically elected by themselves, the ultimate controlling power."

Although the concept of representation is ancient and was considered a common political mechanism by the Middle Ages, historians have noted that it was INTEREST GROUPS, not individuals, that were being represented. Three groups, called *estates*—the church, the nobles, and the commoners—were the bases of the medieval community.

Representative assemblies of the three estates existed in, among other countries, France and Anglo-Saxon England. The concept of the individual as the fundamental building block of the community—and therefore the element that should be represented—first emerged in seventeenth-century Britain. The theorists who evolved it were considered the proselytizers of a dangerous political heresy that had the potential to destroy the established order.

Political thinkers such as Mill, John Locke, and Jean Jacques Rousseau had already moved beyond the concept of pure DEMOCRACY (embodied in the town-meeting idealization of direct rule arising from face-to-face meetings of all citizens) to the awareness that the emerging nation-states were too large, too scattered, and too diverse to allow for this sort of participatory government.

Disregarding undemocratic alternatives (the rule of a benign despot, for example), these philosophers and others reluctantly came to the conclusion that some form of representation was called for if there was to be DEMOCRACY. But while the people's will remained the paramount concern of these theorists, they agonized over how best it could be realized. Was satisfactory representation even possible?

To these theorists, the individual is the basic element of the community, not the estates or corporate interests, and the individual members of the community must be given equal representation in any political body empowered to make that community's laws. Each elected representative should express the will of the group (the constituency) that sent him to the political body, and all the members of that body should, in theory, express the will of all the constituencies in the nation-state—that is, all the people. In the words of the French political writer Honoré Mirabeau, the assembly of representatives should be "a map to scale . . . an exact working model of the mass of people in action."

If, for example, a majority of the people desired that a particular course of action be taken on behalf of the entire community, a like proportion of the representatives also should want it. The democratic theory of representation therefore rested on the beliefs

that an election is a more or less trustworthy expression of public opinion; that while the persons chosen may not hold precisely the same views as their constituents on all the questions that arise, yet they will reflect the general tone of thought of the electorate and its party complexion with some degree of accuracy.

## Delegate or Agent?

The most perplexing of the questions involving representation involves the rights, duties, and obligations of the elected representative to the electors and the constituency. In his *Social Contract*, Rousseau argued that any kind of representation is basically incompatible with the ideal of democracy. But when he had to get down to practicalities Rousseau could not escape the existence and function of representatives in the emerging nation-state, and he grudgingly acquiesced to it as almost a necessary evil.

Accepted reluctantly then, the argument about the nature of representation has, over the centuries, distilled itself into two basic camps: Should the representative serve as the *delegate* of the people or as the *agent* of the people? In the United States and in most constitutional democracies, the former position seems to be the norm—that the people, once they have elected a representative, should consider that they have delegated their

*Edmund Burke (1729–1797), English writer and member of Parliament, conceived of representatives as delegates of their constituents. Source: Library of Congress*

sovereign rights and allow the delegate to function in the assembly as he or she sees fit.

The most eloquent and persuasive of the proponents of the delegate theory was the English political theorist Edmund Burke, who, when first elected to the House of Commons in 1774, wrote a pamphlet to his constituents about what they could expect of him:

It ought to be the happiness and glory of a representative to live in the strictest union, the closest correspondence, and the most unreserved communication with his constituents. Their wishes ought to have great weight with him; their opinion high respect, their business unremitted attention. It is his duty to sacrifice his repose, his pleasure, his satisfaction to theirs—

and above all, ever, and in all cases, to prefer their interests to his own. But his unbiased opinion, his mature judgment, his enlightened conscience, he ought not to sacrifice to you, to any man, to any set of men living. . . . Your representative owes you, not his industry only, but his judgment; and he betrays instead of serving you if he sacrifices it to your opinion.

Burke reasoned that making government decisions was not merely the tallying up of constituents' sentiments for and against something, then voting for the majority viewpoint. Rather, in his view, the making of public policy requires intelligent, enlightened discussion of the best available evidence about the subject at hand, then the application of reasoning and judgment in determining a solution or course of action.

According to Burke, the representative, along with his colleagues sitting in the national assembly, was in a better position than his constituents to arrive at these decisions. He was chosen by them to think about and act on such questions presumably because he had demonstrated a high degree of wisdom, judgment, patriotism or public spiritedness and would continue to do so. He would be acting in the company of others of similar abilities and in a place where the best available evidence on and the widest array of opinions and ideas about a public issue would be available.

Then, acting on his experience and on what he knows and has learned about an issue, the representative as delegate must vote as he thinks best even if such a decision runs counter to his constituents' views. At the next election, the voters can pass judgment on whether the representative's judgments and actions have been truly put to work in their best interests. If the majority answer no and the representative loses the election, the constituents' will has been served and their ultimate sovereignty preserved.

In the opposite view, that of representative as agent, the elected representative should serve, in the words of one political theorist, "as a communications device," acting on the direct instructions of his constituents as to how to vote on any given issue. He exists as their instrument to register their beliefs and opinions at the public forum; if these run counter to his own, he must either disregard his own beliefs and vote as his electors want,

or resign his post. Should a matter arise about which there is no sign of how his constituents want him to vote, he should go home and find out their desire before voting. In the modern era, the agent representative may base his voting decisions on the outcome of POLLS, which can, when desired, provide the answers their designer wants to see, not necessarily an accurate picture of what voters actually want. Also, today it is unlikely that there are many issues on which the constituents' views are not known. Members of Congress, for example, spend much of their time at home trying to get the pulse of the district. And the voters have ample opportunity to let their views be known by telephone, regular and electronic mail, letters to the editor, calls to talk shows, and so forth.

Rousseau, unable to find a practical way to achieve modern democracy without representatives, designed a scheme in which those chosen to serve would be agents of citizen assemblies, each representing a given territorial constituency. The assemblies would meet, elect the representative, and, after discussion of the issues facing the national assembly, would send their representative off to vote with a highly specific list of "yeas" and "nays." He would be judged later by the local assembly by how faithfully he had executed his orders. Left undefined in Rousseau's ideal paradigm was the question of how the delegates to the local assemblies would be chosen and how it would be ascertained that they truly represented their own constituencies.

While some studies have found that the average American voter subscribes to the "representative as agent" belief, and that the voting record of an INCUMBENT is invariably the initial point of attack of his electoral opponents, the representatives themselves, not surprisingly, see their roles differently. On the eve of World War II, nearly a hundred House members were asked to weigh the factors that influenced their vote on the tangled and emotional issue of repeal of the arms-embargo provisions of the Neutrality Act. The first choice by a wide margin was their own independent judgment of what action should be taken; the second was consideration of what their vote would mean to the fortunes of their political party. The third factor, registering only about 30 percent as many responses as "independent judgment," was the views of their constituents. In another study of state legislators' perceptions of their roles, independent judgment also emerged as the primary consideration in determining how a given issue should be voted upon.

## Representation in Practice

Both the delegate and agent theories operate in the rarefied air of idealism, and their eighteenth-century advocates might be hard-pressed to evolve a theory that truly reflects American democracy in the late twentieth century. For example, federal legislation mostly originates in House and Senate committees whose chairmen exercise great discretionary power in deciding whether a proposal should even be brought up for discussion or a vote. The chairmen are chosen, in the Senate now and until recently in the House, on the basis of seniority, giving enormous power to those individuals who have been in office longest.

Until the mid-1960s, senators and representatives from southern states—individuals who by and large favored segregation, which the majority of the nation's electorate opposed—were kept in office by their constituents who also favored segregation. By dint of long service, these members rose to the chairmanships of most important Senate and House committees and, in essence, controlled the country's legislative agenda. Yet their constituencies made up perhaps 10 percent of the entire American electorate, illustrating the "tyranny of the minority," in one view, or, in another view, the prime example of the system of checks and balances at work in preventing a tyranny of the majority.

While internal consensus governed by pragmatism must eventually prevail over what truly must and will be accomplished by legislators and the ultimate "yea" or "nay" still remains with the electorate in the voting booth, there is growing concern that many Americans are becoming alienated from their elected representatives and, by extension, from government itself. If that is the case, their voices remain mute and their desires essentially unknown, or, rightly or wrongly, extrapolated from polls. In the 1996 presidential election, for example, less than 50 percent of eligible voters participated, the lowest turnout in nearly three-quarters of a century, and the winner, Bill Clinton, garnered less than half of that total. The representative of all the people, in other words, was voted in by approximately 25 percent of them.

## Negative Campaigning

The practice of negative campaigning is not new. Candidates took the low road before the American TWO-PARTY SYSTEM was born. Even George Washington was not immune from personal attacks. During the Revolutionary War, the British circulated a phony letter from him "confessing" an affair with a washerwoman's daughter. Ben Franklin's grandson and namesake, Benjamin F. Bache, wrote that "the American nation has been debauched by Washington."

Other presidents, including Bill Clinton, have been the targets of character attacks, as have candidates at all levels. Political SCANDAL is an American tradition—and the grist for editorial cartoonists, comedians, and POLITICAL CONSULTANTS, as well as opposing candidates.

But if negative campaigning is not new, it has flourished in the age of television and the attack ad. POLITICAL ADVERTISING on television, much of it negative, has become the largest single expense of presidential campaigns and a sizable cost for other campaigns of any consequence.

Political use of television began in the 1950s during the Dwight D. Eisenhower administrations, and the first negative TV spots are attributed to Adlai E. Stevenson II, Eisenhower's Democratic opponent in 1952 and 1956. In his second run against the popular "Ike," Stevenson used footage from a 1952 commercial in which Eisenhower pledged a fight against political corruption. Because the White House had experienced some corruption problems during Eisenhower's first term, the Stevenson ads sought to highlight the contrast between promise and reality.

As political television became more commonplace,

*Lyndon B. Johnson's "Daisy" ad so shocked viewers in 1964 that it was withdrawn from the airwaves after a single viewing.*

so did negative ads. A well-known one is the "daisy" commercial that President Lyndon B. Johnson used against Barry Goldwater in 1964. It showed a little girl plucking petals from a daisy, cutting to an atomic explosion in the final scene. The scare sequence, implying Goldwater would be reckless with nuclear warfare, was too controversial. The Johnson camp withdrew it after one showing. Television news programs, however, showed the commercial several times afterward.

## Fast Forward

Not until 1988 was there another negative presidential campaign ad with the impact of the daisy commercial. The new "dubious achievement winner" was the infamous "Willie Horton" ad, which showed a steady stream of prisoners going through a revolving door. Sponsored by supporters of Vice President George Bush's campaign, the ad was intended to portray the Democratic nominee, Massachusetts governor Michael S. Dukakis, as soft on crime because he had signed a bill permitting furloughs from prison. William Robert Hor-

ton Jr., a black convicted murderer, had raped a woman in Maryland while on leave from a Massachusetts prison.

Sen. Al Gore of Tennessee, then a rival candidate for the Democratic presidential nomination, first attacked Dukakis for the furlough program. Bush strategist Lee Atwater picked up the lead, and a California group paid $92,000 to run the Horton ad in the South as an independent expenditure. Although the paid ad appeared only a few times, it—like the anti-Goldwater daisy ad—was shown later on news programs because of the controversy it created.

Atwater, then a political consultant, masterminded Bush's negative campaign. As president, Bush named Atwater chairman of the REPUBLICAN NATIONAL COMMITTEE. Before he died of a brain tumor in 1991, Atwater publicly apologized for any harm his tactics had caused to Dukakis or other opponents.

Other TV spots in Atwater's 1988 strategy attacked Dukakis's patriotism (because he had vetoed a bill requiring school children to pledge allegiance to the flag), his lack of military experience (by showing him looking ludicrous while test driving an army tank), and his record on pollution (by showing debris in Boston harbor).

Some media scholars, including former television reporter Marvin Kalb of Harvard's Joan Shorenstein Center on the Press, Politics, and Public Policy, regard the 1988 use of negative campaigning as the "all-time low" in presidential elections. But despite the backlash against Willie Horton–type spots, attack ads have become a mainstay of modern campaigning.

## Attack Ads and Dirty Tricks

Political consultants reject suggestions that they are to blame for thirty-second attack ads. "It's the fault of a lot of people," said Republican consultant Douglas Bailey. "Consultants have contributed mightily to the mess politics is in, but on the other hand we have dealt with the world as we found it. Prime-time TV is where the numbers [of viewers] are, and they want things in thirty seconds."

Bailey and John Deardourff pioneered in campaign advertising in the 1960s. Their negative spots against Ohio governor John Gilligan in 1974 helped return Jim Rhodes to the statehouse in one of the year's few GOP victories. In 1976 Bailey-Deardourff crafted a media strategy that was praised as effective even though it could not prevent President Gerald R. Ford's narrow loss to Jimmy Carter.

A big change from the 1970s, Bailey said in a 1996 interview, is that there is less risk of turning people off by running negative ads; indeed, the failure to respond to an opponent's negative ad will accord it credibility. "It is much easier," he said, "to run a negative ad to get the voter to go against your opponent than it is to run a positive ad and get the voter to vote for you."

*Massachusetts governor Michael Dukakis, in a Bush/Quayle campaign ad.* Source: Republican National Committee

Bailey and other reputable consultants distance themselves from the ads in which technology has been used to distort or falsify reality. In 1996, for example, Senate Republican John Warner of Virginia fired a consultant who admitted faking a photograph to link the Democratic candidate, Mark Warner (no relation to John Warner), with President Clinton. The ad maker doctored a photo of Sen. Charles Robb and Clinton to make it appear that Mark Warner, not Robb, was standing with the president.

Similarly, in 1992 independent right-wing activist Floyd Brown used doctored photos to make Clinton and Sen. Edward M. Kennedy, Massachusetts Democrat, appear to be raising their joined hands. That same year, consultants working for Republican presidential candidate Patrick J. Buchanan made ads with speeded-up or slowed footage of rival George Bush to make him look physically clumsy.

Although Clinton often was the object of negative advertising, there had been times when he and his handlers were the attackers. Law professor Bradley A. Smith, writing in the *Wall Street Journal* before the 1996 election, said that "Clinton has run one of the most relentlessly negative campaigns in recent memory" against Robert J. Dole.

That is not necessarily bad, however, Smith wrote. "Americans love a negative campaign; always have, always will.... To suggest that a candidate for office should not point out his opponent's shortcomings is preposterous. The question is not whether an ad is negative, but whether it is truthful and relevant."

## Truth in Advertising

The apparent disregard for truth in some political advertising is bothersome to many people. Burt Manning, chairman of the American Association of Advertising Agencies, noted with alarm a PUBLIC OPINION poll showing that the percentage of Americans who want more government regulation on truth in advertising rose from 49 percent in 1993 to 63 percent in 1995. Manning urged political consultants to emulate commercial advertisers by setting up their own self-regulating process to monitor accuracy and fairness.

Others suggest volunteer "truth squads" of ad watchers to expose advertising dishonesty. In 1996 and 1998 the *Washington Post* ran a periodic "Ad Watch" that examined the accuracy of selected TV spots. Each Ad Watch listed the candidate, the producer, the length, a description and picture of the visual, the audio text, and an analysis of the content. A typical analysis—of an ad for James S. Gilmore III, who defeated Donald S. Beyer for governor of Virginia in 1997—concluded that the Gilmore ad was "false" in saying Beyer had no plan to help teachers.

Brown University political scientist Darrell M. West, author of *Air Wars: Television Advertising in Election Campaigns, 1952–1996,* recommends MEDIA COVERAGE as the best antidote to false and misleading campaign ads. An outright ban on campaign ads is unlikely because of free speech protections, West noted, and "government regulation clearly would be inadequate without direct and effective media oversight."

## New Alliance Party (1988– )

The New Alliance Party formed in the late 1980s to promote a combination of minority interests. Self-described as "black-led, multiracial, pro-gay and pro-socialist," the party aggressively filed lawsuits to attain BALLOT ACCESS. In 1988 presidential candidate Lenora B. Fulani, a New York psychologist, drew 217,219 votes nationwide for a fourth-place finish. Her best showing was in the District of Columbia, where she received more than 1 percent of the vote.

In 1992, with the party qualifying for $1.8 million in federal matching funds, Fulani ran again, this time with California teacher Maria Munoz as a RUNNING MATE. Fulani campaigned for equal employment for all. "I believe that a job at a union wage is the right of all Americans," she said. The New Alliance ticket appeared on the ballot in thirty-nine states and the District of Columbia and received 73,714 votes, slightly less than 0.1 percent nationwide.

The New Alliance Party fielded no candidates in 1996.

## New Hampshire Primary

The New Hampshire primary and the IOWA CAUCUS, traditionally the first such events in presidential election years, have positioned those states as "gatekeepers" in the nominating process. Being first and heavily covered by the media—especially the New Hampshire primary—they have a strong influence on the nomination process, deciding which candidates get to be considered by the millions of voters in the primary contests that follow.

As the state that reached gatekeeper status first, New Hampshire holds the edge. With only one exception (Bill Clinton in 1992) every president since Dwight D. Eisenhower in 1952 has won the New Hampshire primary before securing the nomination and the presidency.

By contrast, only two Iowa caucus winners, Jimmy Carter in 1976 and Clinton in 1996, were nominated and elected president during the relatively shorter time, since the PRESIDENTIAL SELECTION REFORMS of the 1960s and 1970s, that Iowa has held comparable gatekeeper status. During that period, Carter (in 1976 and 1980) and Clinton (in 1996) were the only two nominees who won both the Iowa precinct caucuses and the New Hampshire primary in the same year.

A victory in the New Hampshire contest, however, has not guaranteed a lock on the nomination, particularly in recent years when nominations have been won in the primaries and merely ratified at the NATIONAL PARTY CONVENTIONS. In both 1952 and 1956, for example, Estes Kefauver of Tennessee won the Democratic primary in New Hampshire but lost the nomination to Adlai E. Stevenson of Illinois. (Eisenhower, Stevenson's Republican opponent in both elections, did not actively seek his 1952 victory in the New Hampshire primary. Supporters, led by Henry Cabot Lodge Jr. of Massachusetts, placed Eisenhower's name on the ballot without his permission.)

Lodge himself won the New Hampshire primary in 1964 but lost the GOP nomination to Barry Goldwater of Arizona. Other New Hampshire winners who declined or lost the nomination were Democrats: Presi-

*Republican candidate Patrick Buchanan laughing with the press and a patriotically attired dog at his campaign headquarters in Manchester, New Hampshire, February 19, 1996. Source: Jim Bourg, Reuters*

dent Lyndon B. Johnson, who withdrew in 1968 after being embarrassed by the impressive second-place finish of antiwar candidate Eugene J. McCarthy of Minnesota (the eventual nominee, Vice President Hubert H. Humphrey, entered no primaries); Edmund S. Muskie of Maine, who lost the 1972 nomination to George S. McGovern of South Dakota; Gary Hart of Colorado, who lost the 1984 nomination to Walter F. Mondale; and Paul Tsongas of Massachusetts, who lost the 1992 nomination to Clinton.

To lessen the influence of early primaries on the outcome of later races—the so-called BANDWAGON EFFECT—the Democratic Party as part of its presidential selection reforms in 1978 restricted the delegate-selection season to a three-month period stretching from the second Tuesday in March to the second Tuesday in June. New Hampshire, which by state law must hold its primary ahead of other states, and Iowa were permitted to keep their places at the front of the schedule, but they were required to hold their contests closer together in late winter. In 1980 five weeks elapsed between the Iowa caucus and the New Hampshire primary held on February 26. In 1996 the New Hampshire primary followed the February 12 Iowa caucus by only eight days.

The competition of other states for some of the publicity and impact of New Hampshire and Iowa resulted in FRONT-LOADING of the primary and caucus season and earlier identification of major party nominees. In 1996 Senate Majority Leader Robert J. Dole of Kansas won the Iowa caucus, only to lose the New Hampshire primary to television commentator Patrick J. Buchanan. But by quickly sweeping most of the remaining early primaries and caucuses, including the seven mostly southern primaries on SUPER TUESDAY, March 12, Dole was virtually assured of the Republican nomination.

Dole clinched the nomination by winning the California primary, traditionally held in June but moved up in 1996 to March 26. With President Clinton unopposed for the Democratic nomination, the nation knew by the end of March—more than three months before the August party conventions—who the opposing candidates would be in the November presidential election.

Dole's Super Tuesday sweep provided additional evidence that the South, with its habit of voting as a regional bloc, had displaced New Hampshire as the pivot of power in the presidential nominating process. In 1992 Clinton had similarly lost in New Hampshire, recovered in the South, and appeared unstoppable as he headed into the primaries of the industrial Midwest.

Established in 1913, New Hampshire's primary was one of the first created as part of the PROGRESSIVE movement to reform political parties. But as in other parts of the country the primary did not catch on until after World War II, when many of the presidential preference primaries, like New Hampshire's, were of the BEAUTY CONTEST type that did not affect delegate selection. (See PRIMARY TYPES.)

Today's New Hampshire primary is more than a mere beauty contest. National convention delegates bound or committed to particular candidates are awarded in proportion to the candidate's share of the vote, with a threshold of at least 10 percent for Republicans to qualify and 15 percent for Democrats. Both parties' primaries are of the modified closed type. Only registered Republicans or Democrats may vote in their party's primary, but voters undeclared to a party may vote in either primary.

More than 200,000 voters took part in the New Hampshire Republican primary in 1996, a record high number. With President Clinton unopposed for renomination, the Democratic primary drew fewer than 83,000 voters. The state has about 570,000 registered voters, including 240,000 Republican, 200,000 Democratic, 2,700 Libertarian, and the remainder undeclared.

Despite its ability to turn unknowns into FRONT-RUNNERS—notably Jimmy Carter in 1976—the New Hampshire primary can sink promising campaigns. Like Lyndon Johnson in 1968, President Harry S. Truman dropped out after a relatively poor showing, against Kefauver in 1952. (Truman claimed he already had decided not to run.)

In 1972 Edmund S. Muskie of neighboring Maine, well known as Humphrey's running mate in 1968, went to New Hampshire as the front-runner. But in a snowy appearance outside the Manchester *Union-Leader* to protest the newspaper's allegations against his wife, Muskie broke into tears. Although Muskie won the primary, the incident cost him votes and McGovern, the strong second-place finisher, went on to win the Democratic nomination.

At the time the *Union-Leader,* under conservative publisher William Loeb, wielded powerful influence in New Hampshire politics. After Loeb's death in 1981, and with the influx of more liberal voters from the Boston area, the newspaper lost some of its power to persuade.

Loss of the New Hampshire primary, however, is not necessarily the kiss of death. After losing there to Gary Hart in 1984, former vice president Walter F. Mondale rebounded to win the Democratic nomination. Similarly, Vice President George Bush, who lost New Hampshire to Ronald Reagan in 1980, won there in 1988 and went on to score a clear victory over Robert Dole and other candidates for the GOP presidential nomination. Dole himself, after his New Hampshire losses in 1988 and 1996, revived his candidacy to win the 1996 nomination.

New Hampshire's televised candidate DEBATES—notably the one in which Reagan seized the microphone over Bush's protest in 1980—have enlivened the prenomination season and helped to educate voters nationally about the characteristics of the leading candidates.

## Nineteenth Amendment

*See* WOMEN'S SUFFRAGE.

## Nonproportional Representation

*See* PROPORTIONAL REPRESENTATION.

# O

## One Person, One Vote

State legislatures had no constitutional obligation before 1960 to aim at equal populations in drawing legislative and congressional districts. In a series of rulings in the 1960s, however, the Supreme Court held that "substantially equal legislative representation" was a "fundamental principle" under the Constitution. The doctrine, at first known as "one man, one vote" even though the opinion says "one person, one vote," forced legislatures and federal courts to be precise in adjusting the populations of legislative and congressional districts.

The rulings answered the question left open in the Court's first modern REAPPORTIONMENT decision, BAKER V. CARR, in 1962: What standard do federal courts apply in judging the constitutionality of legislative districts? A year later the Court articulated the one-person, one-vote doctrine in a Georgia case, *Gray v. Sanders*, that challenged the state's county-unit primary system for electing statewide officials. Georgia officials insisted that the system—which weighted votes to give advantage to rural districts—was analogous to the ELECTORAL COLLEGE system for choosing the president. But the Court rejected the argument. "The conception of political equality" in American history, Justice William O. Douglas wrote, "can mean only one thing—one person, one vote." Justice John Marshall Harlan was the lone dissenter.

In 1964 the Court applied the same principle to congressional and legislative districting. The first of the decisions came in another Georgia case, *Wesberry v. Sanders*. Voters in the congressional district that included Atlanta claimed in the suit that the population of their district was more than twice the ideal state aver-

*An editorial cartoon showing the loss of political power suffered by rural interests because of decisions such as* Gray v. Sanders. *Source: Reprinted by permission of United Features, Inc.*

age. Writing for a 6–3 majority, Justice Hugo L. Black said that the provision in Article I of the Constitution that members of the House of Representatives be chosen "by the People of the several States" implicitly established the principle of "equal representation for equal numbers."

Four months later, on June 15, 1964, the Court held that the same principle also applied, under the Equal Protection Clause, to both chambers of bicameral state legislatures. The ruling in *Reynolds v. Sims* rejected the argument that a state, by analogy to the federal system, could constitute one house of its legislature on the basis of population and the other on an area basis. "Legislators represent people, not trees or acres," Chief Justice Earl Warren wrote. Harlan was the lone dissenter.

Over the next few years, the Court interpreted the principle to require legislatures to be "as nearly as practicable" equal. In 1969, for example, the Court rejected a Missouri congressional districting plan with a 3.1 percent population variance between districts. The Court has tolerated somewhat greater variance for state legislative districts. In *Hadley v. Junior College District of Metropolitan Kansas City, Mo.* (1970) the Court also applied the equal population principle to all elections—state or local—of persons performing government functions. But in 1973, the Court said the rule did not apply to some special purpose electoral districts, such as those used to regulate water supplies in the West.

## Open Primary

*See* PRIMARY TYPES.

## *Oregon v. Mitchell*

In a 1970 decision, *Oregon v. Mitchell,* the Supreme Court largely backed Congress's effort to override various state-imposed limits on voting. The justices did invalidate, by a 5–4 vote, one important provision of the law that required states to allow eighteen-year-olds to vote in state and local elections. But that ruling was quickly nullified by the TWENTY-SIXTH AMENDMENT.

Congress included the minimum voting age provision for federal, state, and local elections as part of the VOTING RIGHTS ACT Amendments of 1970. The law also suspended LITERACY TESTS nationwide, prohibited states from imposing RESIDENCY REQUIREMENTS in presidential elections, and provided for uniform national rules for ABSENTEE VOTING in presidential elections. Oregon led a number of states in challenging the law as an infringement of state prerogatives over voting.

The justices produced five separate opinions to resolve the various issues. The Court unanimously upheld the suspension of literacy tests. Justice Hugo L. Black explained in the pivotal opinion that the provision fell within Congress's power under the Fifteenth Amendment to outlaw racial discrimination in voting. The Court also upheld, 8–1, the residency and absentee voting provisions for presidential elections. Justice John Marshall Harlan was the lone dissenter. Three other justices who took a narrow view of Congress's power nonetheless found that lawmakers had reason to believe the restriction on residency requirements was necessary to prevent interference with an individual's privilege to take up residency in a state.

On the voting age provision, four justices voted to uphold Congress's enactment in its entirety, while four others voted to strike the provision down completely. Black determined the outcome of the case by voting that the Constitution gave Congress power to prescribe a minimum voting age for federal elections, but not for state and local balloting.

The split decision meant that the states would have to maintain separate voting rolls for federal and state elections. To avert that possibility, Congress proposed and the states quickly ratified the Twenty-sixth Amendment, setting a uniform minimum voting age of eighteen in all elections. (See YOUTH SUFFRAGE.)

# P

## Party Endorsement of Candidates

A political party's nomination is, in effect, its *endorsement* of the recipient candidate. Under the PRIMARY or CAUCUS systems, candidates vie for the nomination/endorsement in the party's primary or caucus election, and the winner appears under the party label in the November general election.

Primaries and caucuses therefore have largely, but not completely, eliminated the controversial practice of parties' bestowing an endorsement before the primary, thereby giving an edge to one of the candidates seeking the nomination. Several states officially recognize preprimary endorsements, and in some cases the endorsement automatically entitles the candidate to a place on the ballot, perhaps at the top of the list. BALLOT ACCESS laws in such states may require unendorsed primary candidates to obtain a specified percentage of the state convention votes or a number of valid voters' signatures to qualify for the ballot.

So-called legal preprimary endorsements are those formally made by the parties as provided by state law. Informal party endorsements are not "illegal," but neither do they have official status. In the 1990s state laws provided for preprimary endorsements in Connecticut, Colorado, Delaware, New Mexico, New York, North Dakota, Rhode Island, and Utah. Parties in other states bestow nonstatutory or extralegal preprimary endorsements. Courts in Massachusetts recognized party rules on preprimary endorsements, and in Illinois, Minnesota, and Wisconsin conventions of one or both parties made informal preprimary endorsements.

Studies have shown that preprimary endorsements are effective mainly in discouraging competition from candidates who failed to get the party's endorsement.

They make little difference to most primary voters. Many challengers to party endorsements have won.

In a 1989 case, *Eu v. San Francisco County Democratic Committee,* the U.S. Supreme Court invalidated California's ban on preprimary endorsements. The Court ruled unanimously that the prohibition violated the First Amendment rights of parties and members to freedom of political speech and association.

Newspapers, organizations, and public figures—including other politicians—also endorse candidates, both before and after the party primaries. Such endorsements, however, are protected by the First Amendment and are not subject to government regulation. Candidates usually seek as many newspaper and personal endorsements as they can get, but whether these "stamps of approval" actually help a candidate depends on many factors that vary from one election to another.

## Party Identification by Voters

Most Americans think of themselves as Democrats, Republicans, or independents. That allegiance is called *party identification,* a long-term, stable influence on voter choice that is not normally subject to sudden shifts from one election to the next.

Political scientists measure voters' party identification through POLLING studies that also gauge the strength of party members' allegiance and the party leanings of independents. The resulting scale of partisanship ranges from strong Democrat through independent to strong Republican. (See NATIONAL ELECTION STUDIES.)

According to this scale, from 1952 to 1995 between

**American Party Systems**

| Party System | Years | Major Parties | Characteristics and Major Events |
|---|---|---|---|
| First | 1789–1824 | Federalist<br>Democratic-Republican | Political parties emerge in 1790s.<br>War of 1812.<br>Democratic-Republicans dominate, 1800–1824. |
| Second | 1828–1854 | Democratic<br>Whig | Factional conflicts develop within Democratic Party, 1828–1836.<br>Whigs emerge as opposition to Democrats in 1830s.<br>Two-party competition results, with the Democrats stronger electorally.<br>Sectional conflicts between North and South intensify and create schisms within Democratic and Whig Parties. |
| Third | 1856–1896 | Democratic<br>Republican | Republican Party emerges as major opposition to Democrats in 1850s.<br>Lincoln elected in 1860; Civil War and Reconstruction follow.<br>Republicans dominate, 1864–1874; two-party competition characterizes 1874–1896.<br>Agrarian unrest surfaces; Populist Party contests 1892 election. |
| Fourth | 1896–1932 | Democratic<br>Republican | Republicans dominate, 1896–1910.<br>Progressive movement develops; Progressives split away from GOP and run Theodore Roosevelt for president, but Democrat Woodrow Wilson is elected.<br>South becomes solidly Democratic.<br>World War I and normalcy of 1920s.<br>Republicans dominate nationally, 1920–1928. |
| Fifth | 1932– | Democratic<br>Republican | Great Depression of 1930s, World War II.<br>New Deal Democratic coalition forms; Democrats dominate electorally in 1930s and 1940s.<br>Korean and Vietnam wars.<br>After 1950s Democratic electoral coalition is weakened, especially among southern whites; the rise of candidate-centered politics and split-ticket voting; Republican domination of the presidency and Democratic control of Congress create an era of divided government; Democrats regain presidency in 1992. |

*Source:* John F. Bibby, *Governing by Consent,* 2d ed. (Washington, D.C.: CQ Press, 1995), 189.

two-thirds and three-fourths of the electorate identified with the DEMOCRATIC or REPUBLICAN Parties, with Democrats long holding the advantage. The margin narrowed in the 1980s, however, resulting in a dead heat by the early 1990s. A 1995 cross-section Gallup poll showed Democrats and Republicans tied nationally at 32 percent and independents ahead with 36 percent.

Staunch partisans seldom defect to the opposition. Strong Republicans in particular show a high level of party loyalty in presidential elections. For those with weaker partisan commitments, short-term influences such as issues and candidate appeal take on greater im-

portance and can cause substantial defections on ELEC-TION DAY.

In 1980, 1984, and 1988, for example, more than 25 percent of weak Democrats failed to support their party's presidential candidate, making it possible for Republicans to win those three presidential elections, even though they had fewer party identifiers than the Democrats. But most partisans do vote for their party's presidential candidates. In 1988 a *New York Times*/CBS EXIT POLL reported that 91 percent of all Republicans and 82 percent of all Democrats voted for their parties' presidential tickets. In the three-way contest in 1992 among

Republican president George Bush, Democrat Bill Clinton, and independent Ross Perot, however, partisan defections were higher than usual, and for the first time since 1964 the Republican defection rate was higher than that of the Democrats: 81 percent of Democrats voted for Clinton compared with 72 percent of Republicans voting for Bush. Exit polls showed the same pattern in 1996: Democrats went 84 percent for Clinton, and Republicans 80 percent for Robert J. Dole.

The tendency of both strong and weak partisans to support their parties' nominees is more pronounced in congressional and state elections. At the presidential level, weakly committed voters, bombarded with saturation news coverage and a deluge of POLITICAL ADVERTISING, may be influenced to desert their party for an appealing candidate or because of a particularly salient issue.

But at the level of House races, with their relative lack of publicity and low-visibility campaigns, weak partisans are more likely to vote in accord with their party identification because less information is available to them.

## Trend to Independence

One of the most notable changes in the electorate's partisanship has been the increase in the proportion of voters labeling themselves INDEPENDENTS. This trend was especially strong from the 1960s through the mid-1970s and was most noticeable among young voters who did not align themselves with a party as quickly as older generations had.

The trend stemmed mainly from a large influx of new voters, the so-called baby boomers who came of voting age in the 1960s and 1970s, and not from partisans adopting the independent label. The tendency of voters to declare themselves independents leveled off after the mid-1970s, and in the 1980s and 1990s partisanship showed a modest resurgence. Even so, the current number of independents is high compared with the number found in the 1950s.

Some political observers have suggested that the growing number of independents has caused a high level of volatility in election outcomes and even provides

the basis for the emergence of a major THIRD PARTY. Independents, however, are not a homogeneous bloc. Instead, they are three quite distinct groups—Republican leaners, Democratic leaners, and pure independents—with the latter by far the smallest group.

Moreover, the three groups behave quite differently in the voting booth. Most self-proclaimed independents are not uncommitted but are in fact closet Democrats and Republicans who generally are more loyal to their party than are weak partisans. Only the pure independents exhibit substantial volatility from one election to the next. Indeed, they vote in a manner that tends to reflect the election outcome in an exaggerated way. For example, in 1980 Ronald Reagan had a modest 5:4 advantage over President Jimmy Carter in the total popular vote, but he had a higher three to one (66 percent to 22 percent) advantage among pure independents.

## Ticket Splitting and Candidate-Centered Politics

Although studies of ELECTORAL BEHAVIOR consistently demonstrate that party identification is the single most important determinant of voter choice, there is also evidence that partisanship's influence has lessened. The incidence of SPLIT-TICKET VOTING for candidates of different parties, instead of voting a straight party ticket, has increased. Ticket splitting was much rarer in 1920, for example, than it is today. That year only 3.2 percent of the CONGRESSIONAL DISTRICTS had split partisan outcomes (in the voting for president and the House), compared with 34.0 percent in 1988, 23.0 percent in 1992, and 25.5 percent in 1996.

To a large degree the high incidence of president/House ticket splitting reflects the pull of incumbency in House races because the INCUMBENT is normally better known, evaluated favorably, well funded, and facing a weak challenger.

Split-ticket voting is further encouraged by the trend in the twentieth century away from party-centered campaigns in which the party organizations controlled nominations, ran campaigns, and appealed to the voters on the basis of partisanship. Today, CANDIDATE-CENTERED CAMPAIGNS predominate, especially for the presidency. With a personal organization and through extensive use of the media, particularly television, candidates sell themselves, not their parties, to the voters.

## Partisan Realignments

Party identification of voters is stable but not static. Over time, the partisan alignment of the electorate may shift, producing a *realignment* or a *dealignment*.

Political scientists have discerned five different party systems in American history, beginning with the first (1789–1824), during which there was basically only one party, the DEMOCRATIC-REPUBLICAN (although the Federalists dominated in 1790,) and ending with the current system (1932 to the present). Since the demise of the WHIGS in the mid-1800s, the Democratic and Republican Parties have alternated dominance during the third through fifth systems. (See table, page 281.)

The weakening of the New Deal Democratic coalition and Republican domination of the presidency during the 1970s and 1980s fueled speculation that the United States was on the verge of another of its periodic electoral realignments and that the fifth party system was coming to an end.

The evidence suggests, however, that a major realignment has not yet occurred: there continue to be slightly more Democratic than Republican identifiers among the voters, despite the decline of the Democratic margin in the 1980s and early 1990s. Although the Democrats broke the Republicans' twelve-year lock on the presidency, the Republicans broke the Democrats' even longer hold on Congress. Also, there has been no major shift in the policy orientation of the voters, who remain basically middle-of-the-road.

Clearly, no realignment has occurred comparable to those of the 1860s and 1930s when the compelling issues of slavery and the Great Depression tore at the fabric of American politics and caused wholesale shifts in voter partisanship. Nevertheless, the nature of the party system has changed significantly; for example, the increase in Republican strength in the South over the last two decades.

Electoral dealignment has taken place as many voters, viewing parties as less relevant, have opted to become independents. The trends toward candidate-centered campaigns and split-ticket voting also indicate more of a dealignment than a realignment at the end of the twentieth century.

---

## Peace and Freedom Party (1967– )

Although founded in Michigan, the radical Peace and Freedom Party has been active largely in California—the only state where it appeared on the ballot in 1996.

From the outset, the party worked with the California Black Panther Party to oppose U.S. involvement in the Vietnam War and espouse black nationalism and other so-called New Left causes. The first Peace and Freedom nominee for president, in 1968, was Black Panther leader Eldridge Cleaver. Running with various vice-presidential candidates, Cleaver received 36,563 votes.

Cleaver's autobiographical, antiracist polemic, *Soul on Ice*, was published in 1968. After the election Cleaver, a paroled convict awaiting trial for murder, went into exile. On his return years later he became a born-again Christian.

Before the 1968 election, black activist-comedian Dick Gregory broke with the Peace and Freedom Party and set up the similarly named Freedom and Peace Party with himself as the presidential nominee. He received 47,133 votes.

After 1968 no Peace and Freedom candidate attracted significant numbers of presidential votes until 1980, when Maureen Smith and Elizabeth Barron received 18,116. In 1972, however, noted pacifist and pediatrician Benjamin Spock, the PEOPLE'S PARTY nominee, ran under the Peace and Freedom banner in California. He received 55,167 votes there and 23,589 votes in other states.

In 1974 the California Peace and Freedom Party declared itself to be socialist. In recent elections its presidential ticket has received at least 10,000 votes: 1988, Herbert Lewin and Vikki Murdock, 10,370; 1992, Ron Daniels and Asiba Tupahache, 27,961; and 1996, Marsha Feinland, 25,332.

## People's Party (1971– )

Delegates from activist and peace groups established the People's Party at a November 1971 convention held in Dallas, Texas. The initial cochairmen were pediatrician Benjamin Spock and author Gore Vidal.

The People's Party first ran a presidential candidate in 1972. They chose Spock for president and black activist Julius Hobson of Washington, D.C., for vice president. Despite hopes for widespread backing from the poor and social activists, the ticket received only 78,756 votes (0.1 percent of the national total). A total of 55,167 of those votes came from California.

At its convention, held in St. Louis, Missouri, August 31, 1975, the People's Party chose black civil rights activist Margaret Wright of California for president and

*Dr. Benjamin Spock. Source: Reuters*

Maggie Kuhn of Pennsylvania, a leader in the Gray Panthers movement for rights for the elderly, for vice president. Kuhn, however, declined the nomination and was replaced on the ticket by Spock.

The party platform focused on cutting the defense budget, closing tax loopholes, and making that money available for social programs. Other planks included redistribution of land and wealth, unconditional amnesty for war objectors and free health care. In her campaign, Wright stressed the necessity for active participation by citizens in the process of government, so that institutions and programs could be run from the grassroots rather than from the top down.

As in 1972 the party's main backing came in California, where it was supported by the state Peace and Freedom Party. Wright's total national vote in 1976 was 49,024, and 85.1 percent (41,731 votes) of those votes came from California. The party has not fielded presidential candidates since 1976.

## People's Party–Populists (1892–1908, 1984– )

The People's Party, also called the Populist Party, was organized at a convention in Cincinnati, Ohio, in May 1891 and climaxed several decades of farm protest against deteriorating economic conditions. Chronically depressed commodity prices, caused by overproduction and world competition, had spurred the politicization of farmers.

Most of the Populist leaders came from the defunct Greenback movement and southern and midwestern farm cooperative associations. The Populists tended to blame their problems on the most visible causes, primarily the high railroad rates and shrinking currency supply, but the platform they adopted at their first national nominating convention in 1892 was far-reaching. As well as advocating the government ownership of railroads and the free coinage of silver, the Populists proposed institution of a graduated income tax and the direct election of senators. Although the Populists proposed labor reforms, such as reducing the working day

*David Duke, a former grand wizard of the Ku Klux Klan, has run for office as a Democrat, a Republican, and a Populist.*
Source: R. Michael Jenkins, Congressional Quarterly

to eight hours, the party never gained appreciable support among industrial workers.

The Populists ran James B. Weaver, the former Greenback candidate, as their presidential nominee in 1892. Weaver received 1,024,280 votes (8.5 percent of the popular vote) and carried five states in the Midwest and West. Increasingly tied to the silver issue, the party showed growing strength in the 1894 congressional races. Especially strong west of the Mississippi River, party congressional candidates polled nearly 1.5 million votes. After the election the Populists had six senators and seven representatives in Congress.

The Democrats surprised Populist leaders in 1896 by writing a free silver PLATFORM and nominating a free silver candidate, William Jennings Bryan. The Populists were faced with the dilemma of either endorsing Bryan and losing their party identity or running a separate ticket and splitting the free silver vote. The Populist convention endorsed Bryan, but ran a separate candidate for vice president, Thomas E. Watson.

After this initial fusion with the Democrats, most Populists remained within the Democratic Party after the 1896 election. The Populist Party remained in existence, running presidential candidates until 1908, but never received more than 0.8 percent of the POPULAR VOTE. The party did not expand its voter appeal beyond an agrarian reform movement, but many of its proposals, particularly in the areas of government and electoral reform, were espoused by progressive politicians in the early twentieth century and enacted into law.

After being absent from the political scene for nearly three-quarters of a century, the Populist Party revived in early 1984 to place former Olympic pole vaulter Bob Richards as a candidate on the presidential ballot in fourteen states. Backers of the new party advocated wiping out the Federal Reserve System, repealing the federal income tax, and protecting U.S. industry from imports. Richards received 66,336 votes. In 1988 the Populists nominated David Duke, a former member of the Ku Klux Klan, who received 47,047 votes nationwide.

In 1992 the Populist Party nominated former Green

Beret commander James "Bo" Gritz for president and Cyril Minett for vice president. On the ballot as the America First Party in eighteen states, the Populists received 107,014 votes or 0.1 percent nationwide. Gritz performed especially well in the West, where he received 3.8 percent of the vote in Utah and 2.1 percent in Idaho.

The 1996 America First candidate, Ralph Forbes of Arkansas, received 932 votes.

## Platform

The adoption of a platform, or statement of party principles, is one of the main functions of a NATIONAL PARTY CONVENTION. The platform committee is charged with the responsibility of writing the document for the convention to consider. The committee's primary challenge is to write a platform all party candidates can use in their campaigns. For this reason, platforms often fit the description given them by Wendell L. Willkie, Republican presidential candidate in 1940: "fusions of ambiguity."

Rarely is a proposed platform rejected in whole, but disputes over a specific section—called a plank—are common. Despite the best efforts of platform-builders to resolve their differences in the comparative privacy of the committee room, they sometimes encounter so controversial a subject that it cannot be compromised.

Under these conditions, dissident committee members may submit a minority report to the convention floor. Open floor fights, like credentials battles, were more likely to occur when two or more candidates were in contention for the nomination and usually reflected the strength of the various candidates. When the party has an incumbent president, the platform often is drafted in the White House or at least is approved by the president.

The Democrats adopted the first platform in 1840. It was a short document, fewer than a thousand words. Since then the platforms with few exceptions have grown longer and longer, covering more issues and appealing to more and more interest groups. One of the exceptions to the growth trend was the 4,500-word

*The presidential campaign of Gov. J. Strom Thurmond of South Carolina was sparked by a disputed civil rights plank in the 1948 Democratic platform.* Source: File photo

Democratic platform of 1988—about one-tenth the length of the 1984 platform, the longest ever. But by 1996 the Democrats' platform had grown again, to about nineteen thousand words, compared with about forty thousand words in its Republican counterpart.

### Influence of Third Parties

Throughout American history, the major parties have embraced THIRD PARTY ideas they initially rejected as too radical. After winning popular acceptance and finding their way into the major party platforms, some controversial proposals became law. Ideas such as the graduated income tax, popular election of senators, WOMEN'S SUFFRAGE, YOUTH SUFFRAGE, minimum wages, and Social Security were advocated by Populists,

Progressives, and other independents long before they were accepted by the nation as a whole.

In contrast, Democrats and Republicans traditionally have been much more chary of adopting extreme platform planks. Trying to appeal to a broad range of voters, the two major parties have tended to compromise differences or to reject controversial planks.

The Democrats have been more ready than the Republicans to adopt once-radical ideas, but there is usually a considerable time lag between their origin in third parties and their eventual adoption in Democratic platforms. For example, although the Democrats by 1912 had adopted many of the Populist planks of the 1890s, the Bull Moose Progressives of that year already were way ahead of them in proposals for social legislation. Not until 1932 did the Democrats adopt many of the 1912 Progressive planks. Similarly, not until the 1960s did Democratic platforms incorporate many of the antiwar and civil rights proposals put forward in 1948 by the party's liberal wing and Henry Wallace's PROGRESSIVE PARTY.

The passage of a strong civil rights plank in the 1948 Democratic platform provoked opposition from southern states and prompted the walkout of the entire Mississippi delegation and thirteen members of the Alabama delegation. Some of the disgruntled southerners then formed their own STATES' RIGHTS DEMOCRATIC PARTY (the Dixiecrats), which held its own convention in Birmingham, Alabama, and nominated South Carolina governor J. Strom Thurmond for president and Mississippi governor Fielding L. Wright for vice president.

## Interest Group Participation

Party platforms offer interest groups a welcome opportunity to influence the direction of the parties. Prior to the national party conventions, about 150 groups appear before each party's platform-writing committee. Rather than appeal only to the party that they think will win, many groups hedge their bets and ask for a hearing before both parties.

Since 1852 most conventions have adopted their platform before nominating their candidates. As a result, platform fights can serve as an indicator of the relative strength of rival candidates, especially when those candidates hold different ideological positions. Platform fights also can signal splits within the party that may prove fatal in the general election. Such was the case for the Republicans in 1964 (divided over extremism, civil rights, and control of nuclear weapons) and the Democrats in 1968 (divided over the Vietnam War and civil rights). (See Major Platform Fights, page 503.)

Twenty years later, consideration of the platform at the 1988 Democratic convention was more a debate than a fight. The approved platform, the party's shortest in fifty years, was filled with generalizations rather than specific promises. Its aim was to promote unity. Republicans assailed the Democrats for vagueness. Their platform was six times longer than the Democrats' (more than thirty thousand words) and reflected a strong conservative stance.

## Thorny Issue: Abortion

The issue of abortion rights has been a particularly difficult one for platform writers since 1973, when the Supreme Court in *Roe v. Wade* established women's constitutional right to abortion. Both parties have had problems finding consensus positions on various aspects of the abortion issue, including a proposed constitutional amendment to overturn the Court decision.

In 1992 Republicans faced one such fight that was over before it began. Abortion rights advocates needed six delegations to challenge the platform committee's conservative right-to-life plank, but they could muster only four. Besides supporting an antiabortion amendment, the platform as adopted stated: "We oppose using public revenues for abortion and will not fund organizations that advocate it." The platform overall was even more conservative than the 1988 version. Its tone, reflected in the rhetoric of several speakers, including television evangelist Pat Robertson, led to widespread journalistic speculation that the 1992 platform was the work of the religious right rather than the George Bush White House. But political scientists concluded after analysis that Bush's advisers drafted the platform and that they had more influence on its final form than the speakers from the party's right wing.

In 1996 both parties adopted their platforms with little rancor and few headlines. Social conservatives at the GOP convention were again pleased with the antiabortion plank, but they were not showcased so prominently as they were four years earlier. Few hard-liners were invited to speak in television prime time, and the moderates who gained the choice speaking slots made no mention of the platform.

Abortion rights advocates tried to have "tolerance language" inserted to acknowledge the right of Republicans to disagree with the party's call for a constitutional ban on abortion. Despite the support of Robert J. Dole of Kansas, the tolerance move was beaten down. Dole said he would not be bound by the platform, which won approval on the first day of the convention that nominated him for president.

By contrast, the Democratic platform adopted later the same month in Chicago contained language recognizing that not everyone agrees with the plank supporting women's right to choose abortion. The new clause said, "The Democratic Party is a party of inclusion. We respect the individual conscience of each American on this difficult issue, and we welcome all our members to participate at every level of our party."

# Plurality

A plurality is the margin by which most U.S. elections are won. In a race of two or more candidates, the candidate who gets the most votes wins. The number of additional votes received by the winner is his or her plurality.

The plurality may amount to a majority (more than 50 percent of the total vote), but a majority is usually not required in American elections. An exception is the RUNOFF system used in some states, where a second or runoff election is held between the two top finishers if no candidate received a majority in the initial PRIMARY election.

Another exception is the ELECTORAL COLLEGE system used for presidential elections. To be elected president, a candidate must receive a majority of the 538 electoral votes—equal to the total number of U.S. senators and representatives, plus three votes that the DISTRICT OF COLUMBIA would have if it were a state. Presidential election actually requires winning an ABSOLUTE MAJORITY of the electoral vote, because presidential electors must cast all 538 votes. The winner therefore must receive at least 270 electoral votes—one-half of 538 plus one. If no candidate receives an absolute majority, the House of Representatives must choose the president. This has happened twice in U.S. history. (See PRESIDENT, NOMINATING AND ELECTING.)

# Pocketbook Voting

Pocketbook voting means making electoral choices according to one's perceived economic interest. In the United States the class conflict that pocketbook voting often implies has been tempered by many other voter concerns and by the political process itself. Nevertheless, public concerns about issues such as taxation and government spending have been evident since the founding of the country.

At times, class differences clearly affected U.S. elections. In the early years of the nineteenth century, the Jeffersonians, many from lower economic strata, successfully challenged the economic power of supporters of the FEDERALIST PARTY. Later in the century Andrew Jackson won the presidency with the broad support of poorer members of the electorate.

After the Civil War many workers became affiliated with the Knights of Labor, which, in the 1880s, entered slates of candidates in numerous state and local elections. But workers' political parties never found a real footing in American politics.

## Role of the Economy

In the twentieth century pocketbook voting reached a high-water mark with President Franklin D. Roosevelt's New Deal. In the midst of the Great Depression, Roosevelt's economic proposals had strong appeal to the jobless and working poor.

*The Virginia gubernatorial race of 1997 turned on Republican Jim Gilmore's pledge to abolish the car tax.*
*Source: Gary Hershorn, Reuters*

Similarly, in 1960 John F. Kennedy promised to "get the country moving again," and in 1980 Ronald Reagan, citing double-digit inflation, asked, "Are you better off today than you were four years ago?" In 1992 the phrase, "It's the economy, stupid," originally meant as a reminder to Bill Clinton's campaign staffers, became his de facto CAMPAIGN SLOGAN.

Closer to home, in state and local elections, people repeatedly vote their pocketbooks on issues such as income and property taxes, bond issues for highway and other public works projects, and land-use and zoning plans. The issue of the annual property tax on automobiles dominated POLITICAL ADVERTISING in the 1997

Virginia gubernatorial race, which was won by the candidate promising repeal. Most states, California especially, regularly put pocketbook issues before the voters in INITIATIVE AND REFERENDUM form.

POLLING has shown consistently that in PUBLIC OPINION the REPUBLICAN PARTY, at least to some extent, favors the rich over the poor. The DEMOCRATIC PARTY generally wins the support of Americans on the lowest rungs of the economic ladder. Political beliefs and opinions, however, are associated with a number of variables besides income. They include education, occupation, race, gender, ethnicity, age, religion, and region. (See PARTY IDENTIFICATION.)

Income disparities may account for differences in voters' perspectives on economic issues, as illustrated by a 1995 Gallup poll. Respondents were asked whether they thought it was more important to reduce the federal budget deficit or to prevent cuts in the federal welfare program. Results indicated that 74 percent of Americans in households with annual incomes above $50,000 thought reducing the deficit was the more important course, compared with 23 percent at that income level who thought it was more important to avoid a cut in welfare. People with annual household incomes under $20,000 were more evenly divided: 52 percent for reducing the deficit and 40 percent for preventing a welfare cut.

Voters across the board, however, usually worry more about economic issues than about social issues. A July 1998 ABC/*Washington Post* poll showed that three of the five issues that people rated "very important" had to do with income, jobs, or taxes. The three were protecting the Social Security system (68 percent), overhauling the tax system (66 percent), and handling the nation's economy (65 percent). The top issue, improving education and the schools (77 percent), indicated voters' willingness to invest money in their children's future. Rated less important were CAMPAIGN FINANCE reform, foreign affairs, teenage smoking, and abortion.

## Little Cohesion

Wide divergences of opinion among income classes seldom translate into unified action at the polls by one group or the other. Although theoretically the more numerous low-income voters could overwhelm opposition in elections and bring about ever-larger social programs and ever-greater costs to the government, results rarely are that clear cut. One reason, according to social and political scientists, is that far larger proportions of middle- and upper-income Americans vote than do those who are poorer. In addition, middle- and upper-income Americans are far more likely to join and support INTEREST GROUPS than are lower-income citizens. Special interests overwhelmingly promote the interests of wealthier voters.

What is clear is that pocketbook voting by poorer Americans has failed to produce a substantial redistribution of national income. Although the federal income tax is progressive, other federal taxes, including the Social Security payroll tax, are regressive. They proportionately take more from wage earners than from salaried executives and others who are far wealthier. When citizens vote their pocketbooks, the rich and not-so-rich often find that their interests are more in harmony than in conflict.

## Political Action Committees

Political action committees (PACs) enable INTEREST GROUPS to raise and distribute money to candidates for elective office. Outright gifts to candidates from corporate or union treasuries are illegal, but contributions from PACs are not. This has made PACs popular with groups hoping to influence the outcome of elections. Rapid growth has made PACs one of the most controversial aspects of the CAMPAIGN FINANCE system.

PACs fall into three main categories: business, labor, and ideological or single-issue. Business PACs, such as those sponsored by the National Association of Realtors and the American Bankers Association, generally favor Republican candidates. Labor PACs, such as those of the National Education Association and the Teamsters Union, give primarily to Democrats. Among the single-issue or ideological PACs, the National Rifle Association's PAC gives more to the Republicans, while that of the National Abortion and Reproductive Rights Action League contributes most heavily to Democrats.

During the 1995–1996 election cycle, PACs contributed $217.8 million to federal (mostly congressional) candidates, an increase of $28.5 million or 15 percent over the 1993–1994 MIDTERM ELECTION cycle. Corporate PACs gave the most, $78.2 million, with labor PACs placing third at $48.0 million. PACs associated with trade, membership, or health groups exceeded the labor PACs' amount with contributions totaling $60.2 million.

Reflecting the Republican takeover of Congress in

*Newt Gingrich, with his wife, Marianne, at his side appears before GOPAC, a political action committee he started. Source: Robert Giroux, Reuters*

1994, GOP House and Senate candidates received the larger share of PAC contributions for the first time since the FEDERAL ELECTION COMMISSION (FEC) began keeping such records in 1978. Republicans took $118.2 million compared with $98.8 million for Democrats. Most of the disparity was in Senate races. In House contests, PACs divided their contributions almost evenly: $79.7 million for Republicans and $79.4 million for Democrats. Corporate PACs gave more than twice as much ($56.9 million) to Republican candidates than to Democrats ($21.1 million). Labor PACs gave even more disproportionately to Democrats ($44.3 million) than to Republicans ($3.4 million).

PACs have little involvement in presidential elections. They provide only a small share of funds needed by candidates seeking their party's presidential nomination, and they are barred from contributing to general election campaigns, which receive PUBLIC FINANCING. Presidential candidates often create their own PACs years before the election to help pay for primary campaigns in several states. In 1996 PACs gave only $2.5

million to presidential candidates, and almost all of that went to President Bill Clinton's Republican challenger, Robert J. Dole, the former Senate majority leader.

Clinton had rejected PAC contributions to his 1996 reelection campaign. Nevertheless, the Clinton candidacy was scarred by SCANDAL over another controversial source of campaign funds, the so-called SOFT MONEY given to the political parties rather than directly to the candidates. In the wake of the scandal, the DEMOCRATIC NATIONAL COMMITTEE returned almost $3 million in questionable contributions, including those from foreign nationals. Although the law on PACs applies mostly to federal candidates and elections, foreign nationals are prohibited from making contributions or expenditures in connection with any U.S. election— federal, state, or local. Even U.S. subsidiaries of foreign-owned companies may not establish a federal PAC if the parent foreign company helps to finance or otherwise participates in operation of the PAC.

Under federal law most PACs are permitted to contribute $5,000 per candidate, per election. There is no limit on the total amount they can give to all candidates. They also can spend as much as they want to help candidates—for example, with heavy television advertising—so long as they operate independently of the candidates' campaigns.

Most states also limit contributions by PACs or individuals to candidates for state or local office. There is no uniformity to the limitations, and amounts vary from state to state. Typically, the state limits are well below the $1,000 ceiling on individual contributions to federal candidates—for example, $100 for legislature candidates and $500 for statewide office.

Although PACs date back to the 1940s, their significance in political campaigns began with the passage in 1971 and 1974 of laws to reform campaign financing. The laws, along with later court decisions, allowed PACs to become a major factor in the financing of congressional elections. In 1974 only about six hundred PACs were registered, and they gave less than $20 million to House and Senate candidates. By 1996 the number of PACs had increased to 4,528. Of that number, 3,035 PACs accounted for the $217.8 million in PAC money contributed to House and Senate candidates in 1995 and 1996. Most of the contributions come from a small number of large PACs, and about a third of all contributions came from the fifty largest PACs. The largest single contributor was the Democratic Republican Independent Voter Education Committee, which gave $2.6 million.

PAC contributions are particularly important in House races. Although many House candidates regularly receive more than half of their campaign funds from PACs, Senate candidates usually are less reliant on them. PACs give most often to incumbents because they are in a position to support PAC interests when legislation is drafted as well as when it comes to a vote. This is particularly true for committee chairs and party leaders, who have more power than other members to see that legislation is approved.

PACs tend to support current members of Congress regardless of party affiliation. Challengers represent a gamble for PACs because only a few defeat incumbents in any election. By contributing to a challenger, PACs risk alienating a successful incumbent. In 1996 all types of PACs gave overwhelmingly more to incumbents than to challengers. Incumbents of both parties received $146.4 million or 67 percent, against $31.6 million or 15 percent for challengers. The remaining $39.8 million or 18 percent went to candidates for open seats in Congress. PAC support helped to reelect a near-record 95 percent of incumbent members.

Many people criticize the role played by PACs, arguing that they allow well-financed interest groups to gain too much political influence. By accepting contributions from PACs, critics say, members of Congress become dependent on them. The need for PAC support may make the members reluctant to vote against the interests of the PAC, either from fear of losing the PAC's contributions or from fear of having the PAC help finance their political opponents.

Senate races have become multimillion-dollar endeavors, financed in part by PACs. An example is the 1996 contest between two House members, Democrat

**Top PAC Contributors, 1995–1996 Election Cycle**

| | |
|---|---|
| Democratic Republican Independent Voter Education Committee | $2,611,140 |
| American Federation of State, County, and Municipal Employees—PEOPLE | $2,505,021 |
| UAW-V-CAP (UAW Voluntary Community Action Program) | $2,467,319 |
| Association of Trial Lawyers of America PAC | $2,362,938 |
| Dealers Election Action Committee of the National Automobile Dealers Association (NADA) | $2,351,925 |
| National Education Association PAC | $2,326,830 |
| American Medical Association PAC | $2,319,197 |
| Realtors PAC | $2,099,683 |
| International Brotherhood of Electrical Workers Committee on Political Education | $2,080,587 |
| Active Ballot Club (United Food and Commercial Workers International Union) | $2,030,795 |

*Source:* Federal Election Commission

Robert C. Torricelli and Republican Dick Zimmer, who competed for an open Senate seat in New Jersey. Torricelli narrowly won the tight race in which he and Zimmer spent a combined total of $25 million, mostly for television advertising. PACs accounted for $993,000 or 10.8 percent of Torricelli's $9.2 million total receipts. Zimmer raised $8.2 million, of which PACs gave $1.3 million or 14.3 percent. Both candidates received additional funds from their parties and from individuals, including many who lived outside New Jersey.

The 1996 elections also provided an example of stepped-up activity on Capitol Hill by an embattled industry seeking to stave off further government regulation. According to the public affairs lobby Common Cause, an advocate of campaign finance reform, the tobacco industry gave $10 million in soft money and PAC contributions in 1995–1996, nearly double its 1992 giving. The Philip Morris cigarette company alone gave $4 million—$3 million in soft money and $1 million from its affiliated PACs. Among the proposals of concern to the industry was one to define nicotine as a controlled substance subject to strict food and drug laws.

A Republican PAC (GOPAC), formerly headed by House Speaker Newt Gingrich of Georgia, figured prominently in an ethics investigation that nearly cost him the speakership. Gingrich admitted telling untruths to the committee about GOPAC's involvement in a televised course he taught and about the use of tax-exempt foundations for partisan purposes. On January 21, 1997, the House voted 395–28 to reprimand Gingrich and fine him $300,000.

Proposals to curb the misuse and influence of PACs have been debated by Congress over the years, but none had become law by the close of the 105th Congress. One way to weaken PACs would be to provide public funds for congressional campaigns, as the federal government has done for presidential campaigns since 1974. President George Bush vetoed a public-financing bill passed in 1992 by Congress, then controlled by the Democrats. Bush and other Republicans opposed public financing and wanted to outlaw most PACs instead.

Defenders argue that PACs provide a legitimate means by which citizens can join together to support candidates. PACs encourage people to participate in politics, they say, and offer the most efficient method for channeling campaign contributions. PAC officials say their groups are seeking not to buy votes but to gain access to members of Congress, so that their views will be heard on legislative decisions affecting them.

## Political Advertising

Election time in America is hard to miss. Yard signs suddenly blossom on front lawns. Political posters become familiar sights (and sometimes eyesores) on fences and utility poles. Mailboxes bulge with candidates' flyers and parties' appeals for money. Cars and lapels become vehicles for bumper stickers and CAMPAIGN BUTTONS.

The signs are everywhere. Especially in local races, these traditional artifacts of electioneering are still very much in evidence when the time comes for candidates to try to sell themselves to the voters. But in the electronic age the term *political advertising* usually means just one thing—political television commercials. Spending on TV spots dwarfs other expenses of campaigns for most major offices.

President Bill Clinton and his Republican challenger, Robert J. Dole, spent $112.9 million between them on television ads in their 1996 contest, according to FEDERAL ELECTION COMMISSION (FEC) data. The two candidates' next highest combined expense was $32.0 million for nonmedia campaigning. Advertising, almost entirely on television, took 60 percent of their postconvention campaign budgets.

The figures include about $19 million the parties spent on TV spots for their presidential nominees—$6.7 million by the Democrats and $12.0 million by the Republicans. In addition, the parties spent some $69 million on so-called issue ads that indirectly supported the nominees—$45 million by the Democrats and $24 million by the Republicans. REFORM PARTY candidate Ross Perot also spent heavily to air half-hour infomercials in his second bid for the presidency.

Parties and INTEREST GROUPS used millions of dol-

*In the 1992 presidential campaign, Ross Perot spent some of his extensive personal wealth on thirty-minute-long, prime-time in-fomercials. Here, he attacks Bill Clinton's job-creation record in Arkansas. Source: File photo*

lars more to buy radio and television ads in behalf of candidates for Congress. Many of these were independent expenditures not coordinated with campaigns and therefore exempt from contribution limits.

Despite all the money and energy devoted to political ads on television, the experts are divided on whether they have any significant effect on election outcomes. Too few studies have been made, they say, to provide any definitive answers. There is some agreement, however, that TV spots might be influential for lower political offices where the candidates and their positions on issues are not well known and for primaries when candidates from the same party are vying for a nomination.

"Ads have their strongest impact with little-known candidates and electoral settings of low visibility, and when journalistic coverage reinforces the ad message," writes political scientist Darrell M. West in *Air Wars: Television Advertising in Election Campaigns, 1952–1996.*

West found that commercials influence how voters learn about candidates, what they identify as priorities, their standards of assessment, and attributions of blame. Timing and content of ads, and decisions on when and where to attack, help to determine viewers' response to the ads.

## Ads Versus Reportage

Political scientists speak of political ads as *unmediated messages* because candidates pay for them and dictate what they say. The newspaper or station carrying the ads do not edit or censor them, except to avoid libel or bad taste. *Mediated messages,* on the other hand, originate with the news media. The press, print or electronic, acts as intermediary. It generates its own MEDIA COVERAGE of the candidate and the campaign. If the candidate's message happens to be passed on in the news story or broadcast, it is the reporter's or commentator's version of that message—which may or may not match what the candidate intended.

Political ads lack the credibility or persuasiveness of news stories. Most people realize the paid ads are self-serving and therefore, as the saying goes, they let them go in one ear and out the other. In the words of political scientist Doris Graber, "Commercials are perceiver-determined. People see in them pretty much what they want to see—attractive images for their favorite candidate and unattractive ones for the opponent."

Because a favorable news story is worth more than several paid commercials, POLITICAL CONSULTANTS go to great lengths to attract press attention that will show their candidate in the best possible light. A few candidates, however, prefer to bypass the press. Perot, for example, hired and fired several political consultants before deciding to manage his own campaigns.

In 1992 Perot's talk show appearances, along with his infomercials, videos, and books, provided one of the least-mediated campaigns in modern history. Perot never hesitated to express his disdain for the working press. Rather than talk to voters through the print and broadcast reports, he set up his own information system. He used it again in 1996, when he was excluded from the Clinton-Dole presidential DEBATES.

The computer provided an even newer and more direct way to reach the voters than talk shows. In 1996 the two major parties, most presidential candidates, and many other candidates provided sites on the Internet's World Wide Web where online users could obtain schedules, speech texts, and other handouts from the various campaigns. The Web sites have since become a staple of the political parties' public relations apparatus. (See appendix, page 498.)

The theory that television ads can outweigh press coverage received a boost after publication of Joe McGinniss's *The Selling of the President 1968,* which suggested that Richard Nixon in effect "bought" the election with slick and expensive advertising. Political scientists, however, have not uncovered persuasive evidence that paid media advertising has a significant effect on voter choice in presidential elections. In a study of the 1988 presidential campaign, media scholar

Michael Robinson compared the George Bush campaign's week-by-week paid media buys with the candidate's standing in the POLLS and found no significant correlations.

In elections that receive little press attention, paid media can make a difference. Challengers for House seats, for example, can use them to build name recognition and compete with the generally more visible and familiar congressional INCUMBENTS. As challengers' expenditures increase, their share of the vote also goes up.

## Statewide Races

The cost of political advertising on television is particularly high for candidates in states where large numbers of their voters are clustered in or near expensive metropolitan TV markets. In 1996 and 1997 two races in Virginia offered examples of the effect such locations have on campaign costs.

A "same name" contest pitted veteran Republican senator John W. Warner against a wealthy challenger, Democrat Mark Warner. To reach voters in the populous northern Virginia region, both candidates had to spend heavily for spots on television stations in Washington, D.C., where media rates reflect coverage of viewers not only in nearby Virginia but also in the DISTRICT OF COLUMBIA itself and in the Maryland suburbs, neither area of use to the Warner media strategies. The result was two very expensive campaigns. Mark Warner's losing race to John Warner was the priciest Senate campaign of 1996, costing $11.5 million, largely for TV spots. Senator Warner's reelection campaign cost $5.2 million.

The 1997 Virginia governor race was the costliest in the state's history, again largely because of television commercials. Republican James S. Gilmore III, the winner, spent a total of $10 million and was helped by $2 million in SOFT MONEY from outside the state. Democrat Donald S. Beyer Jr., a millionaire auto dealer, spent $8 million.

The Gilmore-Beyer contest was a clear example of POCKETBOOK VOTING. Gilmore's successful TV campaign focused on his promise to abolish Virginia's unpopular personal property tax on cars and trucks. Republican strategists viewed the campaign as a model for 1998, prompting a search in other states for issues that affect voters' pocketbooks.

## Free Air Time

To level the political advertising playing field and make television more accessible to candidates, President Clinton and some members of Congress proposed that broadcasters be required to provide free or low-cost air time for political messages. In his 1998 State of the Union address, Clinton called media advertising the "real reason for the explosion in campaign costs." He asked the Federal Communications Commission (FCC) to act to provide "free or reduced cost television time for candidates who observe spending limits voluntarily."

Broadcasters opposed the idea. They were already required by the FCC's EQUAL TIME RULE to provide rebuttal time to persons maligned on programs or commercials other than news programs. No such requirement could be made of print media because of press freedom rights, but the broadcast spectrum is a public resource that the government regulates through its licensing authority.

Broadcasters also were required to give discounts for political advertising. Shortly before the Virginia state elections in 1997, major Washington television stations cut back on the discounted political spots in favor of the more profitable full-cost commercials.

Political consultants say the reasons that TV commercials are expensive also explain why the costs are unlikely to come down: the ads require technological know-how, time buying is a specialty, and the buyers have little incentive to reduce costs. "Mrs. Jones and her teenage kids can't go down to the congressman's corner headquarters and volunteer to make his TV spots," said veteran consultant Doug Bailey.

"Too many consultants, both Democratic and Republican, hire inexperienced 'buyers' to spend millions of dollars," Jan Ziska Crawford, a board member of the American Association of Political Consultants, told Congress in 1996. "Strategic time-buying includes knowing the law and maximizing every dollar raised.

Given that most consultants are paid on a percentage basis, there is no incentive to keep media expenditures down."

Even if Congress passes new laws limiting advertising expenses, consultants will find loopholes in them, said Washington public relations man Victor Kamber. Makers of political spots, for example, base their fees on what a candidate spends for air time, not on their creative or production costs. If new laws required networks to provide free air time, the consultants would simply begin charging for creating and producing the candidates' ads.

At the state level, some officials already enjoy free air time as a perquisite of incumbency. For example, Maryland governor Parris N. Glendening taped at state expense several public service and tourism spots featuring his name and picture. Some TV stations ran them free at the state's request. As in other states, the governor also got free publicity from his name and likeness in state publications and his name on highway signs. Would-be rivals both inside and outside Glendening's Democratic Party protested the exposure as unfair. Glendening was elected to a second term in 1998.

## Issue Advocacy

In the 1996 elections, issue ads emerged as a controversial means of circumventing CAMPAIGN FINANCE restrictions in efforts to elect or defeat political candidates. Interest groups argued that the ads in question did not violate disclosure laws or contribution limits because they did not name any particular candidate. But opponents countered that it was possible to frame an ad to target a candidate whose stand on an issue— abortion or gun control, for example—is well known without actually using the person's name.

In October 1997 the Supreme Court declined to clarify whether government restrictions on issue ads violate free speech rights. It rejected an FEC request for a review of conflicting lower court decisions on issue ads that indirectly advocate election or defeat of particular candidates.

The Court gave no reason for not considering *Federal Election Commission v. Maine Right to Life,* in which a lower court had struck down the FEC's 1995 rule on issue ads as too vague. The FEC said the resulting confusion "threatens significantly to impair the effectiveness of the nation's election laws."

A related controversy concerned so-called soft money, unlimited contributions to the political parties, ostensibly for party-building activities but widely used to assist candidates. Proponents of campaign reform feared that elimination of soft money for the parties would divert more interest group money to issue ads where it would be even more unregulated.

The Clinton administration said that unless the FEC is allowed to regulate issue ads, the door would be opened "for corporations, unions, and others . . . to influence federal elections by spending large amounts of money in independent advertisements that unambiguously attack clearly identified candidates." POLITICAL ACTION COMMITTEES are limited to $5,000 per candidate in campaign contributions.

A study by the Annenberg Public Policy Center estimated that political parties and interest groups spent between $135 million and $150 million on issue advertising in 1996 and that most of their efforts could be described as NEGATIVE CAMPAIGNING.

Paid advertising seems to be most effective in campaigns for and against ballot propositions—lawmaking by popular INITIATIVES AND REFERENDUMS, which is permitted in some states (most notably in California). Especially where the public is unfamiliar with the pros and cons of an issue, ads can help to educate voters and crystallize public opinion.

*Air Wars* author Darrell West states:

What started as a trickle of issue advocacy has become a torrent on every conceivable topic. In the last few years, groups interested in health care, tort reform, term limits, and a balanced budget have blanketed the airwaves with commercials promoting their point of view. Once the exception more than the rule, television ads have become the latest form of political volleyball on controversial issues.

The lack of disclosure rules for issue advocacy campaigns, West states, "takes us back to the secrecy and deception of the pre-Watergate system for contesting American elections."

## Political Consultants

Since its rise to acceptance in the 1960s, political consulting has ballooned into a billion-dollar-a-year industry servicing up to fifty thousand national, state, and local campaigns in every election cycle. Around the country, some seven thousand professional consultants market expertise in CAMPAIGN FINANCE and management, direct mail, POLITICAL ADVERTISING, and public relations. Counting part-timers, the number of consultants may be closer to thirty-five thousand.

Given their number and influence, it is only a slight exaggeration to say that paid consultants wage more political battles in modern-day America than do candidates themselves. Gone are the days when faceless advisers stood discreetly behind candidates and whispered folksy suggestions. Today's consultants are conspicuously out front and outspoken, often becoming celebrities themselves.

But consultants—who rose to influence along with television—are also blamed for many of the political system's problems, including voter apathy. Critics say the professionalization of politics encourages NEGATIVE CAMPAIGNING, escalates campaign costs, reduces debate on the issues to sound bites, distorts the findings of PUBLIC OPINION polling, and even reduces once-eager campaign volunteers to spectators. Consultants respond that responsibility for their decisions must be borne by the candidate, and that they are paid, first and foremost, to win.

"The most significant change in consultants is their indispensability," said Larry J. Sabato, a University of Virginia government professor and author of *The Rise of Political Consultants* (1981). "Back in the 1950s, they were rare, except at the presidential level. Then in the '70s you got consultants for senators and governors, and in the '80s, consultants in House races. Now you have them for ballot referendums, and every race for state legislature and city council."

The influence of consultants on politics is evident in the frequent use by the press of phrases that began as insider-speak: "sound bites," "spin doctors," "theme of the

*Campaign consultants, who once worked in the shadows of the candidates, are now media celebrities themselves. Dick Morris, a one-time adviser to President Bill Clinton, is shown here promoting his book,* Behind the Oval Office: Winning the Presidency in the Nineties. *Source: Jeff Christensen, Reuters*

day," and "photo opportunity." Of the nearly half-billion dollars spent on congressional elections in 1994, 46 percent went to consultants, according to Dwight Morris, a Virginia researcher on campaign spending.

Campaign consultants have their own organization, and consulting has even become an academic program. At American University in Washington, D.C., the Campaign Management Institute offers a two-week course taught by strategists and professors imparting insight into CAMPAIGN STRATEGY, scheduling, theme, and message. George Washington University, also in Washington, offers advanced degrees at its Graduate School of Political Management.

## Birth of an Industry

The first political consultants, according to the American Association of Political Consultants, were Aristotle, Plato, and other philosophers of ancient Greece and Rome. Quintus Cicero wrote a "Handbook of Electioneering" for Romans in 63 B.C. The more modern historical model for a political strategy paper was *The Prince,* written in 1532 by Italian philosopher Niccolo Machiavelli.

In the United States, political campaigns traditionally have been noteworthy for their domination by party machines and volunteers. When William Henry Harrison and John Tyler won the White House in 1840, their "Tippecanoe and Tyler, Too" campaign was run by handlers, who relied on volunteers lured by free whiskey to pack their rallies.

Credit for bringing Abraham Lincoln to the national stage in 1860 went to political clubs called the Wide Awakes. "After the campaign opened," wrote one biographer, "there was scarcely a county or village in the North without its organized and drilled association of Wide Awakes . . . to spread the fame of, and solicit votes for, the Republican presidential candidate."

During the next century, the national parties gained supremacy, developing powerful machines in cities such as Chicago and Albany. Only occasionally did ad hoc entrepreneurs become national players. In 1940, for example, the presidential candidacy of Indiana businessman Wendell L. Willkie was primarily the fruit of a draft movement set in motion by a petition circulated in *Fortune* magazine by a young New York lawyer.

The first consulting business in the United States is thought to be the firm established in the 1930s in California by a husband and wife team of advertising professionals, Clem Whitaker and Leone Baxter. For two decades, their firm presided over some seventy-five major campaigns, among them state ballot INITIATIVES AND REFERENDUMS and the gubernatorial campaigns of Republican Earl Warren.

In the late 1930s and 1940s George Gallup and Elmo Roper set up shops as full-time analysts of electoral trends. Their elite fraternity was joined by regional poll takers such as Mervin Field in California, who formed a group that began to meet annually at Gallup's New Jersey farm.

By the 1950s, the presidential campaigns of Dwight D. Eisenhower and Adlai E. Stevenson were employing advertising men and ghostwriters. But these early consultants toiled mostly outside the public eye.

Not until the 1960s were the internal workings of a political campaign unveiled to the public in all their moral complexity. Journalist Theodore H. White, in the first of what became the quadrennial series *The Making of the President*, documented the 1960 presidential race between John F. Kennedy and Richard M. Nixon with more behind-the-scenes detail than ever before, such as Kennedy's voice lessons and Nixon's decision not to wear TV makeup during the first presidential DEBATE.

The 1968 election was a turning point for political consulting. Nixon, seeking to reinvent his image as the exiled loser of the 1960 race, brought in a team of advisers not from politics but from the news media and Madison Avenue. Luminaries such as CBS News executive Frank Shakespeare and TV producer Roger Ailes persuaded Nixon that television—far from being a cheap gimmick—was the key to winning elections.

Nixon's opponent, Vice President Hubert H. Humphrey, hired Springfield, Massachusetts, consultant Joe Napolitan, who had helped Kennedy to win crucial primaries in 1960. A specialist in survey techniques, Napolitan made dramatic recommendations that Humphrey could not agree to, such as breaking with President Lyndon B. Johnson's efforts to continue the Vietnam War; and he pleaded unsuccessfully with Humphrey to debate Nixon on TV.

Following Nixon's narrow victory, the new political handlers, now subject to increased public scrutiny, were saddled with a negative image. It was Napolitan who spotted the need for a professional organization to counter the criticism and develop bipartisan industry guidelines. He teamed with Republican strategists F. Clifton White and Stuart Spencer and several Democrats, among them consultants Robert Squier and Matt Reese and pollster Bill Hamilton, to form both the American Association of Political Consultants and the International Association of Political Consultants.

With some three hundred firms plying the trade by the 1970s, more consultants came to prominence. Hal Evry, a Republican public relations man who also worked for presidential candidate George Wallace, gained a reputation as the "enfant terrible" of consulting for openly defending campaign gimmicks and unrestrained spending. "The more money a candidate spends, the more likely he is to win," Evry once said.

Jimmy Carter's campaigns were guided by two men who became household names: media adviser Gerald Rafshoon (satirized by Garry Trudeau for manipulative "Rafshoonery" in the comic strip "Doonesbury") and pollster Patrick Caddell, who had polled for leaders of the Florida legislature while a high school senior in 1968. Caddell is credited with providing overarching themes for Carter. His polling during the 1980 campaign showed that attacks from the detail-oriented Carter against Ronald Reagan's perceived ignorance on the issues would backfire.

The Reagan camp's pollster, Richard Wirthlin, gave consultancy the "hierarchical values map," which divided polling data on issues into color-coded charts. In 1984 his research showed that Democratic candidate Walter F. Mondale would win if the main issues were the proposed Equal Rights Amendment to the Constitution, abortion, poverty, and fairness. Reagan would win if the top issues were working to build "a better America and preserve world peace" and "make U.S./World a better place for future generations."

After losing the election, Mondale declared bitterly that "American politics is losing its substance. . . . It's losing the depth that tough problems require to be discussed, and more and more it is that twenty-second [sound bite] snippet."

## Effect on the Electoral Process

The consultants' new-found role as unelected power brokers or "preselectors" of candidates is widely viewed as a mixed blessing. One problem, said Sabato, is that consultants make candidates "too responsive to public opinion" rather than encouraging them to lead. "They rely on negative campaigning that drives down turnout, and they produce homogenized campaigns, like Holiday Inns and McDonald's, where a campaign in Idaho is like one in Pennsylvania, with the same consultant, the same slogans."

Evidence that negative advertising diminishes turnout was supplied in an academic study of Senate races in twelve states during 1992. In states where candidates ran basically positive campaigns, turnout was 57.0 percent; in states with a mixture of positive and negative campaigns, turnout dropped to 52.4 percent; and in states with basically negatively run races, turnout was only 49.7 percent.

Consultants also are criticized by advocates of campaign finance reform, who see them as driving up the cost of campaigns. "Consultants certainly benefit from unrestricted spending," said Paul Hendrie, managing editor at the Center for Responsive Politics. "They push the prevalent theory that large blocks of TV ads" are the way to campaign, and in "states with major media markets, the high costs of campaigning will make candidates there less receptive to spending caps."

Consultants defend their freedom to spend a candidate's money in ways they think will win elections. They go to great lengths to market their expertise in the highly technical area of campaign finance disclosure law and ad buying. But they also admit they are one of the reasons that politicians constantly have to chase money.

Opinion polling methods increasingly are being slanted by pollsters to gain an advantage for a candidate or to provide backing for a preconceived notion. Some pollsters are viewed as advocates rather than dispassionate takers of the public pulse.

Among them is conservative pollster Frank Luntz, who gained fame for "test-driving" the legislative planks under consideration for the House Republicans' "Contract With America" in 1994. Luntz announced at the time that each of the contract's ten items had about 70 percent popular support, but the *Miami Herald* later reported that Luntz had not actually polled on the contract's provisions but had merely conducted focus groups, which primarily had been asked for their reaction to highly charged assertions. For example, according to the newspaper, the groups were asked if "we should stop excessive legal claims, frivolous lawsuits,

and overzealous lawyers." That became a less incendiary contract plank calling for "'loser pays' laws, reasonable limits on punitive damages, and reform of product liability laws to stem the tide of litigation." An industry group, the American Association for Public Opinion Research, later censured Luntz (a nonmember) for refusing to disclose the full wording of his poll or focus group questions. (See Contract with America box, page 261.)

Finally, there is the ever-present issue of consultants who shield their candidate from unscripted contact with the news media. Dan Balz, a *Washington Post* reporter who covered the 1996 presidential campaign, found it astonishing a month before the election that GOP nominee Robert J. Dole had not appeared on NBC's *Meet the Press* since December 1995, when previously he had been the show's most frequent guest. A Dole spokesperson denied that the candidate had been inaccessible.

A point in the consultants' favor is that candidates clearly value them. "I like having a manager who runs my campaigns, and if I don't have someone who is clearly in charge, I have problems," said 1988 Democratic presidential nominee and former Massachusetts governor Michael S. Dukakis. "You have to have someone for advice on things like media, and we had an in-house polling operation that was as accurate as any you could hire. I never felt hemmed in or frustrated by handlers."

On the contrary, Dukakis's chief regret about his unsuccessful campaign was the failure to respond to the Bush campaign's attacks on unforeseen issues such as prison furloughs, which the Republicans dramatized with TV spots based on the case of Willie Horton, a Massachusetts prisoner who raped a woman while on furlough. "That issue was as phony as a $3 bill, but obviously we did not handle it right because of our inexperience, which is partly my fault," Dukakis said.

## Celebrity Consultants

"I had star quality, and I had people interested in meeting me as much as meeting the candidate," Republican strategist Ed Rollins told an interviewer in explaining why he boasted, untruthfully, he later said, of spending money to suppress black voter turnout in the 1993 New Jersey governor's race. Rollins angered many in the political world with his 1996 tell-all memoir, *Bare Knuckles and Back Rooms: My Life in American Politics.* In the book Rollins heaped scorn on some candidates whose campaigns he had mentored. He branded Ross Perot "an extremely dangerous demagogue who would have been a disaster in the White House." He called California businessman Michael Huffington, who ran unsuccessfully for a Senate seat in 1994, and his then-wife, Arianna, "two of the most unprincipled political creatures I'd ever encountered."

In their 1994 campaign memoir, *All's Fair: Love, War, and Running for President,* Clinton strategist James Carville and his wife, Mary Matalin, a former political director to President Bush, wrote that MEDIA COVERAGE of their intraparty romance became a factor in the 1992 election. Matalin recalled resentfully that her political enemy and future husband used the news media to "look like a good guy, saying nice things about me, but it was really a backhanded way to keep the [romance] story alive and keep the [Bush] campaign off our game and off our message."

Consultants generally work exclusively for either Democrats or Republicans, but a few have worked for candidates of different parties. For example, several well-known consultants—Rollins, Luntz, and former Carter operative Hamilton Jordan—worked for Perot's presidential effort in 1992. And when Luntz left, disgusted (and unpaid), Democrats tried to recruit him.

The most notable example of crossover consultants is Dick Morris. After working with Democrat Clinton when he was Arkansas governor in the 1980s, Morris signed on with prominent Republicans such as Sen. Jesse Helms of North Carolina, Sen. Trent Lott of Mississippi, and Gov. Pete Wilson of California. Indeed, in 1991, Morris worked simultaneously (in separate contests) for Mississippi Republican gubernatorial candidate Pete Johnson and Democratic lieutenant governor Brad Dye.

Morris was widely credited with crafting Clinton's successful centrist strategy in 1996. In its September 2 cover story, *Time* magazine called Morris "the most in-

fluential private citizen in America." A week later, Morris again made the magazine's cover, this time after a SCANDAL involving a prostitute forced him to resign. In the weeks thereafter, commentators continued their debates over whether Morris, Rasputinlike, had been too influential in moving a liberal-leaning Clinton to the political center.

In the rival campaign of Republican Bob Dole, the consultants made their presence felt after Dole raised eyebrows with some unscripted comments. For example, he expressed uncertainty about the dangers of tobacco and refused an invitation to address the NAACP. "I've taken my vow of silence," the former Senate majority leader said with a grimace as he followed his handlers' command to avoid taking questions from reporters.

It appeared to Doug Bailey, who helped run President Gerald R. Ford's 1976 campaign, that Dole had too many consultants, with no one of them in charge of the others. Bailey, publisher of "Hotline," an online political news service, said that Dole had "every consultant known to man tied up in some way to his campaign."

## Consultancy's Future

With campaigns stretching ever-longer over the calendar, consultants have stepped in with more in-depth and detailed research. Some is aggressive, delving into opponents' credit histories, adoption records, or sex lives, using information from ex-spouses and "moles" inside opposing campaigns. There are now more than forty firms specializing in opposition research, a number that grew 200 percent in the 1990s, according to Sabato.

Many observers say it is no coincidence that the consulting field exploded in the same period that the country saw a loosening of PARTY IDENTIFICATION, an electorate made passive through television, and a drastic decline in VOTER TURNOUT. The percentage of eligible voters who participate fell from 63 percent in 1960 to 49 percent in 1996. Only 5 percent of adults are politically active, and the percentage of Americans who designate $3 on their tax returns for PUBLIC FINANCING of presidential elections was only 13.0 percent in 1996, down from 29.0 percent in 1980.

Whether this alienation can be linked to the rise of consultants is an often-asked question. Critics decry the strategists' encouragement of candidates to speak in CAMPAIGN SLOGANS and sound bites, which television news shows have reduced from an average of forty-three seconds in 1960 to about eight seconds in 1996, according to the Free TV for Straight Talk Coalition, a group advocating free air time for candidates. (See EQUAL TIME AND REBUTTAL RULES.)

Critics also note how campaigns now devote most of their budgets to thirty-second TV spots. Spending on television political ads rose from $24.5 million in 1972 to $299.6 million in 1992, and was estimated at a half-billion dollars in 1996 by the National Association of Broadcasters. The *Washington Post* reported in January 1998 that the Clinton reelection campaign had spent almost $100 million for TV ads, providing millions in commissions for the team's media advisers. Consultant Dick Morris estimated that he alone received $1.5 million.

"Voters are fed up with TV politics," two former leaders of both major parties, Republican Frank J. Fahrenkopf Jr. and Democrat Charles T. Manatt, wrote in 1996. "The media, too, are critical of the system they helped create. And we, as former chairmen of the Republican and Democratic parties, can attest that politicians themselves don't like the current situation."

Consultants argue that they are merely stepping into a gap opened by the decline in party loyalty, the increase in party PRIMARIES, and technological changes in communication. One reason for the consultants' prominence, said Victor Kamber, president of the Kamber Group, a Washington public relations firm, "is that we live in an age of news." Decades ago, the TV news used to be a half-hour or an hour, counting national and local, but today there are two and three hours of time to fill with features.

Paul Taylor, a former *Washington Post* political reporter who launched the Free TV for Straight Talk Coalition for the Pew Charitable Trusts, was reluctant to blame consultants or any other single group for the de-

terioration of political debate. For consultants, he said, "all the rewards are in thirty-second attack ads. More often than not, it works, and if I were in the consultants' shoes, I would want to win the election. That's the political marketplace."

## Political Culture in America

The term *political culture* refers to people's fundamental beliefs and assumptions about how government and politics should operate. Among such beliefs, five are deeply rooted in the American psyche: popular sovereignty, an obligation of political participation, individual rights, individualism, and equality.

Even though Americans as a whole believe deeply in individual rights and individualism, it is unrealistic to expect that their political thinking would be uniform—and it is not. Within even the five fundamental beliefs there are shadings and gradations. Some hold such beliefs and assumptions more deeply than others. And some, as is their right, do not hold to them at all.

Political culture also varies from group to group. Racial, ethnic, and religious backgrounds can affect people's attitudes toward political parties, candidates, and issues. A city with a large population of northern European ancestry may have political leanings that are different from a city with a mostly Asian population. Financial class also causes variations in political culture and behavior.

A combination of core political beliefs and different backgrounds influence people's ELECTORAL BEHAVIOR and their expectations and evaluations of politicians and policies. They also impose limits on the number of alternatives that policy makers can seriously consider. A policy that violates a basic value—such as the right to own private property—does not have a realistic chance of being adopted.

### Fundamental Beliefs

The Declaration of Independence proclaims that governments derive "their just powers from the consent of the governed." And the Preamble to the Constitution

*Immigration patterns historically have affected, and continue to affect, political attitudes and party identification. Here, new citizens pledge their allegiance to the United States at the U.S. Courthouse in Washington, D.C. Source: R. Michael Jenkins, Congressional Quarterly*

begins, "We the People of the United States." Embedded in these words is the belief that the people, not some hereditary monarch, are the source of government power.

Abraham Lincoln's phrase in the Gettysburg address about the nation being a "government of the people, by the people, and for the people" captures Americans' fundamental belief in popular sovereignty. The primacy of this belief is reflected in the importance we attach to periodic free elections and the role of PUBLIC OPINION in policy making.

Americans nevertheless have some reservations about DEMOCRACY. Many fear that voters may be misled by demagogues—leaders who play on voters' prejudices, fears, and baser emotions. And the value attached

to strong presidential leadership is further proof that people believe they may not always be capable of choosing the best policies by themselves.

As for the widespread belief in individual rights, the Declaration of Independence proclaims that it is "self-evident, that all men are . . . endowed by their Creator with certain unalienable Rights, that among these are Life, Liberty and the pursuit of Happiness." "Liberty" is the right to make one's own decisions and live one's life freely without undue government restraints. The people's basic right to liberty constitutes a limitation on the power of the majority over individuals and groups.

Also well ingrained in American thinking is the belief in the fundamental right to hold private property.

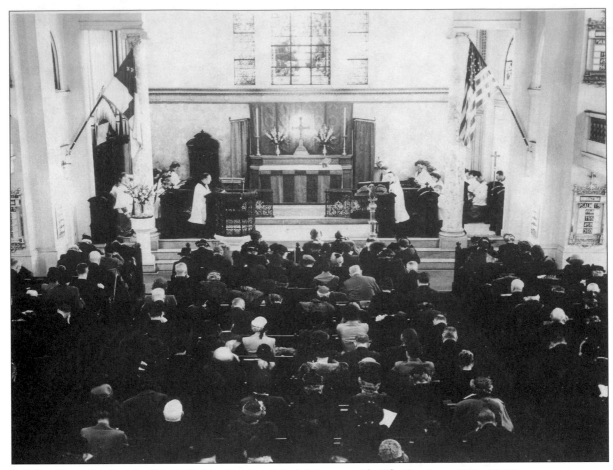

*Religion, like national origin, historically has played a role in defining party identification. Source: National Archives*

The commitment to private property and individual economic initiative has been so strong in the United States that socialism has made little headway, unlike in some other Western democracies. The largest share of votes ever gained by a SOCIALIST candidate for president was the 6 percent (900,369 votes) won by Eugene V. Debs in 1912. No socialist presidential candidate has ever carried a single state.

Individualism is deeply embedded in the American culture. When asked in 1992 to assess the relative importance of various characteristics for getting ahead in life, Americans gave clear priority to three: ambition, hard work, and education. It was what "I do" that mattered—not family background, race, religion, or other factors extraneous to personal effort and commitment.

Recognizing the pervasiveness of individualism, the United States has been more reluctant than most Western nations to institute national social welfare programs. Moreover, it spends a lower share of its national income on these programs than most industrialized nations.

## Equal Opportunity

Even before asserting that people have "unalienable Rights," the Declaration of Independence states that "all men are created equal." In American thinking, equality and individual rights are closely linked—if all people are equal, they must have the same rights.

Equality has several dimensions. In the Declaration of Independence, Thomas Jefferson was referring to political equality. To provide for this kind of equality, the Constitution and statutes contain provisions ensuring that all citizens of legal age have the RIGHT TO VOTE, and the Fourteenth Amendment requires the states to grant all people the "equal protection of the laws."

Many Americans also care about equality of opportunity—that is, they want to help those who are disadvantaged through race, gender, ethnicity, disability, or poverty to compete more effectively. This concern is manifested in the government's expanded role in providing the poor with money, food, housing, education, health care, and legal services.

But despite a commitment to equality of opportunity, most Americans do not believe that everyone should be equally well off; rather, everyone should have a relatively equal chance to become better off than his or her neighbors. Americans are quite prepared in fact to accept large disparities in the economic status of their fellow citizens.

A commitment to equality also implies racial equality, although the Constitution did not provide it until ratification of the Civil War amendments. The goal of racial equality still has not been met, and this failing is a source of continuing frustration, particularly for minority groups. There have been some accomplishments—for example, the barriers intended to prevent racial minorities from exercising their voting rights have been largely eliminated since the 1960s, leading to increased BLACK SUFFRAGE and the election of black officials. Overt discrimination based on government statutes and rules, such as requiring segregated schools, restaurants, and theaters, is no longer tolerated, but minorities have not yet achieved full social and economic equality in America. Moreover, there is no consensus on how to deal with the plight of racial minorities.

One government-sponsored remedy, affirmative action programs, has stirred deep emotions in both its proponents and opponents. These programs seek to ensure that minorities (and women) are fairly considered for employment and college admission; in their most controversial form, they use procedures that give minorities a greater chance of being hired or admitted to educational institutions than their credentials alone would give them. Proponents see these programs as a way to compensate for past acts of discrimination and to give minorities a chance to live the American dream. Opponents, however, see affirmative action programs as reverse discrimination and violations of society's commitment to rewarding people on the basis of merit.

## Demographics

American politics, besides being affected by the country's unique political culture, is no less shaped by the prevailing socioeconomic conditions such as the distribution of wealth within society; the ethnic, racial, and religious composition of the population; and changes in lifestyles ranging from how Americans earn a living to where they live.

### Distribution of Wealth

The prevailing distribution of wealth and income provides one of American society's most important characteristics: the vast majority of Americans are not poor. According to CENSUS data, in 1990 the median household income—the point that separates the upper 50 percent of families from the lower 50 percent—was $29,943. In the same year 13.5 percent of families had incomes that fell below the official government poverty level.

These data help to identify and explain the basic forces influencing American politics. First, a substantial proportion of people (including 22 percent of all children in 1992) are living in poverty; they are not living the American dream. As a result, there is continuing pressure on the government to develop programs to enable the less fortunate to improve their circumstances. Second, there is a wide gap between the living standards of the average white person and that of the average African American or Hispanic. Third, the poor are a distinct minority in the United States: they cannot rely on the traditional weapon of the underprivileged—superior numbers—to achieve their political goals. Instead, they must make alliances with and gain the support of the nonpoor. Indeed, government programs to assist the needy must be supported by large segments of the middle class and by interests that are not poor.

## National Origin

Although more than 90 percent of the American population was born in the United States, the nation, except for Native Americans, descended from immigrants. Until the late 1800s, immigrants came primarily from northern and western Europe, with the largest percentage from Great Britain and Ireland.

The wave of "new immigration" in the late nineteenth century and early twentieth was quite different, however. It was dominated by former inhabitants of eastern and southern Europe—Italians, Poles, Czechs, Slavs, Greeks, and Russian Jews. Their ethnicity tended to set them apart from native-born Americans and constituted a source of psychological identification. But as the descendants of immigrants from eastern and southern Europe have become assimilated into American life and better off economically, their voting patterns have become less distinct and their traditional support of Democratic candidates is no longer assured.

An estimated 6 million legal and 2 million undocumented immigrants entered the country between 1981 and 1990 when the population grew by 22 million. This level of immigration is second only to the 8.8 million immigrants who arrived between 1901 and 1910.

The latest wave of immigration is dramatically changing the ethnic and racial composition of the nation. Primarily from Latin America and Asia, these new immigrants are concentrated in California, Florida, New York, and Texas. Indeed, it is expected that by 2015 or 2020 non-Hispanic whites will become a minority in California.

The influx of Asian and Latin American immigrants is transforming American politics. Hispanic voters, for example, are critical in states with large numbers of electoral votes such as California, Florida, New York, and Texas. And as the Hispanic American population has increased, so too has its representation in the House of Representatives (from eleven to nineteen between the 1990 and 1998 elections). With their increasing numbers, Hispanics in the House have become more influential in shaping legislation, especially bills that affect immigrants. (See table, page 526.)

Hispanic immigrants, who can be of any race, hail from countries where Spanish is the dominant language. Because of their high immigration and birth rates, the number of Hispanic Americans is increasing rapidly—today they make up 14 percent of the population. As BILINGUAL VOTERS, their heavy concentrations in some areas require that ballots and other election materials be in both English and Spanish.

The political orientations of Hispanics vary widely, even though many of them (28 percent) live below the poverty level. Those of Mexican and Puerto Rican heritage tend to be heavily Democratic in their voting patterns. Cuban Americans, however, who are better off economically and ardent anticommunists, tend to be Republicans. According to EXIT POLLS, Hispanic voters as a whole overwhelmingly voted Democratic in 1996, with 79 percent supporting President Bill Clinton against 19 percent for Republican Robert J. Dole.

Race is another feature of American society. African Americans, most of whom are descendants of African slaves, constitute 12 percent of the U.S. population. Unlike Europeans, for whom ethnicity has declining political relevance, African Americans are highly conscious of their ethnicity. They have done less well economically than European immigrants, and more than 31 percent live below the poverty level.

African Americans tend to be concentrated in inner-city neighborhoods and poor rural areas, and many feel the continuing effects of racial discrimination. Government policies that combat poverty and deal with civil rights issues are high on the list of political concerns for African Americans, who are a critical element of the Democratic Party's electoral coalition. The African American vote went almost entirely to Clinton in 1996, with Dole receiving 1 percent and Ross Perot, 2 percent.

The growth of minority populations has profound implications for the census, which is used to reallocate House seats to the states every ten years and also is the distribution basis for some federal programs. In 1998 the Republican Congress and Democratic administration were at odds over the Bureau of the Census's plan to use modern sampling techniques to reduce the minority undercount in the 2000 census. Congressional Republicans sued to block the plan and won a partial victory. The Supreme Court in January 1999 barred use of sampling numbers for distribution of House seats, but not for allocation of federal aid.

## Other Demographic Factors

Age variations also determine the issues government must confront. The U.S. population, on the whole, is aging, which puts heavy pressure on the government to provide the elderly with services, particularly pensions and health care. These pressures can only be expected to intensify. For example, in 1993, 3.3 million people were over the age of eighty-five; the Census Bureau expects this number to double to 6.5 million by 2020 and soar to 17.7 million by 2050.

Religion, too, can affect voting patterns. Protestants are predominantly Republican; Catholics have traditionally been strongly Democratic, although in the 1980s a majority voted Republican for president; and Jews have been overwhelmingly Democratic. In recent elections Protestant evangelists have become increasingly active in politics and have tended to support Republican candidates for president.

Place of residence is yet another factor in America's political equation. For a large part of its history, the United States has been a predominantly rural nation with most of its citizens living on farms and in small towns. But today more than three-fourths of Americans live in a metropolitan area (a central city of at least fifty thousand and its surrounding suburbs), and almost 60 percent of the nation's population resides in metropolitan areas with a population exceeding 1 million.

These and many other factors determine the U.S. political culture, which in turn helps to chart the course of American politics. Stripped to its basics, politics is the pursuit and exercise of power as well as the process through which society expresses and manages its conflicts. But American politics does not play itself out in a vacuum. It is affected on a daily basis by the legal structure imposed by the Constitution, society's cultural values and socioeconomic characteristics, and the government's past policy decisions.

---

## Political Parties

*See* TWO-PARTY SYSTEM.

---

## Political Socialization of the Public

Political socialization—the acquisition of facts about and values related to politics—is a lifelong process. Among its agents are the family, schools, peers, the mass media, and leaders.

The influence of the family is profound. It is the family that first interprets the world for a child and, presumably, acquaints him or her with certain moral, religious, social, economic, and political values. If parents are interested in politics, this interest tends to be passed on to their children.

Parents often impart to their children a political attitude, called PARTY IDENTIFICATION, that is important in understanding ELECTORAL BEHAVIOR. Party identification is a feeling of attachment to and sympathy for a political party. As early as the third grade children frequently think of themselves as Democrats or Republicans.

Family influence on party identification is greatest when both parents identify with the same party. When the father and mother have different party preferences, mothers are likely to have a greater influence than fathers (reflecting the traditional tendency of mothers to spend more time with children than fathers). The maternal influence is especially strong on the daughters of college-educated, politically active mothers. Parents' influence on party identification is strengthened when it is reinforced, or at least not contradicted, by the messages received from other participants in the child's environment, such as friends or neighbors.

Parental influence on party identification decreases as children get older and are subjected to other, outside

*Schools, although they try to be nonpartisan, make a conscious effort to promote citizenship and political awareness. These New Hampshire high school students are conducting a mock convention. Source: File photo*

influences. Children are more likely to change from partisans to independents, however, than they are to go through a conversion process and affiliate with the other party. When the conversion does occur, it normally can be attributed to economic issues.

Political learning occurs in the schools as well. Schools normally do not make a conscious effort to promote a preference for a political party or a specific viewpoint on issues. Rather, they tend to present children with the facts about their country and its political

system and, in the process, foster patriotism and support for the institutions of government. The picture presented of American government in the early grades is beneficent and positive, with the president often viewed as a benevolent leader. Although the high schools continue the process of political education through American history and civics courses, such courses have been found to have only a modest influence on students' political interest, tolerance for differing opinions, trust in government, or inclination to participate in politics.

Adolescents' desire to conform—as seen in their clothing and hair-styles, as well as their musical tastes—is strong evidence of the power of peer pressure on young people's attitudes and behavior. This influence is more limited, however, in the realm of political attitudes. One of the factors contributing to the modest influence that peers have on adolescent political attitudes is the relatively low salience of politics to most adolescents' lives. Politics has little to do with their day-to-day concerns or their status in the peer group.

Politics is apt to take on greater relevance at the college level where peer pressures can affect students' political attitudes. In his classic study of peer group influence, Theodore Newcombe examined the political attitudes of women attending Bennington College, an exclusive liberal arts college in Vermont, in the 1930s. These students' political attitudes were affected significantly by Bennington's liberal POLITICAL CULTURE.

Indeed, during their years there many of the women students became a great deal more liberal in their IDEOLOGY than their generally well-to-do and conservative parents. Twenty-five years later in a follow-up study Newcombe found that Bennington alumnae retained the liberalism of their college days because it was reinforced by their spouses and adult peers.

The mass media—television, newspapers, magazines, and radio—are another influential agent of political socialization. Teachers, especially, rely heavily on the media for the information and values they transmit to their students. Outside the classroom children's direct exposure to the media is extensive. In winter, children from ages two to eleven log an average thirty-one hours a week watching television, and average high school graduates spend fifteen thousand hours during their secondary school years watching television, compared with eleven thousand hours in the classroom. When asked to identify sources of information on which they base their attitudes, high school students mention the mass media more often than families, teachers, friends, or personal experiences.

## Adult Socialization

The shaping of basic political beliefs, values, and attitudes does not stop with graduation from high school or college. But the influences that were the most prominent in youth—parents, school, childhood peers—recede and are replaced by daily events and experiences, the mass media, political leaders, and new peer groups such as coworkers, neighbors, friends, and fellow church and club members.

As people grow older their politically relevant experiences abound. They encounter the Internal Revenue Service, military recruiting, government-influenced mortgage rates, Social Security and Medicare, and economic setbacks. The impressions gained from these experiences and interactions with peers continue to shape people's political attitudes. The daily hardships of the Great Depression of the 1930s, for example, caused people to change their views about the role of government. Unlike in earlier times, they now expected the government to manage the economy and provide social services.

Personal experiences, however, are quite limited compared with the range of politically relevant experiences that the mass media provide. Throughout adulthood, as in childhood, people consume the media in huge doses: in a day the average adult spends more than four hours in front of a television, more than two hours listening to a radio, and eighteen to forty-five minutes reading a newspaper.

As a result, much of what the average person learns about politics is absorbed from the media's factual news programs as well as its fictional sitcoms, soap operas, and late night talk show comedians. Viewers may well conclude that most politicians are buffoons, crooks, or lechers because that is how most are depicted on such programs.

MEDIA COVERAGE OF CAMPAIGNS is a major force in shaping the people's perceptions of reality. For example, the public's perception that the economy was in desperate straits during the 1992 presidential election campaign was a major factor in Bill Clinton's defeat of President George Bush. Objective economic data indicated, however, that the economy was beginning to grow in late 1991 and more robustly in 1992. Yet content analysis showed that news coverage of the economy by ABC, CBS, and NBC was overwhelmingly (96 percent) negative and pessimistic in the July-September quarter of 1992.

PUBLIC OPINION analyst Everett Carll Ladd has concluded that this almost uninterrupted stream of negative press reports and commentary on the nation's economy was the "most important political event of the 1992 campaign." He stresses, however, that this kind of reporting was not caused by some media plot to elect Clinton but rather by the coming together of three elements: journalists feeling closer to the stands of Democrats than those of Republicans; a sense that after twelve years the Republicans and their economic policies had become an old, tired news story; and the fact that "the economy in shambles" was an inherently more interesting story than "some problems, but also many economic strengths."

People's attitudes are affected as well by the actions and statements of political leaders, particularly the president. One of the most dramatic changes in public opinion began in the early 1970s when President Richard Nixon, a man whose entire public career had been built on staunch anticommunism, began the process of normalizing diplomatic relations with the communist government of the People's Republic of China. Virtually overnight, American opinion changed from that of overwhelming opposition to that of heightened tolerance toward and interest in the communist government on mainland China. The actions of successive presidents to strengthen diplomatic, economic, and cultural ties with China continued to garner widespread public support until June 1989 when the communist government brutally repressed pro-democracy demonstrations.

Presidential leadership of public opinion is most effective when the president is riding a crest of popularity. During times of declining popular support, the president finds it difficult to sway the public. Even so effective a communicator as Ronald Reagan could not—as his popularity fell during the 1982 recession—muster support for a constitutional amendment to permit prayer in the public schools.

## The Effect of Social Backgrounds

No two Americans have identical political socialization experiences. People with similar social backgrounds, however, are apt to share some political opinions, which are likely to differ from the views of people with different backgrounds. Differences in education, income or class, ethnicity, race, religion, region, and gender can produce distinctive political orientations.

Education increases people's interest in and understanding of politics and affects the political attitudes that they develop. College graduates profess greater support for civil liberties and have more tolerant racial attitudes than people who attended but did not graduate from college. The better-educated also are more likely to support environmental protection measures, space research, and affirmative action hiring programs for women and minorities. They are less likely to back conservative social policy agenda items such as permitting prayer in the public schools or banning abortion counseling. But the more highly educated also appear to be less supportive of extending the government's role in providing social services.

Income and social class affect people's views on a range of issues. Those in the higher-income bracket are somewhat more supportive of racial and sexual equality, tolerant of diverse views, internationalist in foreign affairs, and conservative on social welfare issues. The higher education level characteristic of the well-to-do appears to be a major factor in their liberalism on noneconomic issues; income affects their views on social welfare issues.

In contrast to the situations found in many western nations, class-based differences do not greatly divide American society. For example, a recent nine-nation study showed that, in spite of great income disparities in the United States, only 29 percent of Americans supported the notion that it is government's responsibility to reduce the differences between those at the upper and lower ends of the income scale. In other countries, by contrast, income redistribution was supported by 82 percent of the respondents in Italy, 65 percent in the Netherlands, and 64 percent in Great Britain.

## Ethnicity and Race

America is frequently called a nation of immigrants, and with each new wave of immigration the mix of nationalities becomes more varied. Most of the earliest settlers came from England, Scotland, and Wales, followed by those from Ireland, Germany, and Scandinavia. During the late nineteenth and early twentieth centuries, immigrants from eastern and southern Europe—Poles, Italians, and Russians—predominated.

The cultural and religious differences between Americans with east and south European backgrounds and those of English heritage have often been a basis for political division within the United States. For example, the immigrants from eastern and southern Europe provided essential support for the New Deal Democratic coalition forged by President Franklin Roosevelt in the 1930s, and those of British heritage traditionally have constituted an important base of Republican voting strength.

Although differences in voting patterns among voters of European heritage are still detectable, the differences are diminishing as older immigrant groups become assimilated into American society. Public opinion surveys show modest differences in thinking, however, among European ethnic groups on issues of government responsibility for health care, improved living standards for the poor, and a more equitable distribution of income. For example, persons with British ancestry are less likely to support government social welfare programs than those with south and east European roots.

The current tide of immigrants from Spanish-speaking (Hispanic) countries in this hemisphere—particularly Mexico and Central America—and from Asia is showing distinctive political attitudes and partisan preferences as well. Reflecting the relatively less well-off economic positions of these "new ethnics," Mexican Americans, for example, are more highly supportive of extending government services and of the Democratic Party than are the "old ethnics" from eastern and southern Europe. The political attitudes of Mexican Americans also differ from those of another Hispanic group, the Cuban Americans, who, with their fierce anticommunist stance and generally higher standard of living, are predominantly Republican.

African Americans constitute the country's largest racial minority (more than 12 percent) with other nonwhites (Asians and Native Americans) making up approximately 3 percent. African Americans and Asians are expanding segments of the population. According to numerous surveys conducted by the National Opinion Research Center, African Americans and other racial minorities tend to have some political attitudes in common. But in contrast to older European ethnics and Hispanics, African Americans are more likely to believe that government should assume a larger responsibility for solving the country's problems, helping the poor, reducing income differences between rich and poor, and providing health care. Asian Americans, in contrast, tend toward more conservative political positions.

## Religious Background

America is a predominantly Protestant nation with 56 percent professing a Protestant religious preference, followed by Catholics, 25 percent; Jewish, 2 percent; other religions, 6 percent; and no religious preference, 11 percent in 1997. Some of the differences in attitudes and partisan preferences found among people of various faiths can be traced to historic causes. Most Catholic immigrants, for example, arrived in the United States at a time when Protestants and Republicans dominated the nation's political and economic life. This fact, as well as the discrimination to which Catholics were once subjected, has left traces of liberal and pro-Democratic sentiment among Catholics. The 1928 election also helped

to forge an electoral bond between Catholics and the Democratic Party, as New York governor Al Smith became the first Catholic presidential nominee of a major party.

The unique history of Jews as a persecuted minority also has influenced their political views; centuries of anti-Semitism have tended to drive them in a liberal direction, especially on civil liberties issues.

Doctrinal differences among religions have political relevance as well. The Catholic church has taken a strong stand against abortion and birth control, and the emphasis Protestants place on individual responsibility for one's economic and spiritual well-being may predispose them toward conservative positions on economic issues. Fundamentalist Protestants show a particularly conservative orientation. They overwhelmingly favor prayer in public schools and oppose abortion.

One of the most striking recent developments about religion and politics is the close relationship between frequency of church attendance and partisan choice. According to the 1992 election data, among whites Republicans fare much better with the "churched" portion of the electorate than with the "less churched" and "unchurched." African Americans, including regular churchgoers, however, are overwhelmingly Democratic, as are Jewish voters.

## Regional Divisions

Regional differences of opinion have been periodic sources of conflict since the earliest days of the American political system. The Civil War was the most dramatic of such instances, and that war and its aftermath left their marks on American politics for more than a century. After the war, small-town, white Protestant, middle-class conservatives, who might otherwise have been Republicans, created a one-party Democratic stronghold in the South.

But as Civil War memories faded, northerners migrated to the South, and the region's per capita income disadvantages began to diminish after World War II. The partisanship of whites changed, and some of the distinctiveness of southern attitudes receded. Southerners, however, continue to hold more conservative views on most issues than people from other regions. They are more likely to consider themselves conservatives, to trust the Republicans to deal with the country's most important problems, to oppose abortion, to favor prayer in the public schools, to oppose homosexual relations, and to support defense expenditures.

Liberalism on social issues tends to be bicoastal, with the Northeast and the Pacific Coast standing out as being the most supportive of women's rights, the right to an abortion, and other issues on the social agenda. The East is also more liberal on economic issues. On civil rights the South is more conservative than the rest of the nation.

Although the unique histories and cultures of the states have an impact on the political outlooks of their residents, powerful forces in American society are undermining these regional influences. For example, the mobility of Americans (approximately 20 percent move each year) is diluting the homogeneity of regional populations, and the national media, which have made their way into living rooms across the country, are diminishing the uniqueness of regional influences.

## The Gender Gap

Men and women, even those who share common racial, social class, ethnic, and religious backgrounds, do not have the same attitudes about some issues. The most frequently noted difference in attitude has been toward the Democratic Party: in the 1980s and 1990s a higher proportion of women than men supported Democratic candidates. As a result, the term *gender gap* entered the political vocabulary.

Women are less apt than men to support military expenditures and the use of force in international affairs and are more apt to support gun control and social welfare spending. Not all issues, however, are gender-sensitive. On the questions of increased spending for education and family leave legislation, the views of men and women are much the same.

## From Socialization to Participation

Once adulthood is reached and political attitudes are largely formed, the next step for the politically active is to put those beliefs to work through political participation. Men and women with higher social and economic status—whether measured by level of education, income, occupation, or government benefits received—participate more actively in politics than those with lower social and economic status.

Education is the single most important socioeconomic characteristic determining political participation. The better educated are more likely to understand how the political process works, to be aware of how the machinations of government might affect their lives, to move in social environments in which politics is discussed, and to be subjected to social pressures to participate. In addition, education helps people to acquire the skills necessary to participate.

Age affects participation as well. Young people are less likely to vote and engage in election-related activities than middle-aged and older citizens, but they are more likely than their elders to take part in unconventional forms of political participation such as protest demonstrations.

In the past, significant differences in political participation were related to gender and race, with women and blacks lagging behind men and whites. Today, however, the differences between men and women have diminished. And the gap between white and black participation rates has been narrowed as African Americans' RIGHT TO VOTE has been protected, black educational attainment and economic mobility have been enhanced, and black political awareness has increased with accompanying increases in BLACK SUFFRAGE. Black participation rates are now similar to those of whites, when differences between the races in educational attainment and socioeconomic status are taken into consideration.

Among the attitudes related to participation are a sense of civic duty (a feeling of obligation to participate), an interest in politics, a sense of political efficacy (a feeling of personal political effectiveness), and a sense of party identification. Although these attitudes are indicators of whether a person is predisposed to participate in politics, they do not, aside from party identification, indicate which issues or candidates will receive that person's attention. Short-term influences—such as the salient issues of the day and the qualities of particular candidates—also help determine whether a person's political socialization will manifest itself in political participation, and in what form.

## Poll Taxes

The *poll tax,* a fee required for voting, once was commonplace in the United States. Originally a head tax, its use waned in the nineteenth century as more people became property owners and therefore could be assessed real estate taxes.

But in the South after the Civil War, the reigning Democratic Party seized upon the poll tax as a device to deter voting by blacks who were flocking to the party of Lincoln and building Republican strength. Later, as the trend to primaries took hold, the poll tax along with GRANDFATHER CLAUSES, LITERARY TESTS, and the WHITE PRIMARY proved effective in limiting voting by poor blacks and whites in the Democrats' SOUTHERN PRIMARIES, the most significant elections in the region.

The fee generally ranged from $1 to $2, but in Alabama, Georgia, Mississippi, and Virginia before 1945 the poll tax was cumulative. A new voter in Georgia could face up to $47 in fees. For impoverished sharecroppers, black or white, even a dollar or two was a hardship.

Various regulations as to the time and manner of payment of the tax also substantially reduced the number of voters. In Mississippi, for example, a person wanting to vote in the Democratic primary (usually held in August) had to pay the poll tax on or before the first day of the two preceding Februarys—long before most voters had even begun to think about the election.

After years of controversy about it, many states dropped the poll tax. But it lingered in much of the South until it was effectively barred by ratification of the Twenty-fourth Amendment to the Constitution in January 1964. The amendment simply stated that the "right of citizens of the United States to vote in any primary or other election [for federal office] . . . shall not be denied or abridged by the United States or any other State by reason of failure to pay any poll tax or other tax."

In 1966 in *Harper v. State Board of Elections* the Supreme Court reversed an earlier decision and ruled that poll taxes were unconstitutional for state and local elections as well. Striking down Virginia's $1.50 poll tax, the Court said that "Wealth, like race, creed, or color is not germane to one's ability to participate intelligently in the electoral process."

## Polling

Polls of PUBLIC OPINION are a big part of modern-day American politics. Candidates and their POLITICAL CONSULTANTS rely on them to identify popular issues, test voter reaction to the candidate's image and programs, and help plan CAMPAIGN STRATEGIES.

Polling companies sell the results of their work to clients—newspapers, corporations, and interest groups—that need information on the public's thinking. The Gallup, Roper, Harris, and Yankelovich organizations are the best known of the nation's pollsters. Some smaller firms specialize in polling for candidates, usually Democrats or Republicans but not both. Few serious candidates for a major elected office undertake campaigns without the advice of pollsters. Often the pollster is the chief campaign adviser.

Major newspapers, news magazines, and television networks also do extensive polling, and the results have become a staple of MEDIA COVERAGE OF CAMPAIGNS as well as an important tool in MEDIA USE BY CAMPAIGNS. Academic institutions, such as the Center for Political Studies (CPS) at the University of Michigan, survey opinion regularly in an effort to develop a database for theoretical explanations of political behavior. Political scientists use all of these sources in their work and rely heavily on the CPS studies of ELECTORAL BEHAVIOR. A CPS adjunct, the NATIONAL ELECTION STUDIES, surveys the electorate in connection with every presidential and MIDTERM election.

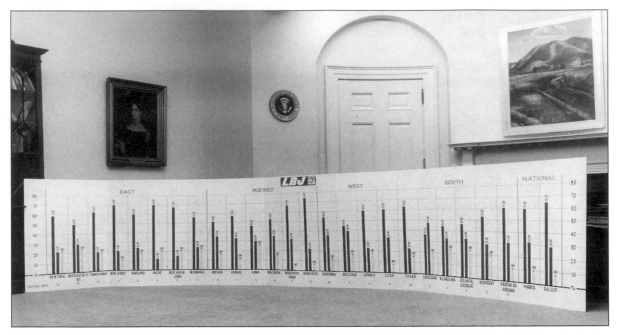

*In the Fish Room (now called the Roosevelt Room), across from the Oval Office, President Lyndon Johnson set up charts displaying his private polls before the 1964 election. Source: Library of Congress*

## Techniques and Ratings

Scientific methods of public opinion polling are a relatively recent development, dating only to the early twentieth century. Before scientific polling, it was almost impossible to measure public sentiment reliably.

George Gallup was the founder of modern polling. His surveys helped his mother-in-law win election as Iowa secretary of state in 1932. Gallup wrote a doctoral thesis on sampling techniques and in 1935, with Elmo Roper and Archibald Crossley, he founded the independent Gallup poll, the leader in scientific polling for decades and still one of the major polling organizations.

Since 1945 the Gallup Organization has asked members of the public monthly—and sometimes more often—whether they approve or disapprove the president's handling of the job. Although other firms do similar polls, Gallup's is the standard gauge of how the public rates presidential performance.

Franklin D. Roosevelt was the first president to take polling data routinely into account when weighing de-

cisions about his administration's policies and actions. With war looming in Europe in the late 1930s, Roosevelt sought advice from Gallup on how to frame his rhetoric concerning U.S. involvement in what became World War II.

It was about that time that the term *pollster* came into existence, according to *New York Times* language columnist William Safire. The word first appeared in *Time* magazine in a 1939 article quoting Gallup's findings that 43 percent of voters favored FDR's running for an unprecedented third term.

After Roosevelt's death in his fourth term, the polls seriously misjudged President Harry S. Truman's chances of defeating Republican Thomas E. Dewey in 1948. The pollsters' error was forever memorialized by the famous picture of a smiling Truman holding up the headline, "Dewey Defeats Truman."

By the 1960s public opinion polling was an accepted White House tool. Lyndon B. Johnson was the first president to have a staff pollster. He hired Albert Cantril, who provided LBJ with polling data from every state. Johnson used the polls both to defend his escalation of the Vietnam War and his decision in 1968 not to seek re-election in the face of mounting opposition to the war. Before the Vietnam War took its toll on his popularity, Johnson had one of the highest approval ratings in the Gallup poll history—80 percent in January 1964. He won in a LANDSLIDE that year, but by the end of his term his ratings were in the 40 percentile area.

George Bush scored the highest rating of any president, 89 percent in 1991 following victory in the Persian Gulf War. But he also had one of the lowest, 30 percent in 1992 because of his administration's problems with the economy.

Truman and Nixon tied at 23 percent as the presidents who at one point received the lowest ratings in Gallup's approval poll. The only other president to score in the twenties was Jimmy Carter, who dipped to 29 percent at several crisis points in his presidency.

Although Bush was the first president to appoint a pollster (Robert M. Teeter) as his reelection campaign manager, Bush campaigned against "those crazy pollsters" in the same 1992 campaign. He accused the poll takers of trying to make him a loser to Clinton before he actually was.

Pollsters for presidential candidates tend to specialize in one party or the other. For example, Richard Wirthlin and Teeter polled for Republicans Ronald Reagan and Bush, respectively. Patrick Caddell polled for Democrats George McGovern, Jimmy Carter, Gary Hart, and Joseph R. Biden Jr. During Clinton's first year in the White House, pollster Stanley Greenberg was paid $1,986,410 by the Democratic National Committee to conduct frequent focus groups and polls for the president's use.

As president in early 1998, Clinton achieved a remarkable ratings feat. Despite a sensational SCANDAL involving his alleged (later admitted) affair with a young female White House intern, Clinton received approval scores ranging as high as 79 percent for his job as president. His job approval rating remained high a year later, even after the House impeached him for perjury and obstruction of justice in connection with the extramarital affair.

## Polling Methods

Polls, with the exception of those conducted by partisan organizations, are seldom challenged as being purposely biased. Skepticism about the results usually centers on the sophisticated, computerized sampling techniques that draw broad conclusions from surveys of small cross sections of the public.

To reach the people in the population sample, most polling organizations today use telephones instead of in-person interviews. Telephone polls are economical and do not significantly distort survey results. The reluctance of many people to be interviewed over the phone, however, is worrisome to public opinion analysts.

For election surveys pollsters are turning more and more to EXIT POLLS on ELECTION DAY—surveying voters as they leave the polling place about how they voted.

Pollsters normally interview only one thousand to two thousand people in a national survey. But even such a small group of respondents can accurately reflect the nation's views if the people being interviewed constitute a representative sample of the population whose opinion is being sought. To create such a sample, pollsters use a probability procedure in which every person in the population being surveyed has the same chance of being chosen for an interview as everyone else.

A classic example of a nonrepresentative sample that resulted in a distorted picture of public opinion was the 1936 *Literary Digest* poll that predicted Kansas governor Alfred Landon would defeat President Franklin Roosevelt in the presidential election. The sample had been selected from phone books and automobile registrations, overlooking the fact that in the depths of the Great Depression people with telephones and cars were only a fraction of the electorate and certainly not a cross section of American voters.

Responsible polling organizations take great care to determine that they have a representative sample of the population they are studying. Preelection polls pose special problems because not all those eligible will actually vote. So a poll that reports the preferences of all eligible voters presents a potentially inaccurate prediction. To deal with this problem, polling organizations try to determine which people are most likely to vote.

Most polling organizations rely on random-digit-dialing to overcome the problems associated with unlisted telephone numbers—30 percent or more in some areas. Random-digit-dialing typically involves using a computer random-number generator or table of random numbers to select the last four digits of the phone numbers to be called after the area codes and exchanges (the first three digits of a seven-digit phone number) in the survey area have been identified.

Survey interviews can last from a few minutes to as long as an hour, depending on the amount of information being sought. Most questions are closed-ended—that is, the respondent chooses from a predetermined set of possible answers, thereby enhancing the comparability of the responses. A small number of questions may be open-ended, with respondents allowed to answer questions in their own words. Open-ended questions may elicit subtle distinctions in people's opinions, but they substantially complicate interpretation and analysis of interview data.

Particular care must be taken that the wording of questions does not bias or influence respondents' answers, which would affect the poll's results. For example, a 1992 *New York Times*/CBS poll asked respondents: "Are we spending too much, too little, or about the right amount on assistance to the poor?" Only 13 percent said we were spending "too much." But when "welfare" was substituted for "assistance to the poor," 44 percent said we were spending "too much."

## Polling Accuracy

As polling techniques have improved, so has the accuracy of polls. The Gallup poll, for example, had an average deviation from the actual winning vote in the ten presidential elections from 1960 through 1996 of only 2.0 percentage points.

Polls can be correct and still vary widely. In August 1992, for example, polls by ten organizations showed Clinton leading in the presidential race by a high of 19 percentage points (ABC/*Washington Post*) to a low of 5 points (Lou Harris). The polls had a margin of error of 3 to 5 points for each candidate.

Inaccurate polls might stem from a sampling error—the degree to which the sample can be expected to vary from the total population being studied. National surveys typically have a sampling error of about 4 percent. This means that if 55 percent of the respondents prefer the Republican candidate, the actual value is likely to be in the range of 51 percent to 59 percent (55 percent plus or minus 4 percent).

Inaccurate poll results also might stem from a faulty questionnaire, sloppy interview procedures, and mistakes in interpreting and analyzing survey responses. An analytical error, for example, occurred in the Gallup poll's final estimate of the 1992 presidential vote because of the unprecedented independent candidacy of Ross Perot, who received equal status with the major party nominees in the presidential DEBATES and had a record advertising budget. Based on the past performance of independent candidates, the Gallup organization decided to allocate none of the undecided voters to Perot. As a result, Gallup underestimated Perot's vote by 6 percentage points.

It is hazardous to predict on the basis of polls what the public's opinions or behavior will be at some time in the future; the public's views can change dramatically and quickly. A poll is only a snapshot of opinions at the time it was taken, and its validity cannot be extended into time.

## Popular Vote

The popular vote—the vote of the people—was less important in early American elections than it is today. Then, as now, the president and vice president were elected by the ELECTORAL COLLEGE rather than by direct popular vote. State legislatures chose the electors in most cases, although in the first presidential election (1789) electors in four states were selected by popular vote. South Carolina was the last state to switch to popular vote in choosing electors, in 1868. Colorado, however, used legislative appointment in 1876, the year it became a state. (See DIRECT ELECTION.)

The House of Representatives, as the "people's

branch," has always been popularly elected, but direct election of Senate members did not become universal until ratification of the Seventeenth Amendment in 1913. Popular election of governors in some states predates the 1789 election because the states existed earlier under the Articles of Confederation. Thirteen of them became the original states under the Constitution when they ratified it, beginning with Delaware on December 7, 1787.

## Wider Participation

As the RIGHT TO VOTE was gradually extended to more and more people through state actions and constitutional amendments, the popular vote grew in significance for all elections. By 1972 virtually all law-abiding American citizens over age eighteen had the FRANCHISE. (See BLACK SUFFRAGE; WOMEN'S SUFFRAGE; YOUTH SUFFRAGE.)

How many actually exercised the franchise, however, was difficult to determine until the latter half of the twentieth century. Reliable popular vote returns for presidential and congressional elections before 1824 are not available; and many of those for later years did not come into existence until after 1962, when a small army of social scientists, supported by grants from the Social Science Research Council and the National Science Foundation, began scouring the nation for old newspapers, state archives, historical society records, and anything else that could help reconstruct the vote tallies of early federal and state elections.

The result was the Historical Elections Returns File of the Inter-university Consortium for Political and Social Research (ICPSR) at the University of Michigan, Ann Arbor. The historical file was the basis for the *Guide to U.S. Elections*, published in 1975 by Congressional Quarterly and updated with new editions in 1985 and 1994. The ICPSR, part of the Institute for Social Research, disseminates the in-depth voting studies of a newer institute affiliate, the NATIONAL ELECTION STUDIES.

The U.S. CENSUS Bureau publishes popular vote returns for contemporary presidential elections, and it conducts VOTER TURNOUT and other surveys of the electorate. Since the 1970s the FEDERAL ELECTION COMMISSION has compiled presidential election results, although its figures sometimes disagree with the Census Bureau's. There is no one "official" set of election results outside of those maintained in each state.

Compilation of reliable popular vote returns for elections after 1824 became feasible because by then the TWO-PARTY SYSTEM was beginning to develop and more states were choosing presidential electors by popular election. Scholars' efforts to compile earlier returns have been thwarted by a lack of records.

As it happened, the 1824 election marked a HISTORIC MILESTONE in the role of the popular vote in presidential elections. When none of the four major candidates, all from different factions of the Democratic-Republican Party, received a majority of the electoral vote, the election had to be decided by the House of Representatives for only the second time in history. Although Andrew Jackson led in the popular vote with 41.3 percent, the House elected John Quincy Adams, who had run second with 30.9 percent.

As a result, Adams became the first "minority president," one who gained the office without a majority of the popular vote. Since then, through 1996, there have been sixteen other minority presidents. (See table, page 133.)

With one exception the other minority presidents, including Bill Clinton in 1992 and 1996, won a majority of the states' electoral votes without winning a majority of the total popular vote. The exception was Rutherford B. Hayes, who ran behind the winner of the popular vote majority, Samuel Tilden, in their 1876 CONTESTED ELECTION. After a protracted partisan dispute over who won the electoral vote majority, a congressional compromise settled the matter in Republican Hayes's favor.

## Voting Trends

The popular vote is useful for measuring ebbs and flows in voter participation and preference in the United States. The figures show, for example, that each major liberalization of election laws resulted in a sharp increase in the number of people voting. From 1824 to 1856, a period in which states gradually relaxed property and taxpaying qualifications, voter participation in presidential elections increased from 3.8 percent to 16.7 percent of the total population. In 1920, when the Nineteenth Amendment giving women the franchise went into effect, voter participation increased to 25.1 percent.

Between 1932 and 1976 both the voting-age population and the number of voters in presidential elections almost doubled. Except for the 1948 presidential election, when just a little over half of the voting-age population was estimated to have gone to the polls, the turnout in the postwar years through 1968 was approximately 60 percent, according to Census Bureau surveys. This relatively high percentage was due partly to passage of the VOTING RIGHTS ACT and CIVIL RIGHTS ACTS protecting African Americans' voting privilege.

Despite a steady increase in the number of persons voting in the 1970s, voter turnout declined as a percentage of eligible voters. Turnout reached a modern peak of 62.8 percent in the 1960 presidential election. It declined steadily over the next decade, falling to 61.9 percent in 1964, 60.9 percent in 1968, 55.2 percent in 1972, and 52.8 percent in 1980. Voting in the congressional MIDTERM ELECTION, always lower than in presidential years, also declined during this period, dropping from 45.4 percent in 1962 to 34.9 percent in 1978.

The decline in presidential voting continued during the 1980s and 1990s, except for upticks to 53.3 percent in 1984 and 55.1 percent in 1992. The 1992 election was the first in which more than 100 million Americans voted for president. The total vote was 104,425,014.

In 1996, however, participation fell again, dropping to 49.0 percent, the lowest mark since 1924. The total presidential vote also fell, to 96,277,223. (See table, page 517.)

## Postconvention Bounce

As a gigantic campaign rally that showcases the candidate in a favorable light, the NATIONAL PARTY CONVENTION often gives a "postconvention bounce" to the nominee's PUBLIC OPINION rating.

Occasionally the bounce is enough to leapfrog the lagging nominee's popularity over that of the preconvention leader. As a rule, however, the candidate who led in the final Gallup POLL before the convention is the one who wins the presidential election.

From 1948 to 1996, nine of thirteen preconvention FRONT-RUNNERS went on to win. In the first exception, President Harry S. Truman came from behind to defeat Republican governor Thomas E. Dewey of New York by 5 percentage points. Dewey had been 11 percentage points ahead before the 1948 party conventions.

Dewey's election had been so expected that beforehand *Life* magazine captioned his picture "the next president," and on ELECTION DAY the *Chicago Daily Tribune* rushed into print with a "Dewey Defeats Truman" headline. Truman gleefully held up the front page the next day for a famous news photograph.

In 1988 Vice President George Bush rebounded from a 6-point ratings deficit to an 8-point victory over Democratic governor Michael S. Dukakis of Massachusetts.

As president in 1992, Bush was the preconvention poll leader by 5 points. But Democratic governor Bill Clinton of Arkansas, who had been in third place behind Bush and independent Ross Perot of Texas, rebounded to win in November by 6 points over Bush and 21 points over Perot.

President Clinton's 1996 victory followed the traditional pattern. He was both the poll leader before the conventions and the ultimate winner over Republican Robert J. Dole of Kansas.

## Populist Party

*See* PEOPLE'S PARTY–POPULIST.

## Precinct

*See* DISTRICTS, WARDS, AND PRECINCTS.

## President, Nominating and Electing

The election of a U.S. president is always costly, often rancorous, sometimes messy, seldom boring. The system is perhaps more complicated than it needs to be, but it has worked with few major repairs for more than two hundred years, generally satisfying the citizenry and meeting the nation's changing needs.

The election occurs every four years and permits the peaceful transfer of power or continuation of the status quo for four more years, no matter how bitter or divisive the campaign that preceded it. Indeed, the American electoral system differs from those of other nations and, for all its flaws, is the envy of many other countries. (See INTERNATIONAL AND U.S. ELECTIONS COMPARED.)

As the nation and the electorate have grown and technology has evolved, presidential elections have become more expensive, costing an estimated $700 million in 1996. Because of the high costs, money and its abuses account for the biggest continuing stain on the system, despite the myriad CAMPAIGN FINANCE reforms enacted since the 1970s to avoid corruption and reduce the influence of special interests.

On the more positive side, presidential nominations have become more open and representative of the voters at large. Party bosses no longer dictate the choice of nominees. Instead, the nominations are won through a hard-fought series of PRIMARY elections and party CAUCUSES, where rank-and-file party members have an opportunity to express their preference. Once forums for determining who would head the presidential ticket, NATIONAL PARTY CONVENTIONS today perform different functions, but among them is the ratification of the nominations won in the primaries.

As televised spectaculars, the conventions remain important to the parties' public relations efforts during the intense weeks before the November election. Although ratings have dropped in recent years, the millions who watch the conventions on television are too big an audience for the parties to ignore, and they do not. With expert advice they have streamlined the pro-

*Rep. Patricia Schroeder, Democrat of Colorado, declined to run for the presidency despite high public standing, citing the "Byzantine state filing rules." Source: Paul Conklin, Congressional Quarterly*

ceedings to showcase their nominees in prime time as the countdown begins to ELECTION DAY.

In these final CAMPAIGN STAGES, today's nominees usually keep intact the organizations they built to help them survive the primaries. These increasingly professional organizations are made up of the candidate, his or her family, a RUNNING MATE, POLLING and POLITICAL CONSULTANTS, fund raisers, MEDIA COVERAGE and MEDIA USE consultants, issues advisers, schedulers, advance persons, and others. CAMPAIGN STRATEGIES must be carefully managed if the candidate is to move successfully through the primary season, the nominating conventions, and the general election campaign.

## Who Runs for President

Candidates for president and vice president must meet the same few constitutional requirements. They

*Colin Powell, shown here as head of the Joint Chiefs of Staff, said he would not run because of the strains a campaign would place on his family. Source: Department of Defense*

must be at least thirty-five years old and natural-born citizens who have "been 14 years a Resident within the United States." (See PRESIDENT, QUALIFICATIONS; VICE PRESIDENT.)

Another requirement, one that affects very few people, is that the candidate must *not* have been elected president twice before. The Twenty-second Amendment, ratified in 1951, limits presidents to two four-year terms. A vice president who succeeds to the presidency and serves more than two years may be elected president only once. Franklin D. Roosevelt, whose breaking of the two-term tradition prompted the term limitation, is the only president who served more than eight years. He died in 1945 while in his fourth term.

The decision to seek the presidency is a difficult one. The candidates must make complicated calculations about financial and time requirements. They must sort out the tangle of party and state rules and the makeup of the electorate in each state. And they must assess their own ability to attract endorsements, recruit a competent staff, and develop an "image" suitable for media presentation. They must also consider the effect a campaign will have on their families, the psychological demands of the office, and possible revelations about their personal lives that might hinder a campaign.

The 1996 election provided two examples of such considerations. One arose from the popularity of retired general Colin L. Powell, who had been the first African American to head the Joint Chiefs of Staff. Polls showed Powell would have been a strong contender for the Republican presidential nomination. He declined to seek it, however, saying he had promised his wife he would stay out of politics. In the other example, the man who won the GOP nomination, Robert J. Dole, worried that the press would disclose an affair he had while married to his first wife. In his televised DEBATES with President Bill Clinton, who had faced a similar SCANDAL in 1992, Dole did not raise the character issue, reportedly fearing it would open himself to the same criticism. Although Dole's affair was disclosed before the election, it received scant attention and was not a major factor in Dole's defeat.

## The Exploratory Stage

There are several STAGES IN AN ELECTION, especially a presidential election. The first, for any office, is the exploratory stage. Since 1976, when Jimmy Carter won the presidency after a two-year campaign, candidates have tended to announce their intentions well ahead of the election, in part to have time to build a strong public profile and in part because early fund raising can be crucial to a campaign. In 1996, with Clinton unopposed within his own party, the race for the Republican nomination drew a large field of candidates. The first to announce was Sen. Phil Gramm of Texas on February 24, 1995. The eventual GOP nominee, Dole, then Senate majority leader, formally entered the race almost two months later, on April 10.

Before announcing, candidates routinely establish a POLITICAL ACTION COMMITTEE (PAC) to raise money and an exploratory committee to help "test the waters" for a campaign. The exploratory advisers identify likely opponents, consider funding prospects and other preliminary factors, and, if conditions appear favorable, the committee may form the nucleus of the candidate's campaign organization.

## The Primary and Caucus Schedule

If a candidate decides to seek a major party nomination, the next step is to enter the primaries and caucuses where DEMOCRATIC and REPUBLICAN party members select DELEGATES to their national conventions. The states and the parties have a wide variety of rules for BALLOT ACCESS qualifications and allocation of delegates. Candidates must follow legal requirements to qualify for state contests, and they also have to adapt their campaign strategies to each state's particular circumstances.

The complexity can be daunting. Colorado representative Patricia Schroeder cited the complexity of state rules as a major factor in her decision not to seek the Democratic presidential nomination in 1988. Independent Ross Perot made it a condition of his 1992 candidacy that his supporters obtain enough signatures to get his name on the ballot in all fifty states. They succeeded.

Traditionally, the NEW HAMPSHIRE PRIMARY and the IOWA CAUCUS are the first delegate-selection events, which gives the two states extraordinary influence over the selection process. (Clinton was the first candidate since 1952 to be elected without winning the New Hampshire primary.) Critics have complained that the system is unrepresentative because both states are predominantly rural, with largely white, Anglo-Saxon, Protestant populations. But no serious efforts have been made to change the pattern.

Democratic Party rules prevent other states from scheduling their primaries earlier than the New Hampshire and Iowa events. Republican caucuses are permitted earlier in Alaska, Hawaii, Louisiana, and Guam. For other states and territories, the primary and caucus period begins in late February or early March and ends in early June. The early primaries have grown in importance. Especially when the campaign does not have an obvious FRONT-RUNNER, the early contests single out a possible leader. After several early tests, the field of candidates shrinks.

This winnowing process was most evident in the Democratic contest in 1984, when five candidates withdrew less than three weeks after the New Hampshire primary. Lack of adequate funding is a deciding factor for many of these early dropouts. Not surprisingly, contributors tend to back only those candidates who appear to have a good chance of winning the nomination.

PUBLIC FINANCING is available for primary campaigns, but only if the candidate raises $5,000 in matchable contributions in each of twenty states. PAC contributions are not matchable.

After the initial flurry of primaries, the goal of the remaining candidates is to attract media attention by winning or performing better than expected in the rest of the contests. Candidates who do not perform as well as expected typically withdraw. The number of delegates at stake, particularly in states that award delegates on the basis of PROPORTIONAL REPRESENTATION, begins to be important. All Democratic primaries use proportional representation. Republican primaries in some states award delegates by WINNER TAKE ALL.

When most of the primaries have been held, attention begins to turn to the questions of which candidate leads in the delegate race and how many delegates are needed for a first-ballot convention victory. A candidate who enjoys a delegate lead late in the race usually focuses more on accumulating as many delegates as possible in the remaining primaries and caucuses than on actually winning the contests. Candidates also woo the delegates who were once allied to candidates who have dropped out as well as those delegates, including elected officials, who have not yet announced a preference.

## The Presidential Nomination

The primary season culminates in the two national party conventions, usually held in late July or August. At these conventions, attended by thousands of delegates and even more guests and reporters, the presidential and vice-presidential nominees are formally selected and a party PLATFORM, setting out the party's goals for the next four years, is approved. In recent elections, the convention also has become an important occasion for showcasing party unity after the sometimes divisive primary battles.

The first national convention was held in 1831, and for more than a century afterward state party leaders had the ultimate say in deciding who the presidential nominee would be. As direct primaries took hold in the twentieth century, this influence began to wane. Then in the 1970s and 1980s, the Democrats initiated a series of PRESIDENTIAL SELECTION REFORMS that opened the nominating process. The reforms were expected to re-

sult in more open conventions, but instead they led to even more primaries.

Victory in the primaries, however, does not mean the primary leader faces no opposition at the convention. Other candidates may stay in the race because they hope to benefit if the leader falters, or they may use the bloc of delegates committed to them to bargain for specific planks in the platform or to influence the selection of the vice-presidential nominee.

Before the widespread use of primaries, the conventions were more competitive and frenetic than they are today. All the candidates still in the race had substantial campaign operations at the conventions. Campaign managers and strategists kept in close contact with state delegations. Candidates deployed floor leaders and "whips" to direct voting on the convention floor and to deal with any problems that arose among state delegations. In addition, "floaters" wandered the crowded floor in search of any signs of trouble. Floor leaders, whips, and floaters often wore specially colored clothing or caps so that they could be spotted easily on the convention floor.

This spectacle, however, has become a rarity at the conventions. It has been decades since either major party took more than one ballot to nominate a president. But in 1996 REFORM PARTY founder Ross Perot faced opposition from former Colorado governor Richard D. Lamm. In a two-step procedure the party nominated Perot at the second of two conventions.

Nominating speeches mark the beginning of the formal selection process. These remarks are usually followed by a series of short seconding speeches, and all of the speeches are accompanied by floor demonstrations staged by delegates supporting the candidate. For many years a good deal of convention time was taken up by the nomination of FAVORITE SONS, candidates nominated by their own state's delegation. Such nominations were seldom taken seriously, and since 1972 both parties have instituted rules that have effectively stopped them.

In recent years, the balloting for the presidential nominee has been anticlimactic. More attention focuses on whom the presidential nominee will select as a running mate. Even then, much of the suspense has been removed because the leading presidential candidates may have named their running mates before the convention begins.

With the young, politically moderate, all-southern ticket of Clinton and Al Gore in 1992 an obvious exception, the choice of the vice-presidential candidate often has been motivated by an effort to balance the ticket geographically. For years, a balanced ticket was one that boasted an easterner and a midwesterner. More recently, the balance has shifted so that the split is more often between a northerner and a southerner. Some examples: Democrats John F. Kennedy of Massachusetts and Lyndon B. Johnson of Texas in 1960, Johnson and Hubert H. Humphrey of Minnesota in 1964, Jimmy Carter of Georgia and Walter F. Mondale of Minnesota in 1976; and Republicans Barry Goldwater of Arizona and William Miller of New York in 1964.

IDEOLOGY also plays a part in the balance. A liberal presidential candidate may be paired with a more conservative running mate to attract a broader base of votes. Or the choice of the vice-presidential candidate may be used to appease party factions who are unhappy with the presidential candidate. Further, governors generally choose running mates with Washington credentials, such as senators. With the increasing number of vice presidents who go on to be president, more attention is given to the abilities of the person who is chosen, and more prominent figures are willing to accept the nomination.

The method for nominating the vice-presidential candidate mirrors the procedure for presidential nominations. The climax of the convention then occurs with the two nominees' acceptance speeches and their first appearance together, with their families, on the podium.

## General Election Campaign

The traditional opening of the presidential election campaign is Labor Day, just two months before the general election on the first Tuesday after the first Monday in November. In recent years, however, candidates have been unwilling to wait until Labor Day to capitalize on their POSTCONVENTION BOUNCE in the polls. After the 1992 Democratic convention, for example, Clinton and Gore and their wives boarded buses for campaign swings through Pennsylvania and other must-win states. Their opponent, President George Bush, went from the GOP convention to Florida, which was recovering from the devastation of Hurricane Andrew. Bush won Florida's twenty-five electoral votes.

The campaign organization for the general election is usually an extension of the nomination organization, and it is separate from the national and state party organizations. Nominees normally have the prerogative of naming their party's national committee chair to help coordinate the campaign.

The national campaign committee, usually based in Washington, D.C., receives its funding from the FEDERAL ELECTION COMMISSION (FEC). In exchange for federal funding, the campaign must agree not to spend more than it receives from the FEC. Since 1975, when federal funding of elections began, all major party nominees have chosen to accept the government funds rather than raise their own money. In 1996 the Clinton and Dole campaigns each received $61.8 million from the FEC. Neither party, however, lived within that income. Both raised millions of dollars in unlimited SOFT MONEY for party activities that indirectly supported the nominees' campaigns.

An INCUMBENT president running for reelection has inherent advantages that may tilt the balance in his favor. The incumbent already has the stature of the presidency and is able to influence MEDIA COVERAGE with official presidential actions and to use pork-barrel politics to appeal to specific constituencies. The president also benefits from the public's reluctance to reject a tested national leader for an unknown quantity.

In times of economic or foreign policy difficulties, however, the president's prominence can have negative effects on the campaign. Jimmy Carter's bid for a second term was plagued by both a sagging economy and the continued holding of U.S. citizens as hostages in Iran. In 1992, after achieving record-high approval ratings for success in the Gulf War, George Bush saw his reelection hopes dashed by an economic recession, which he was slow to acknowledge, and the Democrats' emphasis on "it's the economy, stupid."

Postconvention strategies shift according to circumstances, but one element that usually remains intact is the decision about where to campaign. The winner-take-all ELECTORAL COLLEGE system, in which the leading vote-getter in a state wins all that state's electoral votes, encourages nominees to win as many populous states as possible rather than to build up strength in states where they are weak. Nominees generally spend most of their time in closely contested states, and just enough time in "likely win" states to ensure victory. Appearances in unfavorable states are usually symbolic efforts to show that the candidate is not conceding anything.

Competing in all regions of the country can be difficult. Richard Nixon in 1960 fulfilled his vow to make at least one campaign appearance in every state but lost the election. If he had spent less time in states that heavily favored Kennedy and more time in close states such as Illinois and Missouri, he might have won. In 1984 Democrat Walter F. Mondale and his running mate, Geraldine Ferraro, missed the opportunity to increase their support in northeastern states when they campaigned in the solidly Republican South and West.

The ideological tone of the presidential campaign usually moderates once the parties have determined their nominees. To win the nomination, Democrats must appeal to the more liberal sections of their party; Republicans, to the more conservative sections of theirs. But during the general election campaign, the nominees must try not only to unify their parties but also to attract independents and voters from the other party. The candidates usually can depend on the support of the most ideological members of their own party, so they are able to shift their sights in the fall.

The exceptions come when a third-party candidate appeals to the conservative or liberal elements of one or both parties or when a major party nominee has suffered a bruising nomination battle and must persuade the backers of the defeated candidates to go to the polls. (See THIRD PARTIES.)

Whether to highlight specific issue stances or adopt a "fuzzy" ideological stance is a major question in every campaign. Campaign consultants often advise against being too specific. Mondale's attempt to be frank in 1984 by saying that taxes would have to be raised whether he or President Reagan were elected shows both the opportunity and the risk of adopting a specific position. For a while, the statement put Reagan, who presided over historic budget deficits, on the defensive. But Mondale's strategy backfired when Reagan regained the offensive and charged Democrats with fiscal and taxing irresponsibility.

Campaign debates between the presidential and the vice-presidential candidates have been a mainstay of the fall election campaign since 1976. Although political pundits are quick to declare a winner at the end of each debate, most debates have not fundamentally changed the voters' perceptions of the candidates.

All of the campaign hoopla culminates on election day, when Americans go to the polls. In recent years about 100 million Americans have voted for president, about half the number eligible to register.

Although ballots are tallied electronically in most parts of the United States, the major television networks have developed ways to make their own counts of the election in all states and report the results as soon as they come in. In 1980 the three broadcast networks declared Ronald Reagan the winner before the polls had closed on the West Coast. President Carter then publicly conceded defeat. This spurred complaints that the premature announcement discouraged westerners from voting and may have affected the races for members of Congress and state and local officials. Since then, the networks have refrained from announcing a winner until all the polls have closed.

## Electoral College

Even though the winner has declared victory and the loser conceded defeat, at least two more steps must be taken before a president-elect is officially declared. The first occurs on the first Monday after the second Wednesday in December. On that day electors meet in their respective state capitals to cast their votes for president.

Each state has as many electors as it has members of Congress. Typically, slates of electors are pledged before the popular election to each of the presidential nominees. The presidential nominee who wins the state wins that state's electors. However, there have been several instances in which "faithless electors" did not vote for their party's nominee.

The second step occurs when the electors' ballots are opened and counted before a joint session of Congress in early January. The candidate who wins a majority of the vote is declared the president-elect and is inaugurated three weeks later on January 20.

In the rare event that no presidential candidate receives a majority of the electoral college vote, the election is thrown into the House of Representatives. If no vice-presidential candidate receives a majority of the electoral college vote, the Senate is called upon to make the selection.

## Term of Office

A president's term begins with inauguration at noon on January 20 following the November election. Until the Twentieth Amendment was ratified in 1933, presidents were not inaugurated until March 4, leaving a four-month hiatus between the election and the inauguration. The briefer interval established by the so-called lame-duck amendment shortened the period in which the nation had, in effect, two presidents—the outgoing president and an incoming president-elect. Yet the amendment allowed time for an orderly transition between the old and the new administrations.

The Twentieth Amendment took effect in 1933 after President Franklin Roosevelt and Vice President John Nance Garner had been sworn in. In 1937, at the beginning of their second terms, they became the first president and vice president inaugurated on January 20.

Whether by tradition, TERM LIMITS, or voter action, turnover of administrations is characteristic of the U.S. presidential election system. Of the forty-one men who have been president—George Washington through Bill Clinton—only eighteen have served more than four years. Of those, only Franklin Roosevelt served more than two full terms, for a total of slightly more than twelve years. As of early 1997 twelve presidents served one full term, ten served less than a full term, ten served

two full terms, and eight (including Clinton at this writing) served for more than four years but less than eight years.

Clinton is the forty-second president because one man, Grover Cleveland, is counted twice. Cleveland is the only president who served two nonconsecutive terms.

The Constitution as originally written in 1787 contained no limit on reelection of presidents. George Washington stepped down from the presidency voluntarily after two terms, saying in his farewell address that he had done so not as a matter of principle but because he longed for "the shade of retirement."

Thomas Jefferson was the first president to argue that no president should serve more than two terms. "If some termination to the services of the Chief Magistrate be not fixed by the Constitution, or supplied by practice, his office . . . will in fact become for life, and history shows how easily that degenerates into an inheritance," Jefferson wrote to the Vermont state legislature in 1807, declining its request that he run for a third term.

Jefferson's defense of a two-term limit took root quickly. Indeed, the WHIG PARTY and many Democrats soon argued for a one-term limit. Andrew Jackson was the last president until Abraham Lincoln to be elected to two terms, and even Jackson said he would prefer a constitutional amendment barring more than one six-year presidential term.

Of the first thirty presidents—Washington to Herbert Hoover—twenty served one term or less, and the issue of a third term arose only occasionally. Ulysses S. Grant in 1876 and Woodrow Wilson in 1920 probably would have liked to serve another four years, but both were too unpopular at the end of their second terms even to be renominated by their political parties.

Theodore Roosevelt's situation was more complicated. He had succeeded to the presidency upon the assassination of William L. McKinley, serving all but six months of McKinley's term. In 1904 he won the presidential election in his own right. But in 1908 he declined certain renomination and almost certain reelection, calling the two-term limit a "wise custom." His objection, however, was to a third *consecutive* term, not a third term as such. In 1912 Roosevelt ran for president again, first as a Republican, then as a third-party candidate. He was unsuccessful.

As early as 1937 TR's distant cousin Franklin Roosevelt announced that he did not plan to seek a third term in 1940. But as his second term wore on, he became increasingly frustrated by congressional resistance to his policies and programs. In 1939 World War II broke out in Europe, and there was little hope that the United States would be able to remain aloof from the fray. Waiting until the Democratic convention in July 1940, Roosevelt finally signaled his willingness to be renominated. The delegates overwhelmingly approved.

Polls showed that the public was deeply divided over the propriety of Roosevelt's candidacy. Republicans took up the CAMPAIGN SLOGAN "no third term" in behalf of their nominee, Wendell L. Willkie. Roosevelt won the election, but his POPULAR VOTE margin was 5 million, compared with 11 million in 1936.

In 1944, with the United States and its allies nearing victory in the war, Roosevelt won his fourth term, this time by 3 million votes. He was ill at the time and died less than three months after the inauguration.

## President: Qualifications

To be the president or VICE PRESIDENT of the United States, a person must meet only the few qualifications set forth in the Constitution. The occupant of either office must be at least thirty-five years old, a native-born U.S. citizen, and have lived in the United States for fourteen years.

As a practical matter, however, the constitutional qualifications in Article II, section 1, have proven to be the least of what it takes to be elected to the nation's highest offices. The voters are the ultimate judges, and they typically measure presidential candidates and RUNNING MATES by their political skills, speaking ability, moral character, leadership qualities, physical appearance, and other yardsticks not found in any law or constitutional provision.

At first the framers of the Constitution did not think

it necessary to spell out qualifications for the presidency. They assumed that Congress would select the president, and that anyone it chose would at least meet the minimal age, citizenship, and residency requirements for service in the House of Representatives or the Senate.

But as the delegates settled on the idea of having an ELECTORAL COLLEGE elect the president and vice president, the need to specify the qualifications became apparent. The states would choose the electors and there was no guarantee that so diverse a group would be mindful of the basic standards that the delegates thought the electors should apply. Accordingly, the Constitutional Convention's Committee on Postponed Matters proposed the presidential qualifications, and the convention unanimously approved them on September 7, 1787. The qualifications specified were basically like those for representatives and senators, but with a higher minimum age and longer residency in the United States. (See HOUSE OF REPRESENTATIVES, QUALIFICATIONS; SENATE, QUALIFICATIONS.)

The framers had a reason for each of the presidential qualifications. Age was thought to ensure maturity and a record of personal and political accomplishment on which the electors could base their evaluations of the presidential candidates.

The fourteen-year residency requirement excluded British sympathizers who had fled to the country during the Revolution. And the exclusion of persons who were not born in America or were not citizens when the Constitution was adopted ensured that there would be no move to invite a foreign monarch to accept the presidency as some feared might happen.

No separate qualifications for the vice presidency were listed in the original Constitution. Under the convention's system of selection, the vice president would be the candidate with the second-highest number of votes in the electoral college. The delegates assumed, therefore, that the vice president would meet the specifications to be president.

The original system proved unworkable, however, and the Twelfth Amendment (1804) established the current practice of separate electoral voting for president and vice president. The amendment also specified that the vice president have the same qualifications as the chief executive.

For the most part, the age, citizenship, and residency requirements for the presidency have not seriously limited the voters' choices of qualified candidates. Few persons are likely to have the stature and political support needed for a credible run for the White House before they are in their mid-thirties. Of the three restrictions, native-born citizenship is one that may have precluded the candidacy of otherwise highly qualified persons. For example, former secretary of state Henry A. Kissinger, who was born in Germany, was frequently mentioned as a U.S. citizen whose foreign birth ruled out a potentially strong candidacy. There was never any indication, however, that Kissinger would have run if he could.

All of the early presidents were born as British subjects in the colonial period, but they qualified for the office because they were U.S. citizens in 1788 when the Constitution was ratified. Martin Van Buren, born in 1782, was the first president born after the United States declared its independence from Britain in 1776.

## Age Factor

Most presidents have been considerably older than the thirty-five minimum age, but two have taken office in their early forties. Theodore Roosevelt was the youngest, forty-three when he succeeded the assassinated William F. McKinley. John F. Kennedy was the youngest when elected—forty-three in 1960.

Ronald Reagan was the oldest president—sixty-nine when he was sworn in and seventy-seven when he left office in 1989. The next oldest, Dwight D. Eisenhower, was seventy when he was succeeded in 1961 by the much younger Kennedy. Had Robert J. Dole been elected in 1996, he would have exceeded Reagan's record. He was seventy-three when he won the Republican nomination for president.

Bill Clinton was the first president born in the "baby boom" era, after World War II.

## Geography

The Constitution as amended does impose somewhat of a geographic restriction on the president. The

*John F. Kennedy, the youngest man and the only non-Protestant to be elected president, shared a number of characteristics with other modern presidents: legal training, well-honed political skills, and service in the military and Congress. Source: Library of Congress*

Twelfth Amendment requires the electors to "vote by ballot for President and Vice-President, one of whom, at least, shall not be an inhabitant of the same state with themselves." This language, similar to the wording it replaced, has the effect of preventing the election of a president and vice president from the same state.

Almost all of the forty-one men who have served as president have been elected from the Northeast (fifteen), the Midwest (eleven), and the South (thirteen). Several were born elsewhere but were residing in those regions when elected. They include the only two presidents from the West (California), Herbert Hoover and Ronald Reagan. Hoover was born in Iowa, Reagan in

Illinois. Richard Nixon, the only president born in California, was elected from New York.

By birthplace, Virginia leads as the home of presidents (eight), followed closely by Ohio (seven). Of the twelve presidents since Hoover, seven were born west of the Mississippi River.

## Backgrounds

In theory, anyone who meets the constitutional criteria can become president, and in fact several did rise from humble beginnings to attain the highest office. But as a practical matter a person who becomes president must have demonstrated leadership qualities and political skills—not the least of which is the ability to win enough primaries and caucuses nationally to lock up the nomination of a major political party.

All presidents have been white males, and with one exception (the Catholic Kennedy) all have been Protestant. Most have been lawyers, generally from a large industrial state. Military or public service has been the usual path to the White House. Nineteen presidents were governors of states or territories. Twenty-four presidents served in either or both chambers of Congress. Fourteen were vice presidents and attained the presidency through death of the predecessor or election in their own right.

The only president to serve more than two terms was Franklin D. Roosevelt. He was elected to a fourth four-year term but died in office after being president for twelve years, thirty-nine days.

The Twenty-second Amendment, ratified in 1951, limited future presidents to two terms, consecutive or nonconsecutive. The amendment exempted Harry S. Truman, elected in 1948 after serving out the remainder of FDR's term, but Truman declined to seek a second full term in 1952.

Although George Washington began the two-term tradition, Thomas Jefferson formalized it in 1807 with a letter explaining his rejection of a third term. Reflecting his view that the original Constitution should have had a term limit, Jefferson wrote that if the omission is not fixed by amendment or practice the office of presidency "will, in fact, become for life, and history shows how easily that degenerates into an inheritance."

In addition to the constitutional qualifications, presidents must meet a number of unwritten, informal requirements. Americans demand that their chief executive meet standards of political and managerial expertise as well as moral and social standing. Sometimes, however, the voters are willing to soften those demands if the candidate has compensating appeal. Voters regularly list foreign policy expertise as an important consideration, yet the only international experience several recent presidents have had was their efforts as governors to attract foreign trade to their states.

Divorce formerly was an unwritten bar to the presidency, but Ronald Reagan broke that barrier with his 1980 election. He was divorced and remarried at the time.

Failure to meet moral standards has been troublesome for recent would-be presidents. In 1987 former senator Gary Hart's front-runner status collapsed within a week after the appearance of newspaper reports alleging that he had committed adultery. Soon after, media reports that Sen. Joseph R. Biden Jr. of Delaware had plagiarized a law school paper and parts of campaign speeches led to his early exit from the campaign. But Bill Clinton overcame questions about his character to win the presidency in 1992 and reelection in 1996. (See SCANDALS.)

## Oath of Office

Besides citizenship, age, and residency, the same section of the Constitution (Article II, section 1) sets one other requirement for the president. He or she must take an oath of office, pledging to uphold the law. The section reads:

Before he enter on the Execution of his Office, he shall take the following Oath or Affirmation—"I do solemnly swear (or affirm) that I will faithfully execute the Office of President of the United States, and will do the best of my Ability, preserve, protect and defend the Constitution of the United States."

George Washington added "so help me God" after reciting the oath, and all other presidents have done the same.

Only Franklin Pierce in 1853 chose to affirm the oath rather than swear it. Believing that it was God's punishment that he and his wife survived a recent train wreck that took their eleven-year-old son, Pierce declined to place his hand on a Bible.

## Presidential Draft

Genuine drafts of unwilling presidential nominees are rare. They are rarer still—even nonexistent—in the era of hard-fought, expensive PRESIDENTIAL PRIMAR- IES that eliminate any candidate who is the least bit equivocal about wanting the nomination.

Before primaries replaced NATIONAL PARTY CON- VENTIONS as the place where nominations are really won, presidential drafts were difficult but not impossi- ble. In several instances, deadlocked conventions turned to alternative candidates. Most of these, however, were not considered genuine drafts. In 1880, for example, the Republicans nominated James A. Garfield on the thirty- sixth ballot after the convention deadlocked over other candidates, including former president Ulysses S. Grant. Garfield's protests against being considered, after re- maining silent earlier, only served to attract the delegate votes he needed to win.

Often cited as the first bona fide draft is that of New York governor Horatio Seymour, chosen by the Dem- ocrats in 1868 after protracted balloting. Despite his having made clear earlier that he did not want the nom- ination, the tide turned toward Seymour on the twenty- second ballot. He rushed to the platform shouting, "Your candidate I cannot be!" Hustled off to a private club, Seymour responded to his nomination with tears streaming down his cheeks saying, "Pity me! Pity me!"

Since then there have been two other drafts of balky candidates: the Republicans' selection of Supreme Court justice Charles Evans Hughes in 1916 and the Democrats' selection of Illinois governor Adlai E. Stevenson in 1952.

Stevenson's reluctant acceptance brought to mind Seymour's plea for consolation. Quoting Jesus, Steven- son said he asked the Almighty Father "to let this cup pass from me. . . . So, if this cup may not pass from me except I drink it, Thy will be done."

The most famous statement of presidential non-

*New York governor Horatio Seymour.* Source: *Library of Congress*

availability, however, came from Civil War general William Tecumseh Sherman, who wired the GOP con- vention in 1884: "I will not accept if nominated, and will not serve if elected." The passage of time has since amended Sherman's words to the cryptic: "If nominated I will not accept; if elected I will not serve."

## Presidential Primaries

Woodrow Wilson, the first president elected in the era of presidential primaries, foresaw their potential to replace the NATIONAL PARTY CONVENTIONS and give voters a more direct role in choosing candidates for the

*Although Woodrow Wilson favored the primary system, he owed his election in 1912 to the nominating convention, where he outmaneuvered many other candidates.* Source: Library of Congress

nation's highest office. Elected in 1912, the first year that a substantial number of states (thirteen) held primaries, Wilson promptly asked Congress to establish a system "of primary elections throughout the country at which the voters of several parties may choose their nominees for the presidency without the intervention of nominating conventions." Wilson proposed keeping the conventions as a means to declare the results of the primaries and adopt the parties' PLATFORMS.

Although Congress never enacted a national primary law, the U.S. political system in effect adopted Wilson's idea. Most states in 1996 held presidential primaries, and the conventions had become places where platforms are formulated and nominations are formalized. Every major party nominee since 1976 has gone to the convention with the nomination in his pocket, having won at least a plurality in the party's primaries.

Wilson himself owed his election in part to the inequities of the old nominating convention system. Then the governor of New Jersey, he had entered primaries in twelve states and won only five of them. Nevertheless, he won the Democratic nomination for president on the forty-sixth ballot. On the Republican side in the same election, former president Theodore Roosevelt won nine of twelve primaries but lost the nomination to President William Howard Taft in a bruising convention fight. Roosevelt then formed his own PROGRESSIVE (BULL MOOSE) Party to challenge both Taft and Wilson. The GOP split helped to ensure Wilson's election.

The Progressive fervor had spurred the spread of primaries, which originated with a Florida law in 1901. But after Wilson's election that spirit began to die out. Not until after World War II, when widespread pressures for change touched both parties but especially the Democratic, was there a rapid growth in presidential primaries.

That growth was steady, except for a brief period in the 1980s when some states reverted to the CAUCUS method of DELEGATE selection. In the 1992 and 1996 elections, primary states far outnumbered caucus states.

## Impact of Progressives

In the early twentieth century, Progressives, populists, and reformers in general objected to the links between political bosses and big business. They advocated returning the government to the people.

Part of this "return to the people" was a turn away from boss-dominated conventions. It was only a matter of time before the primary idea spread from state and local elections to presidential contests. Because there was no provision for a nationwide primary, state primaries were initiated to choose delegates to the national party conventions (delegate-selection primaries) and to register voters' preferences on their parties' eventual presidential nominees (preference primaries). (See PRIMARY TYPES.)

Florida's 1901 primary gave party officials an option of holding a party primary to choose any party candidate for public office, as well as delegates to the national conventions. There was no provision, however, for placing names of presidential candidates on the ballot—either in the form of a preference vote or with information indicating the preference of the candidates for convention delegates.

Wisconsin's Progressive Republican politician, Gov. Robert M. La Follette, gave a major boost to the presidential primary following the 1904 Republican National Convention. There the credentials of La Follette's Progressive delegation had been rejected and a regular Republican delegation from Wisconsin seated. Angered, La Follette returned to his home state and began pushing for a presidential primary law. The result was a 1905 Wisconsin law mandating the DIRECT ELECTION of national convention delegates, but making no provision for indicating the delegates' presidential preference.

In 1906 Pennsylvania followed Wisconsin with a statute providing that candidates for delegate could have their names printed on the official ballot beside the name of the presidential candidate the delegate would support at the national convention. However, no member of either party exercised this option in the 1908 primary.

The next step in presidential primaries—the preferential vote for president—took place in Oregon. In 1910, Sen. Jonathan Bourne, a Progressive Republican colleague of La Follette (by then a U.S. senator), sponsored a referendum to establish a presidential preference primary, with delegates legally bound to support the winner of the preference primary. By 1912, with Oregon in the lead, twelve states had enacted presidential primary laws that provided for either direct election of delegates, a preferential vote, or both. The number had expanded to twenty-six states by 1916.

## Primaries and Conventions

As the 1912 election showed, victories in the presidential primaries did not ensure a candidate's nomination. One of former president Theodore Roosevelt's nine victories included a defeat of President Taft in Ohio, Taft's home state. Roosevelt lost to Taft by a nar-

*Bob Dole and his wife, Elizabeth, celebrate his sweep of the seven Republican primaries of March 12, 1996. Source: Rick Wilking, Reuters*

row margin in Massachusetts and to La Follette in North Dakota and Wisconsin. Despite this impressive string of primary victories, the convention rejected Roosevelt in favor of Taft.

Taft supporters dominated the REPUBLICAN NATIONAL COMMITTEE, which ran the convention, and the convention's credentials committee, which ruled on contested delegates. Moreover, Taft was backed by many state organizations, especially in the South, where most delegates were chosen by caucuses or conventions dominated by party leaders.

On the Democratic side, the convention more closely reflected the results of the primaries. Governor Wilson of New Jersey and House Speaker Champ Clark of Missouri were closely matched in total primary votes, with Wilson only 29,632 votes ahead of Clark. Wilson emerged with the nomination after a long struggle with Clark at the convention.

Likewise, in 1916 Democratic primary results foreshadowed the winner of the nomination, although Wilson, the incumbent, had no major opposition for renomination. But once again Republican presidential primaries had little impact upon the nominating process at the convention. The eventual nominee, Supreme Court justice Charles Evans Hughes, had won only two primaries.

In 1920 presidential primaries did not play a major role in determining the winner of either party's nomination. Democrat James M. Cox, the eventual nominee, ran in only one primary, his home state of Ohio. Most of the Democratic primaries featured FAVORITE-SON candidates or write-in votes. And at the convention Democrats took forty-four ballots to make their choice.

Similarly, the main entrants in the Republican presidential primaries that year failed to capture their party's nomination. Sen. Warren G. Harding of Ohio, the compromise choice, won the primary in his home state but lost badly in Indiana and garnered only a handful of votes elsewhere. The three primary leaders—Sen. Hiram Johnson of California, Gen. Leonard Wood of New Hampshire, and Gov. Frank O. Lowden of Illinois—lost out in the end.

After the first wave of enthusiasm for presidential primaries in the early years of the century, interest waned. By 1935, eight states had repealed their presidential primary laws. The diminution of reform zeal during the 1920s and the preoccupation of the country with the Great Depression in the 1930s and war in the 1940s appeared to have been leading factors in the decline. Also, party leaders were ambivalent about primaries; the cost of conducting them was relatively high, both for the candidates and the states. Many presidential candidates ignored the primaries, and voter participation often was low.

But after World War II interest picked up again. Some politicians with presidential ambitions, knowing the party leadership was lukewarm about their candidacies, entered the primaries to try to generate a BANDWAGON effect.

In 1948 Harold Stassen, Republican governor of Minnesota from 1939 to 1943, entered presidential primaries in opposition to the Republican organization and made some headway before losing in Oregon to Gov. Thomas E. Dewey of New York. And in 1952 Tennessee senator Estes Kefauver, riding a wave of public recognition as head of the Senate Organized Crime Investigating Committee, challenged Democratic Party leaders by winning several primaries, including an upset of President Harry S. Truman in New Hampshire. The Eisenhower-Taft struggle for the Republican Party nomination that year also stimulated interest in the primaries.

With the growing demand for political reform in the 1960s and early 1970s, the presidential primaries became more attractive as a path to the nomination. John F. Kennedy, then a relatively obscure U.S. senator from Massachusetts, helped to popularize that route with his successful uphill fight for the Democratic nomination in 1960. Kennedy used the primaries to prove to party leaders that he, a Roman Catholic, could be elected. An unbroken string of Kennedy victories persuaded his chief rival in the primaries, Sen. Hubert H. Humphrey of Minnesota, to withdraw.

Republicans Barry M. Goldwater of Arizona in 1964 and former vice president Richard Nixon in 1968 and Democrat George S. McGovern of South Dakota in

1972—all party presidential nominees—were able to use the primaries to show their vote-getting and organizational abilities. Having failed to win the presidency in 1960 and the California governorship in 1962, Nixon needed a strong primary showing to overcome his "loser" image among GOP leaders. McGovern, too liberal for the Democratic establishment, won the nomination through the primaries.

## Democratic Rules Changes

Despite the Progressive reforms, party leaders until 1968 remained in firm control of the nominating process. With only a handful of the fifteen to twenty primaries regularly contested, candidates could count on a short primary season. They began with the NEW HAMPSHIRE PRIMARY in March, then tested their appeal during the spring in Wisconsin, Nebraska, Oregon, and California before resuming their courtship of party leaders.

But in 1968 the Democrats began tinkering with the nominating rules, resulting in presidential nominating campaigns that were predictable only in their unpredictability. The reforms were launched in an effort to reduce the alienation of liberals and minorities from the Democratic nominating system and to allow the people to choose their own leaders. The Republicans seldom made any changes in their rules. (See PRESIDENTIAL SELECTION REFORMS.)

The Democrats' era of grassroots control produced presidential candidates such as Senator McGovern, a liberal from South Dakota who lost in a LANDSLIDE to Nixon in 1972, and former Georgia governor Jimmy Carter, who beat incumbent president Gerald R. Ford in 1976.

With a then-record high of thirty-seven primaries held in 1980, the opportunity for mass participation in the nominating process was greater than ever before. President Carter and former California governor Ronald Reagan, the Republican nominee, were the clear winners of the long primary season. Carter amassed a plurality of nearly 2.7 million votes over his major rival, Sen. Edward M. Kennedy of Massachusetts. With no opposition in the late primary contests, Reagan emerged as a more one-sided choice of GOP primary voters. He

finished nearly 4.6 million votes ahead of George Bush, who eventually withdrew.

Disheartened by Carter's massive loss to Reagan in 1980, the Democrats revised their nominating rules for the 1984 election. The party created the so-called SUPERDELEGATES; that is, delegate seats were reserved for party leaders who were not formally committed to any presidential candidate. This reform had two main goals. First, Democratic leaders wanted to ensure that the party's elected and appointed officials would participate at the convention. Second, they wanted to ensure that these uncommitted party leaders could play a major role in selecting the presidential nominee if no candidate was a clear FRONT-RUNNER.

While the reforms of the 1970s had been designed to give more influence to grass-roots activists and less to party regulars, the 1980s revisions were intended to bring about a deliberative process in which experienced party leaders could help select a consensus Democratic nominee with a strong chance to win the presidency and then govern effectively.

The Democrats' new rules had some expected, as well as unexpected, results. For the first time since 1968, the number of primaries declined and the number of caucuses increased. The Democrats held only twenty-five primaries in 1984. Yet, like McGovern in 1972 and Carter in 1976, Colorado senator Gary Hart used the primaries to pull ahead (temporarily) of former vice president Walter F. Mondale, an early front-runner whose strongest ties were to the party leadership and its traditional core elements. In 1984 the presence of superdelegates was important because about four out of five backed Mondale.

Some critics regarded the seating of superdelegates as undemocratic, and there were calls for reducing their numbers. Instead, by adding seventy-five superdelegate seats, the DEMOCRATIC NATIONAL COMMITTEE (DNC) increased their numbers from 14 percent of the delegates in 1984 to 15 percent for 1988. Moreover, another 150 new superdelegate seats were set aside for party leaders. All members of the DNC are guaranteed superdelegate seats, as are all Democratic governors, and about 80 percent of the Democrats in Congress.

Still more seats were added to the various superdelegate categories in 1992, bringing the total to 772 or 18 percent of the 4,288 delegates to the Democratic convention in New York City. Having won 51.8 percent of the Democratic primary vote, Arkansas governor Bill Clinton went to the convention with the nomination virtually ensured. He was nominated by acclamation after receiving 3,372 votes on the first ballot. In 1996 the Democrats' superdelegate total dropped slightly to 769. (See DELEGATES.)

The Republican Party does not guarantee delegate seats to its leaders, nor has the party created superdelegates. Its rules, however, permit less rigid pledging of delegates and generally have led to substantial participation by Republican leaders, despite the absence of such guarantees.

## Regional Primaries and Super Tuesday

Problems of presidential primaries included the length of the primary season (nearly twice as long as the general election campaign), the expense, the physical strain on the candidates, and the variations and complexities of state laws. Several states in 1974 and 1975 discussed the feasibility of creating regional primaries, to reduce the candidates' expense and strain of travel and permit their concentration on regional issues. The idea achieved some limited success in 1976 when states in the West and South decided to organize regional primaries. Both groups, however, chose May 25 to hold their primaries, which defeated one of the main purposes of the plan by forcing candidates to shuttle across the country to cover both areas. The western states participating were Idaho, Nevada, and Oregon; the southern states were Arkansas, Kentucky, and Tennessee.

Attempts also were made in New England to construct a regional primary. But New Hampshire did not want to take part and could not because its law requires the state to hold its primary at least one week before any other state. Hesitancy by the other New England state legislatures defeated the idea.

In 1988 the southern states' goal of a regional primary finally was realized. Fourteen states below the Mason-Dixon line—Alabama, Arkansas, Florida, Georgia, Kentucky, Louisiana, Maryland, Mississippi, Missouri,

North Carolina, Oklahoma, Tennessee, Texas, and Virginia—held primaries on what came to be known as SUPER TUESDAY. Two northern states, Massachusetts and Rhode Island, also held their primaries that day (March 8).

The Democrats selected nearly 67 percent of their 1988 convention delegates through primaries. That figure was up from 52 percent in 1984, but nine percentage points less than the 76 percent set in 1976, the record to that time.

The Republicans chose 77 percent of their delegates via primaries, up six points from 1984. George Bush's win in New Hampshire proved to be the turning point in his campaign, and because most Republican primaries were the winner-take-all kind, Bush had the Republican nomination all but locked up after Super Tuesday. He went over the top with the Pennsylvania primary, April 26. In contrast, the Democratic candidates were awarded delegates based on the proportion of votes cast for them in each primary. Democrat Michael S. Dukakis won enough delegates by June 7 to become his party's nominee.

## "March Madness"

By 1992 Super Tuesday had become part of a general rush among states to hold their primaries as early as possible and thus help to determine the ultimate nominees. Dubbed "March Madness," the early clustering or FRONT LOADING of primaries was viewed with dismay by some political analysts. They said it could lead to nominees being locked in before most voters knew what was happening, resulting in less informed and deliberative voting in the general election.

As winners in the eight Super Tuesday primaries March 10, President Bush and Governor Clinton were already well on their way to nomination. Bush had half the delegates he needed for renomination, and Clinton with 707 delegates held a commanding lead over his nearest rival, former senator Paul Tsongas of Massachusetts. In all, roughly half the states held their primaries before the end of March 1992.

In 1996 Arizona and Nevada joined the ranks of states and other jurisdictions holding GOP primaries, where 87.9 percent of the party's convention delegates were chosen. With President Clinton unopposed for renomination, the Democrats elected 65.3 percent of their delegates in primaries and 16.8 percent in caucuses. The remaining 17.9 percent were superdelegates.

In the wide-open Republican race, front-runner Robert J. Dole lost to conservative columnist Patrick J. Buchanan in the February 20 New Hampshire primary, but through victories in subsequent primaries Dole had the GOP nomination clinched by March 26. Only thirteen primaries were held after that date.

The 1996 election saw the misnamed JUNIOR TUES-DAY week surpassing Super Tuesday in the number of participating states. Fourteen states and Puerto Rico held Republican primaries or caucuses March 2 through March 9, compared with seven primaries on Super Tuesday, March 12.

## Approaches to Reform

In an effort to alleviate March Madness and reverse the bunching of primaries in the early months of presidential election years, the 1996 Republican National Convention approved rules changes that would reward states holding later primaries, beginning in 2000. States holding primaries after March 15 would receive 10 percent more delegates, with an additional 5 percent increase for each month of delay until May 15.

Since 1911 hundreds of bills have been introduced in Congress to reform the presidential primary system. Most of them appeared after the 1912, 1952, and 1968 nominating campaigns. These three campaigns produced the feeling among many voters that the will of the electorate, as expressed in the primaries, had been thwarted by national conventions. But since 1911 the only legislation of this type enacted by Congress concerned the presidential primary in the DISTRICT OF COLUMBIA.

Various other suggestions for changing the primary system have been made. One would establish a direct national primary. But a Democratic study commission as well as several academic groups rejected the idea. The consensus was that such a process would strip the party leadership of any role in the nominating process, enable presidential candidates to run factional or regional campaigns, and increase the primacy of media "image" over serious discussion of the issues.

## Presidential Selection Reforms

The last three decades of the twentieth century witnessed many changes in the presidential nominating process, almost all of them originating with the Democratic Party. Where once average voters had little say in the choice of a president until the November election, now they help to narrow the field to the two final major party contenders and perhaps one or more THIRD PARTY nominees. The instrument by which this is done is the PRESIDENTIAL PRIMARY, and the Democratic reforms all dealt with the primary or CAUCUS election of DELEGATES to the NATIONAL PARTY CONVENTION.

While the Democrats made their delegate-selection changes by amending the rules, the Republicans and the third parties have less formally adopted many of the same reforms. In some cases the Republicans never had followed the restrictive rules that the Democrats' changes affected; or the other parties had no choice but to follow the Democrats' lead because state legislatures voted the changes into law.

Ironically, the reforms that were intended to open the nominating conventions to more women and minorities resulted in their having less to do. The changes helped to transform both parties' conventions into archaic events where preordained nominations were declared rather than fought out on the floor. And the Democrats so overcompensated in reducing the power of political bosses that they had to find a new way to give party leaders at least a face-saving role in the nominating process. They did so by creating the SUPERDELEGATE position, which guaranteed certain elected and party officials seats at the Democratic National Convention.

## Rooted in the 1960s

The Democrats' overhaul of the nominating system can be traced in part to the tumultuous political climate of 1968, when protests against the Vietnam War were reaching a peak and Martin Luther King Jr. and Robert F. Kennedy were assassinated. There were race riots in major cities, student uprisings throughout the country, and bitter confrontations between demonstrators and police.

North Vietnam's Tet offensive against South Vietnam in January 1968 brought massive U.S. casualties and provoked renewed opposition to the war. A leading opponent of the war, Sen. Eugene J. McCarthy of Minnesota, challenged President Lyndon B. Johnson in the New Hampshire primary and campaigned against his Vietnam policies. Although Johnson won by a narrow margin, McCarthy's impressive showing dealt a mortal blow to Johnson's reelection campaign. Two weeks afterward the president withdrew his candidacy.

Johnson's heir apparent, Vice President Hubert H. Humphrey, delayed his formal entry into the race to avoid primary contests with McCarthy and Robert Kennedy, who was assassinated June 5 after winning the California primary. With the backing of party regulars, Humphrey assumed correctly that he would be nominated at the Democratic National Convention. But Humphrey's nomination was won at a price. State delegations who opposed his nomination felt shut out, and they let their bitterness be known.

Before the convention, McCarthy supporters had formed the ad hoc Commission on the Democratic Selection of Presidential Nominees, chaired by Iowa governor Harold E. Hughes. The Hughes Commission report, issued just before the convention began, told of unfair representation of McCarthy during the delegate-selection process. Nearly one-third of the convention delegates already had been chosen before McCarthy announced his candidacy. In short, the Hughes Commission report concluded that the Democratic Party's delegate-selection process displayed "considerably less fidelity to basic democratic principles than a nation which claims to govern itself can safely tolerate."

Supporters of McCarthy and Sen. George S. McGovern of South Dakota won one significant reform early in the convention: rejection of the UNIT RULE, which allowed a split state delegation to cast all of its votes for the candidate favored by the delegation majority. Although Humphrey stood to gain from retention of the unit rule, he had long favored more open and democratic conventions, and his supporters helped to defeat the rule. About ten BORDER and southern states—notably Texas—were still using the unit rule in 1968. Texas governor John Connally, a Humphrey supporter, fought a vigorous losing battle to keep the rule.

## McGovern-Fraser Commission

After the 1968 convention many elements of the Democratic Party were determined to change the rules of the game. The report of the convention's Credentials Committee echoed that sentiment. The report alleged unfair and exclusionary practices in the delegate-selection process and proposed the establishment of a committee to examine the problem and offer recommendations. As a result in February 1969 the party established the Commission on Party Structure and Delegate Selection, chaired by Senator McGovern and, later, by Rep. Donald M. Fraser of Minnesota. (The commission came to be known as the McGovern-Fraser Commission.) Its report, issued a little more than a year later, set forth eighteen detailed "guidelines" for the state delegate-selection processes.

The commission's guidelines were designed to counteract rules and practices that either inhibited access to the processes or diluted the influence of those who had access. They condemned discrimination because of race, color, creed, sex, or age and required that affirmative steps be taken to give delegate representation to minorities, women, and young people in proportion to their population in each state. The guidelines further required that restrictive fees (defined as those exceeding $10) and petition requirements for delegate candidates be eliminated and they "urged" elimination of undue restrictions on voter registration (such as literacy tests, lengthy residency requirements, and untimely registration periods).

The guidelines banned the unit rule and "proxy voting" (which allowed votes to be cast for someone who was absent) at every level of the delegate-selection process; set minimum quorum provisions for party committees; and disallowed ex officio delegates (who were automatically appointed because of their public or party position). In addition, the guidelines limited the influence of party committees in the selection of delegates, required written rules for governing the process, demanded adequate public notice of all meetings pertaining to delegate selection, and called for a standardized formula for apportioning delegates among states.

Stressing that most of its guidelines were mandatory, the McGovern-Fraser Commission finished its work early. By the time the 1972 Democratic National Convention met, the commission was able to claim that virtually all the states were in at least substantial compliance with the guidelines, that only 1.1 percent of the convention delegates were still elected by state party committees, and that the percentages of black, females, and young delegates had increased three to four times over their percentages in 1968.

The guidelines' effects were considerable. On the one hand, compliance substantially democratized the system by opening avenues for citizen participation. On the other hand, it greatly reduced the power of party leaders, prompting some observers to say that the reforms had "dismantled" the party. In the process, delegate-selection systems were fundamentally altered. For example, "party caucuses" and "delegate primaries" were abolished in favor of "participatory conventions" and "candidate primaries."

In the party caucus system, low-level party officials chose delegates who in turn chose national convention delegates. In the participatory convention, selection of the intermediary delegates was not limited to party officers but was open to any party member. In the delegate-primary system, members voted for delegates to the national convention (rather than for presidential candidates, whose names did not appear on the ballot). The candidate primary required that the names of presidential candidates, instead of just the names of their potential delegates, be listed on the ballot.

The McGovern-Fraser guidelines also urged a move toward the PROPORTIONAL REPRESENTATION—or what they called "fair representation"—commonly found in European electoral systems but unusual in the United States. Under proportional representation, delegates were assigned in proportion to the percentage of the total that each candidate received. (The usual alternative was a WINNER-TAKE-ALL system, in which the candidate who won a plurality of the POPULAR VOTE received all of the delegate votes in the electoral district.) Furthermore, the guidelines were interpreted as requiring mandatory "quotas" for the representation of minority groups in proportion to their share of the population.

Although states were in substantial compliance with the guidelines by the 1972 Democratic convention, there was considerable resistance to the reforms. More than 40 percent of the convention's membership and more than half of the states challenged some aspect of the guidelines. But complete compliance was achieved because a state's delegation at the convention could not be seated unless the state had followed the guidelines.

Criticism of the reforms increased after the Democratic Party's debacle in the 1972 election. Some observers argued that the new rules contributed to George McGovern's overwhelming loss to Richard Nixon. They argued that a demographically balanced slate of delegates was not necessarily representative of the party's constituency.

## Mikulski Commission

The 1972 Democratic convention called for the establishment of another delegate-selection commission. The call was largely in response to the controversy over some of the McGovern-Fraser reforms. By the time it was actually appointed, the new Commission on Delegate Selection and Party Structure (chaired by Baltimore city councilwoman Barbara Mikulski) was facing a Democratic Party even more badly split than in 1968 between those who wanted a return to traditional procedures and those advocating further reforms. The commission responded by trying, at least rhetorically, to appease both sides.

Because the strongest reaction against the McGovern-Fraser Commission had been over quotas, the Mikulski Commission sought to placate critics by making it clear that quotas were not required, although they were permitted. (Indeed, the McGovern-Fraser Commission had not originally intended for them to be mandatory.) The Mikulski Commission dictated, however, that "affirmative action programs" be adopted to expand the participation of women and minority groups in party affairs.

As further concessions to the critics of McGovern-Fraser, the Mikulski Commission allowed party regulars to appoint up to 25 percent (instead of 10 percent) of a state's delegation; partly removed the ban on proxy voting and eased quorum requirements; extended convention privileges (not including voting rights) to public officials and party regulars (although it retained the ban on ex officio delegates); and loosened the formula for apportioning delegates within states.

Nevertheless, reform advocates won a major victory in the Mikulski Commission's decision to require proportional representation of all candidates receiving at least 10 percent of the vote (later changed to "from 10 to 15 percent," to be decided by individual state parties)—something that McGovern-Fraser had "urged" but not required. In short, the Mikulski Commission advanced, to the extent that it could, the goals of the McGovern-Fraser Commission. In loosening earlier requirements, it tried to make them more palatable to party members who objected to the reforms.

In the wake of the Democratic Party's reforms, the number of presidential primaries mushroomed. Between 1968 and 1976 they nearly doubled (increasing from seventeen to thirty). Most state party leaders felt that the adoption of a presidential primary was the easiest way to conform to the rules and thereby prevent a challenge to their delegates at the next national convention. Party regulars also feared that reformed caucuses would bring activists into wide-ranging party decision making—a consequence that they felt was worse than turning to a primary system.

Members of the McGovern-Fraser Commission had not intended for there to be such an increase in primaries. Political scientist Austin Ranney, a member of the commission, later wrote, "We hoped to prevent any such development [a national primary or more state primaries] by reforming the delegate-selection rules so

that the party's nonprimary processes would be open and fair, participation in them would greatly increase, and consequently the demand for more primaries would fade away. . . ." Instead, he said, "we achieved the opposite of what we intended."

## Winograd Commission

Whatever its cause, the proliferation of presidential primaries was disturbing to party regulars because primary elections tend to weaken the role of state political parties in selecting candidates. The result was the party's formation in 1975 of the Commission on the Role and Future of Presidential Primaries (later changed to the Commission on Presidential Nomination and Party Structure), headed by Michigan Democratic chairman Morley Winograd.

Despite its original purpose, the Winograd Commission ultimately skirted the question of primaries. With the election of Jimmy Carter in 1976, the commission was recast to reflect at least partially the interests of President Carter (which included protecting the incumbent). When it produced its final report, the commission stated that it could not reach a consensus on primaries, and it offered no recommendations in that area.

A number of the commission's recommendations seemed to favor Carter's expectations. First, the nominating season was shortened to three months, from the second Tuesday in March to the second Tuesday in June (although exemptions to go earlier were given later to several states, including Iowa and New Hampshire). This change tended to favor the incumbent president because it diminished the effect of early primaries and caucuses, which give long-shot candidates more time to gain name recognition and money.

Second, the Winograd Commission proposed that filing deadlines for a candidate to enter a primary or a caucus be at least fifty-five days before the selection of delegates. This, too, favored an incumbent by discouraging last-minute challengers. The DEMOCRATIC NATIONAL COMMITTEE (DNC) later amended the proposal and allowed deadlines to fall within a more flexible thirty- to ninety-day range, according to each state.

Third, the commission proposed that the THRESH-

OLD for a candidate to be eligible for a proportional share of delegates be based on an increasing scale of from 15 percent to 25 percent as the nominating season progressed. Although it was argued that this system would give a fair chance to long shots in the early phase of the campaign, the proposal made it extremely difficult for a candidate to wage a successful challenge to a FRONT-RUNNER or incumbent over the entire course of the season. Again, the DNC overruled the proposal and set a threshold range of from 15 to 20 percent.

Finally, the commission proposed the "bound-delegate" rule, which required that a delegate who was elected in behalf of a particular candidate be bound to vote for that candidate at the national convention. This became a major point of contention at the 1980 Democratic convention when Sen. Edward M. Kennedy of Massachusetts—hoping to upset the renomination of Carter—forced a floor fight over the rule. Kennedy's argument was that the bound-delegate rule prevented delegates from taking into account events since their selection (such as the entry of a new candidate into the field).

Other proposals of the Winograd Commission included a ban on open primaries (meaning that a registered Republican could no longer vote in a Democratic primary); a suggestion that state party committees be able to appoint an additional 10 percent of the delegates to the national convention; continued support of affirmative action programs to represent women and minorities; and a rejection of the idea that state delegations should be equally divided between men and women because such a recommendation too closely resembled quotas. The Democratic National Committee later overturned this last point in its call to the 1980 convention.

Finally, the commission eliminated so-called loophole primaries, which had served to undermine proportional representation. In such primaries, citizens voted directly for individual delegates in each district (instead of having the delegates distributed in proportion to the statewide vote tallies of the presidential candidates). Because such primaries generally produced winner-take-

all results, they were a "loophole" to the proportional representation requirement of the party rules. (See PRIMARY TYPES.)

## Hunt Commission

In June 1982 the Democratic National Committee adopted rules changes recommended by yet another party group, the Commission on Presidential Nomination, chaired by North Carolina governor James B. Hunt Jr. The Hunt Commission, as it came to be known, suggested revisions to increase the power of party regulars and give the convention more freedom to act. It was the fourth time in twelve years that the Democrats had rewritten their party rules in an attempt to repair their nominating system without repudiating earlier reforms.

One major Hunt Commission change was the creation of the new superdelegate category—party and elected officials who would go to the 1984 convention uncommitted and would cast about 14 percent of the ballots. The DNC also adopted a commission proposal to weaken the rule binding delegates to vote for their original presidential preference on the first convention ballot. The new rule allowed a presidential candidate to replace any disloyal delegate with a more faithful one.

Another significant revision relaxed proportional representation at the convention and ended the ban on the loophole primary—winner take all by district. Proportional representation of delegates was blamed by some Democrats for the protracted 1980 primary fight between President Carter and Senator Kennedy. Because candidates needed only about 20 percent of the vote in most places to qualify for a share of the delegates, Kennedy was able to remain in contention until he lost the nomination at the convention.

The Hunt Commission raised the threshold for receiving proportional representation to 20 percent in caucus states and to 25 percent in primary states, and states were allowed to give "bonus delegates" to the primary winner to better reflect that candidate's strength (the "winner-take-more" option).

In addition, the Hunt Commission repealed the bound-delegate rule that had caused controversy between Carter and Kennedy forces at the 1980 convention. This action returned delegates to the pre-Winograd Commission "good conscience" standard. Finally, the Hunt Commission retained the affirmative action rule; maintained the policy that delegations be equally divided between men and women (the "equal division" rule); continued to allow candidates to approve their delegates; and reaffirmed the Winograd Commission's shortening of the nominating season to three months. (The commission gave specific exemptions—notably to Iowa and New Hampshire—but with strict limits as to how much earlier than the other states they could be.)

## Fairness Commission

The most recent of the long series of reform efforts within the Democratic Party, the Fairness Commission, was headed by Donald L. Fowler, the party chairman in South Carolina. Its report, adopted by the DNC in March 1986, provided an opportunity for some states (such as Wisconsin and Montana) to hold open primaries. The rule, however, was tightly worded so that states that traditionally had restricted participation to Democrats could not move to open systems.

The Fairness Commission also eased the mechanism for loophole primaries, but it lowered the threshold for "fair" (proportional) representation to 15 percent. In addition, it further increased the number of delegate slots reserved for unpledged superdelegates, giving them about 16 percent of the votes.

In 1988, two years after the commission finished its work, African American civil rights activist Jesse L. Jackson won primaries in ten states plus the District of Columbia, Puerto Rico, and the Virgin Islands. At the Democratic National Convention, however, Jackson won only two states (South Carolina and Mississippi), the District of Columbia, and the Virgin Islands because of the votes of superdelegates. As a concession to Jackson, the convention's Rules Committee recommended that the number of superdelegates be reduced in the future. Instead, the Democrats added more superdelegates, raising the total to about 18 percent of the delegates to the 1992 and 1996 conventions.

After 1986 the Democratic Party continued to adjust its presidential nominating process without the equivalent of a Fairness Commission. In 1990 the DNC banned winner-reward systems, which gave extra delegates to the winner of a primary or caucus. Fifteen states had used some form of winner-reward system in 1988. The Democrats required all states in 1992 and 1996 to divide their publicly elected delegates proportionally among candidates who drew at least 15 percent of the primary or caucus vote.

## Rules Changes in the Republican Party

Although the proliferation of primaries that accompanied the Democratic Party reforms also affected the Republicans, they did not experience the same kind of internal pressures to reform. While liberal insurgents within the Democratic Party found the party's rules to be a barrier to their participation, prompting them to push for reform in 1968, the Republicans faced no such problem. To a large degree, this was because the Republicans were a smaller, more ideologically cohesive party than the Democrats. The Republicans also had far fewer minority or feminist members, which meant that there was less internal demand for equal representation.

To the extent that ideological factions did exist within the Republican Party, they did not find the rules problematic. Indeed, conservative insurgents had been quite successful in 1964. In short, a grass-roots movement promoting specific policy goals was apparently more feasible among the Republicans than among the Democrats. It was the failure of a similar "amateur" movement against party "professionals" within the Democratic ranks that helped to spawn that party's reform.

There also were differences in the structures of the two parties. Republican rules were strictly codified and could be changed only with the national convention's approval. In contrast, the Democrats' rules were loose and uncodified. Changes did not have to be approved by the national convention, making revision easy and inviting reform.

Finally, the Republicans already had achieved several reforms sought by Democrats. Use of the unit rule at the Republican national conventions had been banned since the mid-nineteenth century. A similar ban on proxy voting at the national convention had long been in force.

But clearly the Democrats' reforms went beyond the GOP's existing rules. Nevertheless, rank-and-file Republicans were not overly anxious to keep up the pace. The Democrats were more amenable to the centralization of national party control, and a number of the Democrats' farther-reaching efforts—such as quotas or strictly enforced affirmative action programs—were discouraged by the conservative ideology of the Republican Party.

Nonetheless, the Republicans did institute some reforms in the post-1968 era, often along the same lines as the Democrats. At the same time, Republicans wanted to avoid "McGovernizing" their party through what they perceived as the debilitating aspects of the Democrats' early reforms. The Republican National Convention amended its rules in 1976 so that a subcommittee of the REPUBLICAN NATIONAL COMMITTEE (RNC) would undertake all future rules review—an effort to prevent "runaway" commissions.

Finally, the Democratic Party reforms often prompted changes in state laws that also affected the Republicans. As a result, Republicans had to accommodate those changes—whatever their own rules may have been. More recently, they have tried to anticipate Democratic rules changes that would affect them.

In 1968 the Republican convention called for the establishment of a committee to consider party rules changes. All sixteen members of the Committee on Delegates and Organization (DO Committee, chaired by Rosemary Ginn of Missouri) came from the RNC. Unlike the recommendations of the McGovern-Fraser Commission, the DO Committee's recommendations were not binding. Indeed, the report contained no enforcement or compliance mechanism, which reflected the states' rights orientation of the Republican Party.

Among the DO Committee's recommendations were proposals to ban ex officio delegates, to eliminate proxy voting in meetings on delegate selection, and to "attempt" to have an equal number of men and women in each state's delegation to the national convention. The 1972 convention later approved these recommenda-

tions but rejected a DO Committee proposal that delegations try to include people under the age of twenty-five in proportion to their population in each state. Nevertheless, the convention strengthened the rule to end discrimination and increase participation. It also established a new reform committee under Rule 29 of its bylaws.

The Rule 29 Committee was chaired by Rep. William A. Steiger of Wisconsin. Its fifty-eight members included not only members of the RNC but also state party leaders, governors, members of Congress, young people, and other representatives of the Republican Party. Among its recommendations was a proposal that state parties be required to take "positive action" to broaden participation and, most important, that state action be reviewed by the RNC. Although no sanctions were attached to the review procedure, and quotas were not a part of the recommendation, the RNC objected to the proposal on the grounds that it interfered with the states' rights outlook of the party. The 1976 national convention rejected the establishment of any compliance procedures.

Since 1976 subcommittees of the RNC have undertaken all rules reviews. The first significant change resulting from such a review was approved by the 1996 Republican National Convention. Designed to reduce the FRONT LOADING of primaries in early March, the change effective in 2000 will award bonus delegates to states holding primaries between March 15 and May 15. (See DELEGATES; PRESIDENTIAL PRIMARIES.)

## Primary Types

Most states today use primary elections to narrow candidate fields and choose the party nominees who will compete in the general election for congressional, state, and local offices. They also use primaries to allow voters to participate in the presidential nominating process. The PRESIDENTIAL PRIMARIES fall into two basic categories: the *preference* primary in which voters vote directly for the person they want to see nominated for president and the *delegate-selection* primary in which the voters elect DELEGATES to the NATIONAL PARTY CONVENTIONS.

Within the two basic types, a wide and often confusing array of variations makes it difficult to categorize primaries. How they operate may differ somewhat from state to state and from party to party within the same state. Because primaries are partisan events, state legislatures and election boards conform their primary laws and ballots largely to the wishes of the major political parties. PRESIDENTIAL SELECTION REFORMS within the DEMOCRATIC PARTY have been particularly influential in shaping the U.S. primary election system.

With the available options for presidential primaries, a state may:

• Have a preference vote but choose delegates at state party conventions. The preference vote may or may not be binding on the delegates. Idaho, Montana, North Dakota, and Vermont have nonbinding preference votes for one or both parties. Votes of this type that do not affect the allocation of delegates are known as BEAUTY CONTEST primaries.

• Combine the preference and delegate-selection primaries by electing delegates pledged or favorable to a candidate named on the ballot. Under this system, however, state party organizations may run unpledged slates of delegates. Most states use this system or a variation of it.

• Have an advisory preference vote and a separate delegate-selection vote in which delegates may be listed three ways: pledged to a candidate, favorable to a candidate, or unpledged.

• Have a mandatory preference vote with a separate delegate-selection vote. In these cases, the delegates are required to reflect the preference primary vote. Colorado and Oregon use this system. For 1996, Oregon was the first state to plan a presidential primary conducted by mail. (See ABSENTEE VOTING.)

For those primaries in which the preference vote is binding, state laws may vary as to how many ballots at the national convention are binding on the affected delegates. In recent years, however, this issue has been moot. Not since the 1952 Democratic convention, when

Adlai Stevenson was nominated on the third ballot, has either party taken more than one ballot to nominate a presidential candidate.

Most primary states hold presidential preference votes, in which voters choose among the candidates who have qualified to be on the ballot. The preference vote usually is binding on the delegates, who are elected in the primary itself or chosen outside of it by a CAUCUS process, by a state committee, or by the candidates who have qualified to win delegates.

Delegates may be bound for one ballot or for as long as a candidate remains in the race. National Democratic Party rules in effect only in 1980 required delegates to be bound for one ballot unless released by the candidate they were elected to support. Before it was repealed that year, the rule enabled Sen. Edward M. Kennedy of Massachusetts to sustain until the national convention a losing primary challenge to President Jimmy Carter.

Until 1980 the REPUBLICAN PARTY required delegates bound to a specific candidate by state law to vote for that candidate at the convention regardless of their personal presidential preferences. That rule was repealed at the July 1980 GOP convention.

Delegates from primary states are allocated to candidates in various ways. Most of the methods are based on the preference vote—PROPORTIONAL REPRESENTATION, statewide WINNER TAKE ALL (in which the candidate winning the most votes statewide wins all the delegates), congressional district and statewide winner take all (in which the high vote-getter in a district wins that district's delegates and the high vote-getter statewide wins all the AT-LARGE delegates), or some combination of the three. Most primary states use proportional representation, at least for Democratic primaries because it is mandatory. Some fifteen states allocate Republican delegates on a statewide or district winner-take-all basis, or a combination of the two. They include California, Florida, Ohio, and Wisconsin.

Still another method is the selection of individual delegates in a "loophole," or DIRECT ELECTION, primary. Then the preference vote is either nonbinding or there is no preference vote at all. Among states choosing delegates this way are Illinois, New Jersey, New York, and Pennsylvania. In the proportional representation system, the qualifying threshold for candidates to win delegates can vary.

After a decade of intensive debate, Democratic leaders voted to require proportional representation in all primary and caucus states in 1980. This requirement was made optional in 1984 and 1988, with qualifying thresholds of 20 percent and 15 percent, respectively. For 1992 and 1996 the Democrats again made proportional allocation mandatory, with candidates awarded delegates if they received at least 15 percent of the vote. Along with winner-take-all systems, the Democrats also banned winner-reward systems that gave extra delegates to primary or caucus victors. In addition, the Democrats instituted a new class of unpledged SUPERDELEGATES, who go to the convention by virtue of the elective or party offices they hold.

The Republicans permit winner-take-all primaries and allow states to set their own proportional representation thresholds, which in many states were lower than what the Democrats specified. In Massachusetts, for example, a GOP candidate in 1996 had to receive only 2.703 percent of the vote to win a delegate.

In nearly half the primary states, major presidential candidates are placed on the ballot by the secretary of state or a special nominating committee. The consent of the candidate is required in only three states—Kentucky, Michigan, and North Carolina.

Elsewhere, candidates must take the initiative to get on the ballot. The filing requirements range from sending a letter of candidacy to election officials—the case in Puerto Rico—to filing petitions signed by a specified number of registered voters and paying a filing fee—the case in Alabama. On many primary ballots, voters have the opportunity to mark a line labeled "uncommitted" if they choose not to vote for any of the candidates.

Primaries may be *open, closed,* or *modified.* In an open primary, any registered voter may participate. Closed primaries are restricted to voters registered as members of the political party holding the election. In 1996 states were divided about equally between open or closed primaries. In a few states one or both parties held modified closed primaries that were open, for example,

to INDEPENDENTS or voters who expressed no party preference during VOTER REGISTRATION. About a dozen states nominate candidates in party caucuses rather than primaries.

Some states do not register voters by party affiliation and therefore have open primaries. CROSSOVER VOTING may occur in such states as voters take advantage of the opportunity to help nominate the opposing party's weakest candidates. Election officials take precautions to prevent voters from voting in both the Democratic and Republican primaries. If both parties' candidates are on the same ballot, the ballot is void if marked for both primaries.

The Supreme Court in December 1997 rejected Louisiana's unique open primary system, in which a congressional candidate is elected if he or she receives a majority of votes in the primary. By unanimous vote in *Foster v. Love* the Court upheld a lower court's ruling that the system "thwarts the congressional purpose of establishing a uniform day to prevent earlier elections from influencing later voters." Gov. Mike Foster, Republican, suggested that the state move its open primary to the federal ELECTION DAY and hold RUNOFF elections afterward if necessary.

Another type of open primary won approval of California voters on an INITIATIVE (Proposition 198) in 1996. The highly controversial measure, opposed by the major political parties, permits voters to pick and choose between the parties, office by office, on a single ballot. Known as the *jungle* type because of its wide open, few-holds-barred structure, the primary was patterned after one long used in Washington State. *Blanket* and jungle primaries are similar. Proposition 198 did not affect the 1996 California primary at which it was approved by voters of both parties. The new law took effect in 1998.

In May 1997 the Supreme Court let stand a decision upholding Alaska's similar open primary law. Republicans had challenged the law in an effort to bar Democrats (but not independents) from GOP primaries.

Since the 1970s, states in different parts of the country have scheduled their presidential primaries on the same date to have more influence on the nominating process. These *regional* primaries have become known informally by names such as SUPER TUESDAY, a group of mostly southern primaries, and JUNIOR TUESDAY, mostly in the Northeast. (See PRESIDENTIAL PRIMARIES.)

For much of the first half of the twentieth century, SOUTHERN PRIMARIES held greater importance in U.S. elections than they do today. Because the Democratic Party dominated the South as the states began to adopt the primary system, a plurality victory in the party's primary for governor or senator was tantamount to election. Consequently, most southern states adopted the runoff system to make the election more competitive and representative. If no candidate received a majority or specified percentage in the primary, the two top vote-getters were matched again in the runoff a few weeks later. As the Republican Party gained strength in the South after World War II, some GOP governors and senators were elected and the runoff became less important.

Also in the South, blacks were excluded from so-called WHITE PRIMARIES in some states and counties. The Democratic Party in these areas designated itself as a private organization to circumvent the Fifteenth Amendment's prohibition against states' denying the right to vote because of race or color. In 1944 the Supreme Court declared white primaries illegal.

The POLL TAX, LITERACY TESTS, and complex VOTER REGISTRATION laws were also used to keep the southern Democratic primaries essentially whites-only affairs.

## Progressive Party (1924)

Like the Bull Moose Party of Theodore Roosevelt, the Progressive Party that emerged in the mid-1920s was a reform effort led by a Republican. Wisconsin senator Robert M. La Follette led the new Progressive Party, a separate entity from the Bull Moosers. Unlike the mid-

*Robert M. La Follette (right) gives his son, Bob, advice before the Cleveland convention in 1924.*
Source: *Library of Congress*

dle- and upper-class Roosevelt party of the previous decade, the La Follette party had its greatest appeal among farmers and organized labor.

The La Follette Progressive Party grew out of the Conference for Progressive Political Action (CPPA), a COALITION of railway union leaders and a remnant of the Bull Moose effort that was formed in 1922. The Socialist Party joined the coalition the following year. Throughout 1923 the Socialists and labor unions argued over whether their coalition should form a THIRD PARTY, with the Socialists in favor and the labor unions against it. They finally decided to run an independent presidential candidate, La Follette, in the 1924 election but not to field candidates at the state and local levels. La Follette was given the power to choose his RUNNING MATE and selected Montana senator Burton K. Wheeler, a Democrat.

Opposition to corporate monopolies was the major issue of the La Follette campaign, although the party advocated various other reforms, particularly aimed at farmers and workers, that had been proposed earlier by either the Populists or Bull Moosers. But the Progressive Party itself was a major issue in the 1924 campaign, as the Republicans attacked the alleged radicalism of the party.

Although La Follette had its endorsement, the American Federation of Labor (AFL) provided minimal support. The basic strength of the Progressives, like that of the Populists in the 1890s, derived from agrarian voters west of the Mississippi River. La Follette received 4,832,532 votes (16.6 percent of the POPULAR VOTE) but carried just one state, his native Wisconsin. When La Follette died in 1925, the party collapsed as a national force. It was revived by La Follette's sons on a statewide level in Wisconsin in the mid-1930s.

## Progressive Party (1948)

Henry A. Wallace's Progressive Party resulted from the dissatisfaction of liberal elements in the DEMOCRATIC PARTY with the leadership of President Harry S. Truman, particularly in the realm of foreign policy.

*Henry A. Wallace. Source: Library of Congress*

The Progressive Party was one of two groups that bolted from the Democratic Party in 1948; conservative southern elements withdrew to form the STATES' RIGHTS DEMOCRATIC PARTY.

Henry Wallace, the founder of the Progressive Party, was secretary of agriculture, vice president, and finally secretary of commerce under President Franklin Roosevelt. He was considered one of the most liberal idealists in the Roosevelt administration. Fired from the Truman cabinet in 1946 after breaking with administration policy and publicly advocating peaceful coexistence with the Soviet Union, Wallace began to consider the idea of a liberal THIRD PARTY candidacy. Supported by the American Labor Party, the Progressive Citizens of America, and other progressive organizations in California and Illinois, Wallace announced his third party candidacy in December 1947.

The Progressive Party was launched formally the following July at a convention in Philadelphia, which ratified the selection of Wallace for president and Sen. Glen H. Taylor, D-Idaho, as his running mate. The party adopted a platform that emphasized foreign policy—opposing the cold war anticommunism of the Truman administration and specifically urging abandonment of the Truman Doctrine and the Marshall Plan. These measures were designed to bolster noncommunist nations and contain the spread of communism. On domestic issues the Progressives stressed humanitarian concerns and equal rights for both sexes and all races.

Minority groups—women, youth, African Americans, Jews, Hispanic Americans—were active in the new party, but the openness of the Progressives brought Wallace a damaging endorsement from the COMMUNIST PARTY. Believing the two parties could work together, Wallace accepted the endorsement while characterizing his philosophy as "progressive capitalism."

In 1948 the Progressives appeared on the presidential ballot in forty-five states, but the Communist endorsement helped keep the party on the defensive the entire campaign. In the November election Wallace received only 1,157,326 votes (2.4 percent of the national popular vote), with nearly half of the votes from the state of New York. Not only were the Progressives unable to carry a single state, but in spite of their defection from the Democratic Party President Truman won reelection. The Progressives had poor results in the congressional races, failing to elect one representative or senator.

The Progressive Party's opposition to the Korean War in 1950 drove many moderate elements out of the party, including Henry Wallace. The party ran a national ticket in 1952, but received only 140,023 votes nationwide or 0.2 percent of the national popular vote. The party crumbled completely after the election.

*When Theodore Roosevelt remarked to a reporter during the 1912 GOP convention, "I'm feeling like a bull moose," his vigorous campaign had a symbol. TR lost the GOP nomination and formed the Progressive Party. Source: Library of Congress*

## Progressive Party–Bull Moose (1912)

A split in Republican ranks, spurred by the bitter personal and ideological dispute between President William Howard Taft (1909–1913) and former president

Theodore Roosevelt (1901–1909), resulted in the withdrawal of the Roosevelt forces from the REPUBLICAN PARTY after the June 1912 convention and the creation of the Progressive Party two months later. The new party was known popularly as the Bull Moose Party, a name resulting from Roosevelt's assertion early in the campaign that he felt as fit as a bull moose. While the Taft-Roosevelt split was the immediate reason for the new party, the Bull Moosers were an outgrowth of the progressive movement that was a powerful force in both major parties in the early years of the twentieth century.

In 1908 Roosevelt had handpicked Taft as his successor, but his disillusionment with Taft's conservative philosophy came quickly, and, with the support of progressive Republicans, Roosevelt challenged the incumbent for the 1912 Republican presidential nomination. Roosevelt outpolled Taft in the presidential primary states. Taft nevertheless won the nomination with nearly solid support in the South and among party conservatives, providing the narrow majority of DELEGATES that enabled him to win the bulk of the important credentials challenges.

Although few Republican politicians followed Roosevelt in his bolt, the new party demonstrated a popular base at its convention in Chicago in August 1912. Thousands of delegates, basically middle- and upper-class reformers from small towns and cities, attended the convention that launched the party and nominated Roosevelt for president and California governor Hiram Johnson as his running mate. Roosevelt appeared in person to deliver his "Confession of Faith," a speech detailing his nationalistic philosophy and progressive reform ideas. The Bull Moose platform reflected the crucial tenets of the Progressive movement, calling for more extensive government antitrust action and for labor, social, government, and electoral reform.

Roosevelt was wounded in an assassination attempt while campaigning in Milwaukee, Wisconsin, in October, but he finished the campaign. In the general election Roosevelt received more than 4 million votes (27.4 percent of the POPULAR VOTE) and carried six states. His percentage of the vote was the highest ever received by a THIRD PARTY candidate in American history, but his candidacy split the Republican vote and enabled the Democrats' nominee, Woodrow Wilson, to win the election. The Progressive Party had minimal success at the state and local levels, winning thirteen House seats but electing no senators or governors.

Roosevelt declined the Progressive nomination in 1916 and endorsed the Republican candidate, Charles Evans Hughes. With the defection of its leader, the decline of the progressive movement, and the lack of an effective party organization, the Bull Moose Party ceased to exist.

## Prohibition Party (1869– )

The Prohibition Party existed longer than any third party in American history. It was formed in September 1869 at a convention in Chicago, which attracted approximately five hundred delegates from twenty states. For the first time in U.S. politics, women had equal status with men as delegates. By a narrow majority the convention decided to form an independent party, and three years later the new party put forth its first national ticket. The party's basic goal was enactment of laws prohibiting the manufacture and sale of intoxicating liquor, but its platforms have included other reform proposals. The 1872 Prohibition Party platform included the first WOMEN'S SUFFRAGE plank.

For all but one election between 1884 and 1916, the party's presidential candidate received at least 1.0 percent of the popular vote. The party's best showing came in 1892, when its presidential nominee, John Bidwell, received 270,770 votes (2.2 percent of the popular vote). The party has run a national ticket in every presidential election since 1872, but its candidates have never carried a single state. After the 1976 election the Prohibition Party changed its name to the National Statesman Party, and its 1980 candidate registered using that party name. The 1984 candidate, Earl F. Dodge of Colorado, emphasized that his party—on the ballots once again as Prohibitionists—no longer focused on a single issue: the party backed religious freedom and an antiabortion amendment. Dodge again was the party's standard-bearer in 1988, 1992, and 1996. In 1992 the party could muster only 961 votes nationwide. It did slightly better in 1996, receiving 1,298 votes.

The temperance movement succeeded in gaining prohibition legislation in numerous states in the late nineteenth and early twentieth centuries, and its efforts were capped in 1919 by passage of national prohibition legislation (the Eighteenth Amendment to the U.S. Constitution, repealed fourteen years later by the Twenty-first Amendment). The achievements of the temperance movement were due as much to independent organizations, such as the Women's Christian Temperance

Union (WCTU) and the Anti-Saloon League, as to the Prohibition Party, which had limited success at the polls. These organizations allowed active Democrats and Republicans to remain in their parties while working for prohibition.

## Proportional Representation

Democratic theorists have long argued that the WIN-NER-TAKE-ALL system of elections used in the United States and in other democracies fails to satisfy the requirements of the NATURE OF REPRESENTATION. They contend that in a single-member constituency system persons who did not vote for the winner are not truly represented.

To these theorists, notably John Stuart Mill, each vote in a DEMOCRACY should result in an equal share in the legislature; each voter, so to speak, should have a representative fully and honestly speaking for him or her. But in the U.S. electoral system the majority and the minority are not legislatively represented in any proportion that reflects their actual strength in the DISTRICT. Small minorities are not represented in any way, giving rise to a question: If 50.1 percent of voters elect a representative, are the other 49.9 percent of voters really represented by that person?

*Proportional representation* would make the legislature an exact mirror of the voting strength of the multiple interests within the electorate. To do this requires a multiple-member constituency system. Instead of one representative serving a congressional district, there might be eight or fifteen, or any likely number arising from a system that encourages more than two parties. What is of paramount importance to the advocates of proportional representation is that the legislature be, in essence, a photographic "snapshot" of the electorate—providing a "mathematically exact representation of the various segments of opinion among the electorate," as one political analyst writes.

MULTIMEMBER DISTRICTS are still found in some cities and states, and they once existed as congressional districts in some states until Congress abolished them in 1842. African American and other minority groups have argued that multiple-member districts, instead of guaranteeing their representation, actually deny it by submerging them into the district majority. The Supreme Court has agreed that a multimember district may be unconstitutional if it discriminates against a minority, and the 1965 VOTING RIGHTS ACT contained protection against such districting. (See RACIAL REDISTRICTING; REAPPORTIONMENT AND REDISTRICTING.)

### Complex Formulas

Two basic forms of proportional representation exist: the predominant *"party list" system*, in which political parties are awarded seats in the legislature in proportion to the number of votes cast for their differing party rosters (or "lists") on the ballot; and the *single transferable vote system*, used in some American cities, in which voters cast ballots for individual candidates instead of party lists.

In the single-transferable vote system, where voters choose individual candidates, the question becomes one of determining how candidates rank in terms of voter preference, then using a quota to determine, say, the three winners out of five candidates.

It is obvious that whatever formula determines the winners of seats in proportional representation electoral systems, the systems themselves encourage the formation of multiple parties to faithfully represent the varied interests and concerns of the electorate as a whole and of its absolutely essential component, the individual voter. In the American TWO-PARTY SYSTEM, the Democratic and Republican Parties attempt to draw these varied interests, with varying degrees of success, into mass party organizations with competing wings, for example "moderate Republicans" and "liberal Democrats." The mass party organizations vie with one another for legislative success and the factions within them contend for control of the party's agenda and ideology.

Reforms of the U.S. presidential system have centered on the question of proportional representation, particularly in the selection of DELEGATES to the NA-

TIONAL PARTY CONVENTIONS. The Democratic Party has banned all types of winner-take-all PRIMARIES, but the Republican Party still permits them in some states.

Delegates are allocated to Democratic presidential candidates in proportion to their percentage of the total vote, provided they meet a THRESHOLD of at least 15 percent statewide and in each district. For example, in New Jersey in 1992 Bill Clinton received 62.1 percent of the vote and eighty delegates; Edmund G. "Jerry" Brown won 20.3 percent of the vote and twenty-three delegates; and Paul E. Tsongas was awarded two delegates for having met the threshold requirements.

Proportional representation has not been universally popular among Democratic leaders, and the party has attempted to blunt it by the appointment of so-called SUPERDELEGATES, elected and party officials who go to the conventions in addition to those elected in the primaries and CAUCUSES. Democrats in some states also have used "loophole" primaries, electing delegates directly in each district, to get around the ban on winner-take-all delegate selection. (See PRIMARY TYPES.)

## Critics' Arguments

Proportional representation also has its fair share of critics. Some cite the example of what happened in Germany's Weimar Republic between 1919 and 1930. Proportional representation was adopted at the end of World War I to maintain a political balance between the parties that still existed after the dissolution of the German Empire.

In the 1919 election, the first in which proportional representation was employed, some six major parties polled nearly a million votes with the Social Democrats on the left winning about a third of that total. In union with the two major parties of the center, a strong majority was achieved. Eleven years later, in the sixth election governed by proportional representation, ten parties polled more than a million votes and six others made respectable showings. The result was that no party emerged dominant or even in a position to exert effective leadership as the head of a stable majority coalition.

Such fractionalization was also evident in New York

*John Stuart Mill (1806–1873), an English philosopher, economist, political theorist, journalist, and member of Parliament, believed that the United States was a false democracy in which the numerical majority ruled despotically. Source: Library of Congress*

City when, in 1936, proportional representation was adopted for city council elections. It was at first hoped that the new system would make it possible for reform groups to realistically contest elections against entrenched political machines. The result, one writer wryly noted, was the election to the council of, besides Democrats and Republicans, "Fusionists, American Laborites, Liberals, Communists, and, of course, Independents." By the end of ten years, when proportional representation "had given a lion's roar to irresponsible fleas," the system was abolished, with many agreeing with the assessment of one political observer that proportional representation, in most of America, was, at best, "a fad." Another called it the "choice between democracy and anarchy."

Many critics of proportional representation argue that it encourages splinter groups, thus overrepresenting minorities at the expense of majorities. In Israel, for example, extremely small parties of ultra-Orthodox Jews, some adopting extremist positions not at all in accord with predominant national sentiment or secular needs, form the balance of power between the two major parties, Likud and Labor, and are able to make political demands and exert political leverage far in excess of their actual strength in numbers.

Critics also note that proportional representation offers voters, by and large, a complicated formula to master, one that is susceptible to manipulation by the parties contesting the election. They note that the system tends to reduce the personal contact between voters and their elected representative because the party machinery dictates the order of candidates, sometimes offering only mediocre candidates, and therefore ignoring the vital question of quality of representation, instead opting only for quantity.

The most serious charges are that proportional representation, by basically weakening reasonably stable prodemocratic forces in Italy and Germany and fractionalizing the political process in the years after World War I, made possible the rise of the fascist dictatorships in both nations. As one political analyst noted of this period, "So preoccupied are the adherents [of proportional representation] with the technique of representation—which is only one part of the structure of popular government—that they continue to agitate for a device which not only fails to improve representation but even destroys popular government itself."

## Public Financing of Campaigns

The objective of public funding of election campaigns is to "level the playing field" for candidates so that each, at least in theory, has the same financial advantages as the other. Some states subsidize their major campaigns, and U.S. presidential elections have been publicly funded since 1976. (See PRESIDENT: NOMINATING AND ELECTING.)

Congress's action to provide funding grew out of concerns raised by the 1968 election, in which Richard Nixon outspent Hubert H. Humphrey by two to one. The election of 1972 again produced excesses of spending, leading to abuses that eventually drove President Nixon from office.

Passage of the funding legislation, the Revenue Act of 1971, did not come easily. It followed a long and partisan struggle between congressional Democrats and the Republican Nixon administration.

The act did not affect the 1972 election, but it created the Presidential Election Campaign Fund for future nomination and general election campaigns. In every presidential election since 1976 the major party nominees have accepted the federal funding and the spending cap that goes with it.

The amount that candidates receive during the nominating process is determined by a per-voter spending formula. A candidate qualifies for matching federal funds by raising at least $100,000 in twenty or more states, with at least $5,000 from each state in individual contributions of $250 or less. Candidates receiving federal funds may not accept private contributions for their general election campaigns, and they must pledge not to spend more than $50,000 from personal funds on their campaigns. They are limited to spending $200,000 in each state, with an adjustment for inflation.

Presidential candidates of minor parties receive funding based on their parties' vote in the general election as a percentage of the major parties' average vote. Major parties are defined as those that received 25 percent or more of the vote in the previous election. Minor or THIRD PARTIES are those receiving between 5 percent and 25 percent. A nominee of a new party (defined as one that is neither a major party nor a minor party) can obtain partial funding retroactively if he or she receives 5 percent or more of the vote.

No provision was made for INDEPENDENT candidates, but in 1980 a ruling by the FEDERAL ELECTION COMMISSION (FEC) enabled John Anderson of Illinois to receive partial funding after his independent candidacy drew 6.6 percent of the presidential vote. The commission ruled that Anderson qualified under the provision for new-party retroactive funding, which is based on the ratio of the candidate's POPULAR VOTE to the average popular vote of the two major party candidates. Twelve years later Texas billionaire Ross Perot financed his own campaign, but his 18.9 percent of the vote qualified his new REFORM PARTY to receive funding at about half the level of the major parties for his repeat try for the presidency in 1996.

Under the Revenue Act, the federal campaign money is raised through a "checkoff" option on income tax forms. Taxpayers can designate that $3 (originally $1) of their tax payment be put into the presidential campaign fund. Couples filing joint returns can designate $6 (originally $2) to go into the fund. Congress raised the checkoff in 1993 because the campaign fund was facing a shortage.

Although the checkoff does not increase the tax payment or decrease any refund due, its use has never been popular. The number of Americans opting to earmark tax money for the fund fell from a high of 29.0 percent in 1980 to a low of 13.0 percent in 1996.

In pushing for creation of the fund, the Democrats, long the debt-ridden party, contended it was needed to control the amount of influence that the wealthy could exert in a presidential campaign. Republicans, looking forward to a bountiful presidential election in 1972 with one of their own seeking reelection, opposed the measure. The legislation passed but with the 1972 election exempted. President Nixon signed it into law.

Despite the public's lukewarm attitude toward the checkoff, the two parties now accept its role in the electoral process. Part of their acceptance stems from the loopholes that provide ways to ease the HARD MONEY restrictions of federal CAMPAIGN FINANCE laws. The restrictions include contribution limits for all federal candidates and spending limits for presidential candidates who accept public funding.

One loophole allows groups or individuals to make unlimited "independent expenditures" in behalf of favorite candidates. Another permits the BUNDLING of numerous small contributions into one big one that otherwise would be prohibited. And the parties may receive unregulated SOFT MONEY that indirectly benefits their nominees' campaigns. In 1996 millions of dollars in soft money contributions were at the heart of a campaign finance SCANDAL centering on the DEMOCRATIC NATIONAL COMMITTEE and President Bill Clinton's reelection campaign. Both parties, however, were found to have misused the soft money and were required to return some of it. (See CAMPAIGN FINANCE.)

Another loophole that aroused considerable controversy in 1996 concerned "issue advocacy," the use of advertising that clearly supports a particular candidate without mentioning his or her name. INTEREST GROUPS spend millions of dollars on such ads dealing with abortion, gun control, and other issues where a candidate's position is likely to be well known. At the opening of its 1997–1998 session the Supreme Court rejected an FEC request that the Court review the practice to determine if it violates campaign spending limits or free speech rights. (See MEDIA USE BY CAMPAIGNS.)

In sum, the tax checkoff has not ended private influence. But the expansion of public financing into the nomination process has allowed numerous candidates to compete, at least in the early campaign stages.

## The "Watergate" Election

The last completely privately financed presidential election was the 1972 race. Although spending on broadcast ads fell, overall campaign costs soared. President Nixon's campaign organization spent $61.4 million, while the Democratic campaign of George S. McGovern spent $21.2 million.

The Committee for the Reelection of the President (or "CREEP," as it became known) relied mostly on large contributions, many of them solicited and received before April 7, 1972, the date when disclosure of such gifts would begin under the Federal Election Campaign Act (FECA).

Despite its heavy spending, the Nixon campaign had money left over after he was reelected, leading to reckless attempts to cover up the crime that gave the Watergate scandal its name: the burglary of the Democratic national headquarters in the Watergate Hotel office complex. Congressional investigations into the cover-up, including payment of "hush money" to the perpetrators, resulted in Nixon's resignation in 1974 to avoid his almost certain impeachment by the House.

## Post-Watergate Finance Laws

In the wake of Nixon's resignation Congress passed the sweeping campaign finance legislation that still governs presidential and congressional elections. Gerald Ford, who succeeded to the presidency, reluctantly signed into law the Federal Election Campaign Act Amendments in October 1974. The amendments established limits for contributions to federal candidates and their POLITICAL ACTION COMMITTEES (PACs). (See table, page 39.)

States also became involved in campaign finance reform. By the time Nixon left office, some seventeen states had imposed contribution limitations. New Jersey's limit of $600, which was eligible for state matching funds, was the lowest in the nation.

The federal law was most important for presidential politics. Technically just an amendment to the 1971 law, the post-Watergate statute superseded some of the pre-vious law's provisions and expanded others. The Federal Election Campaign Act Amendments contained the following provisions relating to public financing of presidential elections:

• National spending limits of $10 million for presidential primary candidates and $20 million for major party nominees' general election campaigns. Spending in the nominating process also would be limited in each state to $200,000 or sixteen cents times the state's voting-age population, whichever is greater. These sums have since risen through inflation adjustments. (See table below.)

In 1996 the limits for each presidential candidate were $30.9 million in the primaries and $61.8 million in the general election. The campaigns of President Bill Clinton and Republican nominee Robert J. Dole each received the full amount. Under the law, the campaigns were prohibited from spending any more than that. Perot received $29.0 million, based on his attaining at least 5 percent of the popular vote in 1992. Unlike Clinton and Dole, Perot was allowed to supplement the 1996

### Expenditure Limits for Publicly Funded Candidates

| | Primary Candidates | General Election | |
| --- | --- | --- | --- |
| | | Major Party Nominees | Minor or New Party Nominees |
| National spending limit | $10 mil. + COLA[a] | $20 mil. + COLA[b] | $20 mil. + COLA |
| State spending limit | The greater of $200,000 + COLA or 16¢ x state VAP[b] + COLA | None | None |
| Exempt fundraising limit | 20% of national limit | Not applicable | 20% of national limit |
| Maximum public funds candidate may receive | 50% of national limit | Same as national limit | Percentage of national limit based on candidate's popular vote |
| National party spending limit for candidate[c] | Not applicable | 2¢ x VAP of U.S. + COLA | 2¢ x VAP of U.S. + COLA |
| Limit on spending from candidate's personal funds | $50,000 | $50,000 | $50,000 |

*Source:* Federal Election Commission

    a. Spending limits are increased by the cost-of-living adjustment (COLA), which the Department of Labor calculates annually using 1974 as the base year.
    b. VAP is the Voting Age Population, which the Department of Commerce calculates annually.
    c. The national committee of a political party may make special, limited expenditures, called coordinated party expenditures, on behalf of its presidential nominee, even if the nominee does not accept public funds. Coordinated party expenditures are not considered contributions and do not count against a publicly funded campaign's candidate expenditure limit.

grant with private contributions up to the $61.8 million level.

• Extension of public funding to presidential primaries, with matching grants for candidates who qualify. The requirements were intended to demonstrate that the candidate has broad national support. Contributions from individuals of up to $250 are matched dollar for dollar. The FECA amendments also established the formulas for amounts awarded to the parties for their conventions. The amounts rise with inflation. In 1996 each NATIONAL PARTY CONVENTION received $12.4 million.

## Court Cases and Constitutional Issues

The 1974 FECA amendments faced an important federal court challenge, BUCKLEY V. VALEO, soon after they took effect. The Supreme Court's final 1975 ruling reduced congressional authority over campaign activity.

The Court approved disclosure requirements and limitations on how much individuals and organizations could contribute to national candidates. The Court also approved the federal financing of presidential nominating campaigns and general election campaigns. But one of the most controversial elements of the reform—limits on independent expenditures on behalf of candidates—was overturned. The Court agreed with the plaintiffs' First Amendment argument that restrictions on spending amounted to abridgment of free speech. The Court ruled, however, that campaign organizations could be required to honor spending limits if they accepted federal money. The Court stated:

A restriction on the amount of money a person or group can spend on political communication during a campaign necessarily reduces the quantity of expression by restricting the number of issues discussed, the depth of their exploration, and the size of the audience reached. This is because every means of communicating ideas in today's mass society requires the expenditure of money.

Only Justice Byron White rejected the reasoning. White noted the "many expensive campaign activities that are not themselves communicative or remotely related to speech."

## State Election Funding

By the late 1990s twenty-two states were operating some form of tax-assisted funding for political parties and candidates. About half used a state income tax checkoff system similar to the federal checkoff. Most provided funding only for gubernatorial candidates but a few—notably Minnesota and Wisconsin—also assisted campaigns for the state legislature.

A few states, including Arizona, California, Hawaii, Minnesota, Montana, North Carolina, and Oregon, offered state income tax credits or deductions to encourage political participation through contributions. All the states that regulated political finances required disclosure of contribution sources.

About half the states allow voters to originate laws through ballot INITIATIVES. More states allow referendum votes on certain proposals originating in the state legislature. Some public funding programs began as initiatives or were approved in referendums.

In the 1996 elections Maine voters approved of public funding of campaigns beginning in 2000. Voters in Arkansas, California, and Colorado approved new contribution limits for state and local races.

## Public Opinion

The use of scientific POLLING to determine the public's opinion of candidates and issues has deep implications for politics and elections in the United States. Political campaigns keep a close watch on public opinion for guidance on how to proceed or whether to stay in the race at all.

Candidates who stay and win will, as officeholders, keep abreast of trends in public opinion, both as a tool for formulating government policy and as a guide to prepare for the next election. Few INCUMBENTS or serious candidates ignore the polls in the highly competitive realm of modern politics.

Polling can help determine both the direction and depth of public opinion. The direction is simply whether people view an issue, action, or performance

*President George Bush shares a meal with the troops. His public approval ratings soared during and immediately following the 1991 Persian Gulf War, but in less than a year they tumbled 59 percent. Source: National Archives, Bush Presidential Materials Project*

favorably or unfavorably. Surveys can provide information on the yes-no dimension: how people align themselves on issues such as the death penalty, affirmative action, abortion, tax increases for Medicare and Social Security, or military intervention in Iraq.

A related and critical aspect of public opinion is the distribution, or extent, of agreement or consensus on an issue, with opinions clustering on one side or the other of the yes-no dimension. Some evoke high levels of agreement, such as keeping drugs illegal. Other issues are highly divisive, such as gays in the military. When a high level of consensus exists, government policy makers usually find it wise to follow public opinion.

For example, when crime became a prime concern in

1993 and the Gallup poll showed that 88 percent of the public was in favor of imposing a waiting period for the purchase of a handgun, Congress finally overcame its long-standing reluctance to offend the pro-gun lobby. By wide margins both chambers enacted the long-delayed Brady bill. Named for former presidential press secretary James Brady, who was permanently disabled by a handgun bullet during the 1981 attempt to assassinate Ronald Reagan, the legislation required a five-day waiting period for the purchase of a handgun.

When opinions divide and the public's feelings are strong, outcomes are less certain. In the first days of his presidency, Bill Clinton proposed to implement a campaign pledge to lift the ban on homosexuals in the military, He created a firestorm of controversy that revealed a deeply divided public. Stands were adamantly taken— 87 percent of those opposed to his policy felt strongly about the issue, as did 63 percent of those who supported it. The public's emphatic response and the opposition of senior military personnel and influential senators such as Sam Nunn, Georgia Democrat, who was the chairman of the Armed Services Committee, forced Clinton to back down. He settled for a revised "don't ask, don't tell" policy under which homosexual conduct would still be prohibited, but recruits would no longer be asked if they were gay.

## Importance and Stability

People differ in the extent to which they find an issue salient, or important. National Rifle Association (NRA) members, for example, consider opposition to gun control extremely salient. In the same way, retired people care more about cost-of-living adjustments to Social Security benefits than do working parents, who find tax deductions for child care expenses more important than do retirees.

For the public as a whole the saliency of issues changes over time. At the beginning of the Reagan administration in 1981 the Gallup poll reported that 72 percent of Americans believed inflation to be the most important problem facing the nation. But by 1988, when the inflation rate was down to 4.1 percent from 13.5 percent, only 2 percent of the people gave it such importance.

The intensity of public opinion can vary as well: people may feel strongly about some issues and not so strongly about others. Issues such as abortion, which involve moral questions, are likely to generate the most impassioned opinions. Those who feel strongly are more likely to act on their sentiments and participate in the political process than those whose views are weakly held.

The effect of public opinion is influenced by the strength of commitment people give to a cause, with the result that small but energetic minorities often have an influence well out of proportion to their numbers. Understanding the intensity with which people hold and act on their opinions helps to explain why policy positions opposed by a majority of the people can become public policy.

For example, polls show that at least two-thirds of the public support tougher gun control legislation. But deeply committed opponents, led by the NRA, have blocked new bills (except the Brady bill) that would strengthen gun control laws and have even succeeded in weakening previously passed laws. The NRA efforts have included advertising campaigns, campaign contributions, and aggressive lobbying, with NRA members deluging members of Congress with mail against gun control. By contrast, people favoring tougher gun laws have generally not felt strongly enough about the issue to act on their convictions.

Public opinion can be contradictory on separate aspects of the same issue. A prime example arose from the White House sex SCANDAL that rocked the nation in early 1998. Although President Clinton's acknowledged relationship with Monica Lewinsky, a young intern, involved morality—normally a hot-button issue—polls showed the public considered that less important than allegations that Clinton may have lied under oath about the relationship and urged Lewinsky to do the same. Moreover, the public regarded both issues less important than the president's job performance, and his approval ratings actually rose to a high of 79 percent.

Another dimension of public opinion is its stability. The public can change its mind, occasionally with amazing rapidity. For example, President George Bush's public approval ratings resembled a roller coaster ride. His rating dropped 23 points in the fall of 1990 from 76 percent to 53 percent after he reneged on his "Read my lips, no new taxes" campaign pledge and negotiated a budget compromise with congressional Democrats. In the aftermath of victory in the 1991 Persian Gulf War, he rebounded to a record 89 percent approval rating, which then fell precipitously to 30 percent by August 1992 as the public's anxiety over the economy grew.

Although these examples suggest a high level of volatility in public opinion, studies show that American opinion on many issues exhibits substantial stability and that change in public attitudes tends to occur gradually. Since 1972 the public has overwhelmingly supported a woman's right to have an abortion when there is a strong chance of a serious birth defect or when the pregnancy stems from rape. At the same time, most Americans have consistently opposed permitting abortions sought when, for example, a married woman does not want any more children.

Another aspect of the stability dimension is that a public once divided on an issue can over time achieve a high level of agreement. In 1942 only 30 percent of whites said that they thought white and black students should go to the same schools. Yet by 1984, 90 percent of whites said that they accepted integrated schools.

Analysis of these data, however, showed that whites were not monolithic in their racial attitudes. Differences stemmed from people's diverse social backgrounds and life experiences. An exploration of public opinion, therefore, must consider POLITICAL SOCIALIZATION —the learning process through which people acquire political attitudes.

## Effect on Policy

Public opinion has its most obvious impact on government decision making through elections. In the United States, elections are usually held to vote for candidates for public office and not for specific policies, except in those states that permit voters to enact laws through INITIATIVE AND REFERENDUM.

Clear electoral MANDATES from the voters are rare because candidates take stands on scores of issues and therefore collect voters for different and even conflicting reasons; elections are seldom dominated or decided by just one or two issues. Moreover, the candidates' positions are not always clear, nor are their positions necessarily in opposition to each other.

But even if it is hard to discern a clear policy mandate from the voters on ELECTION DAY, a verdict on the past performances of incumbent officeholders is frequently rendered. Indeed, the public can affect the general direction of government policy by changing the people and parties in control of government institutions.

In the 1992 election, for example, the public gave a negative verdict on President George Bush's handling of

the economy and on divided party control of the government. But in rejecting Bush and replacing him with Bill Clinton, the public did not necessarily signal its approval of Clinton's policy proposals. It did, however, indicate that it was prepared to give him a chance to solve the nation's problems, and Clinton's Democratic administration had a policy agenda of government activism that was markedly different from that of its Republican predecessor.

Public opinion can determine not only who governs but also the context within which political leaders must act. Periodic swings in Americans' IDEOLOGY— changes in their policy mood—provide the setting for and affect government policy making.

The liberal winds that began blowing during the latter 1950s provided the basis for the government activism that characterized the Kennedy-Johnson era of the 1960s. But these breezes died down in the mid-1970s as Americans became more conservative in their general disposition toward government's role in society. Indeed, this conservative policy mood was already in place before Ronald Reagan, the most conservative president since Herbert Hoover, took office and initiated policies designed to restrict the role of government.

Public opinion has its greatest impact on policy when people have clear preferences and feel strongly about an issue. A study by political scientist Alan Monroe found that on issues particularly important to the public, government policy and public opinion were in agreement more than two-thirds of the time. Research also has demonstrated that government policy moves in the direction of a change in public opinion 87 percent of the time when the shift is substantial and not temporary.

One of the most striking examples of the effect of public opinion on national policy was the congressional pay raise controversy of 1989. Overwhelming and vehement public opposition caused a reluctant Congress to reject the 50 percent salary increase proposed by a bipartisan, blue-ribbon commission and endorsed by Presidents Reagan and Bush.

Naturally, there are times when public opinion and government policy are not consistent. Such inconsistencies may stem from the influence of well-organized and energetic INTEREST GROUPS. For example, a popular majority favored tougher air pollution laws throughout the 1980s, yet Congress was unable to enact such legislation. This inaction reflected the ability of auto makers, utilities, several unions, and influential legislators to mobilize opposition to clean air bills.

Inconsistencies between public opinion and government policy also occur when the public cares little about an issue. Polls have shown repeatedly, for example, that Americans favor abolishing the ELECTORAL COLLEGE system for electing the president, but this issue is not high on their list of concerns. As a result, the likelihood of Congress's proposing a constitutional amendment to abolish the electoral college seems remote.

Public opinion influences public policy in the United States only through a complicated and often indirect process. It takes more than a majority of the public registering its approval or disapproval in a poll to affect policy. People's policy preferences are translated into government policy only when individuals act on opinions—that is, when they actually participate in politics. (See CITIZENSHIP AND VOTING.)

## Push Poll

The controversial practice known as *push polling* is actually a type of NEGATIVE CAMPAIGNING. It traces its roots to Richard Nixon's first run for Congress in the late 1940s, when Nixon campaign workers made anonymous calls telling voters that Nixon's opponents were communists. In more recent times push polling was used in the 1994 Florida gubernatorial race, to the embarrassment of the winner, Democrat Lawton Chiles.

In the 1996 election President Bill Clinton's campaign pledged not to use push polling. The Robert J. Dole campaign, which paid more than $1 million to New York City-based Campaign Tel Ltd. to do push polling during the primaries, declined to make such a promise concerning the general election.

In a February 1996 appearance on the *Larry King Weekend* show, a group of Republican campaign managers in Des Moines for the IOWA CAUCUS acknowledged that some of their contractors had phoned households under the guise of conducting an opinion poll, and then planted negative information about an opposing candidate.

Modern push polling is made possible by computer technology that permits rapid dialing to thousands of households, then efficiently routes only the consummated calls to a campaign employee ready to read from a script. Phone banks can cover entire areas at a third of the cost of such operations just a few years ago.

Push polling is not easily detectable. If a caller asked a voter if he would still vote for a candidate knowing, for example, that he cheated on his taxes, no one would know about it unless the call recipient complained to the authorities or the press.

The National Council on Public Polls and the national and international political consultants associations have condemned "this abuse of legitimate public polling" as thinly disguised telemarketing.

# R

## Racial Redistricting

Racial and ethnic considerations have long been a factor in the drawing of legislative and congressional DISTRICTS in the United States, which happens every ten years in the REAPPORTIONMENT AND REDISTRICTING processes that follow each CENSUS. After the 1990 census several states, acting under pressure from the federal government, created a number of new congressional districts that included majority African American or Hispanic populations. In a series of legal challenges, the Supreme Court later forced the redrawing of some of the districts by ruling that racially motivated redistricting could, in some circumstances, violate constitutional rights of nonminority voters.

Historically, the pattern of racially and ethnically identifiable neighborhoods in many urban centers made it possible for lawmakers to draw district lines in a way likely to result in the election of candidates of a particular race or ethnic background—Irish Americans or Italian Americans, for example, from predominantly Irish or Italian districts. Very few blacks, however, were elected to Congress, even from states such as those in the South where they constituted a sizable proportion of the population. Likewise, Hispanic Americans had only a few representatives in Congress, despite the rapid growth in their numbers in the 1980s and 1990s.

To remedy the underrepresentation of these two minority groups in Congress, the Justice Department decreed that states with histories of minority voting rights violations were required under the VOTING RIGHTS ACT to create so-called MAJORITY-MINORITY DISTRICTS—districts where African American or Hispanic populations were in the majority. The Voting Rights Act, as amended in 1982, prohibited election practices

that had a disproportionate impact on minority group voting rights.

The newly drawn majority-minority districts resulted in the election of a larger number of African American and Hispanic members to the House of Representatives in the 1992 election. The elections cheered minority groups and traditional civil rights organizations. But some of the districts were sharply criticized as a form of racial GERRYMANDERING because of their irregular shapes. White voters challenged them in court as a violation of their rights under the Fourteenth Amendment's Equal Protection Clause. (See tables, pages 525, 526.)

One of the first challenges came in North Carolina. African Americans made up about 20 percent of the population, but despite increased BLACK SUFFRAGE the state had sent no blacks to Congress since Reconstruction. When the state gained a new House seat after the 1990 census, the state legislature initially created one majority-black district, but then yielded to Justice Department pressure to create a second. One of the new congressional districts was relatively compact, but the second wound 160 miles through the center of the state to link black neighborhoods in four urban areas. Both districts elected black representatives, both Democrats.

The redistricting plan was challenged in federal court, first by the state's Republican Party and then by a group of white voters. The suits contended that the plan set up a "racially discriminatory process" and deprived white voters of the right to vote "in a color-blind election." The Justice Department joined the state in defending the plan. They argued that the majority-minority districts were necessary to comply with the Voting Rights Act and to remedy past discrimination against black voters. The suits were dismissed by a three-judge federal district court, but reinstated by the Supreme Court in a 5–4 decision, *shaw v. reno* (1993).

In her opinion for the Court, Justice Sandra Day O'Connor acknowledged that racial considerations could not be excluded from the redistricting process. But she said that in "some exceptional cases" a plan could be "so highly irregular that, on its face, it rationally cannot be understood as anything other than an effort to segregate voters on the basis of race." A district that ignores geographical and political boundaries to concentrate members of a particular race, she said, "bears an uncomfortable resemblance to political apartheid" and risks perpetuating "the very patterns of racial bloc voting that majority-minority districting is sometimes said to counteract."

The dissenting justices sharply questioned the logic of the opinion. Justice Byron White argued that white voters had not been harmed by the redistricting because whites constituted 79 percent of the state's population and constituted majorities in ten of the twelve congressional districts. Justice John Paul Stevens called it "perverse" to permit redistricting plans drawn to provide adequate representation of other groups—mentioning rural voters, union members, Hasidic Jews, Polish Americans, and Republicans—but not for blacks.

The ruling returned the case to the lower court to determine whether the redistricting plan met the "strict scrutiny" test used in other racial challenges: that is, whether it was narrowly tailored to serve a compelling government interest. As the case continued, challenges to racially drawn redistricting plans were proceeding in other states, including Georgia and Texas. The Supreme Court used those cases over the next few years to refine its position on racial redistricting.

In its next ruling, the Court in 1995 struck down a Georgia plan that had created three majority-black districts, including one that stretched from the Atlanta suburbs across half the state to the coastal cities of Augusta and Savannah. The 5–4 vote in *Miller v. Johnson* was the same as in the North Carolina case, but the Court laid down a different rule for judging the use of race in redistricting plans.

Writing for the majority, Justice Anthony M. Kennedy said that the earlier decision had not limited challenges to plans with irregularly shaped districts. Instead, he said, redistricting plans were subject to challenge if race was "the predominant factor motivating the legislature's decision to place a significant number of voters within or without a particular district." Racial motivation could be shown, he said, by evidence that the legislature "subordinated" traditional districting principles such as "compactness," "contiguity," or "respect for political subdivisions or communities" to racial considerations.

Applying that test, Kennedy said the Georgia plan was racially motivated and could be upheld only if it satisfied the strict scrutiny test. And he said that the state could not justify the plan on grounds that it was necessary to comply with the Voting Rights Act because the Justice Department had incorrectly interpreted the law to require the maximum number of majority-black districts. Writing for the four dissenters, Justice Ruth Bader Ginsburg warned that the ruling would entangle the federal judiciary in what she called the "highly political business" of legislative districting and leave state legislators uncertain how to comply.

The decision was also criticized outside the Court. President Bill Clinton called the ruling "a setback in the struggle to ensure that all Americans participate fully in the electoral process." One civil rights leader said the decision could "resegregate our political institutions." But a black House member praised the ruling. "We have black districts, red districts, brown districts, yellow districts," said Rep. Gary Franks, Connecticut Republican. "We should have only American districts."

The criticism did not sway the Court's majority. A year later, the same five-justice majority rejected the North Carolina redistricting plan after it had been upheld by a lower court. The suit in *Shaw v. Hunt* challenged the same congressional districts the Court had struck down in *Shaw v. Reno*. The Court also found that Texas had improperly used racial considerations in the drawing of three congressional districts—predominantly black districts in Houston and Dallas and a predominantly Hispanic district in Houston (*Bush v. Vera*). In both cases, the majority rejected arguments by the two states, the Justice Department, and civil rights groups that the plans could be justified on grounds of complying with the Voting Rights Act or remedying past discrimination. In the Texas case, the Court also discounted evidence that some of the irregularity of the districts resulted from changes aimed at benefiting incumbent lawmakers in adjoining districts.

Civil rights groups again complained that the rulings would make it harder for African American or Hispanic candidates to be elected to Congress. But their warnings were tempered by election results in Georgia in November 1996. The two African Americans elected in 1992 from newly drawn majority black districts won reelection even though their districts had been redrawn and no longer had a majority of black voters. Critics of racial redistricting said the results indicated that racial bloc voting was lessening and would continue to decline in importance if the Supreme Court's stance against racial line-drawing stood.

## Radical Republicans

*See* BLACK SUFFRAGE.

## Realignments and Dealignments

The American electorate is not static. From time to time it regroups in response to certain conditions or crises in a phenomenon known as *realignment*. Or it fragments in what is sometimes called *dealignment*.

Both phenomena concern how the voters ally themselves with a political party, the duration and strength of their allegiance, and—in the case of dealignment— whether parties matter much to the majority of the voters at a particular time. Most indications at the end of the twentieth century were that the United States was in a period of dealignment, except for the South, which has realigned.

Political scientist V. O. Key Jr. developed the basic theory of realignment in 1955 as the after-effect of "critical" elections "in which new and durable groupings are

*A growing rift between urban—and mainly northern—workers and the Democratic Party widened when the national convention nominated William Jennings Bryan, a rural Nebraskan, for president in 1896. That rift propelled Republican William McKinley into the White House.* Source: Library of Congress

formed." More recently Lawrence G. McMichael and Richard J. Trilling defined realignment as "a significant and durable change in the distribution of party support over relevant groups within the electorate."

In his 1970 examination of critical elections, political scientist Walter Dean Burnham observed that realignments "recur with rather remarkable regularity approximately one in a generation, or every thirty to thirty-eight years." They tend to happen, he said, when "politics as usual" is inadequate to deal with serious problems in society or the economy.

There is general agreement among political historians that the United States has had five *party systems* in its history, each one characterized by its unique alignment of voters, the combination of parties, and the degree of competition among them. Except for the first alignment, each party system began with a realignment.

The five party systems and their approximate time periods are as follows:

• First, 1789–1824. Despite the founders' reservations about factionalism, two parties quickly emerged during the nation's first decade. The Federalists led by Alexander Hamilton and John Adams favored a strong national government and drew support mostly from business interests. Thomas Jefferson's Democratic-Republicans opposed centralization of government and were supported by farmers and the less affluent. After the Jeffersonians' victory in 1800 the Federalists went into decline, setting the stage for the first realignment.

• Second, 1828–1854. Jefferson's party had evolved into the Democrats, who elected populist Andrew Jackson in 1828 and were opposed by the anti-Jackson Whigs. Although the Democrats were the dominant party, the Whigs gave strong opposition throughout this period until division over the slavery issue took its toll of both parties. The Democrats survived, but the Whigs elected their last president, Zachary Taylor, in 1848.

• Third, 1856–1896. This party system resulted from the first of three realignments that political historians classify as "major." With the Whigs dissolved, the Republican Party emerged from the so-called Civil War realignment as the second major party. It elected its first president, former Whig Abraham Lincoln, in 1860. This realignment was the last to bring forth a new party. Both of the subsequent major realignments were characterized by shifts in power between the two major parties. Throughout the third party system the Republicans dominated the Democrats, who were weakened by their split into northern and southern factions.

• Fourth, 1896–1932. The second major realignment began with the watershed reelection of Republican

William McKinley over William Jennings Bryan, a Populist nominated by the Democrats following the depression of 1893. By now Civil War animosities had faded, and economic issues dominated voter choices between the two parties. The agrarian South became solidly Democratic. The Republicans became the party of the industrialized North. The GOP continued to dominate, although a split in its ranks allowed a Democrat, Woodrow Wilson, to be elected president in 1912 and 1916.

• Fifth, 1932–present. The third major realignment produced a party system that still existed at the end of the twentieth century, in the opinion of most political scientists. It began with the New Deal election of Franklin D. Roosevelt in the Great Depression year of 1932 and led to a long period of Democratic Party dominance. Despite some setbacks, such as the elections of Republican Dwight D. Eisenhower in the 1950s, the New Deal COALITION of southern whites, union members, Catholics, blacks, and Jews basically held together long after World War II.

## Time for Realignment?

By Burnham's rule of thumb that realignments take place every thirty to thirty-eight years, the United States was due for a realignment in the 1960s or 1970s. Election analysts generally agreed, however, that it did not happen, even in the 1980s with the Republican victories of Ronald Reagan and George Bush or the 1990s with the GOP takeover of Congress.

It appeared more likely in the late 1990s that the United States was in a prolonged period of dealignment, which in itself could be significant. "In order for the system to realign, it would have to dealign, and such a process was clearly taking place," political scientist Martin P. Wattenberg wrote in 1991.

A concurring view was published in 1998 by political scientists William H. Flanigan and Nancy H. Zingale in *Political Behavior of the American Electorate*. Acknowledging that there has been a lot of voter movement and electoral volatility since the 1960s, Flanigan and Zingale characterize much of that movement as a "sorting out process" in which "a sizable number of voters have found neither political party a congenial place to be" and instead have avoided PARTY IDENTIFICATION and become INDEPENDENTS. As a result, they conclude, neither party can claim to be the new majority party. "In this situation, we find it more useful to consider the current situation as a continuation of a period of *dealignment*."

The evidence of dealignment includes increases in the number of independent voters and the prevalence of SPLIT-TICKET VOTING. In 1992, the NATIONAL ELECTION STUDIES showed that 38 percent of American voters identified themselves as independents, the highest level in fourteen years. The 18.9 percent of the presidential POPULAR VOTE received by independent Ross Perot also indicated widespread dissatisfaction with the existing two parties. In the 1996 election, in 25.5 percent of CONGRESSIONAL DISTRICTS, voters split their tickets, voting for a presidential candidate of one party and a House candidate of another party. The percentage was down from 43.7 in the Reagan landslide year of 1984 but up slightly from 23.0 in 1992.

In addition, campaigns are far more CANDIDATE-CENTERED than they were in the past. A 1980 National Election Study showed that almost 75 percent of self-described independent voters said they decide how to vote on the basis of the candidate rather than the party.

## Existing Alignments

Within the existing party system American voters align themselves with political parties in differing proportions according to age, religion, sex, socioeconomic status, ethnic or racial background, and other demographic characteristics. As coalitions rather than monoliths, both major parties draw considerable support from every subdivision of U.S. society.

A study of the Democratic and Republican coalitions by political scientist John R. Petrocik indicates that the composition of both changed from the 1950s to 1992. The Republican Party became more southern and white, while the Democratic Party became less southern and more black and Hispanic.

In 1992 African Americans accounted for 22 percent of Democratic supporters, up from 9 percent in the 1950s. Hispanic adherents increased from 1 percent to 11 percent. In the same period, northern union households favoring Democrats dropped from 22 percent to 12 percent, and white southern Democrats fell from 31 percent to 19 percent.

Among components of Republican support, Catholics rose from 10 percent to 15 percent, while white Protestants fell from 51 percent to 38 percent. White southerners increased from 15 percent of the GOP base to 23 percent.

EXIT POLLS and other studies show that since 1980 there has been a "gender gap," with women voting Democratic more than men. In 1995, for example, a Gallup poll showed that 36 percent of women and 28 percent of men identified themselves as Democrats.

In the fifty and over group—voters whose political identity was formed by the Democratic 1930s and 1940s—36 percent were Democrats compared with 24 percent of those eighteen to twenty-nine. With Republicans it was the reverse, with 34 percent in the younger group and 31 percent over age fifty.

---

# Reapportionment and Redistricting

*Reapportionment* and *redistricting* are the two processes that allocate the 435 seats in the House of Representatives, as well as seats in state legislatures and many city councils. Both processes help to determine the partisan and geographic makeup of such bodies, and whether racial or ethnic minorities will receive fair representation.

Reapportionment is the redistribution of seats to reflect shifts in population as indicated by the national CENSUS, which is conducted every ten years. As it applies to Congress, reapportionment gives additional House seats to states that have gained population over the previous decade, and it takes seats away from states that have lost population or have grown more slowly than the national average. The process works similarly in state, county, or city legislative DISTRICTS, the areas from which STATE LEGISLATORS and local council members are elected.

Redistricting means that the district boundaries are redrawn to adjust to the population changes and reallocation of seats. Most U.S. House members represent a specific area within a state, although seven states with sparse populations have only one House member for the entire state. (See HOUSE OF REPRESENTATIVES, ELECTING.)

Redistricting usually occurs in the two years following reapportionment. GOVERNORS and state legislators normally control the mapping process, for CONGRESSIONAL DISTRICTS as well as for state election districts. Counties or cities that have HOME RULE—full or limited independence from the state legislature—may be empowered to draw their own DISTRICT, WARD, AND PRECINCT boundaries.

No matter which body does the redistricting, the process may not be over when that body finishes its work. Affected persons or groups often file legal challenges to the maps. The courts sometimes order a second round of redistricting in the middle of a decade, and on occasion they even draw new district maps on their own.

Reapportionment and redistricting have been subjects of debate throughout U.S. history because the Constitution did not specify how they should be done. The framers decreed that House seats would be divided among the states on the basis of population, and that House members would be elected by the people. Beyond that, the Constitution gave little guidance on these subjects, leaving Congress, the courts, and state governments to wrestle with them.

In contrast to the House, the Senate never undergoes reapportionment or redistricting. The Constitution gave each state two Senate seats, and senators are always chosen on a statewide basis. Moreover, the two-senator minimum cannot be changed. Article V states "that no State, without its Consent, shall be deprived of its equal Suffrage in the Senate."

State senators, however, are elected from smaller districts that are apportioned according to population, much like congressional districts. MULTIMEMBER DISTRICTS, no longer permitted for the U.S. House, are still common in state elections.

After many decades of debate, the Supreme Court settled the basic goal of reapportionment and redistricting with rulings in the 1960s. The current guiding principle is ONE PERSON, ONE VOTE, which requires that each citizen have approximately the same representation. For Congress, this means that the 435 congressional districts should be as close to equal in population as possible.

Many other questions about reapportionment and redistricting have yet to be settled. Most important, the courts have not decided definitively whether the Constitution permits GERRYMANDERING, the drawing of district boundaries to favor one party or group.

## Reapportionment of the U.S. House

Reapportionment determines the relative strength of states and regions in the House according to a mathematical formula that distributes seats to states on the basis of population. It has not been easy to pick the best formula for the distribution. Congress has tried different methods over the years, but none, including the one currently in use, has worked perfectly. Many experts believe it is impossible to devise a method of allocating House seats that does not give some states more or less representation than they deserve.

The cause of the difficulty is simple: no state can have a fraction of a representative. Each state must have a whole number of House members, from one to as many as fifty-two (California) in the 1990s. Even with the complex reapportionment formula currently used, there is some variation in the amount of representation states receive based on their populations.

The framers settled the distribution question for the first Congress by specifically listing the number of seats each of the thirteen original states would have. This was necessary because at that time there were no accurate statistics on the populations of the states. The Constitution directed that after the first census in 1790 each congressional district should have at least 30,000 residents. (If that ratio were still in effect, the House today would have about 8,500 members. After the 1990 reapportionment, the average population of a congressional district was 573,394.)

The Constitution made an exception for small states, which were guaranteed at least one representative no matter what their population. In a compromise between the slave-owning South and the rest of the country, the Constitution provided that each slave would be counted as three-fifths of a person.

At first Congress followed the Constitution in basing representation on an ideal population size of a congressional district. As a result, the total number of House members at any time varied widely. In 1832, for example, the standard size of a congressional district was set at 47,700 people, producing a House of 240 members. None of the different allocation methods used in those days could solve the problem of fractional representation, so congressional districts varied widely in population. The early reapportionment methods also failed to deal with the rapid growth in the nation's population. No matter what method was used, there seemed to be unanticipated effects that went against common sense.

Finally, around 1850, Congress settled on a method that seemed to solve many reapportionment problems—expanding the membership. The size of the House was supposed to be fixed by the most recent apportionment law at 233 members, but Congress regularly voted to add more members as new states entered the Union. The addition of members allowed the House to sidestep the difficult task of cutting back on the representation of existing states to accommodate the new states.

By the beginning of the twentieth century, however, the process threatened to make the House too large to be a workable legislative body. In 1911 Congress fixed the size of the House at 435, where it has remained except for a brief period (1959–1963) when the admission of Alaska and Hawaii raised the total temporarily to 437.

The decision to freeze the size of the House set the stage for the reapportionment battles of the 1920s. The 1920 census was a landmark event in the nation's history because it showed that for the first time there were more Americans living in cities than in rural areas. States with large cities therefore were entitled to many more representatives, while rural states faced sharp cutbacks in their House representation.

Arguing that people who lived on farms and in small towns were the heart and soul of America, rural representatives fought hard to prevent their loss of power. They managed to block reapportionment throughout the 1920s. Redistribution of House seats did not take place until after the 1930 census. That reapportionment led to drastic shifts in power, with California nearly doubling its House delegation, from eleven to twenty, while twenty-one other states lost a total of twenty-seven seats.

The current method of reapportionment, called "the method of equal proportions," was adopted after the 1940 census, effective after the 1950 census, but it was made retroactive to January 1941 to save a Democratic seat Arkansas would have lost to Michigan under a different formula that otherwise yielded identical results for the rest of the country. The equal proportions method allocates House seats according to a complicated mathematical formula designed to minimize population variation among districts. Its adoption put an end to most controversy over reapportionment until the early 1990s, when Massachusetts and Montana mounted legal challenges. Both succeeded in the lower federal courts but the Supreme Court rejected their arguments in 1992.

Massachusetts argued that it deserved another seat because the census had counted overseas military personnel inaccurately. Montana, which had lost one of its two seats in the 1990 reapportionment, challenged the reapportionment formula on grounds that it was unfair to less populous states. The Supreme Court refused to support either claim.

Reapportionment every ten years has continued to exert a major influence on political strength in the House. Because Americans move so often, the populations of many states change substantially in ten years. The political strength of those states in the House can change considerably as well. The most important change in state populations in recent years has been the shift of people away from the older, industrial states of the Northeast and Midwest to the newly developing states along the nation's southern tier, from Florida to California (the Sun Belt).

As a result of the 1980 census, seventeen House seats shifted from the Northeast and Midwest to the Sun Belt. The state that benefited most was Florida, which picked up four seats, followed by Texas with three and California with two. New York, on the other hand, lost five seats—the sharpest drop in House representation for any state since 1840. Illinois, Ohio, and Pennsylvania lost two seats each.

The 1990 census showed that the trend had continued. California picked up seven seats, reflecting a dramatic westward population shift, while Florida gained another four seats and Texas gained three. New York once again was the big loser, dropping three seats. Illinois, Ohio, and Pennsylvania again lost two seats each, as did Michigan.

Many political observers predicted that the 1980 reapportionment would alter the ideological makeup of the House. Most of the states that lost seats tended to favor liberal Democrats, while the states that gained seats were more likely to favor Republicans or conservative Democrats. Because of Democratic successes in the state redistricting battles that followed reapportionment, however, the effects were less significant than expected.

Similarly, Republicans were disappointed in their hopes to substantially reduce the Democrats' majorities in Congress in the 1992 election, the first to reflect reapportionment following the 1990 census. The Republicans did not have to wait long, however, to see their hopes realized. They gained control of the House in 1994 and retained it in 1996 and, with smaller margins, in 1998. In both elections they also won and held majorities in the Senate.

## Redistricting

The early years of debate over redistricting were dominated by the question of whether there needed to be congressional districts within states at all. The Constitution does not say so, and several states favored the multimember district system of AT-LARGE elections in which all the voters in the state chose all the state's House members. Use of the system declined because it did not encourage the close ties between representatives and citizens that developed when a member of Congress represented a specific area.

Congress banned at-large House elections in 1842, except in one-member states, although the ban sometimes was violated until the 1960s. The 1842 law also established the basic principle that House districts should be contiguous—that is, a single, connected area rather than several separate areas scattered across a state.

Redistricting has become a subject of intense debate in recent decades as a result of Supreme Court decisions in the 1960s, major population shifts within states, and the development of computer-based technology. The national Republican and Democratic Parties devote immense resources to the effort to persuade state legislatures and the courts to approve redistricting plans favorable to their own candidates.

Some political scientists believe that redistricting is the single most important factor determining partisan control of the House. They argue that the former dominance of the Democratic Party, which controlled the House continuously from 1955 to 1995, was a result of Democratic control of the redistricting process. Republicans claimed that Democratic-dominated state legislatures devised district plans that gave the advantage to Democratic House candidates.

But in 1994, besides gaining control of Congress, the Republicans gained near-parity with the Democrats in control of state legislatures for the first time since 1968. More than half the states had divided control, with a governor of one party and at least one chamber controlled by the other party.

## Supreme Court Action

For a hundred years redistricting questions received little attention. State legislatures had to draw new congressional district lines when the state gained or lost House seats because of reapportionment, and occasionally there was a heated dispute over a single House district. But the legislatures usually ignored the population shifts within their states and rarely acted to change their own election district lines. As a result, cities did not gain additional representation in the state legislatures as their populations grew. Partisan fights over district lines were rare, however, and there was little pressure for major alterations in the shape of most districts.

Rural areas were vastly overrepresented, while cities did not have nearly so much representation as their populations warranted—a condition known as *malapportionment*. In every state the most populous state legislative district had more than twice as many people as the least populous district. The population balance was not usually so lopsided in congressional districts, but wide differences between rural and urban representation remained. For example, in Texas one urban congressional district had four times as many people in 1960 as one lightly populated rural district. (Such districts in ancient England were known as *rotten boroughs*.)

The state legislatures, dominated by members from rural areas, refused or neglected to change the existing districts, especially those for their own seats. Frustrated urban dwellers turned to the courts, arguing that the legislatures were denying them fair representation.

The situation changed radically when the Supreme Court began to consider redistricting issues in the 1960s, after refusing for decades to become involved in the matter. By the time the Court began to act, there was clear evidence that something was wrong with the way legislative districts were drawn. In its historic decision in BAKER V. CARR (1962), the Supreme Court ruled that the districts used in the Tennessee state legislature were unconstitutional because they violated the principle of one person, one vote.

In 1964 the Court extended the one-person, one-vote doctrine to the U.S. House in the case of *Wesberry v. Sanders,* which concerned congressional districts in Georgia. That decision stated that congressional districts should be as nearly equal in population "as is practicable."

Since then, the Court has continued to tighten the requirement that congressional districts should have equal populations. In *Kirkpatrick v. Preisler* (1969) the Court struck down Missouri's plan, even though the largest district had a population only 3.1 percent larger than that of the smallest district. Any population difference, "no matter how small," the Court declared, was

unacceptable in all but a few cases. The Court set an even more rigorous standard in *Karcher v. Daggett* (1983). In that case the Court overturned New Jersey's congressional map because the difference between the most populated and the least populated districts was 0.69 percent.

Although the one-person, one-vote principle is now widely accepted in American politics, some political experts criticize the Court's strict standard of population equality. For one thing, the census figures for district populations are not entirely accurate, and they usually are out of date soon after the census has been taken. The 1990 census was especially controversial because studies showed that certain urban and minority populations were seriously undercounted.

For the 2000 census, the Clinton administration proposed using modern sampling techniques—commonly used in POLLING—to correct the undercount problem. Republicans in Congress objected, fearing that sampling would give more House representation to areas that usually elect Democrats. Contending that the Constitution requires an actual head count rather than a projection, several GOP House members filed suit against the sampling plan and won a 5–4 Supreme Court ruling in January 1999. The Court barred use of sampling figures for reapportionment but not for redistricting within states.

As a result of unexpected Democratic gains in the 1998 elections, redistricting after the 2000 census will be performed mostly by Democratic-controlled legislatures. The president's party usually loses seats in MIDTERM ELECTIONS, in state legislatures as well as the U.S. House. But in 1998 the Democrats gained five House seats (not enough to gain control) and a net gain of one legislature, leaving the state legislature lineup at twenty-one Democratic, seventeen Republican, eleven divided, and one nonpartisan (Nebraska).

Whether voluntarily drawn by a legislature or ordered by a court, strict equality of redistricting can produce strangely contorted districts. Those drawn to ensure equal population often cross traditional political boundaries, such as cities, counties, or regions, that help voters develop a sense of identification with and interest in their congressional district. Also, critics have pointed out that the Supreme Court's standard can be satisfied by a districting plan that is a grossly unfair case of political gerrymandering, so long as each district has the same number of people.

RACIAL REDISTRICTING is another potential form of gerrymandering. By dividing up African Americans or other minority voters among several districts, a legislature might be able to ensure that members of a minority group make up no more than half the voters in a district and so prevent election of a minority representative. Conversely, drawing a district to take in several black neighborhoods, to ensure that the minority has a population majority, may be unfair to the nonminority voters who happen to live within the boundaries.

When BLACK SUFFRAGE became a reality in the 1960s, civil rights groups feared that African Americans might be subjected to racial gerrymandering by white-dominated legislatures. To prevent this, Congress added provisions to the 1965 VOTING RIGHTS ACT barring redistricting plans that dilute the voting strength of blacks.

The law required states with histories of racial discrimination to submit their redistricting plans to the U.S. Justice Department to ensure that African American voters were being treated fairly. Other minorities, including Hispanics, Asian Americans, and Native Americans, were later included in the law's protection. The department and the courts have required changes in redistricting plans in several states to ensure that minority candidates have a chance of being elected. The department required fourteen states to submit their redistricting plans for approval after the 1990 census.

In a ruling on districts in North Carolina, *Thornburg v. Gingles* (1986), the Supreme Court said gerrymandering that deliberately diluted minority voting strength was illegal. The burden of proof shifted from minorities, who had been required to show that lines were being drawn to dilute their voting strength, to lawmakers, who had to show that they had done all they could to maximize minority voting strength.

In the 1990s, in a series of decisions beginning with *SHAW V. RENO* (1993), a North Carolina case, the Court

cast doubt on the legitimacy of irregularly shaped congressional districts having minority majorities or others where race appeared to have been the "predominant factor" in drawing the district lines. Although in some cases the intent of such gerrymandering may have been benevolent—to ensure election of an African American or Hispanic representative—the Court said in *Shaw*, it bore "an uncomfortable resemblance to political apartheid."

The Court later invalidated some majority-minority districts and lower federal courts followed suit. In September 1998 the Court announced that it would review (in *Hunt v. Cromartie*) a lower federal court's invalidation of North Carolina's districts.

---

## Recall

*See* REMOVAL FROM OFFICE.

---

## Recount

Most elections produce decisive results. In the relatively few that do not, the apparent loser may demand a recount, officially creating a CONTESTED ELECTION.

Recount procedures vary by state. Close elections in about a dozen states automatically trigger a recounting of the regular and ABSENTEE ballots, a process that can take many weeks in a large state. Unlike VOTING MACHINE ballots that can be tallied quickly, absentee ballots must be verified as genuine and counted one by one.

Not everyone can initiate a recount. In most cases where they are not automatic, recounts can be requested only by the defeated candidate, as the interested party. State officials or the courts may order a recount if there is a possibility that ELECTION FRAUD corrupted the results.

Because states share the conduct of presidential and congressional elections with the federal government, state policies vary concerning jurisdiction over federal elections. Some states assert their authority over them, others prefer minimal involvement. For its part, the federal government leaves all the procedural aspects of elections to the states—VOTER REGISTRATION, preparation of the ballot, operation of the polling places, counting of the votes, and recounts if necessary. In the VOTING RIGHTS ACT of 1965, however, the federal government asserted its power to supervise elections in states where discrimination against minority voters is indicated. (See STATE AND FEDERAL ELECTION RESPONSIBILITIES.)

Federal authorities do not recount the POPULAR VOTE, even in disputes over congressional races. The states do the recounting and certify the winner to the House or the Senate. If the certified result is still in dispute, the affected body may investigate under its constitutional power to judge the qualifications of its own members. (See HOUSE OF REPRESENTATIVES, QUALIFICATIONS; SENATE, QUALIFICATIONS.)

Eligibility for review of a House regular or special election is determined by the Federal Contested Elections Act of 1969, which limits challenges to candidates listed on the official state ballot or certified as WRITE-IN candidates. The Senate has no comparable legislation.

Only once in its history has the Senate been unable to resolve an election dispute. That was in New Hampshire's exceedingly close 1974 contest between Republican Louis C. Wyman and Democrat John A. Durkin. Even then, the Senate did not try to recount the New Hampshire votes. After two unsuccessful recounts by the state, the Senate called for a new election, which Durkin won.

After his narrow 1960 loss to John F. Kennedy, Vice President Richard Nixon considered asking for a recount, which would have been the only general recount of a presidential election. Nixon ultimately decided against it for fear of inciting a constitutional crisis.

State laws prohibit frivolous recounts. The challenger must have grounds, such as evidence of errors, irregularities, or fraud. And the original count must be close enough for a recount to change the result.

Errors may include voting machine malfunctions, the same precinct's vote counted twice, the wrong total read off a machine, or computer breakdown. Irregularities may include polls closed early, invalid signatures on absentee ballot envelopes, or poll officials entering booths with voters to give unwanted assistance.

Evidence of fraud may include unusually high or low VOTER TURNOUT in a precinct, illegal noncitizen votes, or voting in the names of deceased persons.

Some states require the requester to pay for the recount, which may or may not be refunded if the result is overturned. A statewide recount can cost from $50,000 to $200,000.

## Redistricting

*See* REAPPORTIONMENT AND REDISTRICTING.

## Referendums

*See* INITIATIVES AND REFERENDUMS.

## Reform Party (1995– )

The Reform Party emerged almost full grown from independent Ross Perot's self-financed presidential candidacy of 1992. Unlike that campaign, in which the Dallas billionaire spurned public funding to avoid federal campaign spending limits, the Reform Party effort of 1996 qualified for federal funding and went along with the limitations that acceptance of the money entailed. By garnering more than 5 percent of the 1992 presidential vote, Perot qualified in 1996 for some $30 million, less than half the amount he spent from his own pocket four years earlier. (See UNITED WE STAND AMERICA.)

Perot was challenged for the Reform Party nomination by Richard D. Lamm, a former Democratic governor of Colorado, who had shown a willingness to risk voter displeasure. Lamm had called, for example, for deep cuts in Medicare, the popular health care program for the elderly.

Perot defeated Lamm in an unusual two-stage proce-

*Ross Perot greets supporters at the Reform Party's convention, August 11, 1996. Source: Lee Celano, Reuters*

dure, with a preliminary vote after nominating speeches at a convention in Long Beach, California, followed by a mail and electronic vote with the winner announced a week later in Valley Forge, Pennsylvania. Ballots had been sent to 1.3 million voters who were registered party members or signers of its BALLOT ACCESS petitions.

Perot again was on the ballot in all states. He chose as his running mate Pat Choate, a native Texan and economist who had coached Perot in his unsuccessful fight against the North American Free Trade Agreement (NAFTA). The Reform Party also had congressional candidates in ten states.

Locked out of the presidential debates, Perot spent much of his campaign money on television "infomercials" espousing the party's principles. In addition to a balanced budget, these included higher ethical standards for the White House and Congress, campaign and elections reforms, a new tax system, and lobbying restrictions.

Even with the restricted budget, Perot again placed third in the national election after the two major party candidates. However, his 8,085,285 votes (8.4 percent of the national total) came to less than half of his 1992 achievement of 18.9 percent, a THIRD PARTY figure surpassed in the twentieth century only by former president Theodore Roosevelt and his Bull Moose candidacy of 1912. Perot had his best showing in Maine, where he received 14.2 percent of the vote. He won no electoral votes.

At a postelection convention in Nashville in early 1997 the Reform Party began the task of building a permanent new political party rivaling the two major parties. An unresolved issue was the future role of Perot, with many stalwarts arguing that the party needed to emerge from what Lamm termed Perot's "dominating shadow." Denying that Reform had become "the party of personality," Perot nevertheless declined to rule out another try for the presidency in 2000. The Nashville convention ended with Perot supporters still firmly in control of the Reform Party.

---

## Registration Laws

*See* VOTER REGISTRATION.

---

## Removal from Office

Recall and impeachment are the processes that allow the people, directly or through their representatives, to remove from office an official who has broken the law or in some other way has presented grounds for dismissal. At the federal level, impeachment applies to the president, vice president, and all other civil officers. There is no recall of federal officials. Some state constitutions permit impeachment and a dozen also allow recall of GOVERNORS and other officials, including mayors and other municipal officers in some cases.

Both impeachment and recall are used sparingly. But their mere availability serves as a powerful check on the honesty and integrity of elected and appointed officials in the various positions of trust to which the people have assigned them.

### Impeachment

For only the second time in its history, the U.S. House voted December 19, 1998, to impeach a president. Using his full name, the House approved two articles of impeachment against President William Jefferson Clinton, charging perjury and obstruction of justice in the investigation of his admitted affair with White House intern Monica S. Lewinsky. Voting mostly along party lines, the Republican-controlled House approved the perjury charge 228–206 and the obstruction of justice charge 221–212. After a five-week trial, however, the Senate acquitted Clinton on February 12, 1999. Neither article received a majority, failing 45–55 on perjury and 50–50 on obstruction. Five Republicans joined the forty-five Senate Democrats to defeat the latter article.

Clinton was only the third president subjected to a formal impeachment inquiry and the only president besides Andrew Johnson to be impeached by the House and tried by the Senate. Johnson was tried but not convicted. The third president targeted by an impeachment inquiry was Richard Nixon, who resigned August 9, 1974, to avoid almost certain impeachment in connection with the Watergate burglary and cover-up SCANDAL.

Of the sixteen officials impeached before Clinton, only seven—all federal judges—had been convicted and removed from office for the constitutional offenses (Article II, section 4) of "Treason, Bribery, or other High Crimes and Misdemeanors." One of the impeached and convicted judges, Democrat Alcee L. Hastings of Florida, was elected to the House in 1992 after his criminal conviction was overturned in the courts.

Impeachment is a two-stage process in which the House of Representatives makes the formal charge, like a grand jury, and the Senate in closed session decides the accused's guilt or innocence, much as a regular jury would. The Senate may also disqualify the convicted official from holding future federal office, but it has done so in only two of the seven judge convictions. The House inserted such a provision in the articles against Clinton, saying his conduct warrants "disqualification to hold and enjoy any office of honor, trust or profit under the United States."

Under Article I of the Constitution, the House has the sole authority to impeach and the Senate alone tries all impeachments, with a two-thirds majority vote required for conviction. If the president or vice president is being tried, the chief justice of the United States presides.

Johnson, the first impeached president, was tried in 1868 on charges of violating the Tenure of Office Act by removing Secretary of War Edwin M. Stanton without the assent of Congress, then controlled by the Radical Republicans bent on punishing the South for the Civil War. Johnson frequently clashed with Congress as he tried to carry out the "malice toward none" policy of his assassinated predecessor, Abraham Lincoln.

In the Senate trial Johnson escaped conviction by a single vote—that of Edmund Gibson Ross of Kansas.

Ross, a freshman, sided at the last minute with six other Republicans and twelve Democrats to make the vote 35–19, one short of the 36 needed to convict Johnson. Ross's vote is often cited as an example of political courage.

Besides Johnson and Clinton, only one other elected federal official had been impeached and tried. He was Sen. William Blount of Tennessee, impeached by the House in 1797 for having conspired to launch a military expedition to conquer Spanish territory for Great Britain. The Senate dismissed the impeachment charges because it already had expelled Blount.

Impeachment charges are presented to the House by its Judiciary Committee as "articles of impeachment." If approved by the full House, the articles go to the Senate for trial, with House-appointed managers serving as prosecutors.

In Nixon's case, the Judiciary Committee July 27–30, 1974, approved three articles charging obstruction of justice, abuse of power, and contempt of Congress. Two other proposed articles were rejected. On August 5, Nixon by order of the Supreme Court released tran scripts of subpoenaed tapes, including the "smoking gun" tape of June 23, 1972, that made clear Nixon knowingly participated in the cover-up of White House involvement in the burglary of DEMOCRATIC NATIONAL COMMITTEE headquarters in the Watergate Hotel complex. Faced with the new evidence and almost total loss of support in Congress, Nixon resigned.

In the case of Clinton, the House Judiciary Committee, after reviewing the report of independent counsel Kenneth W. Starr, concluded that the president may have committed fifteen possibly impeachable offenses, including obstruction of justice, lying under oath about his relationship with Lewinsky, and witness tampering. By a 258–176 vote October 8, the House directed the committee to investigate whether grounds for impeachment existed.

A problem in impeachment cases other than those for bribery or treason is the definition of "high crimes and misdemeanors." Generally, it has come to mean whatever the prosecution wanted it to mean. Because it involved engaging in and concealing private acts, the Clinton case presented a particularly difficult question of impeachability. But to some four hundred historians and presidential scholars the "current charges against him depart from what the Framers saw as grounds for impeachment." They signed an open letter to Congress saying that impeachment would undermine the presidency and leave it "permanently disfigured."

## Recall

The recall procedure for removing state and local officials gained favor during the Progressive Era of the early 1900s as an antidote to political corruption and irresponsibility. It originated in Switzerland (where it is applicable to the entire legislature, not just an individual official) and was adopted by Los Angeles in 1903. From there it spread quickly to other cities, usually those using the commission form of government in which three to nine commissioners carry out both legislative and executive duties.

Oregon was the first state to adopt recall, in 1908, and California followed suit in 1911. By the late 1990s, twelve states, mostly in the West and Midwest, allowed recall of state officers and many state constitutions permitted it for municipal officers as well. In Kansas, one of the first adopters, appointed as well as elected officers are covered by recall. Many of the adopting states had large numbers of elective officers who were immune to removal by a governor and were, in essence, beyond the control of the electorate during their term of office. A number of the states exempted judges from recall.

Laws governing recall usually provide that, if a specified number of voters sign a petition, a SPECIAL ELECTION must be held to decide whether the targeted official should continue to serve or immediately vacate the office. The number of signers required is normally a percentage of those who voted for the particular office in the previous election. This tends to average about 25 percent of the original electorate. The states all have different rules affecting the gathering of petition signatures and deciding upon their legitimacy; these variances can sometimes influence the recall effort, depending on the partisanship of those judging whether the petition satisfies the criteria.

In some jurisdictions, the question of vacating the office is decided in one election and another is then held to decide upon a replacement. In others, because of cost considerations, the elections are combined and the official whose conduct is under fire may register as a candidate. The vote to remove the current official can be either by simple majority or a higher percentage, such as an ABSOLUTE MAJORITY.

After the initial burst of enthusiasm, recall's popularity waned and its end results have been inconclusive. No other states adopted it after the first twelve did, and it has been applied sporadically.

In January 1988 a recall movement against Republican governor Evan Mecham of Arizona obtained enough signatures to require a vote on his removal. But before the special election could be held, the state legislature impeached and convicted Mecham, which removed him from office. Mecham was convicted of obstructing investigation of a death threat and lending official funds to his auto dealership.

The impeachment process has been used more frequently than recall to remove governors from office. Mecham was the fifth governor in the twentieth century to be removed through impeachment and conviction.

In 1997 a petition drive to recall Wisconsin's two Democratic senators, Herb Kohl and Russell H. Feingold, fell about forty thousand short of the number required for a recall election. Abortion opponents launched the drive in protest against the senators' votes against a ban on so-called partial birth abortions.

Although the U.S. Constitution does not provide for recall of senators, Wisconsin officials said if the signature quota had been met they would have scheduled a special election even if the results were only advisory. In the 1998 MIDTERM ELECTION Feingold won reelection with 51 percent of the vote. Kohl was not up for reelection.

As in the Wisconsin case, recall need not be for illegal actions. In Michigan in 1984 voters angry over a tax increase changed party control of the state senate by recalling several members.

Critics say that recall usually is too cumbersome to be applied at the statewide level. It has been successfully used only once to remove a governor—in 1921 in North Dakota. (See GOVERNOR.) Recall is used most often at the local level of government where petition gathering is relatively manageable.

Political theorists believe, however, that the very existence of recall restrains elected officials who fear its application. For the voters, it reinforces the comforting notion of representative-as-agent, in which the elected representative does the voters' bidding and must be periodically answerable to them if he or she fails this trust. (See NATURE OF REPRESENTATION.)

---

## Republican Government

Although today the terms are almost interchangeable, *republican* government was not the same as DEMOCRACY to the founders of the United States. They equated democracy with mob rule. What they were creating, they believed and intended, was a representative democracy or republican form of government.

In a democracy, they feared, a faction or party could become a tyrannical majority. But a "well-constructed Union" formed along republican lines, James Madison wrote in *The Federalist*, would tend to "break and control the violence of faction."

Besides ensuring a government of wise and patriotic citizens, the founders hoped, their Constitution would separate executive, legislative, and judicial powers sufficiently to prevent any one branch from assuming excessive control. Another of those checks and balances was the federal system, with powers shared between the national government and the states.

The powers of the national government were to be those spelled out or implied in the Constitution. By contrast, the states were to exercise *reserved powers*—that is, those not specifically prohibited to the states and those not granted to the national government. As an example of prohibited activities, the Constitution bars the states from coining money or entering into treaties or alliances with foreign countries.

Reflecting the split that preceded adoption of the Constitution in 1789, the first American political parties divided largely over the issue of national versus state government authority. The Federalists—a loose coalition of merchants, shippers, financiers, and other business interests—favored the strong central government established by the Constitution. The opposition (at first called ANTI-FEDERALISTS or Jeffersonians and later known as DEMOCRATIC-REPUBLICANS) were farmers and frontiersmen intent on preserving the sovereignty of the states.

## Federal Supremacy

In a system in which powers are divided between the federal government and the states, it is inevitable that conflicts will arise. To deal with them, Article VI contains a federal supremacy clause, which makes the Constitution and the laws and treaties passed under it the "supreme Law of the Land." This provision means that all state laws, executive orders, and judicial decisions must conform to the Constitution, treaties, and laws of the United States, or they are invalid.

Such conflicts arose almost immediately after the Constitution was put into effect. They aligned the Federalists, who advocated a strong national government capable of encouraging commercial development and exercising discipline over the states, against the Anti-Federalist advocates of states' rights. In one of its most important early decisions, *McCulloch v. Maryland* (1819), the Supreme Court came down strongly on the side of those who favored a broad interpretation of constitutional grants to the national government.

The *McCulloch* case arose over the refusal of the cashier of the United States Bank branch in Baltimore to pay a tax that the state of Maryland had levied on the bank. Maryland argued that Congress had no right to create the bank because the Constitution makes no mention of such a power in Article I.

In writing the Supreme Court's opinion, Chief Justice John Marshall, an ardent Federalist, rejected Maryland's call for a strict and literal interpretation of the grant of powers to Congress. He noted that it was entirely reasonable for Congress to decide that it was "necessary and proper" to create a national bank to carry out Congress's *delegated powers* to impose taxes, borrow money, and care for U.S. property. Marshall thereby established in *McCulloch* the doctrine of *implied powers,* which means the national government may exercise powers that can be reasonably implied from its delegated powers.

In later years the Supreme Court used this precedent to provide the legal justification for sweeping extensions of the national government's powers. By virtue of the implied powers doctrine, the national government has been empowered to support public schools, welfare programs, farm prices, public housing, community development, crime control, and unemployment compensation; regulate working conditions and collective bargaining; fix a minimum wage; ban discrimination in housing, places of public accommodation, and employment; and even affect highway speed limits and the legal drinking age.

The Constitution gives a special role to the states in the government system by guaranteeing each state equal representation in the Senate, permitting electors chosen by each state (the ELECTORAL COLLEGE) to elect the president, and requiring that three-fourths of the states ratify all constitutional amendments. The permanent bond of the states to the Union was settled once and for all by the Civil War (1861–1865). As the Supreme Court declared in a post–Civil War case, the United States is "an indestructible Union composed of indestructible states."

When powers are not granted exclusively to the national government by the Constitution, the states may exercise those powers concurrently, provided there is no conflict with federal law. Among the states' *concurrent powers* are the power to levy taxes, borrow money, and establish courts.

But there is no specific listing of states' reserved powers in the Constitution. In practical terms, this has meant that the states have the major responsibility for government activities such as public education, local government, intrastate highway transportation, protection of public health and safety, and family relations.

## Role of the Courts

The national-state relationship of American federalism is constantly evolving, largely because of the JUDICIAL SYSTEM and its unending interpretation of the Constitution and the validity of laws passed by Congress or the state legislatures. Indeed, the frequency with which the Supreme Court has ruled on such laws, going back to *McCulloch v. Maryland,* points up an important feature of the Constitution-mandated federal system.

The courts' vehicle for their jurisdiction in the national-state relationship is their power of judicial review—an authority not mentioned in the Constitution but one asserted by Chief Justice Marshall in *Marbury v. Madison* in 1803, sixteen years before *McCulloch.*

Federalism has enlarged judicial power and influence because a system that divides power among governments requires an umpire able to resolve disputes. In the United States the courts often perform this function, making decisions that affect generations of Americans.

---

## Republican National Committee

For all but ten of the years 1969–1999, the Republican National Committee (RNC) enjoyed the advantage of having a Republican in the White House. One of those presidents was George Bush, the only former national party chair to hold the nation's highest office.

Although national party involvement in presidential politics is weaker than it used to be, the interests of the national committees and the White House remain inextricably linked. And being the "in" party lends prestige and strength to the national committee allied with the president.

For Bush, however, that link was not sufficient to prevent his defeat by Bill Clinton in 1992. And Clinton, in making the DEMOCRATIC NATIONAL COMMITTEE a close partner in his 1996 reelection campaign, if only for fund raising, crossed CAMPAIGN FINANCE boundaries and risked losing a second term. Had Republican nominee Robert J. Dole won, he would have become the second former national chair to win the presidency. Dole held the post from 1971 to 1973, followed by Bush, 1973–1974. (See Appendix, National Party Chairs, 1848–1999.)

In general, besides their differing fortunes in presidential elections, the RNC and DNC are dissimilar. The RNC is smaller, less bound by complex rules, and has been less active in PRESIDENTIAL SELECTION REFORMS. Its members serve two-year terms versus four years for DNC members. In both parties, the NATIONAL PARTY CONVENTION is the supreme governing body, with the national committee and chair conducting party business between conventions. Like the DNC, the RNC is responsible for issuing the *Call,* which announces the particulars of the party's quadrennial convention. Unlike the DNC, the RNC cannot change party rules. Changes proposed by the Standing Committee on Rules must be approved by GOP convention. Other RNC committees include finance and the convention *Call,* site, and arrangements committees.

A major responsibility of the national committees is the filling of vacancies on the presidential ticket after the nominating conventions. Both the DNC and RNC have had to make substitutions for vice-presidential nominees. (See RUNNING MATE; VICE PRESIDENT.)

Besides the chair and cochair, the RNC elects a secretary and treasurer. Four regional caucuses each elect a man and a woman as vice chairs. The eleven-member Executive Council is made up of three RNC members appointed by the chair and eight elected by the regional caucuses. The Executive Council is authorized to act for the RNC between meetings. An executive committee, which includes the Executive Council, advises the chair.

The 1997–1999 GOP chair, Colorado developer Jim Nicholson, presides over a 165-member national committee headquartered at 310 First Street, S.E., on Capitol Hill in Washington, D.C. The committee staff numbers about 250.

With no Republican in the White House to dictate a choice, a race developed for the party chair after the 1996 election. Haley Barbour of Mississippi, credited with helping to bring about the Republican sweep of Congress in 1994, declined a third two-year term. Nicholson, a West Point graduate and Vietnam War veteran, won as a compromise candidate after multiple ballots, defeating several others who had campaigned for the leadership position.

GOP rules call for the cochair to be the opposite sex of the chair. In 1997 the RNC elected businesswoman Patricia S. Harrison of Arlington, Virginia, for the post.

*Haley Barbour (right) hands the gavel to his successor Jim Nicholson, the new chairman of the Republican National Committee.*
Source: *Jeff Mitchell, Reuters*

The national committee is made up of three people (the national committeeman, national committeewoman, and the chair) from each state and from American Samoa, District of Columbia, Guam, Puerto Rico, and Virgin Islands. Methods of electing those members vary according to state laws and party rules.

Both parties have had only one woman chair. Jean Westwood of Utah served as DNC chair in 1972, and Mary Louise Smith of Iowa was the RNC chair from 1974 to 1977.

Ronald Reagan was the first president of either party to name a part-time general chair to work in tandem with the full-time, salaried national party chair. Reagan's general chair from 1983 to 1986 was Sen. Paul Laxalt of Nevada, while the chair was Frank Fahrenkopf of the same state until 1989.

Bush's aggressive 1988 campaign manager, Lee Atwater of South Carolina, was the first professional POLITICAL CONSULTANT to chair a national party committee. After Atwater became ill with a brain tumor, President

Bush made him general chair with reduced duties. Clayton Yeutter of Nebraska became national chair in 1991. Atwater died in March of that year.

Vacancies in the national chair occur occasionally when the president gives the incumbent another assignment. Richard Nixon, for example, tapped Rogers C. B. Morton to head the Interior Department in 1971, and two years later he sent George Bush to the People's Republic of China as U.S. liaison.

As national chairmen during the second Nixon administration, 1973–1974, Dole and Bush were burdened with the party's worst public relations crisis, Watergate, which ultimately drove Nixon from office. Throughout the emergency, first Dole and then Bush was forced on a daily basis to fend off questions about the break-in at DNC headquarters in the Watergate Office Building on June 17, 1972, and the later discovery of White House tapes that ultimately exposed the "smoking gun" tape proving Nixon's knowledge of the burglary and the conspiracy to cover it up.

The abuses of Watergate, made possible in part by excessive contributions to Nixon's reelection campaign and uncontrolled use of the money, led to PUBLIC FINANCING of presidential campaigns and limits on individual and POLITICAL ACTION COMMITTEE (PAC) contributions to candidates for federal office. The reforms, however, did not limit so-called SOFT MONEY contributions by corporations and other groups to political parties. It was the pursuit of soft money that raised questions about the DNC's fund-raising success in 1996. But the Republicans actually raised $18.9 million more in soft money ($141.2 million) than the Democrats' $122.3 million.

The Republican-controlled Congress authorized overlapping investigations of the 1996 fund raising. Rather than have joint hearings as in the Watergate investigation, the House insisted on probing only the Democrats' finances while the Senate said it would look for possible abuses by both parties.

## Republican National Convention

*See* NATIONAL PARTY CONVENTIONS.

## Republican Party (1854– )

Born in 1854 in the upper Midwest, the Republican Party grew out of the antislavery forces' bitter dissatisfaction with the Kansas-Nebraska Act. The act overturned earlier legislation (the Missouri Compromise of 1820 and the Compromise of 1850), limiting the extension of slavery into the territories, and instituted the concept of popular sovereignty, by which each territory decided its position on slavery. While historians generally credit residents of Ripon, Wisconsin, with holding the party's first organizational meeting in March 1854 and citizens of Jackson, Michigan, with running the party's first electoral ticket in July 1854, the birth of the party was nearly simultaneous in many communities throughout the northern states. The volatile slavery issue was the catalyst that created the party, but the political vacuum caused by the decline of the WHIG PARTY and the failure of the KNOW-NOTHING and FREE SOIL Parties to gain a stable national following allowed the Republicans to grow with dramatic rapidity.

The constituency of the new party was limited to the northern states, since opposition to slavery was the basic issue of the Republicans. But the party did attract diverse elements in the political spectrum—former Whigs, Know-Nothings, Free Soilers, and dissident Democrats.

In its first year the party took the name Republican. Horace Greeley is credited with initiating the name in a June 1854 issue of his newspaper, the *New York Tribune.* In pushing the name, he referred to the Jeffersonian Republicans of the early nineteenth century and Henry Clay's National Republican Party of the 1830s, an early rival of the Democrats.

The Republicans ran candidates throughout the North in 1854 and, in combination with other candidates opposed to the Kansas-Nebraska Act, won a majority in the House of Representatives. Two years later the Republicans ran their first national ticket. Although their presidential candidate, John C. Fremont, did not win, he polled one-third of the vote in a three-man race and carried eleven states. The Republicans were established as a major party.

Although founded on the slavery question, the Republican Party was far from a one-issue party. They presented a nationalistic platform with appeal to business and commercial interests as well as rural antislavery elements. The Republicans proposed legislation for homesteading (free land), the construction of a transcontinental railroad, and the institution of a protective tariff.

Firmly established by the late 1850s, the Republican Party benefited from the increasing sectional factionalism in the DEMOCRATIC PARTY over the slavery issue. In 1858 the party won control of the House of Representatives. Two years later, with Abraham Lincoln as its candidate, the Republicans won the White House and retained control of the House. Lincoln, benefiting from a sectional split in the Democratic Party, won an unusual four-way race and captured the presidency with 39.9 percent of the popular vote.

THE UNION MUST AND SHALL BE PRESERVED

FREE SPEECH, FREE HOMES, FREE TERRITORY.

PROTECTION TO AMERICAN INDUSTRY

FOR PRESIDENT
**ABRAHAM LINCOLN**
OF ILLINOIS.

FOR VICE PRESIDENT
**HANNIBAL HAMLIN**
OF MAINE

*The Lincoln-Hamlin ticket won a decisive electoral college victory in 1860 despite receiving no electoral college votes in the South, even though Lincoln was no abolitionist. In fact, Lincoln had won the nomination in part due to his moderation on the question of abolition. Source: Library of Congress*

Lincoln was a wartime president, and his success in preserving the Union helped the party for the next generation. After the Civil War the Republicans projected a patriotic image, which, coupled with the party's belief in national expansion and limited federal involvement in the free enterprise system, helped make it the dominant party over the next three-quarters of a century. For most of the seventy-two years between 1860 and 1932, the Republicans were the majority party, occupying the White House for fifty-six years and controlling the Senate for sixty years and the House for fifty years. Except for the South, where the party basically was limited to the small number of black voters, the Republicans were strong throughout the nation.

Congressional leaders exercised the dominant power during this period of Republican hegemony. Presidents had little success in challenging the authority wielded by the GOP's congressional leadership.

Just as the party vaulted to power on the divisive slavery issue, its history was altered by a traumatic event—the Great Depression, which began in 1929. As the incumbent party during the economic collapse, the Republicans suffered the political blame, and their fall from power was rapid. In 1928 the Republican presidential candidate (Herbert Hoover) carried forty states; in 1936, during Franklin D. Roosevelt's New Deal days, the Republican standard-bearer (Alfred M. Landon) won just two states. In 1928 the party held a clear majority of seats in both the House and Senate, 267 and 56 respectively; eight years later the party's numbers had shrunk dramatically, with the Republicans holding only 89 seats in the House and 17 in the Senate.

The party eventually made a comeback from this low point but remained the minority party in Congress through the 1980 elections. Between 1932 and 1988 the Republicans won seven of fifteen presidential elections but controlled both chambers of Congress for just four years.

While the Republicans struggled to find the formula for a new majority, the party's basic conservatism made it increasingly appealing, especially in presidential races, to segments of the electorate that previously were firm parts of the Democratic coalition—notably blue-collar workers and the once-Democratic South. Beginning in 1952 the party was able to attract a winning combination when it ran presidential candidates with a moderate conservative image, such as Dwight D. Eisenhower, Richard Nixon, or Ronald Reagan. However, the GOP enjoyed less success at the state and local levels where Democratic majorities, established during the New Deal, remained largely intact.

The Republican difficulties in establishing a new majority were compounded after the 1972 election by the Watergate SCANDAL, which brought down the Nixon administration. Gerald R. Ford, who became president after Nixon resigned August 9, 1974, lost his 1976 election bid to former Georgia governor Jimmy Carter, giving the Democrats control of the White House as well as Congress.

Republican fortunes improved dramatically in 1980 when former California governor Reagan won a landslide electoral vote victory over Carter. Republicans also took control of the Senate for the first time in twenty-eight years and made substantial gains in the House. Although a resurgence of Democratic political strength in the 1982 MIDTERM ELECTION swept more Democrats into the House, the Republicans retained control of the Senate.

In a Gallup poll taken shortly before the 1984 national elections, 28 percent of the respondents identified themselves as Republicans. Although Republicans remained the minority party (42 percent of respondents

identified themselves as Democrats), the party clearly was recovering from the lows it had experienced during the Watergate era. Not since the Eisenhower presidency had more voters called themselves Republicans. The party enjoyed a second landslide victory for Reagan, gaining even more strength and making Reagan one of the most popular presidents of the twentieth century.

In the 1986 election the Democrats regained control of the Senate—despite a nationwide campaign by Reagan to promote Republican senatorial candidates—giving the Democrats full control of Congress and the GOP a sizable obstacle in policy making. A few weeks later the Iran-contra scandal broke. An independent counsel was appointed, and congressional investigations, including months of public hearings, lasted for almost all of 1987.

The setback to the party, if any, did not keep Reagan's vice president, George Bush, from winning big in 1988—53.4 percent of the vote and 426 electoral votes. Bush became the first sitting vice president to win the White House since Martin Van Buren in 1836. Bush also was the first candidate since John F. Kennedy to win the presidential election while his party lost seats in the House. His inability to carry others into office may have been partly due to his message, which was essentially a call to "stay the course."

In seeking a second term in 1992, Bush was burdened with an economy slowly recovering from the recession of 1990–1991. Bush took only 37.4 percent of the nationwide vote and received 168 electoral votes. Although Bill Clinton won the White House for the Democrats after twelve years of GOP presidents, the Republicans posted victories elsewhere, gaining ten seats in the House in 1992 and one Senate seat and two gubernatorial seats in 1993.

In 1994 the Democratic setbacks turned into a rout, with the GOP taking control of both houses of Congress. Grateful House Republicans elected as Speaker Newt Gingrich of Georgia, who had engineered their victory with a ten-point "Contract with America" setting forth conservative goals for the GOP Congress. For the next two years the Republican Congress tried to dismantle decades-old social programs, with repercussions for both parties in the following presidential election.

As the "out" party in 1996, the Republicans faced a wide-open race for its presidential nomination. After a shaky start in which he lost the New Hampshire primary to columnist Patrick J. Buchanan, Senate Majority Leader Robert J. Dole of Kansas emerged as the front-runner among several major candidates. Despite some questions about his age (at seventy-three he would have been the oldest new president), Dole clinched the nomination and launched an energetic campaign against the incumbent Clinton. Dole chose an ex-rival as his running mate, former House member Jack F. Kemp of New York.

Clinton nevertheless stayed far ahead in the preelection polls. The president appeared to benefit from a public opinion backlash against the Republican Congress for its attacks on cherished Democratic programs. Although he narrowed the expected margin of defeat, Dole lost to Clinton with 39.2 million votes or 40.7 percent of the total. He won 159 electoral votes.

Despite the voters' reservations about Congress, and particularly House Speaker Newt Gingrich of Georgia, the GOP kept control of Congress while losing nine seats in the House but gaining two in the Senate. Under an ethics cloud for which he was later reprimanded, Gingrich in 1997 nevertheless became the first Republican Speaker reelected since 1929.

The president's party almost always suffers losses in the midterm election, especially in the sixth year of an administration. With President Clinton under a cloud of scandal that threatened to end with his impeachment, the GOP expected to make even larger gains than normal. In 1998, however, the voters did not behave as expected, and the Republicans found their already slim majority in the House whittled to just five seats, although their margin in the Senate was unchanged. Gingrich resigned not only the speakership but also his House seat in the wake of the poor showing.

## Residency Requirements

*See* ABSENTEE VOTING; HOUSE OF REPRESENTATIVES, QUALIFICATIONS.

## Retrospective Voting

In the process known as *retrospective voting*, voters make decisions about the future based on judgments of the past. A candidate with a record in office is likely to be evaluated on that as to his or her chances of success in another term or a higher office. For an INCUMBENT, retrospection by the voters usually means reelection, but it can also mean rejection.

In 1980 and 1992 voters issued negative verdicts on the performances of presidents Jimmy Carter and George Bush, each of whom saw their public support plummet as economic problems overwhelmed their administrations.

By contrast, in 1984 President Ronald Reagan's performance was judged favorably on the whole, and he rolled to a LANDSLIDE reelection victory. With Reagan ineligible to run again in 1988, his vice president, Bush, clearly benefited from the public perception that Reagan had performed well and that Bush would stay the course.

As Bush's challenger in 1992 and as the incumbent in 1996, Bill Clinton benefited from retrospective voting, as Reagan had in 1980 and 1984. Facing a choice of reelecting Clinton or trading him for Robert J. Dole, another known entity in U.S. politics, the voters again chose Clinton.

In electing him twice, however, the electorate did not give Clinton a MANDATE for drastic change in government policy. Both times he won with less than a majority of the POPULAR VOTE, and in the 1994 MIDTERM ELECTION he received a setback to his program with loss of Democratic Party control of both chambers of Congress. Four years later, however, in the middle of his second term, Clinton and his party defied expectations by gaining five seats in the House and keeping the existing party balance in the Senate. Although the results did not remove Congress from GOP hands, they were all the more remarkable because Clinton was in the midst of a sex SCANDAL that threatened his presidency.

Voters are notoriously skeptical of campaign promises. For them, past performance is a more credible indicator of prospective performance. An experienced politician is likely to be kept on the job if he or she has a record of accomplishment and an IDEOLOGY acceptable to the general public. But if the public feels an incumbent has stumbled in significant ways, it might be inclined to give someone else a chance.

An example of the former is the 1964 Democratic landslide that extended Lyndon Johnson's White House stay a year after the assassination of John F. Kennedy. The landslide greatly strengthened Democratic majorities in the House and Senate and enabled the president to gain congressional approval for a wide range of social welfare legislation, including Medicare, Medicaid, and the War on Poverty. Many of Johnson's "Great Society" programs had been on Kennedy's agenda, but in his brief presidency Kennedy had been unable to push them through. With his mandate and mastery of legislative arm-twisting, Johnson gained enactment of much of the Kennedy-Johnson program.

Similarly, Ronald Reagan's election in 1980 resulted in a reordering of government priorities as the share of funds allocated to the military was increased, the rate of growth in domestic social spending was restricted, income tax rates were reduced, the budget deficit was allowed to grow, deregulation of the economy began, and the Supreme Court became more conservative as a result of three Reagan appointees.

President Carter had advocated some of the same policies, but in light of the Iran hostage crisis, high inflation, and other problems of Carter's administration, the voters felt that Reagan offered better prospects of managing the economy and lifting the national morale. Yet the voting was more retrospective than prospective. It was a rejection of Carter rather than an endorsement of Reagan and his somewhat radical "supply-side economics."

As in these cases, elections often serve as a referendum on the past and enable the voters to make educated guesses about the goals and policies of the candidates who are saying "it's time for a change."

## *Reynolds v. Sims*

*See* ONE PERSON, ONE VOTE.

## Right to Vote

The U.S. Constitution never explicitly mentions the right of a citizen to vote, but it does contain implicit indications that Americans could elect their leaders. Article I, section 2, states that members of the House of Representatives "will be chosen . . . by the People of the Several States."

In the early days of the country, the states exercised complete sway over the question of voter qualifications in all elections. These qualifications were highly restrictive, reflecting the collective faith of the nation's first leaders that only the most virtuous and enlightened among them should lead the new nation. The states enfranchised only men with property and excluded all women, Native Americans, indentured servants, and slaves.

Since then, the FRANCHISE has been expanded by class, race, sex, and age. In the 1824 presidential election, the first for which reliable statistics are available, only 3.8 percent of the population was allowed to vote, but by 1856, after states had relaxed taxpaying and property-owning qualifications, voter participation reached nearly 17 percent. By 1920, after women won the franchise, the figure rose to 25.1 percent. Since 1930 voter participation in presidential elections has averaged approximately 50 percent of those eligible to vote.

The history of American elections has been a story of strenuous efforts by various groups to tear down legal barriers to voting and to expand the size of the electorate. Another side to the story is the dogged fight by opponents to keep these groups from voting at all or, later, to render their votes meaningless. Of the seventeen new amendments added to the Constitution since the passage of the Bill of Rights, nine concern the way citizens participate in elections. The Supreme Court has frequently addressed the topic, and some of the nation's legendary legislative battles have been fought over the regulation of elections. Voting rights, in short, have been a continual source of contention in U.S. politics for both the nation as a whole and for the individual states.

Three constitutional amendments—the Fifteenth,

Nineteenth, and Twenty-sixth—broadened the suffrage. Two others—the Twenty-third and Twenty-fourth—have changed some of the rules for voting in presidential and other federal elections.

## The Fifteenth Amendment

Before the Civil War, only nine states allowed African Americans to vote: the nine northernmost states of New England and the Upper Midwest that had the fewest blacks. After the war ended, the eleven states of the Confederacy were forced by the Reconstruction Act of 1867 (passed by the Republican-controlled Congress) to extend the suffrage to blacks as a condition for readmission to the Union. These new votes were indispensable to the POPULAR VOTE plurality of Ulysses S. Grant, the 1868 Republican candidate for president.

But fearing that southern blacks might lose their franchise to white politicians in these states, and eager for the votes of blacks in those northern and BORDER STATES that did not have universal male suffrage, the Republicans pushed the Fifteenth Amendment through a lame-duck session of Congress in 1869. It provided that neither the United States nor any individual state could deprive a citizen of the right to vote "on account of race, color, or previous condition of servitude." The amendment was ratified a year later by a combination of New England, upper midwestern, and black-controlled southern legislatures.

While the amendment secured the Republicans' short-term goal of safeguarding the voting rights of northern blacks, it produced a virulent reaction in the southern states, one that would bedevil the nation for many years. After federal troops left the region in 1876, white politicians found a host of extraconstitutional ways to keep blacks from voting. The Fifteenth Amendment, seemingly so clear and unambiguous, was virtually ignored. In 1940, for example, only about 3 percent of the 5 million southern blacks of voting age were registered to vote. Of the amendment's effect in the South, one historian noted, "Ninety-five years after its passage, most southern blacks still could not vote."

The methods employed in the South ranged from outright violence and intimidation to legal subterfuges such as POLL TAXES, LITERACY TESTS (from which il-

literate whites were exempted by the so-called GRANDFATHER CLAUSE, if their ancestors had been eligible to vote before 1867), and WHITE PRIMARIES (political parties, as "private" organizations, could exclude blacks from membership and participation).

Although the Supreme Court eventually declared both the grandfather clause (in 1915) and the white primary (in 1944) unconstitutional, voter registration among eligible southern blacks remained well below 30 percent as late as 1960. Not until passage of the Voting Rights Act in 1965 was the Fifteenth Amendment effectively implemented in the South. The act suspended literacy tests—they were permanently banned in 1970—and authorized the federal government to take over the registration process in any county in which less than 50 percent of the voting age population was registered or had voted in the most recent presidential election. Since 1960 the registration rate for southern blacks has doubled.

Blacks, grateful to the party of Abraham Lincoln for freeing the slaves, voted Republican until the Great Depression of the 1930s when Franklin D. Roosevelt and the Democrats won about two thirds of their votes with New Deal social and economic programs. The civil rights laws sponsored by the Democratic Party and the Great Society social programs of the 1960s made African American voters into a monolithic Democratic constituency; in 1992, for example, Bill Clinton won 77 percent of the black vote. (See BLACK SUFFRAGE.)

## The Nineteenth Amendment

Securing the vote was a primary goal of the women's movement from the moment of its birth at the first women's rights convention in Seneca Falls, New York, in 1848. In 1890 women were granted full suffrage by Wyoming, and by 1919 women had the franchise in fifteen states and the right to vote in presidential elections in fourteen others. In time, the only significant opposition to granting women the vote came from the liquor industry, which feared that women would support Prohibition. But even without national WOMEN'S SUFFRAGE, Prohibition, in the form of the Eighteenth Amendment, became the law of the land in 1919. With liquor's opposition greatly reduced, the Nineteenth

Amendment passed easily through both chambers of Congress in the spring of 1919 and was ratified by the required number of states by the summer of 1920, in time for the fall elections of that year.

For more than fifty years after ratification of the amendment, women and men usually voted very much alike with the only "gender gap" being that fewer women than men went to the polls. By the 1980s, however, this gap had closed and a new one—significant differences between the sexes' views on certain issues and candidates—had developed. Women tend to be more concerned about and have more liberal views than men on issues such as social welfare, public policies concerning families, and policies about war and peace.

## The Twenty-Sixth Amendment

The Fourteenth Amendment, ratified in 1868, established twenty-one as the highest minimum age that a state could require for a voter's eligibility. By 1970 only four states had exercised their right to establish a lower voting age.

Political pressure to reduce the voting age by constitutional amendment rose during the late 1960s, spurred on by an unusually large number of young people in the population (the post–World War II "baby boom" generation) and the Vietnam War, a highly controversial conflict that conscripted hundreds of thousands of eighteen-year-olds into the military. Congress, bowing to the cry of "Old enough to fight, old enough to vote," passed a law in 1970 to lower the voting age in all elections to eighteen. The Supreme Court ruled in OREGON V. MITCHELL (1970) that the law was constitutional in its application to federal elections but not to state elections. The decision, which would have required states to establish two sets of voting procedures for state and federal elections, threatened to throw the 1972 election into turmoil.

Responding quickly to the Court, Congress passed the Twenty-sixth Amendment in early 1971. As had the Nineteenth Amendment, it followed the form of the Fifteenth Amendment: the right to vote for citizens who are eighteen years of age or older shall not be denied or abridged by the United States or any state "on account

of age." Ratification by the required number of states took only 107 days, less than half the usual time needed.

As women voters had some fifty years earlier, young voters registered and voted at a much lower rate than other segments of the population—barely one-third of eighteen- to twenty-year-olds have voted in recent elections as compared with two-thirds of those forty-five and older. These results upset the pre-amendment forecasts of many political experts, who believed that masses of young people would turn out in the 1972 election and move the political system dramatically to the left.

## Other Suffrage Amendments

The Twenty-third Amendment, ratified in 1961, gave the presidential vote to a special group of voters—eligible residents of the DISTRICT OF COLUMBIA, the nation's capital. The amendment gave the district three electoral votes in the ELECTORAL COLLEGE. Since the 1964 election, Washington has never given less than 75 percent of its vote to the Democratic candidate for president.

The Twenty-fourth Amendment, ratified in 1964 at the height of the nation's civil rights movement, abolished the poll tax, once used as a tool to disenfranchise blacks and poor whites, in federal elections. At the time of ratification, only five states still levied the tax. In 1966 the Supreme Court extended the ban on poll taxes to state and local elections under the Fourteenth Amendment's "equal protection" provision.

While an individual American's right to vote has been secured, the Supreme Court has come to recognize that, in the words of a legal scholar, "citizens were politically effective only as members of groups." Group voting rights underlay the "ONE-PERSON, ONE-VOTE" issue of legislative REAPPORTIONMENT AND REDISTRICTING. In the mid-1960s, several cases reached the Court involving subjects such as MULTIMEMBER legislative districts, at-large voting, and redistricting plans, issues that the Court saw as fragmenting minority voting strength and reducing the likelihood of black officeholding. Later, the question expanded beyond blacks to Latinos, Native Americans, and Asian Americans; even the use of an English-only BALLOT form was considered by the Court to be a disenfranchising device. In *Thornburg v. Gingles* (1986) the Court, ruling in a case involving the 1982 amendment to the VOTING RIGHTS ACT of 1965, came close to "equating proportionate electoral success with minority inclusion in the political process," according to a legal analyst.

In a true DEMOCRACY, each vote cast should have importance. But the "meaning of a meaningful ballot has radically altered over time," this analyst concludes, and the Court's rulings on cases involving minority votes are part of a continuing political process that shows no signs of ending.

## Rule 29 Committee

*See* PRESIDENTIAL SELECTION REFORMS.

## Running Mate

The wait for a presidential nominee to announce the name of a running mate has lost much of its suspense in recent years. Sometimes, the person chosen was a rival in the PRIMARIES and CAUCUSES where the top spot on the ticket was won. And the nominee may disclose the name early to gain maximum benefit from the announcement.

But even a little suspense is more than there originally was in the completion of a presidential team. During the country's first years, the runner-up for the presidency automatically became the VICE PRESIDENT.

That system did not last long. In 1800 Thomas Jefferson and Aaron Burr found themselves in a tie for electoral votes. Neither man's supporters were willing to settle for the lesser office. The deadlock went to the House of Representatives, where Jefferson needed thirty-six ballots to clinch the presidency, making Burr his vice president.

The unintended misfire of the Constitution's original method of presidential selection led to the Twelfth Amendment to the U.S. Constitution, ratified in 1804, providing for separate ELECTORAL COLLEGE balloting for presidents and vice presidents. With the emergence of political parties by 1800, candidates ran as teams. Once NATIONAL PARTY CONVENTIONS began in 1831, DELEGATES, with the guidance of party bosses, began to do the choosing.

It was only in 1940 that presidential nominees began regularly handpicking their running mates. That year Franklin D. Roosevelt rejected his two-term vice president, John Nance Garner, with whom he had a falling out. After failing to persuade Secretary of State Cordell Hull to run in Garner's place, Roosevelt forced Secretary of Agriculture Henry A. Wallace on a reluctant Democratic convention by threatening to refuse his own nomination if Wallace were rejected.

The only exception to the practice Roosevelt established came in 1956, when Democrat Adlai E. Stevenson left the choice up to the convention, which chose Sen. Estes Kefauver of Tennessee.

In an otherwise unique situation that in one way resembled Roosevelt's dropping Garner, President Gerald R. Ford found a new running mate in his unsuccessful 1976 election against Jimmy Carter. Neither Ford nor his vice president, Nelson A. Rockefeller, had been elected by POPULAR VOTE. Both were elected by Congress under the Twenty-fifth Amendment—Ford as vice president when Spiro T. Agnew resigned in 1973 and Rockefeller as vice president in 1974 after Ford became president following Richard Nixon's resignation. To appease the party's right wing, with whom he had been unpopular, moderate Republican Rockefeller did not seek the vice presidency in 1976. Ford then chose a new partner, Sen. Robert J. Dole of Kansas, for the race to succeed himself in the presidency to which he had not been nationally elected.

Nixon himself survived an effort to drop him from the ticket as Dwight D. Eisenhower's running mate in 1952. After it was disclosed that a wealthy California couple had supplemented Nixon's Senate pay, he went on television with an emotional defense of his actions. In what came to be known as his "Checkers speech" he vowed to keep a gift cocker spaniel by that name and referred to his wife's "respectable Republican cloth coat" as evidence of their modest life style. The appeal

*In the early months of the first Clinton administration, Vice President Al Gore was given the high-visibility mandate to "reinvent government." The two gave a progress report on the White House lawn in September 1993. Source: The White House*

worked. Thousands of viewers telegraphed their support, and Eisenhower kept Nixon as his running mate for two terms.

## Nominations Refused

Occasionally the person chosen as a running mate declines the candidacy. If the refusal comes during the nominating convention, the presidential nominee makes another choice, subject to the convention's approval.

In the preconvention era there were two occasions when the party's congressional caucus ("King Caucus") made substitutions after the nominees declined. In 1812 the Democratic-Republican caucus selected Elbridge Gerry of Massachusetts after John Langdon of New Hampshire rejected the nomination. In the 1824 elec-

tion that marked the end of King Caucus, John C. Calhoun of South Carolina accepted the vice-presidential nomination after Albert Gallatin of Pennsylvania declined. Calhoun became John Quincy Adams's vice president in only the second election decided by the House of Representatives. (See ELECTORAL COLLEGE AND VOTES.)

During the convention era, two nominees declined in time to be replaced by vote of the delegates. Silas Wright of New York turned down the Democratic nomination in 1844, and George M. Dallas of Pennsylvania, who accepted, became vice president to James K. Polk. Frank O. Lowden of Illinois refused the Republican nomination in 1924, and it went to Charles G. Dawes, also of Illinois, vice president under Calvin Coolidge.

If the vice-presidential nominee withdraws after the

convention, the vacancy is filled by the party's national committee. This happened in 1860 when Benjamin Fitzpatrick of Alabama refused the Democratic nomination and the DEMOCRATIC NATIONAL COMMITTEE (DNC) replaced him with Gov. Herschel V. Johnson of Georgia as Stephen A. Douglas's running mate.

In 1912 Vice President James S. Sherman of New York died the week before ELECTION DAY, and the REPUBLICAN NATIONAL COMMITTEE (RNC) nominated Columbia University president Nicholas Murray Butler as President William Howard Taft's running mate. It was too late to put Butler's name on the state ballots, but he received Sherman's eight electoral votes. Taft lost to Woodrow Wilson.

In 1972 Sen. Thomas F. Eagleton of Missouri withdrew as running mate to Sen. George S. McGovern of South Dakota after it was disclosed that Eagleton had been treated in the past for depression. The DNC gave the nomination to McGovern's substitute choice, R. Sargent Shriver of Maryland.

Currently, as in the Ford and Rockefeller cases, vacancies in the vice presidency itself are filled under procedures of the Twenty-fifth Amendment, ratified in 1967. (See VICE PRESIDENT.)

## A Once-Maligned Office

If the selection of a running mate often seemed like something of an afterthought, it could be because until recently the position was not especially coveted. John Adams, the first man to hold the job, once complained, "My country has in its wisdom contrived for me the most insignificant office that ever the intention of man contrived or his imagination conceived."

More than a century later, Thomas R. Marshall, Woodrow Wilson's vice president, expressed a similarly dismal view: "Once there were two brothers. One ran away to sea; the other was elected Vice President. And nothing was ever heard of either of them again." Still later, Vice President Garner gave the office its most memorable put-down. It was, he said, "not worth a bucket of warm spit." (He actually used the vulgar term for another bodily fluid, but editors thought it unfit for family newspapers.)

Writing in *Atlantic* in 1974, historian Arthur Schlesinger Jr. suggested the office be done away with. "It is a doomed office," he commented. "The Vice President has only one serious thing to do: that is, to wait around for the President to die." But there is a reasonable chance that whoever fills the position will get a chance to move up, either by succession or election. As of 1996, fourteen presidents had held the second-ranking post, seven in the twentieth century.

Also, since the 1970s the vice presidency has evolved from the somnolent office it once was; during this period four vice presidents enjoyed responsibility their predecessors did not. President Ford gave Vice President Rockefeller considerable authority in domestic policy coordination. Walter F. Mondale and George Bush helped to set policy for their respective presidents, Carter and Ronald Reagan. And Bill Clinton placed Al Gore in charge of a "reinventing government" task force.

## Factors in Selection

Whoever is selected as a running mate is scrutinized not so much as a policy maker, but for how well the choice balances (or unbalances) the ticket. One important factor is geography, which Clinton of Arkansas used unconventionally in choosing Gore of neighboring Tennessee to form the first successful all-southern ticket in 164 years.

Other traditional factors weighed by nominees are religion and ethnicity. In modern national politics, however, those considerations seemed to be losing their place to race, gender, and age. In 1984, for example, the Democrats chose Rep. Geraldine A. Ferraro of New York to be their vice-presidential candidate, the first woman to receive a major party nomination.

Although no African American has so far been selected by either party, many Democrats thought that Jesse L. Jackson deserved second place on the ticket in 1988. Jackson had received 29 percent of the primary vote to 43 percent for Michael Dukakis. Instead, the fifty-four-year-old Dukakis chose Sen. Lloyd Bentsen of Texas, then sixty-seven, balancing the Democratic ticket by age as well as geographically and philosophically.

George Bush selected Sen. Dan Quayle of Indiana, a choice that proved extremely controversial, even among Republicans. Quayle, born in 1947, had served two terms in the House of Representatives before his election to the Senate in 1980. The brevity of his experience in politics and his avoidance of Vietnam War duty by serving in the Indiana National Guard fostered doubts that he was qualified to serve as president, should that become necessary.

Because of Quayle's youth and good looks, it was even suggested by some critics that Bush had selected him to appeal to young voters and women. Moreover, Quayle seemed ill at ease before the television camera and often misspoke when giving a speech or answering questions. But Bush vigorously defended his choice of running mate, and the two swept to victory in November.

For his 1992 running mate, Clinton, in another unbalancing act, selected someone in his own age group (forty-six versus forty-four for Gore) rather than an elder statesman like Bentsen, who became secretary of the Treasury in the first Clinton administration. In 1996 Clinton and Gore became the first Democratic running mates to win reelection since Roosevelt and Garner in 1936. (Although FDR was reelected in 1940 and 1944, it was with two different vice presidents. He abandoned Wallace in 1944 in favor of Harry S. Truman.)

The Twelfth Amendment prohibits any one state from monopolizing the presidency and vice presidency. In roundabout fashion the amendment requires the electors to "vote by ballot for President and Vice President, one of whom, at least, shall not be an inhabitant of the same state with themselves." No matter what state has the winning president or vice president, the electors there must vote for an outsider for one of the two offices. (See VICE PRESIDENT.)

## Runoff Primary

The runoff primary is an integral part of the SOUTH-ERN PRIMARY system, which until recent years was dominated by the DEMOCRATIC PARTY and helped to

**Preference and Runoff Primaries**

| State | Preferential Primary | Runoff Primary Adopted |
|---|---|---|
| Alabama | Until 1931 | 1931 |
| Arkansas | — | 1939[a] |
| Florida | Until 1929 | 1929 |
| Georgia | — | 1917[b] |
| Louisiana[c] | Until 1922 | 1922 |
| Mississippi | — | 1902 |
| North Carolina | — | 1915 |
| South Carolina | — | 1915 |
| Tennessee[d] | — | — |
| Texas | — | 1918 |
| Virginia[e] | — | — |

*Sources:* Alexander Heard and Donald S. Strong, *Southern Primaries and Elections* (1950; reprint, Salem, N.H.: Ayers, 1970); V. O. Key Jr., *Southern Politics in State and Nation* (New York: Alfred A. Knopf, 1949); Virginia secretary of state.

a. Arkansas adopted the runoff in 1933, abandoned it in 1935, and reinstituted it in 1939.

b. Runoff held under county unit system.

c. Louisiana used the runoff "for a time prior to 1916," according to political scientist V. O. Key Jr.; in 1975 Louisiana adopted an initial non-partisan primary followed by a general election runoff.

d. Tennessee has never used the preferential or runoff primary. Candidates are nominated by winning a plurality.

e. Virginia adopted the runoff primary in 1969 and repealed it in 1971.

ensure the election of its nominees to state and federal posts throughout the South.

Developed to ensure election by majority rather than PLURALITY, the runoff matches the two top finishers a few weeks after the first PRIMARY. It is also used widely in the BORDER STATES and in city and county elections throughout the country.

In the early decades of the twentieth century the RE-PUBLICAN PARTY posed only token opposition to the Democrats in the South. Most serious candidates ran in the Democratic primary, sometimes in such large numbers that a very small plurality could win the nomination for a fringe candidate who otherwise would have been out of the running.

Beginning in the 1930s most of the southern states adopted the runoff system. Virginia was the last, in 1969. With only two candidates in the runoff, one was bound to get a majority vote (more than 50 percent). Of the eleven states of the old Confederacy, only Tennessee never adopted the runoff system. It came closest to being a two-party state.

With the emergence of the Republican Party as a power in the South, the Democratic runoff primary has lost much of its significance. For both major parties, however, the runoff helps to ensure that in the final election the opposing nominees were the choices of most of the party members in the DISTRICT or other constituency.

Now that blacks no longer are excluded from southern primaries, African American leaders disagree on whether the runoff helps or hurts their candidates. Some, notably Jesse L. Jackson, argue that a black is almost certain to lose the runoff if the opponent is white. Others contend that the black vote could be split in a nonrunoff primary, allowing a white candidate to win by plurality.

# S

## Safe Seat

*See* INCUMBENCY.

## Scandals

Political scandals have affected many an American election. Some have led to the withdrawal or defeat of candidates; others have led to the removal of officials after they have been elected. A few of the more significant scandals involving elected officials or their administrations are listed here.

Omitted are presidents' extramarital affairs that were rumored—such as those of Woodrow Wilson, Warren G. Harding, Franklin D. Roosevelt, and John F. Kennedy—but not confirmed or publicly exposed until after their deaths.

### 1802

President Thomas Jefferson is publicly accused of being the father of several children of a slave, Sally Hemings. During Jefferson's second term, six years after the accusations surfaced, Hemings has another son, Eston. For almost two hundred years, historians debate inconclusively about whether Jefferson fathered Hemings's children. On November 5, 1998, genetics researchers in Massachusetts publish DNA findings that they say strongly indicate Jefferson was Eston's father. Other experts, however, say the study merely shows that Jefferson, among other male members of his family, could have been the father.

### 1831

The so-called petticoat wars of Andrew Jackson's administration end with the resignation of Secretary of War John Eaton. Wives of other cabinet members had refused to accept Eaton's wife, Peggy, because of her allegedly promiscuous past. Eaton's resignation enabled Jackson to shake up his cabinet and halt the two-year disruption. In 1832 Jackson rewards his former secretary of state Martin Van Buren, who resigned along with Eaton, by making him his second-term RUNNING MATE in place of Vice President John C. Calhoun. Van Buren wins the presidency four years later.

### 1859

Rep. Daniel Sickles, New York Democrat, shoots and kills Phillip Barton Key, son of *Star-Spangled Banner* author Francis Scott Key, on Washington's Lafayette Square. Sickles's wife, Teresa, had publicly confessed her affair with Key. Sickles later pleads temporary insanity and is acquitted of murder.

### 1873

The House censures Rep. Oakes Ames, Massachusetts Republican, and Rep. James Brooks, New York Democrat, for corruption in connection with the Crédit Mobilier scandal. Crédit Mobilier, the construction arm of Union Pacific Railroad, was suspected of using underhanded means to complete the last link of the transcontinental railroad in 1869. To head off a congressional inquiry, Ames, a shareholder, arranged to sell $33 million of the company's stock at low prices to members and executive branch officials. House Speaker James G. Blaine, Maine Republican, and Rep. James A. Garfield, Ohio Republican, are among those implicated but not disciplined. The scandal has political repercussions in 1872 as Schuyler Colfax loses renomination as Ulysses S. Grant's vice president. In 1880 Garfield is elected president.

1875

The breakup of the Whiskey Ring during the Grant administration leads to the conviction of 110 officials. The ring was a conspiracy of revenue officials to defraud the government of excise taxes on liquor and distilled spirits. It included the collector of internal revenue in St. Louis, Gen. John A. McDonald, along with Treasury officials and Grant's private secretary, Gen. Orville E. Babcock. Grant's support helps to acquit Babcock but Treasury Secretary Benjamin A. Bristow's efforts to break up the ring lead to his being eased from the cabinet. Bristow loses the 1876 GOP presidential nomination to Rutherford B. Hayes.

1884

Grover Cleveland wins election as president after admitting that he fathered a child out of wedlock. He supports the child financially. Elected again in 1892 (after being defeated in 1888) he becomes the only president to serve nonconsecutive terms.

1922–1923

Senate investigation of the Teapot Dome, Wyoming, oil-leasing scandal exposes corruption in the administration of President Warren G. Harding. Interior Secretary Albert B. Fall, convicted of bribery, becomes the first cabinet member sent to prison.

*Captioned "Another Voice for Cleveland," this 1884 cartoon played on Grover Cleveland's admission that he had fathered an illegitimate son. Source: Library of Congress*

## 1947

Rep. James Michael Curley, Democrat and former governor of Massachusetts, enters jail June 26 on a mail fraud conviction. President Truman commutes the sentence November 26.

## 1954

The Senate "condemns" (censures) Joseph R. McCarthy, Wisconsin Republican, on December 1 for actions that "tended to bring the Senate into dishonor and dispute." The resolution cites McCarthy for reckless statements in connection with the Senate's investigation of the controversial Army-McCarthy hearings held earlier in the year. McCarthy loses his chairmanships when the Democrats take over the Senate in 1955. He dies in office in 1957.

## 1958

Sherman Adams, former governor of New Hampshire, resigns as Eisenhower's chief of staff amid accusations that he interceded with federal regulators in behalf of Bernard Goldfine, a Boston industrialist who had given Adams expensive gifts.

## 1964

Walter W. Jenkins, special assistant to and longtime associate of President Lyndon B. Johnson, resigns October 14 following his arrest for soliciting sex at the Washington, D.C., YMCA. The White House says Jenkins was hospitalized for "extreme fatigue."

## 1967–1970

The House's attempt to exclude flamboyant Adam Clayton Powell Jr., New York Democrat, results in a landmark Supreme Court case, *Powell v. McCormack*. Powell, an African American, blames the House action on racism. The Court rules in 1969 that Powell met the constitutional qualifications for House membership. Powell regains his seat but rarely attends sessions. He fails to gain renomination in 1970. (See HOUSE OF REPRESENTATIVES, QUALIFICATIONS.)

## 1967

The Senate censures Thomas J. Dodd, Connecticut Democrat, on June 23 for spending campaign contributions for personal purposes. Dodd does not seek his party's renomination in 1970.

## 1969

A young woman, Mary Jo Kopechne, dies when a car driven by Sen. Edward M. Kennedy, Massachusetts Democrat, plunges off a narrow bridge on Chappaquiddick Island after midnight on July 19. Kennedy swims to safety but does not report the accident until nine hours later. Kennedy pleads guilty to leaving the scene of an accident and receives a suspended jail sentence. The incident leaves many unanswered questions about Kennedy's behavior and his activities with Kopechne, a former secretary and campaign worker for Kennedy's brother Robert, who was assassinated the previous year while running for president.

## 1972–1974

A June 17, 1972, break-in at Democratic national headquarters in Washington's Watergate Hotel escalates into a major scandal that drives President Richard Nixon from office on August 9, 1974. Nixon and top officials of his administration are implicated in the cover-up of the burglary, which was committed by persons with ties to the White House or Nixon's 1972 reelection committee. A Supreme Court decision requires Nixon to relinquish secret audio tapes that prove he was aware of the cover-up. Among those jailed is Nixon's first attorney general, John N. Mitchell. Vice President Gerald R. Ford becomes president and pardons Nixon for any crimes he may have committed.

## 1973

Spiro T. Agnew resigns as vice president October 10 to avoid trial on tax evasion charges dating to his time as governor of Maryland. Congress approves Nixon's nomination of Gerald Ford to fill the vacancy.

## 1974

House Ways and Means Chairman Wilbur D. Mills, Arkansas Democrat, is stopped in his car the night of October 9 with Anabell Battistella, an Argentine stripper known as Fanne Foxe. Police rescue the woman after she jumps into the nearby Potomac River Tidal Basin. Mills is reelected despite the incident but later admits to alcoholism and relinquishes his chairmanship. He does not seek reelection in 1976.

## 1976

Ohio Democrat Wayne L. Hays resigns as chairman of the House Administration Committee amid publicity about his relations with Elizabeth Ray, a former committee clerk. Ray says Hays gave her the job in exchange for sexual favors. Hays denies the charge but admits having a "personal relationship" with Ray. He does not seek reelection but later wins a seat in the Ohio legislature.

Donald W. Riegle Jr., formerly a Republican, is elected to the Senate in Michigan as a Democrat. During the campaign it is disclosed that Riegle had an affair with a younger woman in 1969. He later divorced to marry a different younger woman.

## 1977–1978

The House reprimands three California Democrats in connection with the South Korean lobbying scandal. John J. McFall, Edward R. Roybal, and Charles H. Wilson are disciplined in October 1978 for failing to report campaign or personal gifts from lobbyist Tongsun Park. McFall resigns, and Wilson is censured on another matter after losing his 1980 primary race. Roybal serves until 1993.

## 1977

Maryland governor Marvin Mandel, Democrat, is convicted of federal mail fraud and racketeering charges and serves time in prison. In 1979 his conviction is overturned and he is allowed to return to office for a few days before the newly elected governor is sworn in.

## 1979

For the first time since 1921 (when a member was censured for inserting indecent material in the *Congres-*sional Record*) the House approves a censure resolution. Rep. Charles C. Diggs Jr., Michigan Democrat, is publicly chastised July 31 for diverting clerk-hire funds to his own use. Diggs resigns in June 1980 after the Supreme Court refuses to overturn his 1978 conviction on related criminal charges.

In the Senate, Georgia Democrat Herman E. Talmadge is "denounced" (censured) October 11, 1979, for abuses in the collecting, reporting, and handling of expense vouchers and campaign contributions. Talmadge is denied reelection in 1980.

## 1980

FBI agents posing as Arab sheiks ensnare seven members of Congress in a sting operation that becomes known as Abscam. The seven, including Sen. Harrison A. Williams Jr., New Jersey Democrat, are later convicted for their apparent willingness to accept the "sheiks'" false bribes. All leave Congress, some involuntarily. Rep. Michael J. "Ozzie" Myers, Pennsylvania Democrat, becomes the first House member expelled for corruption. Williams resigns to avoid expulsion from the Senate.

One of the Abscam victims, Rep. John W. Jenrette Jr., South Carolina Democrat, is further embarrassed when his wife, Rita, tells the press that he and she once had sex on the Capitol steps. Rita poses for *Playboy,* and Jenrette enters an alcoholism program. He resigns December 10.

Rep. Robert E. Bauman, Maryland Republican, pleads innocent October 3 to sexually soliciting a teenage boy. The charge is dropped as Bauman agrees to counseling for alcoholism. Bauman is defeated for reelection.

Also in 1980, the House censures Charles Wilson, who had been reprimanded in 1978 in connection with the South Korean lobbying scandal. Wilson is censured for financial misconduct a week after losing his bid for renomination in California.

## 1981

Jon C. Hinson, Mississippi Republican, resigns from the House April 13 after being arrested in a Capitol Hill men's room on a misdemeanor charge of attempted sodomy. He receives a suspended sentence.

### 1982

Fred W. Richmond, New York Democrat, resigns from the House after pleading guilty to marijuana possession and other charges.

### 1983

The House July 20 censures Gerry E. Studds, Massachusetts Democrat, and Daniel B. Crane, Illinois Republican, for having sexual relations with House pages, Studds with a male and Crane with a female. Crane loses reelection, but Studds wins several more terms.

### 1984

Rep. George V. Hansen, Idaho Republican, is the first member of Congress convicted for noncompliance with financial disclosure laws. He is reprimanded by the House July 31 and is defeated for reelection in November.

### 1987

House and Senate committees jointly investigate the so-called Iran-contra affair concerning undercover U.S. arms sales to Iran and the diversion of the proceeds to anticommunist "contra" guerrillas in Nicaragua. The committees conclude that President Ronald Reagan allowed a "cabal of zealots" to take over significant aspects of U.S. foreign policy. Congress had prohibited arms sales to Iran, which held U.S. embassy personnel hostage during the Carter administration, as well as continued aid to the contras. Several high-ranking officials are convicted in the affair but others, including former defense secretary Caspar Weinberger, are pardoned by Reagan's successor, George Bush.

Two leading candidates for the 1988 Democratic presidential nomination, former senator Gary Hart of Colorado and Sen. Joseph R. Biden Jr. of Delaware, drop out amidst widely differing scandals. Hart is the first to go, following reports that model Donna Rice spent the night at his townhouse while his wife was away. Hart withdraws on May 8, reenters the race in December, but quits for good after the SUPER TUESDAY primaries in spring 1988.

Biden's fledgling campaign is undermined by a video showing that he plagiarized a speech by British Labor leader Neil Kinnock. Biden drops out in September. The man who assembled the video, John Sasso, resigns as manager of the rival campaign by Massachusetts governor Michael S. Dukakis.

The House on December 18 reprimands Austin J. Murphy, Pennsylvania Democrat, for financial misconduct and allowing another member for vote for him on the House floor. Murphy is reelected to three more terms.

### 1988

The Arizona Senate convicts Republican governor Evan Mecham and removes him from office April 4. A recall movement against Mecham obtained sufficient signatures in January, but his removal obviates the need for a recall election. Mecham is convicted of obstructing investigation of a death threat and lending official funds to his automobile dealership. (See REMOVAL FROM OFFICE.)

### 1989

The Senate rejects President George Bush's nomination of former senator John G. Tower, Texas Republican, as secretary of defense. Hearings before the Armed Services Committee, which Tower formerly headed, focus on his reputation as a "womanizer" and heavy drinker. The committee recommends rejection of the appointment, the first of a cabinet nominee since 1959.

Jim Wright, Texas Democrat, resigns as Speaker of the House amid ethics questions about his profits from a book deal. It is the first time a Speaker has been forced by scandal to leave the office at midterm. His chief accuser, Georgia Republican Newt Gingrich, is himself rebuked by the House in January 1997 for misleading ethics investigators.

### 1990

Washington, D.C., mayor Marion S. Barry Jr. is videotaped using crack cocaine in a hotel where he had been lured by a former girl friend. Convicted of cocaine possession, Barry serves six months in prison. Returned to office in 1994, Barry declines to seek another term in 1998. (See DISTRICT OF COLUMBIA.)

The Senate denounces Dave Durenberger, Minnesota Republican, July 25 for "unequivocally unethical" conduct in connection with a book deal and acceptance of Senate reimbursement for rent on a Minnesota condominium. Durenberger did not seek reelection in 1994.

Barney Frank, Massachusetts Democrat, is reprimanded by the House on July 26 for improperly using his office to help a male prostitute. Frank, who acknowledged his homosexuality in 1987, is reelected to several more terms.

Donald E. "Bud" Lukens, Ohio Republican, resigns from the House October 24 facing accusations of sexual advances to a congressional elevator operator. He had been convicted in May 1989 of having sex with a sixteen-year-old Ohio girl.

## 1991

A scandal concerning practices at the House bank erupts in September when the General Accounting Office reports that members had cashed thousands of bad checks without penalty. The bank covered the checks that were "floated" before salaries were deposited. Public indignation leads to the defeat of many of the check-kiters, whose names are made public in April 1992.

The Senate Ethics Committee, acting in the name of the full Senate, reprimands Alan Cranston, California Democrat, on November 20 for his role in the so-called Keating Five affair. The punishment is the harshest handed out to the five senators investigated for possible intervention with federal regulators to save a savings and loan headed by Charles H. Keating Jr., a major contributor to political campaigns and causes. The other four senators are Democrats Dennis DeConcini of Arizona, John Glenn of Ohio, and Donald Riegle of Michigan, and Republican John McCain of Arizona. The committee rebukes the four for poor judgment but says that only Cranston's actions were "substantially linked" to his fund raising. Cranston, ill with prostate cancer, already had announced his decision to retire from the Senate.

Also in 1991, an old sex scandal is revived against Sen. Charles S. Robb, Virginia Democrat and son-in-law of the late president Lyndon B. Johnson. Former beauty queen Tanquil "Tai" Collins alleges that she and Robb had a love affair in 1983 when she was twenty and he was forty-four. Robb again denies the allegations, but Collins repeats them in a *Playboy* article and photo spread.

## 1991–1992

An investigation of thefts from the House Post Office leads to exposure of lax procedures that allow members, who may mail official mail without postage, to exchange stamp vouchers for cash. By late 1992 the House postmaster resigns, and several clerks plead guilty to various charges. A grand jury subpoenas records of Ways and Means Committee chairman Dan Rostenkowski, Illinois Democrat, one of the major purchasers of stamps. Rostenkowski loses his seat in 1994.

## 1992

Sen. Brock Adams, Washington Democrat, decides against seeking reelection after the *Seattle Times* reports finding eight women (none identified by name) claiming sexual abuse or harassment by Adams. In 1987 a woman family friend filed suit against Adams, claiming he drugged and fondled her while his wife was away. The case was closed with each side accusing the other of initiating settlement.

## 1992–1996

Scandals dog the administration of President Bill Clinton even before it begins. In February 1992 an Arkansas state employee, Gennifer Flowers, goes public with her story that she was Clinton's lover for twelve years. On television she plays tapes of intimate conversations with Clinton, then the governor. Flowers loses her state job but cashes in on the celebrity with her exposé in the tabloid *Star* and an article and photo spread in *Penthouse*.

Clinton and his wife, Hillary, appear on CBS's *Sixty Minutes*, where he acknowledges "problems in our marriage" but does not confirm Flowers's allegations. He goes on to win the Democratic nomination and defeat President George Bush.

Other scandals of Clinton's first term include the firing of the White House travel office staff, possible misuse of limited burial plots in Arlington National Cemetery, and the Whitewater realty development in Arkansas.

## 1994

In February 1994 former Arkansas state employee Paula Corbin Jones alleges that Clinton exposed himself to her in a Little Rock hotel while he was governor. She files a sexual harassment suit.

In August, Kenneth W. Starr is named independent counsel to investigate the Whitewater matter, which also involves Mrs. Clinton and her former law firm.

## 1995

Sen. Bob Packwood, Oregon Republican, resigns October 1 facing expulsion after a three-year Senate investigation of complaints by women staffers that Packwood sexually harassed them. Oregon conducts the special election to replace Packwood entirely by mail. (See ABSENTEE VOTING.)

## 1996

Clinton campaign strategist Dick Morris resigns following reports of his relationship with prostitute Sherry Rowlands. The story breaks during the Democratic National Convention at Chicago.

The news media disclose that Republican presidential nominee Robert J. Dole had an affair with Phyllis Wells, an employee in his Kansas City senatorial office, while he was still married to his first wife, also named Phyllis. The affair apparently was a factor in Dole's December 1970 decision to end his twenty-three-year marriage. Although the scandal is disclosed before the November election, it apparently is not the cause of Dole's loss to President Bill Clinton. Dole married Elizabeth Hanford in December 1975.

## 1997

Newt Gingrich becomes the first sitting House Speaker sanctioned for ethics violations. The House reprimands him January 21 and fines him $300,000 after he admits misleading the ethics (Standards of Official Conduct) committee about the relationship between a college course he taught and GOPAC, a POLITICAL ACTION COMMITTEE he headed until 1995. The fine is for the ethics committee's costs in sorting out Gingrich's conflicting statements. In April Gingrich announces he will pay the fine with a loan from 1996 Republican presidential nominee Robert Dole, but in 1998 Gingrich says he will not need Dole's money.

Rep. Jay Kim, California Republican, pleads guilty in August to federal charges of accepting $250,000 in illegal foreign and corporate campaign contributions in 1992. His wife and fund raiser, June Kim, also pleads guilty. In March 1998 Kim is sentenced to one year of probation and two months of home detention, which allows him to continue his House duties. Kim, the first Korean American elected to Congress, loses his 1998 reelection primary.

Arizona's Republican governor, J. Fife Symington, resigns after his September 3 bank fraud convictions for false statements to obtain loans for his failing real estate empire. One of the seven convictions is later dropped. In February 1998 he is sentenced to two and a half years in prison.

## 1998: Clinton Impeachment

Independent counsel Starr obtains tapes in which a former White House intern, Monica S. Lewinsky, claims to have had sexual relations with Clinton several times between November 15, 1995, and March 29, 1997. Starr receives court permission to expand his intervention in the Paula Jones case to cover the Lewinsky allegations. Clinton is deposed January 17 in the Jones case and gives secret testimony about his relationship with Lewinsky. On January 21 the media break the news of the Lewinsky tapes and Starr's investigation of her allegations. In media interviews Clinton flatly denies sexual relations with "that woman, Ms. Lewinsky."

He later admits to an "inappropriate relationship" with Lewinsky but continues to deny a sexual relationship until the night of August 17, after he testified before a federal grand jury. Having admitted to the grand jury that he lied, Clinton appears on television to apologize

*House Speaker Newt Gingrich's personal dramas—ethics woes, spats with the president, an abortive coup by younger members of Congress—made him an issue the way most of his predecessors never were and contributed to his consistently low public opinion ratings. Source: Douglas Graham, Congressional Quarterly*

to his family and to the American people. His relationship with Lewinsky, he says, "was not appropriate. In fact, it was wrong." In his grand jury testimony, later made public, he also acknowledges having sex with Gennifer Flowers.

Starr sends his voluminous report to Congress September 9, and the House votes October 8 to begin a formal impeachment inquiry against Clinton. He joins Andrew Johnson (who was impeached but not convicted) and Richard Nixon (who resigned before impeachment) as one of only three presidents subjected to this indignity.

On November 13 the Paula Jones sexual harassment suit is settled with Clinton's agreeing to pay her $850,000 with no admissions or apologies.

The Clinton-Lewinsky affair brings forth disclosure of extramarital affairs by members of Congress, including one by Henry J. Hyde, Illinois Republican, who as chairman presides over the House Judiciary Commit-

tee's impeachment inquiry. Also confessing marital infidelity is Rep. Robert L. Livingston, Louisiana Republican, the FRONT-RUNNER to become Speaker following Gingrich's resignation after the GOP's poor showing in the 1998 House elections. As the House prepares to vote on Clinton's impeachment, Livingston declines to run for Speaker and announces he will shortly resign his seat.

On December 19 the House votes to impeach Clinton on charges of perjury and obstruction of justice in connection with the Starr investigation. Chairman Hyde delivers the articles of impeachment to the Senate for trial, which begins in January 1999.

## 1998: Other Scandals

The Maryland Senate votes January 16 to expel an African American member, Larry Young, for using his office to obtain business from health companies and a state college for which he did little work. The 36–10 vote is largely along racial lines, with none of the nine black senators supporting it. It is the first expulsion in the Maryland Senate's 221-year history.

With his wife at his side, Colorado governor and Democratic national chairman Roy Romer tells a February 8 news conference that he has a continuing "very affectionate" relationship with longtime aide B. J. Thornberry, but he denies ever having sex with her.

Citing adverse publicity about him and other family members, Rep. Joseph F. Kennedy II, Democrat, announces August 28 that he will not run for governor of Massachusetts or for reelection to the House. He had received bad publicity because of the annulment of his marriage, and his brother, Michael, was in the news for having sex with a teenage baby sitter. Michael later dies in a skiing accident.

In Georgia, the Republican gubernatorial campaign of front-runner Mike Bowers is set back by news reports that Bowers had a ten-year adulterous affair with a former employee. Bowers loses the July 21, 1998, primary to Guy Millner.

Veteran state senator Tommy Burks is found dead October 19 in Monterey, Tennessee, an apparent murder victim. His controversial Republican opponent, Putnam County tax assessor Byron Looper, is charged with the close-range shooting. Looper is already under indictment for theft and misuse of county property.

Both African American candidates in Florida's Third CONGRESSIONAL DISTRICT are touched by scandal. The incumbent, Democrat Corrine Brown, fends off several allegations of unethical conduct. Her Republican opponent, Bill Randall, admits October 21 to having a son out of wedlock in the 1980s while he was separated from his wife. Randall later became a minister and began paying child support to the mother. Brown wins reelection in November.

Former Louisiana governor Edwin Edwards, Democrat, is indicted November 6 by a federal grand jury on racketeering and conspiracy charges stemming from the awarding of riverboat casino licenses. Edwards, who was acquitted of other racketeering charges in the 1980s, was famed for boasting that he could be convicted only if police caught him "with a dead woman or a live boy."

Former U.S. Senate candidate Ruthann Aron, ac-

cused of trying to hire a hit man to kill her husband and a lawyer, pleads no contest November 22 and is sentenced to three years in jail. Aron, who originally pleaded insanity, is ordered to receive psychiatric treatment during her sentence and five years of probation. In 1994 Aron unsuccessfully opposed William E. Brock, former senator (from Tennessee) and GOP national chairman, for the party's Senate nomination in Maryland. The lawyer Aron wanted killed testified against her in a lawsuit stemming from her failed campaign.

Former Rhode Island governor Edward D. DiPrete, Republican, pleads guilty December 11 to bribery and racketeering charges for steering contracts to political donors. His one-year minimum-security prison sentence permits him to work weekdays at the family insurance business.

Clinton's first agriculture secretary, former House member Mike Espy, Mississippi Democrat, is acquitted by a federal district court jury December 2 on thirty corruption counts. Espy had been charged with accepting gratuities from agricultural producers. Nine others were convicted in the investigation.

Oklahoma's Republican governor Frank A. Keating is accused of hypocrisy for calling for President Clinton's resignation while refusing to criticize publicly Lt. Gov. Mary Fallin for her relationship with Greg Allen, one of her security guards. Allen resigns in early December for admitted "unprofessional conduct" with Fallin but asks for his job back. Fallin and Allen deny any sexual relationship. Keating's double standard is said to hurt his presidential ambitions.

## 1999: Clinton Trial

On January 7 the Senate opens the impeachment trial of President Clinton. With Chief Justice William H. Rehnquist presiding, House managers (prosecutors) lay out the House's case against Clinton, followed by rebuttal from the president's defense team. No witnesses are called, but the Senate—and the public—see excerpts of videotaped testimony by Lewinsky, White House aide Sidney Blumenthal, and lawyer and Clinton friend Vernon Jordan. Henry Hyde, chairman of the House managers, concedes that Lewinsky's testimony "wasn't harmful, but it wasn't helpful."

*Former White House Intern Monica Lewinsky's affair with President Bill Clinton led to his impeachment by the House and trial in the Senate. Source: Mark Wilson, Reuters*

On February 12 the Senate acquits Clinton, voting 45–55 on perjury and 50–50 on obstruction of justice. Five Republicans join the forty-five Senate Democrats in defeating the latter article. They and others say Clinton's offenses did not rise to the level of "high crimes and misdemeanors" required for conviction and removal from office. Neither article receives a majority vote, let alone the two-thirds vote required for an impeachment conviction.

## Senate, Electing

For more than half of its first two centuries of existence, the United States chose senators indirectly, through the state legislatures. Since 1914, however, the people have filled Senate seats by DIRECT ELECTION.

The change came about through the Seventeenth Amendment to the Constitution, ratified in 1913 following years of dissatisfaction with the original method of Senate elections. The amendment left the president and vice president as the only indirectly elected officials of the federal government, chosen by the ELECTORAL COLLEGE rather than direct POPULAR VOTE.

Senators serve six-year terms, and one-third of them come up for election every other year. Members of the House of Representatives serve two-year terms, and all must stand for election every even-numbered year. They have always been elected by direct vote of the people. (See HOUSE OF REPRESENTATIVES, ELECTING.)

The original, indirect method of Senate elections arose from a fundamental disagreement about the nature of Congress, which was settled by the so-called Great Compromise at the Constitutional Convention in 1787. Delegates from the small states wanted equal representation in Congress, while the larger states argued for a legislature based on population, where their strength would prevail.

As a compromise the framers split the basis for representation between the two legislative chambers—population for the House and equal representation for the Senate, with two senators for each state regardless of its size. House members were to be representatives of the people, elected by the voters. Senators were to be, in effect, ambassadors representing the sovereign states to the federal government. As such, the framers felt, senators should be chosen by the states through their legislatures, rather than directly by the voters.

The argument was that legislatures would be able to give more sober and reflective thought to the kind of persons needed to represent the states' interests. The delegates to the Constitutional Convention also thought the state legislatures, and therefore the states, would take a greater interest in the fledgling national government if they were involved in its operations this way. The delegates already were familiar with the procedure: they themselves had been chosen by the state legislatures, as had members of the Continental Congress (the Congress under the Articles of Confederation).

Before settling on the legislatures, however, delegates

*Sen. Blair Lee, Democrat of Maryland, photographed in 1939. Elected in November 1913, Lee was the first U.S. senator to be popularly elected. Source: Columbia Historical Society*

to the Constitutional Convention considered and abandoned several alternatives. One was that senators be elected by the House. Another was that they be nominated by the state legislatures and appointed by the president. The delegates discarded both ideas as making the Senate too dependent on another part of the federal government. They also turned down a system of senatorial electors, similar to presidential electors. And they rejected direct election as too radical and inconvenient.

Another problem was the length of the senatorial term. In settling on staggered six-year terms the framers tried to balance the belief that relatively frequent elections were necessary to promote good behavior against the need for steadiness and continuity in government.

In the early decades of legislative appointment, the notion of senators' being ambassadors was deeply entrenched. Some state legislatures even told senators how to vote. Occasionally the affected senators balked and resigned rather than vote against their consciences.

For example, in 1836 future president John Tyler, then a U.S. senator from Virginia, was instructed to vote in favor of expunging the Senate's censure of President Andrew Jackson for removing federal deposits from the Bank of the United States. Tyler, a bitter opponent of Jackson, had voted for the censure, and he resigned rather than comply. In another instance, Sen. Hugh Lawson White of Tennessee, a Whig, resigned in 1840 after his state legislature told him to vote for an economic measure supported by the Democratic Van Buren administration.

Legislative appointment, however, also produced some titans who were looked to for guidance in national affairs. The 1858 Illinois race between Abraham Lincoln and Democratic senator Stephen A. Douglas, for example, remains the most famous Senate election of all time. Lincoln, then a House member of the new Republican Party, engaged Douglas in seven nationally publicized DEBATES on the issues of slavery, states' rights, and the admission to the Union of pro-slavery territories. Although the Illinois legislature reelected Douglas, the debates paved the way for Lincoln's election as president in 1860.

## Flawed System

Methods used by the legislatures to elect senators sometimes caused problems, particularly the requirement in most states that the candidates had to win majorities in both houses of the legislature. Because the two chambers often disagreed, the system produced many deadlocks. Frequently, all other legislative business halted as members struggled to agree on a candidate. Sometimes the legislature was simply unable to elect anyone, leaving the state without full representation in the Senate.

Although the Constitution (Article I, section 4) empowered Congress to make or change state rules for electing senators, the national legislature took a hands-off approach for many years. Not until 1866 did Congress step in with a Senate election law. It required the two houses of a state legislature first to vote separately on candidates. If no candidate received a majority in both houses, then members of both chambers were to meet together and vote jointly, until one candidate received a majority of all votes.

Unfortunately, the 1866 law did little to correct the election problems. Deadlocks and election abuses continued to occur as political factions in each state fought for control of its two Senate seats. The stakes were high because senators customarily controlled much of the federal patronage—government jobs and contracts—available in the state.

A dispute in Delaware at the end of the nineteenth century illustrates how bitter and prolonged the fights over Senate elections could be. Divisions in the Delaware legislature were so fierce that no Senate candidate was elected for four years. Senate terms are staggered, and the state had only one senator for part of that time. For two years, from 1901 to 1903, Delaware was left entirely without representation in the Senate.

The system also encouraged corruption. Because of the importance of Senate seats, and the relatively small numbers of state legislators who controlled them, candidates frequently were tempted to use bribery and intimidation to win. Controversies over alleged ELECTION FRAUD often had to be resolved by the Senate, which, like the House, is the judge of its own members under the Constitution (Article I, section 5).

One of the most sensational cases concerned the election of William Lorimer, Republican, who won on the ninety-ninth ballot taken by the Illinois legislature in 1909. A year after he had taken his seat, the Senate cleared Lorimer of charges that he had won election by bribery. But new evidence prompted another investigation, and in 1912 the Senate invalidated Lorimer's election and excluded him from the chamber.

Towering over all criticisms of legislative elections of senators, however, was the complaint that they did not reflect the will of the people. For more than a century the American political system had gradually tended to give voters more power. By the early years of the twentieth century the Senate was the most conspicuous case in which the people had no direct say in choosing those who would govern them.

As pressure mounted to change the system, the House voted five times between 1893 and 1902 for a constitutional amendment to provide for Senate elections by popular vote. But each time the Senate refused to act. All the incumbent senators had been elected by the legislatures, and most were adamantly opposed to direct election.

Frustrated, reformers began implementing various formulas for preselecting Senate candidates, trying to reduce the legislative balloting to something approaching a mere formality. In some cases party conventions endorsed nominees for the Senate, allowing the voters at least to know who the members of the legislature were likely to support.

Southern states, then known as the Solid South because of their strong allegiance to the DEMOCRATIC PARTY, adopted the party primary to choose Senate nominees. The SOUTHERN PRIMARY, as it came to be known, was the only election that mattered in that region. Even in the South, however, state legislators could not be legally bound to support anyone because the Constitution gave them the unfettered power of electing to the Senate the candidate of their choice.

Oregon, which had a strong tradition of political reform, made the most determined efforts to guarantee the popular choice of senators. Under a nonbinding 1901 law, Oregon voters expressed their preference for senator in popular ballots. While the election results had no legal force, the law required that the popular returns be formally announced to the state legislature before it elected a senator. At first the law did not work—the legislature did not elect the winner of the informal popular vote in 1902—but the reformers increased their pressure. They demanded that candidates for the legislature sign a pledge to vote for the winner of the popular vote. By 1908 the plan was successful. Oregon's Republican legislature elected to the U.S. Senate a Democrat, George Chamberlain, the winner of the popular contest. Several other states—including Colorado, Kansas, Minnesota, Montana, Nevada, and Oklahoma—adopted Oregon's plan. By 1910 nearly half the senators elected by the legislatures already had been "select-ed" by popular vote.

### The Seventeenth Amendment

The state reform plans put more pressure on the Senate to agree to a constitutional amendment for direct elections. Proponents began pushing for a convention to propose this amendment and perhaps others. (Article V of the Constitution provides two methods of proposing amendments—passage by two-thirds of both houses of Congress or through the calling of a special convention if requested by the legislatures of two-thirds of the states. An amendment proposed by either method must be ratified by three-fourths of the states.)

Conservatives began to fear an unprecedented amending convention more than they did popular election of senators. They worried that it might be dominated by liberals and progressives who would propose numerous amendments and change the very nature of the government. Consequently, conservatives' opposition to popular election of senators diminished.

At the same time progressives of both parties made strong gains in the midterm elections of 1910. Some successful Senate candidates had pledged to work for adoption of a constitutional amendment providing for popular election. In this atmosphere the Senate debated and finally passed the amendment on June 12, 1911, by a vote of 64–24. The House concurred in the Senate version on May 13, 1912, by a vote of 238–39. Ratification of the Seventeenth Amendment was completed by the requisite number of states on April 8, 1913, and was proclaimed a part of the Constitution by Secretary of State William Jennings Bryan on May 31, 1913.

The first popularly elected senator was Blair Lee, Maryland Democrat, in November 1913. He was elected for the three years remaining in the term of a senator who had died.

No wholesale changeover in membership occurred when the Seventeenth Amendment became effective. Every one of the twenty-three senators seeking reelection to full terms in November 1914 was successful. All had been elected by state legislatures in their previous terms.

*This cover story from* Cosmopolitan magazine, *dated April 1906, linked many senators to large corporations and political machines and provided another reason for passage of the Seventeenth Amendment.* Source: Senate Historical Office

The transition to direct elections, however, did not eliminate Senate election disputes. One of the most bitterly fought took place in New Hampshire in 1974 between Republican Louis C. Wyman and Democrat John A. Durkin. It was the closest election in Senate history. Wyman had won by two votes, but Durkin appealed and ultimately won after the Democratic Senate called for a new election. (See CONTESTED ELECTIONS; ZZZ.)

### Special Elections

Unlike House vacancies, which require the holding of a special election, Senate vacancies usually are filled by temporary appointment by the GOVERNOR. The

Constitution grants this authority in Article I, section 3, paragraph 2, which, before it was amended, stated: "If Vacancies happen by Resignation, or otherwise, during the Recess of the Legislature of any State, the Executive thereof may make temporary Appointments until the next Meeting of the Legislature, which shall then fill such Vacancies."

The Seventeenth Amendment revised the governors' authority to fill vacancies. In such cases, the amendment says, "the executive authority of such State shall issue writs of election to fill such vacancies: *Provided,* That the legislature of any State may empower the executive thereof to make temporary appointments until the people fill the vacancies by election as the legislature may direct."

Special elections held under this provision usually took place in November of even-numbered years, coincident with other federal or state elections, which meant in some cases that the unexpired term had only two months to run. Some states, however, held special elections shortly after the vacancy occurred. Governors quite often appoint themselves to fill Senate vacancies.

In the case of New Hampshire's Wyman-Durkin contest, the governor appointed former senator Norris H. Cotton to serve until the special election was held to resolve the disputed election. Cotton, whose retirement created the vacancy in the first place, served more than a month in 1975 until Durkin was sworn in.

## Senate's Three Classes

To bring one-third of the Senate up for election every two years, rather than all at the same time, the founders divided the Senate into three classes or groups of members. A member's class depends on the year in which he or she is elected. Article I, section 3, paragraph 2, of the Constitution states, "Immediately after they shall be assembled in Consequence of the first Election, they shall be divided as equally as may be into three Classes. The Seats of the Senators of the first Class shall be vacated at the Expiration of the second Year, of the second Class at the Expiration of the fourth Year, and of the third Class at the Expiration of the sixth Year, so that one-third may be chosen every Second year."

Therefore, senators belonging to class one began their regular terms in the years 1789, 1791, 1797, 1803, and so on, continuing through the present day to 1995 and coming up for reelection in 2000. Senators belonging to class two began their regular terms in 1789, 1793, 1799, 1805, and so on, continuing through to the present day in 1997 and up for election in 2002. And senators belonging to class three began their regular terms in 1789, 1795, 1801, 1807, and so on, continuing through the present day to 1999, and up for reelection in 2004.

## Sessions and Terms

In the fall of 1788, the expiring Continental Congress established a schedule for the incoming government under the new Constitution. The Congress decided that the new government was to commence on the first Wednesday in March 1789—March 4. Even though the House did not achieve a quorum until April 1 and the Senate April 6, and President Washington was not inaugurated until April 30, the terms of the Senate, House, and president were still considered to have begun March 4. The term of the First Congress continued through March 3, 1791. Because congressional and presidential terms were fixed at exactly two, four, and six years, March 4 became the official date of transition from one administration to another every four years and from one Congress to another every two years.

## "Long" and "Short" Sessions

The Constitution did not mandate a regular congressional session to begin March 4. Instead, Article I, section 4, paragraph 2, called for at least one congressional session every year, to convene on the first Monday in December unless Congress by law set a different day. Consequently, except when called by the president for special sessions, or when Congress itself set a different day, Congress convened in regular session each December, until the Twentieth Amendment took effect in late 1933.

The original December date resulted in a long and short session. The first (long) session would meet in December of an odd-numbered year and continue into the next year, usually adjourning some time in the summer. The second (short) session began in December of an even-numbered year and continued through March 3 of the next year, when its term ran out. It also became customary for the Senate to meet in brief special session on March 4 or March 5, especially in years when a new president was inaugurated, to act on presidential nominations.

To illustrate with an example of a typical Congress, the Twenty-ninth (1845–1847): President James K. Polk, Democrat, was inaugurated on March 4, 1845. The Senate met in special session from March 4 to March 20 to confirm Polk's cabinet and other appointments. Then the first regular session convened December 1, 1845, working until August 10, 1846, when it adjourned. The second, a short session, lasted from December 7, 1846, through March 3, 1847. Because it was not clear whether terms of members of Congress ended at midnight March 3 or noon March 4, the custom evolved of extending the legislative day of March 3, in odd-numbered years, to noon March 4.

## The Twentieth Amendment

Like House members, senators were affected by ratification of the Twentieth Amendment, the so-called Lame-Duck Amendment, in 1933. The amendment moved up the beginning of congressional sessions to January 3. It also changed the date of presidential inaugurations from March 4 to January 20. (See PRESIDENT, NOMINATING AND ELECTING; VICE PRESIDENT.)

The short session had encouraged filibusters and other delaying tactics by members determined to block legislation that would die upon the automatic adjournment of Congress on March 3. Moreover, the Congresses that met in short session always included a substantial number of lame-duck members who had been defeated at the polls, yet were able quite often to determine the legislative outcome of the session.

Dissatisfaction with the short session began to mount after 1900. During the Wilson administration (1913–1921), each of four such sessions ended with a Senate filibuster and the loss of important bills including several funding bills. Sen. George W. Norris, Nebras-

ka Republican, became the leading advocate of a constitutional amendment to abolish the short session by starting the terms of Congress and the president in January instead of March.

The Senate approved the Norris amendment five times during the 1920s, only to see it blocked in the House each time. It was finally approved by both chambers in 1932 and became the Twentieth Amendment upon ratification by the thirty-sixth state in 1933. The amendment provided that the terms of senators and representatives would begin and end at noon on the third day of January of the year following the election. It provided also that Congress should meet annually on January 3 "unless they shall by law appoint a different day."

The second session of the Seventy-third Congress was the first to convene on the new date, January 3, 1934. The amendment was intended to permit Congress to extend its first session for as long as necessary and to complete the work of its second session before the next election, thus avoiding legislation by a lame-duck body.

## Senate, Qualifications

The United States Senate is often called the nation's most exclusive club. Yet under the Constitution Senate membership is open to most adult Americans. To be a senator, according to Article I, section 3, a person need only be at least thirty years old, a U.S. citizen for nine years, and an inhabitant of the state from which he or she is elected.

The Senate is also referred to erroneously as the "upper body," even though the House of Representatives has equal power and requires similar qualifications for election. (See HOUSE OF REPRESENTATIVES, ELECTING; HOUSE OF REPRESENTATIVES, QUALIFICATIONS.)

One reason for the Senate's greater prestige is its smaller size. Out of a nation of 260 million, only 100 men and women can be senators, compared with 435 representatives. And a state's two senators each represent the entire state, where all but the least populated states are carved into two or more DISTRICTS, each represented by a House member.

The consequences of the Senate's compact size and individuals' greater opportunities to affect legislation are the intense competition and high costs of statewide campaigning for each seat. In the television age the competition is expressed by heavy spending for advertising to reach the maximum number of voters. (See CAMPAIGN FINANCE; MEDIA USE BY CAMPAIGNS.)

In a large state such as California (29.8 million population) or New York (18.0 million), a race for the Senate can cost several millions of dollars, and for incumbents defending their seats raising that much money is almost a full-time job. When the 1998 elections were more than a year away, sixteen Senate candidates had amassed huge war chests. Topping the list with $8.6 million was incumbent New York Republican Alphonse M. D'Amato, followed closely by one of his expected Democratic challengers, Rep. Charles E. Schumer, with $6.5 million. Schumer won the election.

## Senate Characteristics

By quirks of history, both the Senate and House have had members who did not meet the constitutional minimum age requirements. The youngest senator was John H. Eaton, Tennessee Republican, who was twenty-eight years, four months, and twenty-nine days in 1818 when he was sworn in. The other underage senators were Henry Clay of Kentucky (no party), twenty-nine years, eight months, when he first entered the Senate in 1806, and Armistead Mason, Virginia Republican, twenty-eight years, five months, and eighteen days in 1816. Because no one challenged their election, all three were duly sworn in.

A West Virginian, Democrat Rush D. Holt, was underage when elected at twenty-nine in 1934, but he did not claim his seat until his thirtieth birthday in June 1935. The Senate later rejected an effort to invalidate Holt's election.

The oldest senator in history is Strom Thurmond, South Carolina Republican, who was born December 5, 1902. Thurmond surpassed Theodore Francis Green, Rhode Island Democrat, born October 2, 1867. Green

*Sen. Hiram R. Revels, Republican of Mississippi, was the first black senator, serving 1870–1871. The Fifteenth Amendment gave former slaves the right to vote in national elections.* Source: Library of Congress

was ninety-three and seven months old when he retired in 1961, and he lived five years longer.

Thurmond also set records as the oldest member of Congress and as the longest-serving senator, surpassing the forty-two-year mark set by Carl T. Hayden, Arizona Democrat, who retired in 1969. As of early 1999, however, Thurmond had not matched Hayden's total of fifty-seven years in Congress, including fifteen years in the House.

In the 105th Congress (1997–1999) the average senator was fifty-seven and a half years old. Republican members tended to be slightly younger than Democrats.

The first black senator was Hiram R. Revels, Mississippi Republican, who served in 1870 and 1871. After the Civil War the Fifteenth Amendment, ratified in 1870, gave former slaves the right to vote in national elections. The POLL TAX, WHITE PRIMARIES, and similar impediments to BLACK SUFFRAGE continued, however, until passage of the VOTING RIGHTS ACT OF 1965 and subsequent amendments.

Since adoption of the Fifteenth Amendment, scores of African Americans have served in the House, but only four have been senators. One of the four, Carol Moseley-Braun, Illinois Democrat, was one of nine woman senators in the 105th Congress and the only black senator. The Senate never has had more than one African American member at a time.

The first woman senator, Rebecca L. Felton, Georgia Democrat, was also the oldest new senator and served the shortest term. At age eighty-seven she was appointed October 1, 1922, to fill a vacancy, but she was not sworn in until November 21, 1922. She was replaced the following day by Walter F. George, who had been elected to fill the seat .

Although the Constitution did not bar women from Congress, their election was a rarity until the Nineteenth Amendment made WOMEN'S SUFFRAGE universal in 1920. The first elected female senator was Hattie W. Caraway, Arkansas Democrat, in 1931.

The first woman to serve in both the House and Senate was Margaret Chase Smith, Maine Republican, who served twenty-four years (1949–1973) in the Senate, longer than any other woman. By 1997 three other woman senators also had House service: Democrats Barbara Mikulski of Maryland and Barbara Boxer of California and Republican Olympia J. Snowe of Maine.

## Qualification Disputes

Since the founding of the nation there have been six formal efforts to disqualify senators-elect on the constitutional requirements of age, citizenship, or residence. Only two of those resulted in exclusion from the Senate, both on grounds of citizenship.

In the first case, in 1793, the Senate excluded Geneva-born Albert Gallatin of Pennsylvania, who had been a citizen less than the required nine years. He argued unsuccessfully that he in effect became a citizen when he took part in the Revolution. Gallatin later served six years in the House and was Treasury secretary from 1801 to 1814. In 1812 he was nominated for the vice presidency but declined. (See RUNNING MATE.)

In the other case, the Senate voided the election of Ireland native James Shields of Illinois after he was seated briefly in 1849 before he reached the ninth year of his naturalized citizenship. He was then elected to the vacancy created by his disqualification and served until 1855. He later was a senator from Minnesota (1858–1859) and Missouri (January-March 1879), making him the only senator to serve three states.

A third citizenship case concerned the first black senator, Hiram Revels. The Senate admitted him, however, ruling that the Fourteenth Amendment, ratified two years before his election, had made him a citizen retroactively.

The unsuccessful disqualification effort against Rush Holt in 1935 was the only one based on age.

Two senators challenged on grounds of nonresidence—Stanley Griswold of Ohio in 1809 and Adelbert Ames of Mississippi in 1870—won their cases and were admitted. Charges of nonresidence are more common, however, in senatorial campaigns than in Senate floor challenges. In 1988, for example, Sen. Frank Lautenberg, Democrat, fended off a celebrity challenge from former army general and Heisman Trophy winner Pete Dawkins, in part by questioning Dawkins's claim to New Jersey residence.

The Supreme Court has struck down efforts by INTEREST GROUPS, and Congress itself, to add to the Senate and House qualifications set forth in the Constitution. The one additional qualification still in effect is in the Fourteenth Amendment, ratified in 1868, which excludes from Congress anyone who "has engaged in rebellion against the United States or given aid or comfort to its enemies."

The only senator-elect excluded as one of the Civil War cases was Philip F. Thomas, Maryland Democrat, in 1867. He was charged with aiding the enemy because he gave his son $100 as he left to fight for the Confederacy. Although the Fourteenth Amendment had not yet been ratified, the Senate excluded Thomas on grounds of noncitizenship.

Efforts of almost half the states to impose TERM LIMITS on members of Congress have been nullified by the Supreme Court. In his opinion in *U.S. Term Limits v. Thornton* (1995), Justice John Paul Stevens explained that it was unconstitutional for individual states to change the qualifications for election to Congress.

## Seventeenth Amendment

*See* SENATE, ELECTING.

## Shaw v. Reno

The Supreme Court's 1993 decision in *Shaw v. Reno* established the right of white voters to challenge CON-GRESSIONAL DISTRICTS drawn to include a majority black population. The ruling, which threatened a number of so-called MAJORITY-MINORITY districts around the country, was hailed by advocates of "color-blind" districting but criticized by minority groups and traditional civil rights organizations.

The case involved a RACIAL REDISTRICTING plan approved by the North Carolina legislature after the state gained one new congressional seat through REAP-PORTIONMENT following the 1990 CENSUS. Under pressure from the U.S. Justice Department, the legislature created two districts with African American majorities. One relatively compact district lay in the state's Piedmont region. The other—the Twelfth District—combined black neighborhoods in four urban areas by means of a snakelike, 160-mile-long corridor across the center of the state.

Both districts elected black representatives in the 1992 election. White voters then challenged the plan. They claimed it set up a "racially discriminatory voting process" and deprived them of the right to vote in "a color-blind" election.

A three-judge federal district court, in a split decision, rejected the white voters' suit. But by a 5–4 vote, the Supreme Court reinstated the suit, ruling that white voters could challenge racially drawn districts under the Equal Protection Clause of the Fourteenth Amendment if the districts were "highly irregular" and "lacked sufficient justification."

Writing for the majority, Justice Sandra Day O'Connor said that in some cases a redistricting plan could be "so highly irregular that, on its face, it rationally cannot

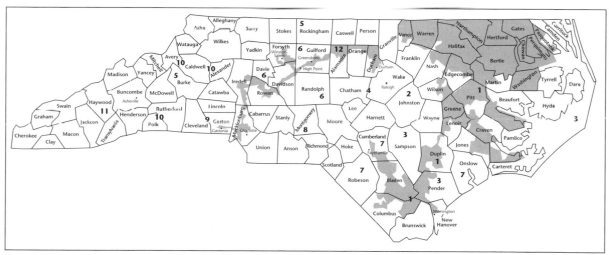

*The irregular shapes of North Carolina's First and Twelfth Congressional Districts were challenged in* Shaw v. Reno.

be understood as anything other than an effort to segregate voters on the basis of race." The Court's four most conservative members joined in the opinion: Chief Justice William H. Rehnquist and Justices Antonin Scalia, Anthony M. Kennedy, and Clarence Thomas.

In a dissenting opinion, Justice Byron R. White contended that the white voters had suffered no legal injury. "Though they might be dissatisfied at the prospect of casting a vote for a losing candidate, surely they cannot complain of discriminatory treatment." Justices Harry A. Blackmun and John Paul Stevens joined White's dissent; Justice David H. Souter dissented separately.

The decision returned the case to the three-judge court to determine whether the state had sufficient justification for the districting plan. O'Connor said the panel should weigh whether the plan met the "strict scrutiny" test used in other racial challenges: whether it was narrowly tailored to meet a compelling government interest.

In its second ruling, the three-judge court again upheld the districting scheme. The panel held the state had a compelling interest in overcoming past racial discrimination and in creating separate majority-black districts with rural and urban populations. But the Supreme Court disagreed. In its second ruling in the case, *Shaw v. Hunt* (1996), the Court by a 5–4 vote said the state could not justify the plan on grounds of overcoming past discrimination or complying with the federal VOTING RIGHTS ACT.

*Protesters concerned about the future of Social Security join a September 24, 1998, rally against tax cuts.* Source: Scott Ferrell, Congressional Quarterly

## Single-Issue Voting

Some people feel so strongly about an issue that they base their voting decisions solely on candidates' stands on that issue. This way of making electoral choices is called *single-issue voting,* and election studies indicate that its occurrence is on the rise. In contrast, PARTY IDENTIFICATION is waning among modern voters, making political affiliation less of a factor in how they vote. (See ISSUE VOTING.)

Issues that arouse voters' passions are apt to be

volatile subjects that do not lend themselves to compromise, middle-of-the-road solutions. Before the Civil War, the abolition of slavery was one such issue. Today's "hot button" issues include abortion rights and gun ownership. People are usually for or against either one, with little in between.

The NATIONAL ELECTION STUDIES (NES) after the

1992 election showed that pro-life (antiabortion) voters favored George Bush over Bill Clinton, while pro-choice voters strongly favored Clinton over Bush. The third candidate, Ross Perot, did better among pro-choice voters than among pro-life voters.

For an issue to be a factor in voter choice, however, the voter must be informed about the candidates' positions. The NES studies indicated that, despite the time and money Perot spent on his television "infomercials," voters were not clear about his issue stands. Many Perot supporters apparently voted against "politics as usual" rather than for or against an issue.

Single-issue voting has benefited from CAMPAIGN FINANCE laws that exempt controversial issue-advocacy POLITICAL ADVERTISING from limits on contributions to candidates. So long as the issue ad does not name the candidate and is run independently, it does not count as a contribution. In the 1998 California primary, for example, single-issue ads on abortion and TERM LIMITS dominated the expensive media advertising related to the campaigns. Because the candidates' stands on those issues were well known, the INTEREST GROUPS involved were able to help or hurt candidates with barrages of mostly NEGATIVE CAMPAIGNING without financial cost to the candidates.

## Single-Member District

Most legislators in the United States, including members of the House of Representatives, are elected from single-member DISTRICTS by PLURALITY vote. For the seven states entitled by population to only one representative, the entire state is the district and the candidates for the seat run AT LARGE.

In the early nineteenth century some states elected U.S. representatives from MULTIMEMBER DISTRICTS. Congress banned the practice in 1842, however, when it decreed that no district could elect more than one representative. Some multimember districts or wards are still used in state and local elections. (See DISTRICTS, WARDS, AND PRECINCTS.)

The WINNER-TAKE-ALL characteristic of congressional and other single-member elections stands in contrast to PROPORTIONAL REPRESENTATION, in which parties receive a share of the seats based on their share of the vote. Winner-take-all favors the TWO-PARTY SYSTEM because THIRD PARTIES have little realistic chance of sharing in the political power, and the major parties have little to gain by forming COALITIONS with weaker parties.

Racial and ethnic minorities generally prefer single-member districts over multimember districts covering a wider geographical area. A compact district that is predominantly African American has a better chance of electing a black representative than does a predominantly white district where candidates must run at large for two or more seats. The Supreme Court has frowned, however, on efforts to ensure minority representation by creating MAJORITY-MINORITY DISTRICTS through artificially contorted district lines. (See CUMULATIVE VOTING; RACIAL REDISTRICTING.)

## Smith v. Allwright

See PRIMARY TYPES; WHITE PRIMARIES.

## Soccer Moms

See WOMEN'S SUFFRAGE.

## Socialist Labor Party (1888– )

The Socialist Labor Party, the first national socialist party in the United States, ranks second only to the PROHIBITION PARTY among third parties in longevity. Formed in 1874 by elements of the Socialist International in New York, it was first known as the Social Democratic Workingmen's Party. In 1877 the group adopted the name Socialist Labor Party. Throughout the 1880s the party worked in concert with other left-wing third parties, including the Greenbacks.

The Socialist Labor Party ran national tickets in

every presidential election from 1892 through 1976. The party collected its highest proportion of the national vote in 1896, when its candidate received 36,356 votes (0.3 percent of the popular vote).

Led by the autocratic Daniel DeLeon (1852–1914), a former Columbia University law lecturer, the Socialist Labor Party became increasingly militant and made its best showing in local races in 1898. But DeLeon's insistence on rigid party discipline and his opposition to the organized labor movement created a feeling of alienation among many members. Moderate elements bolted from the party, joining the SOCIALIST PARTY of Eugene V. Debs, which formed in 1901.

The Socialist Labor Party continued as a small, tightly organized far-left group bound to DeLeon's uncompromising belief in revolution. As late as 1976 the party advocated direct worker action to take over control of production and claimed five thousand members nationwide.

*The Socialists have been among the most persistent and successful votegetters of America's third parties. Eugene Debs was the Socialist candidate in five of the first six presidential elections in the twentieth century. Source: Library of Congress*

## Socialist Party (1901– )

The Socialist Party was established officially in July 1901 at a convention in Indianapolis, Indiana, which joined together former American Railway Union president Eugene V. Debs's Social Democratic Party with a moderate faction of the SOCIALIST LABOR PARTY. The two groups had begun discussions a year before and in the 1900 presidential campaign jointly supported a ticket headed by Debs that received 86,935 votes (0.6 percent of the popular vote).

The 1901 unity convention identified the new Socialist Party with the working class and described the party's goal as "collective ownership . . . of the means of production and distribution." The party grew rapidly in the early twentieth century, reaching a peak membership of approximately 118,000 in 1912. That year also proved to be the party's best at the polls. Debs, a presidential candidate five times between 1900 and 1920, received 900,369 votes (6.0 percent of the popular vote). The Socialists elected 1,200 candidates to local offices, including 79 mayors.

With the outbreak of World War I, the party became a vehicle for antiwar protest. In 1917 pacifist Socialists converted a number of mayoral elections into referendums on the war, winning 34 percent of the vote in Chicago, more than 25 percent in Buffalo, and 22 percent in New York City.

The following year Debs was convicted of sedition for making an antiwar speech and was sentenced to a term in the Atlanta federal penitentiary, from which he ran for president in 1920 and received 915,490 votes (3.4 percent of the popular vote).

Four years later the Socialists endorsed Wisconsin

senator Robert M. La Follette's presidential candidacy, an unsuccessful attempt to establish a farm-labor coalition. In 1928 the Socialists resumed running a presidential ticket. With the death of Debs in 1926, the party selected Norman Thomas, a former minister and social worker, to be the party's standard-bearer for the next six elections. The Great Depression brought a brief surge for the Socialists in 1932, with Thomas polling 884,649 votes (2.2 percent of the popular vote).

But 1932 proved to be only a temporary revival for the Socialists. Roosevelt's New Deal stole their thunder, and the Socialist Party failed to attract even one-half of 1 percent of the vote in any succeeding presidential election. In 1976 the party ran its first presidential ticket in two decades. The candidates received 6,038 votes, 0.01 percent of the popular vote.

Although Socialist Party candidates received a few more votes in the 1980 elections, 6,898, their percentage share of the total vote remained 0.01. The old-line Socialist Party faded again from the presidential candidate scene in 1984 but reappeared in 1988, 1992, and 1996. The Socialist candidates, Willa Kenoyer and Ron Ehrenreich in 1988 and J. Quinn Brisben and Barbara Garson in 1992, however, experienced a precipitous drop in support, receiving only 3,882 nationwide votes in 1988 and 3,057 in 1992. The 1996 candidate, Mary Cal Hollis of Colorado, did slightly better with 4,764 votes.

## Socialist Workers Party (1938– )

The Socialist Workers Party was formed in 1938 by followers of the Russian revolutionary Leon Trotsky. Originally a faction within the U.S. COMMUNIST PARTY, the Trotskyites were expelled in 1936 on instructions from Soviet leader Joseph Stalin. A brief Trotskyite coalition with the SOCIALIST PARTY ended in 1938 when the dissidents decided to organize independently as the Socialist Workers Party. Through its youth arm, the Young Socialist Alliance, the Socialist Workers Party was active in the anti-Vietnam War movement and contributed activists to civil rights protests.

Since 1948 the party has run a presidential candidate, but its entries have never received more than 0.1 percent of the popular vote. In 1992 presidential candidate James Warren was on the ballot in thirteen states and the District of Columbia and drew 23,096 votes nationwide. The party's 1996 candidate, James Harris of Georgia, received 8,463 votes.

## Soft Money

A 1979 federal law allows political parties to raise and spend money for general political activities outside the legal limits on contributions. This "soft money" supplements the HARD MONEY governed by stricter CAMPAIGN FINANCE regulations.

Soft money quickly became a major source of revenue for the parties and a giant loophole in the laws that were meant to lessen the influence of INTEREST GROUPS in U.S. elections. Aggressive pursuit of soft money, particularly by President Bill Clinton's 1996 reelection campaign, prompted congressional investigations and calls for further reforms of the campaign finance system.

Democratic and Republican Party committees reported raising a total of $263.5 million in soft money for the 1995–1996 election cycle, according to the FEDERAL ELECTION COMMISSION (FEC). The figures were up substantially for both parties since the 1992 presidential election. Republican committees raised $141.2 million and spent $149.7 million. Democratic committees raised $122.3 million and spent $117.5 million.

Despite the Republicans' higher totals, the Democrats' soft money tactics drew more MEDIA COVERAGE and were the primary focus of hearings by the Republican-controlled 105th Congress (1997–1999). The FEC itself came under fire for not doing more to police the soft money situation before it got out of control.

The Clinton White House was criticized for overzealous solicitation of soft money contributions to the DEMOCRATIC NATIONAL COMMITTEE (DNC). Supposedly to be used for party-building activities, some of the money reportedly was converted to hard

*Protesters from the National Campaign Finance Reform Coalition wave signs and shout slogans at guests attending a Bush/Quayle fund raiser at the Washington Convention Center in April 1992. Source: R. Michael Jenkins, Congressional Quarterly*

money for the reelection of Clinton and Vice President Al Gore. Under the 1974 Federal Election Campaign Act (FECA) as amended, the Clinton-Gore general election campaign was restricted to spending the $61.8 million it received in PUBLIC FINANCING under FECA. (The Republican ticket of Robert J. Dole and Jack F. Kemp received the same amount, with the same limitations.)

Following disclosure of the sources, the DNC returned several millions of dollars in contributions. Some came from Chinese and other foreign nationals who are barred from contributing to U.S. elections. Other donors were guests at White House coffees or overnight stays in the historic Lincoln Bedroom or other guest rooms.

Reformers view soft money as a backdoor entrance for corporations and unions that have long been prohibited from giving money to political candidates. Corporate and labor POLITICAL ACTION COMMITTEES, as well as other PACs and individuals, are permitted to donate money but are limited in the amounts they can give to candidates for federal office. (See table, Contribution Limits, page 39.)

The 1979 soft money law, however, allowed donations of $100,000 or more to the parties, which are per-

## Growth in Soft Money

In 1979 Congress amended campaign finance law to encourage contributions to state and local political parties. New regulations by the Federal Election Commission in 1991 and a Supreme Court decision in 1996 have led to rapid growth in the amount of money received by national parties.

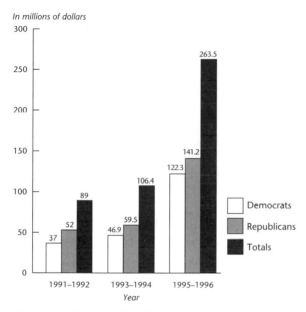

*In millions of dollars*

- Democrats
- Republicans
- Totals

*Source:* Center for Responsive Politics.

mitted to spend without limit for voter registration, turnout drives, and other activities to benefit the party rather than specific federal candidates. A portion of the "nonfederal money," as it is technically known, is transferred by the national committees to their state and local committees. Some goes to help candidates in nonfederal races.

Soft money also may be used for generic party advertising and for a controversial form of MEDIA USE BY CAMPAIGNS—paid issue-advocacy ads that clearly support or oppose a particular candidate without actually naming him or her.

Some reformers would eliminate or drastically restrict soft money, but others caution that if used properly it is beneficial in stimulating citizen awareness of issues and participation in elections. Proposals to strike a compromise between the two positions were pending in Congress, but no action was forthcoming in 1998.

## Sophisticated Voting

Also known as strategic voting, *sophisticated voting* occurs when a person casts a vote he thinks will help the candidate he prefers, even if it means voting for one of the opponents. In a three-way race, for example, a Democrat may vote for the INDEPENDENT candidate if it appears that the independent has no chance of winning but could split the Republican vote.

*Sincere* voters, on the other hand, do not take into consideration the strategic consequences of their ballots. They simply vote for the candidates who are their first choice for the elective office at stake.

The plurality system of American elections fosters sophisticated voting, particularly in multicandidate races, such as a PRIMARY election for a political party nomination. Usually the candidate who receives the largest share of the vote is the winner, even if it is not a majority share (more than 50 percent). There seldom is any incentive for strategic voting in a two-way race because a CROSSOVER VOTE could help elect the candidate the voter wants to defeat. Exceptions might be cases where a majority vote is required and the voter wants to ensure a RUNOFF ELECTION between the two candidates, or the voter is lukewarm about his or her first choice and does not want to "waste" a vote on a likely loser. (See THERMOMETER RATINGS.)

WINNER-TAKE-ALL elections also lend themselves to sophisticated voting. In presidential nominating contests, the DEMOCRATIC PARTY has banned winner-take-all primaries in favor of PROPORTIONAL REPRESENTATION, in which convention delegates are distributed to candidates in proportion to their share of the vote above a certain THRESHOLD for qualification. The REPUBLICAN PARTY in some states, however, still permits winner-take-all primaries.

In presidential elections, the winner-take-all nature of the ELECTORAL COLLEGE system can lead to strategic voting on ELECTION DAY if there are more than two major candidates. To be elected president, a candidate must receive an ABSOLUTE MAJORITY of the 538 electoral votes. If no candidate receives 270 electoral votes (half of the total plus one) the election devolves to the House of Representatives for decision.

Because the presidential candidate who receives a plurality in a state receives all of its electoral votes, some voters may engage in strategic voting to gain an advantage for their candidate. They may try to use their individual votes to try to split the vote between the perceived strongest opponent and the one who poses the least threat to their preferred candidate.

Political scientists Paul R. Abramson, John H. Aldrich, and David W. Rohde believe that strategic voting took place in the 1992 presidential race of incumbent Republican George Bush, Democrat Bill Clinton, and independent Ross Perot. In their book *Change and Continuity in the 1992 Elections,* they say that "the results strongly suggest that at least some voters who preferred Perot strategically voted for Clinton or Bush."

For their analysis Abramson, Aldrich, and Rohde used the NATIONAL ELECTION STUDIES (NES) thermometer ratings of voters toward the three candidates, ranging from "very warm or favorable feeling" to "very cold or unfavorable feeling." The authors report that these preelection ratings "are usually a very accurate reflection of the vote." On that basis they conclude that "apparently Clinton would have been the preferred candidate of a majority if he had run against either Bush or Perot alone." Most of those who favored Bush or Clinton overwhelmingly voted for them. But of the 16 percent of respondents who placed Perot highest in the thermometer ratings, only 77 percent actually voted for him, indicating that Perot lost some votes to strategic voting.

Somewhat related to sophisticated or strategic voting is use of the BULLET VOTE. Bullet voting is different, however, because the voter does vote his or her top preference in a MULTICANDIDATE DISTRICT contest. But it is strategic in that the voter relinquishes the opportunity to vote for more than one candidate in an effort to take votes away from other candidates who might have a better chance of winning one of the seats to be filled.

## Sore Loser Laws

About half the states have laws that in a given election year prevent PRIMARY losers from entering another party's primary or the general election in another try for the office to be filled. Such laws are known as *sore loser laws.*

Although the laws have been challenged as an unconstitutional denial of BALLOT ACCESS, the U.S. Supreme Court has upheld them as a fair and reasonable way to limit the length of election battles while still giving the voters a sufficient choice of candidates. In a 1974 case, *Storer v. Brown,* the Court upheld the California sore loser law as being in harmony with the state's goal of having political parties use primaries to settle their internal differences and limit the ballot to primary winners and qualified independents. Besides giving the people "understandable choices," the Court said, this system should give the general election winner "sufficient support to govern effectively."

The Court also upheld a related "disaffiliation" law that prevented California candidates from running as independents if they had been registered with a party less than a year before the primary. Both actions strengthened the parties' role in winnowing out candidates and avoiding the dangers of what the Court called "unrestrained factionalism."

Until 1959 California had permitted cross-filing of candidates in other parties' primaries, which some saw as a dilution of the parties' distinctive identities. Repeal of cross-filing, the Court said, made the primary "not merely a warm-up for the general election, but an integral part of the entire election process."

Presidential candidate John B. Anderson encountered sore loser laws in several states in 1980 when he sought to run as an independent in the general election after losing several early primaries to the eventual nominee, Ronald Reagan. Anderson ultimately was able to get on the ballot in every state, largely because he had tried to remove his name from the primary ballot in some states before the primary was held.

At first, however, the early filing deadlines in some states threatened to keep Anderson off the November ballot. Anderson brought suit in one such state, challenging Ohio's early deadline as an unconstitutional restriction on independent candidates. He won in federal district court and received 5.9 percent of Ohio's vote on ELECTION DAY. The state appealed, however, and in 1982 the Supreme Court in *Anderson et al. v. Celebrezze* overturned a federal appeals court that had reversed the district court action. The Supreme Court ruled that early filing deadlines for independents put them at a disadvantage and deny a choice to voters not satisfied with the candidates put forth by existing political parties.

Although the *Anderson* ruling seemed to contradict the Court's earlier decision in *Storer*, the Court said Ohio's early deadline approach was more burdensome to independents than California's sore-loser approach.

In January 1998 Ohio's supreme court ruled that the state's sore loser law applied even to a nonpartisan election for the Ohio board of education. Persons who had run in a partisan primary the previous May were ineligible to run in November for a seat on the board, the court said. It upheld the sore loser law as preventing "intraparty conflicts, voter confusion, and candidacies prompted by short-range goals."

*Jefferson Davis, president of the Confederate States of America.*
Source: Library of Congress

## Southern Democrats

Agitation over the slavery issue, building for a generation, reached a climax in 1860 and produced a sectional split in the DEMOCRATIC PARTY. Throughout the mid-nineteenth century the Democrats had remained unified by supporting the various pieces of compromise legislation that both protected slavery in the southern states and endorsed the policy of popular sovereignty in the territories. But in 1860 Southern Democrats wanted the Democratic convention (meeting in Charleston, South Carolina) to insert a PLATFORM plank specifically protecting slavery in the territories. When their plank was defeated, delegates from most of the southern states walked out.

The Charleston convention stalemated over a presidential choice and, after recessing for six weeks, reconvened in Baltimore, where Illinois senator Stephen A. Douglas was nominated. Most of the southern delegates, plus those from California and Oregon, bolted the convention and nominated their own ticket in a rump convention held after Douglas's selection. Vice President John C. Breckinridge of Kentucky was chosen for president, and Joseph Lane, a states' rights advocate from Oregon, was selected as his RUNNING MATE. A platform was adopted that recognized the right of slavery to exist in the territories. After the formation of the two sectional tickets, two separate Democratic national committees operated in Washington, D.C., to oversee their campaigns.

Although in the 1860 election the combined Douglas and Breckinridge votes amounted to a majority of the ballots cast, the split in Democratic ranks was a boon to the campaign of the Republican candidate, Abraham Lincoln, who won with a plurality of the vote. The

Breckinridge ticket received 848,019 votes (18.1 percent of the POPULAR VOTE) and carried nine southern and BORDER STATES.

During the Civil War the Southern Democrats provided much of the leadership for the Confederate government, including its president, Jefferson Davis. At the end of the conflict the Southern Democrats made no attempt to continue as a separate sectional entity and rejoined the national Democratic Party.

## Southern Primary

Throughout much of the time after the PRIMARY came into widespread use in the early twentieth century, the DEMOCRATIC PARTY primaries were the only elections that counted in the South. The party so dominated the region that to win its nomination was in effect to win the election.

But that changed in recent years as the REPUBLICAN PARTY gained strength in the South and indeed came to dominate the area much as the Democrats once did. By the end of the century Republicans outnumbered Democrats in the southern statehouses and congressional delegations, two of their number held the top House and Senate leadership posts, and in presidential politics the South usually voted solidly Republican.

Nevertheless, the southern primary holds a special place in U.S. political history and deserves separate discussion in any examination of primaries and how they work. Also, because they were so lopsided politically, the southern primaries spawned a regional addition to the nominating process: the RUNOFF primary.

In a 1949 study of politics in the region, political scientist V. O. Key Jr. concluded, "In fact, the Democratic primary is no nominating method at all. The primary is the election." The area of his study comprised the eleven states—all members of the Civil War Confederacy—traditionally known as the Old South: Alabama, Arkansas, Florida, Georgia, Louisiana, Mississippi, North Carolina, South Carolina, Tennessee, Texas, and Virginia.

Through World War II and the postwar years, the Democratic primary predominated in the South. Of the 114 gubernatorial elections held there between 1919 and 1948, the Democratic nominee won 113 times. The exception was Tennessee's election of a Republican governor in the Harding presidential LANDSLIDE of 1920. In the same period, the Democratic nominee won 131 of 132 southern Senate elections, the only exception being a SPECIAL ELECTION in Arkansas in 1937 when the Democratic nominee lost to an independent Democrat.

The first popularly elected Republican U.S. senator from the South, John G. Tower of Texas, won a special election in 1961. Thereafter, Republicans gradually won Senate seats in all southern states except Louisiana. Likewise, Republicans picked up governorships slowly after 1949, their first victories in the South coming in Arkansas and Florida in 1966.

As recently as 1994 Republicans were still a distinct minority in southern state and congressional offices. They were outnumbered eight to three in governorships, twelve to ten in Senate seats, and seventy-seven to forty-eight in U.S. House seats. The Democratic primaries continued to be the deciding election in most southern states.

The Democrats' numerical strength in the South, however, did not ensure a liberal Congress. Although elected under the Democratic label, southern House and Senate members tended to vote more like conservative Republicans. They often sided with Republicans to form the so-called conservative COALITION on crucial floor votes in Congress. When it came together as a majority of Republicans and a majority of southern Democrats, the conservative coalition often had a high success rate against northern Democrats.

The Republican takeover of Congress in 1995 dramatically increased the coalition's victory rate to a near-perfect 98.9 percent while at the same time diminishing the coalition's importance. On many of the coalition votes, the southern Democrats' support was superfluous because the majority Republicans would have won anyway. Some political scientists dismissed the usefulness of continuing to analyze the coalition's performance. "It's a concept designed to measure a phenomenon that's no longer there," said one.

In the 105th Congress, 1997–1999, Democrats held only 8 of the 22 southern-state Senate seats and only 54 of the 125 southern House seats. In southern governorships, Republicans outnumbered Democrats in reverse of the 1994 ratio: eight Republicans and three Democrats.

At the presidential level, the South has long since ceased to be a Democratic bastion. Republican nominee Richard Nixon carried each of the eleven states of the Old South with at least 65 percent of the vote in 1972. In 1984 and 1988 Ronald Reagan and George Bush did almost as well, carrying every southern state with at least 58 percent (Reagan) or 54 percent (Bush) of the vote. In 1992 Democrat Bill Clinton won despite the South, losing seven of the eleven states to Bush. He did better in 1996, again losing seven states but trading a loss in Georgia for a win in Florida, for a net gain of twelve southern state electoral votes.

## Runoff Primaries

By 1920 all southern states were choosing their Democratic gubernatorial and senatorial nominees through the primary process. But many legislators found the system flawed because it frequently allowed a candidate in a multicandidate race to win a plurality of the popular vote—and therefore the Democratic nomination that ensured election—even if his vote amounted to only a fraction of the total vote in the primary.

Consequently, most southern states adopted the runoff primary—a second election following the first primary, usually by two to four weeks—that matched only the top two contenders from the first primary. The runoff election ensured a majority nomination. Mississippi was the first to adopt the runoff system, in 1902, followed by North Carolina and South Carolina in 1915, Georgia in 1917 (using a county unit system), Texas in 1918, Louisiana in 1922, Florida in 1929, Alabama in 1931, and Arkansas in 1933. (Arkansas dropped the runoff in 1935 and reestablished it in 1939.) Tennessee never adopted the runoff system. Virginia adopted it in 1969 and repealed it two years later. (With some exceptions, Virginia since 1977 has nominated candidates at state conventions rather than primaries.)

Under Georgia's county unit system, each county was apportioned a certain number of unit votes. The candidate who received the largest number of a county's popular votes was awarded all of its unit votes, even if he won only a plurality. A candidate had to have a majority of the state's county unit votes to win the primary, otherwise a runoff became necessary. The runoff also was held on the basis of the county unit system.

The system was heavily weighted toward sparsely populated rural areas because every county, no matter how small, had at least two unit votes. It sometimes produced winners who received less than a majority of popular votes, even in the runoff. In 1963 the county unit system fell before the Supreme Court's ONE-PERSON, ONE-VOTE doctrine. In *Gray v. Sanders* the Court declared the system unconstitutional because of the disparity in representation between urban and rural areas.

Tennessee remains the only southern state to nominate by plurality of the primary vote. In that state's 1974 gubernatorial race, Ray Blanton won the Democratic nomination with only 22.7 percent of the vote yet went on to win the governorship in November. As in the rest of the South, however, election as governor of Tennessee no longer automatically follows victory in the Democratic primary.

Runoffs are not always obligatory. In most states, if the second-place primary finisher declines a runoff, the first-place candidate is then the nominee.

After using the runoff for fifty-three years, Louisiana modified its system again in 1975. The new law allowed voters to participate in an open nonpartisan primary followed by a general election runoff between the two top finishers. In the primary, all candidates of all parties were to be on the ballot, but party designations were optional at the individual candidate's discretion. A candidate receiving more than 50 percent of the primary vote would be unopposed in the general election. If no candidate received more than 50 percent, the two candidates receiving the greatest number of votes (regardless of party) would oppose each other in the general election. The law went into effect in 1975 for gubernatorial candidates and in 1978 for congressional candidates.

In 1984 Jesse L. Jackson, then a contender for the Democratic presidential nomination, tried unsuccessfully to abolish runoffs, which he claimed hurt black candidates' chances of election. The Democratic National Convention, however, defeated his proposal, 2,500.8 to 1,253.2.

Forty years earlier the Supreme Court struck down another PRIMARY TYPE, the so-called WHITE PRIMARY from which blacks were excluded under the Democrats' guise that they were a private organization not subject to the FIFTEENTH AMENDMENT's protection of the RIGHT TO VOTE. Until LITERACY TESTS and POLL TAXES were struck down, they too were widely used in the South to deter voting by blacks.

## Preferential Primaries

Before switching to the runoff system, Alabama, Florida, and Louisiana experimented for several years with a preferential system of primary voting. Under this system a voter indicates his first and second choices by writing a 1 or a 2 beside two candidates' names. To determine the winner, without a runoff, second-choice votes are added to the first-choice votes, and the candidate with the highest combined total wins.

The preference system, however, faded out by 1931. Apparently it was too confusing for voters, most of whom did not bother to cast second-choice votes. In Alabama's 1920 Democratic primary for the Senate, for example, there were 130,814 first-choice votes but only 34,768 second-choice votes.

## Special Elections

Vacancies in congressional seats or governorships often create the need for special elections. House vacancies, especially, must be filled as soon as possible to maintain the affected state's full representation based on population. (See HOUSE OF REPRESENTATIVES, ELECTING.)

Special elections are not always required, however, for Senate or governorship vacancies. The GOVERNOR may be empowered to appoint an interim senator to fill the unexpired term. Or, if a governor dies, the LIEUTENANT GOVERNOR may take over the job.

But when special elections for senator or governor are held in the South, the runoff system may complicate matters. There may not be time to go through the lengthy runoff primary process. The primary filing deadline may have passed, or it may be a year when no

regular primary is scheduled. In such cases, the state committee sometimes selects the party nominee without holding a primary.

In the heyday of the Democratic southern primary, this process led to some unexpected results. In Arkansas in 1937, for example, a bypassed House member, John E. Miller, won as an independent Democrat after the state committee nominated Gov. Carl E. Bailey for a vacant Senate seat.

In another case, in 1954, former governor Strom Thurmond became a write-in candidate for the Senate after South Carolina Democratic leaders chose another candidate to succeed a renominated senator who had died. Thurmond, who later switched to the Republicans, became the only senator ever elected by WRITE-IN VOTE. In 1997 Thurmond achieved two other distinctions. At age ninety-four he became the longest serving U.S. senator as well as the oldest senator. (See SENATE, QUALIFICATIONS.)

To avoid the pitfalls of no-primary party nominations, Texas adopted an unusual method of filling congressional vacancies. All candidates, regardless of party, compete in a free-for-all special primary. (Similar "jungle" primaries have been adopted in other states.) If no one receives a majority, a special runoff election is held between the top two candidates. The Texas system was used in 1961 when Lyndon B. Johnson left the Senate to become vice president. In the first contest, Republican John Tower and Democrat William Blakley finished first and second without a majority. Tower defeated Blakley in the second election.

The system was used again in 1993 after Sen. Lloyd Bentsen resigned to become Treasury secretary. In the special runoff election, Republican Kay Bailey Hutchison became Texas's first woman senator by defeating the interim incumbent, Democrat Bob Krueger, who had run a close second to Hutchison in the special primary.

## The "Solid South" Meltdown

For decades the term "solid South" meant solidly Democratic and solidly white. Today it means solidly Republican in ideology and less solidly white in voting participation.

With the abolition of poll taxes, literacy tests, and

other bars to voting by blacks, the racial mixture of VOTER TURNOUT in southern elections is not much different from that in the rest of the country. African Americans in the South, however, still tend to be loyal to the Democratic Party, which pushed the civil rights reforms of the 1960s and later mandated more DELEGATE slots for women and minorities at its own national conventions.

Conservative reaction to the Democrats' antiwar and equal rights policies, however, helped to transform the South into a Republican stronghold. After the 1996 elections, the country was more closely divided than at any time in four decades. While no party owned the map nationally, the Republicans had a solid lock on the South, where GOP House candidates outpolled their Democratic opponents by 2.8 million votes.

Whatever the geographic polarization meant nationally, in the South it signified the dethroning of the Democratic primary.

## Special Elections

A special election, known in British usage as a *by-election,* is an election held at a different time from the regular election, usually to fill a vacancy.

In Congress, special elections are more common for House seats than for Senate seats. It is the usual practice for the GOVERNOR to call a special election in case of a House vacancy. Some states empower the governor to make an interim appointment when a Senate vacancy occurs, although special elections are not uncommon in such cases. (See HOUSE OF REPRESENTATIVES, ELECTING; SENATE, ELECTING.)

Special elections are never held for president or vice president. Succession to the presidency is provided for in the Twenty-fifth Amendment to the Constitution, ratified in 1967. If the president dies, resigns, or is removed from office, the vice president becomes president. If the president is unable to serve, the vice president becomes acting president. If there is no vice president, the president names a replacement subject to confirmation by Congress. (See PRESIDENT, NOMINATING AND ELECTING; VICE PRESIDENT.)

In most states the LIEUTENANT GOVERNOR becomes the governor if the office becomes vacant. Laws vary from state to state for the holding of special elections to fill vacancies in state or local offices.

## Spending Limits

*See* CAMPAIGN FINANCE; PUBLIC FINANCING.

## Split- and Straight-Ticket Voting

Voting for candidates of different political parties on the same ballot is known as *split-ticket voting.* Voting for candidates of only one party is called *straight-ticket voting.*

Except in a PRIMARY, where all the candidates are of the same party, the BALLOT TYPES used in most states permit either split- or straight-ticket voting. A few states, however, prohibit straight-ticket voting and their ballots are designed accordingly.

The "party-column" ballot used in some states facilitates straight-ticket voting because each party's candidates for various offices are arranged vertically under the party label. Marking a single block or pulling a single lever on the VOTING MACHINE casts votes for all of a party's candidates for all offices. The party-column ballot also encourages a COATTAILS effect. A strong candidate at the top may draw a vote for the whole ticket.

The "office-group" ballot is more conducive to split-ticket voting. Candidates are identified by party, and their names are arranged alphabetically under the office being sought, requiring the voter to pick and choose individually.

Even though it takes more effort than straight-ticket voting, split-ticket voting is more prevalent than in the past. Reasons include a decline in PARTY IDENTIFICATION and increases in the number of INDEPENDENT voters and CANDIDATE-CENTERED CAMPAIGNS.

In national elections, split-ticket voting usually is measured by the percentage of voters who divide their votes between the presidential candidate of one party and the House candidate of another party. By that measure about 25 percent of voters split their tickets in 1996. That figure was up sharply from decades earlier, when most campaigns were party-centered and fewer voters considered themselves independents.

---

## Stages in an Election

Elections for major federal and state offices can be roughly divided into two segments: the prenomination stage and the general election stage. But within those broad categories the typical election passes through several other phases.

For the candidate, the prenomination stage is the longer and perhaps more crucial. An early start and the gathering of PARTY ENDORSEMENTS and financial support can go a long way toward obtaining the party's nomination. Lack of preparation and inattention to the necessary steps can doom a candidacy almost before it starts.

Running for office usually is a long process; too long, it is often said. The American election season extends over more months than its counterpart in most other nations, testing the stamina and patience of the candidates and the voters. PUBLIC OPINION polls taken late in the CAMPAIGN show a general weariness with the whole process and a wish that "they" would hurry up and get it over with.

At the presidential level, campaigns begin a full year or more before the November election. In the 1996 election, for example, the eventual Republican nominee, Robert J. Dole of Kansas, declared his candidacy on April 10, 1995. But early as Dole was, five other GOP candidates already had tossed their hats in the ring. Unopposed for renomination, President Bill Clinton officially became a candidate when he met the December 15, 1995, filing date for the first-in-the-nation NEW HAMPSHIRE PRIMARY.

By contrast, Prime Minister John Major announced in March 1997 that Britain would hold parliamentary elections in May. British elections are much shorter—six weeks is the maximum—and less expensive than U.S. congressional elections, even though Britain does

not have an equivalent to the restrictive American CAMPAIGN FINANCE system. Spending for a U.S. House seat can exceed a million dollars, and multimillion-dollar Senate campaigns have become commonplace. Spending for a seat in Parliament may be less than $20,000. (See INTERNATIONAL AND U.S. ELECTIONS COMPARED.)

## Prenomination Stage

For the candidate, the first step in an election is deciding if he or she really wants to go through with the arduous campaign for the office under consideration. If the answer is yes, the candidate must look at the checklist of requirements and qualifications. Age may be a factor. Some offices require the candidate to be older than the minimum voting age of eighteen. The Constitution, for example, requires the president and vice president to be at least thirty-five years old. House members must be at least twenty-five and senators, thirty. (See specific office for other qualifications.)

Age and residency requirements vary from office to office and state to state. The candidate must be a registered voter and, here again, VOTER REGISTRATION laws differ. Twenty-eight states register voters by party or as INDEPENDENTS. The rest do not require party registration or, if they do, do not break down the rolls by party.

Becoming a candidate often entails paying a filing fee and may require the submission of petitions signed by specified numbers of qualified voters. BALLOT ACCESS is more difficult for THIRD-PARTY or independent candidates than it is for those running under a major party label. To get on the ballot in all fifty states in 1992, for example, independent presidential candidate Ross Perot had to rely on his supporters to obtain millions of signatures nationwide.

Usually the filing deadline is set well ahead of the actual PRIMARY or CAUCUS to give the CANVASSING BOARD, elections board, or other authority sufficient time to check the signatures, prepare the ballot, and make the other necessary arrangements for the election.

As in New Hampshire, state filing deadlines for primaries or caucuses may be in the calendar year preceding the election year. Most often, however, the deadlines are early in the election year.

A sampling for the 1996 election shows the wide variety of rules and dates that presidential candidates had to observe:

• Alaska Democratic Caucuses—Filing deadline, January 22; filing fee to the state Democratic Party, $2,500.

• Colorado Primaries—Filing deadline, January 2 (same for both parties); filing fee to secretary of state, $500 or signatures of 5,000 registered voters; candidates also had to be qualified to receive federal matching funds.

• Hawaii Democratic Caucuses—Filing deadline, February 9; filing fee to state party, $1,500, or submit 100 signatures of party members.

• New Hampshire Republican Primary—Filing deadline, December 15, 1995; filing fee to secretary of state, $1,000; no petitions required.

• South Carolina Republican Primary—Filing deadline, December 31, 1995; filing fee to the state party, $7,500.

• Nebraska Primaries—Filing deadline, March 13 (both parties); names of nationally recognized candidates placed on the ballot; other candidates needed 300 voters' signatures (at least 100 from each of the state's congressional districts).

Running for office is expensive and FUND RAISING is an ever present activity in every stage of an election. One of the first things a candidate may do is form a PO-LITICAL ACTION COMMITTEE (PAC) to receive and dispense funds for his or her election or reelection campaign.

To test the waters before plunging into a costly campaign, a potential candidate may hire a POLLING firm to ask voters their opinion of the candidate. If the poll indicates the candidate has a reasonable chance of winning, the candidate may hire a professional POLITICAL CONSULTANT to plan the campaign strategy. Other paid staff may be hired for the duration of the campaign, but unpaid volunteer supporters do much of the work in a typical campaign.

PUBLIC FINANCING OF CAMPAIGNS from the $3 federal income tax checkoff is restricted to presidential campaigns, and spending limits apply only to candidates who accept the public funds. In its 1976 *BUCKLEY V. VALEO* decision, the Supreme Court struck down spending limits for candidates using their own money.

Donations to political campaigns, however, are limited by federal CAMPAIGN FINANCE laws regulated by the FEDERAL ELECTION COMMISSION (FEC). Some states also have campaign finance laws and public financing. Most federal and state party committees, and some local units, must register with the FEC and report regularly on their finance activities.

Campaigns for governor or the state legislature may begin months or years before the election. In Maryland, for example, Gov. Parris N. Glendening took office in 1995 and immediately began raising money for reelection in 1998. A campaign for the Maryland General Assembly, which cost about $5,000 twenty years earlier, required some $100,000 in 1998. Would-be legislators routinely began fund raising two years before the polls opened.

Depending on the office and size of the state, city, or DISTRICT, running in a primary can be a grueling process. To try to shake as many hands as possible, the candidate might go door to door or spend hours greeting voters outside factory gates or in shopping centers. He or she must maintain a full schedule of speaking to groups or campaign rallies. And in between there are media interviews and advertising spots to be squeezed in, along with efforts to distribute campaign buttons, lawn signs, and bumper stickers.

In some states, RUNOFF ELECTIONS are held if no candidate receives a majority of the primary vote. Such elections add another stage to the prenomination phase of the elections process.

## General Election

The scope of an election widens after the primaries are held and the parties have selected their nominees. For the presidential candidates and their RUNNING MATES, this process is not official until the NATIONAL PARTY CONVENTIONS have acted on the nominations.

Now the successful candidates must look beyond the

*Eight aspirants for the 1996 Republican presidential nomination meet before a debate in New Hampshire. From the left, they are Alan Keyes, Morry Taylor, Steve Forbes, Robert Dornan, Bob Dole, Richard Lugar, Lamar Alexander, and Pat Buchanan. Phil Gramm dropped out of the race too soon to pose with the others.* Source: *Jim Bourg, Reuters*

party members who nominated them and try to persuade independent and undecided voters to vote for them in the general election. For federal and most state elections the general election takes place on ELECTION DAY in November of even-numbered years. Off-year elections for nonfederal offices in some states may be in other months. Losers in the primaries must decide whether they want to remain in the race as independents. (See SORE LOSER LAWS.)

Televised DEBATES among presidential and other candidates have become standard fixtures in political campaigns. The broadcasts and preparation for them now provide an important campaign benchmark.

Financial and human energy costs rise sharply in the general election phase. A candidate who was contending with fellow party members in the primaries and caucuses now must face the resources of another party, which may be better bankrolled. In a large state or congressional district, a candidate may have to spend heavily to reach the voters, by television or personal visits. A New Jersey candidate, for example, may have to buy television time in the expensive New York market to reach voters in northern New Jersey. In a large state such as Texas a candidate may have to fly from city to city to make campaign stops, in addition to buying time in the populous Dallas-Fort Worth area, because no one television station covers the whole state. Both types of campaigning are expensive.

*Bill and Hillary Clinton at a Democratic National Committee fundraising dinner for business executives in Washington on September 10, 1998.*
Source: Mark Wilson, Reuters

Running for president is a massive and costly operation. President Clinton and challenger Dole spent an estimated $150.2 million on their general election campaigns in 1996 ($76.7 million by Dole and $73.5 million by Clinton). Counting their primary campaigns, the two candidates spent a combined total of about $232 million. Television and radio advertising was the largest single expense for both candidates, accounting for almost half ($113.0 million) of the combined total. More than half ($150 million) of the campaign money came from public funding. The remaining 35 percent came from contributions and party spending.

Especially in presidential election years, the public's interest in politics picks up as the general election approaches. It is a busy time for people responsible for voter registration, which is almost always a state and local operation. But the federal and state governments share in the conduct of elections, especially those for president and Congress. (See STATE AND FEDERAL ELECTION RESPONSIBILITIES.)

For example, federal law protects the ABSENTEE VOTING rights of military personnel and other U.S. citizens who are away from the polls on election day. The date for federal elections was also set by Congress. It is the first Tuesday after the first Monday in even-numbered years.

Another federal law, the so-called MOTOR VOTER ACT, made it possible to register as a voter while renewing a driver's license. This law has greatly increased the number of registered voters in most if not all states. In addition, a number of federal laws and constitutional amendments protect voting rights and extend suffrage, including the CIVIL RIGHTS ACTS, laws and Supreme Court decisions on the RIGHT TO REPRESENTATION, the RIGHT TO VOTE, the VOTING RIGHTS ACT, WOMEN'S SUFFRAGE, and YOUTH SUFFRAGE.

In a congressional, state, or local election the voters ballot directly for the candidates. But in a presidential election, the voters are actually choosing members of the ELECTORAL COLLEGE—men and women who will cast their state's electoral votes for the presidential or vice-presidential candidate who won the POPULAR

VOTE in their state. To be elected president or vice president, the candidate must win an ABSOLUTE MAJORITY (at least 270) of the 538 total electoral votes. Except in Maine and Nebraska, electoral votes are awarded on a WINNER-TAKE-ALL basis. Whoever wins the most popular votes (a plurality) gains all of that state's electoral votes. Maine and Nebraska award electoral votes by special presidential election districts. (See DIRECT ELECTION.)

The electoral college does not meet as one body. Rather, the electors meet in their respective states to cast their ballots and transmit the results to Congress for counting. After Congress counts the votes and declares the election of the president and vice president, the presidential election is effectively over.

If there is a change of administrations, however, the transition process begins soon after the election to ensure that the change goes smoothly, without serious disruption to domestic or foreign affairs. Typically, the incoming president appoints a transition team to work with the outgoing administration to plan the changeover, seek qualified appointees for the top executive branch jobs, and plan the inauguration ceremonies.

On a smaller scale, a similar transition takes place after the election of governors, mayors, county executives, and other state and local administrators. Fund raising may continue if there are campaign debts to be paid, and for federal offices reports on finances must be made to the FEC.

Newly elected members of Congress travel to Washington to organize their leadership and committees and to set up their offices. By the time the new Congress convenes in January, most of the preliminaries have been taken care of, and the new members and staffs are ready to begin governing.

## Stalking Horse

A stalking horse is a candidate running as a decoy for another, perhaps stronger, candidate. The term comes from the hunting trick of hiding behind a horse to get in close for a shot at the prey.

In the age of the PRESIDENTIAL PRIMARY and PUBLIC OPINION POLLING, the stalking-horse strategy is rare. Those institutions now perform one of the stalker's main functions: testing voter reaction to the candidate relative to the one for whom he is fronting. And presidential nominations are now won in the primaries, not at the NATIONAL PARTY CONVENTION where the nomination is formalized. In the preprimary era of BROKERED CONVENTIONS, a stalking horse might have had some usefulness as a way to deadlock the convention.

The last presidential nominees to avoid full participation in the primaries were Richard Nixon and Hubert H. Humphrey in 1968. Nixon entered few primaries and Humphrey, none. Four years later Humphrey entered some primaries but was outpolled by George S. McGovern, whom some observers regarded as a stalking horse for Edward M. Kennedy. But McGovern received the Democratic nomination himself and waged an ill-fated attempt to dislodge Nixon. In 1976 many Humphrey backers thought that Edmund G. "Jerry" Brown Jr. was a stalking horse for Kennedy, but Brown insisted he was running on his own. That year Humphrey dropped out after Jimmy Carter won the important NEW HAMPSHIRE PRIMARY.

In these cases, as in earlier elections, the candidates accused of being stalking horses did not admit to being such, if that is what they were.

## State and Federal Election Responsibilities

Operation of the American election system is a dual responsibility shared by the federal and state governments. In some ways the states have the larger share of the burden because of their broad constitutional authority to regulate elections.

Even for federal elections, states do most of the work and make many of the major decisions. They or their

*State governments have broad constitutional authority to regulate elections, including voter registration. Source: AARP News Bulletin*

subdivisions are in charge of VOTER REGISTRATION, operating the polling stations, counting the votes, and certifying the results. Within limits prescribed by the Constitution or acts of Congress, the states decide the qualifications for voting in the general election and participation in political party events such as PRIMARIES or CAUCUSES.

The federal government, on the other hand, plays mainly a monitoring role. It regulates CAMPAIGN FINANCE in federal elections and some aspects of state and local fund raising. It watches for illegal denial of the constitutional RIGHT TO VOTE, through racial discrimination or other means. It sets the times for federal elections and it determines the winner in cases of CONTESTED ELECTIONS for the presidency and House and Senate seats.

Article I, section 4, of the U.S. Constitution authorizes the states to set the "Times, Places and Manner of holding Elections for Senators and Representatives," but the same section empowers Congress to make laws superseding such regulations. Under that authority or through constitutional amendments, the national government has overridden state laws by setting a uniform federal ELECTION DAY (the first Tuesday after the first Monday in November of even-numbered years), extending the FRANCHISE to women and eighteen-year-olds, protecting BLACK SUFFRAGE, and requiring easier voter registration.

At the same time, states on their own initiative have acted in recent years to give voters more candidate choices through easier BALLOT ACCESS, to make voting more convenient by extended ABSENTEE VOTING or postal elections. States also have opened primaries and caucuses to voters excluded from such events by rules limiting participation to party members.

The federal and state responsibilities for elections

overlap each other a good deal, making it difficult to label any one area as exclusively "national" or "state." Instead it is useful to sort out the roles of each within the major parts of elections regulation.

## Regulation of Parties

Except in the area of campaign finance there is little regulation of political parties at the national level. Party regulation is largely a state function that varies considerably from state to state.

Introduction of the state-provided, secret Australian BALLOT TYPE in the late nineteenth century brought widespread changes in public policy toward parties, which until then had distributed their own ballots. The government ballots designated candidates by party labels, giving a justification for regulating what had been considered private organizations.

At first, however, regulation did not extend to the then-new mechanism of party primaries for the nomination of candidates. Under a 1921 Supreme Court ruling, primaries were internal affairs not subject to government interference. After the Court reversed itself in *United States v. Classic* (1941) more and more states required primary nominations, with significant effects for partisan politics.

Over the years the Democratic and Republican National Committees grew in staff size and influence, resulting in top-down changes in state laws on primaries. PRESIDENTIAL SELECTION REFORMS in the Democratic Party, particularly, affected state rules for the selection of delegates to the NATIONAL PARTY CONVENTIONS.

State regulations define party membership and eligibility to vote in *closed* primaries—those in which only party members can vote. About twenty states register voters by political party affiliation, in effect maintaining the parties' membership rolls.

States also determine ballot access, which may ensure a place on the general election ballot for major party candidates but may require that new or THIRD PARTIES obtain large numbers of valid voters' signatures on petitions to be listed on the ballot.

Almost three-quarters of the states dictate how members of the parties' state central committees are chosen. Selection by party officials is the most common method.

A 1986 study by the Advisory Committee on Intergovernmental Relations (ACIR) provided one of the most recent state-by-state assessments of the degree of party regulation. ACIR categorized thirty-six states as heavy to moderate regulators and only fourteen as light regulators.

Some state regulations help to preserve the U.S. TWO PARTY SYSTEM. For example, some states have SORE LOSER LAWS that prevent defeated primary candidates from running in the general election under another label. Some also permit prenomination PARTY ENDORSEMENTS of selected candidates, which tilt the primary or caucus playing field toward favorites of the party establishment. In a 1989 case, *Eu v. San Francisco Democratic Committee,* the Supreme Court invalidated California's attempt to prohibit parties from endorsing or opposing primary candidates.

## Voter Registration

Registration of voters is the most important of the states' responsibilities in the regulation of elections. Maintenance of clean voting rolls free of fictitious or duplicate names, noncitizens, nonresidents, deceased persons, and persons under age eighteen is essential to the prevention of ELECTION FRAUD and loss of confidence in the electoral process.

Requirements for registration vary from state to state. Most states have a registration deadline well in advance of the election but a few permit election day registration at the polls. About twenty states register voters according to party affiliation but only one state, North Dakota, does not require prior registration for voting.

Although the states have wide discretion in setting the terms for voting, the federal government has imposed mandatory guidelines that affect some aspects of voter registration. The VOTING RIGHTS ACT of 1965 and its extensions, for example, barred LITERACY TESTS for voting and required federal clearance of election law changes in states where registration levels were below 50 percent. It also provided for federal monitors at the polls in low-registration states.

The 1993 MOTOR VOTER ACT required states to provide voter registration forms and assistance at vehicle or driver registries, welfare bureaus, and other state offices serving large segments of the public.

Various constitutional amendments that originated in Congress also have limited states' rights in determining eligibility to vote. For example, the Fifteenth Amendment (1870) provided voting rights for all races, the Nineteenth Amendment (1920) gave the vote to women, the Twenty-fourth Amendment (1964) abolished POLL TAXES, and the Twenty-sixth Amendment (1971) lowered the voting age to eighteen.

## Campaign Finance

Federal regulation of elections is confined mostly to the fund-raising aspect of candidates' campaigns in federal elections. The Federal Elections Campaign Act of 1971 (FECA) and its extensions require disclosure of contributions to presidential, House, and Senate campaigns. FECA also limits contributions from individuals and POLITICAL ACTION COMMITTEES (PACs) and sets spending limits for presidential campaigns that receive PUBLIC FINANCING. Spending for House and Senate campaigns is not limited in amounts but must be reported.

The law requires certain types of expenditures by state and local party committees to be reported to the FEDERAL ELECTION COMMISSION. FECA takes precedence over state campaign finance laws regarding contributions from foreign nationals, who are barred from making gifts or expenditures in any U.S. election—federal, state, or local. The federal law also takes precedence over any state law affecting the financing of federal election campaigns.

## Ballots and Voting Methods

The states determine the types of ballots used and the methods by which the voters indicate their choices. The two most common types are the *party-column ballot* and the *office-group ballot*. In the former, all the candidates of one party are listed in the same column or row. This type discourages SPLIT-TICKET VOTING because a voter can vote a straight party ticket by pulling a single lever or marking a single block. The office-group ballot, used in more than half the states, lists candidates

by the office being sought, which makes split-ticket voting easier.

Most states use VOTING MACHINES rather than paper ballots, or a combination of the two in which a computer "reads" the ballot fed into it and keeps a running tally of the votes. States may choose from a number of different systems, but those used in federal elections must meet standards set by the Federal Election Commission.

## Apportionment and Districting

The dual federal/state nature of U.S. elections also extends to the important task of apportioning seats in the House of Representatives and seats in state legislatures that are distributed on a population basis.

The CENSUS taken every ten years by the federal Census Bureau identifies population shifts among and within states, and the House of Representatives then reallocates its 435 seats on the basis of that information. State legislatures do the same with their legislative seats.

The legislatures then redraw the CONGRESSIONAL DISTRICT boundaries to make them as nearly equal as possible under the Supreme Court's ONE PERSON, ONE VOTE mandatory guidelines. State legislative districts also must meet the same requirements. Frequently there are partisan battles over the redistricting, sometimes because of conflicting federal and state interests, and a few of these require court settlement. (See REAPPORTIONMENT AND REDISTRICTING.)

Another function of the Census Bureau is to estimate the size of the voting age population for each election, to help in measuring the VOTER TURNOUT as a percentage of those eligible to vote. Because voter registration rules differ from state to state, the Census Bureau does not try to calculate the national total of registered voters.

---

## State Legislator

The fifty state legislatures make up a fundamental building block of American DEMOCRACY, representing their constituencies on issues and concerns that range from local to national. State legislatures deal with

POCKETBOOK questions such as taxation, the allocation of state aid to schools, the building of public works, master plans and regional zoning questions, and the regulation of businesses. But they also influence the overall future political design of the U.S. Congress.

Although the legislatures, with their long histories and established traditions, all face common problems of governance, they exhibit a wide range of differing characteristics. Among these differences is what the state legislative bodies call themselves. In Massachusetts and New Hampshire, for example, they call themselves the General Court. In other states they are the general assembly or the legislative assembly or, simply, the legislature.

In all but Nebraska, which has a UNICAMERAL legislature, there are so-called upper houses (always called senates) and lower houses, which go under varying titles including house of representatives, house of delegates, and assembly.

Almost all the state legislatures are required to meet annually, but some, generally in the smaller states, have established limits on the length of any legislative session. For example, Alabama restricts its annual session to thirty legislative days (days in which legislative business is transacted); in Virginia, the sessions last thirty legislative days in odd years, sixty in even years. Other states stipulate that their legislatures conclude their business by a specific date. Still others, mostly the larger states, have much longer sessions, presumably because of the complexity and continuing nature of their tasks.

A headcount in early 1996 showed that there are 7,424 state legislators across the nation, with Democrats holding a slight edge in numbers over Republicans. Party control of state legislatures is important to the federal government because after each national CENSUS, the state legislatures use the new numbers for REAPPORTIONMENT AND REDISTRICTING, an inherently political process that helps to determine the broad political makeup of the U.S. House of Representatives for a ten-year period.

After the census is concluded, the national party organizations devote immense resources to persuading the state legislatures to approve congressional district-ing plans favorable to their interests. In the past, Democratic-dominated state legislatures have devised district plans that gave advantages to Democratic House candidates, making it difficult for Republicans to win.

Republican advances in the 1990s, however, particularly in the legislatures of the South and the Sun Belt states, could reverse the situation. Both parties were skirmishing over the issue in advance of the 2000 census, with Democrats favoring the use of statistical sampling to reduce undercounts in urban areas. Republicans won the upper hand, however, when the Supreme Court in January 1999 barred the use of sampling estimates for reapportionment of House seats.

Turnover rates for legislators vary greatly from state to state. In 1996 turnover was only 3 percent in the New Jersey house and 2 percent in the Mississippi senate. The same year, turnover was 55 percent in the Kansas senate and nearly 45 percent in the Maine house. In many of the larger states, the legislatures are populated by professional politicians whose primary business is government; in many of the smaller states with shorter legislative sessions, so-called "citizen legislators" serve and then return to their homes and businesses once the legislature's work is done.

Enactment of TERM LIMITS in twenty states between 1990 and 1995, with limits on service ranging from six years to twelve for house and senate members, has already had an impact on the Maine and California legislatures, where many incumbents chose not to run for reelection or resigned their seats. In 1998, for example, nearly 25 percent of California's assembly members and senators were ineligible to run for reelection. Half the members of the 100-seat Arkansas house and 67 of Michigan's 110 house members were ineligible to run.

The long-run results of term-limit laws are unknown, but it appeared likely that the laws would reduce the number of full-time politicians seeking legislative seats. Term-limit critics decry the expected loss of some veteran lawmakers' expertise in highly complex areas such as taxation and technology.

The states have no standard set of qualifications for candidates. Most require a period of residency, however. Age requirements vary widely, from eighteen in some fifteen states for candidates to both chambers, to thirty for the senate (generally considered, as it is in the federal government, the more deliberative of the two houses) in New Hampshire, New Jersey, and Tennessee. Most states, except the fifteen that established eighteen as the minimum age for candidacy, have lower age limits for house candidates than for those running for seats in the upper house. These age limits run from twenty-one to twenty-seven, with twenty-one being the most common qualifying age.

Many states set two-year terms for both chambers, with some preferring two-year terms for the lower house and four-year terms for the upper house. Some also require that half the senate membership stand for reelection every two years. Most state GOVERNORS are elected for four-year terms.

The legislatures themselves set their number of seats, and all seats are apportioned on the basis of population. In many states, the houses are twice as large as the senates, with senate districts equaling two house districts. The size of the bodies varies widely among the states. As might be expected, some of the less-populous have the smallest houses. Alaska, for example, has 40 members; Delaware, 41; and Nevada, 42. But New Hampshire, a small state, has 400 members, far more than the next largest legislature, Pennsylvania, with 203. Alaska, Delaware, and Nevada also have the smallest senate memberships.

Legislators in populous states have year-round staff serving them and their constituents at the capitol and at their district offices. Most legislatures have set salary limits on these staff positions, generally corresponding to those of other state employees. Some of the smaller states, however, make no financial provision for district office staffing, and a number of others limit the hiring of staff to the period of the actual legislative session. Almost all states provide travel allowances so that the legislators can regularly return home to their districts; many pay per diem expenses.

As government's role in everyday life expands, state legislators have increasingly been called upon to intervene on behalf of constituents with state agencies, including welfare bureaus, motor vehicle agencies, and boards charged with determining unemployment and disability compensation.

Yet several studies have shown that constituents in many states are poorly informed about what their state legislators do, are not very interested in the legislature's business, and are somewhat cynical about how it does it. It is not uncommon for a voter not to know the name of his or her state senator or representative. Seven studies of voter attitudes toward state legislatures indicated that these evaluations had much to do with partisan affinity—individuals whose PARTY IDENTIFICATION corresponded to the majority party in the state legislature tended to see the political body more favorably—and with voters' appraisal of their governor's performance, if the governor was also a member of their party.

Compensation for state legislators spans a wide range. New Hampshire's four hundred representatives are paid $200 for their two-year term. California's legislators make $72,000 annually. The larger states also reward the leadership positions in both houses (president of the senate, Speaker of the house) with extra pay and allowances. Louisiana's Speaker, for example, earns an additional $32,000 annually. For many state legislators, however, service represents a degree of financial and personal sacrifice. One study found that even part-time legislators are spending more than half their working time on legislative matters with no corresponding financial reward.

Although California terminated its retirement program in 1991 when it also approved term limits, many of the states have pension programs for qualified, contributing legislators. These range from a modest percentage of the representative's salary to a high of 85 percent of an Illinois representative's final salary after twenty years of service.

The workload of legislatures also varies widely. A study of New York's state assembly spanning the first six months of 1992 showed that 17,667 bills were introduced by its 150 members. Of the proposals, 846 were enacted into law. A correspondingly high number of resolutions also were brought to the floor with a proportionate number passed. On average, 146 separate pieces of legislation were considered in Albany on any given day of that particular legislative session, and 7 were passed.

In Wyoming, in contrast, in a three-week session in 1994, 303 bills were introduced, and 102 of them were enacted before the legislators adjourned for the year.

## States' Rights Democratic Party (1948)

The States' Rights Democratic Party was a conservative southern faction that bolted from the Democrats in 1948. The immediate reason for the new party, popularly known as the Dixiecrats, was dissatisfaction with President Harry Truman's civil rights program. But the Dixiecrat effort to maintain a segregated way of life was also an attempt to demonstrate the political power of the twentieth century southern Democrats and to reestablish their importance in the DEMOCRATIC PARTY.

The Mississippi Democratic Party's state executive committee met in Jackson in May 1948 to lay the groundwork for the Dixiecrat secession. The meeting called for a bolt by southern delegates if the Democratic National Convention endorsed Truman's civil rights program. When the convention did approve a strong civil rights plank, the entire Mississippi delegation and half the Alabama delegation left the convention. Gov. Fielding L. Wright of Mississippi invited all anti-Truman delegates to meet in Birmingham three days after the close of the Democratic convention to select a states' rights ticket.

Most southern Democrats with something at stake—national prominence, seniority in Congress, patronage privileges—shunned the new Dixiecrat Party. The party's leaders came from the ranks of southern governors and other state and local officials. The Birmingham convention chose two governors to lead the party: J. Strom Thurmond of South Carolina for president and Fielding Wright of Mississippi for vice president.

Other than the presidential ticket, the Dixiecrats did not run candidates for any office. Rather than try to develop an independent party organization, the Dixiecrats, whenever possible, used existing Democratic Party apparatus.

The party was on the ballot in only one state outside the South and in the November election received 1,157,326 votes (2.4 percent of the popular vote). The Thurmond ticket carried four Deep South states where it ran under the Democratic Party label, but it failed in its basic objective to prevent the reelection of President Truman.

After the election the party ceased to exist almost as abruptly as it had begun, with most of its members returning to the Democratic Party. In a statement upon reentering the Democratic fold, Thurmond characterized the Dixiecrat episode as "a fight within our family." (While serving in the U.S. Senate sixteen years later, Thurmond switched to the Republican Party.)

## Straight-Ticket Voting

*See* SPLIT-TICKET AND STRAIGHT-TICKET VOTING.

## Straw Vote

One of the early types of preelection polls, the straw vote got its name from the farmers' trick of throwing a handful of straw in the air to see which way the wind was blowing. For more than a century, newspaper and magazine straw polls were the leading predictors of major elections.

The first published presidential poll was in the *Harrisburg Pennsylvanian* on July 24, 1824. The publication's straw vote among people in Wilmington and Newark, Delaware, showed a preference for Andrew Jackson over John Quincy Adams. Jackson did win the popular vote but lost to Adams in the second presidential election decided by the U.S. House. (See PRESIDENT, NOMINATING AND ELECTING.)

In 1866 the *Cleveland Leader* reported that a straw vote taken on a train showed passengers favoring Congress over President Andrew Johnson in their conflicting views on Reconstruction. Two years later the conflict peaked when Johnson became the first president to be impeached.

By 1896 straw polling had become fairly scientific. For the presidential election that year the *Chicago Tribune* polled railroad and factory workers and found 80 percent supporting Republican William McKinley over Democrat William Jennings Bryan, who had been expected to win the labor vote.

Another Chicago paper, the *Record,* conducted an even more scientific poll. It mailed ballots to all 300,000 registered voters in the city and, based on the responses, predicted McKinley would win in Chicago with 57.95 percent of the vote—matching almost exactly the actual vote of 57.91 percent.

Basically there were three ways to conduct a straw vote: by printing a ballot in the newspaper; mailing ballots to all registered voters or to a random sample of them, such as every twelfth voter; or sending canvassers into communities to have residents fill out ballots then and there. Of the three methods, the first was the least reliable because it was subject to ballot stuffing: people could buy extra papers and "vote" many times. Mailed ballots were safer but they could be counterfeited, and sometimes were. Personal canvassing was the most reliable method.

Newspapers became quite skilled in taking straw votes. Polls by the *Cincinnati Enquirer,* for example, mirrored actual results in presidential elections from 1908 to 1928.

The most famous straw poll, however, was by a magazine, the *Literary Digest.* It began presidential polling in 1924 and gained a reputation for uncanny accuracy by correctly predicting that election and the next two, including Franklin D. Roosevelt's unexpected defeat of incumbent Herbert Hoover in 1932.

The *Digest* poll was a massive undertaking, requiring millions of ballot mailings. The mailing list, however, was derived mostly from telephone directories and motor vehicle registrations, which were unrepresentative of the U.S. population in the Great Depression year of 1936 because only the wealthier households had phones or cars. The *Digest* suffered a major embarrassment that year with its erroneous prediction that Kansas governor Alfred M. Landon would unseat Roosevelt.

In the same election a newcomer, George Gallup, gained credibility at the *Digest's* expense with his prediction that Roosevelt would win a second term. Although Gallup underestimated Roosevelt's 60.8 percent vote—the biggest presidential LANDSLIDE up to that time—his methodology worked and his reputation was established.

The *Digest's* wrong call was the beginning of the end for straw polls and the magazine itself. Not long after 1936 the *Literary Digest* went out of business.

---

## Succession

*See* LIEUTENANT GOVERNOR; VICE PRESIDENT.

---

## Suffrage

*See* BLACK SUFFRAGE; RIGHT TO VOTE; WOMEN'S SUFFRAGE; YOUTH SUFFRAGE.

---

## Super Tuesday

What began as basically a regional PRIMARY in the South came to fruition in 1988 after years of discussion. The same-day primary early in the nominating season quickly gained the unofficial name *Super Tuesday.*

Southern advocates of the idea hoped to draw some attention away from the first-in-the-nation NEW HAMPSHIRE PRIMARY by scheduling simultaneous primaries a few weeks after New Hampshire's. The main goal of the sponsors was to bring forth moderate presidential candidates of national stature who were from the South or were at least acceptable to southern voters.

The 1988 Super Tuesday, however, proved more helpful to liberal Democrats Michael Dukakis and Jesse Jackson than to any moderate or conservative southerners. The one southern Republican who had emerged as a contender, TV evangelist Pat Robertson, saw his candidacy collapse after a poor showing in Super Tuesday Republican primaries. Vice President George Bush, a Connecticut Yankee transplanted to Texas, did well on Super Tuesday and eventually won election as Ronald Reagan's successor.

Super Tuesday fell on March 8 in 1988, when fourteen southern or BORDER STATES held their presidential primaries. However, the northern states of Massachusetts and Rhode Island also held Super Tuesday primaries, and victories there boosted Dukakis's campaign for the Democratic nomination, which he ultimately won.

The heavy black VOTER TURNOUT in the South on Super Tuesday largely benefited Jackson, who outpolled Dukakis in eight of the fourteen southern and border state primaries. Although Al Gore of Tennessee and Richard Gephardt of Missouri won their own states, only Gore's overall Super Tuesday performances was impressive.

In 1992, with incumbent president Bush expected to overcome television commentator Patrick J. Buchanan's challenge to his renomination by the Republicans, the Democratic primaries provided most of the Super Tuesday suspense. Only eight states held primaries on March 10, and they again included Massachusetts and Rhode Island.

Having lost the New Hampshire primary to former senator Paul Tsongas of Massachusetts, Bill Clinton of Arkansas needed a big win on Super Tuesday. He got it, with victories in five of the eight contests, losing Massachusetts, Rhode Island, and Texas to Tsongas. Former California governor Jerry Brown, the runner-up to Clinton in the total 1992 Democratic primary vote, won none of the Super Tuesday primaries that year.

In 1996 Republican contests dominated the primaries scene because President Clinton faced only token opposition for renomination by the Democrats. Front-runner Robert J. Dole and several other GOP stalwarts competed for the party's nomination to oppose Clinton.

Super Tuesday was somewhat upstaged, however, by a newcomer: JUNIOR TUESDAY Week, thirteen primaries or caucuses held March 2–9, mostly in the Northeast. Four of the original 1988 Super Tuesday states—Georgia, Maryland, Massachusetts, and Rhode Island—moved their 1996 primaries up to Junior Tuesday Week. With all but one (New Hampshire) of the six New Eng-

land states participating, Junior Tuesday, March 5, became largely a regional primary.

Six other of the original participants—Florida, Louisiana, Mississippi, Oklahoma, Tennessee, and Texas—stayed with Super Tuesday, March 12. They were joined by Oregon. The two remaining original participants—Missouri and Virginia—did not hold presidential primaries.

Although Dole lost the February 20 New Hampshire primary to Buchanan, he quickly regained front-runner status with a sweep of all the Junior Tuesday Week contests. Two of Dole's rivals, former Tennessee governor Lamar Alexander and Sen. Richard G. Lugar of Indiana, dropped out.

The following week Dole repeated his success, taking all of the southern-oriented Super Tuesday contests. With Dole appearing unstoppable, one of his last remaining rivals, publishing magnate Malcolm S. "Steve" Forbes Jr., withdrew. By March 26, after victories in the Midwest and California, Dole had clinched the Republican nomination. Buchanan nevertheless stayed in the race.

Both Super Tuesday and Junior Tuesday were part of a phenomenon known as FRONT-LOADING or "March Madness"—the rush among states to hold their primaries as early as possible and help to determine the ultimate nominees. Some political analysts and the 1996 Republican national chairman, Haley Barbour, viewed the trend with dismay. They said it could lead to nominees' being locked in before most voters knew what was happening, resulting in less-informed and less-deliberative voting in the general election.

Under Barbour's leadership, the 1996 GOP convention approved rules changes to relieve the congestion by giving bonus delegates to states that delay their primaries, beginning in 2000. But California, the most populous state, did not find the bonus enticing. It moved up its 2000 primary to March 7, the same as New York and several New England states, and one week before Super Tuesday.

## Superdelegate

Also known as an automatic delegate, a superdelegate is an elected or appointed official who attends the Democratic NATIONAL PARTY CONVENTION as an unpledged DELEGATE by virtue of his or her leadership position. The Republican Party does not use superdelegates.

PRESIDENTIAL SELECTION REFORMS in the Democratic Party after the 1968 election, when Hubert H. Humphrey won the party's nomination without entering any PRIMARY contests, almost totally excluded party leaders from meaningful participation at the 1972, 1976, and 1980 conventions. Some in the party felt that the reforms, which shifted delegate selection entirely to the primary and CAUCUS system, had gone too far. They lobbied for bringing the leadership back into the nominating process.

In response, the Hunt Commission, one of several Democratic rules revision committees in the 1970s and 1980s, proposed creation of the superdelegate category in 1984. At the party convention that year 568 superdelegates cast about 14 percent of the ballots. They voted overwhelmingly for Walter F. Mondale over Gary Hart and Jesse L. Jackson. Without his 450 superdelegate votes Mondale would have fallen short of the convention majority that gave him the nomination on the first ballot.

In 1988 Jackson complained that superdelegate votes at the convention cost him some of the states he had won in primaries. Although Michael Dukakis won the nomination, the convention Rules Committee recommended fewer superdelegates in the future. Instead, however, the party added more, raising the proportion of superdelegates to about 16 percent of the delegate total in 1988 and 18 percent in 1992 and 1996. The superdelegates included 80 percent of the Democratic members of Congress, all Democratic governors, Democratic National Committee members, and state party chairs and vice chairs. (See figure, page 140.)

Republicans traditionally have selected party leaders as nominating convention delegates, making it unnecessary for them to have a counterpart to the Democrats' superdelegate category.

## Swing District

*See* CONGRESSIONAL DISTRICT.

## Swing Voter

*See* REALIGNMENTS AND DEALIGNMENTS.

# T

## Term Limits

The PRESIDENT, the GOVERNOR in most states, and executive officials in many local governments are limited to a fixed number of terms in office—most commonly, two four-year terms. The limits, most of which were enacted in the twentieth century, reflected a widespread popular concern with allowing a single individual to gain too much power in office over time.

A strong movement emerged in the 1990s to impose similar term limits on STATE LEGISLATORS and members of Congress. Voters in twenty-three states approved ballot measures to impose such limits, but the Supreme Court in 1995 invalidated the congressional term limits by ruling that they could be enacted only by an amendment to the U.S. Constitution. All of the twenty-three states, except Alaska and North Dakota, limited the terms of their state legislators, and those limits remained in effect.

Advocates said the idea of term limits—or "rotation in office"—had historical precedents in ancient Greece and Rome, the Renaissance city-states of Florence and Venice, and at least three of the American colonies. The Articles of Confederation included a provision limiting delegates to the Continental Congress to three years in office over a six-year period.

An early draft of the Constitution also included a tenure limitation for members of what was to become the House of Representatives, but the provision was dropped without dissent or debate. Alexander Hamilton also persuaded the delegates to the Constitutional Convention not to require rotation for the presidency. Anti-Federalists complained about the lack of a rotation provision in their unsuccessful effort to prevent ratification of the Constitution.

Despite the lack of mandatory tenure restrictions, voluntary retirement from federal office was common through the nineteenth century. George Washington unintentionally established a precedent by voluntarily stepping down from the presidency after completing his second four-year term; no president until Franklin D. Roosevelt chose to seek a third term. Turnover in Congress was high through the 1800s, above 40 percent for the House in most years.

Longer congressional careers became more common in the twentieth century. The national government had only limited impact on day-to-day life in the country before 1900. But the rise of the federal administrative state and the emergence of the United States as a major military and diplomatic power made Washington a much more important place for Congress and president alike.

### Presidents' Two-Term Limit

Congress had always been discontented with the Constitution's failure to restrict the number of presidential terms. From 1789 to 1947, 270 resolutions to limit the president's tenure had been introduced in the House and Senate, 60 of them since 1928. But the Roosevelt years added a partisan dimension to this longstanding concern.

Roosevelt's decision to seek a third term in the White House in 1940 was controversial despite his personal popularity. He won reelection for a third term and then again in 1944 but died in April 1945 only a few months into his fourth term. After his death, Republicans in Congress began advocating a constitutional amendment to limit the president to two four-year terms.

In 1947 the Republican-controlled Congress approved the proposal by substantial majorities: 285–121 in the House and 59–23 in the Senate. All of the votes against the amendment in each chamber came from Democrats. After three years and eleven months the requisite three-fourths of the states had ratified the amendment, and it was added as the Twenty-second Amendment on February 27, 1951. (Only the Twenty-seventh Amendment, concerning congressional pay raises, took longer to ratify.)

So few presidents have served even two full terms since the Twenty-second Amendment was enacted that its effects on the modern presidency are difficult to measure. As the INCUMBENT, Roosevelt's successor, Harry S. Truman, was exempt from the amendment but declined to seek a second full term in 1952.

John Kennedy was assassinated in the third year of his first term. His successor, Lyndon Johnson, was eligible to run for two full terms on his own. But Johnson's political unpopularity in 1968 led him to abandon his attempt to win a second full term.

Richard Nixon was elected to a second full term in 1972, but his role in the Watergate SCANDAL forced him to resign less than two years later. Gerald R. Ford served more than half of Nixon's second term, which limited Ford to only one elected term as president. But Ford failed to win even that. The candidate who defeated him in 1976, Jimmy Carter, was defeated in turn by Ronald Reagan in 1980. Reagan was reelected in 1984 and served until the end of his second term in 1989.

Through the 1996 election the constraints of the two-term limit had been felt by only two presidents, both of them Republicans: Dwight D. Eisenhower and Ronald Reagan. Bill Clinton, the only Democrat since Roosevelt to win a second term, was under siege in 1998 and 1999 for an improper sexual relationship and was considered fortunate if he managed to serve out the remainder of that term.

Both Eisenhower and Reagan disliked the two-term idea. After leaving office Eisenhower backed a change to three terms, as did Truman. Reagan during his second term campaigned for repeal of the limit, although in a way that would not have applied to him. He argued that the voters should be able to extend a future president's tenure for as long as they liked.

*Thomas R. Foley, Democrat of Washington, was the first sitting Speaker of the House to lose a reelection bid in 134 years.*
Source: R. Michael Jenkins, Congressional Quarterly

Other presidents have proposed that the president be limited to a single term of six years. Advocates, including Andrew Jackson, Lyndon Johnson, and Carter, claimed that a single six-year term would free the president from the political pressures of reelection and grant the administration more time to accomplish its long-term goals. Opponents noted that under a six-year term an unpopular president would serve two more years than under the current system, and a popular president, two fewer years. Another argument was that the president would in effect be a LAME DUCK for the full six years, rather than only in the second term as is now the case.

## Proposed Congressional Limits

During debate on the Twenty-second Amendment, one senator offered an alternative to limit both the president and members of Congress to a single six-year term. It failed, 82–1. But support for term limits for members of Congress began to emerge after ratification of the amendment. President Truman endorsed twelve-year limits for lawmakers in 1951. Public opinion polls found increasing support for the idea: a plurality of 49 percent favored the idea in a 1964 survey; polls in 1977 and 1981 found 59 percent majorities in support.

Congress finally gave the idea official attention in the late 1970s. Lawmakers from both major parties introduced a flurry of constitutional amendments aimed at increasing congressional effectiveness either by limiting tenure, increasing House terms to four years, or both. A Senate Judiciary subcommittee held hearings on the term-limit issue in 1978, but no further action was taken.

Republicans took up the issue in the 1980s, in part out of frustration with the Democrats' dominance of Congress since the 1950s. The Republican Party platform in 1988 called for limiting congressional terms. A year later, two Republican political consultants created a national term-limits group. Two more national groups were formed in 1990. In the same year, voters in three states—California, Colorado, and Oklahoma—approved measures to limit the tenure of state lawmakers. The Colorado measure also included a provision to limit members of the state's congressional delegation to twelve years in office.

The Colorado proposal became the model for congressional term limit measures in other states. Supporters campaigned for the proposals by contending that long-term members of Congress lost touch with constituents and abused their positions by approving dubious "pork-barrel" spending to benefit their states or districts. They also argued that term limits would make congressional elections more competitive, noting that the reelection rate of members of Congress since the end of World War II had been high—above 90 percent for House members. Opponents responded that the proposals would restrict voter choice, deprive Congress of its most experienced and knowledgeable members, and weaken Congress vis-à-vis the president.

Through 1994, term limit supporters won approval of measures to restrict congressional tenure in twenty-two states; state legislators were also term-limited in all but two of those states. All but one of the congressional term limit measures were contained in ballot INITIATIVES approved by voters; most were approved by substantial majorities of more than 60 percent. The earlier measures imposed twelve-year limits on members of the House or the Senate; later measures tightened the tenure restriction for House members to six years.

The term limits issue also appeared to influence the outcome of several individual races for Congress in November 1994. Republican candidates for the House included congressional term limits as part of their ten-point "Contract with America." (See box, page 246.)

Republicans recaptured control of both houses of Congress in the election, for the first time since 1954. GOP candidates also defeated a number of prominent, long-serving Democrats, including the Speaker of the House, Thomas R. Foley, of Washington State, who had been a vocal opponent of his own state's congressional term limits.

Despite the popular support for term limits, Congress refused to act on the issue prior to the 1994 election. A House Judiciary subcommittee held hearings in 1993 and 1994, but proposals for a constitutional amendment on the issue were not brought to a vote. In addition, members of Congress and citizens' groups opposed to congressional term limits filed suits against the measures in two of the states: Washington and Arkansas. They contended that the states had no power to add to the qualifications for serving in Congress established in Article I of the Constitution: a minimum age, U.S. citizenship, and state residency for a specified period of time. (See HOUSE OF REPRESENTATIVES, QUALIFICATIONS; SENATE, QUALIFICATIONS.)

The Supreme Court ruled on the issue in 1995 in the Arkansas case, *U.S. Term Limits Inc. v. Thornton.* In a 5–4 decision on May 22, the Court held that the states indeed had no power to change the qualifications for serving in Congress. "Allowing individual States to adopt their own qualifications for congressional service would be inconsistent with the framers' vision of a uniform National Legislature representing the people of the United States," Justice John Paul Stevens wrote for the majority.

Writing for the four dissenters, Justice Clarence Thomas responded: "Nothing in the Constitution deprives the people of each State of the power to prescribe eligibility requirements for the candidates who seek to represent them in Congress."

The ruling was the year's second blow to the term-limits movement. In March the House had brought four separate term-limit constitutional amendments to a vote, but each one fell well short of the two-thirds majority required for approval. After the Supreme Court ruling, supporters vowed to continue their efforts to elect members of Congress committed to voting for term limits. But at a news conference on the day of the ruling, Foley said he believed the term limit issue was dead.

The limits on state lawmakers, however, remained on the books and began to force the retirement of veteran legislators in many states. Supporters claimed the term-limit measures were resulting in increased electoral competition, but opponents disagreed and instead claimed the measures were weakening state legislatures.

Opponents also mounted legal attacks against the limits on state lawmakers in some of the states. Generally, courts sustained the state term limits. But in 1997, a federal appeals court in California struck down the limits on state lawmakers, saying that voters had not been clearly informed that the measure imposed a lifetime ban on serving more than eight years in the state senate or six years in the state assembly. Supporters vowed to appeal the ruling to the Supreme Court.

The debate over congressional term limits also prompted reconsideration of the effects of the Twenty-second Amendment on the presidency. Some political scientists contended that the amendment had weakened presidents during their second, lame-duck terms in office. But no movement emerged to repeal the amendment.

## Terms of Office

*See* ELECTION CYCLE IN AMERICA; SPECIFIC OFFICE

## Thermometer Ratings

Political scientists measure voters' feelings toward candidates with thermometer ratings, ranging from 100 degrees or "very warm or favorable feeling" to zero or "very cold or unfavorable feeling." No rating is recorded if the voter does not recognize the politician's name.

Before presidential elections, the NATIONAL ELECTION STUDIES (NES) conducts surveys of voter attitudes concerning the candidates. Each respondent is shown a drawing of a "feeling thermometer" that looks like a standard temperature thermometer. The respondent is then asked to show on that scale the level of his or her feelings toward a particular candidate. After the election NES asks the same voters who they supported.

The thermometer rankings are usually a very accurate reflection of the actual vote. In 1992, for example, 93 percent of those who ranked President George Bush highest on the thermometer also voted for him. Similarly, 95 percent of those high on Bill Clinton also gave him their votes. Of the 16 percent warmest to Ross Perot, 77 percent voted for him.

The thermometer ratings are a tool for measuring whether a portion of the electorate voted its feelings or instead engaged in strategic or SOPHISTICATED VOTING to support another candidate.

## Third Parties

Despite heavy odds, third parties have tried from time to time to make headway against the United States' TWO-PARTY SYSTEM. For the most part, it has been a losing cause. The system favors the dominant political organizations, which for more than a century have been the DEMOCRATIC and REPUBLICAN Parties.

Never in that time has an INDEPENDENT or third party candidate won the presidency. Only twice since 1832 have third parties or independents won more than 20 percent of the POPULAR VOTE in presidential elections. Eight times they have won 10 percent or more, most recently in 1992.

Third parties and independents have been somewhat

Top Vote-Winning Third Parties, 1832–1996

| Party | Election Year | Popular Vote Candidate | Popular Vote (percent) | No. Electoral Votes |
|---|---|---|---|---|
| Anti-Masonic | 1832 | William Wirt | 7.8 | 7 |
| Free Soil | 1848 | Martin Van Buren | 10.1 | 0 |
| American ("Know-Nothing") | 1856 | Millard Fillmore | 21.5 | 8 |
| Southern Democrats | 1860 | John C. Breckinridge | 18.1 | 72 |
| Constitutional Union | 1860 | John Bell | 12.6 | 39 |
| Populist | 1892 | James B. Weaver | 8.5 | 22 |
| Socialist | 1912 | Eugene V. Debs | 6.0 | 0 |
| Progressive (Bull Moose) | 1912 | Theodore Roosevelt | 27.4 | 88 |
| Progressive | 1924 | Robert M. La Follette | 16.6 | 13 |
| American Independent | 1968 | George C. Wallace | 13.5 | 46 |
| Independent | 1980 | John B. Anderson | 6.6 | 0 |
| Independent | 1992 | Ross Perot | 18.9 | 0 |
| Reform Party | 1996 | Ross Perot | 8.4 | 0 |

*Source*: Michael Nelson, ed., *Guide to the Presidency,* 2d ed. (Washington, D.C.: Congressional Quarterly, 1996), 300. Updated by the author.

*Note:* These parties (or independents) received more than 5.6 percent of the popular vote, the average third party vote historically cast for president. Daniel A. Mazmanian, *Third Parties in Presidential Elections* (Washington, D.C.: Brookings, 1974), 4–5.

more successful at lower levels, electing some members of Congress, governors, mayors, and other state or local officials.

BALLOT ACCESS and CAMPAIGN FINANCE laws, the ELECTORAL COLLEGE system, as well as tradition and mainstream party loyalties all make it difficult for third parties to organize and survive. Most are born of short-term conflict and dissatisfaction with the major parties, and most die quickly.

But third parties occasionally have influenced elections despite their small share of the vote. For example, in 1848 the LIBERTY PARTY, a movement dedicated to the abolition of slavery, received less than 3 percent of the popular vote and no electoral votes. Yet the party drained enough votes from the WHIG PARTY to guarantee the election of Democratic candidate James K. Polk.

Antislavery sentiments also helped the Republican Party to grow quickly from a new third party in the 1850s into the second major party, replacing the Whigs. Six years after its founding the GOP elected a president, Abraham Lincoln, in 1860. The older Democratic Party traces its origins back to Thomas Jefferson's DEMO-CRATIC-REPUBLICAN PARTY.

From time to time, there has been concern that a third party presidential candidate would attract enough votes to throw the election into the House of Representatives. When none of the presidential candidates wins a majority of the votes in the electoral college, the election automatically goes to the House for decision. In 1968, when Alabama governor George C. Wallace ran as the standard bearer of the AMERICAN INDEPENDENT PARTY, it was feared that he would win enough southern states to deny either of the major party candidates victory in the electoral college. But the Republican candidate, Richard Nixon, managed to outpoll Wallace in several southern states and win a solid electoral vote majority. (See CAMPAIGN STRATEGIES.)

More recently, in 1992, it seemed that the independent presidential candidacy of Texas billionaire Ross Perot might draw enough votes from President George Bush or Democratic challenger Bill Clinton to throw the election to the House. Perot himself gave that as one of his reasons for temporarily dropping out of the race. In the end Perot drew 18.9 percent of the popular vote, the largest ever for an individual, but he won no electoral votes.

Third parties also exert influence by publicizing important issues or options that the major parties have ignored. Because the major parties do not want to lose support to third parties, they may adopt positions they otherwise might not have taken.

Often, however, the third party PLATFORM has been too radical for the political temper of the day. Such platforms have been denounced as impractical, dangerous, destructive of moral virtues, and even traitorous. The advocates have been more anti-establishment and more far-reaching in their proposed solutions to problems than the major parties have dared to be.

Some observers view third parties as a threat to the stability of the democratic system in the United States. Others see them as a vital element in expressing minority sentiments and as a testing ground for new ideas and policies. Many of the ideas originally viewed as extreme—WOMEN'S SUFFRAGE, for example—eventually have gained acceptance and been adopted into law.

## Types of Third Parties

Political scientist James Q. Wilson has identified four types of third parties: ideological, one-issue, economic protest, and factional.

*Ideological parties,* according to Wilson, have a "comprehensive view of American society and government that is radically different from that of the established parties." They can be found at both ends of the political spectrum and include in the present day both the SO-CIALIST and the LIBERTARIAN Parties. Although ideological parties appeal to a narrow base of support, they have proved to be the most enduring type of third party, largely because of the ideological commitment of their members.

*One-issue parties* may grow out of dissatisfaction with the major parties' stance on a particular issue, such as slavery, states' rights, currency, opposition to immigration, abortion, and even hostility to lawyers. Once the issue ceases to be of importance, the basis for the party's existence disappears.

Because most issues provoke either intense feelings for a relatively short period of time—or, if they persist, eventually are addressed adequately by the major parties—one-issue parties tend to be short-lived. An excep-

tion is the PROHIBITION PARTY, which has run a presidential candidate in each election since its founding in 1869. It is the longest-running third party in U.S. history. Although primarily dedicated to banning the sale of liquor, the party was closely linked to the early feminist movement. Indeed, it was the first party to endorse women's suffrage.

*Economic protest parties* evolve in opposition to depressed economic conditions. A sour economy, for example, prompted formation of the PEOPLE'S PARTY, better known as the Populists. In 1891 the Populists nominated presidential and vice-presidential candidates at a national convention in Cincinnati. Calling for free coinage of silver (the country was then on a gold standard), the party won 8.5 percent of the popular vote in the 1892 presidential election.

Four years later, however, the Democrats embraced many of the Populists' issues and nominated William Jennings Bryan on a free-silver platform. Populists continued to run in presidential elections through 1908 but with no appreciable accumulation of support.

Perot's REFORM PARTY, which grew out of his 1992 movement entitled United We Stand America, was another example of an economic protest party. But by 1996, with the economy healthy, Perot's message had lost much of its appeal, and he mustered only 8.4 percent of the vote against President Clinton and challenger Robert J. Dole.

*Factional parties* evolve from a split in one of the major parties. According to Wilson, they usually form to protest "the identity and philosophy of the major party's presidential candidate." In the twentieth century, factional parties drew more votes than any other type of third party.

The most successful was the PROGRESSIVE PARTY, formed in 1912 to support the candidacy of former president Theodore Roosevelt after he lost the Republican nomination to President William Howard Taft. In November Roosevelt won 27.5 percent of the popular vote to Taft's 23.2 percent, but both men lost to Democrat Woodrow Wilson. When Roosevelt later defected from the Progressives, the party disintegrated.

In 1924 Sen. Robert M. La Follette of Wisconsin split

Fate of Third Parties and Independent Candidates

| Year | Third Party | Percent of Popular Vote for President | No. of Electoral Votes | Status in Next Election |
|------|-------------|------|------|------|
| 1832 | Anti-Masonic | 7.8 | 7 | Endorsed Whig candidate |
| 1848 | Free-Soil | 10.1 | 0 | Received 4.9% of vote |
| 1856 | American (Know-Nothing) | 21.5 | 8 | Party dissolved |
|      | Republican | 33.1 | 114 | Won presidency |
| 1860 | Southern Democrat | 18.1 | 72 | Party dissolved |
|      | Constitutional Union | 12.6 | 39 | Party dissolved |
| 1892 | Populist | 8.5 | 22 | Endorsed Democratic candidate |
| 1912 | Progressive (T. Roosevelt) | 27.4 | 88 | Returned to Republican Party |
|      | Socialist | 6.0 | 0 | Received 3.2% of vote |
| 1924 | Progressive (R. La Follette) | 16.6 | 13 | Returned to Republican Party |
| 1948 | States' Rights Democratic | 2.4 | 39 | Party dissolved |
|      | Progressive (H. Wallace) | 2.4 | 0 | Received 0.23% of vote |
| 1968 | American Independent (G. Wallace) | 13.5 | 46 | Received 1.4% of vote |
| 1980 | John B. Anderson | 6.6 | 0 | Did not run |
| 1992 | Ross Perot | 18.9 | 0 | Ran on Reform Party ticket |

*Source:* John F. Bibby, *Governing by Consent*, 2d ed. (Washington, D.C.: CQ Press, 1985), 198. Updated by the author.

off from the Republican Party and revived the Progressive Party label. The liberal La Follette went on to receive 16.6 percent of the popular vote. But when he died in 1925 the party again collapsed.

Another party formed briefly under the Progressive banner in 1948, this time splitting off from the liberal wing of the Democratic Party. But the third party with more impact that year was the STATES' RIGHTS DEMOCRATIC PARTY, formed by southerners who walked out of the Democratic convention in opposition to President Harry S. Truman's civil rights program. Led by South Carolina governor J. Strom Thurmond, the party captured four southern states and thirty-nine electoral votes.

Civil rights was again the issue in 1968, when Governor Wallace bolted from the Democratic Party to form the American Independent Party. Wallace was supported by many whites, especially blue-collar workers who were fed up with civil rights activism, Vietnam War protests, urban riots, and what they saw as the liberal ideology of the Democratic Party. Wallace won 13.5 percent of the popular vote and forty-six electoral votes.

Running again in May 1972, this time for the Demo-

cratic nomination, Wallace was shot by would-be assassin Arthur Bremer while campaigning in Laurel, Maryland. Wallace was paralyzed from the waist down. He lost the nomination and never returned to presidential politics.

In 1980 Illinois representative John B. Anderson formed the NATIONAL UNITY PARTY as the vehicle for his independent candidacy after he lost the Republican nomination to Ronald Reagan. Anderson received a good deal of attention but only 6.6 percent of the popular vote and no electoral votes.

As of the 1996 election, Wallace was the last third party candidate to receive any electoral votes. Since 1968 only five independent or minor candidates, including Anderson in 1980 and Perot in 1992 and 1996, have received even 1 percent of the popular vote for president. The others are John G. Schmitz, AMERICAN PARTY, 1.4 percent in 1972, and Edward Clark, Libertarian, in 1980, 1.1 percent.

## Obstacles to Success

Third parties face considerable legal, political, and cultural barriers. Often voters do not cast their ballots for third parties because of their allegiance to a major party. Indeed, loyal members tend to work within their party to promote change. They leave the party only as a last resort.

Some voters disillusioned with their party simply do not vote. When third parties prosper, voter participation nationwide usually declines. People with weak PARTY IDENTIFICATION, such as new voters, are more likely to vote for third party candidates.

The fact that third parties have little chance of winning further diminishes their support. People often feel that a vote for a third party is a wasted vote. Some also have the sense that third parties are somehow illegitimate, a belief that the major parties try to encourage.

The legal barriers facing third parties may seem daunting. To appear on the election ballots in the fifty states and the District of Columbia, third parties must pass a series of hurdles, including petition requirements, filing deadlines, and fees. The requirements vary from state to state.

Forty states prohibit FUSIONISM, under which candidates may run for office under several different party names. The practice, allowed in New York and nine other states, permits voters to vote for the candidate under the party label most compatible with their own views. The Supreme Court, however, ruled in a Minnesota case, *McKenna v. Twin Cities Area New Party*, in April 1997 that states have a right to bar the multiple listings. Fusion advocates had argued that the prohibition violated their First Amendment rights.

The 1974 Federal Election Campaign Act also has been a barrier to third party presidential candidates. The act allows major party candidates to receive PUBLIC FINANCING during the campaign. But third parties are allowed public funds only after the election is over and only if they appear on the ballot in at least ten states and receive at least 5 percent of the popular vote nationwide.

In 1996 Perot qualified for public funds on the strength of his showing four years earlier. He had rejected the federal grants in 1992, thereby avoiding spending limits; instead, he financed his campaign with a reported $72.9 million of his own money.

Receiving public funds only after the campaign is ended puts third party candidates at a significant disadvantage. The money is not available when it is most needed, and valuable time must be spent on fund raising rather than on other campaign activities. Fund raising itself is more difficult because third parties do not have the organizational structure or expertise of the major parties.

Third parties are also at a disadvantage because their party organizations are weaker than those of the major parties and their candidates are usually less experienced in politics and less known to the public. Third party candidates receive less free MEDIA COVERAGE than the major party candidates. In 1996 the commission in charge of presidential DEBATES barred Perot from participation in the Clinton-Dole forums, a valuable source of publicity for the major candidates.

In sum, the POLITICAL CULTURE in the United States is not particularly conducive to third parties. The American political tradition of moderation, consensus, and compromise does not lead to the formation of vigorous and persistent third party movements.

Nevertheless, minor parties continue to come and go. In 1996, nineteen presidential candidates besides Clinton and Dole received more than four hundred votes each. Of the nineteen, however, only Perot received more than 1 percent of the vote. (See table, page 517.)

---

## Thornburg v. Gingles

*See* REAPPORTIONMENT AND REDISTRICTING

---

## Threshold Rules

In presidential nominating politics the Democratic Party employs a *threshold rule* to determine which PRIMARY candidates are entitled to any delegates to the NATIONAL PARTY CONVENTION. A candidate must get at least a certain percentage of the primary vote to receive a share of that state's delegates. Since 1988 the threshold has been 15 percent.

Unlike the Republicans, the Democrats have banned WINNER-TAKE-ALL primaries in which the plurality winner gains all of the state's delegates. The Democrats award delegates by a form of PROPORTIONAL REPRESENTATION, with candidates who meet the threshold receiving the share of delegates that is the same as his or her share of the primary POPULAR VOTE.

In true proportional representation there would be no threshold. Any candidate who received 1 percent of the vote would receive 1 percent of the delegates. The Democrats imposed a threshold to keep the delegations from splintering into too many small factions.

After banning winner-take-all systems in 1976, the Democrats continued on and off to accept some state rules that allowed candidates to receive more than their proportionate share of the delegates. These "bonus" or "winner-take-more" plans were prohibited in 1980 but allowed again in 1984 and 1988. They were banned in 1992 and 1996.

In 1976 the Winograd Commission, one of several commissions the Democrats appointed to study their rules, recommended a 15 percent threshold rule that would increase to 25 percent later in the primary season. The DEMOCRATIC NATIONAL COMMITTEE reduced the higher percentage from 25 percent to 20 percent. (See PRESIDENTIAL SELECTION REFORMS.)

In 1984 the Hunt Commission raised the threshold to 20 percent in CAUCUS states and 25 percent in primary states. After one of that year's major candidates, Jesse L. Jackson, argued that the 20 percent threshold was too high, the Fairness Commission lowered it to 15 percent for the 1988 primaries. It remained at that level in 1992 and 1996.

## Turnout

*See* VOTER TURNOUT.

## Twelfth Amendment

*See* PRESIDENT, NOMINATING AND ELECTING; VICE PRESIDENT.

## Twentieth (Lame Duck) Amendment

*See* PRESIDENT, NOMINATING AND ELECTING; SENATE, ELECTING; VICE PRESIDENT.

## Twenty-Fifth Amendment

*See* PRESIDENT, NOMINATING AND ELECTING; VICE PRESIDENT.

## Twenty-Fourth Amendment

*See* RIGHT TO VOTE.

## Twenty-Second Amendment

*See* PRESIDENT, NOMINATING AND ELECTING.

## Twenty-Sixth Amendment

The Twenty-sixth Amendment, ratified in 1971, established a uniform national voting age of eighteen for federal, state, and local elections. The amendment was proposed and ratified after the Supreme Court upheld Congress's power to lower the voting age for federal elections but blocked it from establishing the same voting age for state and local balloting.

Before 1970 all but four states set the minimum voting age at twenty-one; the exceptions were Georgia and Kentucky (eighteen), Alaska (nineteen), and Hawaii (twenty.) The drive to lower the voting age to eighteen gained momentum during the Vietnam War. Proponents raised the battle cry, "Old enough to fight, old enough to vote!" They argued that it was unfair to draft young men for military service but deny them the RIGHT TO VOTE. Also, the post–World War II baby boom meant that in the 1960s the eighteen to twenty-year-old population was unusually large. By 1970 there was a broad consensus in Congress in favor of allowing eighteen-year-olds to vote. But supporters differed on whether the change could be accomplished by statute or required a constitutional amendment.

Congress eventually inserted a statutory provision setting a uniform voting age of eighteen for federal, state, and local elections into an omnibus extension of the VOTING RIGHTS ACT in 1970. President Richard Nixon signed the measure into law but expressed doubts about the constitutionality of the voting-age change.

Several states immediately challenged the law. In OREGON V. MITCHELL, the Supreme Court on December 21, 1970, upheld all of the law except the provision lowering the voting age for state and local elections. Justice Hugo L. Black wrote the pivotal opinion in the 5–4 decision on the voting age change. He said that the Constitution gave Congress supervisory power over the conduct of presidential and congressional elections. But he said the Fourteenth Amendment gave Congress authority to override state voting standards only to combat discrimination based on race, not on age.

Supporters of the lower voting age immediately said they would seek a constitutional amendment to achieve their goal. They were joined by state election officials, who said the Court's ruling would impose a costly administrative burden of maintaining separate voting lists for federal and state elections.

The amendment, only thirty-six words long, provided that the right to vote of citizens at least eighteen years of age could not be "denied or abridged by the United States or any state on account of age." Congress completed action on the amendment on March 23, 1971, and submitted it to the states for approval. Ratification by the needed thirty-eight states was completed by June 30—a record time for approval of a constitutional amendment.

The newly enfranchised young voters, however, showed little enthusiasm for the privilege of voting. Only 48.3 percent of eighteen- to twenty-year-olds turned out to vote in 1972, the first presidential election in which they were eligible to vote in all states. Since then their turnout rate has declined steadily, to a low of 31.2 percent in 1996.

## Twenty-Third Amendment

*See* DISTRICT OF COLUMBIA; RIGHT TO REPRESENTATION.

## Two-Party System

The phrase "two-party system" accurately describes the overall pattern of electoral competition in the United States. But it also masks a great deal of variation in the nature and extent of interparty competition.

Most statewide elections—contests for a state's ELECTORAL COLLEGE votes and for the Senate and governorships—tend to be confrontations between the DEMOCRATS and the REPUBLICANS. A large proportion of congressional (House) districts, however, are safe havens for one party. In elections during the 1980s an average of seventy-one House seats (16 percent) went uncontested by one of the major parties. In 1996, 73.6 percent of House incumbents seeking reelection won with at least 60 percent of the major-party vote.

Elections for some state offices often lack authentic two-party competition. Uncontested elections are commonplace in state legislative elections, as is a lack of interparty competition, for example, in traditional Democratic strongholds in big city districts or in states where Republicans have long dominated. But these neat distinctions are becoming blurred. Along with the decline in PARTY IDENTIFICATION, Republican inroads in the South and Democratic gains in some conservative areas have made the electoral mixture more difficult to categorize. Moreover, races for state constitutional offices such as attorney general and secretary of state frequently are not competitive. For example, in 1992 in the South only half of the contests for these offices were genuinely competitive.

Comparative state studies have shown that socioeconomic diversity within a state's population contributes to two-party competition. A socially diverse population provides a basis for differences over government policy and allows both parties to build up support among selected groups.

---

### How the Parties Got Their Names

Our understanding of political party development in the United States is complicated by considerable confusion surrounding the names of the parties. Contemporary Democrats trace their partisan ancestry back to Thomas Jefferson. In Jefferson's day, however, the party went by two different names, either *Republican* or *Democratic-Republican*. By 1830 the dominant wing of a divided Democratic-Republican Party, led by President Andrew Jackson, abandoned the *Republican* portion of their label, leaving *Democratic* standing alone ever since.

A quarter-century later, in 1854, antislavery sympathizers forming a new party appropriated the name *Republican*. Today's Republicans are their descendants.

The term *democrat* comes from the Greek word *democratia*, a combination of *demos*, meaning "common people," and the suffix *-kratia*, denoting "strength, power." Thus *democratia* means "power of the people," or "the people rule."

The term *republican* derives from the Latin phrase *res publica*. It literally means "public thing," or "public affair," and it connotes a government in which citizens participate. Both party names suggest the Democrats' and Republicans' common belief in popular government, conducted by representatives of the people and accountable to them.

Gilded Age political cartoonist Thomas Nast endowed the two major political parties with enduring symbols: the Democratic donkey and the Republican elephant. The association of the Democrats with the donkey actually dates back to the 1830s when Andrew Jackson was characterized by his opponents as a jackass. In the 1870s Nast resurrected this image in a series of compelling political cartoons appearing in *Harper's Weekly*. The donkey aptly symbolized the rowdy, outrageous, tough, durable Democrats. Nast portrayed the Republican Party as an elephant. His initial employment of this symbol lampooned the foolishness of the Republican vote. Nast and other cartoonists later likened the elephant's size and strength advantages over other animals to the GOP's domination of the post–Civil War political landscape. The symbol came to suggest such elephant-like attributes as cleverness, majesty, ponderousness, and unwieldiness.

In an age when literacy rates were much lower than today, and when information about specific party candidates and their policies was in short supply for the mass public, these party symbols came to serve as valuable cues to prospective voters, providing them with an easy way to distinguish candidates of one party from those of another. For modern electorates, these traditional symbols have diminished significance, but they endure as part of the popular culture.

*Source:* Michael Nelson, ed., *Guide to the Presidency*, 2d ed. (Washington, D.C.: Congressional Quarterly, 1996), 778.

---

The changeover of the South from a one-party Democratic region to one characterized by increased interparty competition and much stronger Republican showings in both national and statewide elections illustrates what happens when a society becomes more diverse. Until the 1950s the southern electorate was relatively homogeneous, sharing common ethnic, religious, and economic characteristics. It was overwhelmingly white, Anglo-Saxon, and Protestant. The economy of the South was primarily agrarian, and its people tended to live in rural areas and small towns.

Such homogeneity, therefore, offered little basis for the development of two parties. Real two-party competition did not come to the region until industrialization, unionization, urbanization, the immigration of northerners, and increased BLACK SUFFRAGE created divisions within southern society that enabled the Republicans to gain a basis of support.

## Origins

The two major parties have dominated American politics and Congress since the mid–nineteenth century. Scholars have posed various theories for the dualistic national politics of a country as diverse as the United States. Some trace the origins of the national two-party system to early conflicts between Federalists (advocates of a strong central government) and Anti-Federalists, who took the opposite view. This difference continued in subsequent divisions: North versus South, East versus West, agricultural versus financial and industrial interests, and rural versus urban areas.

Constitutional, political, and legal arrangements are other bases of the two-party system. Plurality elections in single-member districts, for example, encouraged the creation and maintenance of two major parties. Under the WINNER-TAKE-ALL principle, the person who wins the most votes in a state or district is elected to the Senate or House. This principle discourages the formation of THIRD PARTIES. In addition, many states have laws that make it difficult to create new parties. Nonetheless, voters' disillusionment with both major parties and growing independent-mindedness has led some scholars to suggest that conditions are ripe for the formation of another major party.

## Signs of Dissatisfaction

In 1996 voters in 110 of 435 congressional districts, or 25.5 percent, split their tickets, voting for the presidential candidate of one party and the House candidate of another party. In House elections, the growing support for third-party candidates has led to a gap between the number of members who won with 60 percent of the major-party vote and those who won 60 percent of the total vote. The 1994 difference was almost two percentage points.

Besides independence, factors in the increased partisan competitiveness include REAPPORTIONMENT AND REDISTRICTING, anti-incumbent sentiment, fewer uncontested seats, the growth of POLITICAL ACTION COMMITTEES (PACs), and the dramatic changes in MEDIA COVERAGE of campaigns and politics. The latter two factors, particularly, have lessened the importance of the major parties in CAMPAIGN FINANCE and linkage between candidates and the public.

With the growth of PACs, candidates have become less dependent on their national or local parties for financial support. They generally form their own PACs, which solicit contributions from individuals or the PACs of INTEREST GROUPS seeking to influence government policy.

The news media, especially television, now perform many of the duties of the major parties in keeping their members informed about the issues and candidates. With the information available at the click of a remote control, partisan members no longer feel obliged to attend meetings or rallies where enthusiasm can be whipped up by oratory and camaraderie.

## Two-Thirds Rule

Candidates for the DEMOCRATIC presidential or vice-presidential nomination faced an especially high hurdle during the party's first century. Unlike other major parties, the Democrats used a controversial rule that required a two-thirds majority vote of the NATIONAL PARTY CONVENTION to obtain either nomination.

The party adopted the rule at its first convention, in 1832, and followed it until 1936. During those 104 years the rule denied the presidential nomination to two candidates—Martin Van Buren and James Beauchamp "Champ" Clark—who received majorities but not the required two-thirds vote.

On the first ballot in 1844, former president Van Buren won 146 of the 266 convention votes, or 54.9 percent majority. His total fell below a simple majority on succeeding roll calls, and on the ninth ballot the nomination went to former governor James K. Polk of Tennessee. Polk thus became the first DARK-HORSE presidential candidate.

Ironically, Van Buren had benefited twice from the two-thirds rule since its inception. At the 1832 convention, President Andrew Jackson wanted the rule adopted because it ensured the nomination of Van Buren in place of Vice President John C. Calhoun of South Carolina, who had clashed with Jackson on several issues, notably Calhoun's support of southern states' rights to nullify federal laws they deemed unconstitutional. After being dumped from the ticket, Calhoun returned to South Carolina to continue his fight against Jackson as a U.S. senator. He was the first vice president to resign.

As vice president in 1836, Van Buren was Jackson's choice to succeed him as president after two terms in office. Again the two-thirds rule favored Van Buren,

*Vice President John C. Calhoun, celebrated in the South for his eloquent advocacy of slavery and states' rights, was ousted from the ticket at the instigation of ardent nationalist Andrew Jackson. Source: Library of Congress*

who won the nomination and the election. He was defeated for reelection in 1840, however, making him the first INCUMBENT president denied a second term after first completing a full term as vice president. George Bush in 1992 became the second such person.

At the 1912 convention House Speaker Champ Clark of Missouri received a bare 50.8 percent majority on the tenth ballot with 556 of the 1,094 convention votes. He received even lower majorities through the sixteenth ballot. The nomination ultimately went to New Jersey governor Woodrow Wilson on the forty-sixth ballot.

The REPUBLICAN PARTY never adopted the two-thirds rule. In contrast to the typical GOP convention, Democratic conventions often were characterized by turbulence and multiballot contests over nominations. In 1924 it took Wall Street lawyer John W. Davis 103 roll calls to win the Democratic nomination.

With the assistance of Clark's son, Sen. Joel Bennett Clark of Missouri, President Franklin D. Roosevelt won repeal of the two-thirds rule at the 1936 convention. Southern delegations had long fought repeal because the rule gave the South a virtual veto over the selection of national ticket nominees. The issue was settled with a compromise that promised larger southern delegations at future Democratic conventions, with seats allocated on the basis of the party's voting strength in a state rather than solely by population.

# U

## Unicameral

A unicameral legislature is a single-chamber governing body. Only one state, Nebraska, has a unicameral legislature but city, county, and town councils typically consist of a single body.

Under the Articles of Confederation adopted in 1777, the United States had a unicameral Congress and a weak central government. But the Virginia Plan, as modified by the so-called Great Compromise (the Connecticut Plan) at the constitutional convention in 1787, gave the nation a bicameral Congress, with a House of Representatives elected by POPULAR VOTE and a Senate elected (until 1913) by state legislatures. The two-chamber Congress was better suited to the concept of federalism, with the national government sharing powers with the states, and its adoption helped to ensure ratification of the Constitution in 1788.

Since then some states have tried to argue that their legislatures, like Congress, ought to be able to have one chamber (like the U.S. Senate) that is not subject to the Supreme Court's ONE PERSON, ONE VOTE standard of equal representation. But the Court ruled in *Reynolds v. Sims* (1964) that both chambers of a state legislature must be apportioned on the basis of population. The Court rejected the "federal analogy" on grounds that the states are not "sovereign" and were not exempted by the Constitution from equal representation as the U.S. Senate was. (Each state has two senators, regardless of population.)

Three of the original thirteen states had unicameral legislatures, but all three converted to bicameralism: Georgia in 1789, Pennsylvania in 1790, and Vermont in 1836.

Nebraska changed to a unicameral legislature in 1934, largely at the instigation of its Republican senator, George W. Norris. Norris was also the author of the so-called LAME DUCK (Twentieth) Amendment to the U.S. Constitution. The Nebraska legislature has forty-nine members, called "senators," chosen on a nonpartisan basis from districts apportioned according to population.

Several states, most recently California, have considered conversion to unicameralism. In 1996 the California Constitutional Revision Commission, after a year of hearings, recommended that the state have a single-body legislature of 121 members and a TERM LIMIT of three four-year terms. The recommendations, however, were not among the propositions put before the California voters in November 1996 or June 1998. A two-thirds vote of each chamber of the state legislature was required for placement on the ballot.

## Union Party (1936)

Advocating more radical economic measures in light of the Great Depression, several early supporters of President Franklin D. Roosevelt broke with him and ran their own ticket in 1936 under the Union Party label. Largely an outgrowth of the Rev. Charles E. Coughlin's National Union for Social Justice, the new party also had the support of Francis E. Townsend, leader of a movement for government-supported old-age pensions, and Gerald L. K. Smith, self-appointed heir of Louisiana senator Huey P. Long's share-the-wealth program.

Father Coughlin was the keystone of the Union Party and was instrumental in choosing its presidential ticket

*Father Charles E. Coughlin of the Union Party delivers one of his notorious radio addresses. His violent, anti-Semitic oratory contributed to the party's demise. Source: Culver Pictures*

in June 1936—Rep. William Lemke, Republican of North Dakota, for president and Thomas O'Brien, a Massachusetts railroad union lawyer, for vice president. The new party did not hold a convention. The party's platform reportedly was written by Coughlin, Lemke, and O'Brien and was similar to the program espoused by Coughlin's National Union. Among the features of the Union Party platform were proposals for banking and currency reform, a guaranteed income for workers, restrictions on wealth, and an isolationist foreign policy.

Lacking organization and finances during the campaign, the party further suffered from the increasingly violent and often anti-Semitic tone of the oratory of both Coughlin and Smith.

The Union Party failed miserably in its primary goal of defeating Roosevelt. Roosevelt won a LANDSLIDE victory and the Lemke ticket received only 892,267 votes (2 percent of the POPULAR VOTE). The party standard-bearers were unable to carry a single state, and the Union Party's candidates for the House and Senate all were defeated. The party continued on a local level until it was finally dissolved in 1939.

## Unit Rule

The so-called unit rule was one of two controversial nominating rules used for years by the DEMOCRATIC PARTY but never embraced by the Republicans. The other was the TWO-THIRDS RULE, which required a two-thirds majority for nomination as president or vice president.

The unit rule enabled a NATIONAL PARTY CONVENTION delegation to cast all of its votes as the majority wished, regardless of minority objections. The rule prevailed from the earliest Democratic conventions until the turbulent 1968 Chicago convention rejected it. The party subsequently prohibited the unit rule in all phases of party activity. (See PRESIDENTIAL SELECTION REFORMS.)

Not all states followed the unit rule. It was most popular in the South, which until the mid–twentieth century tended to be heavily Democratic. Along with the two-thirds rule, which the party dropped in 1936, the unit rule enhanced the power of the South in choosing party nominees. Although they were less populous than some of the northern industrial states, southern states could deliver—or withhold—crucial blocs of convention votes.

By the time of the 1968 convention, only about a fifth of the states, mostly BORDER and southern states, still used the unit rule. They made up the core of opposition to the motion to abolish the rule, which won 1,351.25 votes to 1,209.

In effect, the unit rule created WINNER-TAKE-ALL possibilities, especially in CAUCUS states. With the rule eliminated, it still remained possible for caucus and

PRIMARY winners in certain states to take all of the delegates by a simple majority victory. The Democratic Party, however, later banned all types of winner-take-all contests.

---

## United We Stand America (Independent Ross Perot) (1992– )

The presidential campaign of Texas billionaire Ross Perot in 1992 drew the highest vote share of any INDEPENDENT or THIRD PARTY candidate in eighty years. Relying heavily on his wealth and on grassroots volunteer efforts to get his name on the ballot in all fifty states and the District of Columbia, Perot received 19,741,657 votes or 18.9 percent of the nationwide vote. He did not win any sizable constituency or receive any electoral votes, but he drew a respectable 10 percent to 30 percent in popular voting across the nation. He ran best in the West, New England, the Plains states, around his Dallas base, in economically distressed parts of the Rust Belt and in high-growth districts on Florida's coasts.

Perot, who announced the possibility of his candidacy in February 1992, ran his early unofficial campaign mainly on one issue—eliminating the federal deficit. He had the luxury of funding his entire campaign, which included buying huge amounts of television time. Drawing on the disenchantment of voters, Perot and his folksy, no-nonsense approach to government reform struck a populist chord. But he also demonstrated his quirkiness by withdrawing from the presidential race in mid-July and then reversing himself and reentering in October. He chose as his RUNNING MATE retired admiral James B. Stockdale, who as a navy flier had been a prisoner during much of the Vietnam War.

United We Stand America (UWSA), formed from the ashes of Perot's candidacy, did not bill itself as an official political party. Promoting itself instead as a nonpartisan educational organization, UWSA called for a balanced budget, government reform, and health care reform. While the group's leaders did not endorse candidates or offer them financial assistance, the leaders attempted to influence elections and hold incumbents accountable through election forums and voter guides ranking candidates on selected issues.

After the election Ross Perot, rather than UWSA, commanded considerable attention on Capitol Hill. From marshaling grassroots support on congressional reform to unsuccessfully opposing the North American Free Trade Agreement (NAFTA), Perot remained highly visible on the political scene. Democrats and Republicans were unable to co-opt his following as they had those of major third party movements in the past. And Perot continued to use his supporters' anger with government and the political process to sustain himself as an independent political force. In the fall of 1995 Perot created a full-fledged political party, the REFORM PARTY, and ran as its nominee in a campaign financed with federal funds.

---

## U.S. Labor Party (Independent Lyndon LaRouche) (1973– )

Formed in 1973 as the political arm of the National Caucus of Labor Committees (NCLC), the U.S. Labor Party made its debut in national politics in 1976. The NCLC, a Marxist group, was organized in 1968 by splinters of the radical movements of the 1960s. New Yorker Lyndon LaRouche, the party's chairman and a self-taught economist who worked in the management and computer fields, became its 1976 presidential nominee and Wayne Evans, a Detroit steelworker, his RUNNING MATE.

The party directed much of its fire at the Rockefeller family. It charged that banks controlled by the Rockefellers were strangling the U.S. and world economies. In an apocalyptic vein, the party predicted a world monetary collapse by election day and the destruction of the country by thermonuclear war by the summer of 1977.

LaRouche's party developed a reputation for harassment because of its shouted interruptions and demonstrations against its political foes, including the COMMUNIST PARTY and the United Auto Workers. It accused some left-wing organizations and individuals, such as linguist Noam Chomsky and Marcus Raskin and his Institute for Policy Studies, of conspiring with the Rockefellers and the Central Intelligence Agency.

During the 1976 campaign, LaRouche was more critical of challenger Jimmy Carter than President Gerald R. Ford. He depicted Ford as a well-meaning man out of his depth in the presidency, but Carter as a pawn of nuclear war advocates and a disgracefully unqualified presidential candidate. LaRouche captured only 40,043 votes, less than 0.1 percent of the national vote. He was on the ballot in twenty-three states and the District of Columbia.

Although the U.S. Labor Party did not run a presidential candidate in the 1980 election, LaRouche ran a strident campaign—as a Democrat. By this time, LaRouche's politics had shifted to the right, and his speeches were fraught with warnings of conspiracy.

He continued his crusade in 1984 but as an "independent Democrat," dismissing Democratic presidential nominee Walter F. Mondale as an "agent of Soviet influence." LaRouche received 78,807 votes, or 0.1 percent of the vote.

In 1988 LaRouche again attempted to run as a Democrat but, failing to get the nomination, garnered 25,562 votes under the banner of the National Economic Recovery Party. On December 16, 1988, LaRouche and six of his associates were convicted on forty-seven counts of mail fraud and conspiracy to commit mail fraud. LaRouche was sentenced to fifteen years in prison.

In 1992 the unflagging LaRouche ran again for president from his jail cell. As a convicted felon, he no longer had the right to vote himself. LaRouche ran as an independent although his name appeared on several state ballots under various party names, including Economic Recovery. His supporters, experienced in winning ballot access, placed him on the ballot in seventeen states and the District of Columbia. He received 26,333 votes nationwide. In 1996 LaRouche's name disappeared from general election ballots.

## U.S. Taxpayers Party (1992– )

Making its second appearance in a presidential election, the U.S. Taxpayers Party was on the ballot in thirty-nine states in 1996. Its nominee, Howard Phillips of Vienna, Virginia, drew 184,359 votes, almost five times as many as his 1992 total of 43,434. Of the eighteen minor parties receiving at least 750 votes in 1996, the U.S. Taxpayers Party received the fourth highest total.

Phillips, longtime chairman of the Conservative Caucus, founded the party to counter what he perceived to be a left-to-center movement by the Republican Party under George Bush. Failing to recruit rightist icons such as Patrick J. Buchanan, Oliver North, or Jesse Helms to be the party's standard bearer, Phillips ran himself. In addition to taxes the party opposed welfare, abortion, and affirmative action.

# V

## Vacancy in Office

*See* specific office.

## Vice President

The vice president is the electoral twin of the PRESI-DENT. Paired on the same ticket, both must meet the same few constitutional requirements: be at least thirty-five in age, a natural-born U.S. citizen, and have lived in the United States for the previous fourteen years.

Those qualifications, spelled out in Article II, section 1, clause 5, of the Constitution, were originally intended for presidents and did not mention vice presidents. The framers stipulated that the vice president would be the runner-up in the presidential contest and therefore would have the necessary qualifications to hold either office. For the first three elections, the ELECTORAL COLLEGE worked as planned, with each elector casting two votes for president and the second-highest vote getter becoming vice president.

But in the fourth presidential election, 1800, the system backfired. Thomas Jefferson and Aaron Burr, running together against other candidates, drew the same number of electoral votes. The tie threw the election to the House of Representatives, which chose Jefferson. Burr became his vice president.

By the time of the fifth election, 1804, Congress and the states had adopted the Twelfth Amendment, which required separate ballots for president and vice president, with electors casting only one vote for each office. That procedure is in effect today.

Under this system, it is possible for the president and vice president to receive different electoral vote totals,

even though as a pair they received the same popular vote. There have been nine instances of *faithless electors* who refused to give their vote to the candidate who won their state, the most recent in 1988. West Virginia elector Margaret Leach voted for the defeated Democratic candidates in reverse order. Instead of each receiving 112 electoral votes nationally, Michael Dukakis wound up with 111 for president and 1 for vice president and his RUNNING MATE, Lloyd Bentsen, received the reverse.

If no vice-presidential candidate receives a majority of electoral votes, the Senate elects the vice president under terms of the Twelfth Amendment. The choice is limited to the two contenders who received the most electoral votes. Two-thirds of the Senate must be present for the vote, but a simple majority of the total Senate membership is enough for election.

The Senate has chosen a vice president only once, in 1837, when Martin Van Buren's running mate, Richard M. Johnson of Kentucky, received only 147 electoral votes—one fewer than a majority. Twenty-three Virginia electors who supported Van Buren, a Democrat, boycotted Johnson because he was known to have kept a succession of black mistresses. The remaining electoral votes were split among three candidates, with Francis Granger, a Whig from New York, having the next highest total. Required to choose between Johnson and Granger, the Senate voted along party lines, electing Johnson on a 33–16 vote. If the Whigs had controlled the Senate, it is conceivable that the president would have been from one party, his vice president from another.

The Twelfth Amendment specified that the vice president must meet the same qualifications as the president. And, by requiring the electors to vote for at least one candidate not from their own state, the amendment retained the Constitution's requirement that the presi-

*Richard M. Johnson, the only vice president to be elected by the Senate, owed his place on the ticket to the popular outgoing president, Andrew Jackson. Source: Library of Congress*

dent and vice president be from different states. Rarely, however, has this deprived a presidential candidate of the first choice of a running mate. Candidates usually try to strengthen the ticket by choosing a popular figure from another part of the country, as well as someone from a different age group or who brings another special quality to the vice-presidential candidacy.

Walter F. Mondale in 1984 tried to balance the Democratic ticket by sex. He chose as running mate Geraldine A. Ferraro of New York, making her the only woman to receive a major party nomination for vice president.

## Vital Statistics on the Vice Presidency

The youngest vice president was John C. Breckinridge, thirty-six when he took office with James Buchanan. The oldest was Harry Truman's vice president, Alben W. Barkley, who was seventy-five when he left office. Barkley was popularly known as the "veep," still a nickname for the vice president.

Dan Quayle, who served with George Bush, was the first "baby boomer" vice president. He was born after World War II.

Like the presidents, most vice presidents prepared for the office with long public service careers, notably in Congress. Thirty-two vice presidents, including Al Gore, served in the House, Senate, or both.

Nine vice presidents became president when the incumbent chief executive died or resigned. They and the presidents they succeeded (in parentheses) are John Tyler (William Henry Harrison, died 1841), Millard Fillmore (Zachary Taylor, died 1850), Andrew Johnson (Abraham Lincoln, assassinated 1865), Chester A. Arthur (James A. Garfield, assassinated 1881), Theodore Roosevelt (William McKinley, assassinated 1901), Calvin Coolidge (Warren G. Harding, died 1923), Harry S. Truman (Franklin Roosevelt, died 1945), Lyndon B. Johnson (John F. Kennedy, assassinated 1963), and Gerald R. Ford (Richard Nixon, resigned 1974).

Five vice presidents were elected president in their own right without first having attained the presidency through succession: John Adams, Thomas Jefferson, Martin Van Buren, Richard Nixon, and George Bush. Six incumbent vice presidents ran for president and lost. They included Nixon, who lost in 1960, and the man he defeated in 1968, Vice President Hubert H. Humphrey.

The longest-serving president, Franklin D. Roosevelt, had three vice presidents: John Nance Garner, Henry A. Wallace, and Truman. Garner was the first vice president sworn in under terms of the Twentieth Amendment, the so-called Lame-Duck Amendment, ratified in 1933. Previously, presidential inaugurations took place on March 4. Roosevelt and Garner were sworn in January 20, 1937, at the start of their second

terms. (See PRESIDENT, NOMINATING AND ELECT-
ING; SENATE, ELECTING.)

## Oath and Duties

Like the president, the vice president is required to
take an oath of office. Unlike the president's, however,
the vice president's oath is not spelled out in the Constitution. It is prescribed by Congress in the *United States
Code* and is the same oath required of all federal officers
except the president:

I, ........., do solemnly swear (or affirm) that I will support and
defend the Constitution of the United States against all enemies, foreign and domestic; that I will bear true faith and allegiance to the same; that I take this obligation freely, without
any mental reservation; and that I will well and faithfully discharge the duties of the office on which I am about to enter, so
help me God.

Besides being the standby president, the vice president has the duty under the Constitution to preside
over the Senate and to vote there as a tie-breaker. In
practice, the Senate president pro tempore (usually the
majority party senator with the longest service) or,
more frequently, a junior senator presides over the day-
to-day sessions in the absence of the vice president.

As of February 1999 vice presidents have voted 226
times to break Senate ties. When the Senate was smaller
than it is today, ties were much more common. The first
vice president, John Adams, decided twenty-nine votes.
By contrast, Lyndon Johnson and Dan Quayle cast no
deciding votes; Spiro Agnew, two; Mondale, one; Bush,
eight; and Gore, three. (See page 528.)

Only two vice presidents have resigned the office.
John C. Calhoun, Andrew Jackson's first vice president,
resigned in 1832 to become a member, from South Carolina, of the Senate he had presided over as vice president. Agnew, Richard Nixon's first vice president, resigned in 1973 after pleading no contest to federal
charges that he evaded income taxes while he was GOV-
ERNOR of Maryland.

In the past, vice presidents had little to do other than
act as Senate president and stand in for the president at
ceremonial and diplomatic functions. Modern presidents, however, have found substantive work for their

*Charles G. Dawes was one of the most accomplished vice presi-
dents: lawyer, businessman, financier, brigadier general, director of the Bureau of the Budget, chairman of the Allied Repa-
rations Commission, and winner of the Nobel Peace Prize.*
*Source: Illinois State Historical Library*

vice presidents. In 1925, the year he took office with
Calvin Coolidge, Charles G. Dawes was awarded the
Nobel Peace Prize for helping Germany to recover after
World War I.

Lyndon Johnson used Senate veteran Hubert
Humphrey as a goodwill ambassador on Capitol Hill.
Jimmy Carter sent Mondale abroad on numerous mis-
sions and relied on him as a general adviser. Ford and

Nelson A. Rockefeller, the only two appointed vice presidents, accepted the job with the understanding that they would be more than figureheads. Bush named Quayle the head of a competitive commission empowered to review and overturn federal regulations. And Bill Clinton put Al Gore in charge of making the government smaller and more efficient.

The vice president also has two statutory roles: member of the National Security Council and member of the Smithsonian Institution's Board of Regents.

But attending funerals of foreign dignitaries remains a part of the vice president's job. George Bush went to so many he coined a slogan: "You die, I fly."

## Succession

Ever since William Henry Harrison became the first president to die in office in 1841, it has been clear that the vice president becomes the new president in such cases. The Constitution was vague on that point, but Vice President John Tyler set that precedent by refusing to become merely the "acting president." He claimed the full powers of the office for the balance of Harrison's term.

But periodically concern arose about what would happen if the president were disabled, or if there were a vacancy in the vice presidency. Most such questions were answered with ratification of the Twenty-fifth Amendment to the Constitution. Approved by the House and Senate in 1965, the amendment took effect February 10, 1967, after ratification by thirty-eight states.

Congressional consideration of the problem had been prompted by President Dwight D. Eisenhower's heart attack in 1955. The ambiguity of the language of the disability clause (Article II, section 1, clause 6) of the Constitution had provoked occasional debate ever since the Constitutional Convention of 1787. But it never had been decided how far the term *disability* extended or who would be the judge of it. (The original wording also included the term *inability*.) Clause 6 provided that Congress should decide who was to succeed to the presidency if both the president and the vice president died, resigned, or became disabled.

---

### Order of Presidential Succession

Vice President
Speaker of the House of Representatives
President Pro Tempore of the Senate
Secretary of State
Secretary of the Treasury
Secretary of Defense
Attorney General
Secretary of the Interior
Secretary of Agriculture
Secretary of Commerce
Secretary of Labor
Secretary of Health and Human Services
Secretary of Housing and Urban Development
Secretary of Transportation
Secretary of Energy
Secretary of Education
Secretary of Veterans Affairs

*Note:* Succession Act of 1947, as modified following the creation of new departments. Any successor to the presidency must meet the qualifications for the office established by the Constitution.

---

Congress has enacted succession laws three times. By the act of March 1, 1792, it provided for succession (after the vice president) of the president pro tempore of the Senate, then of the House Speaker; if those offices were vacant, states were to send electors to Washington to choose a new president. That law stood until passage of the Presidential Succession Act of January 19, 1886, which changed the line of succession to run from the vice president to the secretary of state, secretary of the Treasury, and so on through the cabinet in order of rank. Sixty-one years later the Presidential Succession Act of July 18, 1947, (still in force) placed the Speaker of the House and the president pro tempore of the Senate ahead of cabinet officers in succession after the vice president. (See box, Order of Presidential Succession.)

Before ratification of the Twenty-fifth Amendment, no procedures had been laid down to govern situations arising in the event of presidential incapacity or of a vacancy in the office of vice president. Two presidents had serious disabilities. James A. Garfield was shot in 1881 and confined to his bed until he died two and a half months later; Woodrow Wilson suffered a stroke in 1919 and was incapacitated for several months. In each case the vice president did not assume any duties of the presidency for fear he would appear to be usurping the powers of that office.

## Presidential Disability, Vice-Presidential Vacancy

The United States has been without a vice president eighteen times for a total of forty years through 1998, after the elected vice president succeeded to the presidency, died, or resigned. In 1912 William Howard Taft's vice president, James S. Sherman, died a week before ELECTION DAY. Taft and Sherman's hastily named replacement were defeated. In several other instances, vice-presidential nominees have withdrawn and been replaced. (See RUNNING MATE.)

The Twenty-fifth Amendment established procedures that clarified what happens if the president is disabled or if there is a vacancy in the vice presidency. The amendment provided that the vice president should become acting president if (1) the president informed Congress that he was unable to perform his duties, or (2) if the vice president and a majority of the cabinet, or another body designated by Congress, found the president to be incapacitated. In either case, the vice president would be acting president until the president could resume his duties or informed Congress that his disability had ended.

Congress was given twenty-one days to resolve any dispute among the president, vice president, and cabinet over the president's disability; a two-thirds vote of both chambers was required to overrule the president's declaration that he was no longer incapacitated.

If the vice presidency became vacant by death, succession to the presidency, or resignation, the president was to nominate a vice president, and the nomination was to be confirmed by a majority vote of both chambers of Congress. Within only eight years, that provision of the Twenty-fifth Amendment was put to use.

In 1973 when Vice President Agnew resigned, President Nixon nominated Gerald Ford, the House minority leader, as the new vice president. Both chambers of Congress confirmed Ford, and he was sworn in December 6, 1973. On Nixon's resignation August 9, 1974, Ford succeeded to the presidency, becoming the first president in American history who was elected neither to the presidency nor to the vice presidency. President Ford chose as his new vice president Nelson A. Rockefeller, former governor of New York, who was sworn in December 19, 1974.

With both the president and vice president holding office through appointment rather than election, members of Congress and the public expressed concern about the power of a president to appoint, in effect, his own successor. Accordingly, Sen. John O. Pastore, Democrat of Rhode Island, introduced a proposed constitutional amendment February 3, 1975, to provide for a special national election for president if more than one year remained in a presidential term. Hearings were held before the Senate Judiciary Subcommittee on Constitutional Amendments, but no action was taken.

## The Amendment in Operation

Only two clear situations of presidential disability have arisen since the Twenty-fifth Amendment was adopted, both during the Reagan administration. The first happened when Reagan was shot on March 30, 1981. Although Reagan needed surgery, Vice President Bush was not named acting president. White House aides discouraged any such action for fear that it would make Reagan appear weak or confuse the nation.

Within the White House itself, however, there was brief uncertainty about who is in charge when the president temporarily is unable to function. Soon after news of the shooting became known, the Reagan cabinet gathered in the White House, ready to invoke the amendment's procedures, if necessary. Vice President Bush was airborne, returning to Washington from Texas.

At a televised press briefing that afternoon, Secretary of State Alexander M. Haig Jr. confirmed that Reagan was in surgery and under anesthesia. It was clear that he temporarily was unable to make presidential decisions should a national emergency require them.

Trying to reassure the country, Haig stated that he was in control in the White House pending the return of Vice President Bush, with whom he was in contact. This assertion was followed by a question from the press about who was making administration decisions. Haig responded, "Constitutionally, gentlemen, you have the president, the vice president, and the secretary of state in that order, and should the president decide he wants to transfer the helm to the vice president, he will do so. He has not done that." Actually, Haig was referring to succession before the 1947 act.

Criticism of the administration's failure to act after Reagan was shot shaped its response to the second instance of presidential disability, Reagan's cancer surgery on July 13, 1985. This time Reagan did relinquish his powers and duties to Bush before undergoing anesthesia.

Curiously, however, he did not explicitly invoke the Twenty-fifth Amendment, saying instead that he was not convinced that the amendment was meant to apply to "such brief and temporary periods of incapacity." Still, a precedent was established that the Twenty-fifth Amendment would work as intended in future administrations. This precedent was followed in May 1991 when President Bush said he would turn power over to Vice President Quayle if his irregular heartbeat required electroshock therapy. It did not.

---

## Voter Apathy

*See* zzz.

---

## Voter Registration

To guard against abuses of the American electoral system, states employ a number of devices designed to restrict voting within their jurisdictions to persons legally entitled to do so. Chief among these protections is the voter registration process.

The need for such a system is a reflection of America's growth in population and diversity. According to

the FEDERAL ELECTION COMMISSION, there were 146.2 million registered voters in 1996, or about 66 percent of the voting age population.

When the United States was primarily a rural nation, its scattered communities were small and most people knew each other. Voting was a relatively simple matter: a voter simply had to show up at the polls, be recognized by the election judges, and cast his ballot. If he were challenged, he could either sign or mark an affidavit that swore to his qualifications or produce other voters who were recognized from the area to attest to his standing. (At that time, WOMEN'S SUFFRAGE had not come into existence, so all voters were men.)

But toward the end of the nineteenth century, the country had ceased to be rural in nature. The growth of cities and their concentrations of people made the simple system of voter recognition and approval, while still workable in some places, impractical and highly susceptible to fraudulent voting practices.

In the urban areas, practices such as "repeating" (casting ballots at multiple polling places), and "voting the graveyard" (using the names of dead people to cast ballots), became commonplace. As the FRANCHISE grew, sheer numbers of voters outweighed the ability of election judges to know who was eligible to vote and who was not. States began to turn to systems of registering voters, and, by the beginning of the twentieth century, all the states had a type of registration in place and working. When women gained the RIGHT TO VOTE, more names were added to the burgeoning rolls.

### Fraud Protection

The overriding purpose of the registration systems, whatever their particularities, is to ensure that votes are cast only by eligible voters. To thwart the ELECTION DAY schemes of the unscrupulous, all the systems provided a register, prepared in advance, of all voters in a given DISTRICT eligible to vote in that election. This roster, while not a complete protection against ELECTION FRAUD or corrupt election judges, offers some assurance that, in almost every situation, eligibility questions have been answered and that a voter duly listed on the rolls can vote when he or she reaches the polls. With

*Volunteers from the League of Women Voters provide voter registration forms. Source: Courtesy of League of Women Voters*

passage of the VOTING RIGHTS ACT of 1965, virtually all bars to voting eligibility disappeared. (See BLACK SUFFRAGE.)

The states employ a variety of registration systems, but all follow one of two basic approaches. The first is the *periodic* system, in which the existing voting rolls are cast aside at certain stipulated periods and new lists are drawn up, requiring voters to reregister. The second is the *permanent* system, under which the same list of voters is used indefinitely, with legally specified types of updates regarding additions and deletions of voters' names. Because the permanent system offers states some savings in time and money, and also because it appears to be more immune to fraudulent practices, it is the preferred choice.

In the United States, the burden of registering to vote rests primarily with the individual voter. Except in North Dakota, which has no formal registration system,

registration is a prerequisite to voting, and the citizen of voting age must take the initiative of getting on the rolls. This policy is in contrast to that in most other Western democracies, where registration is virtually automatic. (See INTERNATIONAL AND U.S. ELECTIONS COMPARED.) American voters as a rule must go to a designated office to register or to obtain a registration form that can be mailed in. The federal MOTOR VOTER ACT of 1993, however, now requires all states to provide mail-in voter registration forms in government offices such as motor vehicle bureaus and public assistance agencies. The Motor Voter Act is said to have added 10 million new voters to the rolls. The increase, however, was not reflected in VOTER TURNOUT in 1996, the first presidential election after the act became effective.

The Motor Voter Act is also credited with helping to keep the voting rolls up to date. Voters who fail to respond to election board mailings can be placed on an inactive list and removed from the rolls if they do not vote during a specified period. The requirements for keeping accurate and current voting lists indirectly affect political candidates as well. The registration indicates whether a candidate meets the residency requirements for the office being sought, and there have been numerous instances of candidates being kept off the ballot for being registered in the wrong area.

## Forms and Procedures

Registration forms common in most states are simple and straightforward. An applicant is asked to check off whether the registration is a new one or represents a change of address or name. The applicant then fills in his or her name, address, date of birth, mailing address (if different from residence), a home telephone (optional), and information about the person's previous voter registration, including the county name, if it is in a different voting area.

The potential voter is also asked to "swear or affirm" that he or she is a U.S. citizen, that the address provided is correct, that he or she will be eighteen years of age on or before the next election, and is not on parole, probation, or serving a sentence for any indictable offense under federal or state law. This affidavit form also asks if the signer understands that making a false or fraudulent registration may subject him or her to a fine and/or imprisonment.

Once the form is completed, signed, and received by election officials, the new voter is registered on the election rolls of the appropriate voting precinct. The registration office may then, if the voter is reregistering at a new address, inform the voter's previous voting district that his or her name should be removed from those rolls.

The closing date for registration before an election varies from state to state. Some allow registration up to election day, but on average registration must take place twenty-eight days prior to the election.

Most states register voters according to party affiliation, largely to prevent "party raiding" by limiting closed PRIMARY and CAUCUS elections to party members. Usually the state requires changes in party registration to be made well in advance of the primary or caucus date. Several states, however, including California in 1998, hold open primaries not restricted to party members.

In separate 1997 cases the Supreme Court made two rulings on how long someone switching parties must wait before voting in another party's closed primary. The Court upheld New York's eight- to eleven-month waiting period, but struck down Illinois's twenty-three-month waiting period as excessive. (See CROSSOVER VOTING.)

Voter registration lists are a public record and copies are available to candidates and others, usually for a fee. Some states, however, have passed legislation creating secret voting lists to protect women from abusive partners. Such laws allow the abuse victims to be put on the secret list and vote by mail if they receive a court restraining or "no contact" order against the partner trying to locate them. Civil libertarians have opposed the laws, however, arguing that voter registrations are "the quintessential public record" and should be kept that way.

---

## Voter Turnout

Relatively few Americans exercise their cherished RIGHT TO VOTE. Less than half (49.0 percent) of the voting age population actually cast ballots in 1996—the lowest rate for a presidential election year since 1924. Turnout is even lower in MIDTERM ELECTIONS, when the U.S. House and one-third of the Senate are up for election. In 1998, for example, turnout was 36.0 percent.

Many other countries have higher voter participation rates, and some are much higher. In a 1996 survey of thirty-one nations, Australia (96.0 percent) and Angola (91.3 percent) had the highest turnout rates in recent national elections. Only Niger (34.9), Lebanon (40.0), and Egypt (47.0) had lower turnout percentages than the United States. Direct comparison is difficult, however, because of varied methods of registration and calculation. Some countries, for example, have national registration and voter turnout is based on those figures.

*An American soldier serving in Bosnia casts an absentee ballot, October 29, 1996. Source: Almir Arnaut, Reuters*

In the United States, with no national registration, turnout is calculated on the size of the voting age population, not on the number of registered voters.

Across the country, states vary widely in their rates of voter turnout. In 1996 Maine had a 64.5 percent turnout, and Hawaii, only 40.8 percent. These widely different rates can be attributed to three factors.

The first is a combination of levels of interparty competition, intensity of campaigning, and voter mobilization efforts. When there is genuine electoral competition between the Republicans and Democrats and an intense campaign effort on the part of candidates, parties, and INTEREST GROUPS, a state's voter participation goes up.

A second factor is VOTER REGISTRATION requirements, which differ greatly by state. North Dakota has no voter registration; Maine, Minnesota, and Wisconsin permit ELECTION DAY registration at the polls. Most states require registration about a month before the election.

The third factor affecting voter turnout is the composition of a state's electorate. Associated with high levels of turnout are a high income, a high-status occupation, educational achievement, and being middle-aged, Jewish or Catholic, and white.

## Characteristics of Voters and Nonvoters

Age and education are the two personal characteristics most closely related to voter turnout. Young people tend to have the lowest rates of turnout. In the 1996 presidential election only 31.2 percent of persons eighteen to twenty years old turned out to vote. When the age group is widened, the turnout is even lower. According to EXIT POLLS taken in the same election, only 17.0 percent of eighteen- to twenty-nine-year olds reported that they had voted, compared with 50.0 percent of those between ages forty-five and sixty-four. Registration requirements, attending college away from home, military service, and residential mobility all create obstacles to YOUTH SUFFRAGE.

Although the turnout rates of various age groups differ significantly, by age thirty-five most people vote at least occasionally. Most middle-aged people usually vote. Less than 5 percent of the total electorate almost never vote, according to voting records over the last one hundred years.

Education is the single most important personal characteristic affecting turnout: the higher one's level of education, the greater the likelihood of voting. Better-educated people are likely to recognize how politics affects their lives and the things they care about, to be interested in politics, and to be skilled in dealing with registration requirements.

Higher levels of education also are associated with higher incomes and greater social prestige. When education is held constant, however, income has little effect on voter turnout. In 1996, 70 percent of persons with at least some college education voted.

Racial groups also differ in their turnout rates. African Americans have lower turnout levels than whites, but African Americans vote more frequently than Hispanics. The participation rates tend to reflect the generally lower levels of education of these minorities.

Turnout rates among African Americans have risen steadily as discriminatory barriers to BLACK SUFFRAGE have been outlawed and determined efforts to mobilize black voters have continued. As a result, the African American vote has become a critical factor in determining the outcome of some elections, especially for Democratic candidates because African Americans tend to be overwhelmingly Democratic.

In the past women had lower rates of turnout than men; even after 1920 and ratification of the Nineteenth Amendment giving them the vote (WOMEN'S SUFFRAGE), their participation in politics was neither fully accepted nor encouraged. Today, however, women report slightly higher rates of turnout than men (52 percent versus 48 percent).

## Efforts to Increase Turnout

Because people who rank relatively high in socioeconomic status and educational attainment, who are middle-aged, and who are white have the highest turnout rates, more Republicans than Democrats are likely to go to the polls. For this reason GET-OUT-THE-VOTE campaigns and efforts to increase turnout through easing of registration requirements have been a standard Democratic electoral strategy.

Increased voter turnout does not necessarily benefit the Democrats, however. In the 1988 presidential election, nonvoters—by not voting—probably held down George Bush's margin over Michael Dukakis in the POPULAR VOTE. A 1989 *New York Times*/CBS survey showed that nonvoters preferred Bush 50–34, a wider margin than the 53–46 he actually received.

But when turnout swelled by 13 million in 1992, independent Ross Perot benefited along with Democrat Clinton. First-time voters accounted for 11 percent of the ballots and went strongly Democratic, giving Clinton 48 percent, Bush 30 percent, and Perot 22 percent. In EXIT POLLS 15 percent of Perot voters indicated that they would not have voted had their candidate not been on the ballot.

Early in his first term as president, Clinton signed into law the National Voter Registration Act of 1993. Better known as the MOTOR VOTER ACT, it enables eligible citizens to register as voters when they apply for or renew their driver's licenses. Although the act has added millions of eligible voters to the states' rolls, the increase as of the 1996 election had not translated into a corresponding increase in voter participation.

Congress has also considered a uniform polls closing time for presidential elections. The earlier closing of polls in the East is considered a deterrent to voting in the West because of the television networks' success in FORECASTING ELECTION RESULTS. In 1980, for example, the networks projected Ronald Reagan's defeat of President Jimmy Carter shortly after eastern polls closed. Carter immediately conceded defeat, removing a major incentive for western voters to go to their still-open polls. The networks have since promised not to project winners in a given state until the polls have closed there. But that did not solve the problem of premature naming of presidential election winners.

Neither Congress nor the individual states have seriously considered making voting compulsory by fining nonvoters. Alien as it may seem to the American concept of DEMOCRACY, compulsory or mandatory voting

# Voter Turnout, 1996 Presidential Election

| State | Resident Voting Age Population[1] | 1996 Voter Registration[2] | Total Vote for President | % of Voting Age Who Registered | % of Voting Age Who Voted | % of Registered Who Voted |
|---|---|---|---|---|---|---|
| Alabama | 3,220,000 | 2,470,766 | 1,534,349 | 76.7 | 47.7 | 62.5 |
| Alaska | 425,000 | 414,815 | 241,620 | 97.6 | 56.9 | 58.2 |
| Arizona | 3,145,000 | 2,244,672 | 1,404,405 | 71.4 | 44.7 | 62.7 |
| Arkansas | 1,873,000 | 1,369,459 | 884,262 | 73.1 | 47.2 | 64.6 |
| California | 22,826,000 | 15,662,075 | 10,019,484 | 68.6 | 43.9 | 64.0 |
| Colorado | 2,862,000 | 2,346,253 | 1,510,704 | 82.0 | 52.8 | 64.4 |
| Connecticut | 2,479,000 | 1,881,323 | 1,392,614 | 75.9 | 56.2 | 74.0 |
| Delaware | 548,000 | 421,710 | 270,845 | 77.0 | 49.4 | 64.2 |
| Florida | 11,043,000 | 8,077,877 | 5,303,794 | 73.1 | 48.0 | 65.7 |
| Georgia | 5,418,000 | 3,811,284 | 2,299,071 | 70.3 | 42.4 | 60.3 |
| Hawaii | 890,000 | 544,916 | 360,120 | 61.2 | 40.5 | 66.1 |
| Idaho | 858,000 | 700,430 | 491,719 | 81.6 | 57.3 | 70.2 |
| Illinois | 8,754,000 | 6,663,301 | 4,311,391 | 76.1 | 49.3 | 64.7 |
| Indiana | 4,374,000 | 3,488,088 | 2,135,431 | 79.7 | 48.8 | 61.2 |
| Iowa | 2,138,000 | 1,776,433 | 1,234,075 | 83.1 | 57.7 | 69.4 |
| Kansas | 1,897,000 | 1,436,418 | 1,074,300 | 75.7 | 56.6 | 74.8 |
| Kentucky | 2,928,000 | 2,396,086 | 1,388,708 | 81.8 | 44.4 | 58.0 |
| Louisiana | 3,131,000 | 2,559,352 | 1,783,959 | 81.7 | 57.0 | 69.7 |
| Maine | 945,000 | 1,001,292 | 605,897 | 106.0 | 64.1 | 60.5 |
| Maryland | 3,820,000 | 2,587,978 | 1,780,870 | 67.7 | 46.6 | 68.8 |
| Massachusetts | 4,649,000 | 3,459,193 | 2,556,786 | 74.4 | 55.0 | 73.9 |
| Michigan | 7,072,000 | 6,677,079 | 3,848,844 | 94.4 | 54.4 | 57.6 |
| Minnesota | 3,422,000 | 3,067,802 | 2,192,640 | 89.6 | 64.1 | 71.5 |
| Mississippi | 1,967,000 | 1,715,913 | 893,857 | 87.2 | 45.4 | 52.1 |
| Missouri | 3,995,000 | 3,342,849 | 2,158,065 | 83.7 | 54.0 | 64.6 |
| Montana | 656,000 | 590,751 | 407,261 | 90.1 | 62.1 | 86.9 |
| Nebraska | 1,211,000 | 1,015,056 | 677,415 | 83.8 | 55.9 | 66.7 |
| Nevada | 1,212,000 | 778,092 | 464,279 | 64.2 | 38.3 | 59.7 |
| New Hampshire | 871,000 | 754,771 | 499,175 | 86.7 | 57.3 | 66.1 |
| New Jersey | 6,034,000 | 4,320,866 | 3,075,807 | 71.6 | 51.0 | 71.2 |
| New Mexico | 1,224,000 | 851,479 | 556,074 | 69.6 | 45.4 | 65.3 |
| New York | 13,564,000 | 10,162,156 | 6,316,129 | 74.9 | 46.6 | 62.1 |
| North Carolina | 5,519,000 | 4,318,008 | 2,515,807 | 78.2 | 45.6 | 58.2 |
| North Dakota[3] | 476,000 | — | 266,411 | — | 56.0 | — |
| Ohio | 8,347,000 | 6,879,687 | 4,534,434 | 82.4 | 54.3 | 65.9 |
| Oklahoma | 2,426,000 | 1,979,017 | 1,206,713 | 81.6 | 49.7 | 61.0 |
| Oregon | 2,411,000 | 1,962,155 | 1,377,760 | 81.4 | 57.1 | 70.2 |
| Pennsylvania | 9,197,000 | 6,805,612 | 4,506,118 | 74.0 | 49.0 | 66.2 |
| Rhode Island | 751,000 | 602,692 | 390,284 | 80.3 | 52.0 | 64.8 |
| South Carolina | 2,771,000 | 1,814,777 | 1,151,689 | 65.4 | 41.6 | 63.5 |
| South Dakota | 535,000 | 459,971 | 323,826 | 86.0 | 60.5 | 70.4 |
| Tennessee | 4,035,000 | 2,849,910 | 1,894,105 | 70.6 | 46.9 | 66.5 |
| Texas | 13,597,000 | 10,540,678 | 5,611,644 | 77.5 | 41.3 | 53.2 |
| Utah | 1,333,000 | 1,050,452 | 665,629 | 78.8 | 49.9 | 63.4 |
| Vermont | 445,000 | 385,328 | 258,449 | 86.6 | 58.1 | 67.1 |
| Virginia | 5,083,000 | 3,322,135 | 2,416,642 | 65.4 | 47.5 | 72.7 |
| Washington | 4,115,000 | 3,078,128 | 2,253,837 | 74.8 | 54.8 | 73.2 |
| West Virginia | 1,417,000 | 970,745 | 636,459 | 68.5 | 44.9 | 65.6 |
| Wisconsin[3] | 3,824,000 | — | 2,196,169 | — | 57.4 | — |
| Wyoming | 356,000 | 240,711 | 211,571 | 67.6 | 59.4 | 87.9 |
| District of Columbia | 422,000 | 361,419 | 185,726 | 85.6 | 44.0 | 51.4 |
| United States | 196,511,000 | 146,211,960 | 96,277,223 | 74.4 | 49.0 | 66.0 |

*Sources:* Bureau of the Census, Federal Election Commission, Government Division of the Congressional Research Service, and state election offices.

1. Bureau of Census estimate of all persons over the age of eighteen (includes a significant number of people not allowed to vote in U.S. elections).
2. The total number of registered voters in 1996 as reported by the states.
3. North Dakota has no formal voter registration system; Wisconsin has election day registration at the polls.

Growing Franchise in the United States, 1930–1996

| Year | Estimated Population of Voting Age | Vote Cast for Presidential Electors | | Vote Cast for U.S. Representatives | |
|------|------|------|------|------|------|
| | | Number | Percent | Number | Percent |
| 1930 | 73,623,000 | — | — | 24,777,000 | 33.7 |
| 1932 | 75,768,000 | 39,758,759 | 52.5 | 37,657,000 | 49.7 |
| 1934 | 77,997,000 | — | — | 32,256,000 | 41.4 |
| 1936 | 80,174,000 | 45,654,763 | 56.9 | 42,886,000 | 53.5 |
| 1938 | 82,354,000 | — | — | 36,236,000 | 44.0 |
| 1940 | 84,728,000 | 49,900,418 | 58.9 | 46,951,000 | 55.4 |
| 1942 | 86,465,000 | — | — | 28,074,000 | 32.5 |
| 1944 | 85,654,000 | 47,976,670 | 56.0 | 45,103,000 | 52.7 |
| 1946 | 92,659,000 | — | — | 34,398,000 | 37.1 |
| 1948 | 95,573,000 | 48,793,826 | 51.1 | 45,933,000 | 48.1 |
| 1950 | 98,134,000 | — | — | 40,342,000 | 41.1 |
| 1952 | 99,929,000 | 61,550,918 | 61.6 | 57,571,000 | 57.6 |
| 1954 | 102,075,000 | — | — | 42,580,000 | 41.7 |
| 1956 | 104,515,000 | 62,026,908 | 59.3 | 58,426,000 | 55.9 |
| 1958 | 106,447,000 | — | — | 45,818,000 | 43.0 |
| 1960 | 109,672,000 | 68,838,219 | 62.8 | 64,133,000 | 58.5 |
| 1962 | 112,952,000 | — | — | 51,267,000 | 45.4 |
| 1964 | 114,090,000 | 70,644,592 | 61.9 | 65,895,000 | 57.8 |
| 1966 | 116,638,000 | — | — | 52,908,000 | 45.4 |
| 1968 | 120,285,000 | 73,211,875 | 60.9 | 66,288,000 | 55.1 |
| 1970 | 124,498,000 | — | — | 54,173,000 | 43.5 |
| 1972 | 140,777,000 | 77,718,554 | 55.2 | 71,430,000 | 50.7 |
| 1974 | 146,338,000 | — | — | 52,495,000 | 35.9 |
| 1976 | 152,308,000 | 81,555,889 | 53.5 | 74,422,000 | 48.9 |
| 1978 | 158,369,000 | — | — | 55,332,000 | 34.9 |
| 1980 | 163,945,000 | 86,515,221 | 52.8 | 77,995,000 | 47.6 |
| 1982 | 169,643,000 | — | — | 64,514,000 | 38.0 |
| 1984 | 173,995,000 | 92,652,842 | 53.3 | 83,231,000 | 47.8 |
| 1986 | 177,922,000 | — | — | 59,619,000 | 33.5 |
| 1988 | 181,956,000 | 91,594,809 | 50.3 | 81,786,000 | 44.9 |
| 1990 | 185,812,000 | — | — | 61,513,000 | 33.1 |
| 1992 | 189,524,000 | 104,425,014 | 55.1 | 96,239,000 | 50.8 |
| 1994 | 193,650,000 | — | — | 69,770,000 | 36.0 |
| 1996 | 196,511,000 | 96,277,223 | 49.0 | 92,272,000 | 47.0 |

*Sources*: Bureau of the Census, *Statistical Abstract of the United States 1996* (Washington, D.C.: U.S. Government Printing Office, 1996); Federal Election Commission, *Federal Elections 96* (Washington, D.C.: Federal Election Commission, 1997).

is the law in several democracies including Australia, which helps account for that nation's exceptionally high turnout rate. (See INTERNATIONAL AND U.S. ELECTIONS COMPARED.)

To encourage voter participation some states, notably Oregon, have experimented with elections conducted entirely by mail. Postal voting, formerly limited to ABSENTEE VOTING, has both its champions and its detractors and is too new to assess as a cure for nonvoting.

## Nonvoting: Cause for Concern

Nonvoting is not primarily a matter of cumbersome voter registration holding down turnout. Rather, it is caused by personal attitudes—a lack of interest, a distrust of government, a low sense of civic duty, a feeling that elections are not important or that an individual's vote will not matter, and weak attachments to a political party. (See PARTY IDENTIFICATION.)

With a voter turnout rate just under 50 percent, well below those of most Western democracies, the American Republic appears unhealthy. But any comparison with other democratic systems must take into account how most nations compute their turnout rates: based on the percentage of registered voters who actually cast ballots on election day.

In the United States, which does not have uniform national registration requirements and where the federal government does not assume responsibility for registering voters, turnout rates are normally based on the percentage of the voting age population. Our split system of STATE AND FEDERAL RESPONSIBILITIES for elections makes it difficult to use registered voters as a basis for comparison.

A private organization, the Committee for the Study of the American Electorate, tries to calculate the U.S. turnout rate among registered voters. On that basis, American participation compares more favorably with that in other countries. The committee estimates that 73.4 percent of eligible Americans were registered to vote in 1996 and that 66.8 percent of those did vote.

To date, there is no convincing evidence that the low U.S. turnout rates are distorting the public's policy and candidate preferences. In general, nonvoters have candidate preferences much like those of voters. Analyses of presidential elections held between 1964 and 1988 by political sociologist Ruy Teixeira indicated that if all the eligible citizens had actually voted in those elections, the outcomes would have remained the same.

This finding does not mean that nonvoting never makes a difference. But it does mean that relatively unusual conditions must be met for turnout to play a determining role in election outcomes. For example, the election must be close to begin with because of partisan balance or other circumstances; a very large turnout increase must be generated; and a large group of nonvoters with heavily lopsided candidate preferences must be available for mobilization.

Such conditions—and turnout—probably determined the outcome when Chicago elected its first African American mayor, Harold Washington, in 1983. In that election African Americans voted overwhelmingly (99 percent) for Washington, and their historically low turnout rate swelled by 30 percent.

Voter turnout rates provide only a limited perspective on the electoral and more general political participation within a society. There is more to political participation than casting a ballot, and Americans tend to have higher rates of nonvoting participation in politics than do the citizens of most democracies. Nor do turnout rates reflect the amount of electing—frequency of elections, the range of offices, and type of electoral decisions—that can take place in a country.

Therefore, although Americans have a turnout rate below that of most other democracies, they do not necessarily do less voting than other citizens; in fact, they probably do more. Americans' relatively low rates of turnout also may reflect general satisfaction with the political order and a belief that the next election will not bring major and threatening changes because both the Republican and Democratic Parties usually espouse essentially middle-of-the-road policies.

Although nonvoting in America is perhaps less worrisome than it might appear at first glance, reasons for concern still exist. With the educated, more well-to-do, and influential having the highest turnout rates, universal suffrage does not provide the kind of counterweight to power and wealth once envisioned by the advocates of universal suffrage. A high incidence of nonvoting also can threaten the legitimacy of democratic government. As fewer and fewer people vote, there is the danger that people will withdraw their support from the government as the principle of government by the consent of the governed is called into question.

## Voting Machine

The mechanical voting machine made its debut more than a century ago. Today half of American voters in three-fourths of the states cast their ballots on such machines or their electronic successors.

Although Thomas A. Edison invented the voting machine and received his first patent for it in 1869, it was twenty-three years later that a similar machine was

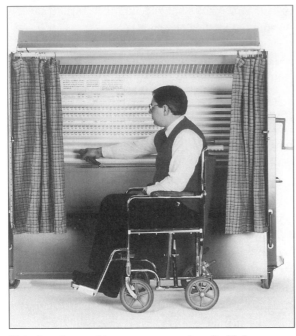

*Today's voting machines can accommodate disabled voters.*
Source: Courtesy of Sequoia Pacific Voting Equipment Inc.

first used, at a Lockport, New York, town meeting on April 15, 1892. The creator was Jacob H. Myers, a Rochester safemaker, who built the machine to "protect mechanically the voter from rascaldom, and make the process of casting the ballot perfectly plain, simple and secret."

Unlike the Edison device, which was meant for recording and counting votes in Congress, Myers's machine was intended for public use. As Myers continued to develop his machine, his company expanded to become the Automatic Voting Machine Co. of Jamestown, New York. Its AVM machines are still in use throughout the United States, along with mechanical voting machines built by other companies.

In the 1980s manufacturers introduced electronic voting machines that used computer technology to make the recording, tallying, and delivery of voting results faster and more accurate. Among the new systems was the AVC Advantage made by the AVM successor company, Sequoia Pacific Voting Equipment Inc.

Electronic systems were soon replacing older voting technologies. In Florida, for example, only eight counties in 1998 were using mechanical voting machines, and only one was using manually tabulated paper ballots. The remaining fifty-eight counties were using electronic systems certified by the state Division of Elections. In all, eleven voting systems were certified in Florida, including Sequoia's AVC Advantage.

Although the makers insisted that the electronic machines kept ballots secret and secure, conservative critics were openly skeptical of that claim. In Clark County, Nevada, Republican congressional candidate Pat MacMillan filed a federal lawsuit to disqualify the Sequoia Pacific DRE (direct recording electronic) machines used by the county. MacMillan said the machines did not meet FEDERAL ELECTION COMMISSION standards and that they allowed the "fixing" of elections. Sequoia, however, said that its machines were FEC certified and that "no system has been more publicly and thoroughly examined and tested than the AVC Advantage."

The FEC sets standards for voting systems but does not certify them. Instead, it recommends use of systems tested and certified by the National Association of State Election Directors (NASED). Sequoia Pacific said its AVC Advantage was certified after testing by one of NASED's independent test authorities and had been approved for use by twenty states.

Sequoia Pacific literature said Clark County had 1,800 machines in 802 precincts "accommodating early voting and utilizing a complete networked Windows-based election management system." Early voting permits a single machine to accept votes from up to two thousand precincts. Several states have early voting laws that allow ballots to be cast before ELECTION DAY by mail or at designated polling places. (See ABSENTEE VOTING.)

One complaint of the critics was that unlike older technologies the electronic machines did not leave a "paper trail" to verify results in case of a CONTESTED ELECTION, RECOUNT, or suspected ELECTION FRAUD, a charge that the manufacturers deny. Sequoia, for example, said that its machine "stores an electronic randomized record of all votes cast" and that this "Audit Trail can be printed on demand."

Nevertheless, suspicion of the electronic, networked direct recording devices could be found on the Internet Web sites of several organizations. One group called Voting Integrity Project Inc. (VIP) said it was exploring "the potential for a national institute of electronic voting" to certify the machines and programs in use throughout the country. (See page 131.)

---

## Voting Rights Act

Passage of the Voting Rights Act of 1965 authorized direct federal action to help African Americans register and vote. Earlier BLACK SUFFRAGE legislation required affected groups or individuals to seek court action to obtain the rights being protected.

Other than the Fourteenth Amendment to the Constitution, which guaranteed equal protection of the laws, perhaps no single document matched the Voting Rights Act in righting the wrongs of discrimination against the descendants of slaves. Within months of the act's passage, a million southern black voters had been added to the rolls. And within a few years black elected officials numbered in the thousands, mostly in the South.

President Lyndon B. Johnson pushed through the bill over the strenuous states' rights opposition of southern delegations in Congress. He signed it into law on August 6, 1965.

The act suspended the use of LITERACY TESTS and similar devices that had been used to keep African Americans from voting. It authorized the U.S. attorney general to supervise elections in states and their political subdivisions where voting registration had fallen below 50 percent or where the VOTER TURNOUT was below that level in the 1964 presidential election.

Initially, the act brought the federal machinery to bear in seven states, mostly in the South—Alabama, Georgia, Louisiana, Mississippi, South Carolina, and Virginia; the seventh was Alaska. Parts of Arizona, Idaho, and North Carolina were included, and other states

were later brought under the act's provisions. By 1989 it covered all or parts of sixteen states.

## Pressure for Enactment

Impetus for the Voting Rights Act came from events in Selma, Alabama, on March 7, 1965, when state and local election officials interfered with African American demonstrations against discriminatory voting practices. Led by Martin Luther King Jr., civil rights activists set out to march from Selma to the capital at Montgomery. They hoped to dramatize their drive to register voters in Dallas County, where only 2.1 percent of the eligible black voters were on the rolls.

Six blocks into the fifty-mile march the civil rights demonstrators were confronted by police and white protesters. When the marchers tried to retreat, they were clubbed and teargassed as national news media televised the scene.

Ten days later, on March 17, President Johnson went before Congress to deliver a tough new voting rights bill. Adopting the slogan of the civil rights movement, Johnson vowed, "We will overcome."

Johnson and his predecessor, John F. Kennedy, had been under pressure from black leaders since the 1960 election. Kennedy's narrow victory over Richard Nixon had been achieved with crucial help from black voters, who were growing impatient for help in return. The 1963 assassinations of Mississippi civil rights leader Medgar Evers and Kennedy himself added impetus to the black leaders' efforts.

The Kennedy and Johnson administrations had won passage of CIVIL RIGHTS ACTS banning discrimination in areas of public accommodation such as hotels, restaurants, and theaters. The new laws also brought minorities somewhat closer to realization of their RIGHT TO VOTE. For example, a 1960 law authorized the appointment of federal officials to monitor elections. And the 1964 Civil Rights Act eased procedures for federal authorities to look into voting rights cases. Also, the Twenty-fourth Amendment (1964) banned the use of POLL TAXES in federal elections.

But civil rights leaders criticized the 1960 law as too cumbersome to be effective. Its complicated procedures

*Voting rights was one of many reforms sought by the civil rights supporters, including Martin Luther King Jr. (front row, second from left), who marched from the Washington Monument to the Lincoln Memorial on August 28, 1963. Source: National Archives.*

for registering black voters required the attorney general to first win a civil suit for deprivation of civil rights. Other steps then had to follow before a black voter could apply for a court order that would require state officials to let the applicant vote. Thurgood Marshall, then an official of the National Association for the Advancement of Colored People (NAACP) and later the first African American on the Supreme Court, called the law "a fraud."

Against this background Congress went to work on Johnson's voting rights proposal. An expected Senate filibuster never materialized. Instead, southern oppo-

nents tried to weaken the bill with a series of amendments, most of which were defeated by margins of 2 to 1 or 3 to 1.

One of the most controversial provisions was a flat ban on poll taxes, which were still permissible in state and local elections despite the Twenty-fourth Amendment. To win the bill's passage over adamant southern opposition to the poll tax ban, the floor managers dropped the outright ban. The bill as finally enacted merely called for the attorney general to seek court action against enforcement of poll tax laws. In 1966, however, the Supreme Court ruled that poll taxes were unconstitutional in state and local elections as well as federal elections.

Congress completed action on the Voting Rights Act on August 3, 1965. President Johnson signed it into law three days later in a nationally televised ceremony under the Capitol dome. African Americans, he said, had come to the United States "in darkness and they came in chains. And today we strike away the last major shackle of those fierce, ancient bonds."

## Implementation of the Act

The day after Johnson signed the Voting Rights Act, the Justice Department sued to eliminate Mississippi's poll tax. It took similar action three days later against Alabama, Texas, and Virginia. On August 10 the department suspended literacy tests and similar voter qualification devices in Alaska and the six southern states where registration was below the 50 percent "trigger." The affected states and counties were required to obtain federal approval (preclearance) before changing their voting laws or procedures.

President Johnson announced that in the first nineteen days under the new law, examiners had registered 27,385 blacks in three southern states. In one day alone in Selma, 381 blacks had been put on the rolls—more than all the black registrants there in the previous sixty years. By November the number would rise to nearly eight thousand.

In March 1966 the Supreme Court upheld the Voting Rights Act in *South Carolina v. Katzenbach*. (Nicholas deB. Katzenbach was the U.S. attorney general.) The Court said Congress had acted within its powers under the Fifteenth Amendment (1870), which authorized the enactment of "appropriate legislation" to enforce the right to vote.

Several times in the following two decades Congress amended the Voting Rights Act to extend the section 5 enforcement authority (1970, 1975, 1982), cover Spanish-speaking voters (1975), and overturn a 1980 Court decision that required proof of discriminatory intent (1982). The 1975 amendments required BILINGUAL BALLOTS in jurisdictions where more than 5 percent of the population was non–English speaking.

## Supreme Court Decisions

As the Voting Rights Act continued to revolutionize southern politics, resulting in larger numbers of elected African American officials, states and individuals filed more challenges to the act's legality. After the 1990 CENSUS, some of the challenges dealt with the problems of RACIAL REDISTRICTING.

In 1969 in *Allen v. Virginia Board of Elections* the Supreme Court upheld the government's enforcement authority under section 5, which required renewal by Congress five years after passage of the act. The case concerned two proposed changes in local election procedures, from districtwide elections to AT-LARGE elections, and from elected to appointed county superintendents of education. The Court consolidated the Virginia case with one from Mississippi. Officials of both states had contended that electoral decisions were not covered by the Voting Rights Act.

Five years later in a Texas case, *White v. Regester,* the Court again considered at-large elections, which minority voters said diluted their strength by submerging them into the larger majority pool of voters. The Court said MULTIMEMBER DISTRICTS were not automatically unconstitutional under the Fourteenth Amendment, but that they could be in violation if they were used "invidiously to cancel out or minimize the voting strength of racial groups."

Two years after *White*, in 1975, the Court further refined its views on enforcement in *Beer v. United States.* The issue was whether a New Orleans REAPPORTIONMENT plan providing for two majority-black districts, where there had been none, was acceptable even though a differently drawn map could have provided the chance for election of more black city council members. The Court ruled that an electoral plan from a jurisdiction covered by the Voting Rights Act was acceptable under the law, provided there was "no retrogression in the position of racial minorities with respect to their effective exercise of the electoral franchise."

In 1980 the Court handed voting rights activists another setback by ruling in *Mobile v. Bolden* that intent to discriminate had to be shown for there to have been a violation of section 2 of the act. Unlike section 5, which

Congress had to renew after taking into account registration improvements in the covered jurisdictions, section 2 was permanent and covered the entire nation.

Civil rights lawyers took their complaints to Capitol Hill in 1982 when section 5 was due for renewal. Under a House-Senate compromise, section 2 was revised to overturn the *Mobile* decision.

The compromise retained House wording that an election procedure could violate the act if it "results in the denial or abridgment" of the right to vote. But Senate language was added based on the 1973 *White v. Regester* decision, which required a court to look at the "totality of the circumstances" before determining whether a violation existed. The compromise also stipulated that minority groups did not have a "right" to PROPORTIONAL REPRESENTATION and that lack of such representation was only one circumstance a court could consider in a voting rights case.

Four years later, in *Thornburg v. Gingles* (pronounced "jingles"), the Supreme Court upheld the revised section 2 and set out the criteria needed to prove a violation existed under the provision. The essential elements were whether a MAJORITY-MINORITY DISTRICT could be created, whether minority voters tended to vote for particular candidates, and whether white-bloc voting usually defeated minority-preferred candidates. The Court rejected the argument that once one or more black candidates have been elected from a challenged district, the district is immune from challenges under the Voting Rights Act.

Barely five months after the *Gingles* decision, Mike Espy became the first black elected to Congress from Mississippi since Reconstruction, bringing to four the total number of African American House members from southern states. In the 106th Congress (1999–2001) there were thirty-four black House members, representing districts in twenty states and the DISTRICT OF COLUMBIA.

## Cumulative Voting

The 1993 Supreme Court decision in *SHAW V. RENO* focused new attention on the concept of CUMULATIVE VOTING as an alternative to the existing WINNER-TAKE-ALL system of congressional elections. Under cumulative voting, voters in, for example, a five-member at-large district would each have five votes. They could cast all five votes for one candidate, or they could divide up their votes among the candidates.

In *Shaw* the Court reinstated a challenge to two oddly shaped North Carolina CONGRESSIONAL DISTRICTS drawn to have a black majority in each district. Both districts elected African Americans in 1992, the state's first black members of Congress in ninety years.

North Carolina had drawn the districts under pressure from the Justice Department as enforcer of the Voting Rights Act. The Court said, however, that it appeared the state had engaged in racial GERRYMANDERING.

A better way to ensure minority rights, some voting rights advocates believe, would have been for the state to create three large districts with multiple representatives elected under the cumulative voting system. Federal law, however, requires single-member congressional districts with representatives elected under the winner-take-all method. The only at-large voting for U.S. representatives takes place in states entitled to only one House seat.

Cumulative voting requires multimember districts. Although it is currently barred for federal elections, cumulative voting has been tried for local elections, and some political scientists view it as worth examining in the continuing search for effective minority voting participation at the state and national levels.

In Illinois members of the General Assembly were elected by cumulative voting until 1982. In 1987 Peoria, Illinois, and Alamogordo, New Mexico, adopted cumulative voting for city elections to satisfy court requirements for minority representation.

## Voting Studies

*See* NATIONAL ELECTION STUDIES.

## Ward

*See* DISTRICTS, WARDS, AND PRECINCTS.

## Whig Party (1834–1856)

Organized in 1834 during the administration of President Andrew Jackson, the Whig Party was an amalgam of forces opposed to Jackson administration policies. Even the name "Whig" was symbolic of the intense anti-Jackson feeling among the party's adherents. The name was taken from the earlier British Whig Party, founded in the seventeenth century in opposition to the tyranny of the Stuart monarchs. Likewise, the term was popular during the American Revolution, as the colonists fought against what they considered the despotism of King George III. The new Whig Party was opposed to "King Andrew," the Whig characterization of President Jackson and his strong executive actions.

Southerners, enraged over Jackson's stand against states' rights in the South Carolina nullification dispute, joined the COALITION early. Then came businessmen, merchants, and conservatives, shocked and fearful of Jackson's war on the Bank of the United States. This group, basically a remnant of the National Republican Party, espoused Henry Clay's American Plan, a program of federal action to aid the economy and tie together the sections of the country. The plan included tariff protection for business, a national bank, public works, and distribution to the states of money received for the sale of public lands. The Clay plan became the basis for the Whigs' nationalistic economic program.

Another influential group joining the Whig coalition was the Anti-Masons, an egalitarian movement strong in parts of New England, New York, and Pennsylvania.

Throughout its life, the Whig Party was plagued by factionalism and disunity. In the 1836 presidential election, the first in which the Whigs took part, the party had no national presidential candidate. Rather, three different candidates ran in different parts of the country—Gen. William Henry Harrison, Hugh L. White, and Daniel Webster—each hoping to carry Whig electors in states where they were popular. Then the Whig electors, if a majority, could combine in the ELECTORAL COLLEGE on one candidate or, if that proved impossible, throw the election into the House. But Van Buren, the Democratic nominee, won a majority of the electors.

Befitting their lack of unity, the Whigs adopted no platform in 1840 and nominated Harrison, a military hero, for the presidency. His campaign, emphasizing an apocryphal log cabin and hard cider home life in Ohio, resulted in a LANDSLIDE victory.

But Harrison died only a month after taking office (April 4, 1841). The new president, John Tyler of Virginia, proceeded to veto most elements of the Whig economic program, including the tariff and reestablishment of the national bank. Given Tyler's well-known states' rights position—ignored by the Whigs in 1840 when they capitalized on his southern appeal—the vetoes were inevitable. The cabinet resigned in outrage, and for the rest of his term Tyler remained a president without a party. Because the Whigs controlled the presidency and both houses of Congress just for Tyler's first two years in office, his vetoes spoiled the only chance the Whigs ever had of implementing their program.

The Whigs won the White House for the second and last time in 1848 by running another military hero, Gen. Zachary Taylor. Like Harrison, Taylor was a nonideological candidate who died in office. He was succeeded by Vice President Millard Fillmore.

*An 1840 sheet music cover to "The Log Cabin Song," dedicated to the Whig Party. Source: Library of Congress*

The development of the slavery question in the 1840s and its intensification in the 1850s proved to be the death knell for the Whig Party. A party containing antislavery New Englanders and southern plantation owners was simply unable to bridge the gap between them. The Compromise of 1850, forged by Clay, only briefly allayed the controversy over extension of slavery into the western territories. Many southern Whigs gravitated toward the Democrats, whom they believed more responsive to their interests. In the North, new parties specifically dedicated to opposing the expansion of slavery (Free Soilers, Anti-Nebraskans, Republicans) attracted Whig voters.

The last Whig national convention, in 1856, adopted a platform but endorsed former president Millard Fillmore, already the nominee of the Know-Nothing Party.

The Whig platform deplored sectional strife and called for compromise to save the Union. But it was a futile campaign, with Fillmore carrying only Maryland and winning only 21.5 percent of the national vote.

## Whistle Stop

In the language of elections, the phrase *whistle stop* means to campaign by making brief appearances in many small communities. It originated with President Harry S. Truman's nationwide campaign by train in 1948. Railroaders had long used the word *whistle stop* to mean a town too small for a regularly scheduled stop. To let passengers off, the conductor would have to pull the steam whistle cord to signal the engineer to stop.

*President Ronald Reagan waves to crowds on his whistle stop tour through Ohio on October 12, 1984. Source: Ronald Reagan Library*

Writer and former House member Ken Hechler, West Virginia Democrat, recalled in his book, *Working With Truman: A Personal Memoir of the White House Years,* that in Butte, Montana, Truman made one of his usual attacks on the Republican Congress. He particularly targeted one of its leaders, Sen. Robert A. Taft of Ohio, who had urged people to fight inflation by eating less. "I guess he would let you starve, I don't know," Truman said.

Reported by the press, the remark stung Taft into responding with a speech castigating Truman for "blackguarding Congress at every whistle station in the West." Truman and the Democrats struck back, accusing Taft of insulting Truman's campaign stops by implying they were backward, rural communities. In Los Angeles Truman joked that the city was the biggest whistle stop he had made. He changed Taft's "whistle station" to "whistle stop" and the phrase stuck.

Truman went on to score an upset victory over New York governor Thomas A. Dewey, who according to the POLLS was almost certain to win.

Truman did not invent campaigning by train, however. In 1896 Democrat William Jennings Bryan traveled eighteen thousand miles and made six hundred speeches while his incumbent opponent, William McKinley, campaigned from his front porch in Canton, Ohio. McKinley won.

In 1992 buses replaced trains as the transportation mode of choice by Bill Clinton and his running mate, Al Gore. After the Democrats' NATIONAL PARTY CONVENTION they took off on an intercity bus version of Truman's whistle-stop tour. After the GOP convention, President George Bush went on vacation, and lost the November election. He did, however, win his vacation state, Florida, which was still recovering from the devastation of Hurricane Andrew.

---

## White Primary

Closely connected with the history of the SOUTHERN PRIMARY is the issue of race. A number of exclusionary devices were used to keep blacks from voting in the DEMOCRATIC PARTY primary, which in effect was the election because the party had no real opposition throughout the South. Among those devices was the so-called white primary, in which the party designated itself a private association or club, open only to whites. (See PRIMARY TYPES.)

After primaries came into general use for nominating party candidates, it was not clear that Congress had the authority to regulate primaries as it did regular elections. The Supreme Court added to the confusion in a 1921 ruling, *Newberry v. United States,* that implied Congress lacked such power.

The doubt created by the Court encouraged the eleven states of the old Confederacy to exclude blacks from the primaries. The states or counties holding white primaries defended the practice as constitutional because the Fifteenth Amendment, ratified in 1870, prohibited only *states,* not private associations, from denying the RIGHT TO VOTE to persons on account of race or color.

Five times after the *Newberry* decision the issue of white primaries came before the Supreme Court in cases from Texas and Louisiana. In two Texas cases in 1927 and 1932 the Court agreed with a black man, Dr. L. A. Nixon, that he had been wrongfully excluded from the Democratic primary by the legislature or the party as a delegate of the state. But in 1935 in *Grovey v. Townsend* the Court upheld the right of the Texas Democratic Party, acting on its own as a private association, to close its primaries to nonmembers.

In 1941, however, the Supreme Court discarded the *Newberry* restriction on federal regulation of primaries. It declared in *United States v. Classic,* a Louisiana case unrelated to racial discrimination, that Congress has the power to regulate primaries as it does other elections. Three years later, in *Smith v. Allwright,* the Court declared the white primary unconstitutional, holding that a primary was an integral part of the election machinery for choosing state and federal officials.

Lonnie E. Smith, a black man who sued after Texas officials barred him from the primary, was represented by attorneys from the National Association for the Advancement of Colored People, including Thurgood

Marshall, who later became the first African American on the Supreme Court.

## Winner Take All

Most elections, whether of government officials or officers of private clubs, are decided on the winner-take-all system. It is the simplest kind of election to conduct and the easiest to understand: the person who receives the most votes wins the office being sought.

Members of Congress and most state legislators are elected under the winner-take-all rule. They run in SINGLE-MEMBER DISTRICTS (which may be the whole state in the case of candidates for U.S. Senate and some U.S. House seats) and win if they receive at least a PLURALITY of the vote.

A more complicated system, PROPORTIONAL REPRESENTATION, is more likely to give fair representation to the various racial, ethnic, and other demographic or political groups within a state or district. Under proportional representation seats are distributed among candidates in proportion to their share of the POPULAR VOTE. To do this, however, requires the use of MULTI-MEMBER DISTRICTS or a similar form of multiple representation in the geographical area covered by the election. Then if a ten-member district is 40 percent African American, for example, the black community has a reasonable chance of winning four of the ten seats if it puts up a full complement of candidates.

A few states had multimember CONGRESSIONAL DISTRICTS until Congress abolished them in 1842. Some state legislative districts or city council wards still elect multiple members.

In PRESIDENTIAL PRIMARIES, delegates to the NATIONAL PARTY CONVENTIONS usually are awarded on the basis of proportional representation rather than winner-take-all. In many cases a candidate must meet a THRESHOLD RULE, such as 15 percent of the vote, before winning any delegates. Some Republican primaries use winner-take-all, but the Democratic Party does not allow them.

Presidential elections are won or lost on a winner-take-all basis. The state's popular vote winner receives all of the state's electoral votes. In the ELECTORAL COLLEGE, the leading candidate must receive an ABSOLUTE MAJORITY of the 538 votes to become president.

## Winograd Commission

*See* PRESIDENTIAL SELECTION REFORMS.

## Women's Suffrage

Full voting rights were not extended to all American women until 1920, when the Nineteenth Amendment to the Constitution won ratification from the states. That year, for the first time, women in every state had the right to participate in the November election. The amendment states: "The right of citizens of the United States to vote shall not be denied or abridged by the United States or by any State on account of sex."

Almost one hundred years elapsed between the time the fight for women's suffrage began in earnest, before the Civil War, and the Nineteenth Amendment won approval. Pioneer suffragists were women active in the antislavery movement who were struck by the similarity between their lot, under law, and that of slaves.

Ironically, male former slaves or descendants of slaves gained the RIGHT TO VOTE long before women did, although southern states thwarted that right well into the twentieth century with a variety of devices such as LITERACY TESTS, POLL TAXES, and the WHITE PRIMARY. The Fifteenth Amendment to the Constitution, ratified in 1870, made it illegal to deny the vote "on account of race, color, or previous condition of servitude." At that time, the amendment affected only men. (See BLACK SUFFRAGE.)

### History of the Movement

Before the Civil War, three significant events in women's suffrage took place at about the same time. One was the 1848 Women's Rights Convention called by Lucretia Mott and Elizabeth Cady Stanton at Seneca

*Suffragists and their supporters march for women's rights in front of New York City's Flatiron building. Women would not be granted universal suffrage until 1920. Source: Library of Congress*

Falls, New York, Stanton's hometown. The two women persuaded the convention to take the highly controversial step of including a call for the vote in its declaration of principles. This act marked the unofficial start of the women's suffrage movement.

The second major event was the first national suffrage convention, organized at Worcester, Massachusetts, in 1850 by Lucy Stone, who later founded the American Woman Suffrage Association. Two years later Stanton and Susan B. Anthony jointly organized another convention, this one at Syracuse, New York. Both women, like Lucy Stone, were veterans of the effort to abolish slavery. Anthony had vowed to "ignore all laws

to help the slave, [and] ignore it all to protect an enslaved woman."

Also prominent in both the abolition and suffrage causes were Victoria Claflin Woodhull and Sojourner Truth. Woodhull, a spiritualist and preacher, ran for president in 1872, before women could vote. Her RUNNING MATE was African American leader Frederick Douglass. Truth, a former slave born Isabella, was known for her "Aren't I a woman?" speech to a mid-1800s women's convention. She later fell out with Mott, Stanton, and other white suffragists because she thought black men should have the vote before women.

After the Civil War, Anthony and others contended

that the Fourteenth Amendment (1868), which forbade states to "abridge the privileges or immunities of citizens of the United States," had given women equal rights, including voting rights. The amendment set penalties for any state that denied the vote to its adult male inhabitants, without reference to race. Undeterred by the fact that the amendment specified *male* inhabitants, the militant women seized upon its broader recognition of equality. They also contended that the Fifteenth Amendment's use of the word *race* was not meant to exclude women but was instead meant to suggest a type of forbidden discrimination. The combined effect of the Fourteenth and Fifteenth Amendments undergirded the demand for women's suffrage.

In St. Louis, suffragists Francis and Virginia Minor were among those who argued that the Fourteenth and Fifteenth Amendments implied a national citizenship that included voting rights. They encouraged test cases, and Virginia Minor's own denial of registration reached the Supreme Court. In *Minor v. Happersett* (1875) the Court dismissed the national citizenship theory and declared that the Constitution conferred no suffrage rights. Women's suffrage would have to come from the states or a constitutional amendment.

In 1872 Anthony and fifteen other women were arrested for "voting without a lawful right to vote" in Rochester, New York, after registering under the Fourteenth Amendment's guarantee of protection of citizens' privileges and immunities. Anthony never paid the $100 fine. She and her followers then pressed Congress for a constitutional amendment granting the FRANCHISE to women, but the Senate rejected the proposal 16–34 in 1887.

The suffragists were more successful in the states. By the end of the nineteenth century four western states had extended the franchise to women, beginning with Wyoming in 1890, followed by Colorado in 1893 and Utah and Idaho in 1896. Then, as the PROGRESSIVE movement gained influence, additional states gave women the vote: Washington in 1910; California in 1911; Arizona, Kansas, and Oregon in 1912; Montana and Nevada in 1914; New York in 1917; and Michigan, South Dakota, and Oklahoma in 1918.

Arguments for and against the vote included extravagant claims. Some said women's enfranchisement would end corruption in American politics; others cautioned that it would lead to free love. Those in favor of keeping the status quo argued that women had virtual representation in government through the votes of husbands, fathers, and other men in their lives.

Activist suffragettes (as women suffragists were sometimes called) did not accept that rationale. By 1914 some advocates, led by Alice Paul, president of the National Women's Party, were using more militant tactics. They opposed every Democratic candidate in the eleven states where women could vote, regardless of the candidate's position on women's suffrage. They reasoned that the majority party should be held responsible for the failure of Congress to endorse a constitutional amendment. More than half of the forty-three Democrats running in those races were defeated.

Many suffragists saw President Woodrow Wilson as a major obstacle to their movement, even though he favored women's suffrage. Wilson preferred to let the states handle voting qualifications and was opposed to the idea of a constitutional amendment. Women responded by demonstrating in Washington, and thousands were arrested and jailed.

In January 1918 Wilson finally announced his support for the proposed amendment. The House agreed the next day. Only after a new Congress met in 1919, however, did the Senate join the House in mustering the two-thirds majority required to send the amendment to the states for ratification. The amendment took effect in August 1920, when three-fourths of the states had consented to ratification.

After the Nineteenth Amendment took effect, VOTER TURNOUT rose significantly. The amendment added women in thirty-three states to those in the fifteen states that had already granted the vote to women. The total vote for president in 1916, when Wilson won reelection, was 18.5 million. Four years later, when Republican Warren G. Harding defeated Democrat James M. Cox, the turnout was 26.8 million.

Harding was the first president elected after all American women became eligible to vote. The last president elected entirely by men—before any state had enfranchised women—was Benjamin Harrison, Republican, in 1888.

## Aftermath

In 1921 a marble statue honoring suffragists Anthony, Stanton, and Mott was dedicated in the Rotunda of the U.S. Capitol. Congress had grudgingly accepted the gift at the insistence of Alice Paul.

The day after its dedication the statue was moved to the Crypt area below the main floor level. Irreverently nicknamed "Three Ladies in a Bathtub," the statue has been viewed by millions of Capitol visitors.

Women's rights advocates protested the location, however, and raised private funds to have it moved in 1997 to the Rotunda area for a one-year trial. Some African American women's leaders tried unsuccessfully to stop the move because the statue did not depict Sojourner Truth.

The sculptor, Adelaide Johnson, left an uncarved background to the statue to symbolize the unfinished fight for women's rights. She died in 1955 at age 108.

Today, some eighty years after the Nineteenth Amendment was ratified, women are represented in the Capitol not only by a statue but also by statutes they have helped to enact. As of 1998 more than 150 women had served as senators and representatives. The first woman in Congress was Jeannette Rankin, a Montana Republican elected to the House in 1916 when only a handful of states permitted women to vote. Rankin later served another two-year term, 1941–1943.

The 106th Congress, 1999–2001, had sixty-seven women members—nine in the Senate and fifty-eight in the House. Yet the United States ranked only thirty-ninth among 160 legislatures in female representation, according to the Inter-Parliamentary Union. Sweden ranked first.

In the electorate, women voters drew special attention from candidates and the media in 1996, particularly the young suburban women known as "soccer moms." They were viewed as a swing vote group although they made up only 6 percent of the voting age population.

Women as a whole, however, did have the votes to swing the election. EXIT POLLS indicated that, for the first time, the female vote did not mirror the male vote in presidential choice. Women preferred Bill Clinton 54 percent to 37 percent, while men chose Robert J. Dole 44 percent to 43 percent.

If women could not vote, Dole may have been elected. Election analysts believed that Clinton won the women's vote because he did a better job of addressing so-called women's issues: children, education, community, the future, sex and violence on television, and similar close-to-home concerns.

The League of Women Voters, successor in 1920 to the National American Woman Suffrage Association (formed in 1890 by a merger of the American Woman Suffrage Association and Stanton and Anthony's National Woman Suffrage Association), sponsored televised presidential DEBATES in 1976–1984. Since 1988 the sponsor has been the Commission on Presidential Debates.

Sixty-two years after ratification of the Nineteenth Amendment, the proposed Equal Rights Amendment (ERA) died because it fell three states short of the thirty-eight needed for ratification. In spirit, if not in potential application, the ERA was related to the women's suffrage movement. Alice Paul had proposed an early version of it. The failed amendment, as sent to the states by Congress in 1972, said in part, "Equality of rights under the law shall not be abridged or denied by the United States or by any state on account of sex."

---

# Workers World Party (1959– )

With the Hungarian citizen revolt and other developments in Eastern Europe providing some impetus, the Workers World Party in 1959 split off from the SOCIALIST WORKERS PARTY. The party theoretically supports worker uprisings in all parts of the world. Yet it backed the communist governments that put down rebellions in Hungary during the 1950s, Czechoslovakia in the 1960s, and Poland in the 1980s. Workers World is an activist revolutionary group that, up until 1980, concentrated its efforts on specific issues, such as the antiwar and civil rights demonstrations during the 1960s and 1970s. The party has an active youth organization, Youth Against War and Fascism.

In 1980 party leaders saw an opportunity, created by the weakness of the U.S. economy and the related high unemployment, to interest voters in its revolutionary ideas. That year it placed Deirdre Griswold, the editor of the party's newspaper and one of its founding members, on the presidential ballot in ten states. Together with her RUNNING MATE Larry Holmes, a twenty-seven-year-old black activist, Griswold received 13,300 votes. In 1984 Holmes ran as the presidential candidate, getting on the ballot in eight states and receiving 15,329 votes. In 1988 Holmes ran with Gloria La Riva, and they garnered 7,846 votes. La Riva ran as the presidential candidate in 1992 and was on the ballot only in New Mexico, where she received 181 votes.

The Workers World Party dramatically improved its electoral fortunes in 1996. Its candidate, Monica Moorehead of New Jersey, was on the ballot in twelve states and received 29,082 votes.

---

# Write-In Vote

Voters sometimes choose not to vote for any candidate listed on a ballot. At such times they may instead write in the name of another person. This voting option is usually available under regulations that vary from state to state.

Perhaps more than any other aspect of elections, write-in voting has held an uncertain place in the constitutional guarantee of the RIGHT TO VOTE. This ambiguity reflects the perceived inefficiency of counting write-in votes when elections are conducted with printed ballots or VOTING MACHINES.

The U.S. Constitution leaves to each state the administration of its own elections and also gives each state the dominant role in conducting federal elections within its borders. Additionally, the Supreme Court has taken into account the need for substantial state regulation of the electoral process so that elections may be held in a fair and orderly way. (See STATE AND FEDERAL ELECTION RESPONSIBILITIES.)

At the same time, however, the Court in numerous instances has upheld voters' rights and invalidated some state regulations as too restrictive. Many observers therefore were surprised when the Court ruled 6–3 in a Hawaii case June 8, 1992, that states may prohibit write-in voting altogether, rejecting arguments that such action violates citizens' rights to free speech and political association. The Court made it clear, however, that a state is free to provide for write-in voting and that the Court's decision should not be read to discourage such voting.

In the colonial period and in the early decades of the United States, all voting by ballots was, in a sense, write-in voting. Preprinted ballots were not yet in use, and voters wrote on their ballots the name of their choice for public office. Actually, during that time most elections, especially in the South, were decided by voice vote.

## Secret Ballot

In the face of widespread voting corruption, the Australian ballot was introduced in the United States in the 1880s; it filled the need for an absolutely secret and indistinguishable ballot. Its size, shape, and color gave no indication of what candidates or political parties the user voted for. Previously, parties printed and distributed their own ballots, making SPLIT TICKET or THIRD PARTY voting difficult if not impossible. (See BALLOT TYPES.)

By about 1910 most of the states had adopted the Australian system. About that time, too, voting machines were beginning to be used, and in the computer age they play an ever-larger role in elections.

Generally, after the Australian ballot came into use, states made a blank line on the paper ballots available for write-in votes. Then too, manufacturers of voting machines typically included a device that made write-in votes possible, if seldom easy.

The history of elections is replete with failed write-in candidacies. But in at least two instances write-in votes have had national significance. An impressive demonstration of voter sentiment occurred in Minnesota's 1952 Republican PRESIDENTIAL PRIMARY when more than a hundred thousand voters wrote in Dwight D.

Eisenhower's name. That showing of strength gave Eisenhower a commanding lead in his contest with Sen. Robert A. Taft of Ohio for the GOP nomination. Two years later, Strom Thurmond, a former governor of South Carolina, received 143,442 write-in votes in the Democratic primary election for U.S. senator, defeating the PARTY ENDORSED candidate. At that time a Democratic SOUTHERN PRIMARY victory virtually ensured election. Thurmond, who switched to the Republican Party in 1964, is the only U.S. senator to owe election to write-in votes.

Because the Australian ballot tended to diminish the rights of citizens to vote for persons not listed on the printed ballots, many state courts took actions in the late nineteenth century upholding write-in voting. State courts also played a significant role in asserting the option of write-in voting when automated voting became the rule in heavily populated areas.

## Balancing Test

The U.S Supreme Court has provided the states with considerable leeway in their conduct of elections. In an Ohio case, *Anderson v. Celebrezze,* the Court in 1983 established a so-called balancing test for reviewing election rules. The balancing test requires that any court must first determine whether, and to what extent, an election law injures a voter's First Amendment rights. Next, the court must decide whether the state's interests are sufficient to justify the burden imposed on the voter's First Amendment rights.

In the case, brought by INDEPENDENT presidential candidate John B. Anderson in 1980, the Court found in Anderson's favor, overturning a lower federal court that had upheld Ohio's early filing deadline for independent candidates. Despite such deadlines and various SORE LOSER LAWS, Anderson had managed to appear on the ballot in every state in 1980 as an opponent to President Jimmy Carter and his successful Republican CHALLENGER, Ronald Reagan.

The Supreme Court used its balancing test in deciding the 1992 Hawaii write-in case, *Burdick v. Takushi.* The state's prohibition of write-in voting was permissible, the majority said, because the ban imposed only a "very limited burden" on voters' rights.

Hawaii in 1992 was one of three states (the others were Oklahoma and Nevada) that banned write-in voting. Thirty-six other states restricted write-ins in a significant way. In the *Washington Post* April 14, 1991, before the *Burdick* decision, political reporter David Broder wrote, "Hawaii is virtually a one-party state. . . . The ruling Democrats have rigged the laws so that, where there is no opponent the office does not even appear on the general election ballot." Indeed, Alan Burdick, the Honolulu voter who challenged his state's write-in ban, did not want to vote for a Democratic candidate unopposed in his local legislative district.

Writing for the three Supreme Court dissenters, Justice Anthony M. Kennedy said large numbers of Hawaiian voters cast blank ballots in uncontested races. He said that "many Hawaii voters are dissatisfied with the choices available to them. The write-in ban thus prevents these voters from participating in Hawaii elections in a meaningful manner."

# Y

## Yellow Dog Democrat

*See* BLUE DOG DEMOCRAT; BRASS COLLAR DEMO-
CRAT.

## Youth Suffrage

The most recent constitutional change affecting the
RIGHT TO VOTE was the lowering of the voting age to
eighteen. The Twenty-sixth Amendment made the
change in 1971.

Before World War II no state permitted voting by
persons under twenty-one. Led by Georgia's wartime
lowering of the voting age in 1943, after a drive marked
by the CAMPAIGN SLOGAN "Fight at Eighteen, Vote at
Eighteen," several states passed the more liberal requirement. President Dwight D. Eisenhower proposed a constitutional amendment in 1954, but it died in a Senate
committee.

Sixteen years later, in the midst of the Vietnam War,
Congress included an age provision in the 1970 amendments to the 1965 VOTING RIGHTS ACT. The amendments set a minimum voting age of eighteen for all federal, state, and local elections. But later in 1970, by a 5–4
vote in OREGON V. MITCHELL, the Supreme Court declared the age requirement unconstitutional for state
and local elections. Although it upheld most other sections of the act, including the lower voting age in federal elections, the Court said Congress exceeded its authority in attempting to overrule state constitutions that
set the voting age between nineteen and twenty-one.

Congress and the states promptly moved to correct
the situation, which would have required election officials in some states to maintain two sets of VOTER REG-
ISTRATION rolls—one for presidential and congressional elections, and the other for state and local elections. Ratification of the Twenty-sixth Amendment in
1971 took only 107 days—less than half the time needed
to ratify any other amendment.

The amendment states: "The right of citizens of the
United States, who are eighteen years of age or older, to
vote shall not be denied or abridged by the United
States or by any State on account of age."

### Test Case Sought

Although the Constitution leaves presidents out of
the procedure for passing amendments, presidents can
use the "bully pulpit" of their office to try to influence
their approval or defeat by Congress or the states. In the
case of the Twenty-sixth Amendment, President
Richard Nixon urged Congress in 1970 to work on such
an amendment in case the Supreme Court invalidated
Congress's action lowering the voting age in state elections to eighteen—which it ultimately did in *Oregon v.
Mitchell.* At Nixon's direction, Attorney General John N.
Mitchell helped to bring about the suit in which he was
named, resulting in a speedy determination that Congress alone could not lower the vote age for all elections.

Before the amendment was ratified, only four states
permitted voting under age twenty-one. Besides Georgia, they were Kentucky, which also set the minimum at
eighteen; Hawaii, twenty; and Alaska, nineteen. Voters
in three states—New Jersey, Ohio, and Oregon—had recently rejected lower voting ages. Fifteen other states
planned to hold referendums on the issue in the 1970
elections.

The Twenty-sixth Amendment was the fourth
amendment to enlarge the electorate since the Constitution was adopted in 1789. The others were the Fif-

*Democratic presidential candidate Bill Clinton talks with young people on a program hosted by the MTV cable channel in 1992. In spite of efforts to engage youthful voters, their participation has steadily declined since 1972. Source: MTV*

teenth, which gave the vote to former slaves and their descendants (1870); the Nineteenth, which enfranchised women (1920); and the Twenty-third, which permitted Washington, D.C., residents to vote for president (1961). (See BLACK SUFFRAGE; DISTRICT OF COLUMBIA; WOMEN'S SUFFRAGE.)

Some 11 million young Americans gained the right to vote because of the Twenty-sixth Amendment. Another 14 million became eligible to vote for president for the first time in 1972 because in the 1968 election they had been under twenty-one, the minimum voting age then in effect in most states.

## Appeals to Young Voters

In the 1972 election, both President Nixon and his Democratic opponent, Sen. George S. McGovern of

South Dakota, courted the youth vote. An estimated 7.5 million of the newly eligible young voters were students, and McGovern's anti–Vietnam War stance was popular on campuses. The McGovern campaign concentrated its efforts on the student segment of the young voters.

The Nixon campaign aimed its appeal at the larger, nonstudent group of young voters, numbering about 17.5 million. They included workers, housewives, soldiers, and job seekers.

According to a profile by the Commerce Department, a typical young first-time voter in 1972 was white, single, living in a family, not going to school. He or she was a high school graduate, a job holder, and lived in a metropolitan area.

A Gallup POLL before the November 1972 election indicated that college students were almost evenly divided between Nixon and McGovern. Earlier polls had shown McGovern leading Nixon among young voters by a substantial margin. On that basis McGovern's organization initially predicted a 10-million-vote victory, which never happened.

Nixon was reelected with 60.7 percent of the POPULAR VOTE, a LANDSLIDE second only to Lyndon B. Johnson's 61.1 percent in 1964. McGovern and his RUNNING MATE, R. Sargent Shriver, won only Massachusetts and the District of Columbia. (McGovern's original running mate, Sen. Thomas Eagleton of Missouri, had dropped out after it was disclosed he had received treatment for depression years earlier.)

In his reelection statement Nixon attributed his victory partly to the youth vote. He said: "We have accomplished what was thought to be impossible . . . we won a majority of the votes of young Americans."

Nixon's jubilation was short-lived, however. Less than two years later, facing impeachment, he resigned from office for his role in the Watergate SCANDAL stem-ming from a burglary before the 1972 election at the DEMOCRATIC NATIONAL COMMITTEE headquarters.

The youth vote in 1972 also proved to be disappointing to Democratic challengers in a half-dozen House districts containing large universities. Only two of the challengers won, and neither attributed his victory to the student vote.

New voters eighteen to twenty years old showed no great enthusiasm for going to the polls in 1972 or later. Their VOTER TURNOUT rate in the 1972 election was 48.3 percent, compared with 55.2 percent for the population as a whole. Since then voting participation among young people has declined. Their 1996 turnout was 31.2 percent, compared with 54.2 percent for the population as a whole. According to CENSUS figures, there were 10,785,000 Americans in the eighteen-to-twenty age group in 1996, and 4,919,000 of those or 45.6 percent were registered to vote. Of those, only 3,366,000 actually voted.

# Z

## ZZZ

The cartoon symbol of sleep—*ZZZ*—illustrated many Americans' attitude toward politics and elections as the nation slumped toward the twenty-first century. Signs of voter apathy, boredom, and cynicism abounded.

POLL after PUBLIC OPINION poll showed a lack of interest and sense of futility among the electorate. Political reporters Jack Germond and Jules Witcover entitled their book on the 1992 election *Wake Me When It's Over.* Long after it was over, the public was still asleep.

The collective blahs were reflected in declining VOTER TURNOUT rates in the United States. Only 49.0 percent of the voting age population turned out for the 1996 presidential election, the lowest rate in seventy-two years.

As expected in a MIDTERM ELECTION, the turnout rate was still lower for the 1998 congressional races— about 36 percent. Even that figure was somewhat higher than expected. Polls indicated that many voters were energized by the impending House impeachment of President Bill Clinton in connection with the Monica Lewinsky SCANDAL. Although it failed to deter the Republican-controlled House, the election sent an apparent anti-impeachment message. Instead of losing seats as is normally the case at midterm, especially a second midterm, the president's party gained five House seats and maintained the status quo in the Senate.

Among young people, "Get some ZZZ's" is a popular expression meaning, "Get some sleep." And young voters apparently find politics even more boring than their elders do. The youth turnout in the 1996 election was only 31.2 percent, the lowest since the voting age was reduced to eighteen nationwide in 1971.

Many voters feel that their vote does not count, despite the sharply conflicting evidence that a few votes' difference could have changed the outcome of scores of close U.S. elections. "In Maryland, Indifference Is Consensus," read a *Washington Post* headline in August 1998. Never mind that the upcoming election was a replay of the race between Democratic governor Parris N. Glendening, the winner, and Republican Ellen Sauerbrey— one of the closest, most bitterly fought CONTESTED ELECTIONS of 1994. (Glendening won the second matchup by a comfortable margin.)

Other headlines echoed the same: "Many More Non-Voters in '96 Were 'Too Busy.'" "Up from Apathy." "Campaigns as Seen Through a Filter of Cynicism." "Pols on Pins and Needles Worried About Turnout at the Polls." "Are You Apathetic About Fall's Election? You're Written Off."

Although no more evidence was needed, the 1998 elections proved once again that each vote does count. In Nevada, Democrat Harry Reid won reelection to the U.S. Senate by a scant 401 votes out of more than 400,000 cast. A RECOUNT confirmed Reid's defeat of challenger John Ensign, a Republican House member.

Reid's squeaker rivaled the 1974 Senate race in New Hampshire between Republican Louis C. Wyman and Democrat John A. Durkin. On election night Wyman led by 355 votes out of about 222,000 cast. A recount reduced Wyman's lead to ten votes, and another further reduced it to only two votes—the closest Senate race in history.

Durkin's protest of the results led to a bitter, seven-month Senate wrangle and forty-one roll-call votes about who won. Finally, the Senate declared the seat vacant and Durkin handily won the special election.

Local elections in 1998 also produced some single-digit margins of victory. A Maryland House of Dele-

gates nomination was won by five votes. In the same state, only eight votes separated the winner and loser of the Republican primary for comptroller. In the general election, the GOP nominee was overwhelmingly defeated by former governor William Donald Schaefer. Democrat Schaefer's uninhibited antics for the camera enlivened many of his campaigns. He once donned an old-time bathing suit for a plunge into the Baltimore aquarium. The *Washington Post* headlined his surprise bid for the comptroller vacancy "Just the Ticket for a Slow Race."

Not every candidate can swim with seals—or wants to—but many have shown that a memorable CAMPAIGN SLOGAN or a novel CAMPAIGN STRATEGY, such as walking across the state as some governors have done, can go a long way to attracting favorable attention and overcoming voter apathy.

As campaigns have become more expensive and professional, the major political parties have partially forsaken their traditional role as grass roots mobilizers to concentrate on CAMPAIGN FINANCE and candidate consulting. The vacuum they have left has been filled to some extent by labor unions, environmental groups, and Christian political organizations.

In 1998, for example, the AFL-CIO budgeted three times as much money for GET-OUT-THE-VOTE drives as for issue ads, a controversial form of POLITICAL ADVERTISING that allows interest groups to boost favored candidates without exceeding federal or state contribution limits. EMILY's List, a political action committee (PAC) that supports prochoice candidates, spent $3 million in the same election to get women to vote.

Poor as the turnout is in November elections, it is even worse in party primaries. PARTY IDENTIFICA-

TION among voters is down, and the decrease is reflected in lackluster participation in primaries. In 1998 the primary turnout rate was 17.5 percent, the lowest since 1962 when primaries began to peak in number and participation.

Leaving the nominating process only to interested party members may not produce the best candidates and can be downright foolhardy if too few voters pay attention. In an Indiana 1998 primary, for example, Democrats were embarrassed to discover they had nominated a convicted felon to run for Congress. He was not elected.

Some, perhaps most, political and social scientists regard low voter turnout as a sign of weakness, an indication that democracy is not working. Others contend that apathy indicates a satisfied electorate, one that is not angry or eager to "throw the rascals out."

Consequently, there is little agreement about the danger of low turnout and what to do about it. Although other Western democracies have much higher turnout rates than the United States, some of the methods they employ to boost participation—such as fines for nonvoting—likely would not be acceptable to Americans. Others, such as making ELECTION DAY a holiday or moving it to a weekend, have never been seriously considered. (See INTERNATIONAL AND U.S. ELECTIONS COMPARED.)

The biggest step toward making it easier to register and vote was the MOTOR VOTER ACT of 1993, which allows citizens to obtain registration forms at motor vehicle registries and other government offices. But in its first few years of operation the act showed no appreciable effect on voting.

Voting by mail has shown promise at increasing turnout, but it also has its detractors, including Curtis Gans, director of the Committee for the Study of the American Electorate. Comparing recent turnouts in mail votes in Oregon (which voted in 1998 to hold all future elections by mail) and conventional elections in Pennsylvania, Gans noted that the Oregon rate was higher by the same margin that it always was higher than Pennsylvania's. By mailing their ballots as soon as they get them, Gans said, voters deprive themselves of information available to those who vote later.

Some states have instituted early voting or relaxed ABSENTEE VOTING to make it easier for residents to vote. But even these benign measures are opposed by some hardliners who feel that it is a mistake to encourage "lazy, ignorant" people to vote.

Nonvoters, however, understandably bristle at being called lazy or ignorant. According to one poll, 4.6 million nonvoters in 1996 could not take time off from work or were otherwise "too busy." That group outnumbered the 3.5 million cases of simple voter apathy. They said they just did not care about the election.

So if the ZZZ sound is heard on election day it may not be snoring. It may be people who are busy sawing wood.

# Appendices

Constitution of the United States

Changes in Democrats' Nominating Rules

Democratic Party's Reform Commissions on
Presidential Selection

Republican Party's Reform Committees on
Presidential Selection

Election-Related Web Sites

Presidential Nominating Campaigns, 1980–1996

National Party Chairs, 1848–1999

Major Platform Fights

Democratic Conventions, 1832–1996

Republican Conventions, 1856–1996

Chief Officers and Keynote Speakers at Democratic
National Conventions, 1832–1996

Chief Officers and Keynote Speakers at Republican
National Conventions, 1856–1996

General Election Debates, 1960–1996

U.S. Presidents and Vice Presidents

Summary of Presidential Elections, 1789–1996

1996 Popular Vote Summary, Presidential

Distribution of House Seats and Electoral Votes

Law for Counting Electoral Votes in Congress

Party Affiliations in Congress and the Presidency,
1789–2001

Incumbents Reelected, Defeated, or Retired,
1946–1998

Blacks in Congress, 41st–106th Congresses,
1869–2001

Hispanic Americans in Congress, 45th–106th
Congresses, 1877–2001

Women in Congress, 65th–106th Congresses,
1917–2001

Senate Votes Cast by Vice Presidents

State Government

# Constitution of the United States

*The United States Constitution was written at a convention that Congress called on February 21, 1787, for the purpose of recommending amendments to the Articles of Confederation. Every state but Rhode Island sent delegates to Philadelphia, where the convention met that summer. The delegates decided to write an entirely new constitution, completing their labors on September 17. Nine states (the number the Constitution itself stipulated as sufficient) ratified by June 21, 1788.*

*The presidency is the most original feature of the Constitution. Described mainly in Article II, it was created as a strong, unitary office. The president was to be elected by an electoral college to a four-year term.*

*Under Article I, congressional elections were to be held every two years, with all House members and one-third of the senators up for election. Senators, two for each state, were elected by state legislatures for six-year terms. Popular election of senators began with ratification of the Seventeenth Amendment (1913).*

*Several other constitutional amendments have dealt with elections. Among them, the Twelfth (1804) specified separate electoral college voting for president and vice president; the Fourteenth (1868) required states to give full male suffrage or lose House seats; the Fifteenth (1870) enfranchised former slaves; the Nineteenth (1920) gave the vote to women; the Twenty-second (1951) limited presidents to two terms; and the Twenty-sixth (1971) lowered the voting age to eighteen nationally.*

We the People of the United States, in Order to form a more perfect Union, establish Justice, insure domestic Tranquility, provide for the common defence, promote the general Welfare, and secure the Blessings of Liberty to ourselves and our Posterity, do ordain and establish this Constitution for the United States of America.

## ARTICLE I

**Section 1.** All legislative Powers herein granted shall be vested in a Congress of the United States, which shall consist of a Senate and House of Representatives.

**Section 2.** The House of Representatives shall be composed of Members chosen every second Year by the People of the several States, and the Electors in each State shall have the Qualifications requisite for Electors of the most numerous Branch of the State Legislature.

No Person shall be a Representative who shall not have attained to the age of twenty five Years, and been seven Years a Citizen of the United States, and who shall not, when elected, be an Inhabitant of that State in which he shall be chosen.

[Representatives and direct Taxes shall be apportioned among the several States which may be included within this Union, according to their respective Numbers, which shall be determined by adding to the whole Number of free Persons, including those bound to Service for a Term of Years, and excluding Indians not taxed, three fifths of all other Persons.][1] The actual Enumeration shall be made within three Years after the first Meeting of the Congress of the United States, and within every subsequent Term of ten Years, in such Manner as they shall by Law direct. The Number of Representatives shall not exceed one for every thirty Thousand, but each State shall have at Least one Representative; and until such enumeration shall be made, the State of New Hampshire shall be entitled to chuse three, Massachusetts eight, Rhode-Island and Providence Plantations one, Connecticut five, New-York six, New Jersey four, Pennsylvania eight, Delaware one, Maryland six, Virginia ten, North Carolina five, South Carolina five, and Georgia three.

When vacancies happen in the Representation from any State, the Executive Authority thereof shall issue Writs of Election to fill such Vacancies.

The House of Representatives shall chuse their Speaker and other Officers; and shall have the sole Power of Impeachment.

**Section 3.** The Senate of the United States shall be composed of two Senators from each State, [chosen by the Legislature thereof,][2] for six Years; and each Senator shall have one Vote.

Immediately after they shall be assembled in Consequence of the first Election, they shall be divided as equally as may be into three Classes. The Seats of the Senators of the first Class shall be vacated at the Expiration of the second Year, of the second Class at the Expiration of the fourth Year, and of the third Class at the Expiration of the sixth Year, so that one third may be chosen every second Year; [and if Vacancies happen by Resignation, or otherwise, during the Recess of the Legislature of any State, the Executive thereof may make temporary Appointments until the next Meeting of the Legislature, which shall then fill such Vacancies.]³

No Person shall be a Senator who shall not have attained to the Age of thirty Years, and been nine Years a Citizen of the United States, and who shall not, when elected, be an Inhabitant of that State for which he shall be chosen.

The Vice President of the United States shall be President of the Senate, but shall have no Vote, unless they be equally divided.

The Senate shall chuse their other Officers, and also a President pro tempore, in the Absence of the Vice President, or when he shall exercise the Office of President of the United States.

The Senate shall have the sole Power to try all Impeachments. When sitting for that Purpose, they shall be on Oath or Affirmation. When the President of the United States is tried, the Chief Justice shall preside: And no Person shall be convicted without the Concurrence of two thirds of the Members present.

Judgment in Cases of Impeachment shall not extend further than to removal from Office, and disqualification to hold and enjoy any Office of honor, Trust or Profit under the United States: but the Party convicted shall nevertheless be liable and subject to Indictment, Trial, Judgment and Punishment, according to Law.

**Section 4.** The Times, Places and Manner of holding Elections for Senators and Representatives, shall be prescribed in each State by the Legislature thereof; but the Congress may at any time by Law make or alter such Regulations, except as to the Places of chusing Senators.

The Congress shall assemble at least once in every Year, and such Meeting shall [be on the first Monday in December],⁴ unless they shall by Law appoint a different Day.

**Section 5.** Each House shall be the Judge of the Elections, Returns and Qualifications of its own Members, and a Majority of each shall constitute a Quorum to do Business; but a smaller Number may adjourn from day to day, and may be authorized to compel the Attendance of absent Members, in such Manner, and under such Penalties as each House may provide.

Each House may determine the Rules of its Proceedings, punish its Members for disorderly Behaviour, and, with the Concurrence of two thirds, expel a Member.

Each House shall keep a Journal of its Proceedings, and from time to time publish the same, excepting such Parts as may in their Judgment require Secrecy; and the Yeas and Nays of the Members of either House on any question shall, at the Desire of one fifth of those Present, be entered on the Journal.

Neither House, during the Session of Congress, shall, without the Consent of the other, adjourn for more than three days, nor to any other Place than that in which the two Houses shall be sitting.

**Section 6.** The Senators and Representatives shall receive a Compensation for their Services, to be ascertained by Law, and paid out of the Treasury of the United States. They shall in all Cases, except Treason, Felony and Breach of the Peace, be privileged from Arrest during their Attendance at the Session of their respective Houses, and in going to and returning from the same; and for any Speech or Debate in either House, they shall not be questioned in any other Place.

No Senator or Representative shall, during the Time for which he was elected, be appointed to any civil Office under the Authority of the United States, which shall have been created, or the Emoluments whereof shall have been encreased during such time; and no Person holding any Office under the United States, shall be a Member of either House during his Continuance in Office.

**Section 7.** All Bills for raising Revenue shall originate in the House of Representatives; but the Senate may propose or concur with Amendments as on other Bills.

Every Bill which shall have passed the House of Representatives and the Senate, shall, before it become a Law, be presented to the President of the United States; If he approve he shall sign it, but if not he shall return it, with his Objections to that House in which it shall have originated, who shall enter the Objections at large on their Journal, and proceed to reconsider it. If after such Reconsideration two thirds of that House shall agree to pass the Bill, it shall be sent, together with the Objections, to the other House, by which it shall likewise be reconsidered, and if approved by two thirds of that House, it shall become a Law. But in all such Cases the Votes of both Houses shall be determined by yeas and Nays, and the Names of the Persons voting for and against the Bill shall be entered on the Journal of each House respectively. If any Bill shall not be returned by the President within ten Days (Sundays excepted) after it shall have been presented to him, the Same shall be a Law, in like Manner as if he had signed it, unless the Congress by their Adjournment prevent its Return, in which Case it shall not be a Law.

Every Order, Resolution, or Vote to which the Concurrence of the Senate and House of Representatives may be necessary (except on a question of Adjournment) shall be presented to the President of the United States; and before the Same shall take Effect, shall be approved by him, or being disapproved by him, shall be repassed by two thirds of the Senate and House of Representatives, according to the Rules and Limitations prescribed in the Case of a Bill.

**Section 8.** The Congress shall have Power To lay and collect Taxes, Duties, Imposts and Excises, to pay the Debts and provide for the common Defence and general Welfare of the United States; but all Duties, Imposts and Excises shall be uniform throughout the United States;

To borrow Money on the credit of the United States;

To regulate Commerce with foreign Nations, and among the several States, and with the Indian Tribes;

To establish an uniform Rule of Naturalization, and uniform Laws on the subject of Bankruptcies throughout the United States;

To coin Money, regulate the Value thereof, and of foreign Coin, and fix the Standard of Weights and Measures;

To provide for the Punishment of counterfeiting the Securities and current Coin of the United States;

To establish Post Offices and post Roads;

To promote the Progress of Science and useful Arts, by securing for limited Times to Authors and Inventors the exclusive Right to their respective Writings and Discoveries;

To constitute Tribunals inferior to the supreme Court;

To define and punish Piracies and Felonies committed on the high Seas, and Offences against the Law of Nations;

To declare War, grant Letters of Marque and Reprisal, and make Rules concerning Captures on Land and Water;

To raise and support Armies, but no Appropriation of Money to that Use shall be for a longer Term than two Years;

To provide and maintain a Navy;

To make Rules for the Government and Regulation of the land and naval Forces;

To provide for calling forth the Militia to execute the Laws of the Union, suppress Insurrections and repel Invasions;

To provide for organizing, arming, and disciplining, the Militia, and for governing such Part of them as may be employed in the Service of the United States, reserving to the States respectively, the Appointment of the Officers, and the Authority of training the Militia according to the discipline prescribed by Congress;

To exercise exclusive Legislation in all Cases whatsoever, over such District (not exceeding ten Miles square) as may, by Cession of particular States, and the Acceptance of Congress, become the Seat of the Government of the United States, and to exercise like Authority over all Places purchased by the Consent of the Legislature of the State in which the Same shall be, for the Erection of Forts, Magazines, Arsenals, dock-Yards, and other needful Buildings;— And

To make all Laws which shall be necessary and proper for carrying into Execution the foregoing Powers, and all other Powers vested by this Constitution in the Government of the United States, or in any Department or Officer thereof.

**Section 9.** The Migration or Importation of such Persons as any of the States now existing shall think proper to admit, shall not be prohibited by the Congress prior to the Year one thousand eight hundred and eight, but a Tax or duty may be imposed on such Importation, not exceeding ten dollars for each Person.

The Privilege of the Writ of Habeas Corpus shall not be suspended, unless when in Cases of Rebellion or Invasion the public Safety may require it.

No Bill of Attainder or ex post facto Law shall be passed.

No Capitation, or other direct, Tax shall be laid, unless in Proportion to the Census or Enumeration herein before directed to be taken.[5]

No Tax or Duty shall be laid on Articles exported from any State.

No Preference shall be given by any Regulation of Commerce or Revenue to the Ports of one State over those of another; nor shall Vessels bound to, or from, one State, be obliged to enter, clear, or pay Duties in another.

No Money shall be drawn from the Treasury, but in Consequence of Appropriations made by Law; and a regular Statement and Account of the Receipts and Expenditures of all public Money shall be published from time to time.

No Title of Nobility shall be granted by the United States: And no Person holding any Office of Profit or Trust under them, shall, without the Consent of the Congress, accept of any present, Emolument, Office, or Title, of any kind whatever, from any King, Prince, or foreign State.

**Section 10.** No State shall enter into any Treaty, Alliance, or Confederation; grant Letters of Marque and Reprisal; coin Money; emit Bills of Credit; make any Thing but gold and silver Coin a Tender in Payment of Debts; pass any Bill of Attainder, ex post facto Law, or Law impairing the Obligation of Contracts, or grant any Title of Nobility.

No State shall, without the Consent of the Congress, lay any Imposts or Duties on Imports or Exports, except what may be absolutely necessary for executing it's inspection Laws: and the net Produce of all Duties and Imposts, laid by any State on Imports or Exports, shall be for the Use of the Treasury of the United States; and all such Laws shall be subject to the Revision and Controul of the Congress.

No State shall, without the Consent of Congress, lay any Duty of Tonnage, keep Troops, or Ships of War in time of Peace, enter into any Agreement or Compact with another State, or with a foreign Power, or engage in War, unless actually invaded, or in such imminent Danger as will not admit of delay.

ARTICLE II

*Section 1.* The executive Power shall be vested in a President of the United States of America. He shall hold his Office during the Term of four Years, and, together with the Vice President, chosen for the same Term, be elected, as follows

Each State shall appoint, in such Manner as the Legislature thereof may direct, a Number of Electors, equal to the whole Number of Senators and Representatives to which the State may be entitled in the Congress: but no Senator or Representative, or Person holding an Office of Trust or Profit under the United States, shall be appointed an Elector.

[The Electors shall meet in their respective States, and vote by Ballot for two Persons, of whom one at least shall not be an Inhabitant of the same State with themselves. And they shall make a List of all the Persons voted for, and of the Number of Votes for each; which List they shall sign and certify, and transmit sealed to the Seat of the Government of the United States, directed to the President of the Senate. The President of the Senate shall, in the Presence of the Senate and House of Representatives, open all the Certificates, and the Votes shall then be counted. The Person having the greatest Number of Votes shall be the President, if such Number be a Majority of the whole Number of Electors appointed; and if there be more than one who have such Majority, and have an equal Number of Votes, then the House of Representatives shall immediately chuse by Ballot one of them for President; and if no Person have a Majority, then from the five highest on the list the said House shall in like Manner chuse the President. But in chusing the President, the Votes shall be taken by States, the Representation from each State having one Vote; A quorum for this Purpose shall consist of a Member or Members from two thirds of the States, and a Majority of all the States shall be necessary to a Choice. In every Case, after the Choice of the President, the Person having the greatest Number of Votes of the Electors shall be the Vice President. But if there should remain two or more who have equal Votes, the Senate shall chuse from them by Ballot the Vice President.][6]

The Congress may determine the Time of chusing the Electors, and the Day on which they shall give their Votes; which Day shall be the same throughout the United States.

No Person except a natural born Citizen, or a Citizen of the United States, at the time of the Adoption of this Constitution, shall be eligible to the Office of President; neither shall any Person be eligible to that Office who shall not have attained to the Age of thirty five Years, and been fourteen Years a Resident within the United States.

In Case of the Removal of the President from Office, or of his Death, Resignation, or Inability to discharge the Powers and Duties of the said Office,[7] the Same shall devolve on the Vice President, and the Congress may by Law provide for the Case of Removal, Death, Resignation or Inability, both of the President and Vice President, declaring what Officer shall then act as President, and such Officer shall act accordingly, until the Disability be removed, or a President shall be elected.

The President shall, at stated Times, receive for his Services, a Compensation, which shall neither be encreased nor diminished during the Period for which he shall have been elected, and he shall not receive within that Period any other Emolument from the United States, or any of them.

Before he enter on the Execution of his Office, he shall take the following Oath or Affirmation:—"I do solemnly swear (or affirm) that I will faithfully execute the Office of President of the United States, and will to the best of my Ability, preserve, protect and defend the Constitution of the United States."

*Section 2.* The President shall be Commander in Chief of the Army and Navy of the United States, and of the Militia of the several States, when called into the actual Service of the United States; he may require the Opinion, in writing, of the principal Officer in each of the executive Departments, upon any Subject relating to the Duties of their respective Offices, and he shall have Power to grant Reprieves and Pardons for Offences against the United States, except in Cases of Impeachment.

He shall have Power, by and with the Advice and Consent of the Senate, to make Treaties, provided two thirds of the Senators present concur; and he shall nominate, and by and with the Advice and Consent of the Senate, shall appoint Ambassadors, other public Ministers and Consuls, Judges of the supreme Court, and all other Officers of the United States, whose Appointments are not herein otherwise provided for, and which shall be established by Law: but the Congress may by Law vest the Appointment of such inferior Officers, as they think proper, in the President alone, in the Courts of Law, or in the Heads of Departments.

The President shall have Power to fill up all Vacancies that may happen during the Recess of the Senate, by granting Commissions which shall expire at the End of their next Session.

*Section 3.* He shall from time to time give to the Congress Information of the State of the Union, and recommend to their Consideration such Measures as he shall judge necessary and expedient; he may, on extraordinary Occasions, convene both Houses, or either of them, and in Case of Disagreement between them, with Respect to the Time of Adjournment, he may adjourn them to such Time as he shall think proper; he shall receive Ambassadors and other public Ministers; he shall take Care that the Laws be faithfully executed, and shall Commission all the Officers of the United States.

**Section 4.** The President, Vice President and all civil Officers of the United States, shall be removed from Office on Impeachment for, and Conviction of, Treason, Bribery, or other high Crimes and Misdemeanors.

## ARTICLE III

**Section 1.** The judicial Power of the United States, shall be vested in one supreme Court, and in such inferior Courts as the Congress may from time to time ordain and establish. The Judges, both of the supreme and inferior Courts, shall hold their Offices during good Behaviour, and shall, at stated Times, receive for their Services, a Compensation, which shall not be diminished during their Continuance in Office.

**Section 2.** The judicial Power shall extend to all Cases, in Law and Equity, arising under this Constitution, the Laws of the United States, and Treaties made, or which shall be made, under their Authority; — to all Cases affecting Ambassadors, other public Ministers and Consuls; —to all Cases of admiralty and maritime Jurisdiction; —to Controversies to which the United States shall be a Party; —to Controversies between two or more States; —between a State and Citizens of another State;[8] —between Citizens of different States; —between Citizens of the same State claiming Lands under Grants of different States, and between a State, or the Citizens thereof, and foreign States, Citizens or Subjects.[8]

In all Cases affecting Ambassadors, other public Ministers and Consuls, and those in which a State shall be Party, the supreme Court shall have original Jurisdiction. In all the other Cases before mentioned, the supreme Court shall have appellate Jurisdiction, both as to Law and Fact, with such Exceptions, and under such Regulations as the Congress shall make.

The Trial of all Crimes, except in Cases of Impeachment, shall be by Jury; and such Trial shall be held in the State where the said Crimes shall have been committed; but when not committed within any State, the Trial shall be at such Place or Places as the Congress may by Law have directed.

**Section 3.** Treason against the United States, shall consist only in levying War against them, or in adhering to their Enemies, giving them Aid and Comfort. No Person shall be convicted of Treason unless on the Testimony of two Witnesses to the same overt Act, or on Confession in open Court.

The Congress shall have Power to declare the Punishment of Treason, but no Attainder of Treason shall work Corruption of Blood, or Forfeiture except during the Life of the Person attainted.

## ARTICLE IV

**Section 1.** Full Faith and Credit shall be given in each State to the public Acts, Records, and judicial Proceedings of every other State. And the Congress may by general Laws prescribe the Manner in which such Acts, Records and Proceedings shall be proved, and the Effect thereof.

**Section 2.** The Citizens of each State shall be entitled to all Privileges and Immunities of Citizens in the several States.

A Person charged in any State with Treason, Felony, or other Crime, who shall flee from Justice, and be found in another State, shall on Demand of the executive Authority of the State from which he fled, be delivered up, to be removed to the State having Jurisdiction of the Crime.

[No Person held to Service or Labour in one State, under the Laws thereof, escaping into another, shall, in Consequence of any Law or Regulation therein, be discharged from such Service or Labour, but shall be delivered up on Claim of the Party to whom such Service or Labour may be due.][9]

**Section 3.** New States may be admitted by the Congress into this Union; but no new State shall be formed or erected within the Jurisdiction of any other State; nor any State be formed by the Junction of two or more States, or Parts of States, without the Consent of the Legislatures of the States concerned as well as of the Congress.

The Congress shall have Power to dispose of and make all needful Rules and Regulations respecting the Territory or other Property belonging to the United States; and nothing in this Constitution shall be so construed as to Prejudice any Claims of the United States, or of any particular State.

**Section 4.** The United States shall guarantee to every State in this Union a Republican Form of Government, and shall protect each of them against Invasion; and on Application of the Legislature, or of the Executive (when the Legislature cannot be convened) against domestic Violence.

## ARTICLE V

The Congress, whenever two thirds of both Houses shall deem it necessary, shall propose Amendments to this Constitution, or, on the Application of the Legislatures of two thirds of the several States, shall call a Convention for proposing Amendments, which, in either Case, shall be valid to all Intents and Purposes, as Part of this Constitution, when ratified by the Legislatures of three fourths of the several States, or by Conventions in three fourths thereof, as the one or the other Mode of Ratification may be proposed by the Congress; Provided [that no Amendment which may be made prior to the Year One thousand eight hundred and eight shall in any Manner affect the first and fourth Clauses in the Ninth Section of the first Article; and][10] that no State, without its Consent, shall be deprived of its equal Suffrage in the Senate.

## ARTICLE VI

All Debts contracted and Engagements entered into, before the Adoption of this Constitution, shall be as valid against the United States under this Constitution, as under the Confederation.

This Constitution, and the Laws of the United States which shall be made in Pursuance thereof; and all Treaties made, or which shall be made, under the Authority of the United States, shall be the supreme Law of the Land; and the Judges in every State shall be bound thereby, any Thing in the Constitution or Laws of any State to the Contrary notwithstanding.

The Senators and Representatives before mentioned, and the Members of the several State Legislatures, and all executive and judicial Officers, both of the United States and of the several States, shall be bound by Oath or Affirmation, to support this Constitution; but no religious Test shall ever be required as a Qualification to any Office or public Trust under the United States.

## ARTICLE VII

The Ratification of the Conventions of nine States, shall be sufficient for the Establishment of this Constitution between the States so ratifying the Same.

Done in Convention by the Unanimous Consent of the States present the Seventeenth Day of September in the Year of our Lord one thousand seven hundred and Eighty seven and of the Independence of the United States of America the Twelfth. IN WITNESS whereof We have hereunto subscribed our Names,

George Washington,
*President and deputy from Virginia.*

[The language of the original Constitution, not including the Amendments, was adopted by a convention of the states on September 17, 1787, and was subsequently ratified by the states on the following dates: Delaware, December 7, 1787; Pennsylvania, December 12, 1787; New Jersey, December 18, 1787; Georgia, January 2, 1788; Connecticut, January 9, 1788; Massachusetts, February 6, 1788; Maryland, April 28, 1788; South Carolina, May 23, 1788; New Hampshire, June 21, 1788.

Ratification was completed on June 21, 1788.

The Constitution subsequently was ratified by Virginia, June 25, 1788; New York, July 26, 1788; North Carolina, November 21, 1789; Rhode Island, May 29, 1790; and Vermont, January 10, 1791.]

## AMENDMENTS

### Amendment I

*(First ten amendments ratified December 15, 1791.)*

Congress shall make no law respecting an establishment of religion, or prohibiting the free exercise thereof; or abridging the freedom of speech, or of the press; or the right of the people peaceably to assemble, and to petition the Government for a redress of grievances.

### Amendment II

A well regulated Militia, being necessary to the security of a free State, the right of the people to keep and bear Arms, shall not be infringed.

### Amendment III

No Soldier shall, in time of peace be quartered in any house, without the consent of the Owner, nor in time of war, but in a manner to be prescribed by law.

### Amendment IV

The right of the people to be secure in their persons, houses, papers, and effects, against unreasonable searches and seizures, shall not be violated, and no Warrants shall issue, but upon probable cause, supported by Oath or affirmation, and particularly describing the place to be searched, and the persons or things to be seized.

### Amendment V

No person shall be held to answer for a capital, or otherwise infamous crime, unless on a presentment or indictment of a Grand Jury, except in cases arising in the land or naval forces, or in the Militia, when in actual service in time of War or public danger; nor shall any person be subject for the same offence to be twice put in jeopardy of life or limb; nor shall be compelled in any criminal case to be a witness against himself, nor be deprived of life, liberty, or property, without due process of law; nor shall private property be taken for public use, without just compensation.

### Amendment VI

In all criminal prosecutions, the accused shall enjoy the right to a speedy and public trial, by an impartial jury of the State and district wherein the crime shall have been committed, which district shall have been previously ascertained by law, and to be informed of the nature and cause of the accusation; to be confronted with the witnesses against him; to have compulsory process for obtaining witnesses in his favor, and to have the Assistance of Counsel for his defence.

### Amendment VII

In Suits at common law, where the value in controversy shall exceed twenty dollars, the right of trial by jury shall be preserved, and no fact tried by a jury, shall be otherwise re-examined in any Court of the United States, than according to the rules of the common law.

## Amendment VIII

Excessive bail shall not be required, nor excessive fines imposed, nor cruel and unusual punishments inflicted.

## Amendment IX

The enumeration in the Constitution, of certain rights, shall not be construed to deny or disparage others retained by the people.

## Amendment X

The powers not delegated to the United States by the Constitution, nor prohibited by it to the States, are reserved to the States respectively, or to the people.

## Amendment XI *(Ratified February 7, 1795)*

The Judicial power of the United States shall not be construed to extend to any suit in law or equity, commenced or prosecuted against one of the United States by Citizens of another State, or by Citizens or Subjects of any Foreign State.

## Amendment XII *(Ratified June 15, 1804)*

The Electors shall meet in their respective states and vote by ballot for President and Vice-President, one of whom, at least, shall not be an inhabitant of the same state with themselves; they shall name in their ballots the person voted for as President, and in distinct ballots the person voted for as Vice-President, and they shall make distinct lists of all persons voted for as President, and of all persons voted for as Vice-President, and of the number of votes for each, which lists they shall sign and certify, and transmit sealed to the seat of the government of the United States, directed to the President of the Senate; — The President of the Senate shall, in the presence of the Senate and House of Representatives, open all the certificates and the votes shall then be counted; — The person having the greatest number of votes for President, shall be the President, if such number be a majority of the whole number of Electors appointed; and if no person have such majority, then from the persons having the highest numbers not exceeding three on the list of those voted for as President, the House of Representatives shall choose immediately, by ballot, the President. But in choosing the President, the votes shall be taken by states, the representation from each state having one vote; a quorum for this purpose shall consist of a member or members from two-thirds of the states, and a majority of all the states shall be necessary to a choice. [And if the House of Representatives shall not choose a President whenever the right of choice shall devolve upon them, before the fourth day of March next following, then the Vice-President shall act as President, as in the case of the death or other constitutional disability of the President. —][11] The person having the greatest number of votes as Vice-President, shall be the Vice-President, if such number be a majority of the whole number of Electors appointed, and if no person have a majority, then from the two highest numbers on the list, the Senate shall choose the Vice-President; a quorum for the purpose shall consist of two-thirds of the whole number of Senators, and a majority of the whole number shall be necessary to a choice. But no person constitutionally ineligible to the office of President shall be eligible to that of Vice-President of the United States.

## Amendment XIII *(Ratified December 6, 1865)*

**Section 1.** Neither slavery nor involuntary servitude, except as a punishment for crime whereof the party shall have been duly convicted, shall exist within the United States, or any place subject to their jurisdiction.

**Section 2.** Congress shall have power to enforce this article by appropriate legislation.

## Amendment XIV *(Ratified July 9, 1868)*

**Section 1.** All persons born or naturalized in the United States, and subject to the jurisdiction thereof, are citizens of the United States and of the State wherein they reside. No State shall make or enforce any law which shall abridge the privileges or immunities of citizens of the United States; nor shall any State deprive any person of life, liberty, or property, without due process of law; nor deny to any person within its jurisdiction the equal protection of the laws.

**Section 2.** Representatives shall be apportioned among the several States according to their respective numbers, counting the whole number of persons in each State, excluding Indians not taxed. But when the right to vote at any election for the choice of electors for President and Vice President of the United States, Representatives in Congress, the Executive and Judicial officers of a State, or the members of the Legislature thereof, is denied to any of the male inhabitants of such State, being twenty-one years of age,[12] and citizens of the United States, or in any way abridged, except for participation in rebellion, or other crime, the basis of representation therein shall be reduced in the proportion which the number of such male citizens shall bear to the whole number of male citizens twenty-one years of age in such State.

**Section 3.** No person shall be a Senator or Representative in Congress, or elector of President and Vice President, or hold any office, civil or military, under the United States, or under any State, who, having previously taken an oath, as a member of Congress, or as an officer of the United States, or as a member of any State legislature, or as an executive or judicial officer of any State, to support the Constitution of the United States, shall have engaged in insurrection or rebellion against the same, or given aid or comfort to the enemies thereof. But Congress may by a vote of two-thirds of each House, remove such disability.

*Section 4.* The validity of the public debt of the United States, authorized by law, including debts incurred for payment of pensions and bounties for services in suppressing insurrection or rebellion, shall not be questioned. But neither the United States nor any State shall assume or pay any debt or obligation incurred in aid of insurrection or rebellion against the United States, or any claim for the loss or emancipation of any slave; but all such debts, obligations and claims shall be held illegal and void.

*Section 5.* The Congress shall have power to enforce, by appropriate legislation, the provisions of this article.

*Amendment XV (Ratified February 3, 1870)*

*Section 1.* The right of citizens of the United States to vote shall not be denied or abridged by the United States or by any State on account of race, color, or previous condition of servitude.

*Section 2.* The Congress shall have power to enforce this article by appropriate legislation.

*Amendment XVI (Ratified February 3, 1913)*

The Congress shall have power to lay and collect taxes on incomes, from whatever source derived, without apportionment among the several States, and without regard to any census or enumeration.

*Amendment XVII (Ratified April 8, 1913)*

The Senate of the United States shall be composed of two Senators from each State, elected by the people thereof, for six years; and each Senator shall have one vote. The electors in each State shall have the qualifications requisite for electors of the most numerous branch of the State legislatures.

When vacancies happen in the representation of any State in the Senate, the executive authority of such State shall issue writs of election to fill such vacancies: *Provided,* That the legislature of any State may empower the executive thereof to make temporary appointments until the people fill the vacancies by election as the legislature may direct.

This amendment shall not be so construed as to affect the election or term of any Senator chosen before it becomes valid as part of the Constitution.

*[Amendment XVIII (Ratified January 16, 1919)*

*Section 1.* After one year from the ratification of this article the manufacture, sale, or transportation of intoxicating liquors within, the importation thereof into, or the exportation thereof from the United States and all territory subject to the jurisdiction thereof for beverage purposes is hereby prohibited.

*Section 2.* The Congress and the several States shall have concurrent power to enforce this article by appropriate legislation.

*Section 3.* This article shall be inoperative unless it shall have been ratified as an amendment to the Constitution by the legislatures of the several States, as provided in the Constitution, within seven years from the date of the submission hereof to the States by the Congress.][13]

*Amendment XIX (Ratified August 18, 1920)*

The right of citizens of the United States to vote shall not be denied or abridged by the United States or by any State on account of sex.

Congress shall have power to enforce this article by appropriate legislation.

*Amendment XX (Ratified January 23, 1933)*

*Section 1.* The terms of the President and Vice President shall end at noon on the 20th day of January, and the terms of Senators and Representatives at noon on the 3d day of January, of the years in which such terms would have ended if this article had not been ratified; and the terms of their successors shall then begin.

*Section 2.* The Congress shall assemble at least once in every year, and such meeting shall begin at noon on the 3d day of January, unless they shall by law appoint a different day.

*Section 3.*[14] If, at the time fixed for the beginning of the term of the President, the President elect shall have died, the Vice President elect shall become President. If a President shall not have been chosen before the time fixed for the beginning of his term, or if the President elect shall have failed to qualify, then the Vice President elect shall act as President until a President shall have qualified; and the Congress may by law provide for the case wherein neither a President elect nor a Vice President elect shall have qualified, declaring who shall then act as President, or the manner in which one who is to act shall be selected, and such person shall act accordingly until a President or Vice President shall have qualified.

*Section 4.* The Congress may by law provide for the case of the death of any of the persons from whom the House of Representatives may choose a President whenever the right of choice shall have devolved upon them, and for the case of the death of any of the persons from whom the Senate may choose a Vice President whenever the right of choice shall have devolved upon them.

*Section 5.* Sections 1 and 2 shall take effect on the 15th day of October following the ratification of this article.

*Section 6.* This article shall be inoperative unless it shall have been ratified as an amendment to the Constitution by the legislatures of three-fourths of the several States within seven years from the date of its submission.

*Amendment XXI (Ratified December 5, 1933)*

**Section 1.** The eighteenth article of amendment to the Constitution of the United States is hereby repealed.

**Section 2.** The transportation or importation into any State, Territory, or possession of the United States for delivery or use therein of intoxicating liquors, in violation of the laws thereof, is hereby prohibited.

**Section 3.** This article shall be inoperative unless it shall have been ratified as an amendment to the Constitution by conventions in the several States, as provided in the Constitution, within seven years from the date of the submission hereof to the States by the Congress.

*Amendment XXII (Ratified February 27, 1951)*

**Section 1.** No person shall be elected to the office of the President more than twice, and no person who has held the office of President, or acted as President, for more than two years of a term to which some other person was elected President shall be elected to the office of the President more than once. But this Article shall not apply to any person holding the office of President when this Article was proposed by the Congress, and shall not prevent any person who may be holding the office of President, or acting as President, during the term within which this Article becomes operative from holding the office of President or acting as President during the remainder of such term.

**Section 2.** This article shall be inoperative unless it shall have been ratified as an amendment to the Constitution by the legislatures of three-fourths of the several States within seven years from the date of its submission to the States by the Congress.

*Amendment XXIII (Ratified March 29, 1961)*

**Section 1.** The District constituting the seat of Government of the United States shall appoint in such manner as the Congress may direct:

A number of electors of President and Vice President equal to the whole number of Senators and Representatives in Congress to which the District would be entitled if it were a State, but in no event more than the least populous State; they shall be in addition to those appointed by the States, but they shall be considered, for the purposes of the election of President and Vice President, to be electors appointed by a State; and they shall meet in the District and perform such duties as provided by the twelfth article of amendment.

**Section 2.** The Congress shall have power to enforce this article by appropriate legislation.

*Amendment XXIV (Ratified January 23, 1964)*

**Section 1.** The right of citizens of the United States to vote in any primary or other election for President or Vice President, for electors for President or Vice President, or for Senator or Representative in Congress, shall not be denied or abridged by the United States or any State by reason of failure to pay any poll tax or other tax.

**Section 2.** The Congress shall have power to enforce this article by appropriate legislation.

*Amendment XXV (Ratified February 10, 1967)*

**Section 1.** In case of the removal of the President from office or of his death or resignation, the Vice President shall become President.

**Section 2.** Whenever there is a vacancy in the office of the Vice President, the President shall nominate a Vice President who shall take office upon confirmation by a majority vote of both Houses of Congress.

**Section 3.** Whenever the President transmits to the President pro tempore of the Senate and the Speaker of the House of Representatives his written declaration that he is unable to discharge the powers and duties of his office, and until he transmits to them a written declaration to the contrary, such powers and duties shall be discharged by the Vice President as Acting President.

**Section 4.** Whenever the Vice President and a majority of either the principal officers of the executive departments or of such other body as Congress may by law provide, transmit to the President pro tempore of the Senate and the Speaker of the House of Representatives their written declaration that the President is unable to discharge the powers and duties of his office, the Vice President shall immediately assume the powers and duties of the office as Acting President.

Thereafter, when the President transmits to the President pro tempore of the Senate and the Speaker of the House of Representatives his written declaration that no inability exists, he shall resume the powers and duties of his office unless the Vice President and a majority of either the principal officers of the executive departments or of such other body as Congress may by law provide, transmit within four days to the President pro tempore of the Senate and the Speaker of the House of Representatives their written declaration that the President is unable to discharge the powers and duties of his office. Thereupon Congress shall decide the issue, assembling within forty-eight hours for that purpose if not in session. If the Congress, within twenty-one days after receipt of the latter written declaration, or, if Congress is not in session, within twenty-one days after Congress is required to assemble, determines by two-thirds vote of both Houses that the President is unable to discharge the powers and duties of his office, the Vice President shall continue to discharge the same as Acting President; otherwise, the President shall resume the powers and duties of his office.

*Amendment XXVI (Ratified July 1, 1971)*

**Section 1.** The right of citizens of the United States, who are eighteen years of age or older, to vote shall not be denied or abridged by the United States or by any State on account of age.

**Section 2.** The Congress shall have power to enforce this article by appropriate legislation.

*Amendment XXVII (Ratified May 7, 1992)*

No law varying the compensation for the services of the Senators and Representatives shall take effect, until an election of Representatives shall have intervened.

SOURCE: U.S. Congress, House, Committee on the Judiciary, *The Constitution of the United States of America, as Amended,* 100th Cong., 1st sess., 1987, H Doc 100–94.

NOTES:  1. The part in brackets was changed by section 2 of the Fourteenth Amendment.

2. The part in brackets was changed by the first paragraph of the Seventeenth Amendment.

3. The part in brackets was changed by the second paragraph of the Seventeenth Amendment.

4. The part in brackets was changed by section 2 of the Twentieth Amendment.

5. The Sixteenth Amendment gave Congress the power to tax incomes.

6. The material in brackets was superseded by the Twelfth Amendment.

7 This provision was affected by the Twenty-fifth Amendment.

8. These clauses were affected by the Eleventh Amendment.

9. This paragraph was superseded by the Thirteenth Amendment.

10. Obsolete.

11. The part in brackets was superseded by section 3 of the Twentieth Amendment.

12. See the Nineteenth and Twenty-sixth Amendments.

13. This amendment was repealed by section 1 of the Twenty-first Amendment.

14. See the Twenty-fifth Amendment.

## Changes in Democrats' Nominating Rules

Between 1972 and 1992 Democrats tinkered with their nominating rules every four years, producing a system that, if not better than before, was always different. In 1996 the party left its rules unchanged for the first time in twenty years. The following chart shows the ebb and flow of the Democratic Party's rules changes, with a "✔" indicating the years these major rules were in effect.

| | 1972 | 1976 | 1980 | 1984 | 1988 | 1992 | 1996 |
|---|---|---|---|---|---|---|---|
| **Timing:** Restrict delegate-selection events to a three-month period (the "window"). | | | ✔ | ✔ | ✔ | ✔ | ✔ |
| **Conditions of Participation:** Restrict participation in delegate-selection events to Democrats. | | ✔ | ✔ | ✔ | ✔ | ✔ | ✔ |
| **Proportional Representation:** Ban all types of winner-take-all contests. | | | | ✔ | | ✔ | ✔ |
| Ban all types of winner-reward contests (where winner receives extra delegates). | | | | | | ✔ | ✔ |
| **Delegate Loyalty:** Give candidates the right to approve delegates identifying with their candidacy. | | ✔ | ✔ | ✔ | ✔ | ✔ | ✔ |
| Bind delegates to vote for their original presidential preference at convention on first ballot. | | | | ✔ | | | |
| **Party and Elected Officials:** Expand each delegation to include pledged party and elected officials. | | | | ✔ | ✔ | ✔ | ✔ |
| Further expand each delegation to include uncommitted party and elected officials ("superdelegates"). | | | | ✔ | ✔ | ✔ | ✔ |
| **Demographic Representation:** Encourage participation and representation of minorities and traditionally under-represented groups (affirmative action). | | | | ✔ | ✔ | ✔ | ✔ |
| Require delegations to be equally divided between men and women. | | | ✔ | ✔ | ✔ | ✔ | ✔ |

## Democratic Party's Reform Commissions on Presidential Selection

| Known as | Formal name | Years in operation | Chair | Size | Mandating body |
|----------|-------------|--------------------|-------|------|----------------|
| McGovern-Fraser Commission | Commission on Party Structure and Delegate Selection | 1969–1972 | Sen. George McGovern (S.D.), 1969–1970; Rep. Donald M. Fraser (Minn.), 1971–1972[a] | 28 | 1968 national convention |
| Mikulski Commission | Commission on Delegate Selection and Party Structure | 1972–1973 | Barbara A. Mikulski, Baltimore city councilwoman | 81 | 1972 national convention |
| Winograd Commission | Commission on Presidential Nomination and Party Structure | 1975–1976 1976–1980[b] | Morley Winograd, former chairman of Michigan Democratic Party | 58 | 1976 national convention |
| Hunt Commission | Commission on Presidential Nomination | 1980–1982 | Gov. James B. Hunt Jr. of North Carolina | 70 | 1980 national convention |
| Fairness Commission | Fairness Commission | 1984–1986 | Donald Fowler, chairman of South Carolina Democratic Party | 53 | 1984 national convention |

SOURCE: William J. Crotty, *Party Reform* (New York: Longman, 1983), 40–43. Updated by the author.

NOTES: a. Fraser assumed chair January 7, 1971.    b. The original Winograd Commission was not authorized by the national convention. It was created by the national chairman, Robert Strauss. The post-1976 committee membership was expanded.


## Republican Party's Reform Committees on Presidential Selection

| Known as | Formal name | Years in operation | Chair | Size | Mandating body |
|----------|-------------|--------------------|-------|------|----------------|
| DO Committee | Committee on Delegates and Organization | 1969–1971 | Rosemary Ginn, member, Republican National Committee, from Missouri | 16 | 1968 national convention |
| Rule 29 Committee | Rule 29 Committee | 1973–1975 | Rep. William A. Steiger (Wis.) | 57 | 1972 national convention |

| Major recommendations | Distinctive features | Principal report |
|---|---|---|
| "Quotas"; rules for opening delegate selection to 1972 national convention | First, most ambitious, and most important of reform groups. Completely rewrote rules for presidential selection; made them mandatory for state parties and state practices; changed power distribution within Democratic Party; set model other reform commissions attempted to follow. | *Mandate for Change* (1970) |
| Modified McGovern-Fraser rules; revised quotas; provided for proportional representation of presidential candidates' strength; increased role of party regulars in delegate selection | Commission had a stormy, if brief, life. Its principal recommendations were intended to placate regulars and modify most controversial aspects of McGovern-Fraser rules. Its major achievement, however, was in *not* seriously revising the McGovern-Fraser provisions. With the work of this commission, the assumption underlying the reforms became generally accepted within the party. | *Democrats All* (1973) |
| 10% "add-on" delegates for party officials; steps to close system at top | Vehicle of party regulars and Carter administration to tighten system, increase role of party regulars, and adopt rules expected to help Carter's renomination. Developed complicated procedures that are heavily dependent on national party interpretation. | *Openness, Participation and Party Building: Reforms for a Stronger Democratic Party* (1978) |
| 25% quota for party officials | Expanded role of party and elected officials in national conventions. | *Report of the Commission on Presidential Nomination* (1982) |
| Loosened restrictions on "open primaries"; lowered the threshold for "fair representation" to 15%; increased number of "superdelegates." | Tried to satisfy both wings of the party by simultaneously increasing the power of party leaders (by increasing the number of superdelegates) and by lowering the threshold for fair representation. | No formal report. |

| Major recommendations | Distinctive features | Principal report |
|---|---|---|
| Proposals for increasing participation in delegate selection process. | The committee's recommendations were not binding; designed "to implement the Republican Party's Open Door policy." | No formal report. |
| Implement "positive action" to open delegate selection process; institute RNC review of such action | Most ambitious reform effort by the Republican Party. The committee's major recommendations, however, were rejected by the RNC and by the 1976 national convention. | No formal report. |

# Election-Related Web Sites

Thousands of Internet sites provide information about elections and politics. The following are among the best:

## AllPolitics
*http://cnn.com/allpolitics*

*Time* magazine and CNN operate this site, which offers hundreds of news stories about elections and politics from various sources, including Congressional Quarterly. It also has detailed results from recent state and federal elections.

## Ballot Access News
*http://www.ballot-access.org*

The full text of the newsletter *Ballot Access News* from early 1994 to the present is available at this site. The newsletter publishes information about efforts around the country to overturn laws that restrict ballot access by candidates.

## Census: Voting and Registration Data
*http://www.census.gov/population/www/socdemo/voting.html*

The U.S. Census Bureau operates this site, which has data about registration and voting by various demographic and socioeconomic groups. Data are available from 1964 to the present.

## Center for Responsive Politics
*http://www.crp.org*

The heart of this site is its databases containing detailed campaign finance data. One of the most interesting databases provides information about contributors to federal political campaigns. Users can search the database by contributor name, Zip Code, employer, or recipient. Other databases offer information about contributions by political action committees to federal candidates, financial disclosure statements filed by all members of Congress, detailed campaign finance profiles of each member of Congress, and related information.

## Congressional Quarterly's American Voter
*http://voter.cq.com*

The "On the Job" section of this site has extensive information about each member of Congress. For each member, the site provides results of primary and general elections, a record of recent key votes, the text of recent floor speeches, a list of bills and resolutions introduced during the current session, records of committee votes, a list of principal staff contacts, and more.

## ELECnet
*http://www.iupui.edu/~epackard/eleclink.html*

ELECnet provides hundreds of links to Web sites operated by state, county, and city elections offices around the country. It also has links to federal agencies that provide election-related information and national organizations that host election-oriented Web sites.

## Election Central
*http://www.lwv.org/elect.html*

The League of Women Voters Education Fund operates this site, which has links to information about state and local candidates around the country, details about how to register to vote, voter registration contact numbers for every state, and links to other election sites.

## Election Notes
*http://www.klipsan.com/elecnews.htm*

This site's highlight is its links to current election news from around the world. It also has the full text of a book titled *Atlas of United States Presidential Elections,* links to worldwide election calendars, links to election results, and much more. It is operated by Klipsan Press.

## FECInfo
*http://www.tray.com/fecinfo*

FECInfo, which is operated by a private individual, offers an extraordinary collection of federal campaign finance data. The site has lists of the top contributors from each state, lists of the leading political action committees in various categories, data on soft money contributions, numerous databases that provide itemized information about receipts and expenditures by federal candidates and political action committees, and much more.

## Federal Election Commission
*http://www.fec.gov*

This site's highlight is a database of campaign finance reports filed from May 1996 to the present by House and presidential candidates, political action committees, and political party committees. Senate reports are not included because they are filed with the secretary of the Senate. The site also has summary financial data for House and Senate candidates in the current election cycle, abstracts of court decisions pertaining to federal election law, data regarding the number of political action committees in existence from 1974 to the present, and a directory of national and state agencies that are responsible for releasing information about campaign financing, candidates on the ballot, election results, lobbying, and other issues.

## Federal Voting Assistance Program (FVAP)
*http://www.fvap.gov*

The Federal Voting Assistance Program (FVAP) site has a calendar of upcoming elections, information about how to apply for an absentee ballot, details about legislative initiatives affecting elections, links to state government sites that offer election results, and the *Voting Assistance Guide,* which has information about the procedures for registering and voting in each state. The site is operated by the Office of the Secretary of Defense.

## Geographic Information Center: Election Maps
*http://www.lib.virginia.edu/gic/elections/index.html*

Color-coded national maps at this site show which presidential candidate won the popular vote in each state in elections from 1860 to the present and also list the percentage of the popular vote that the candidate received. A second set of maps shows the number of electoral votes that candidates received in each state for elections from 1900 to the present. The site is operated by the Social Sciences Data Center at the University of Virginia.

## International Foundation for Election Systems
*http://www.ifes.org/index.htm*

One of this site's highlights is its collection of links to Web sites operated by election commissions and other election-related organizations in countries around the world. It also provides a worldwide elections calendar, links to news about current elections, and a newsletter titled *Elections Today.*

## National Election Studies
*http://www.umich.edu/~nes*

This site, which is operated by the University of Michigan's Institute for Social Research, provides a wealth of polling data regarding electoral behavior and public opinion from 1952 to the present.

## Office of the Clerk On-line Information Center
*http://clerkweb.house.gov/histrecs/history/history.htm*

This site, which is operated by the Office of the Clerk in the U.S. House of Representatives, has popular vote totals for presidential, U.S. Senate, and U.S. House of Representatives candidates. The candidates are arranged by state. Data are available for elections from 1920 to the present.

## Pew Research Center for the People and the Press
*http://www.people-press.org*

The Pew site presents the results of polls regarding elections and political issues. Results of polls conducted from late 1995 to the present are available online, and paper copies of older polls can be ordered.

## Political Resources on the Net
*http://www.agora.stm.it/politic*

Links to more than 18,000 election and politics sites on the Internet are presented at this site. The links are sorted by country.

## Political Science Resources: United States Politics
*http://www.lib.umich.edu/libhome/documents.center/ psusp.html*

This site from the University of Michigan Documents Center offers links to hundreds of Web sites about politics and elections. The listings are divided into more than twenty categories, including campaign finances, elections, lobby groups, news sources, political parties, primaries, public policy issues, statistics, and think tanks.

## Politics1
*http://www.politics1.com*

Politics1 provides a huge set of links to Web sites operated by candidates, political parties, election offices, and election news sources in states around the country. It also has links to sites for presidential candidates, the two major parties, third parties, and political news sources.

## PoliticsOnline
*http://www.politicsonline.com*

This site's highlight is its large collection of links to news stories about how the Internet is being used in elections and politics around the world.

## Project Vote Smart
*http://www.vote-smart.org*

The Project Vote Smart site provides biographies of more than 13,000 candidates and elected officials in offices ranging from state legislator to president, annotated samples of the voting records of members of Congress on numerous issues, detailed campaign finance data for members of Congress, links to thousands of other politics-related Web sites, and lots more.

Rock the Vote
*http://www.rockthevote.org*

Rock the Vote lets users apply for voter registration on-line. It also has calendars of primary and general election dates and links to other political Web sites.

Soft Money Laundromat
*http://www.commoncause.org/laundromat*

Common Cause's Soft Money Laundromat is a searchable database of soft money contributions by special interests to the Democratic and Republican national party committees. Users can search the database by donor name, donor location, and industry. The site also has profiles of the largest soft money donors, lists of the top soft money donors, and background information about the soft money issue.

State Vote '98
*http://www.ncsl.org/statevote98*

This site from the National Conference of State Legislatures has extensive results from state elections around the country. The site has maps showing partisan control of state legislatures, election profiles for each state, and a searchable database of results of state initiative and referenda votes around the country.

Washingtonpost.com: Politics
*http://www.washingtonpost.com/wp-srv/politics/front.htm*

The *Washington Post* operates this site, which has political and election news, in-depth reports about key campaigns, and results for U.S. Senate races, U.S. House races, gubernatorial races, and ballot initiatives around the country.

Web White and Blue
*http://www.webwhiteblue.com*

Web White and Blue has links to some of the best election-related sites on the Internet. The sites provide voter information, campaign news, information about issues, state-based data, and election news. Many of the sites are directories that link to lots of other sites about the topic.

# Presidential Nominating Campaigns, 1980–1996

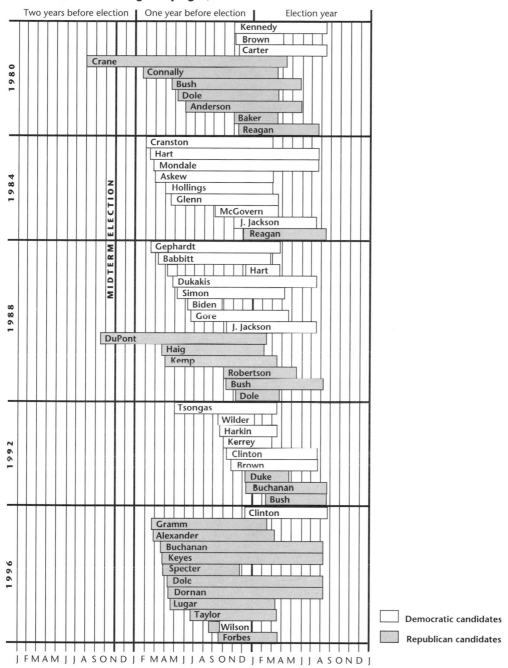

SOURCE: *Selecting the President: From 1789 to 1996* (Washington, D.C.: Congressional Quarterly, 1997), 63.

## National Party Chairs, 1848–1999

| Name | State | Years of Service | Name | State | Years of Service |
|------|-------|------------------|------|-------|------------------|
| **Democratic Party** | | | **Republican Party** (continued) | | |
| B. F. Hallett | Massachusetts | 1848–52 | Zachariah Chandler | Michigan | 1876–79 |
| Robert McLane | Maryland | 1852–56 | J. Donald Cameron | Pennsylvania | 1879–80 |
| David A. Smalley | Virginia | 1856–60 | Marshall Jewell | Connecticut | 1880–83 |
| August Belmont | New York | 1860–72 | D. M. Sabin | Minnesota | 1883–84 |
| Augustus Schell | New York | 1872–76 | B. F. Jones | Pennsylvania | 1884–88 |
| Abram S. Hewitt | New York | 1876–77 | Matthew S. Quay | Pennsylvania | 1888–91 |
| William H. Barnum | Connecticut | 1877–89 | James S. Clarkson | Iowa | 1891–92 |
| Calvin S. Brice | Ohio | 1889–92 | Thomas H. Carter | Montana | 1892–96 |
| William F. Harrity | Pennsylvania | 1892–96 | Mark A. Hanna | Ohio | 1896–1904 |
| James K. Jones | Arkansas | 1896–1904 | Henry C. Payne | Wisconsin | 1904 |
| Thomas Taggart | Indiana | 1904–08 | George B. Cortelyou | New York | 1904–07 |
| Norman E. Mack | New York | 1908–12 | Harry S. New | Indiana | 1907–08 |
| William F. McCombs | New York | 1912–16 | Frank H. Hitchcock | Massachusetts | 1908–09 |
| Vance C. McCormick | Pennsylvania | 1916–19 | John F. Hill | Maine | 1909–12 |
| Homer S. Cummings | Connecticut | 1919–20 | Victor Rosewater | Nebraska | 1912 |
| George White | Ohio | 1920–21 | Charles D. Hilles | New York | 1912–16 |
| Cordell Hull | Tennessee | 1921–24 | William R. Willcox | New York | 1916–18 |
| Clem Shaver | West Virginia | 1924–28 | Will Hays | Indiana | 1918–21 |
| John J. Raskob | Maryland | 1928–32 | John T. Adams | Iowa | 1921–24 |
| James A. Farley | New York | 1932–40 | William M. Butler | Massachusetts | 1924–28 |
| Edward J. Flynn | New York | 1940–43 | Hubert Work | Colorado | 1928–29 |
| Frank C. Walker | Pennsylvania | 1943–44 | Claudius H. Huston | Tennessee | 1929–30 |
| Robert E. Hannegan | Missouri | 1944–47 | Simeon D. Fess | Ohio | 1930–32 |
| J. Howard McGrath | Rhode Island | 1947–49 | Everett Sanders | Indiana | 1932–34 |
| William M. Boyle Jr. | Missouri | 1949–51 | Henry P. Fletcher | Pennsylvania | 1934–36 |
| Frank E. McKinney | Indiana | 1951–52 | John Hamilton | Kansas | 1936–40 |
| Stephen A. Mitchell | Illinois | 1952–54 | Joseph W. Martin Jr. | Massachusetts | 1940–42 |
| Paul M. Butler | Indiana | 1955–60 | Harrison E. Spangler | Iowa | 1942–44 |
| Henry M. Jackson | Washington | 1960–61 | Herbert Brownell Jr. | New York | 1944–46 |
| John M. Bailey | Connecticut | 1961–68 | B. Carroll Reece | Tennessee | 1946–48 |
| Lawrence F. O'Brien | Massachusetts | 1968–69 | Hugh D. Scott Jr. | Pennsylvania | 1948–49 |
| Fred Harris | Oklahoma | 1969–70 | Guy George Gabrielson | New Jersey | 1949–52 |
| Lawrence F. O'Brien | Massachusetts | 1970–72 | Arthur E. Summerfield | Michigan | 1952–53 |
| Jean Westwood | Utah | 1972 | C. Wesley Roberts | Kansas | 1953 |
| Robert Straus | Texas | 1972–77 | Leonard W. Hall | New York | 1953–57 |
| Kenneth Curtis | Maine | 1977–78 | H. Meade Alcorn Jr. | Connecticut | 1957–59 |
| John White | Texas | 1978–81 | Thruston B. Morton | Kentucky | 1959–61 |
| Charles Manatt | California | 1981–85 | William E. Miller | New York | 1961–64 |
| Paul Kirk | Massachusetts | 1985–89 | Dean Burch | Arizona | 1964–65 |
| Ronald H. Brown | Washington, D.C. | 1989–93 | Ray C. Bliss | Ohio | 1965–69 |
| David Wilhelm | Illinois | 1993–94 | Rogers C. B. Morton | Maryland | 1969–71 |
| Christopher Dodd (general chair) | Connecticut | 1994–97 | Robert Dole | Kansas | 1971–73 |
| | | | George Bush | Texas | 1973–74 |
| Donald Fowler | South Carolina | 1994–97 | Mary Louise Smith | Iowa | 1974–77 |
| Roy Romer (general chair) | Colorado | 1997– | William Brock | Tennessee | 1977–81 |
| | | | Richard Richards | Utah | 1981–83 |
| Steven Grossman | Massachusetts | 1997– | Paul Laxalt (general chair) | Nevada | 1983–86 |
| **Republican Party** | | | Frank Fahrenkopf Jr. | Nevada | 1983–89 |
| Edwin D. Morgan | New York | 1856–64 | Lee Atwater | South Carolina | 1989–91 |
| Henry J. Raymond | New York | 1864–66 | Clayton Yeutter | Nebraska | 1991–92 |
| Marcus L. Ward | New Jersey | 1866–68 | Rich Bond | New York | 1992–93 |
| William Claflin | Massachusetts | 1868–72 | Haley Barbour | Mississippi | 1993–97 |
| Edwin D. Morgan | New York | 1872–76 | Jim Nicholson | Colorado | 1997– |

SOURCES: Hugh A. Bone, *Party Committees and National Politics* (Seattle: University of Washington, 1958), 241–243; Congressional Quarterly, *The President, the Public, and the Parties*, 2d ed. (Washington, D.C.: Congressional Quarterly, 1997), 21.

**1860, Democratic.** A minority report on the slavery plank, stating that the decision on allowing slavery in the territories should be left to the Supreme Court, was approved, 165 to 138. The majority report (favored by the South) declared that no government—local, state or federal—could outlaw slavery in the territories. The acceptance of the minority report precipitated a walkout by several dozen Southern delegates and the eventual sectional split in the party.

**1896, Democratic.** The monetary plank of the platform committee, favoring free and unlimited coinage of silver at a ratio of 16 to 1 with gold, was accepted by the convention, which defeated a proposed gold plank, 626 to 303. During debate William Jennings Bryan made his famous "Cross of Gold" speech supporting the platform committee plank, bringing him to the attention of the convention and resulting in his nomination for president.

**1908, Republican.** A minority report, proposing a substitute platform, was presented by Sen. Robert M. La Follette of Wisconsin. Minority proposals included increased antitrust activities, enactment of a law requiring publication of campaign expenditures and popular election of senators. All the proposed planks were defeated by wide margins; the closest vote, on direct election of senators, was 114 for, 866 against.

**1924, Democratic.** A minority plank was presented that condemned the activities of the Ku Klux Klan, then enjoying a resurgence in the South and some states in the Midwest. The plank was defeated $542^{7}/_{20}$ to $543^{3}/_{20}$, the closest vote in Democratic convention history.

**1932, Republican.** A minority plank favoring repeal of the Eighteenth Amendment (Prohibition) in favor of a state-option arrangement was defeated, $460^{2}/_{9}$ to $690^{19}/_{36}$.

**1948, Democratic.** An amendment to the platform, strengthening the civil rights plank by guaranteeing full and equal political participation, equal employment opportunity, personal security and equal treatment in the military service, was accepted, $651^{1}/_{2}$ to $582^{1}/_{2}$.

**1964, Republican.** An amendment offered by Sen. Hugh Scott of Pennsylvania to strengthen the civil rights plank by including voting guarantees in state as well as in federal elections and by eliminating job bias was defeated, 409 to 897.

**1968, Democratic.** A minority report on Vietnam called for cessation of the bombing of North Vietnam, halting of offensive and search-and-destroy missions by American combat units, a negotiated withdrawal of American troops and establishment of a coalition government in South Vietnam. It was defeated, $1,041^{1}/_{4}$ to $1,567^{3}/_{4}$.

**1972, Democratic.** By a vote of 1,852.86 to 999.34, the convention rejected a minority report proposing a government guaranteed annual income of $6,500 for a family of four. By a vote of 1,101.37 to 1,572.80, a women's rights plank supporting abortion rights was defeated.

**1980, Democratic.** The platform battle, one of the longest in party history, pitted President Jimmy Carter against his persistent rival, Sen. Edward M. Kennedy of Massachusetts. Stretching over seventeen hours, the debate focused on Kennedy's economics plank, which finally was defeated by a voice vote. Yet Carter was forced to concede on so many specific points, including Kennedy's $12 billion anti-recession jobs programs, that the final document bore little resemblance to the draft initially drawn up by Carter's operatives.

**1992, Democratic.** A tax fairness plank offered by former senator Paul E. Tsongas of Massachusetts was defeated by a vote of 953 to 2,287. The plank called for a delay in any middle-class tax cut and tax credit for families with children until the deficit was under control.

# Democratic Conventions, 1832–1996

| Years | City | Dates | Presidential Nominee | Vice Presidential Nominee | No. of Pres. Ballots |
|-------|------|-------|---------------------|--------------------------|---------------------|
| 1832 | Baltimore | May 21–23 | Andrew Jackson | Martin Van Buren | 1 |
| 1835 | Baltimore | May 20–23 | Martin Van Buren | Richard M. Johnson | 1 |
| 1840 | Baltimore | May 5–6 | Martin Van Buren | —[1] | 1 |
| 1844 | Baltimore | May 27–29 | James K. Polk | George M. Dallas | 9 |
| 1848 | Baltimore | May 22–25 | Lewis Cass | William O. Butler | 4 |
| 1852 | Baltimore | June 1–5 | Franklin Pierce | William R. King | 49 |
| 1856 | Cincinnati | June 2–6 | James Buchanan | John C. Breckinridge | 17 |
| 1860 | Charleston | April 23–May 3 | Deadlocked | | 57 |
| | Baltimore | June 18–23 | Stephen A. Douglas | Benjamin Fitzpatrick Herschel V. Johnson[2] | 2 |
| 1864 | Chicago | Aug. 29–31 | George B. McClellan | George H. Pendleton | 1 |
| 1868 | New York | July 4–9 | Horatio Seymour | Francis P. Blair | 22 |
| 1872 | Baltimore | July 9–10 | Horace Greeley | Benjamin G. Brown | 1 |
| 1876 | St. Louis | June 27–29 | Samuel J. Tilden | Thomas A. Hendricks | 2 |
| 1880 | Cincinnati | June 22–24 | Winfield S. Hancock | William H. English | 2 |
| 1884 | Chicago | July 8–11 | Grover Cleveland | Thomas A. Hendricks | 2 |
| 1888 | St. Louis | June 5–7 | Grover Cleveland | Allen G. Thurman | 1 |
| 1892 | Chicago | June 21–23 | Grover Cleveland | Adlai E. Stevenson | 1 |
| 1896 | Chicago | July 7–11 | William J. Bryan | Arthur Sewall | 5 |
| 1900 | Kansas City | July 4–6 | William J. Bryan | Adlai E. Stevenson | 1 |
| 1904 | St. Louis | July 6–9 | Alton S. Parker | Henry G. Davis | 1 |
| 1908 | Denver | July 7–10 | William J. Bryan | John W. Kern | 1 |
| 1912 | Baltimore | June 25–July 2 | Woodrow Wilson | Thomas R. Marshall | 46 |
| 1916 | St. Louis | June 14–16 | Woodrow Wilson | Thomas R. Marshall | 1 |
| 1920 | San Francisco | June 28–July 6 | James M. Cox | Franklin D. Roosevelt | 44 |
| 1924 | New York | June 24–July 9 | John W. Davis | Charles W. Bryan | 103 |
| 1928 | Houston | June 26–29 | Alfred E. Smith | Joseph T. Robinson | 1 |
| 1932 | Chicago | June 27–July 2 | Franklin D. Roosevelt | John N. Garner | 4 |
| 1936 | Philadelphia | June 23–27 | Franklin D. Roosevelt | John N. Garner | Acclamation |
| 1940 | Chicago | July 15–18 | Franklin D. Roosevelt | Henry A. Wallace | 1 |
| 1944 | Chicago | July 19–21 | Franklin D. Roosevelt | Harry S. Truman | 1 |
| 1948 | Philadelphia | July 12–14 | Harry S. Truman | Alben W. Barkley | 1 |
| 1952 | Chicago | July 21–26 | Adlai E. Stevenson | John J. Sparkman | 3 |
| 1956 | Chicago | Aug. 13–17 | Adlai E. Stevenson | Estes Kefauver | 1 |
| 1960 | Los Angeles | July 11–15 | John F. Kennedy | Lyndon B. Johnson | 1 |
| 1964 | Atlantic City | Aug. 24–27 | Lyndon B. Johnson | Hubert H. Humphrey | Acclamation |
| 1968 | Chicago | Aug. 26–29 | Hubert H. Humphrey | Edmund S. Muskie | 1 |
| 1972 | Miami Beach | July 10–13 | George McGovern | Thomas F. Eagleton R. Sargent Shriver[3] | 1 |
| 1976 | New York | July 12–15 | Jimmy Carter | Walter F. Mondale | 1 |
| 1980 | New York | Aug. 11–14 | Jimmy Carter | Walter F. Mondale | 1 |
| 1984 | San Francisco | July 16–19 | Walter F. Mondale | Geraldine A. Ferraro | 1 |
| 1988 | Atlanta | July 18–21 | Michael S. Dukakis | Lloyd Bentsen | 1 |
| 1992 | New York | July 13–16 | Bill Clinton | Albert Gore Jr. | 1 |
| 1996 | Chicago | Aug. 26–29 | Bill Clinton | Albert Gore Jr. | 1 |

NOTES:

1. The 1840 Democratic convention did not nominate a candidate for vice president.

2. The 1860 Democratic convention nominated Benjamin Fitzpatrick, who declined the nomination shortly after the convention adjourned. On June 25 the Democratic National Committee selected Herschel V. Johnson as the party's candidate for vice president.

3. The 1972 Democratic convention nominated Thomas F. Eagleton, who withdrew from the ticket on July 31. On August 8 the Democratic National Committee selected R. Sargent Shriver as the party's candidate for vice president.

## Republican Conventions, 1856–1996

| Years | City | Dates | Presidential Nominee | Vice Presidential Nominee | No. of Pres. Ballots |
|-------|------|-------|----------------------|---------------------------|----------------------|
| 1856 | Philadelphia | June 17–19 | John C. Fremont | William L. Dayton | 2 |
| 1860 | Chicago | May 16–18 | Abraham Lincoln | Hannibal Hamlin | 3 |
| 1864 | Baltimore | June 7–8 | Abraham Lincoln | Andrew Johnson | 1 |
| 1868 | Chicago | May 20–21 | Ulysses S. Grant | Schuyler Colfax | 1 |
| 1872 | Philadelphia | June 5–6 | Ulysses S. Grant | Henry Wilson | 1 |
| 1876 | Cincinnati | June 14–16 | Rutherford B. Hayes | William A. Wheeler | 7 |
| 1880 | Chicago | June 2–8 | James A. Garfield | Chester A. Arthur | 36 |
| 1884 | Chicago | June 3–6 | James G. Blaine | John A. Logan | 4 |
| 1888 | Chicago | June 19–25 | Benjamin Harrison | Levi P. Morton | 8 |
| 1892 | Minneapolis | June 7–10 | Benjamin Harrison | Whitelaw Reid | 1 |
| 1896 | St. Louis | June 16–18 | William McKinley | Garret A. Hobart | 1 |
| 1900 | Philadelphia | June 19–21 | William McKinley | Theodore Roosevelt | 1 |
| 1904 | Chicago | June 21–23 | Theodore Roosevelt | Charles W. Fairbanks | 1 |
| 1908 | Chicago | June 16–19 | William H. Taft | James S. Sherman | 1 |
| 1912 | Chicago | June 18–22 | William H. Taft | James S. Sherman<br>Nicholas Murray Butler[1] | 1 |
| 1916 | Chicago | June 7–10 | Charles E. Hughes | Charles W. Fairbanks | 3 |
| 1920 | Chicago | June 8–12 | Warren G. Harding | Calvin Coolidge | 10 |
| 1924 | Cleveland | June 10–12 | Calvin Coolidge | Charles G. Dawes | 1 |
| 1928 | Kansas City | June 12–15 | Herbert Hoover | Charles Curtis | 1 |
| 1932 | Chicago | June 14–16 | Herbert Hoover | Charles Curtis | 1 |
| 1936 | Cleveland | June 9–12 | Alfred M. Landon | Frank Knox | 1 |
| 1940 | Philadelphia | June 24–28 | Wendell L. Willkie | Charles L. McNary | 6 |
| 1944 | Chicago | June 26–28 | Thomas E. Dewey | John W. Bricker | 1 |
| 1948 | Philadelphia | June 21–25 | Thomas E. Dewey | Earl Warren | 3 |
| 1952 | Chicago | July 7–11 | Dwight D. Eisenhower | Richard M. Nixon | 1 |
| 1956 | San Francisco | Aug. 20–23 | Dwight D. Eisenhower | Richard M. Nixon | 1 |
| 1960 | Chicago | July 25–28 | Richard M. Nixon | Henry Cabot Lodge | 1 |
| 1964 | San Francisco | July 13–16 | Barry Goldwater | William E. Miller | 1 |
| 1968 | Miami Beach | Aug. 5–8 | Richard M. Nixon | Spiro T. Agnew | 1 |
| 1972 | Miami Beach | Aug. 21–23 | Richard M. Nixon | Spiro T. Agnew | 1 |
| 1976 | Kansas City | Aug. 16–19 | Gerald R. Ford | Robert Dole | 1 |
| 1980 | Detroit | July 14–17 | Ronald Reagan | George Bush | 1 |
| 1984 | Dallas | Aug. 20–23 | Ronald Reagan | George Bush | 1 |
| 1988 | New Orleans | Aug. 15–18 | George Bush | Dan Quayle | 1 |
| 1992 | Houston | Aug. 17–20 | George Bush | Dan Quayle | 1 |
| 1996 | San Diego | Aug. 12–15 | Robert Dole | Jack Kemp | 1 |

NOTES:

1. The 1912 Republican convention nominated James S. Sherman, who died on October 30. The Republican National Committee subsequently selected Nicholas Murray Butler to receive the Republican electoral votes for vice president.

## Chief Officers and Keynote Speakers at Democratic National Conventions, 1832–1996

| Year | Chair National Committee | Temporary Chair | Permanent Chair | Keynote Speaker |
|---|---|---|---|---|
| 1832 | | Robert Lucas, Ohio | Robert Lucas, Ohio | |
| 1836 | | Andrew Stevenson, Va. | Andrew Stevenson, Va. | |
| 1840 | | Isaac Hill, N.H. | William Carroll, Tenn. | |
| 1844 | | Hendrick B. Wright, Pa. | Hendrick B. Wright, Pa. | |
| 1848 | Benjamin Hallet, Mass. | J.S. Bryce, La. | Andrew Stevenson, Va. | |
| 1852 | Robert M. McLane, Md. | Gen. Romulus M. Saunders, N.C. | John W. Davis, Ind. | |
| 1856 | David A. Smalley, Vt. | Samuel Medary, Ohio | John E. Ward, Ga. | |
| 1860 | August Belmont, N.Y. | Francis B. Flournoy, Ark. | Caleb Cushing, Mass. | |
| 1864 | August Belmont, N.Y. | William Bigler, Pa. | Horatio Seymour, N.Y. | |
| 1868 | August Belmont, N.Y. | Henry L. Palmer, Wis. | Horatio Seymour, N.Y. | |
| 1872 | Augustus Schell, N.Y. | Thomas Jefferson Randolph, Va. | James R. Doolittle, Wis. | |
| 1876 | Abram Stevens Hewitt, N.Y. | Henry M. Watterson, Ky. | John A. McClernand, Ill. | |
| 1880 | William H. Barnum, Conn. | George Hoadly, Ohio | John W. Stevenson, Ky. | |
| 1884 | William H. Barnum, Conn. | Richard B. Hubbard, Texas | William F. Vilas, Wis. | |
| 1888 | William H. Barnum, Conn. | Stephen M. White, Calif. | Patrick A. Collins, Mass. | |
| 1892 | William F. Harrity, Penn. | William C. Owens, Ky. | William L. Wilson, W.Va. | |
| 1896 | James K. Jones, Ark. | John W. Daniel, Va. | Stephen M. White, Calif. | |
| 1900 | James K. Jones, Ark. | Charles S. Thomas, Colo. | James D. Richardson, Tenn. | |
| 1904 | Thomas Taggart, Ind. | John Sharp Williams, Miss. | Champ Clark, Mo. | |
| 1908 | Norman E. Mack, N.Y. | Theodore A. Bell, Calif. | Henry D. Clayton, Ala. | |
| 1912 | William F. McCombs, N.Y. | Alton B. Parker, N.Y. | Ollie M. James, Ky. | |
| 1916 | Vance C. McCormick, Pa. | Martin H. Glynn, N.Y. | Ollie M. James, Ky. | |
| 1920 | George H. White, Ohio | Homer S. Cummings, Conn. | Joseph T. Robinson, Ark. | |
| 1924 | Clem Shaver, W.Va. | Pat Harrison, Miss. | Thomas J. Walsh, Mont. | |
| 1928 | John J. Raskob, Md. | Claude G. Bowers, Ind. | Joseph T. Robinson, Ark. | |
| 1932 | James A. Farley, N.Y. | Alben W. Barkley, Ky. | Thomas J. Walsh, Mont. | |
| 1936 | James A. Farley, N.Y. | Alben W. Barkley, Ky. | Joseph T. Robinson, Ark. | Alben W. Barkley, Ky. |
| 1940 | Edward J. Flynn, N.Y. | William B. Bankhead, Ala. | Alben W. Barkley, Ky. | William B. Bankhead, Ala. |
| 1944 | Robert E. Hannegan, Mo. | Robert S. Kerr, Okla. | Samuel D. Jackson, Ind. | Robert S. Kerr, Okla. |
| 1948 | J. Howard McGrath, R.I. | Alben W. Barkley, Ky. | Sam Rayburn, Texas | Alben W. Barkley, Ky. |
| 1952 | Stephen A. Mitchell, Ill. | Paul A. Dever, Mass. | Sam Rayburn, Texas | Paul A. Dever, Mass. |
| 1956 | Paul M. Butler, Ind. | Frank G. Clement, Tenn. | Sam Rayburn, Texas | Frank Clement, Tenn. |
| 1960 | Henry Jackson, Wash. | Frank Church, Idaho | LeRoy Collins, Fla. | Frank Church, Idaho |
| 1964 | John M. Bailey, Conn. | John O. Pastore, R.I. | John W. McCormack, Mass. | John O. Pastore, R.I. |
| 1968 | Lawrence F. O'Brien, Mass. | Daniel K. Inouye, Hawaii | Carl B. Albert, Okla. | Daniel K. Inouye, Hawaii |
| 1972[1] | Lawrence F. O'Brien, Mass. | | Lawrence F. O'Brien, Mass. | Reubin Askew, Fla. |
| 1976 | Robert S. Strauss, Texas | | Lindy Boggs, La. | John Glenn, Ohio Barbara C. Jordan, Texas |
| 1980 | John C. White, Texas | | Thomas P. O'Neill Jr., Mass. | Morris K. Udall, Ariz. |
| 1984 | Charles T. Manatt, Calif. | | Martha Layne Collins, Ky. | Mario M. Cuomo, N.Y. |
| 1988 | Paul G. Kirk Jr., Mass. | | Jim Wright, Texas | Ann W. Richards, Texas |
| 1992 | Ronald H. Brown, D.C. | | Ann W. Richards, Texas | Bill Bradley, N.J. Zell Miller, Ga. Barbara C. Jordan, Texas |
| 1996 | Donald Fowler, S.C. | | Thomas A. Daschle, S.D. Richard A. Gephardt, Mo. | Evan Bayh, Ind. |

NOTES:
1. A rule change eliminated the position of temporary chair.

# Chief Officers and Keynote Speakers at Republican National Conventions, 1856–1996

| Year | Chair National Committee | Temporary Chair | Permanent Chair | Keynote Speaker |
|------|--------------------------|-----------------|-----------------|-----------------|
| 1856 | Edwin D. Morgan, N.Y. | Robert Emmet, N.Y. | Henry S. Lane, Ind. | |
| 1860 | Edwin D. Morgan, N.Y. | David Wilmot, Pa. | George Ashmun, Mass. | |
| 1864 | Edwin D. Morgan, N.Y. | Robert J. Breckinridge, Ky. | William Dennison, Ohio | |
| 1868 | Marcus L. Ward, N.J. | Carl Schurz, Mo. | Joseph R. Hawley, Conn. | |
| 1872 | William Claflin, Mass. | Morton McMichael, Pa. | Thomas Settle, N.C. | |
| 1876 | Edwin D. Morgan, N.Y. | Theodore M. Pomeroy, N.Y. | Edward McPherson, Pa. | |
| 1880 | J. Donald Cameron, Pa. | George F. Hoar, Mass. | George F. Hoar, Mass. | |
| 1884 | Dwight M. Sabin, Minn. | John R. Lynch, Miss. | John B. Henderson, Mo. | |
| 1888 | B.F. Jones, Pa. | John M. Thurston, Neb. | Morris M. Estee, Calif. | |
| 1892 | James S. Clarkson, Iowa | J. Sloat Fassett, N.Y. | William McKinley Jr., Ohio | |
| 1896 | Thomas H. Carter, Mont. | Charles W. Fairbanks, Ind. | John M. Thurston, Neb. | |
| 1900 | Marcus A. Hanna, Ohio | Edward O. Wolcott, Colo. | Henry Cabot Lodge, Mass. | |
| 1904 | Henry C. Payne, Wis. | Elihu Root, N.Y. | Joseph G. Cannon, Ill. | |
| 1908 | Harry S. New, Ind. | Julius C. Burrows, Mich. | Henry Cabot Lodge, Mass. | |
| 1912 | Victor Rosewater, Neb. | Elihu Root, N.Y. | Elihu Root, N.Y. | |
| 1916 | Charles D. Hilles, N.Y. | Warren G. Harding, Ohio | Warren G. Harding, Ohio | |
| 1920 | Will H. Hays, Ind. | Henry Cabot Lodge, Mass. | Henry Cabot Lodge, Mass. | Henry Cabot Lodge, Mass. |
| 1924 | John T. Adams, Iowa | Theodore E. Burton, Ohio | Frank W. Mortdell, Wyo. | |
| 1928 | William M. Butler, Mass. | Simeon D. Fess, Ohio | George H. Moses, N.H. | |
| 1932 | Simeon D. Fess, Ohio | L. J. Dickinson, Iowa | Bertrand H. Snell, N.Y. | |
| 1936 | Henry P. Fletcher, Pa. | Frederick Steiwer, Ore. | Bertrand H. Snell, N.Y. | Frederick Steiwer, Ore. |
| 1940 | John Hamilton, Kan. | Harold E. Stassen, Minn. | Joseph W. Martin Jr., Mass. | Harold E. Stassen, Minn. |
| 1944 | Harrison E. Spangler, Iowa | Earl Warren, Calif. | Joseph W. Martin Jr., Mass. | Earl Warren, Calif. |
| 1948 | Carroll Reece, Tenn. | Dwight H. Green, Ill. | Joseph W. Martin Jr., Mass. | Dwight H. Green, Ill. |
| 1952 | Guy George Gabrielson, N.J. | Walter S. Hallanan, W.Va. | Joseph W. Martin Jr., Mass. | Douglas MacArthur |
| 1956 | Leonard W. Hall, N.Y. | William F. Knowland, Calif. | Joseph W. Martin Jr., Mass. | Arthur B. Langlie, Wash. |
| 1960 | Thruston B. Morton, Ky. | Cecil H. Underwood, W.Va. | Charles A. Halleck, Ind. | Walter H. Judd, Minn. |
| 1964 | William E. Miller, N.Y. | Mark O. Hatfield, Ore. | Thruston B. Morton, Ky. | Mark O. Hatfield, Ore. |
| 1968 | Ray C. Bliss, Ohio | Edward W. Brooke, Mass. | Gerald R. Ford, Mich. | Daniel J. Evans, Wash. |
| 1972 | Robert Dole, Kan. | Ronald Reagan, Calif. | Gerald R. Ford, Mich. | Richard G. Lugar, Ind. |
| | | | | Anne L. Armstrong, Texas |
| 1976 | Mary Louise Smith, Iowa | Robert Dole, Kan. | John J. Rhodes, Ariz. | Howard H. Baker Jr., Tenn. |
| 1980 | Bill Brock, Tenn. | Nancy Landon Kassebaum, Kan. | John J. Rhodes, Ariz. | Guy Vander Jagt, Mich. |
| 1984 | Frank J. Fahrenkopf Jr., Nev. | Howard H. Baker Jr., Tenn. | Robert H. Michel, Ill. | Katherine Ortega, N.M. |
| 1988 | Lee Atwater, S.C. | Elizabeth Hanford Dole, N.C. | Robert H. Michel, Ill. | Thomas H. Kean, N.J. |
| 1992 | Richard N. Bond, N.Y. | Kay Bailey Hutchison, Texas | Robert H. Michel, Ill. | Phil Gramm, Texas |
| 1996 | Haley Barbour, Miss. | Christine Todd Whitman, N.J. | Newt Gingrich, Ga. | Susan Molinari, N.Y. |
| | | George W. Bush, Texas | | |

## General Election Debates, 1960–1996

| Date | Location | Participants | Moderator | Sponsor |
|------|----------|--------------|-----------|---------|
| September 26, 1960 | WBBM studio, Chicago, Illinois | Sen. John F. Kennedy and Vice President Richard M. Nixon | Howard K. Smith, CBS News | CBS |
| October 7, 1960 | NBC studio, Washington, D.C. | Sen. John F. Kennedy and Vice President Richard M. Nixon | Frank McGee, NBC | NBC |
| October 13, 1960 | Nixon in Hollywood, California, and Kennedy in New York City | Sen. John F. Kennedy and Vice President Richard M. Nixon | Bill Shadel, ABC | ABC |
| October 21, 1960 | ABC studio, New York City | Sen. John F. Kennedy and Vice President Richard M. Nixon | Quincy Howe, ABC News | ABC |
| September 23, 1976 | Walnut Theater, Philadelphia, Pennsylvania | Former governor Jimmy Carter and President Gerald R. Ford | Edwin Newman, NBC News | League of Women Voters |
| October 6, 1976 | Palace of Fine Arts, San Francisco, California | Former governor Jimmy Carter and President Gerald R. Ford | Pauline Frederick, NPR | League of Women Voters |
| October 22, 1976 | Phi Beta Kappa Hall, College of William and Mary, Williamsburg, Virginia | Former governor Jimmy Carter and President Gerald R. Ford | Barbara Walters, ABC News | League of Women Voters |
| September 21, 1980 | Baltimore Convention Center, Baltimore, Maryland | Rep. John Anderson and former governor Ronald Reagan | Bill Moyers, PBS | League of Women Voters |
| October 28, 1980 | Convention Center Music Hall, Cleveland, Ohio | President Jimmy Carter and former governor Ronald Reagan | Howard K. Smith, ABC News | League of Women Voters |
| October 7, 1984 | Kentucky Center for Arts, Louisville, Kentucky | Former vice president Walter Mondale and President Ronald Reagan | Barbara Walters, ABC News | League of Women Voters |
| October 21, 1984 | Music Hall, Kansas City, Missouri | Former vice president Walter Mondale and President Ronald Reagan | Edwin Newman, retired NBC News | League of Women Voters |
| September 25, 1988 | Wait Chapel, Wake Forest University, Winston-Salem, North Carolina | Gov. Michael Dukakis and Vice President George Bush | Jim Lehrer, McNeil-Lehrer News Hour | Commission on Presidential Debates |
| October 13, 1988 | Pauley Pavilion, University of California at Los Angeles, Los Angeles, California | Gov. Michael Dukakis and Vice President George Bush | Bernard Shaw, CNN | Commission on Presidential Debates |
| October 11, 1992 | Washington University, St. Louis, Missouri | President George Bush, Gov. Bill Clinton, and independent candidate Ross Perot | Jim Lehrer, McNeil-Lehrer News Hour, PBS | Commission on Presidential Debates |
| October 15, 1992 | University of Richmond, Richmond, Virginia | President George Bush, Gov. Bill Clinton, and independent candidate Ross Perot | Carole Simpson, ABC News | Commission on Presidential Debates |
| October 19, 1992 | Michigan State University, East Lansing, Michigan | President George Bush, Gov. Bill Clinton, and independent candidate Ross Perot | Jim Lehrer, McNeil-Lehrer News Hour, PBS | Commission on Presidential Debates |
| October 6, 1996 | Bushnell Theatre, Hartford, Connecticut | President Bill Clinton and Sen. Robert Dole | Jim Lehrer, McNeil-Lehrer News Hour, PBS | Commission on Presidential Debates |
| October 16, 1996 | Shiley Theatre at the University of San Diego, San Diego, California | President Bill Clinton and Sen. Robert Dole | Jim Lehrer, McNeil-Lehrer News Hour, PBS | Commission on Presidential Debates |

SOURCES: Joel L. Swerdlow, *Presidential Debates: 1988 and Beyond* (Washington, D.C.: Congressional Quarterly, 1987); and the Commission on Presidential Debates.

# U.S. Presidents and Vice Presidents

| President and Political Party | Born | Died | Age at Inauguration | Native of | Elected from | Term of Service | Vice President |
|---|---|---|---|---|---|---|---|
| George Washington (F) | 1732 | 1799 | 57 | Va. | Va. | April 30, 1789–March 4, 1793 | John Adams |
| George Washington (F) | | | 61 | | | March 4, 1793–March 4, 1797 | John Adams |
| John Adams (F) | 1735 | 1826 | 61 | Mass. | Mass. | March 4, 1797–March 4, 1801 | Thomas Jefferson |
| Thomas Jefferson (DR) | 1743 | 1826 | 57 | Va. | Va. | March 4, 1801–March 4, 1805 | Aaron Burr |
| Thomas Jefferson (DR) | | | 61 | | | March 4, 1805–March 4, 1809 | George Clinton |
| James Madison (DR) | 1751 | 1836 | 57 | Va. | Va. | March 4, 1809–March 4, 1813 | George Clinton |
| James Madison (DR) | | | 61 | | | March 4, 1813–March 4, 1817 | Elbridge Gerry |
| James Monroe (DR) | 1758 | 1831 | 58 | Va. | Va. | March 4, 1817–March 4, 1821 | Daniel D. Tompkins |
| James Monroe (DR) | | | 62 | | | March 4, 1821–March 4, 1825 | Daniel D. Tompkins |
| John Q. Adams (DR) | 1767 | 1848 | 57 | Mass. | Mass. | March 4, 1825–March 4, 1829 | John C. Calhoun |
| Andrew Jackson (D) | 1767 | 1845 | 61 | S.C. | Tenn. | March 4, 1829–March 4, 1833 | John C. Calhoun |
| Andrew Jackson (D) | | | 65 | | | March 4, 1833–March 4, 1837 | Martin Van Buren |
| Martin Van Buren (D) | 1782 | 1862 | 54 | N.Y. | N.Y. | March 4, 1837–March 4, 1841 | Richard M. Johnson |
| W. H. Harrison (W) | 1773 | 1841 | 68 | Va. | Ohio | March 4, 1841–April 4, 1841 | John Tyler |
| John Tyler (W) | 1790 | 1862 | 51 | Va. | Va. | April 6, 1841–March 4, 1845 | |
| James K. Polk (D) | 1795 | 1849 | 49 | N.C. | Tenn. | March 4, 1985–March 4, 1849 | George M. Dallas |
| Zachary Taylor (W) | 1784 | 1850 | 64 | Va. | La. | March 4, 1849–July 9, 1850 | Millard Fillmore |
| Millard Fillmore (W) | 1800 | 1874 | 50 | N.Y. | N.Y. | July 10, 1850–March 4, 1853 | |
| Franklin Pierce (D) | 1804 | 1869 | 48 | N.H. | N.H. | March 4, 1853–March 4, 1857 | William R. King |
| James Buchanan (D) | 1791 | 1868 | 65 | Pa. | Pa. | March 4, 1857–March 4, 1861 | John C. Breckinridge |
| Abraham Lincoln (R) | 1809 | 1865 | 52 | Ky. | Ill. | March 4, 1861–March 4, 1865 | Hannibal Hamlin |
| Abraham Lincoln (R) | | | 56 | | | March 4, 1865–April 15, 1865 | Andrew Johnson |
| Andrew Johnson (R) | 1808 | 1875 | 56 | N.C. | Tenn. | April 15, 1865–March 4, 1869 | |
| Ulysses S. Grant (R) | 1822 | 1885 | 46 | Ohio | Ill. | March 4, 1869–March 4, 1873 | Schuyler Colfax |
| Ulysses S. Grant (R) | | | 50 | | | March 4, 1873–March 4, 1877 | Henry Wilson |
| Rutherford B. Hayes (R) | 1822 | 1893 | 54 | Ohio | Ohio | March 4, 1877–March 4, 1881 | William A. Wheeler |
| James A. Garfield (R) | 1831 | 1881 | 49 | Ohio | Ohio | March 4, 1881–Sept. 19, 1881 | Chester A. Arthur |
| Chester A. Arthur (R) | 1830 | 1886 | 50 | Vt. | N.Y. | Sept. 20, 1881–March 4, 1885 | |
| Grover Cleveland (D) | 1837 | 1908 | 47 | N.J. | N.Y. | March 4, 1885–March 4, 1889 | Thomas A. Hendricks |
| Benjamin Harrison (R) | 1833 | 1901 | 55 | Ohio | Ind. | March 4, 1889–March 4, 1893 | Levi P. Morton |
| Grover Cleveland (D) | 1837 | 1908 | 55 | N.J. | N.Y. | March 4, 1893–March 4, 1897 | Adlai E. Stevenson |
| William McKinley (R) | 1843 | 1901 | 54 | Ohio | Ohio | March 4, 1897–March 4, 1901 | Garret A. Hobart |
| William McKinley (R) | | | 58 | | | March 4, 1901–Sept. 14, 1901 | Theodore Roosevelt |
| Theodore Roosevelt (R) | 1858 | 1919 | 42 | N.Y. | N.Y. | Sept. 14, 1901–March 4, 1905 | |
| Theodore Roosevelt (R) | | | 46 | | | March 4, 1905–March 4, 1909 | Charles W. Fairbanks |
| William H. Taft (R) | 1857 | 1930 | 51 | Ohio | Ohio | March 4, 1909–March 4, 1913 | James S. Sherman |
| Woodrow Wilson (D) | 1856 | 1924 | 56 | Va. | N.J. | March 4, 1913–March 4, 1917 | Thomas R. Marshall |
| Woodrow Wilson (D) | | | 60 | | | March 4, 1917–March 4, 1921 | Thomas R. Marshall |
| Warren G. Harding (R) | 1865 | 1923 | 55 | Ohio | Ohio | March 4, 1921–Aug. 2, 1923 | Calvin Coolidge |
| Calvin Coolidge (R) | 1872 | 1933 | 51 | Vt. | Mass. | Aug. 3, 1923–March 4, 1925 | |
| Calvin Coolidge (R) | | | 52 | | | March 4, 1925–March 4, 1929 | Charles G. Dawes |
| Herbert Hoover (R) | 1874 | 1964 | 54 | Iowa | Calif. | March 4, 1929–March 4, 1933 | Charles Curtis |
| Franklin D. Roosevelt (D) | 1882 | 1945 | 51 | N.Y. | N.Y. | March 4, 1933–Jan. 20, 1937 | John N. Garner |
| Franklin D. Roosevelt (D) | | | 55 | | | Jan. 20, 1937–Jan. 20, 1941 | John N. Garner |
| Franklin D. Roosevelt (D) | | | 59 | | | Jan. 20, 1941–Jan. 20, 1945 | Henry A. Wallace |
| Franklin D. Roosevelt (D) | | | 63 | | | Jan. 20, 1945–April 12, 1945 | Harry S. Truman |

*(Continued)*

## U.S. Presidents and Vice Presidents *(Continued)*

| President and Political Party | Born | Died | Age at Inauguration | Native of | Elected from | Term of Service | Vice President |
|---|---|---|---|---|---|---|---|
| Harry S. Truman (D) | 1884 | 1972 | 60 | Mo. | Mo. | April 12, 1945–Jan. 20, 1949 | |
| Harry S. Truman (D) | | | 64 | | | Jan. 20, 1949–Jan. 20, 1953 | Alben W. Barkley |
| Dwight D. Eisenhower (R) | 1890 | 1969 | 62 | Texas | N.Y. | Jan. 20, 1953–Jan. 20, 1957 | Richard Nixon |
| Dwight D. Eisenhower (R) | | | 66 | | Pa. | Jan. 20, 1957–Jan. 20, 1961 | Richard Nixon |
| John F. Kennedy (D) | 1917 | 1963 | 43 | Mass. | Mass. | Jan. 20, 1961–Nov. 22, 1963 | Lyndon B. Johnson |
| Lyndon B. Johnson (D) | 1908 | 1973 | 55 | Texas | Texas | Nov. 22, 1963–Jan. 20, 1965 | |
| Lyndon B. Johnson (D) | | | 56 | | | Jan. 20, 1965–Jan. 20, 1969 | Hubert H. Humphrey |
| Richard Nixon (R) | 1913 | 1994 | 56 | Calif. | N.Y. | Jan. 20, 1969–Jan. 20, 1973 | Spiro T. Agnew |
| Richard Nixon (R) | | | 60 | | Calif. | Jan. 20, 1973–Aug. 9, 1974 | Spiro T. Agnew |
| | | | | | | | Gerald R. Ford |
| Gerald R. Ford (R) | 1913 | | 61 | Neb. | Mich. | Aug. 9, 1974–Jan. 20, 1977 | Nelson A. Rockefeller |
| Jimmy Carter (D) | 1924 | | 52 | Ga. | Ga. | Jan. 20, 1977–Jan. 20, 1981 | Walter F. Mondale |
| Ronald Reagan (R) | 1911 | | 69 | Ill. | Calif. | Jan. 20, 1981–Jan. 20, 1985 | George Bush |
| Ronald Reagan (R) | | | 73 | | | Jan. 20, 1985–Jan. 20, 1989 | George Bush |
| George Bush (R) | 1924 | | 64 | Mass. | Texas | Jan. 20, 1989–Jan. 20, 1993 | Dan Quayle |
| Bill Clinton (D) | 1946 | | 46 | Ark. | Ark. | Jan. 20, 1993–Jan. 20, 1997 | Albert Gore Jr. |
| Bill Clinton (D) | | | 50 | | | Jan. 20, 1997– | Albert Gore Jr. |

NOTE: D—Democrat; DR—Democratic-Republican; F—Federalist; R—Republican; W—Whig.

## Summary of Presidential Elections, 1789–1996

| Year | No. of states | Candidates | Party | Electoral vote | Popular vote |
|---|---|---|---|---|---|
| 1789[a] | 10 | **George Washington** | **Fed.** | **69** | —[b] |
| | | John Adams | Fed. | 34 | |
| 1792[a] | 15 | **George Washington** | **Fed.** | **132** | —[b] |
| | | John Adams | Fed. | 77 | |
| 1796[a] | 16 | **John Adams** | **Fed.** | **71** | —[b] |
| | | Thomas Jefferson | Dem.-Rep. | 68 | |
| 1800[a] | 16 | **Thomas Jefferson** | **Dem.-Rep.** | **73** | —[b] |
| | | Aaron Burr | Dem.-Rep. | 73 | |
| | | John Adams | Fed. | 65 | |
| | | Charles Cotesworth Pinckney | Fed. | 64 | |
| 1804 | 17 | **Thomas Jefferson** *George Clinton* | **Dem.-Rep.** | **162** | —[b] |
| | | Charles Cotesworth Pinckney *Rufus King* | Fed. | 64 | |
| 1808 | 17 | **James Madison** *George Clinton* | **Dem.-Rep.** | **122** | —[b] |
| | | Charles Cotesworth Pinckney *Rufus King* | Fed. | 64 | |
| 1812 | 18 | **James Madison** *Elbridge Gerry* | **Dem.-Rep.** | **128** | —[b] |
| | | George Clinton *Jared Ingersoll* | Fed. | 89 | |
| 1816 | 19 | **James Monroe** *Daniel D. Tompkins* | **Dem.-Rep.** | **183** | —[b] |
| | | Rufus King *John Howard* | Fed. | 34 | |
| 1820 | 24 | **James Monroe** *Daniel D. Tompkins* | **Dem.-Rep.** | **231**[c] | —[b] |
| 1824[d] | 24 | **John Quincy Adams** *John C. Calhoun* | **Dem.-Rep.** | **99** | **113,122 (30.9%)** |
| | | Andrew Jackson *Nathan Sanford* | Dem.-Rep. | 84 | 151,271 (41.3%) |
| 1828 | 24 | **Andrew Jackson** *John C. Calhoun* | **Dem.-Rep.** | **178** | **642,553 (56.0%)** |
| | | John Quincy Adams *Richard Rush* | Nat.-Rep. | 83 | 500,897 (43.6%) |

*(Continued)*

| Year | No. of states | Candidates | Party | Electoral vote | Popular vote |
|---|---|---|---|---|---|
| 1832[e] | 24 | **Andrew Jackson** *Martin Van Buren* | **Dem.** | **219** | **701,780 (54.2%)** |
| | | Henry Clay *John Sergeant* | Nat.-Rep. | 49 | 484,205 (37.4%) |
| 1836[f] | 26 | **Martin Van Buren** *Richard M. Johnson* | **Dem.** | **170** | **764,176 (50.8%)** |
| | | William Henry Harrison *Francis Granger* | Whig | 73 | 550,816 (36.6%) |
| 1840 | 26 | **William Henry Harrison** *John Tyler* | **Whig** | **234** | **1,275,390 (52.9%)** |
| | | Martin Van Buren *Richard M. Johnson* | Dem. | 60 | 1,128,854 (46.8%) |
| 1844 | 26 | **James K. Polk** *George M. Dallas* | **Dem.** | **170** | **1,339,494 (49.5%)** |
| | | Henry Clay *Theodore Frelinghuysen* | Whig | 105 | 1,300,004 (48.1%) |
| 1848 | 30 | **Zachary Taylor** *Millard Fillmore* | **Whig** | **163** | **1,361,393 (47.3%)** |
| | | Lewis Cass *William O. Butler* | Dem. | 127 | 1,223,460 (42.5%) |
| 1852 | 31 | **Franklin Pierce** *William R. King* | **Dem.** | **254** | **1,607,510 (50.8%)** |
| | | Winfield Scott *William A. Graham* | Whig | 42 | 1,386,942 (43.9%) |
| 1856[g] | 31 | **James Buchanan** *John C. Breckinridge* | **Dem.** | **174** | **1,836,072 (45.3%)** |
| | | John C. Fremont *William L. Dayton* | Rep. | 114 | 1,342,345 (33.1%) |
| 1860[h] | 33 | **Abraham Lincoln** *Hannibal Hamlin* | **Rep.** | **180** | **1,865,908 (39.8%)** |
| | | Stephen A. Douglas *Herschel V. Johnson* | Dem. | 12 | 1,380,202 (29.5%) |
| 1864[i] | 36 | **Abraham Lincoln** *Andrew Johnson* | **Rep.** | **212** | **2,218,388 (55.0%)** |
| | | George B. McClellan *George H. Pendleton* | Dem. | 21 | 1,812,807 (45.0%) |
| 1868[j] | 37 | **Ulysses S. Grant** *Schuyler Colfax* | **Rep.** | **214** | **3,013,650 (52.7%)** |
| | | Horatio Seymour *Francis P. Blair Jr.* | Dem. | 80 | 2,708,744 (47.3%) |

| Year | No. of states | Candidates | Party | Electoral vote | Popular vote |
|------|------|------------|-------|----------------|--------------|
| 1872 | 37 | **Ulysses S. Grant** *Henry Wilson* | **Rep.** | **286** | **3,598,235 (55.6%)** |
| | | Horace Greeley *Benjamin Gratz Brown* | Dem. | —[k] | 2,834,761 (43.8%) |
| 1876 | 38 | **Rutherford B. Hayes** *William A. Wheeler* | **Rep.** | **185** | **4,034,311 (47.9%)** |
| | | Samuel J. Tilden *Thomas A. Hendricks* | Dem. | 184 | 4,288,546 (51.0%) |
| 1880 | 38 | **James A. Garfield** *Chester A. Arthur* | **Rep.** | **214** | **4,446,158 (48.3%)** |
| | | Winfield S. Hancock *William H. English* | Dem. | 155 | 4,444,260 (48.2%) |
| 1884 | 38 | **Grover Cleveland** *Thomas A. Hendricks* | **Dem.** | **219** | **4,874,621 (48.5%)** |
| | | James G. Blaine *John A. Logan* | Rep. | 182 | 4,848,936 (48.2%) |
| 1888 | 38 | **Benjamin Harrison** *Levi P. Morton* | **Rep.** | **233** | **5,443,892 (47.8%)** |
| | | Grover Cleveland *Allen G. Thurman* | Dem. | 168 | 5,534,488 (48.6%) |
| 1892[l] | 44 | **Grover Cleveland** *Adlai E. Stevenson* | **Dem.** | **277** | **5,551,883 (46.1%)** |
| | | Benjamin Harrison *Whitelaw Reid* | Rep. | 145 | 5,179,244 (43.0%) |
| 1896 | 45 | **William McKinley** *Garret A. Hobart* | **Rep.** | **271** | **7,108,480 (51.0%)** |
| | | William J. Bryan *Arthur Sewall* | Dem. | 176 | 6,511,495 (46.7%) |
| 1900 | 45 | **William McKinley** *Theodore Roosevelt* | **Rep.** | **292** | **7,218,039 (51.7%)** |
| | | William J. Bryan *Adlai E. Stevenson* | Dem. | 155 | 6,358,345 (45.5%) |
| 1904 | 45 | **Theodore Roosevelt** *Charles W. Fairbanks* | **Rep.** | **336** | **7,626,593 (56.4%)** |
| | | Alton B. Parker *Henry G. Davis* | Dem. | 140 | 5,028,898 (37.6%) |
| 1908 | 46 | **William Howard Taft** *James S. Sherman* | **Rep.** | **321** | **7,676,258 (51.6%)** |
| | | William J. Bryan *John W. Kern* | Dem. | 162 | 6,406,801 (43.0%) |

*(Continued)*

| Year | No. of states | Candidates | Party | Electoral vote | Popular vote |
|------|------|------------|-------|----------------|--------------|
| 1912[m] | 48 | **Woodrow Wilson** *Thomas R. Marshall* | **Dem.** | **435** | **6,293,152 (41.8%)** |
| | | William Howard Taft *James S. Sherman* | Rep. | 8 | 3,486,333 (23.2%) |
| 1916 | 48 | **Woodrow Wilson** *Thomas R. Marshall* | **Dem.** | **277** | **9,126,300 (49.2%)** |
| | | Charles E. Hughes *Charles W. Fairbanks* | Rep. | 254 | 8,546,789 (46.1%) |
| 1920 | 48 | **Warren G. Harding** *Calvin Coolidge* | **Rep.** | **404** | **16,133,314 (60.3%)** |
| | | James M. Cox *Franklin D. Roosevelt* | Dem. | 127 | 9,140,884 (34.2%) |
| 1924[n] | 48 | **Calvin Coolidge** *Charles G. Dawes* | **Rep.** | **382** | **15,717,553 (54.1%)** |
| | | John W. Davis *Charles W. Bryan* | Dem. | 136 | 8,386,169 (28.8%) |
| 1928 | 48 | **Herbert C. Hoover** *Charles Curtis* | **Rep.** | **444** | **21,411,991 (58.2%)** |
| | | Alfred E. Smith *Joseph T. Robinson* | Dem. | 87 | 15,000,185 (40.8%) |
| 1932 | 48 | **Franklin D. Roosevelt** *John N. Garner* | **Dem.** | **472** | **22,825,016 (57.4%)** |
| | | Herbert C. Hoover *Charles Curtis* | Rep. | 59 | 15,758,397 (39.6%) |
| 1936 | 48 | **Franklin D. Roosevelt** *John N. Garner* | **Dem.** | **523** | **27,747,636 (60.8%)** |
| | | Alfred M. Landon *Frank Knox* | Rep. | 8 | 16,679,543 (36.5%) |
| 1940 | 48 | **Franklin D. Roosevelt** *Henry A. Wallace* | **Dem.** | **449** | **27,263,448 (54.7%)** |
| | | Wendell L. Willkie *Charles L. McNary* | Rep. | 82 | 22,336,260 (44.8%) |
| 1944 | 48 | **Franklin D. Roosevelt** *Harry S. Truman* | **Dem.** | **432** | **25,611,936 (53.4%)** |
| | | Thomas E. Dewey *John W. Bricker* | Rep. | 99 | 22,013,372 (45.9%) |
| 1948[o] | 48 | **Harry S. Truman** *Alben W. Barkley* | **Dem.** | **303** | **24,105,587 (49.5%)** |
| | | Thomas E. Dewey *Earl Warren* | Rep. | 198 | 21,970,017 (45.1%) |

| Year | No. of states | Candidates | Party | Electoral vote | Popular vote |
|------|---------------|------------|-------|----------------|--------------|
| 1952 | 48 | **Dwight D. Eisenhower** *Richard M. Nixon* | **Rep.** | **442** | **33,936,137 (55.1%)** |
| | | Adlai E. Stevenson II *John J. Sparkman* | Dem. | 89 | 27,314,649 (44.4%) |
| 1956[p] | 48 | **Dwight D. Eisenhower** *Richard M. Nixon* | **Rep.** | **457** | **35,585,245 (57.4%)** |
| | | Adlai E. Stevenson II *Estes Kefauver* | Dem. | 73 | 26,030,172 (42.0%) |
| 1960[q] | 50 | **John F. Kennedy** *Lyndon B. Johnson* | **Dem.** | **303** | **34,221,344 (49.7%)** |
| | | Richard Nixon *Henry Cabot Lodge* | Rep. | 219 | 34,106,671 (49.5%) |
| 1964 | 50* | **Lyndon B. Johnson** *Hubert H. Humphrey* | **Dem.** | **486** | **43,126,584 (61.1%)** |
| | | Barry Goldwater *William E. Miller* | Rep. | 52 | 27,177,838 (38.5%) |
| 1968[r] | 50* | **Richard Nixon** *Spiro T. Agnew* | **Rep.** | **301** | **31,785,148 (43.4%)** |
| | | Hubert H. Humphrey *Edmund S. Muskie* | Dem. | 191 | 31,274,503 (42.7%) |
| 1972[s] | 50* | **Richard Nixon** *Spiro T. Agnew* | **Rep.** | **520** | **47,170,179 (60.7%)** |
| | | George McGovern *Sargent Shriver* | Dem. | 17 | 29,171,791 (37.5%) |
| 1976[t] | 50* | **Jimmy Carter** *Walter F. Mondale* | **Dem.** | **297** | **40,830,763 (50.1%)** |
| | | Gerald R. Ford *Robert Dole* | Rep. | 240 | 39,147,793 (48.0%) |
| 1980 | 50* | **Ronald Reagan** *George Bush* | **Rep.** | **489** | **43,904,153 (50.7%)** |
| | | Jimmy Carter *Walter F. Mondale* | Dem. | 49 | 35,483,883 (41.0%) |
| 1984 | 50* | **Ronald Reagan** *George Bush* | **Rep.** | **525** | **54,455,074(58.8%)** |
| | | Walter F. Mondale *Geraldine Ferraro* | Dem. | 13 | 37,577,137 (40.6%) |
| 1988[u] | 50* | **George Bush** *Dan Quayle* | **Rep.** | **426** | **48,881,278 (53.4%)** |
| | | Michael S. Dukakis *Lloyd Bentsen* | Dem. | 111 | 41,805,374 (45.6%) |

*(Continued)*

## Summary of Presidential Elections, 1789–1996 *(Continued)*

| Year | No. of states | Candidates | Party | Electoral vote | Popular vote |
|------|------|------|------|------|------|
| 1992 | 50* | **Bill Clinton** *Al Gore* | **Dem.** | 370 | **44,908,233 (43.0%)** |
|  |  | George Bush *Dan Quayle* | Rep. | 168 | 39,102,282 (37.4%) |
| 1996 | 50* | **Bill Clinton** *Al Gore* | **Dem.** | 379 | **47,402,357 (49.2%)** |
|  |  | Robert Dole *Jack Kemp* | Rep. | 159 | 39,1987,755 (40.7%) |

SOURCES: Harold W. Stanley and Richard G. Niemi, *Vital Statistics on American Politics,* 5th ed. (Washington, D.C.: CQ Press, 1995), Table 3-13; 1996 data, Richard M. Scammon, Alice V. McGillvray, and Rhodes Cook, *America Votes 22* (Washington, D.C.: Congressional Quarterly, 1998), 9.

NOTES: In the elections of 1789, 1792, 1796, and 1800, each candidate ran for the office of president. The candidate with the second highest number of electoral votes became vice president. For elections after 1800, italic indicates vice-presidential candidates. Dem.-Rep.—Democratic-Republican; Fed.—Federalist; Nat.-Rep.—National-Republican; Dem.—Democratic; Rep.—Republican.

a. Elections of 1789–1800 were held under rules that did not allow separate voting for president and vice president.

b. Popular vote returns are not shown before 1824 because consistent, reliable data are not available.

c. Monroe ran unopposed. One electoral vote was cast for John Adams and Richard Stockton, who were not candidates.

d. 1824: All four candidates represented Democratic-Republican factions. William H. Crawford received 41 electoral votes, and Henry Clay received 37 votes. Since no candidate received a majority, the election was decided (in Adams's favor) by the House of Representatives.

e. 1832: Two electoral votes were not cast.

f. 1836: Other Whig candidates receiving electoral votes were Hugh L. White, who received 26 votes, and Daniel Webster, who received 14 votes.

g. 1856: Millard Fillmore, Whig-American, received 8 electoral votes.

h. 1860: John C. Breckinridge, Southern Democrat, received 72 electoral votes. John Bell, Constitutional Union, received 39 electoral votes.

i. 1864: Eighty-one electoral votes were not cast.

j. 1868: Twenty-three electoral votes were not cast.

k. 1872: Horace Greeley, Democrat, died after the election. In the electoral college, Democratic electoral votes went to Thomas Hendricks, 42 votes; Benjamin Gratz Brown, 18 votes; Charles J. Jenkins, 2 votes; and David Davis, 1 vote. Seventeen electoral votes were not cast.

l. 1892: James B. Weaver, People's Party, received 22 electoral votes.

m. 1912: Theodore Roosevelt, Progressive Party, received 86 electoral votes.

n. 1924: Robert M. La Follette, Progressive Party, received 13 electoral votes.

o. 1948: J. Strom Thurmond, States' Rights Party, received 39 electoral votes.

p. 1956: Walter B. Jones, Democrat, received 1 electoral vote.

q. 1960: Harry Flood Byrd, Democrat, received 15 electoral votes.

r. 1968: George C. Wallace, American Independent Party, received 46 electoral votes.

s. 1972: John Hospers, Libertarian Party, received 1 electoral vote.

t. 1976: Ronald Reagan, Republican, received 1 electoral vote.

u. 1988: Lloyd Bentsen, the Democratic vice-presidential nominee, received 1 electoral vote for president.

*Fifty states plus the District of Columbia.

## 1996 Popular Vote Summary, Presidential

| State | Electoral Vote Rep. | Electoral Vote Dem. | Electoral Vote Other | Total Vote | Republican | Democratic | Reform | Other | Plurality | | Percentage Rep. | Percentage Dem. | Percentage Reform |
|---|---|---|---|---|---|---|---|---|---|---|---|---|---|
| Alabama | 9 | | | 1,534,349 | 769,044 | 662,165 | 92,149 | 10,991 | 106,879 | R | 50.1% | 43.2% | 6.0% |
| Alaska | 3 | | | 241,620 | 122,746 | 80,380 | 26,333 | 12,161 | 42,366 | R | 50.8% | 33.3% | 10.9% |
| Arizona | | 8 | | 1,404,405 | 622,073 | 653,288 | 112,072 | 16,972 | 31,215 | D | 44.3% | 46.5% | 8.0% |
| Arkansas | | 6 | | 884,262 | 325,416 | 475,171 | 69,884 | 13,791 | 149,755 | D | 36.8% | 53.7% | 7.9% |
| California | | 54 | | 10,019,484 | 3,828,380 | 5,119,835 | 697,847 | 373,422 | 1,291,455 | D | 38.2% | 51.1% | 7.0% |
| Colorado | 8 | | | 1,510,704 | 691,848 | 671,152 | 99,629 | 48,075 | 20,696 | R | 45.8% | 44.4% | 6.6% |
| Connecticut | | 8 | | 1,392,614 | 483,109 | 735,740 | 139,523 | 34,242 | 252,631 | D | 34.7% | 52.8% | 10.0% |
| Delaware | | 3 | | 271,084 | 99,062 | 140,355 | 28,719 | 2,948 | 41,293 | D | 36.5% | 51.8% | 10.6% |
| Florida | | 25 | | 5,303,794 | 2,244,536 | 2,546,870 | 483,870 | 28,518 | 302,334 | D | 42.3% | 48.0% | 9.1% |
| Georgia | 13 | | | 2,299,071 | 1,080,843 | 1,053,849 | 146,337 | 18,042 | 26,994 | R | 47.0% | 45.8% | 6.4% |
| Hawaii | | 4 | | 360,120 | 113,943 | 205,012 | 27,358 | 13,807 | 91,069 | D | 31.6% | 56.9% | 7.6% |
| Idaho | 4 | | | 491,719 | 256,595 | 165,443 | 62,518 | 7,163 | 91,152 | R | 52.2% | 33.6% | 12.7% |
| Illinois | | 22 | | 4,311,391 | 1,587,021 | 2,341,744 | 346,408 | 36,218 | 754,723 | D | 36.8% | 54.3% | 8.0% |
| Indiana | 12 | | | 2,135,842 | 1,006,693 | 887,424 | 224,299 | 17,426 | 119,269 | R | 47.1% | 41.5% | 10.5% |
| Iowa | | 7 | | 1,234,075 | 492,644 | 620,258 | 105,159 | 16,014 | 127,614 | D | 39.9% | 50.3% | 8.5% |
| Kansas | 6 | | | 1,074,300 | 583,245 | 387,659 | 92,639 | 10,757 | 195,586 | R | 54.3% | 36.1% | 8.6% |
| Kentucky | | 8 | | 1,388,708 | 623,283 | 636,614 | 120,396 | 8,415 | 13,331 | D | 44.9% | 45.8% | 8.7% |
| Louisiana | | 9 | | 1,783,959 | 712,586 | 927,837 | 123,293 | 20,243 | 215,251 | D | 39.9% | 52.0% | 6.9% |
| Maine | | 4 | | 605,897 | 186,378 | 312,788 | 85,970 | 20,761 | 126,410 | D | 30.8% | 51.6% | 14.2% |
| Maryland | | 10 | | 1,780,870 | 681,530 | 966,207 | 115,812 | 17,321 | 284,677 | D | 38.3% | 54.3% | 6.5% |
| Massachusetts | | 12 | | 2,556,785 | 718,107 | 1,571,763 | 227,217 | 39,698 | 853,656 | D | 28.1% | 61.5% | 8.9% |
| Michigan | | 18 | | 3,848,844 | 1,481,212 | 1,989,653 | 336,670 | 41,309 | 508,441 | D | 38.5% | 51.7% | 8.7% |
| Minnesota | | 10 | | 2,192,640 | 766,476 | 1,120,438 | 257,704 | 48,022 | 353,962 | D | 35.0% | 51.1% | 11.8% |
| Mississippi | 7 | | | 893,857 | 439,838 | 394,022 | 52,222 | 7,775 | 45,816 | R | 49.2% | 44.1% | 5.8% |
| Missouri | | 11 | | 2,158,065 | 890,016 | 1,025,935 | 217,188 | 24,926 | 135,919 | D | 41.2% | 47.5% | 10.1% |
| Montana | 3 | | | 407,261 | 179,652 | 167,922 | 55,229 | 4,458 | 11,730 | R | 44.1% | 41.2% | 13.6% |
| Nebraska | 5 | | | 677,415 | 363,467 | 236,761 | 71,278 | 5,909 | 126,706 | R | 53.7% | 35.0% | 10.5% |
| Nevada | | 4 | | 464,279 | 199,244 | 203,974 | 43,986 | 17,075 | 4,730 | D | 42.9% | 43.9% | 9.5% |
| New Hampshire | | 4 | | 499,175 | 196,532 | 246,214 | 48,390 | 8,039 | 49,682 | D | 39.4% | 49.3% | 9.7% |
| New Jersey | | 15 | | 3,075,807 | 1,103,078 | 1,652,329 | 262,134 | 58,266 | 549,251 | D | 35.9% | 53.7% | 8.5% |
| New Mexico | | 5 | | 556,074 | 232,751 | 273,495 | 32,257 | 17,571 | 40,744 | D | 41.9% | 49.2% | 5.8% |
| New York | | 33 | | 6,316,129 | 1,933,492 | 3,756,177 | 503,458 | 123,002 | 1,822,685 | D | 30.6% | 59.5% | 8.0% |
| North Carolina | 14 | | | 2,515,807 | 1,225,938 | 1,107,849 | 168,059 | 13,961 | 118,089 | R | 48.7% | 44.0% | 6.7% |
| North Dakota | 3 | | | 266,411 | 125,050 | 106,905 | 32,515 | 1,941 | 18,145 | R | 46.9% | 40.1% | 12.2% |
| Ohio | | 21 | | 4,534,434 | 1,859,883 | 2,148,222 | 483,207 | 43,122 | 288,339 | D | 41.0% | 47.4% | 10.7% |
| Oklahoma | 8 | | | 1,206,713 | 582,315 | 488,105 | 130,788 | 5,505 | 94,210 | R | 48.3% | 40.4% | 10.8% |
| Oregon | | 7 | | 1,377,760 | 538,152 | 649,641 | 121,221 | 68,746 | 111,489 | D | 39.1% | 47.2% | 8.8% |
| Pennsylvania | | 23 | | 4,506,118 | 1,801,169 | 2,215,819 | 430,984 | 58,146 | 414,650 | D | 40.0% | 49.2% | 9.6% |
| Rhode Island | | 4 | | 390,284 | 104,683 | 233,050 | 43,723 | 8,828 | 128,367 | D | 26.8% | 59.7% | 11.2% |
| South Carolina | 8 | | | 1,151,689 | 573,458 | 506,283 | 64,386 | 7,562 | 67,175 | R | 49.8% | 44.0% | 5.6% |
| South Dakota | 3 | | | 323,826 | 150,543 | 139,333 | 31,250 | 2,700 | 11,210 | R | 46.5% | 43.0% | 9.7% |
| Tennessee | | 11 | | 1,894,105 | 863,530 | 909,146 | 105,918 | 15,511 | 45,616 | D | 45.6% | 48.0% | 5.6% |
| Texas | 32 | | | 5,611,644 | 2,736,167 | 2,459,683 | 378,537 | 37,257 | 276,484 | R | 48.8% | 43.8% | 6.7% |
| Utah | 5 | | | 665,629 | 361,911 | 221,633 | 66,461 | 15,624 | 140,278 | R | 54.4% | 33.3% | 10.0% |
| Vermont | | 3 | | 258,449 | 80,352 | 137,894 | 31,024 | 9,179 | 57,542 | D | 31.1% | 53.4% | 12.0% |
| Virginia | 13 | | | 2,416,642 | 1,138,350 | 1,091,060 | 159,861 | 27,371 | 47,290 | R | 47.1% | 45.1% | 6.6% |
| Washington | | 11 | | 2,253,837 | 840,712 | 1,123,323 | 201,003 | 88,799 | 282,611 | D | 37.3% | 49.8% | 8.9% |
| West Virginia | | 5 | | 636,459 | 233,946 | 327,812 | 71,639 | 3,062 | 93,866 | D | 36.8% | 51.5% | 11.3% |
| Wisconsin | | 11 | | 2,196,169 | 845,029 | 1,071,971 | 227,339 | 51,830 | 226,942 | D | 38.5% | 48.8% | 10.4% |
| Wyoming | 3 | | | 211,571 | 105,388 | 77,934 | 25,928 | 2,321 | 27,454 | R | 49.8% | 36.8% | 12.3% |
| Dist. of Col. | | 3 | | 185,726 | 17,339 | 158,220 | 3,611 | 6,556 | 140,881 | D | 9.3% | 85.2% | 1.9% |
| United States | 159 | 379 | | 96,277,872 | 39,198,755 | 47,402,357 | 8,085,402 | 1,591,358 | 8,203,602 | D | 40.7% | 49.2% | 8.4% |

# Distribution of House Seats and Electoral Votes

*(Based on Censuses of 1950, 1960, 1970, and 1990)*

| State | U.S. House Seats | | | | | | | | | Electoral Votes | | | | |
|---|---|---|---|---|---|---|---|---|---|---|---|---|---|---|
| | 1953–1963 | 1960 Census Changes | 1963–1973 | 1970 Census Changes | 1973–1983 | 1980 Census Changes | 1983–1993 | 1990 Census Changes | 1993–2003 | 1952, 1956, 1960 | 1964, 1968 | 1972, 1976, 1980 | 1984, 1988 | 1992, 1996, 2000 |
| Alabama | 9 | −1 | 8 | −1 | 7 | — | 7 | — | 7 | 11 | 10 | 9 | 9 | 9 |
| Alaska | 1 | — | 1 | — | 1 | — | 1 | — | 1 | 3 | 3 | 3 | 3 | 3 |
| Arizona | 2 | +1 | 3 | +1 | 4 | +1 | 5 | +1 | 6 | 4 | 5 | 6 | 7 | 8 |
| Arkansas | 6 | −2 | 4 | — | 4 | — | 4 | — | 4 | 8 | 6 | 6 | 6 | 6 |
| California | 30 | +8 | 38 | +5 | 43 | +2 | 45 | +7 | 52 | 32 | 40 | 45 | 47 | 54 |
| Colorado | 4 | — | 4 | +1 | 5 | +1 | 6 | — | 6 | 6 | 6 | 7 | 8 | 8 |
| Connecticut | 6 | — | 6 | — | 6 | — | 6 | — | 6 | 8 | 8 | 8 | 8 | 8 |
| Delaware | 1 | — | 1 | — | 1 | — | 1 | — | 1 | 3 | 3 | 3 | 3 | 3 |
| District of Columbia | — | — | — | — | — | — | — | — | — | — | 3 | 3 | 3 | 3 |
| Florida | 8 | +4 | 12 | +3 | 15 | +4 | 19 | +4 | 23 | 10 | 14 | 17 | 21 | 25 |
| Georgia | 10 | — | 10 | — | 10 | — | 10 | +1 | 11 | 12 | 12 | 12 | 12 | 13 |
| Hawaii | 1 | +1 | 2 | — | 2 | — | 2 | — | 2 | 3 | 4 | 4 | 4 | 4 |
| Idaho | 2 | — | 2 | — | 2 | — | 2 | — | 2 | 4 | 4 | 4 | 4 | 4 |
| Illinois | 25 | −1 | 24 | — | 24 | −2 | 22 | −2 | 20 | 27 | 26 | 26 | 24 | 22 |
| Indiana | 11 | — | 11 | — | 11 | 1 | 10 | — | 10 | 13 | 13 | 13 | 12 | 12 |
| Iowa | 8 | −1 | 7 | −1 | 6 | — | 6 | −1 | 5 | 10 | 9 | 8 | 8 | 7 |
| Kansas | 6 | −1 | 5 | — | 5 | — | 5 | −1 | 4 | 8 | 7 | 7 | 7 | 6 |
| Kentucky | 8 | −1 | 7 | — | 7 | — | 7 | −1 | 6 | 10 | 9 | 9 | 9 | 8 |
| Louisiana | 8 | — | 8 | — | 8 | — | 8 | −1 | 7 | 10 | 10 | 10 | 10 | 9 |
| Maine | 3 | −1 | 2 | — | 2 | — | 2 | — | 2 | 5 | 4 | 4 | 4 | 4 |
| Maryland | 7 | +1 | 8 | — | 8 | — | 8 | — | 8 | 9 | 10 | 10 | 10 | 10 |
| Massachusetts | 14 | −2 | 12 | — | 12 | −1 | 11 | −1 | 10 | 16 | 14 | 14 | 13 | 12 |
| Michigan | 18 | +1 | 19 | — | 19 | −1 | 18 | −2 | 16 | 20 | 21 | 21 | 20 | 18 |
| Minnesota | 9 | −1 | 8 | — | 8 | — | 8 | — | 8 | 11 | 10 | 10 | 10 | 10 |
| Mississippi | 6 | −1 | 5 | — | 5 | — | 5 | — | 5 | 8 | 7 | 7 | 7 | 7 |
| Missouri | 11 | −1 | 10 | — | 10 | −1 | 9 | — | 9 | 13 | 12 | 12 | 11 | 11 |
| Montana | 2 | — | 2 | — | 2 | — | 2 | −1 | 1 | 4 | 4 | 4 | 4 | 3 |
| Nebraska | 4 | −1 | 3 | — | 3 | — | 3 | — | 3 | 6 | 5 | 5 | 5 | 5 |
| Nevada | 1 | — | 1 | — | 1 | +1 | 2 | — | 2 | 3 | 3 | 3 | 4 | 4 |
| New Hampshire | 2 | — | 2 | — | 2 | — | 2 | — | 2 | 4 | 4 | 4 | 4 | 4 |
| New Jersey | 14 | +1 | 15 | — | 15 | −1 | 14 | −1 | 13 | 16 | 17 | 17 | 16 | 15 |
| New Mexico | 2 | — | 2 | — | 2 | +1 | 3 | — | 3 | 4 | 4 | 4 | 5 | 5 |
| New York | 43 | −2 | 41 | −2 | 39 | −5 | 34 | −3 | 31 | 45 | 43 | 41 | 36 | 33 |
| North Carolina | 12 | −1 | 11 | — | 11 | — | 11 | +1 | 12 | 14 | 13 | 13 | 13 | 14 |
| North Dakota | 2 | — | 2 | −1 | 1 | — | 1 | — | 1 | 4 | 4 | 3 | 3 | 3 |
| Ohio | 23 | +1 | 24 | −1 | 23 | −2 | 21 | −2 | 19 | 25 | 26 | 25 | 23 | 21 |
| Oklahoma | 6 | — | 6 | — | 6 | — | 6 | — | 6 | 8 | 8 | 8 | 8 | 8 |
| Oregon | 4 | — | 4 | — | 4 | +1 | 5 | — | 5 | 6 | 6 | 6 | 7 | 7 |
| Pennsylvania | 30 | −3 | 27 | −2 | 25 | −2 | 23 | −2 | 21 | 32 | 29 | 27 | 25 | 23 |
| Rhode Island | 2 | — | 2 | — | 2 | — | 2 | — | 2 | 4 | 4 | 4 | 4 | 4 |
| South Carolina | 6 | — | 6 | — | 6 | — | 6 | — | 6 | 8 | 8 | 8 | 8 | 8 |
| South Dakota | 2 | — | 2 | — | 2 | −1 | 1 | — | 1 | 4 | 4 | 4 | 3 | 3 |
| Tennessee | 9 | — | 9 | −1 | 8 | +1 | 9 | — | 9 | 11 | 11 | 10 | 11 | 11 |
| Texas | 22 | +1 | 23 | +1 | 24 | +3 | 27 | +3 | 30 | 24 | 25 | 26 | 29 | 32 |
| Utah | 2 | — | 2 | — | 2 | +1 | 3 | — | 3 | 4 | 4 | 4 | 5 | 5 |
| Vermont | 1 | — | 1 | — | 1 | — | 1 | — | 1 | 3 | 3 | 3 | 3 | 3 |
| Virginia | 10 | — | 10 | — | 10 | — | 10 | +1 | 11 | 12 | 12 | 12 | 12 | 13 |
| Washington | 7 | — | 7 | — | 7 | +1 | 8 | +1 | 9 | 9 | 9 | 9 | 10 | 11 |
| West Virginia | 6 | −1 | 5 | −1 | 4 | — | 4 | −1 | 3 | 8 | 7 | 6 | 6 | 5 |
| Wisconsin | 10 | — | 10 | −1 | 9 | — | 9 | — | 9 | 12 | 12 | 11 | 11 | 11 |
| Wyoming | 1 | — | 1 | — | 1 | — | 1 | — | 1 | 3 | 3 | 3 | 3 | 3 |

# Law for Counting Electoral Votes in Congress

*Following is the complete text of Title 3, section 15, of the U.S. Code, enacted originally in 1887, governing the counting of electoral votes in Congress:*

Congress shall be in session on the sixth day of January succeeding every meeting of the electors. The Senate and House of Representatives shall meet in the Hall of the House of Representatives at the hour of 1 o'clock in the afternoon on that day, and the President of the Senate shall be their presiding officer. Two tellers shall be previously appointed on the part of the Senate and two on the part of the House of Representatives, to whom shall be handed, as they are opened by the President of the Senate, all the certificates and papers purporting to be certificates of the electoral votes, which certificates and papers shall be opened, presented, and acted upon in the alphabetical order of the States, beginning with the letter A; and said tellers, having then read the same in the presence and hearing of the two Houses, shall make a list of the votes as they shall appear from the said certificates; and the votes having been ascertained and counted according to the rules in this subchapter provided, the result of the same shall be delivered to the President of the Senate, who shall thereupon announce the state of the vote, which announcement shall be deemed a sufficient declaration of the persons, if any, elected President and Vice President of the United States, and, together with a list of votes, be entered on the Journals of the two Houses. Upon such reading of any such certificate or paper, the President of the Senate shall call for objections, if any. Every objection shall be made in writing, and shall state clearly and concisely, and without argument, the ground thereof, and shall be signed by at least one Senator and one Member of the House of Representatives before the same shall be received. When all objections so made to any vote or paper from a State shall have been received and read, the Senate shall thereupon withdraw, and such objections shall be submitted to the Senate for its decision; and the Speaker of the House of Representatives shall, in like manner, submit such objections to the House of Representatives for its decision; and no electoral vote or votes from any State which shall have been regularly given by electors whose appointment has been lawfully certified to according to section 6* of this title from which but one return has been received shall be rejected, but the two Houses concurrently may reject the vote or votes when they agree that such vote or votes have not been so regularly given by electors whose appointment has been so certified. If more than one return or paper purporting to be a return from a State shall have been received by the President of the Senate, those votes, and those only, shall be counted which shall have been regularly given by the electors who are shown by the determination mentioned in section 5† of this title to have been appointed, if the determination in said section provided for shall have been made, or by such successors or substitutes, in case of a vacancy in the board of electors so ascertained, as have been appointed to fill such vacancy in the mode provided by the laws of the State; but in case there shall arise the question which of two or more of such State authorities determining what electors have been appointed, as mentioned in section 5 of this title, is the lawful tribunal of such State, the votes regularly given of those electors, and those only, of such State shall be counted whose title as electors the two Houses, acting separately, shall concurrently decide is supported by the decision of such State so authorized by its law; and in such case of more than one return or paper purporting to be a return from a State, if there shall have been no such determination of the question in the State aforesaid, then those votes, and those only, shall be counted which the two Houses shall concurrently decide were cast by lawful electors appointed in accordance with the laws of the State, unless the two Houses, acting separately, shall concurrently decide such votes not to be the lawful votes of the legally appointed electors of such State. But if the two Houses shall disagree in respect of the counting of such votes, then, and in that case, the votes of the electors whose appointment shall have been certified by the executive of the State, under the seal thereof, shall be counted. When the two Houses have voted, they shall immediately again meet, and the presiding officer shall then announce the decision of the questions submitted. No votes or papers from any other State shall be acted upon until the objections previously made to the votes or papers from any State shall have been finally disposed of.

NOTES:

*Section 6 provides for certification of votes by electors by state governors.

†Section 5 provides that if state law specifies a method for resolving disputes concerning the vote for presidential electors, Congress must respect any determination so made by a state.

## Party Affiliations in Congress and the Presidency, 1789–2001

| Year | Congress | House Majority party | House Principal minority party | Senate Majority party | Senate Principal minority party | President |
|------|----------|---------|---------|---------|---------|-----------|
| 1999–2001 | 106th | R–223 | D–211 | R–55 | D–45 | D (Clinton) |
| 1997–1999 | 105th | R–227 | D–207 | R–55 | D–45 | D (Clinton) |
| 1995–1997 | 104th | R–230 | D–204 | R–53 | D–47 | D (Clinton) |
| 1993–1995 | 103rd | D–258 | R–176 | D–57 | R–43 | D (Clinton) |
| 1991–1993 | 102nd | D–267 | R–167 | D–56 | R–44 | R (Bush) |
| 1989–1991 | 101st | D–259 | R–174 | D–55 | R–45 | R (Bush) |
| 1987–1989 | 100th | D–258 | R–177 | D–55 | R–45 | R (Reagan) |
| 1985–1987 | 99th | D–252 | R–182 | R–53 | D–47 | R (Reagan) |
| 1983–1985 | 98th | D–269 | R–165 | R–54 | D–46 | R (Reagan) |
| 1981–1983 | 97th | D–243 | R–192 | R–53 | D–46 | R (Reagan) |
| 1979–1981 | 96th | D–276 | R–157 | D–58 | R–41 | D (Carter) |
| 1977–1979 | 95th | D–292 | R–143 | D–61 | R–38 | D (Carter) |
| 1975–1977 | 94th | D–291 | R–144 | D–60 | R–37 | R (Ford) |
| 1973–1975 | 93rd | D–239 | R–192 | D–56 | R–42 | R (Ford) R (Nixon) |
| 1971–1973 | 92nd | D–254 | R–180 | D–54 | R–44 | R (Nixon) |
| 1969–1971 | 91st | D–243 | R–192 | D–57 | R–43 | R (Nixon) |
| 1967–1969 | 90th | D–247 | R–187 | D–64 | R–36 | D (L. Johnson) |
| 1965–1967 | 89th | D–295 | R–140 | D–68 | R–32 | D (L. Johnson) |
| 1963–1965 | 88th | D–258 | R–177 | D–67 | R–33 | D (L. Johnson) D (Kennedy) |
| 1961–1963 | 87th | D–263 | R–174 | D–65 | R–35 | D (Kennedy) |
| 1959–1961 | 86th | D–283 | R–153 | D–64 | R–34 | R (Eisenhower) |
| 1957–1959 | 85th | D–233 | R–200 | D–49 | R–47 | R (Eisenhower) |
| 1955–1957 | 84th | D–232 | R–203 | D–48 | R–47 | R (Eisenhower) |
| 1953–1955 | 83rd | R–221 | D–211 | R–48 | D–47 | R (Eisenhower) |
| 1951–1953 | 82nd | D–234 | R–199 | D–49 | R–47 | D (Truman) |
| 1949–1951 | 81st | D–263 | R–171 | D–54 | R–42 | D (Truman) |
| 1947–1949 | 80th | R–245 | D–188 | R–51 | D–45 | D (Truman) |
| 1945–1947 | 79th | D–242 | R–190 | D–56 | R–38 | D (Truman) |
| 1943–1945 | 78th | D–218 | R–208 | D–58 | R–37 | D (F. Roosevelt) |
| 1941–1943 | 77th | D–268 | R–162 | D–66 | R–28 | D (F. Roosevelt) |
| 1939–1941 | 76th | D–261 | R–164 | D–69 | R–23 | D (F. Roosevelt) |
| 1937–1939 | 75th | D–331 | R–89 | D–76 | R–16 | D (F. Roosevelt) |
| 1935–1937 | 74th | D–319 | R–103 | D–69 | R–25 | D (F. Roosevelt) |
| 1933–1935 | 73rd | D–310 | R–117 | D–60 | R–35 | D (F. Roosevelt) |
| 1931–1933 | 72nd | D–220 | R–214 | R–48 | D–47 | R (Hoover) |
| 1929–1931 | 71st | R–267 | D–167 | R–56 | D–39 | R (Hoover) |
| 1927–1929 | 70th | R–237 | D–195 | R–49 | D–46 | R (Coolidge) |
| 1925–1927 | 69th | R–247 | D–183 | R–56 | D–39 | R (Coolidge) |
| 1923–1925 | 68th | R–225 | D–205 | R–51 | D–43 | R (Coolidge) |
| 1921–1923 | 67th | R–301 | D–131 | R–59 | D–37 | R (Harding) |

N O T E :  (Key to abbreviations: AD—Administration; AM—Anti-Masonic; D—Democratic; DR—Democratic-Republican; F—Federalist; J—Jacksonian; NR—National Republican; Op—Opposition; R—Republican; U—Unionist; W—Whig. Figures are for the beginning of the first session of each Congress.

| Year | Congress | House | | Senate | | President |
|------|----------|-------|---|--------|---|-----------|
| | | Majority party | Principal minority party | Majority party | Principal minority party | |
| 1919–1921 | 66th | R–240 | D–190 | R–49 | D–47 | D (Wilson) |
| 1917–1919 | 65th | D–216 | R–210 | D–53 | R–42 | D (Wilson) |
| 1915–1917 | 64th | D–230 | R–196 | D–56 | R–40 | D (Wilson) |
| 1913–1915 | 63rd | D–291 | R–127 | D–51 | R–44 | D (Wilson) |
| 1911–1913 | 62nd | D–228 | R–161 | R–51 | D–41 | R (Taft) |
| 1909–1911 | 61st | R–219 | D–172 | R–61 | D–32 | R (Taft) |
| 1907–1909 | 60th | R–222 | D–164 | R–61 | D–31 | R (T. Roosevelt) |
| 1905–1907 | 59th | R–250 | D–136 | R–57 | D–33 | R (T. Roosevelt) |
| 1903–1905 | 58th | R–208 | D–178 | R–57 | D–33 | R (T. Roosevelt) |
| 1901–1903 | 57th | R–197 | D–151 | R–55 | D–31 | R (T. Roosevelt) R (McKinley) |
| 1899–1901 | 56th | R–185 | D–163 | R–53 | D–26 | R (McKinley) |
| 1897–1899 | 55th | R–204 | D–113 | R–47 | D–34 | R (McKinley) |
| 1895–1897 | 54th | R–244 | D–105 | R–43 | D–39 | D (Cleveland) |
| 1893–1895 | 53rd | D–218 | R–127 | D–44 | R–38 | D (Cleveland) |
| 1891–1893 | 52nd | D–235 | R–88 | R–47 | D–39 | R (B. Harrison) |
| 1889–1891 | 51st | R–166 | D–159 | R–39 | D–37 | R (B. Harrison) |
| 1887–1889 | 50th | D–169 | R–152 | R–39 | D–37 | D (Cleveland) |
| 1885–1887 | 49th | D–183 | R–140 | R–43 | D–34 | D (Cleveland) |
| 1883–1885 | 48th | D–197 | R–118 | R–38 | D–36 | R (Arthur) |
| 1881–1883 | 47th | R–147 | D–135 | R–37 | D–37 | R (Arthur) R (Garfield) |
| 1879–1881 | 46th | D–149 | R–130 | D–42 | R–33 | R (Hayes) |
| 1877–1879 | 45th | D–153 | R–140 | R–39 | D–36 | R (Hayes) |
| 1875–1877 | 44th | D–169 | R–109 | R–45 | D–29 | R (Grant) |
| 1873–1875 | 43rd | R–194 | D–92 | R–49 | D–19 | R (Grant) |
| 1871–1873 | 42nd | R–134 | D–104 | R–52 | D–17 | R (Grant) |
| 1869–1871 | 41st | R–149 | D–63 | R–56 | D–11 | R (Grant) |
| 1867–1869 | 40th | R–143 | D–49 | R–42 | D–11 | R (A. Johnson) |
| 1865–1867 | 39th | U–149 | D–42 | U–42 | D–10 | R (A. Johnson) R (Lincoln) |
| 1863–1865 | 38th | R–102 | D–75 | R–36 | D–9 | R (Lincoln) |
| 1861–1863 | 37th | R–105 | D–43 | R–31 | D–10 | R (Lincoln) |
| 1859–1861 | 36th | R–114 | D–92 | D–36 | R–26 | D (Buchanan) |
| 1857–1859 | 35th | D–118 | R–92 | D–36 | R–20 | D (Buchanan) |
| 1855–1857 | 34th | R–108 | D–83 | D–40 | R–15 | D (Pierce) |
| 1853–1855 | 33rd | D–159 | W–71 | D–38 | W–22 | D (Pierce) |
| 1851–1853 | 32nd | D–140 | W–88 | D–35 | W–24 | W (Fillmore) |
| 1849–1851 | 31st | D–112 | W–109 | D–35 | W–25 | W (Fillmore) W (Taylor) |
| 1847–1849 | 30th | W–115 | D–108 | D–36 | W–21 | D (Polk) |
| 1845–1847 | 29th | D–143 | W–77 | D–31 | W–25 | D (Polk) |

*(Continued)*

| Year | Congress | House | | Senate | | President |
|------|----------|-------|--|--------|--|-----------|
| | | *Majority party* | *Principal minority party* | *Majority party* | *Principal minority party* | |
| 1843–1845 | 28th | D–142 | W–79 | W–28 | D–25 | W (Tyler) |
| 1841–1843 | 27th | W–133 | D–102 | W–28 | D–22 | W (Tyler) |
| | | | | | | W (W. Harrison) |
| 1839–1841 | 26th | D–124 | W–118 | D–28 | W–22 | D (Van Buren) |
| 1837–1839 | 25th | D–108 | W–107 | D–30 | W–18 | D (Van Buren) |
| 1835–1837 | 24th | D–145 | W–98 | D–27 | W–25 | D (Jackson) |
| 1833–1835 | 23rd | D–147 | AM–53 | D–20 | NR–20 | D (Jackson) |
| 1831–1833 | 22nd | D–141 | NR–58 | D–25 | NR–21 | D (Jackson) |
| 1829–1831 | 21st | D–139 | NR–74 | D–26 | NR–22 | DR (Jackson) |
| 1827–1829 | 20th | J–119 | AD–94 | J–28 | AD–20 | DR (John Q. Adams) |
| 1825–1827 | 19th | AD–105 | J–97 | AD–26 | J–20 | DR (John Q. Adams) |
| 1823–1825 | 18th | DR–187 | F–26 | DR–44 | F–4 | DR (Monroe) |
| 1821–1823 | 17th | DR–158 | F–25 | DR–44 | F–4 | DR (Monroe) |
| 1819–1821 | 16th | DR–156 | F–27 | DR–35 | F–7 | DR (Monroe) |
| 1817–1819 | 15th | DR–141 | F–42 | DR–34 | F–10 | DR (Monroe) |
| 1815–1817 | 14th | DR–117 | F–65 | DR–25 | F–11 | DR (Madison) |
| 1813–1815 | 13th | DR–112 | F–68 | DR–27 | F–9 | DR (Madison) |
| 1811–1813 | 12th | DR–108 | F–36 | DR–30 | F–6 | DR (Madison) |
| 1809–1811 | 11th | DR–94 | F–48 | DR–28 | F–6 | DR (Madison) |
| 1807–1809 | 10th | DR–118 | F–24 | DR–28 | F–6 | DR (Jefferson) |
| 1805–1807 | 9th | DR–116 | F–25 | DR–27 | F–7 | DR (Jefferson) |
| 1803–1805 | 8th | DR–102 | F–39 | DR–25 | F–9 | DR (Jefferson) |
| 1801–1803 | 7th | DR–69 | F–36 | DR–18 | F–13 | DR (Jefferson) |
| 1799–1801 | 6th | F–64 | DR–42 | F–19 | DR–13 | F (John Adams) |
| 1797–1799 | 5th | F–58 | DR–48 | F–20 | DR–12 | F (John Adams) |
| 1795–1797 | 4th | F–54 | DR–52 | F–19 | DR–13 | F (Washington) |
| 1793–1795 | 3rd | DR–57 | F–48 | F–17 | DR–13 | F (Washington) |
| 1791–1793 | 2nd | F–37 | DR–33 | F–16 | DR–13 | F (Washington) |
| 1789–1791 | 1st | AD–38 | Op–26 | AD–17 | Op–9 | F (Washington) |

SOURCES: *Congressional Quarterly Weekly Report,* selected issues; U.S. Bureau of the Census, *Historical Statistics of the United States, Colonial Times to 1970* (Washington, D.C.: Government Printing Office, 1975); and *Congressional Directory,* selected years.

NOTE: (Key to abbreviations: AD—Administration; AM—Anti-Masonic; D—Democratic; DR—Democratic-Republican; F—Federalist: J—Jacksonian; NR—National Republican; Op—Opposition; R—Republican; U—Unionist; W—Whig. Figures are for the beginning of the first session of each Congress.

## Incumbents Reelected, Defeated, or Retired, 1946–1998

| Year | Retired[1] | Total seeking reelection | Defeated in primaries | Defeated in general election | Total reelected | Percentage of those seeking reelection |
|------|---------|---------|---------|---------|---------|---------|
| *House* | | | | | | |
| 1946 | 32 | 398 | 18 | 52 | 328 | 82.4 |
| 1948 | 29 | 400 | 15 | 68 | 317 | 79.3 |
| 1950 | 29 | 400 | 6 | 32 | 362 | 90.5 |
| 1952 | 42 | 389 | 9 | 26 | 354 | 91.0 |
| 1954 | 24 | 407 | 6 | 22 | 379 | 93.1 |
| 1956 | 21 | 411 | 6 | 16 | 389 | 94.6 |
| 1958 | 33 | 396 | 3 | 37 | 356 | 89.9 |
| 1960 | 26 | 405 | 5 | 25 | 375 | 92.6 |
| 1962 | 24 | 402 | 12 | 22 | 368 | 91.5 |
| 1964 | 33 | 397 | 8 | 45 | 344 | 86.6 |
| 1966 | 22 | 411 | 8 | 41 | 362 | 88.1 |
| 1968 | 23 | 409 | 4 | 9 | 396 | 96.8 |
| 1970 | 29 | 401 | 10 | 12 | 379 | 94.5 |
| 1972 | 40 | 390 | 12 | 13 | 365 | 93.6 |
| 1974 | 43 | 391 | 8 | 40 | 343 | 87.7 |
| 1976 | 47 | 384 | 3 | 13 | 368 | 95.8 |
| 1978 | 49 | 382 | 5 | 19 | 358 | 93.7 |
| 1980 | 34 | 398 | 6 | 31 | 361 | 90.7 |
| 1982 | 40 | 393 | 10 | 29 | 354 | 90.1 |
| 1984 | 22 | 409 | 3 | 16 | 390 | 95.4 |
| 1986 | 38 | 393 | 2 | 6 | 385 | 98.0 |
| 1988 | 23 | 408 | 1 | 6 | 401 | 98.3 |
| 1990 | 27 | 406 | 1 | 15 | 390 | 96.0 |
| 1992 | 65 | 368 | 19 | 24 | 325 | 88.3 |
| 1994 | 48 | 387 | 4 | 34 | 349 | 90.2 |
| 1996 | 49 | 384 | 2 | 21 | 361 | 94.0 |
| 1998 | 23 | 404 | 3 | 6 | 395 | 97.8 |
| *Senate* | | | | | | |
| 1946 | 9 | 30 | 6 | 7 | 17 | 56.7 |
| 1948 | 8 | 25 | 2 | 8 | 15 | 60.0 |
| 1950 | 4 | 32 | 5 | 5 | 22 | 68.8 |
| 1952 | 4 | 31 | 2 | 9 | 20 | 64.5 |
| 1954 | 6 | 32 | 2 | 6 | 24 | 75.0 |
| 1956 | 6 | 29 | 0 | 4 | 25 | 86.2 |
| 1958 | 6 | 28 | 0 | 10 | 18 | 64.3 |
| 1960 | 5 | 29 | 0 | 1 | 28 | 96.6 |
| 1962 | 4 | 35 | 1 | 5 | 29 | 82.9 |
| 1964 | 2 | 33 | 1 | 4 | 28 | 84.8 |
| 1966 | 3 | 32 | 3 | 1 | 28 | 87.5 |
| 1968 | 6 | 28 | 4 | 4 | 20 | 71.4 |
| 1970 | 4 | 31 | 1 | 6 | 24 | 77.4 |
| 1972 | 6 | 27 | 2 | 5 | 20 | 74.1 |

*(Continued)*

Incumbents Reelected, Defeated, or Retired, 1946–1998    *(Continued)*

| Year | Retired[1] | Total seeking reelection | Defeated in primaries | Defeated in general election | Total reelected | Percentage of those seeking reelection |
|------|---------|----------|----------|----------|----------|----------|
| 1974 | 7 | 27 | 2 | 2 | 23 | 85.2 |
| 1976 | 8 | 25 | 0 | 9 | 16 | 64.0 |
| 1978 | 10 | 25 | 3 | 7 | 15 | 60.0 |
| 1980 | 5 | 29 | 4 | 9 | 16 | 55.2 |
| 1982 | 3 | 30 | 0 | 2 | 28 | 93.3 |
| 1984 | 4 | 29 | 0 | 3 | 26 | 89.6 |
| 1986 | 6 | 28 | 0 | 7 | 21 | 75.0 |
| 1988 | 6 | 27 | 0 | 4 | 23 | 85.2 |
| 1990 | 3 | 32 | 0 | 1 | 31 | 96.9 |
| 1992 | 7 | 28 | 1 | 4 | 23 | 82.1 |
| 1994 | 9 | 26 | 0 | 2 | 24 | 92.3 |
| 1996 | 13 | 21 | 13 | 1 | 19 | 90.5 |
| 1998 | 5 | 29 | 0 | 3 | 26 | 89.6 |

SOURCE: Norman J. Ornstein, Thomas E. Mann, and Michael J. Malbin, *Vital Statistics on Congress, 1997-1998* (Washington, D.C.: Congressional Quarterly, 1998); updated by the author.

NOTES:

1. Does not include persons who died or resigned before the election.

2. Sheila Frahm, appointed to fill Robert Dole's term, is counted as an incumbent in Kansas's "B" seat.

## Blacks in Congress, 41st–106th Congresses, 1869–2001

| Congress | | House D | House R | Senate D | Senate R | Congress | | House D | House R | Senate D | Senate R |
|---|---|---|---|---|---|---|---|---|---|---|---|
| 41st | (1869) | — | 2 | — | 1 | 81st | (1949) | 2 | — | — | — |
| 42d | (1871) | — | 5 | — | — | 82d | (1951) | 2 | — | — | — |
| 43d | (1873) | — | 7 | — | — | 83d | (1953) | 2 | — | — | — |
| 44th | (1875) | — | 7 | — | 1 | 84th | (1955) | 3 | — | — | — |
| 45th | (1877) | — | 3 | — | 1 | 85th | (1957) | 3 | — | — | — |
| 46th | (1879) | — | — | — | 1 | 86th | (1959) | 3 | — | — | — |
| 47th | (1881) | — | 2 | — | — | 87th | (1961) | 3 | — | — | — |
| 48th | (1883) | — | 2 | — | — | 88th | (1963) | 4 | — | — | — |
| 49th | (1885) | — | 2 | — | — | 89th | (1965) | 5 | — | — | — |
| 50th | (1887) | — | — | — | — | 90th | (1967) | 5 | — | — | 1 |
| 51st | (1889) | — | 3 | — | — | 91st | (1969) | 9 | — | — | 1 |
| 52d | (1891) | — | 1 | — | — | 92d | (1971) | 13 | — | — | 1 |
| 53d | (1893) | — | 1 | — | — | 93d | (1973) | 16 | — | — | 1 |
| 54th | (1895) | — | 1 | — | — | 94th | (1975) | 16 | — | — | 1 |
| 55th | (1897) | — | 1 | — | — | 95th | (1977) | 15 | — | — | 1 |
| 56th | (1899)[a] | — | 1 | — | — | 96th | (1979) | 15 | — | — | — |
| 71st | (1929) | — | 1 | — | — | 97th | (1981) | 17 | — | — | — |
| 72d | (1931) | — | 1 | — | — | 98th | (1983) | 20 | — | — | — |
| 73d | (1933) | — | 1 | — | — | 99th | (1985) | 20 | — | — | — |
| 74th | (1935) | 1 | — | — | — | 100th | (1987) | 22 | — | — | — |
| 75th | (1937) | 1 | — | — | — | 101st | (1989) | 23 | — | — | — |
| 76th | (1939) | 1 | — | — | — | 102d | (1991) | 25 | 1 | — | |
| 77th | (1941) | 1 | — | — | — | 103d | (1993) | 38 | 1 | 1 | — |
| 78th | (1943) | 1 | | — | — | 104th | (1995) | 37 | 2 | 1 | — |
| 79th | (1945) | 2 | — | — | — | 105th | (1997) | 36 | 1 | 1 | — |
| 80th | (1947) | 2 | — | — | — | 106th | (1999) | 36 | 1 | — | — |

SOURCES. *Black Americans in Congress, 1870-1977,* H.Doc. 95-258, 95th Cong., 1st sess., 1977; *Congressional Quarterly Almanac,* various years; *Congressional Quarterly Weekly Report,* November 10, 1984, 2921; November 8, 1986, 2863; November 12, 1988, 3294; November 10, 1990, 3836; November 7, 1992, Supplement, 8; November 12, 1994, Supplement, 10; January 4, 1997, 28; January 9, 1999, 62.

NOTE: Does not include nonvoting delegates.

a. After the Fifty-sixth Congress, there were no black members in either the House or Senate until the Seventy-first Congress.

## Hispanic Americans in Congress, 45th–106th Congresses, 1877–2001

| Congress | | House D | House R | Senate D | Senate R | Congress | | House D | House R | Senate D | Senate R |
|---|---|---|---|---|---|---|---|---|---|---|---|
| 45th | (1877) | — | 1 | — | — | 76th | (1939) | 1 | — | 1 | — |
| 46th | (1879) | — | 1 | — | — | 77th | (1941) | — | — | 1 | — |
| 47th | (1881) | — | 1 | — | — | 78th | (1943) | 1 | — | 1 | — |
| 48th | (1883) | — | — | — | — | 79th | (1945) | 1 | — | 1 | — |
| 49th | (1885) | — | — | — | — | 80th | (1947) | 1 | — | 1 | — |
| 50th | (1887) | — | — | — | — | 81st | (1949) | 1 | — | 1 | — |
| 51st | (1889) | — | — | — | — | 82d | (1951) | 1 | — | 1 | — |
| 52d | (1891) | — | — | — | — | 83d | (1953) | 1 | — | 1 | — |
| 53d | (1893) | — | — | — | — | 84th | (1955) | 1 | — | 1 | — |
| 54th | (1895) | — | — | — | — | 85th | (1957) | 1 | — | 1 | — |
| 55th | (1897) | — | — | — | — | 86th | (1959) | 1 | — | 1 | — |
| 56th | (1899) | — | — | — | — | 87th | (1961) | 2 | — | 1 | — |
| 57th | (1901) | — | — | — | — | 88th | (1963) | 3 | — | 1 | — |
| 58th | (1903) | — | — | — | — | 89th | (1965) | 3 | — | 1 | — |
| 59th | (1905) | — | — | — | — | 90th | (1967) | 3 | — | 1 | — |
| 60th | (1907) | — | — | — | — | 91st | (1969) | 3 | 1 | 1 | — |
| 61st | (1909) | — | — | — | — | 92d | (1971) | 4 | 1 | 1 | — |
| 62d | (1911) | — | — | — | — | 93d | (1973) | 4 | 1 | 1 | — |
| 63d | (1913) | 1 | — | — | — | 94th | (1975) | 4 | 1 | 1 | — |
| 64th | (1915) | 1 | 1 | — | — | 95th | (1977) | 4 | 1 | — | — |
| 65th | (1917) | 1 | — | — | — | 96th | (1979) | 5 | 1 | — | — |
| 66th | (1919) | 1 | 1 | — | — | 97th | (1981) | 6 | 1 | — | — |
| 67th | (1921) | 1 | 1 | — | — | 98th | (1983) | 9 | 1 | — | — |
| 68th | (1923) | 1 | — | — | — | 99th | (1985) | 10 | 1 | — | — |
| 69th | (1925) | 1 | — | — | — | 100th | (1987) | 10 | 1 | — | — |
| 70th | (1927) | 1 | — | — | 1 | 101st | (1989) | 9 | 1 | — | — |
| 71st | (1929) | — | — | — | — | 102d | (1991) | 10 | 1 | — | — |
| 72d | (1931) | 2 | — | — | — | 103d | (1993) | 14 | 3 | — | — |
| 73d | (1933) | 2 | — | — | — | 104th | (1995) | 14 | 3 | — | — |
| 74th | (1935) | 1 | — | 1 | — | 105th | (1997) | 14 | 3 | — | — |
| 75th | (1937) | 1 | — | 1 | — | 106th | (1999) | 15 | 3 | — | — |

SOURCES: *Biographical Directory of the United States Congress 1774–1989; Congressional Quarterly Almanac,* various years; *CQ Weekly,* January 9, 1999, 62.

NOTE: Statistics do not include delegates or commissioners. Since the 17th Congress, there have been three Democrats and five Republicans who have served in the House of Representatives as delegates for territories that would later become states. In addition, Joseph Marion Hernandez (W-Fla.) served as a delegate to the U.S. House of Representatives during the 17th Congress. There have also been nineteen Hispanic Americans who have served as delegates to the House of Representatives representing the territories of Puerto Rico, Guam, and the Virgin Islands since 1901.

## Women in Congress, 65th–106th Congresses, 1917–2001

| Congress | | House D | House R | Senate D | Senate R | Congress | | House D | House R | Senate D | Senate R |
|---|---|---|---|---|---|---|---|---|---|---|---|
| 45th | (1877) | — | 1 | — | — | 76th | (1939) | 1 | — | 1 | — |
| 65th | (1917) | — | 1 | — | — | 86th | (1959) | 9 | 8 | — | 1 |
| 66th | (1919) | — | — | — | — | 87th | (1961) | 11 | 7 | 1 | 1 |
| 67th | (1921) | — | 2 | — | 1 | 88th | (1963) | 6 | 6 | 1 | 1 |
| 68th | (1923) | — | 1 | — | — | 89th | (1965) | 7 | 4 | 1 | 1 |
| 69th | (1925) | 1 | 2 | — | — | 90th | (1967) | 5 | 5 | — | 1 |
| 70th | (1927) | 2 | 3 | — | — | 91st | (1969) | 6 | 4 | — | 1 |
| 71st | (1929) | 4 | 5 | — | — | 92d | (1971) | 10 | 3 | — | 1 |
| 72d | (1931) | 4 | 3 | 1 | — | 93d | (1973) | 14 | 2 | 1 | — |
| 73d | (1933) | 4 | 3 | 1 | — | 94th | (1975) | 14 | 5 | — | — |
| 74th | (1935) | 4 | 2 | 2 | — | 95th | (1977) | 13 | 5 | — | — |
| 75th | (1937) | 4 | 1 | 2 | — | 96th | (1979) | 11 | 5 | 1 | 1 |
| 76th | (1939) | 4 | 4 | 1 | — | 97th | (1981) | 10 | 9 | — | 2 |
| 77th | (1941) | 4 | 5 | 1 | — | 98th | (1983) | 13 | 9 | — | 2 |
| 78th | (1943) | 2 | 6 | 1 | — | 99th | (1985) | 13 | 9 | — | 2 |
| 79th | (1945) | 6 | 5 | — | — | 100th | (1987) | 12 | 11 | 1 | 1 |
| 80th | (1947) | 3 | 4 | — | 1 | 101st | (1989) | 14 | 11 | 1 | 1 |
| 81st | (1949) | 5 | 4 | — | 1 | 102d | (1991) | 19 | 9 | 1 | 1 |
| 82d | (1951) | 4 | 6 | — | 1 | 103d | (1993) | 36 | 12 | 5 | 1 |
| 83d | (1953) | 5 | 7 | — | 1 | 104th | (1995) | 31 | 17 | 5 | 3[b] |
| 84th | (1955) | 10 | 7 | — | 1 | 105th | (1997) | 35 | 16 | 6 | 3 |
| 85th | (1957) | 9 | 6 | — | 1 | 106th | (1999) | 39 | 17 | 6 | 3 |

SOURCES: *Women in Congress*, H. Rept. 94-1732, 94th Cong., 2d sess., 1976; *Congressional Quarterly Almanac*, various years; *Congressional Quarterly Weekly Report*, November 10, 1984, 2921; November 8, 1986, 2863; November 12, 1988, 3294; November 10, 1990, 3836; November 7, 1992, Supplement, 8; November 12, 1994, Supplement, 10; January 4, 1997, 28; January 9, 1999, 62.

NOTE: Includes only women who were sworn in as members and served more than one day. Statistics do not include delegates or commissioners.

a. Includes the late Sala Burton, who died after being sworn into the 100th Congress, and who was replaced by another Democratic woman, Nancy Pelosi.

b. Sheila Frahm (R-Kan.) was appointed to fill the vacancy left by Sen. Robert Dole (R-Kan.) bringing the total to four Republican woman senators. Frahm ran for the open Senate seat but lost in the Kansas Republican primary.

## Senate Votes Cast by Vice Presidents

Following is a list of the number of votes cast by each vice president through January 20, 1999.

| Period | Vice President | Votes Cast | Period | Vice President | Votes Cast |
|--------|----------------|------------|--------|----------------|------------|
| 1789–1797 | John Adams | 29 | 1897–1899 | Garret A. Hobart | 1 |
| 1797–1801 | Thomas Jefferson | 3 | 1901 | Theodore Roosevelt | 0 |
| 1801–1805 | Aaron Burr | 3 | 1905–1909 | Charles W. Fairbanks | 0 |
| 1805–1812 | George Clinton | 11 | 1909–1912 | James S. Sherman | 4 |
| 1813–1814 | Elbridge Gerry | 8 | 1913–1921 | Thomas R. Marshall | 4 |
| 1817–1825 | Daniel D. Tompkins | 5 | 1921–1923 | Calvin Coolidge | 0 |
| 1825–1832 | John C. Calhoun | 28 | 1925–1929 | Charles G. Dawes | 2 |
| 1833–1837 | Martin Van Buren | 4 | 1929–1933 | Charles Curtis | 3 |
| 1837–1841 | Richard M. Johnson | 14 | 1933–1941 | John N. Garner | 3 |
| 1841 | John Tyler | 0 | 1941–1945 | Henry A. Wallace | 4 |
| 1845–1849 | George M. Dallas | 19 | 1945 | Harry S. Truman | 1 |
| 1849–1850 | Millard Fillmore | 3 | 1949–1953 | Alben W. Barkley | 7 |
| 1853 | William R. King | 0 | 1953–1961 | Richard M. Nixon | 8 |
| 1857–1861 | John C. Breckinridge | 10 | 1961–1963 | Lyndon B. Johnson | 0 |
| 1861–1865 | Hannibal Hamlin | 7 | 1965–1969 | Hubert H. Humphrey | 4 |
| 1865 | Andrew Johnson | 0 | 1969–1973 | Spiro T. Agnew | 2 |
| 1869–1873 | Schuyler Colfax | 13 | 1973–1974 | Gerald R. Ford | 0 |
| 1873–1875 | Henry Wilson | 1 | 1974–1977 | Nelson A. Rockefeller | 0 |
| 1877–1881 | William A. Wheeler | 5 | 1977–1981 | Walter F. Mondale | 1 |
| 1881 | Chester A. Arthur | 3 | 1981–1989 | George Bush | 7 |
| 1885 | Thomas A. Hendricks | 0 | 1989–1993 | Dan Quayle | 0 |
| 1889–1893 | Levi P. Morton | 4 | 1993–1999 | Al Gore | 3 |
| 1893–1897 | Adlai E. Stevenson | 2 | | | |
| | | | | **Total** | **226** |

SOURCE: Library of Congress, Congressional Research Service.

# State Government

| State | Governor | Name of Lawmaking Body | Total House | Dem. | Rep. | Other | Total Senate | Dem. | Rep. | Other |
|---|---|---|---|---|---|---|---|---|---|---|
| Alabama | Don Siegelman (D) | Legislature | 105 | 69 | 36 | | 35 | 23 | 12 | |
| Alaska | Tony Knowles (D) | Legislature | 40 | 16 | 24 | | 20 | 5 | 15 | |
| Arizona | Jane Dee Hull (R) | Legislature | 60 | 20 | 40 | | 30 | 14 | 16 | |
| Arkansas | Mike Huckabee (R) | General Assembly | 100 | 77 | 23 | | 35 | 29 | 6 | |
| California | Gray Davis (D) | Legislature | 80 | 48 | 32 | | 40 | 25 | 15 | |
| Colorado | Bill Owens (R) | General Assembly | 65 | 25 | 40 | | 35 | 15 | 20 | |
| Connecticut | John G. Rowland (R) | General Assembly | 151 | 96 | 55 | | 36 | 19 | 17 | |
| Delaware | Thomas R. Carper (D) | General Assembly | 41 | 15 | 26 | | 21 | 13 | 8 | |
| Florida | Jeb Bush (R) | Legislature | 120 | 47 | 73 | | 40 | 15 | 25 | |
| Georgia | Roy Barnes (D) | General Assembly | 180 | 102 | 78 | | 56 | 33 | 23 | |
| Hawaii | Benjamin J. Cayetano (D) | Legislature | 51 | 39 | 12 | | 25 | 23 | 2 | |
| Idaho | Dirk Kempthorne (R) | Legislature | 70 | 12 | 58 | | 35 | 4 | 31 | |
| Illinois | George H. Ryan (R) | General Assembly | 118 | 62 | 56 | | 59 | 27 | 32 | |
| Indiana | Frank L. O'Bannon (D) | General Assembly | 100 | 53 | 47 | | 50 | 19 | 31 | |
| Iowa | Tom Vilsack (D) | General Assembly | 100 | 44 | 56 | | 50 | 20 | 30 | |
| Kansas | Bill Graves (R) | Legislature | 125 | 48 | 77 | | 40 | 13 | 27 | |
| Kentucky | Paul E. Patton (D) | General Assembly | 100 | 66 | 34 | | 38 | 20 | 18 | |
| Louisiana | Mike Foster (R) | Legislature | 105 | 78 | 27 | | 39 | 25 | 14 | |
| Maine | Angus King (I) | Legislature | 151 | 79 | 71 | 1 (Indep) | 35 | 20 | 14 | 1 (Indep) |
| Maryland | Parris N. Glendening (D) | General Assembly | 141 | 106 | 35 | | 47 | 32 | 15 | |
| Massachusetts | Argeo Paul Cellucci (R) | General Court | 160 | 131 | 28 | 1 (Indep) | 40 | 33 | 7 | |
| Michigan | John Engler (R) | Legislature | 110 | 52 | 58 | | 38 | 15 | 23 | |
| Minnesota | Jesse Ventura (REF) | Legislature | 134 | 63 | 71 | | 67 | 42 | 24 | 1 (Indep) |
| Mississippi | Kirk Fordice (R) | Legislature | 122 | 83 | 36 | 3 (Indep) | 52 | 34 | 18 | |
| Missouri | Mel Carnahan (D) | General Assembly | 163 | 86 | 76 | 1 (Indep) | 34 | 17 | 16 | 1 (Vacant) |
| Montana | Marc Racicot (R) | Legislative Assembly | 100 | 41 | 59 | | 50 | 18 | 32 | |
| Nebraska | Mike Johanns (R) | Legislature | n/a | n/a | n/a | | 49 | | | 49 (Other) |
| Nevada | Kenny Guinn (R) | Legislature | 42 | 28 | 14 | | 21 | 9 | 12 | |
| New Hampshire | Jeanne Shaheen (D) | General Court | 400 | 153 | 246 | 1 (Indep) | 24 | 13 | 11 | |
| New Jersey | Christine Todd Whitman (R) | Legislature | 80 | 32 | 48 | | 40 | 16 | 24 | |
| New Mexico | Gary E. Johnson (R) | Legislature | 70 | 40 | 30 | | 42 | 25 | 17 | |
| New York | George E. Pataki (R) | Legislature | 150 | 98 | 52 | | 61 | 26 | 35 | |
| North Carolina | James B. Hunt, Jr. (D) | General Assembly | 120 | 65 | 55 | | 50 | 35 | 15 | |
| North Dakota | Edward T. Schafer (R) | Legislative Assembly | 98 | 34 | 64 | | 49 | 18 | 31 | |
| Ohio | Robert A. Taft, II (R) | General Assembly | 99 | 40 | 59 | | 33 | 12 | 21 | |
| Oklahoma | Frank Keating (R) | Legislature | 101 | 61 | 40 | | 48 | 33 | 15 | |
| Oregon | John Kitzhaber (D) | Legislative Assembly | 60 | 25 | 34 | 1 (Indep) | 30 | 12 | 17 | 1 (Indep) |
| Pennsylvania | Tom Ridge (R) | General Assembly | 203 | 100 | 103 | | 50 | 20 | 30 | |
| Rhode Island | Lincoln C. Almond (R) | General Assembly | 100 | 86 | 13 | 1 (Indep) | 50 | 42 | 8 | |
| South Carolina | James H. Hodges (D) | General Assembly | 124 | 56 | 68 | | 46 | 26 | 20 | |
| South Dakota | William J. Janklow (R) | Legislature | 70 | 18 | 51 | 1 (Undec) | 35 | 13 | 22 | |
| Tennessee | Don Sundquist (R) | General Assembly | 99 | 59 | 40 | | 33 | 18 | 15 | |
| Texas | George W. Bush (R) | Legislature | 150 | 79 | 71 | | 31 | 15 | 16 | |
| Utah | Michael O. Leavitt (R) | Legislature | 75 | 21 | 54 | | 29 | 11 | 18 | |
| Vermont | Howard Dean (D) | General Assembly | 150 | 77 | 67 | 2 (Indep); 4 (Other) | 30 | 17 | 13 | |

*(Continued)*

## State Government *(Continued)*

| State | Governor | Name of Lawmaking Body | Total House | Dem. | Rep. | Other | Total Senate | Dem. | Rep. | Other |
|---|---|---|---|---|---|---|---|---|---|---|
| Virginia | Jim Gilmore (R) | General Assembly | 100 | 50 | 49 | | 40 | 19 | 21 | |
| Washington | Gary Locke (D) | Legislature | 98 | 49 | 49 | | 49 | 27 | 22 | |
| West Virginia | Cecil H. Underwood (R) | Legislature | 100 | 75 | 25 | | 34 | 29 | 5 | |
| Wisconsin | Tommy G. Thompson (R) | Legislature | 99 | 44 | 55 | | 33 | 17 | 16 | |
| Wyoming | Jim Geringer (R) | Legislature | 60 | 17 | 43 | | 30 | 10 | 20 | |

SOURCES: National Council of State Legislatures; Congressional Quarterly.

NOTE: Current as of January 15, 1999.

# Bibliography

Abramson, Paul R., John H. Aldrich, and David W. Rohde. *Change and Continuity in the 1996 and 1998 Elections.* Washington, D.C.: CQ Press, 1999.

Alexander, Herbert E. *Financing Politics: Money, Elections, and Political Reform,* 4th ed. Washington, D.C.: CQ Press, 1992.

Appleton, Andrew M., and Daniel S. Ward, eds. *State Party Profiles: A 50-State Guide to Development, Organization, and Resources.* Washington, D.C.: Congressional Quarterly, 1997.

Asher, Herbert. *Polling and the Public: What Every Citizen Should Know,* 4th ed. Washington, D.C.: CQ Press, 1998.

Baker, Richard A. *The Senate of the United States: A Bicentennial History.* Malamar, Fla.: Krieger Publishing, 1988.

Benjamin, Gerald, and Michael J. Malbin. *Limiting Legislative Terms.* Washington, D.C.: CQ Press, 1992.

Beyle, Thad L. *State Government: CQ's Guide to Current Issues and Activities 1998–1999.* Washington, D.C.: Congressional Quarterly, 1998.

Bibby, John F. *Governing by Consent: An Introduction to American Politics,* 2d ed. Washington, D.C.: CQ Press, 1994.

————. *Politics, Parties, and Elections in America.* Chicago: Nelson-Hall, 1987.

Bogdanor, Vernon, ed. *The Blackwell Encyclopaedia of Political Science.* Cambridge, Mass.: Blackwell Publishers, 1991.

Boller, Paul F. Jr. *Presidential Campaigns,* rev. ed. New York: Oxford University Press, 1996.

Broder, David S. *Behind the Front Page: A Candid Look at How the News Is Made.* New York: Simon and Schuster, 1987.

Cappella, Joseph A., and Kathleen Hall Jamieson. *The Spiral of Cynicism: The Press and the Public Good.* New York: Oxford University Press, 1997.

Cigler, Allan J., and Burdett A. Loomis. *Interest Group Politics,* 5th ed. Washington, D.C.: CQ Press, 1998.

*Congress and the Nation,* vols. 1–9. Washington, D.C.: Congressional Quarterly, 1969–1997.

*Congressional Elections 1946–1996.* Washington, D.C.: Congressional Quarterly, 1998.

*Congressional Quarterly Almanac,* yearly editions. Washington, D.C.: Congressional Quarterly.

Conway, M. Margaret. *Political Participation in the United States,* 2d ed. Washington, D.C.: CQ Press, 1990.

Council of State Governments. *Book of the States, 1994–1995,* Lexington, Ky.: Council of State Governments, 1996.

Currie, James T. *The United States House of Representatives.* Malabar, Fla.: Krieger Publishing, 1988.

Davis, Kenneth C. *Don't Know Much About History.* New York: Avon Books, 1995.

Drew, Elizabeth. *Politics and Money: The New Road to Political Corruption.* New York: Macmillan Publishing, 1983.

Edsall, Thomas Byrne. *The New Politics of Inequality.* New York: W. W. Norton, 1984.

Fallows, James. *Breaking the News: How the Media Undermine American Democracy.* New York: Pantheon Books, 1996.

*Famous Historical Dates.* Philadelphia: Philadelphia and Reading Railroad, 1948.

Fensenthal, Dan. *Topics in Social Choice: Sophisticated Voting, Efficacy and Proportional Representation.* New York: Praeger, 1990.

Flanigan, William H., and Nancy H. Zingale. *Political Behavior of the American Electorate,* 9th ed. Washington, D.C.: CQ Press, 1998.

Fritz, Jean. *Shh! We're Writing the Constitution.* New York: G. P. Putnam's Sons, 1987.

Garment, Suzanne. *Scandal: The Crisis of Mistrust in American Politics.* New York: Times Books, 1991.

Garraty, John A. *1,001 Things Everyone Should Know about American History.* New York: Doubleday, 1989.

Garrison, Webb. *Treasury of White House Tales.* Nashville: Rutledge Hill Press, 1989.

Gilbert, Dennis, and Joseph A. Kahl. *The American Class Structure: A New Synthesis,* 3d ed. Chicago: Dorsey Press, 1987.

Graham, Gene. *One Man, One Vote: Baker v. Carr and the*

*American Levellers.* Boston: Atlantic Monthly Press, 1972.

Guber, Susan. *How to Win Your 1st Election.* Boca Raton, Fla.: St. Lucie Press, 1997.

Gillespie, J. David. *Politics at the Periphery: Third Parties in Two-Party America.* Columbia: University of South Carolina Press, 1993.

Graber, Doris A. *Media Power in Politics,* 3d ed. Washington, D.C.: CQ Press, 1993.

Gray, Virginia, Russell L. Hanson, and Herbert Jacob. *Politics in the American States: A Comparative Analysis,* 7th ed. Washington, D.C.: CQ Press, 1999.

Greenman, Ben, and Kristin Miller. *NetVote: Follow the 1996 Campaign Online.* New York: Michael Wolff Publishing, 1996.

Hagood, Wesley O. *Presidential Sex: From the Founding Fathers to Bill Clinton.* New York: Birch Lane Press, 1995.

Havel, James T. *U.S. Presidential Candidates and the Elections: A Biographical and Historical Guide,* 2 vols. New York: Macmillan Library Reference USA, 1996.

Jamieson, Kathleen Hall. *Packaging the Presidency,* 3d ed. New York: Oxford University Press, 1996.

Kazee, Thomas A., ed. *Who Runs for Congress? Ambition, Context, and Candidate Emergence.* Washington, D.C.: CQ Press, 1994.

King, Anthony Stephen. *Running Scared: Why America's Politicians Campaign Too Much and Govern Too Little.* New York: Martin Kessler Books, 1997.

Kruschke, Earl R. *Encyclopedia of Third Parties in the United States.* Santa Barbara, Calif.: ABC-CLIO, 1991.

Kownslar, Allan O., and Terry L. Smart. *American Government,* 2d ed. New York: Webster Division, McGraw-Hill, 1983.

Kurian, George T. *World Encyclopedia of Parliaments and Legislatures.* Washington, D.C.: Congressional Quarterly, 1997.

Lewis, Charles, and the Center for Public Integrity. *The Buying of the President.* New York: Avon Books, 1996.

Lewis-Beck, Michael S., and Tom W. Rice. *Forecasting Elections.* Washington, D.C.: CQ Press, 1992.

Lipset, Seymour Martin. *Political Man: The Social Bases of Politics.* Expanded ed. Baltimore: Johns Hopkins Press, 1981.

Maddex, Robert L. Jr. *Illustrated Dictionary of Constitutional Concepts.* Washington, D.C.: Congressional Quarterly, 1996.

———. *Constitutions of the World.* Washington, D.C.: Congressional Quarterly, 1995.

Miller, William "Fishbait," as told to Frances Spatz Leighton. *Fishbait: The Memoirs of the Congressional Doorkeeper.* Englewood Cliffs, N.J.: Prentice-Hall, 1977.

Mintz, Morton, and Jerry S. Cohen. *America, Inc.: Who Owns and Operates the United States.* New York: Dial Press, 1971.

Maisel, L. Sandy, ed. *Political Parties and Elections in the United States: An Encyclopedia,* 2 vols. New York: Garland Publishing, 1991.

Maxwell, Bruce. *How to Access the Federal Government on the Internet 1997.* Washington, DC: Congressional Quarterly, 1996.

———. *How to Access the Government's Electronic Bulletin Boards.* Washington, D.C.: Congressional Quarterly, 1995.

Mitchell, Jack. *How to Get Elected: An Anecdotal History of Mudslinging, Red-Baiting, Vote-Stealing and Dirty Tricks in American Politics.* New York: St. Martin's Press, 1992.

Moore, David W. *The Super Pollsters: How They Measure and Manipulate Public Opinion in America.* New York: Four Walls Eight Windows, 1992.

Moore, John L. *Speaking of Washington: Facts, Firsts, and Folklore.* Washington, D.C.: Congressional Quarterly, 1993.

*National Party Conventions 1831–1996.* Washington, D.C.: Congressional Quarterly, 1998.

Nelson, Michael, and others. *The Elections of 1996.* Washington, D.C.: CQ Press, 1997.

———. *The Elections of 1992.* Washington, D.C.: CQ Press, 1993.

———. *The Elections of 1988.* Washington, D.C.: CQ Press, 1989.

Oleszek, Walter J. *Congressional Procedures and the Policy Process,* 4th ed. Washington, D.C.: CQ Press, 1996.

Ornstein, Norman J., Thomas E. Mann, Michael J. Malbin. *Vital Statistics on Congress 1997–1998.* Washington, D.C.: Congressional Quarterly, 1998.

Plano, Jack C., and Milton Greenberg. *The American Political Dictionary,* 8th ed. New York: Holt, Rinehart and Winston, 1989.

*Presidential Elections 1789–1996.* Washington, D.C.: Congressional Quarterly, 1998.

Price, David. *Bringing Back the Parties.* Washington, D.C.: CQ Press, 1984.

Ragsdale, Lyn. *Vital Statistics on the Presidency: Washington to Clinton.* Washington, D.C.: Congressional Quarterly, 1996.

Reader's Digest. *Our Glorious Century.* Pleasantville, N.Y.: Reader's Digest Association, 1994.

———. *When, Where, Why and How It Happened.* Pleasantville, N.Y.: Reader's Digest Association, 1993.

———. *Strange Stories, Amazing Facts of America's Past.* Pleasantville, N.Y.: Reader's Digest Association, 1989.

Rosenstone, Steven J., Roy L. Behr, and Edward H. Lazarus. *Third Parties in America: Citizen Response to Major Party Failure.* Rev. ed. Princeton, N.J.: Princeton University Press, 1995.

Rosenthal, Alan. *The Third House: Lobbyists and Lobbying in the States.* Washington, D.C.: CQ Press, 1993.

Sabato, Larry. *Goodbye to Good-time Charlie: The American Governorship Transformed,* 2d. ed. WAshington, D.C.: CQ Press, 1983.

Safire, William. *Safire's New Political Dictionary: The Definitive Guide to the New Language of Politics.* New York: Random House, 1993.

Scammon, Richard M., Alice V. McGillivray, and Rhodes Cook. *America Votes 22: A Handbook of Contemporary Election Statistics 1996.* Washington, D.C.: Congressional Quarterly, 1998.

Shafritz, Jay M. *The Dorsey Dictionary of American Government and Politics.* Chicago: Dorsey Press, 1988.

Salmore, Stephen A., and Barbara G. Salmore. *Candidates, Campaigns, and Parties: Electoral Politics in America.* Washington, D.C.: CQ Press, 1985.

Southwick, Leslie H. *Presidential Also-Rans and Running Mates, 1788–1980.* Jefferson, N.C.: McFarland, 1984.

Stanley, Harold W., and Richard G. Niemi. *Vital Statistics on American Politics, 1997–1998.* Washington, D.C.: Congressional Quarterly, 1998.

Swerdlow, Joel L. *Presidential Debates: 1988 and Beyond.* Washington, D.C.: Congressional Quarterly, 1987.

*Washington Information Directory 1998–1999.* Washington, D.C.: Congressional Quarterly, 1998.

# Index